No Stress Tech Guide To ACT! 2009

By Dr. Indera E. Murphy

Tolana Publishing
Teaneck, New Jersey

No Stress Tech Guide To ACT! 2009 (Version 11.0)

Published By:
Tolana Publishing
PO Box 719
Teaneck, NJ 07666 USA

Find us online at www.tolanapublishing.com
Inquiries may be sent to the publisher: tolanapub@yahoo.com

Our books are available online at www.amazon.com, www.barnesandnoble.com and www.alibris.com.
Our books can also be ordered from Ingram. Check our website for the best price.

ISBN-13: 978-1-935208-07-5
ISBN-10: 1935208071

Library of Congress Catalog Number: 2009900798

Printed and bound in the United States Of America

Cover by Mary Kramer, Milkweed Graphics, www.milkweedgraphics.com

V2.0

Dedication

This book is dedicated to Frank Brown III, whose ACT! is so together, that I forget that he is only 10 years old.

With Love,
Auntie 'Dera

Why A Book On ACT! 2009

After reading the brief Users Guide that comes with ACT!, I felt that users, especially new users, would prefer to have more assistance in learning how to get the most out of ACT!. The Users Guide provides a starting point of reference, but often the Users Guide refers you to the Help system to get more information. As a professor and author, I do not feel that flipping between a book and the Help system is the most ideal way to learn how to use a software package.

I know that many books claim to have "step-by-step instructions". If you have tried to follow books that make this claim and you got lost or could not complete a task as instructed, it may not have been your fault. When I decided to write computer books, I vowed to really have step-by-step instructions that actually included every step.
This includes steps like which file to open, which menu option to select, when to save a file and more. In my opinion, it is this level of detail that makes a computer book easy to follow.

About The Author

Dr. Indera Murphy is an author, educator and IT professional that has over 20 years of experience in the Information Technology field. She has held a variety of positions including, programmer, consultant, technical writer, web designer, course developer and project leader. Indera has designed and developed software applications and web sites, as well as, manage IT Projects. In addition to being an Executive Director and consultant, Indera is also an online adjunct professor. She teaches courses in a variety of areas including technical writing, information processing, Access, HTML, Windows, project management, spreadsheets, Dreamweaver and critical thinking.

Titles In The Series

	ISBN
ACT! 2007	978-0-9773912-5-7
ACT! 2009	978-1-935208-07-5
ACT! 2010	978-1-935208-09-9
ACT! Pro 2011	978-1-935208-13-6
ACT! Pro 2012	978-1-935208-17-4
Using Crystal Reports 2008 With ACT! 2010 Databases	978-1-935208-10-5
Crystal Reports XI For Beginners (2nd Edition)	978-1-935208-00-6
What's New In Crystal Reports 2008	978-1-935208-01-3
Crystal Reports 2008 For Beginners	978-0-9773912-9-5
Crystal Reports 2011 For Beginners	978-1-935208-15-0
Crystal Reports Beyond The Basics	978-1-935208-18-1
Crystal Reports For Visual Studio 2005	978-0-9773912-6-4
Crystal Reports Basic For Visual Studio 2008	978-0-9773912-8-8
Crystal Reports For Visual Studio 2010	978-1-935208-12-9
Crystal Xcelsius 4.5	978-1-935208-02-0
Xcelsius 2008	978-1-935208-05-1
SAP Crystal Dashboard Design 2011 For Beginners	978-1-935208-11-2
OpenOffice.org 2 Writer	978-0-9773912-4-0
OpenOffice.org 3 Writer	978-1-935208-08-2
Microsoft Office Starter 2010 (Word & Excel)	978-1-935208-14-3
Microsoft PowerPivot For Excel 2010	978-1-935208-16-7
Microsoft Works 7	978-0-9773912-2-6
Microsoft Works 8 & 8.5	978-0-9773912-1-9
Microsoft Works 9	978-0-9773912-7-1
Windows XP	978-0-9773912-0-2

Coming Soon

Alpha Five Desktop Applications For Beginners	978-1-935208-20-4
Crystal Reports For Sage Peachtree Accounting	978-1-935208-19-8

TABLE OF CONTENTS

GETTING STARTED WITH ACT! 2009

The fastest and easiest way to overcome an obstacle is to have someone that has been there, to be by your side every step of the way. That is the goal of this book, to be by your side, while you learn ACT! 2009.

A hands-on approach is usually the best way to learn most things in life. This book is a visual guide that shows you how to create and modify contact, company and group records. There are over 675 illustrations in this book that practically eliminate the guess work and let you know that you are doing the steps correctly. Real world examples are provided to help give you an idea of when to use certain features.

The table of contents takes the "How To" approach because ACT! consists of a series of tasks that overall, do not have to be completed in a specific order. There is more to ACT! than knowing how to enter contact information. ACT! is robust and has a lot of features.

The goal of this book is to show you how to use ACT! for your contact relationship management tasks. From time to time, I will point out functionality that may not work as expected. When I do this, I am not complaining, merely pointing out things that you should be aware of.

By the time that you complete all of the exercises in this book, you will know more than the basics of ACT!. While you can jump from one section of the book to another, mainly because you paid for the book and can do as you please, it is my hope that you complete all of the exercises in the order that they are presented, because that will help you gain a better understanding of the features and functionality that ACT! offers. You will also gain more insight into how the features work together.

It is my sincere hope that whatever your skill level is with ACT!, that you will learn more about features that you may already be familiar with and that you learn about features that you did not know existed. Learning new tips and shortcuts will allow you to work faster and smarter. The more that you know about ACT!, the easier your day to day contact and customer relationship management experiences will be.

So sit back and lets get started.

Thank you for purchasing this book!

What Is ACT! And What Can It Do For Me?

ACT! is a very popular Contact and Customer Relationship Management (CRM) database software package that is used by individuals and companies. In the beginning, ACT! was primarily used by sales people, but over the years the user base and types of companies that use ACT! has expanded. There are more than 2.8 million ACT! users. CRM software provides a way to keep your contacts, which can be business associates, customers, friends, family, vendors, potential customers and any type of contacts that you have, organized. More importantly to many users, ACT! has the ability to create an audit trail or history for each contact. This makes it easier to remember your relationship with each contact.

ACT! is used to store information like addresses, contact type, to-do lists, meeting and sales information, as well as, other information that will help you maintain existing contacts and develop new contacts. ACT! also has built in applications that allow you to do word processing, send faxes, create and send email. One feature that you may find very useful is the variety of ways that you can look up contact information. Additionally, you can put contacts into groups like friends, sales reps and territory. You can also design and run reports. One of the best features of ACT! is that you can customize it to better meet your needs.

There are several versions of ACT!: ACT! 2009, which can support up to 10 simultaneous users per database. ACT! 2009 Premium Solutions and ACT! 2009 Premium for Web, which is the online version. The biggest difference between the two premium versions is that the latter allows you to access your data online.

The list of features that ACT! has for managing contacts is extensive. There are over 40 fields that can be used to store general contact information like name, company, email and address. Not only can you keep your contact information organized, you can attach documents that you create in other software packages to the contacts and activities in the database. That is just the beginning of what ACT! offers. The list below provides some of the functionality that ACT! has.

- ☑ Over 25 pre-built reports that present the data in an easy to understand format.
- ☑ The ability to customize existing reports and create your own reports.
- ☑ Automate the creation of a series of tasks that you have to complete for contacts on a regular basis.
- ☑ Put a copy of the database on your laptop to work remotely. When you return to the office, you can sync your copy with the live copy of the database that is on a server.
- ☑ Create activities and reminders for tasks that you need to complete, on a contact by contact basis.
- ☑ Use dashboards, graphs and pipelines to help make business decisions.

ACT! is relatively easy to learn. One reason that ACT! is easy to learn is because it has many of the same options that are in other software packages that you may have used before. This includes options on menus and keyboard shortcuts. When you first start using ACT!, you may think that there are not a lot of features, but there are more features then meets the eye. The majority of people that use ACT!, use it to manage contacts, but there is nothing stopping you from using it to keep track of your book, movie or music collection. If you already know that you need a custom contact management database, you may find it helpful to take notes on the features that you will need to create a database that meets your needs.

If you have read any reviews of ACT!, you have probably read that using the software will make you more efficient and will save you time when it comes to managing your contacts. That is true. What the reviews do not point out or make obvious is that to get the most out of ACT! or any software package for that matter, one has to know more than the basics of the software.

What's New In ACT! 2009

What's new in ACT! 2009 depends on the version of ACT! that you are upgrading from. The older the version of ACT! that you are upgrading from, the more new features you will notice. The list below contains some of the new or modified features in ACT! 2009.

- ☑ Automate tasks like database maintenance using the ACT! Scheduler.
- ☑ Print calendars using the filters that you select.
- ☑ The search capabilities have been improved. You can switch between contact, company and group lookups without starting over. You can also view previous lookups.

- ☑ Microsoft Outlook can be used in lieu of the email software that comes with ACT!.
- ☑ Emails that are created in Outlook can now be tracked in ACT!.

Overall Objectives

This book is written to accommodate classroom and online training, as well as, to be used as a self-paced training course. While there are no prerequisites to successfully complete the exercises in this book, having a general knowledge of any of the following would be helpful.

- ☑ Prior version of ACT!
- ☑ Windows environment
- ☑ Database structures
- ☑ Report design

Step-by-step instructions are included throughout this book. This book takes a hands-on, performance based approach to teaching you how to use ACT! and provides the skills required to use the software efficiently. After completing this book you will be able to perform the following tasks and more:

- ☑ Customize ACT!
- ☑ Create, edit and duplicate contact, company and group records
- ☑ Use the Lookup command
- ☑ Sort contact records
- ☑ Link company and contact records
- ☑ Run and customize reports
- ☑ Schedule activities and create opportunities
- ☑ Modify report templates and menus
- ☑ Import and export data
- ☑ Perform database maintenance tasks

Lesson 1 Objectives

In this lesson you will learn about the following:

- ☑ What ACT! can do for you
- ☑ The Help system
- ☑ Software support options
- ☑ Creating and copying databases
- ☑ Setting default preferences
- ☑ Changing layouts
- ☑ The views in ACT!
- ☑ The Detail view tabs

Conventions Used In This Book

I designed the following conventions to make it easier for you to follow the instructions in this book.

- ☑ The `Courier font` is used to indicate what you should type.
- ☑ **Drag** means to press and hold down the left mouse button while moving the mouse.
- ☑ **Click** means to press the left mouse button once, then release it immediately.
- ☑ **Double-click** means to quickly press the left mouse button twice, then release the mouse button.
- ☑ **Right-click** means to press the right mouse button once, which will open a shortcut menu.
- ☑ Click **OK** means to click the OK button on the dialog box.
- ☑ Press **Enter** means to press the Enter key on your keyboard.
- ☑ Press **Tab** means to press the Tab key on your keyboard.
- ☑ Click **Save** means to click the Save button in the software.

- ☑ Click **Finish** means to click the Finish button on the dialog box.
- ☑ **SMALL CAPS** are used to indicate an option to click on or to bring something to your attention.
- ☑  This icon indicates a tip or additional information about the topic that is being discussed.
- ☑  This icon indicates a shortcut or another way to complete the task that is being discussed.
- ☑  This icon indicates a warning, like a feature that has been removed or information that you need to be aware of.
- ☑  This icon indicates that after testing the steps several times on different computers, the results vary. This doesn't mean that I have done something wrong, only that there can be differences in the results that you see.
- ☑  This icon represents a question that I posted in the ACT! forum, but either did not receive an answer to, by the time this book went to print or the answer that I received did not resolve the problem or question that I had.
- ☑ The blinking cursor is the marker that is in a field or document and appears to the right of where you are typing. This is also known as the **INSERTION POINT** or **KEYBOARD CURSOR**. This is different then the pointer that is controlled by the mouse. The **MOUSE POINTER** usually looks like an I-beam when not in use.
- ☑ When you see "**YOUR SCREEN SHOULD HAVE THE OPTIONS SHOWN IN FIGURE X.X**", or something similar in the exercises, check to make sure that your screen does look like the figure. If it does, continue with the next set of instructions. If your screen does not look like the figure, redo the steps that you just completed so that your screen does match the figure. Not doing so may cause you problems when trying to complete exercises later in the book.
- ☑ The section heading **EXERCISE X.Y:** (where X equals the lesson number and Y equals the exercise number) represents exercises that have step-by-step instructions that you should complete. You will also see sections that have step-by-step instructions that are not an exercise. Completing them as you go through the book is optional, but recommended.
- ☑ [See Lesson 2, Figure 2-8] refers to an illustration (aka screen shot) that you can use as a reference for the topic that is being discussed.
- ☑ [See Lesson 2, Contact Fields] refers to a section in a lesson that you can use as a reference for the topic that is being discussed.
- ☑ "Clear the (name of option)" means to remove the check mark from the option specified in the instruction.
- ☑ "Save the Contact file as" means to open the Contact file and save it with the new name that is specified in the instruction. Doing this allows you keep the original file unchanged.
- ☑ **VIEW ⇒ CALENDAR ⇒ DAILY**, means to open the **VIEW** menu, select **CALENDAR**, then select **DAILY**, as shown in Figure 1-1.

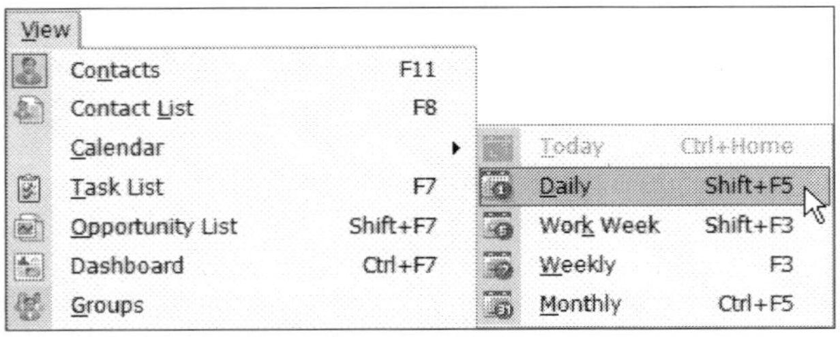

Figure 1-1 Menu navigation technique

Assumptions

(Yes, I know one should never assume anything, but the following assumptions have been made.)
It is assumed that . . . .

- ☑ You know that the operating system used to write this book is Windows XP Professional. If you are using a different version of Windows, some of the illustrations may have a slightly different look.
- ☑ You are familiar with the Windows environment, including Windows Explorer and are comfortable using a mouse.
- ☑ You understand that this book is based on ACT! 2009, version 11.0.

☑ You know that the version of Microsoft Office used and referenced in this book is 2003.

☑  You know that this button will minimize the open window and place an icon for the open window on the Windows taskbar. When you want to view the window again, click the button on the taskbar and the window will reappear.

☑  You know that this button will open the current window to the full size of your computer screen.

☑  You know that this button will close the window that is open.

☑ You understand that references to folders are folders on your computers hard drive and not a server. If your ACT! database is on a server, that is where the default ACT! folders should be located.

☑ You will have the My_ACT2009Demo database open at the beginning of each lesson, starting with Lesson 2, unless instructed otherwise. You will create this database later in this lesson.

☑ You have access to the Internet to download any updates that may be available for ACT! and to download the practice files needed to complete some of the exercises in this book.

☑ When you see <smile>, that signifies my attempt of adding humor to the learning process.

☑ Optional: That you have access to a printer, if you want to print any of the reports that you run or create.

☑ Optional: You have Microsoft Word and Excel, version 2002 or higher, installed, if you want to complete the exercises that use these packages.

Interactive Message Symbols

Like many other software packages, ACT! will display interactive messages on dialog boxes that require a response from you to confirm an action. Table 1-1 explains the three types of interactive message symbols and what they mean.

Symbol	Name	This interactive message type . . . . .
	Information	Provides information about an action that you just performed.
	Warning	Usually requires you to make a decision.
	Critical	Requires you to make a decision before moving on to the next step.

Table 1-1 Interactive message symbols explained

What's Not Covered

Rarely does any one book cover all of the features that a software package has. I cannot speak for every author, but I did not omit features or topics to cheat or mislead you. The size of this book should be proof of that <smile>. It is often a question of time and importance of the topic in relation to what the most used features are of the software. The reason that the following features are not covered in this book is two-fold: They will not prevent you from using over 95% of the features in ACT! and some of the features listed require additional software, hardware or both. Another reason they are not covered is because there are as many different set-ups for the additional software and hardware, as there are people using it.

For example, I may use Brand X PDA and you use Brand Y PDA. What works for me may not work for you. If I wrote instructions that you could not follow, you would think that there is something really wrong with me and even worse, you may think that I did not know what I was doing.

☑ Options only found in the Premium versions of ACT!, which aren't many.

☑ Sending broadcast faxes.

☑ Using ACT! with your PDA.

☑ Using ACT! with Microsoft Outlook.

What Is A Database?

A **DATABASE** is a repository used to store a collection of related information. An ACT! database is used to store contacts and all of the information for each contact that you have. It seems to be human nature to want to enter as little data as possible, often to save time. ACT!, is more useful in the long run if it has more data. A database has records and fields.

A **FIELD** holds one piece of information, like the contact name or title.

A **RECORD** is a collection of fields about one entity like a contact, company or group.

Demo Database

ACT!, like many other software packages, comes with a fully functional demo database that you can use to learn how to use the software. This is the database that you will use to complete the exercises in this book. If you have made changes to the data in the demo database prior to using this book, you should copy the original database to your hard drive (or server if the demo database is on a network). That way, your data and results will match the exercises in this book.

First Time Opening ACT!

If you have not opened ACT! yet, the first time that you do, you will see the dialog box shown in Figure 1-2.

This dialog box is used to select the database that you want to use.

Later in this lesson you will learn how to select a default database that will open automatically, each time that you open ACT!.

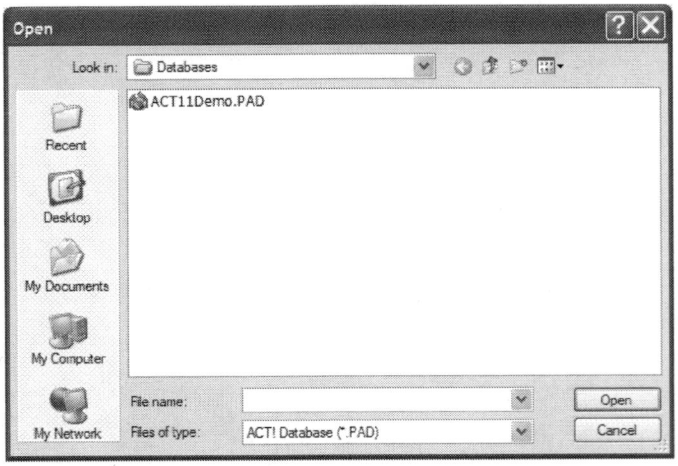

Figure 1-2 Open dialog box

1. Double-click on the ACT11Demo.PAD file. This will open the demo database that comes with ACT!.

> **.PAD** stands for Pointer to ACT! database.

By default, you will see the window shown in Figure 1-3.

This window has links to information about the new features in this version of ACT!, as well as, the new features in previous versions.

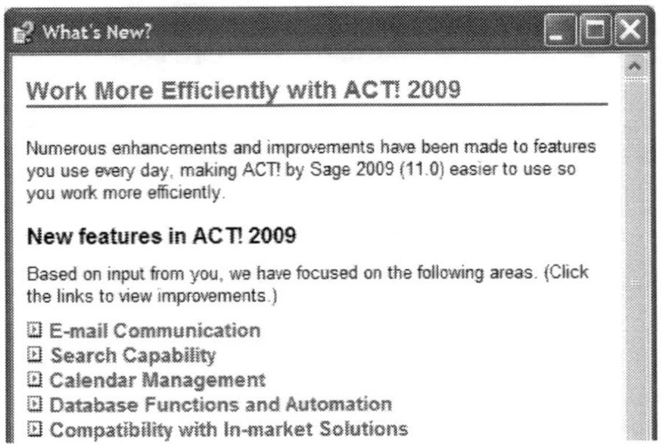

Figure 1-3 What's New help window

2. For now, close the What's New help window.

Getting Help In ACT!

There are several ways to get help for a problem that you may have when using the software. All of the help options approved by Sage Software (the makers of ACT!) are on the Help menu. The exception is the community forums, which are discussed later in this lesson. The more popular options are discussed below.

The Help System

The Help system in ACT! is quite extensive. When you open the Help system, it opens in a new window instead of opening on the right side of the ACT! window. To open the Help system, follow the instructions below.

1. Help ⇒ Help Topics. You will see the window shown in Figure 1-4. There are four buttons on the toolbar at the top of the help window, as shown in Figure 1-5. The toolbar buttons are explained below.

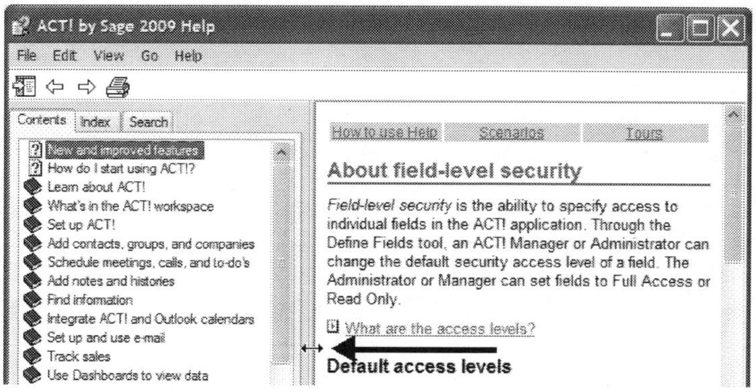

Figure 1-4 Help window

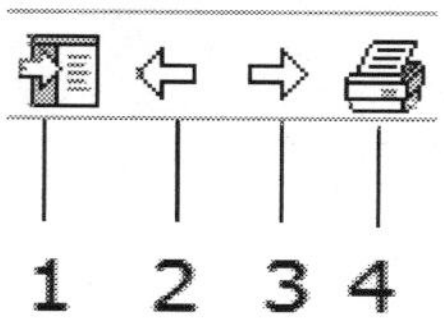

Figure 1-5 Help system toolbar buttons

① The **SHOW/HIDE** button toggles. It will open and close the left side of the Help window, as shown in Figure 1-6.

Compare this to the window shown earlier in Figure 1-4. To close the left side of the window, click this button again.

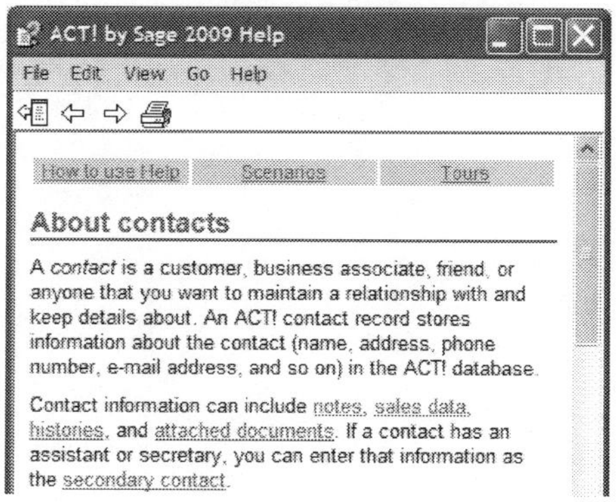

Figure 1-6 Left side of the help window hidden

② The **BACK** button displays the previous topic that you viewed. This option is only available after you have viewed at least two help topics.

③ The **FORWARD** button works similar to the Back button. The Forward button also displays topics that you have already viewed.

④ The **PRINT** button will print the help topic that is currently displayed.

To make the left pane of the window wider, place the mouse pointer in the position illustrated above in Figure 1-4, then drag the mouse to the right.

There is a **FAVORITES TAB** that is not visible by default (View ⇒ Favorites), but it does not work. I added this to my wish list of items that I would like Sage would fix.

> If you leave the Help window open while using ACT!, the contents on the right side of the window will automatically change and display an overview page based on the view that is displayed in the ACT! window. For example, if you switch to the Group List view, the Help page for the Group List view will be displayed.

2. If necessary, click the Show button and make the window larger, then click on the **CONTENTS** tab.

The window looks like the one shown earlier in Figure 1-4. The Contents tab is the online manual. This tab is like a table of contents. Click on the subject that you want to see more topics for, then double-click on a topic to view.

You have probably seen this style of help in other software applications. Each of the tabs (Contents, Index and Search) provide help in a slightly different way.

Figure 1-7 shows the options on the **INDEX** tab. The Index tab is like the index in a book. It provides a list of most features and options in ACT!.

Type in the name of the feature that you are looking for or scroll down the list on the Index tab, which is in alphabetical order. You can also enter a keyword and then click the **DISPLAY** button, illustrated in Figure 1-7, to view more information about the topic.

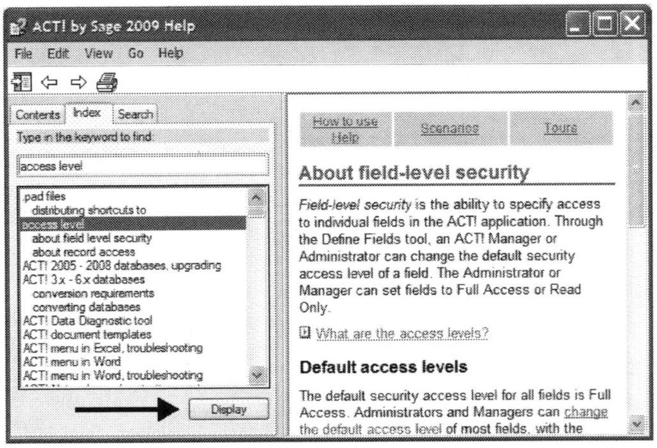

Figure 1-7 Index tab

3. Click on the **SEARCH** tab.

If you type in a keyword on the Search tab and click the **LIST TOPICS** button, illustrated in Figure 1-8, you will see a list of topics that relate to the keyword that you typed in. Select the topic that is closest to what you are looking for, then click the **DISPLAY** button or double-click on the topic in the list of topics on the left.

Notice that the word or phrase that you typed in is highlighted in the body of the help document on the right side of the window.

View ⇒ Highlights, will turn the highlighting on the right side of the window, on and off, as shown in Figure 1-8.

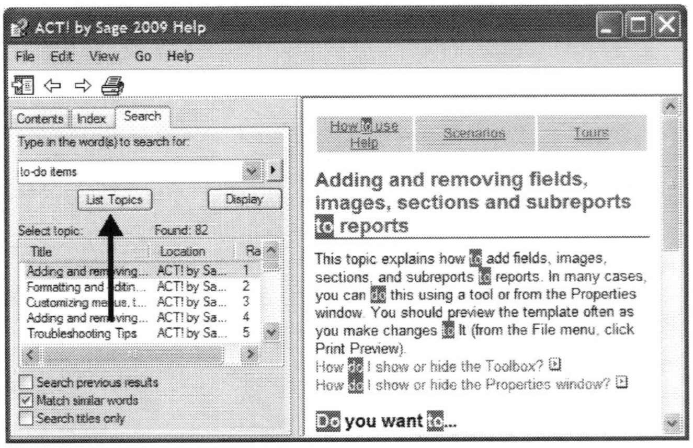

Figure 1-8 Search tab

Boolean Search Options

The right arrow button after the Search field illustrated in Figure 1-9, is used to create a complex search. This allows for several terms or keywords to be searched for at the same time.

Type in the first keyword that you want to search for, then select one of the Boolean options in the drop-down list shown in Figure 1-9. Type in the next keyword that you want to include (or exclude).

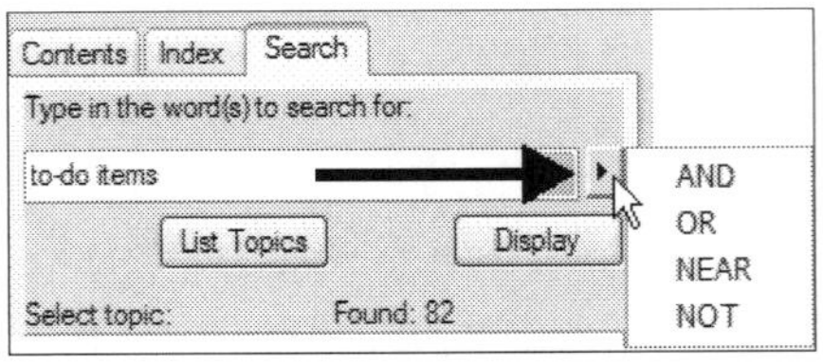

Figure 1-9 Boolean search options illustrated

Once you have entered all of the keywords, click the List Topics button.

The advantage that the Search tab has over the Index tab is that you do not have to know the exact name or phrase of what you are looking for. You should try using both tabs and see which one gives you the best results.

4. Close the Help window.

If you have ACT! open and the Alarms dialog box is getting on your nerves, you can minimize it or click the **CLEAR ALARM** button on the dialog box.

Feature Tours

This option is on the Help menu shown in Figure 1-10. It contains tutorials for some of the popular features in ACT!.

You have to be connected to the Internet to view the tours.

Follow the steps below to run the Activities tour.

1. Help ⇒ Feature Tours ⇒ Activities.

2. The tour will start. When you are finished viewing the tour, close the browser window.

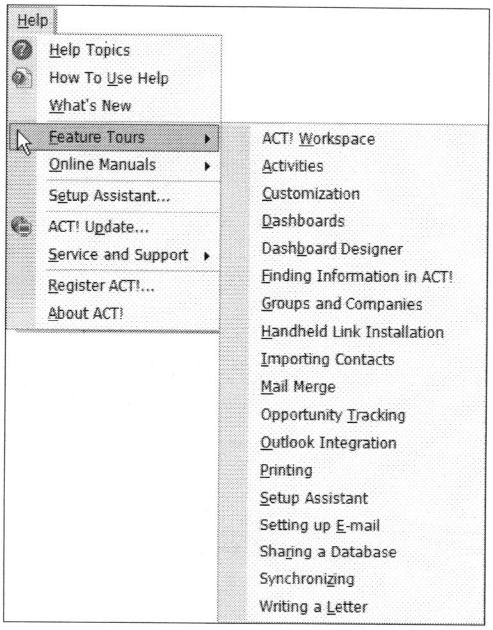

Figure 1-10 Feature Tours menu options

Online Manuals

The manuals that come with the software are installed when ACT! is installed. You can open them from the Help menu shown above in Figure 1-10. To view them, you need to have the free Adobe Acrobat Reader installed on your computer. The Adobe Reader software can be downloaded from the link below. (You do not have to download and install any of the software that comes with the Adobe Reader, for the reader to work.) You can also use the full version of Adobe Acrobat or another software package that can open and view PDF files.

http://www.adobe.com/products/acrobat/readstep2.html

Community Forums

If you have a question about ACT!, you can post a message in the community forum. The link below is for the home page of the forum. If you do not already have an account for the forum, you will be prompted to create one. The account is free. Sage Software does provide staff to answer questions in the forum. The questions are also answered by other ACT! users.

http://community.act.com/sage/

Request A Feature

As you go through this book and think of a feature that you wish ACT! had, or a feature that you think needs to be improved, it is probably a good idea to send the company a message explaining the addition or change that you would like to see in future versions of the software.

They do read the messages, but sadly, it may take a few version releases before a suggestion is implemented, depending on when they receive the request. I have sent them quite a few suggestions after using prior versions of ACT!. They are listed on the "Wish List" page for ACT! on our web site. It is important to note that as far as I can tell, they do not respond to the messages unless they have a question about your suggestion. The link below is where you can submit your request. If the link does not work, look for the "Request A Feature" link on www.act.com.

http://www.act.com/community/feature/index.cfm

Setup Assistant Wizard

In ACT! 2008 and earlier, the Setup Assistant Wizard was called the **GETTING STARTED WIZARD.**

The Setup Assistant option on the Help menu shown above in Figure 1-10 can be used to help you with the following:

① Checking to make sure that your e-mail and word processor preferences are set up correctly.
② Creating a database to store your contact information in.
③ Converting an existing database to work with the current version of ACT!.
④ The setup process to integrate your Outlook calendar with the calendar in ACT!.

While the wizard will complete all of the tasks listed above, you can pick and choose the options that you want to set up.

Exercise 1.1: How To Check For Updates

From time to time, it is a good idea to check to see if there are updates for ACT!. Updates provide changes to the software. Sometimes they are improvements to existing functionality and sometimes they are fixes to features that are not working correctly. This type of update is often called a **BUG FIX**.

You need to be connected to the Internet to check for updates. In a multi-user environment, you probably will not have to check for or install updates because this is usually handled by tech support or a Database Administrator. Before installing any update, you should back up any existing databases that you use.

1. Help ⇒ ACT! Update, as shown above in Figure 1-10, is used to check for updates.

   If there are no updates available, you will see the message shown in Figure 1-11 in the lower right corner of your computer screen.

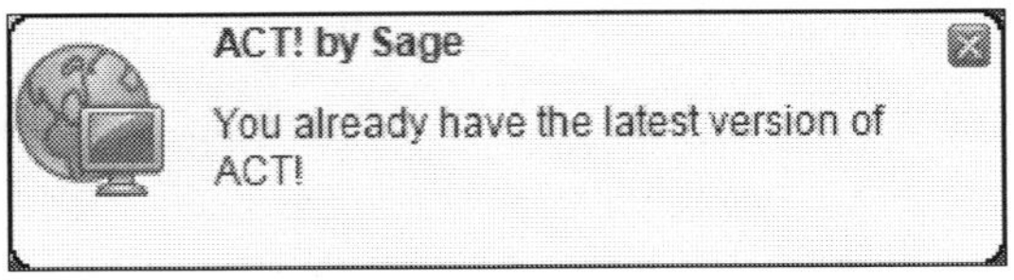

Figure 1-11 Latest version of ACT! installed message

In the lower right corner of your computer screen you may see a message that says to "Click here" for a description and download. If so, click on the option.

You will see a dialog box similar to the one shown in Figure 1-12 if there is an update available.

If you want to read about the update, click on the link on the dialog box otherwise, click the **DOWNLOAD** button. When this book went to print, there were no updates for ACT! 2009. This screen shot is from a prior version of ACT!.

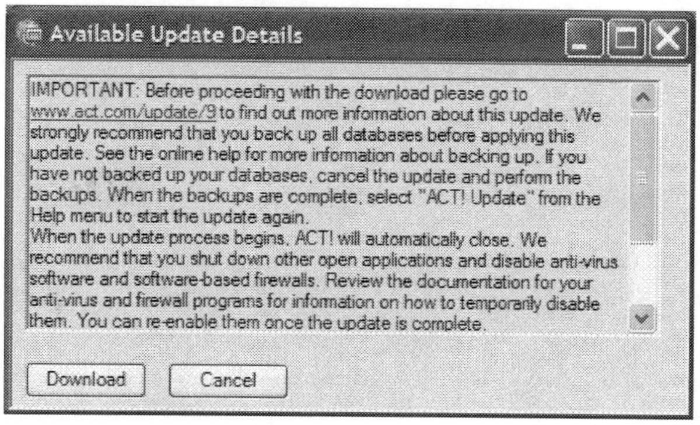

Figure 1-12 Available Update Details dialog box

2. Click Yes when prompted to continue without backing up your data. You can select this option now because you have not created any databases yet.

3. When prompted, close ACT!. The update will be installed and the database will be updated if necessary.

Exercise 1.2: Create A Folder For Your Files

You will create and modify databases in this book. You will also download files and databases. It would be a good idea to store all of the files and databases in the same folder on your hard drive so that you can find them easily. You will create a folder at the root of the C drive. If you want to create the folder in another location or under an existing folder, navigate to that location prior to starting step 2 below. The steps below explain how to obtain and download the practice files that are used in this book.

1. All of the files that are used in this book are in a zip file named act_2009.zip. To have the link for the files sent to you, send an email to act2009@tolanapublishing.com. If you do not receive an email in a few minutes with the subject line ACT! 2009 Files, check the spam folder in your email software.

2. Once you receive the email with the link to the files, open Windows Explorer and click on the Local Disk (C) drive.

3. File ⇒ New ⇒ Folder.

4. Type `ACT 2009 Book` as the folder name. Press Enter, then close Windows Explorer.

> Unless stated otherwise, all of the databases and files that you create in this book should be saved in the folder that you just created. I will refer to this folder as "your folder" throughout the book.

5. Go to the web page listed in the email that you received and download the zip file into the folder that you just created.

6. In Windows Explorer, click on the folder that you created.

   You should see the zip file on the right side of the window.

   Right-click on the zip file and select **EXTRACT TO HERE**, as illustrated in Figure 1-13. The files will be copied to your folder.

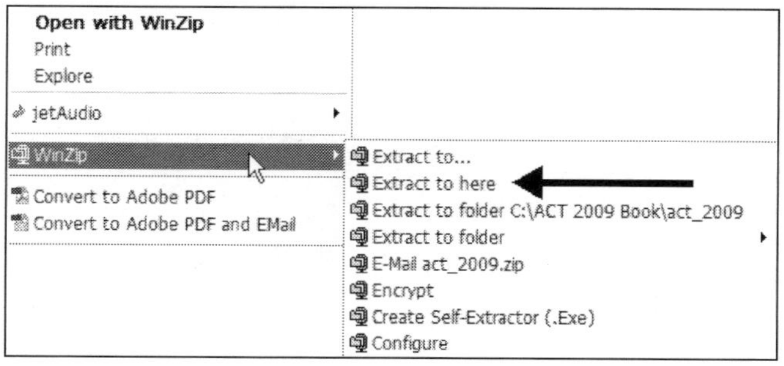

Figure 1-13 How to extract the files

What Is The "My Record"?

The My Record is the contact record that is displayed when you first open a database in ACT!. This record contains information about you and is used when you create documents like letters that require information about you, like your name and address. This saves you a lot of time because you do not have to enter this information for every document that you create.

If the database that you use is also used by other people, your My Record may have already been created for you by the administrator of the database. The first time that you use a database you should make sure that the information on your contact record is accurate and as complete as possible. Having the information filled in on your My Record is really important if you plan to use the templates that come with ACT!. If the information is not filled in on the My Record, a lot of your information that would automatically be filled in, in a mail merge document or template will be missing or inaccurate. Each person that uses the database has a My Record.

The My Record information is also used to track who created a record, who last modified a record and who deleted a record. This is how different users are designated as the owner (which ACT! calls the Record Manager) of a (contact, company, group or opportunity) record in the database. If the database will be used by more than one person, each person should create a My Record, otherwise they will have to log on as someone else. Logging on as someone else is not the best solution, in my opinion, because the other persons name will automatically be filled in when information is added, changed or deleted.

If by chance when the database opens and you do not see your contact record, something may be wrong. The things that come to mind are the following:

① The database could be corrupt.
② You did not log on as yourself.
③ Your contact information has been changed by someone else.

Look at the data on the contact record closely to see if your name has been changed and all of the other information is correct. If you are sure that the record is not yours, you should review the maintenance options covered in Lesson 20, to see if any of them will resolve the issue. If not, post a message in the forum.

Database Naming Conventions

At some point, you may have the need to create a database. Like many other things in life, there are rules that you have to follow. Below are the rules for database names.

① The name cannot be more than 32 characters.
② The name cannot contain spaces or any of the following characters:
~ ! @ # $ % ^ & * ( ) + { } | : " < > ? ` - = [ ] \ ; ' , . /
③ The name can have a combination of letters, numbers and the under score. The underscore is often used in place of a space.

Exercise 1.3: Create A New Database

During the process of creating a database you will create a My Record. The person that creates a database is automatically given administrator security rights to the database. You will learn more about security in Lesson 20. In this exercise you will learn how to create a database from scratch, opposed to using the Setup Assistant Wizard to create the database.

1. Open ACT!, if it is not already open, then click the **NEW DATABASE** button or File ⇒ New Database.

2. Type `My_ACT_Database` in the **DATABASE NAME** field on the New Database dialog box.

3. Click the **BROWSE** button, then navigate to your folder.

   Click on the folder illustrated in Figure 1-15.

   (**Hint**: If necessary, click on the plus sign in front of the My Computer option to see the C drive).

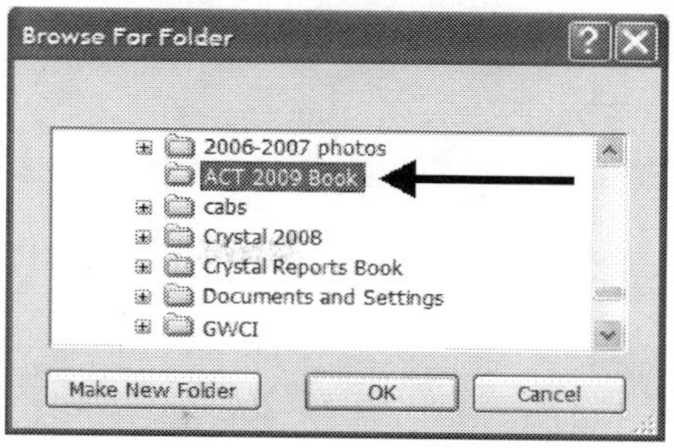

Figure 1-14 Browse For Folder dialog box

4. Click OK. This is the folder that the database will be saved in.

5. Check the **SHARE THIS DATABASE WITH OTHER USERS** option.

Anyone that you plan to share the database with must be using the same version of ACT! that the database was created with. If you (the creator of the database) are using the Standard version of ACT! 2009, other people that want to use your database have to use this version also. For example, they cannot use an older version of ACT! or ACT! 2009 Premium Solutions if you are using the Standard version of ACT!.

6. Type your first and last name in the **USER NAME** field.

   Other then your name, you should have the same options filled in that are shown in Figure 1-15.

   If you wanted the database to be password protected, you would enter the password in the last two fields on the dialog box.

   It is not a requirement for ACT! databases to have a password.

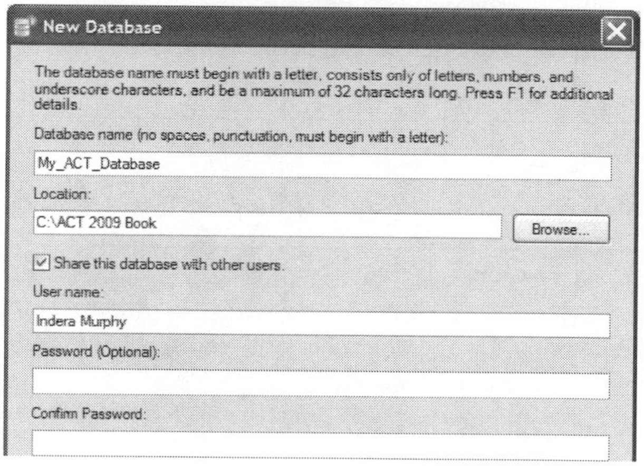

Figure 1-15 Information for a new database

User names are not case sensitive, but passwords are.

7. Click OK. The database will now be created. When it is finished, there will be one contact record in the database, which is the My Record that is automatically created for the user name on the New Database dialog box, shown above in Figure 1-15. You would add your information to the contact record when you see it on the screen.

Password Protected Databases

If the database is used by more than one person, you will see the dialog box shown in Figure 1-16 when you open the database.

You would have to enter your user name and password exactly as it was entered on the dialog box shown above in Figure 1-15 or how it was set up by the Database Administrator (by default, the person that created the database).

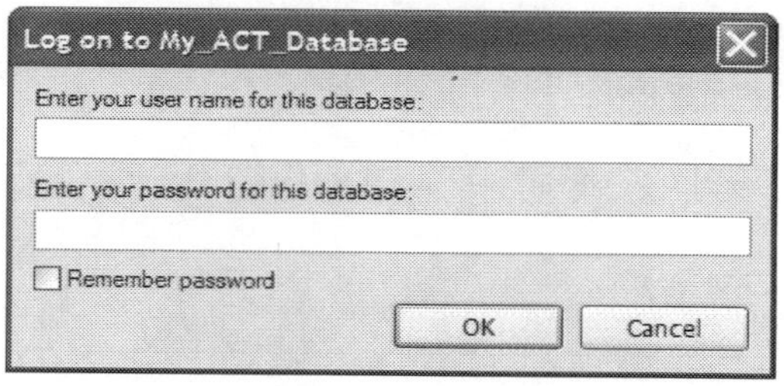

Figure 1-16 Log on dialog box

ACT! Folders

When ACT! is installed, several folders are automatically created. When you create a database, you can use these folders to store files in or you can create your own folders.

Viewing A Database

Earlier you created a database. You may find it helpful to view the structure and folders of databases in ACT!, so that you will know where files are located.

1. Open Windows Explorer.
2. Navigate to and click on your folder. You should see the files and folders shown in Figure 1-17. You will also see the files that you downloaded, even though they are not shown in the figure.

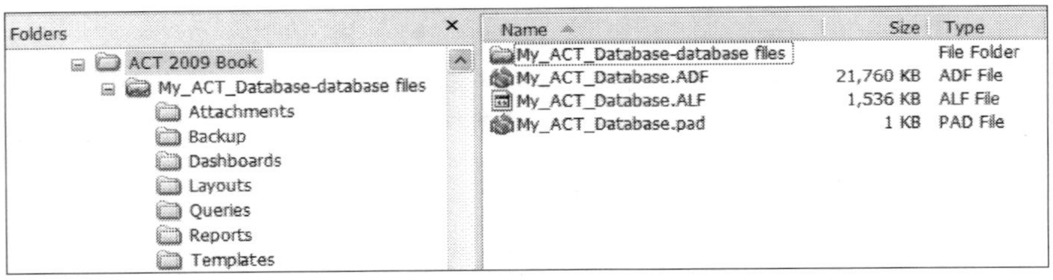

Figure 1-17 Contents of the ACT 2009 Book folder

3. Close Windows Explorer.

Database Tips
Below are some tips that you should know about ACT! databases.

① The folders shown on the left side of Figure 1-17 above, are automatically created when a new database is created. They are used to store files that are created or used by ACT!.
② When a database is created, approximately 20 MB of hard drive space is allocated for it.
③ The **.ADF** file is the database file.
④ The **.ALF** file is the log file for the database. This file should be backed up. If this file becomes corrupt and you do not have a copy of it, you will need to contact Sage in order to be able to use the database again.
⑤ The **.PAD** file is used to open the database. It is a shortcut that points to the database. If you want to share the database with other people, give them a copy of this file.
⑥ ACT! databases store three types of files, as discussed in Table 1-2.

File Type	Description
Database	This is the database file that contains the contact records, notes, activities and all of the data that you see when you use ACT!.
Database Supplemental	These files are automatically created when ACT! is installed. Reports and templates are supplemental files. (1)
Personal Supplemental	These are files that you create and save, like letters or spreadsheets. (1)

Table 1-2 ACT! file types

(1) You will learn more about supplemental files in Lesson 12.

The ACT! Window

When you open a database you will see the window shown in Figure 1-18, unless the **STARTUP VIEW** preference option has been changed. Table 1-3 explains the sections of the window. Parts of the window will change based on the view that is selected.

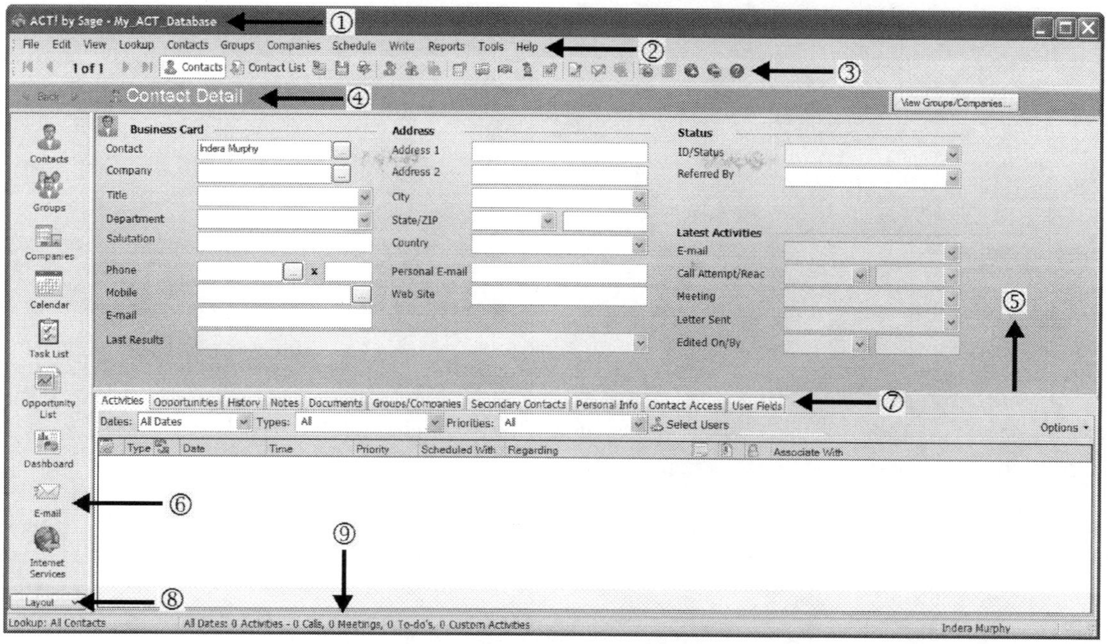

Figure 1-18 ACT! window

	Name	Description
①	Title bar	Displays the name of the database that is open. The icon in the left corner of this section opens the Control menu shown in Figure 1-19. The options on this menu are used to you close, restore, move, size, minimize or maximize the ACT! window.
②	Menu bar	Contains the default menus and commands for the current view. (2)
③	Toolbar	Contains a button for each of the options that you will probably use the most. The buttons are shortcuts to items on the menu bar. The buttons change depending on the view that is selected. (2)
④	Display area	After you switch to a different view, the right and left arrow buttons are enabled. Clicking on the arrow buttons will display the next (right arrow) or previous (left arrow) view that was opened. The name of the current view is also displayed in this section. The **VIEW GROUPS/COMPANIES** button is used to view and filter contacts by group or company name.
⑤	Detail	Contains basic information for the contact, company or group. Many of these fields are used in templates and reports, which means that the information should be as accurate as possible.
⑥	Navigation bar	The buttons in this section are used to change the view. (2)
⑦	Tabs	The fields on each tab contain information about the contact, company or group. The information that you see on the tabs depends on the access rights and security that you have. This means that different people that use the database will see different information. The data on the tabs are related to the contact, company or group record that is displayed in the top half of the window. You can create additional tabs, which you will learn how to do in Lesson 18. (2)
⑧	Layout button	The options on this button contain layouts for the type of view (contact, company or group) that is currently displayed. Each layout for each view can contain different fields. For example the Basic Contact Layout 1024x768 displays more fields than the Basic Contact Layout 800x600.
⑨	Status bar	This section is primarily used to provide additional information about the contact, company or group record that is currently displayed. On the Opportunity List view, totals are displayed in this section.

Table 1-3 Sections of the ACT! window explained

(2) This option can be customized.

Figure 1-19 Control menu

Exercise 1.4: How To Copy A Database

The exercises that you will complete in this book will modify the demo database that comes with ACT!. Therefore, it is a good idea to make a copy of the demo database and use the copy to complete the exercises.

1. File ⇒ Open Database. Navigate to the following location on your hard drive: C:\Documents and Settings\Your Username\My Documents\ACT\ACT For Windows 11\Databases.

   You should see the file illustrated in Figure 1-20.

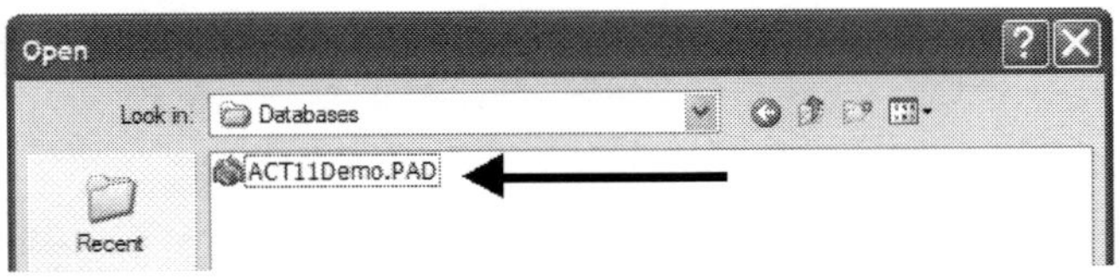

Figure 1-20 ACT! Demo database shortcut file

2. Double-click on the **.PAD** file. If you see a message stating that the database needs to be updated, click Yes to create a back up.

3. Click OK on the Back Up Database dialog box. The update process could take a few minutes.

4. When the database opens, File ⇒ Save Copy As, then type `My_ACT2009Demo` in the **DATABASE NAME** field.

5. Check the option **SHARE THIS DATABASE WITH OTHER USERS**.

   You should have the options shown in Figure 1-21.

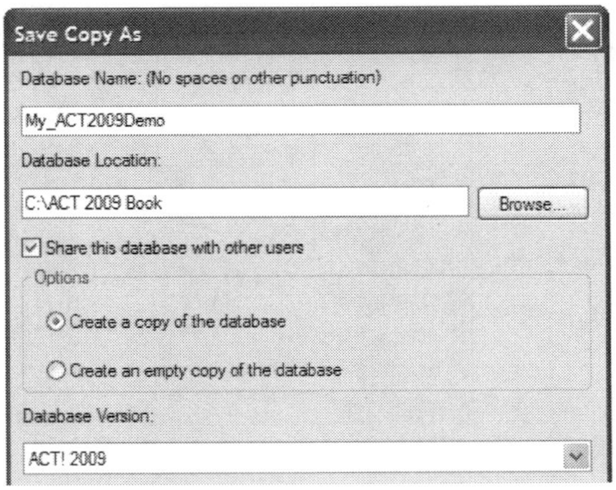

Figure 1-21 Save Copy As dialog box

6. Click OK. It will take what seems like a long time (a few minutes) to save a copy of the database.

7. Click OK when you see the "Save As was successful" message.

Exercise 1.5: View And Modify The Preferences

In this exercise you will learn about the preferences in ACT!. You will also modify some of the preferences for the My_ACT2009Demo database.

Preferences Overview

As you go through the preferences section of this lesson, try to think about how you will use ACT! in terms of how the preferences can be modified to work best for you. It may be a good idea to write down the options that you want to change and what you want to change them to. That way, after you have completed this book, you can make the changes.

For example, if you plan to keep most of the databases that you use in one folder, you could set that folder as the one that ACT! looks in first. The default folder for databases is the My Documents folder in Windows. I have watched many people lose work that was stored in the My Documents folder because they were not aware of the pitfalls of storing work in a folder that Windows creates. ACT! allows you to change the default location for databases, documents, reports, queries and any other type of file that you can create or use in ACT!.

Preferences are used to change ACT! to work the way that you want or need it to. Some of the preferences require administrator rights.

1. Tools ⇒ Preferences.

General Tab Preferences

The options shown in Figure 1-22 are used to select preferences for the database.

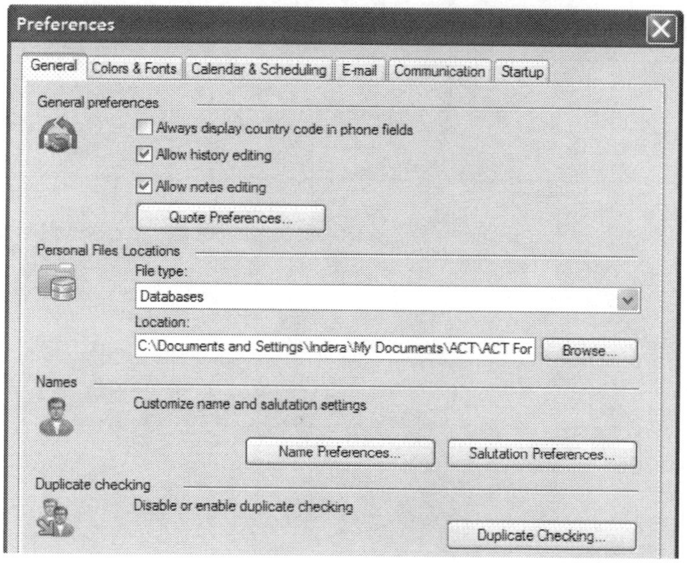

Figure 1-22 General tab preferences

> Administrator or manager rights are needed to change the **DUPLICATE CHECKING** and **ALLOW HISTORY EDITING** options.

The options in the **FILE TYPE** drop-down list shown in Figure 1-23 contain the types of files that you can set a folder location for. This means that you can store the databases in one location (folder) and the documents that you create in a different location. If you want to save different file types in the same folder, you have to select the same folder for each file type.

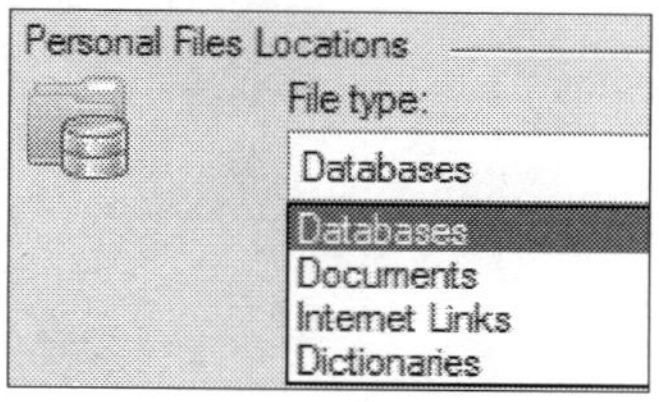

Figure 1-23 File type options

> The **FILE TYPE** and **LOCATION** options are something that you will want to change after you complete the exercises in this book because these options should reflect the location of the database that you use the most.

1. Click the **BROWSE** button shown earlier in Figure 1-22, then navigate to and click on your folder.

2. Click OK to close the Browse For Folder dialog box. The **LOCATION** field should have changed to the folder that you selected in step 1.

3. Select your folder as the location for the Documents file.

4. Click the **SALUTATION PREFERENCES** button. Select the option, **USE CONTACT'S FIRST NAME**, then click OK. In prior versions of ACT!, this was the default salutation option.

5. Click the **DUPLICATE CHECKING** button, then open the **RECORD TYPE** drop-down list and select Company.

6. Change the first **THEN ON** field to <None>, as shown in Figure 1-24.

   Like the salutation options, the default company duplicate checking options have changed from previous versions.

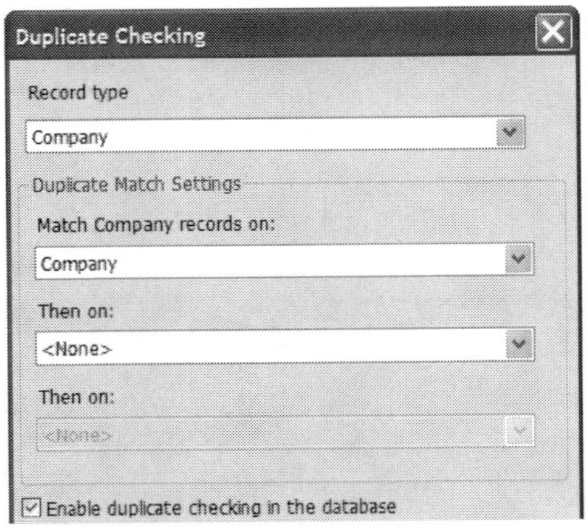

Figure 1-24 Duplicate checking options for company records

7. Click OK, then click the Apply button.

Colors & Fonts Tab Preferences

The options on this tab are used to change the default font, style, text and background colors that are displayed.

The options on the right side of the tab shown in Figure 1-25 are used to customize all of the views (lists), tabs, calendar and compositions (the dialog box that you enter notes on) in the **CUSTOMIZE** list.

Click on the object that you want to modify in the Customize list, then change the options on the right side of the dialog box as needed.

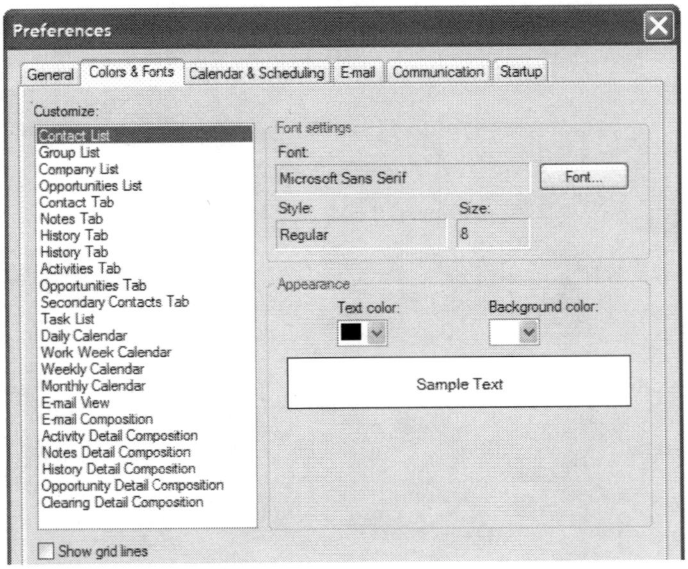

Figure 1-25 Colors & Fonts tab preferences

If you want to make the same change to more than one of the options in the Customize list, click on the first option that you want to change. Press and hold the CTRL key down, then click on the other options that you want to modify, as shown in Figure 1-26.

Once you have selected all of the views and windows that you want to customize, select the font settings, style, appearance and background color options that you want. There is no global change option available, so this is the work around that I came up with. This will provide a consistent look when you go from one part of ACT! to another. This means that you will not have the top half of the Contact Detail view with a green background and the background color of the tabs on the Contact Detail view purple, unless that is what you want.

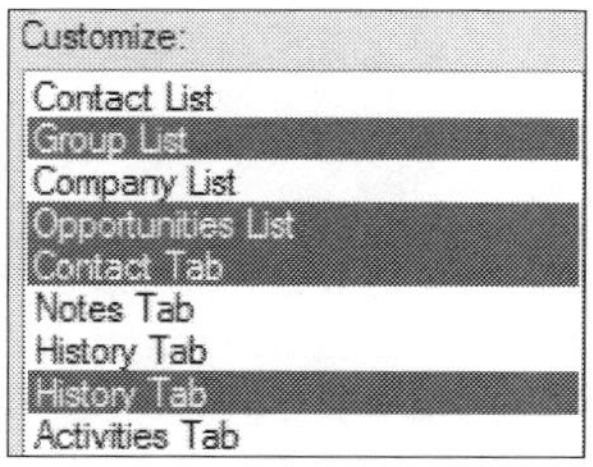

Figure 1-26 Multiple options selected to be customized at the same time

If available and checked, the **SHOW GRID LINES** option will change the layout of data on a tab to look like a spreadsheet, as shown in Figure 1-27.

You may want to change the colors and fonts or add grid lines to the Notes and History tabs because they will contain more data than the other tabs and having color or gridlines may make the entries easier to read.

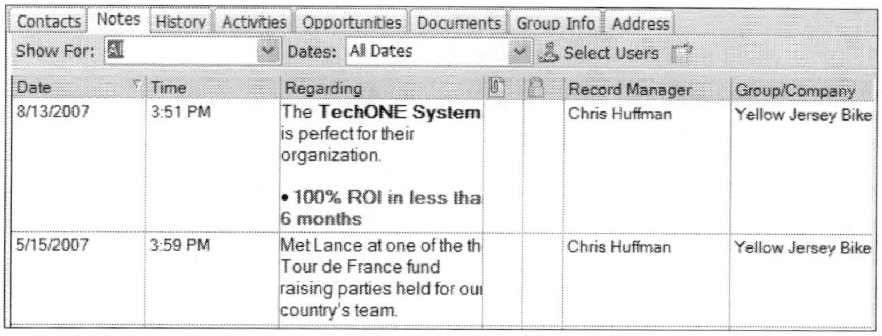

Figure 1-27 Grid lines option turned on

Calendar & Scheduling Tab Preferences

Each of the buttons shown in Figure 1-28 are used to open a dialog box that has options for a specific preference.

The **CALENDAR PREFERENCES** options are used to set the work days and time period increments for the calendars.

The **SCHEDULING PREFERENCES** options are used to set the default values for all of the activity types.

The **CALENDAR INTEGRATION PREFERENCES** options are used to configure how data will be copied between ACT! and Outlook calendars.

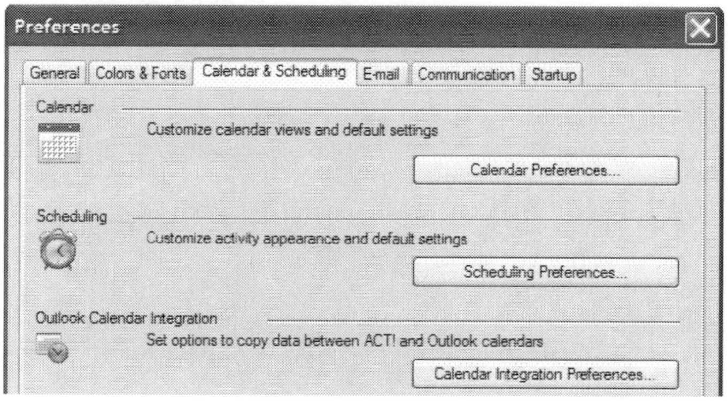

Figure 1-28 Calendar & Scheduling tab preferences

E-mail Tab Preferences

The options shown in Figure 1-29 are the settings for the e-mail software that you will use with ACT!.

It is not a requirement to configure email software because you can use the Email Editor that comes with ACT!. These settings do not change the options that you currently have set in your e-mail software.

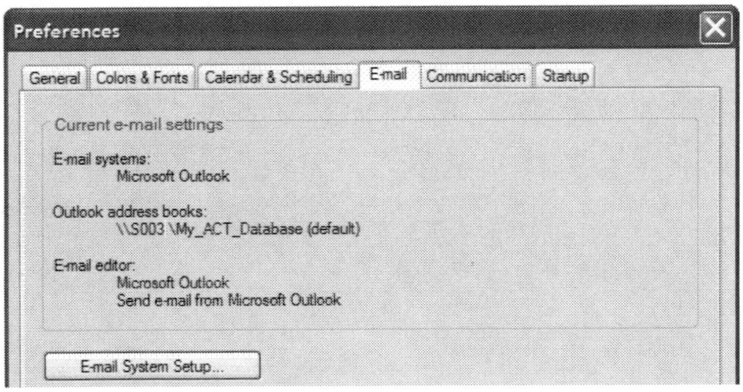

Figure 1-29 E-mail tab preferences

If you do not see any settings on this tab, it means that you have not set up an email package to use with ACT!. The **E-MAIL SYSTEM SETUP** button shown above in Figure 1-29 opens the **E-MAIL SETUP WIZARD**, which is used to configure Internet Mail, Outlook or Outlook Express as the email software that you want ACT! to recognize. The email choices that you see may be different because the choices depend on the email software that ACT! finds and recognizes on your hard drive. I've read that Windows Mail in Vista is not compatible.

ACT! E-mail Editor Tab Preferences

The options shown in Figure 1-30 are used to configure the ACT! Email Editor.

The options on this tab are used to select the incoming and outgoing e-mail settings.

You can even set an option to notify you when you receive e-mail.

If the **CHECK SPELLING BEFORE SENDING E-MAIL** option is selected, emails that you compose will be spell checked automatically before they are sent.

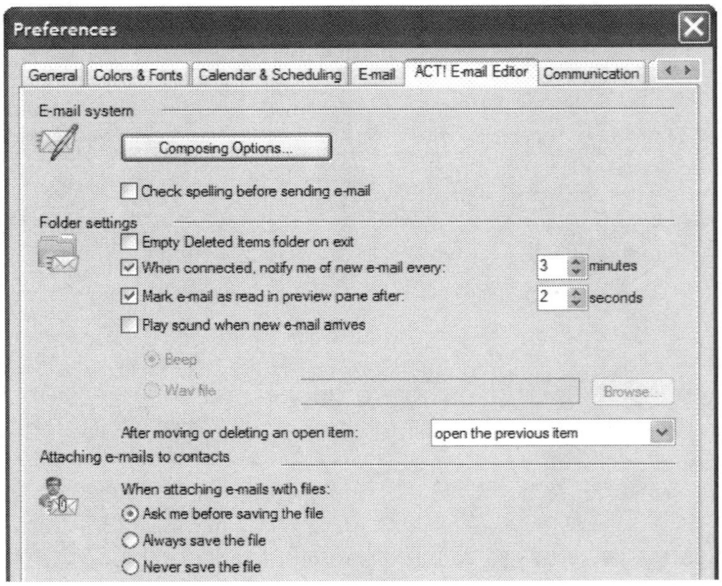

Figure 1-30 ACT! Email Editor tab preferences

The **COMPOSING OPTIONS** button on the ACT! Email Editor tab opens the dialog box shown in Figure 1-31.

This dialog box contains additional e-mail options that can be selected.

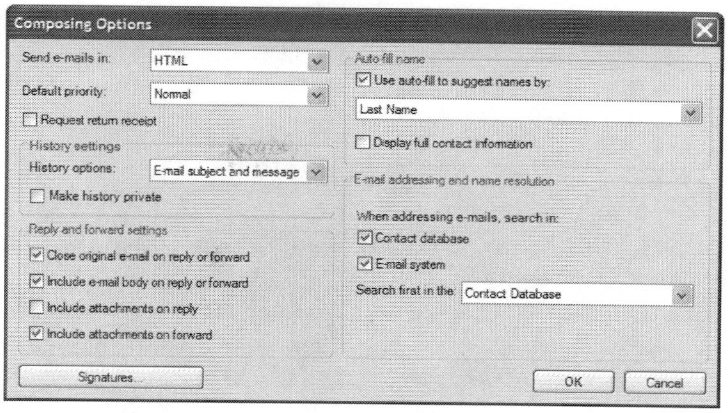

Figure 1-31 Composing Options dialog box

Communication Tab Preferences

The options shown in Figure 1-32 are used to select the default word processor, spell check, fax software and print options that you will use.

The **DIALER PREFERENCES** option requires your computer to be connected to a phone line, similar to using dial-up Internet service. These options allow ACT! to dial phone numbers for you.

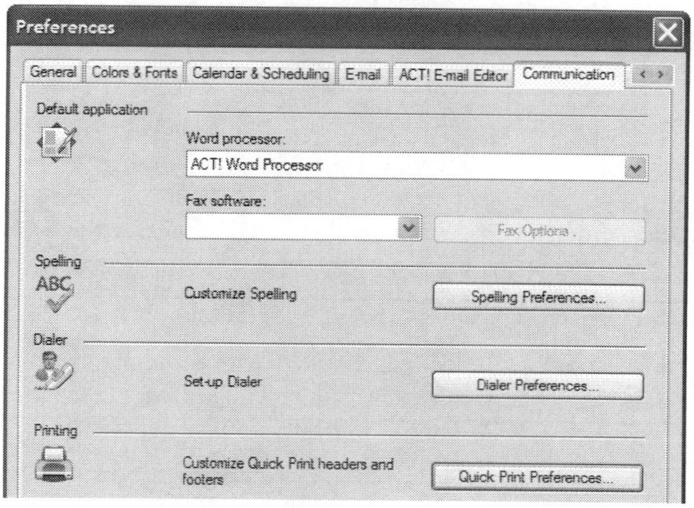

Figure 1-32 Communication tab preferences

The **QUICK PRINT PREFERENCES** button on the Communication tab opens the dialog box shown in Figure 1-33.

These options are used to select the header and footer options for printing the lists that you saw earlier in Figure 1-25.

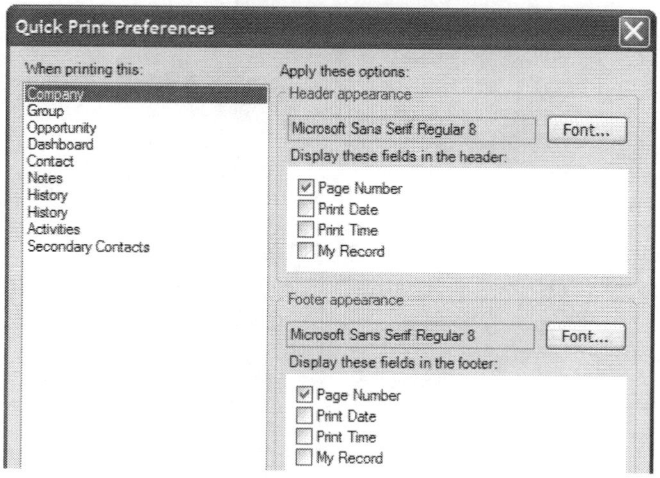

Figure 1-33 Header and Footer print options

1. If the ACT! Word Processor option is not selected, as shown earlier in Figure 1-32, select it now, then click the **SPELLING PREFERENCES** button.

The options in the **UPON SAVING, CHECK SPELLING** section shown in Figure 1-34, are used to select which tabs on the detail views will have spell checking enabled automatically.

If you have a custom dictionary from another application that you want to use in ACT!, you can select it by clicking the Browse button in the **SELECT USER DICTIONARY** section.

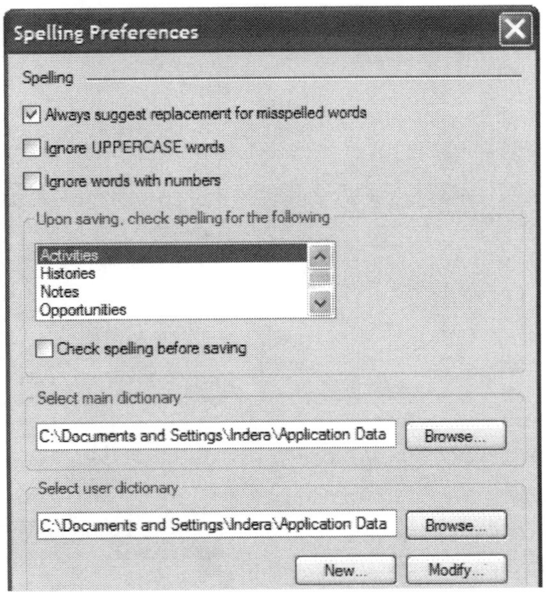

Figure 1-34 Spelling Preferences dialog box

User Dictionaries

User dictionaries are used to save words that are not in the main dictionary. This is helpful because once you save a word in this dictionary, it will not be considered a misspelled word again. If you use Microsoft Office and have created a custom dictionary, you can use it in ACT!.

You can create several user dictionaries. For example, if you are in the legal field you could create a legal dictionary and store the legal words that you need in it. If you need to add or delete words that are in the **USER** dictionary, click the **MODIFY** button.

The options on the dialog box shown in Figure 1-35 are used to add and delete the words in the user dictionary.

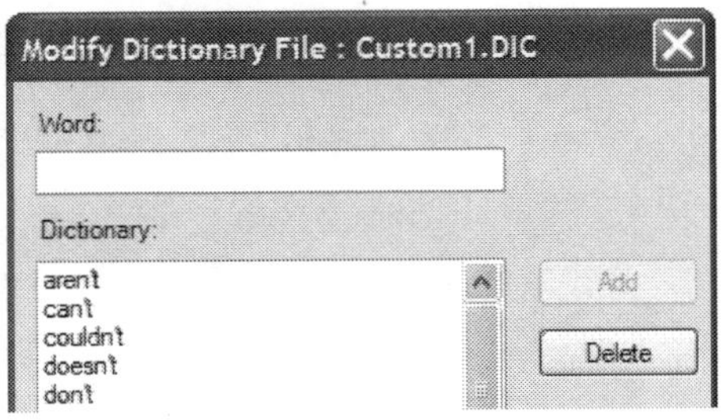

Figure 1-35 Modify Dictionary File dialog box

2. On the Spelling Preferences dialog box, click on the **ACTIVITIES** option in the list, then press and hold down the Shift key.

   Scroll to the end of the list and click on the last option. All of the options should be highlighted, as shown in Figure 1-36.

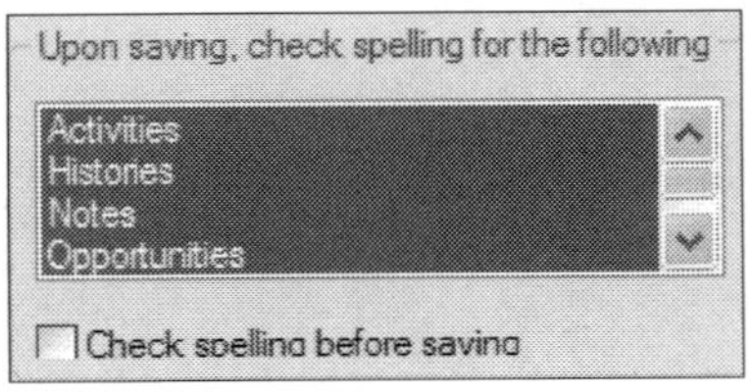

Figure 1-36 ACT! tabs selected

3. Clear the **CHECK SPELLING BEFORE SAVING** option if you do not want to have the spell checker run automatically each time you create an entry one of the tabs that you just highlighted. You can run the spell checker manually as needed.

4. Click OK, then click the Apply button on the Communication tab.

Startup Tab Preferences

The options shown in Figure 1-37 determine what will happen each time ACT! is opened and what happens when records are added to the database.

If you primarily use the same ACT! database, you can click the **STARTUP DATABASE** button and select the database that you want to have open automatically when ACT! is opened.

If you do not want the database to open with the Contact Detail view, select the view that you want from the **STARTUP VIEW** drop-down list. You can also select the Dashboard option, which is covered in Lesson 14.

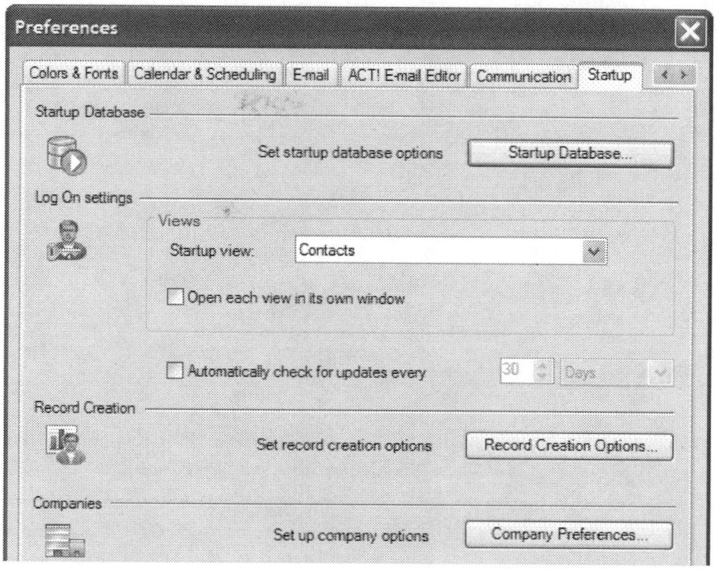

Figure 1-37 Startup tab preferences

If checked, the **AUTOMATICALLY CHECK FOR UPDATES EVERY** option is used to let ACT! know how frequently you want to check for software updates. If your database is on a server, you should not select this option because the administrator needs to update the copy of ACT! and the database that is on the server before the desktop copies of ACT! (the copy that is installed on your computer) are updated.

I disable automatic update options in all software because I prefer to create an image of my hard drive before installing updates, just in case the update doesn't want to play nice with the other software that I have installed, if you know what I mean. The other reason that I disable this option is because ACT! will open faster because it will not have to check for updates before the software opens.

The **CHECK FOR UPDATES** option should be disabled on remote databases because remote databases should only be updated after the main database has been updated. In Lesson 19 you will learn about remote databases.

The **RECORD CREATION** options are covered in detail in Lesson 12.

The **COMPANY PREFERENCES** options are covered in detail in Lesson 4.

Exercise 1.6: Select A Database To Automatically Open With ACT!

Earlier you learned that a database could be selected to open automatically when ACT! is opened. You will select the copy of the database that you just created to open automatically when you open ACT!. This will be the database that you use to complete the majority of exercises in this book.

1. Tools ⇒ Preferences ⇒ Startup tab.

2. Click the **STARTUP DATABASE** button.

3. Select the **NAMED DATABASE** option, then click the button at the end of the drop-down list field.

4. Double-click on the My_ACT2009Demo.pad file in your folder.

   You should have the options selected that are shown in Figure 1-38.

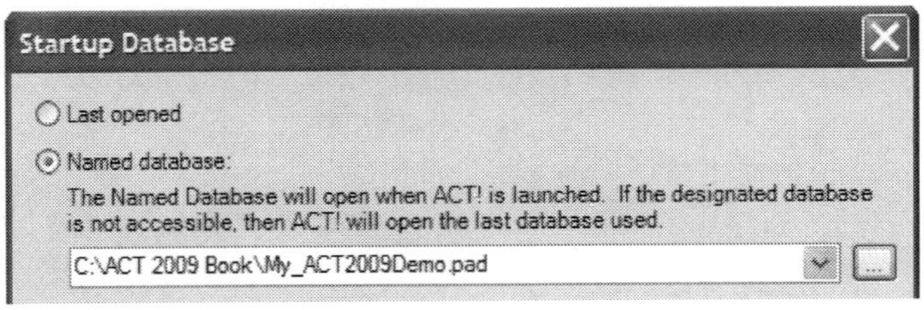

Figure 1-38 Startup Database options

5. Click Apply, then click OK. The next time that you open ACT!, this is the database that will automatically open.

6. File ⇒ Exit, to close ACT!, then reopen it.

The database will be verified. This is only done the first time that a database is opened. Look in the upper left corner of the ACT! window. You should see the name of the database in the Title bar.

If you know that you will use more than one database and have set one database as the default (the one that opens automatically), make sure that you have the one that you need open, before you start adding records. Otherwise, you may find that you have entered data in the wrong database. If you find that this is the case, you can use the Import tool that is covered in Lesson 19 to copy the records to the correct database, then delete the records from the database that they were added to by mistake.

Exercise 1.7: Viewing Layouts

ACT! comes with the two basic layout styles that are shown in Figure 1-39 for the Contact, Group and Company Detail views. The demo database has an additional layout as shown.

Layouts are the background, fields and tabs on the ACT! window. They can be modified to better meet your needs or you can create your own layout. Fields and tabs can be added, re-arranged or hidden as needed.

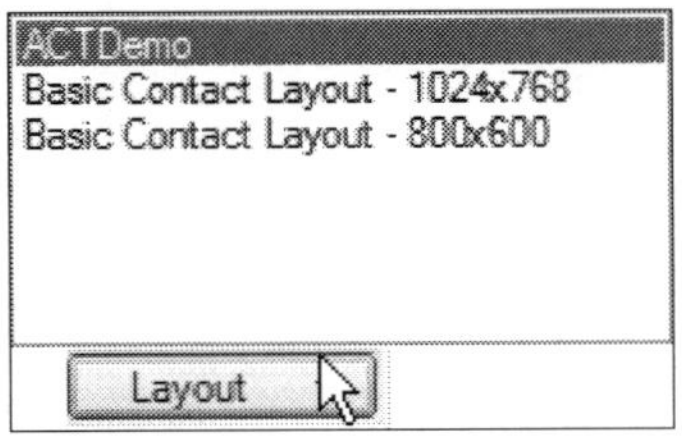

Figure 1-39 Basic layouts

1. Click the **LAYOUT** button in the lower left corner of the ACT! window and select **BASIC CONTACT LAYOUT - 800x600**, if it is not already selected.

2. File ⇒ Save, to save the changes.

It is possible that a database will require more than one layout. Different people or groups of people that are using the database may need to see different fields or may need to have the fields appear in a different order. Images and text can also be added to a layout. You can switch layouts at any time. You will learn how to modify layouts in Lesson 18.

The Views In ACT!

There are seven views in ACT! (Contacts, Groups, Companies, Calendar, Task List, Opportunity List and Dashboard) that you can view records in.

The first seven icons on the left side of the window in the Navigation bar are used to switch to a different view. The last two buttons on the Navigation bar open other applications.

The view can also be changed from the **VIEW** menu, as shown in Figure 1-40.

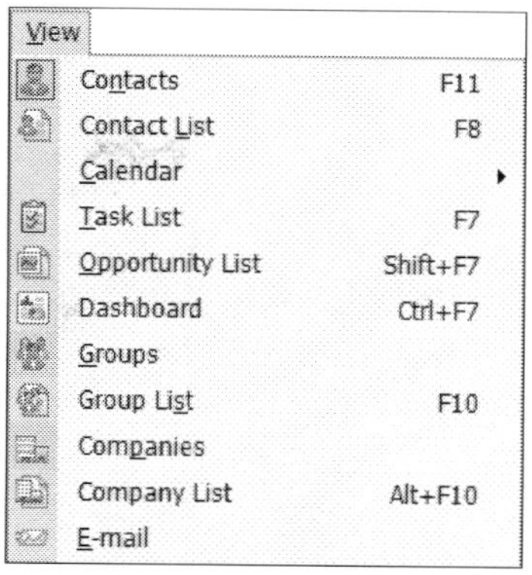

Figure 1-40 View menu options

Like other software, the items on a menu like the one shown above in Figure 1-40 that have an icon in the left column means that the option is on at least one toolbar in the software.

Table 1-4 explains the buttons on the Navigation bar. Figures 1-41 to 1-46 show each of the views.

Button	Description
Contacts	Opens the **CONTACT DETAIL** view shown earlier in Figure 1-18.
Groups	Opens the **GROUP DETAIL** view shown in Figure 1-41.
Companies	Opens the **COMPANY DETAIL** view shown in Figure 1-42.
Calendar	Opens the **CALENDAR** view shown in Figure 1-43.
Task List	Opens the **TASK LIST** view shown in Figure 1-44.
Opportunity List	Opens the **OPPORTUNITY LIST** view shown in Figure 1-45.
Dashboard	Opens the **DASHBOARD** view shown in Figure 1-46.
E-mail	Opens the e-mail software that is set as the default in ACT!.
Internet Services	Opens Internet Explorer.

Table 1-4 Navigation bar buttons explained

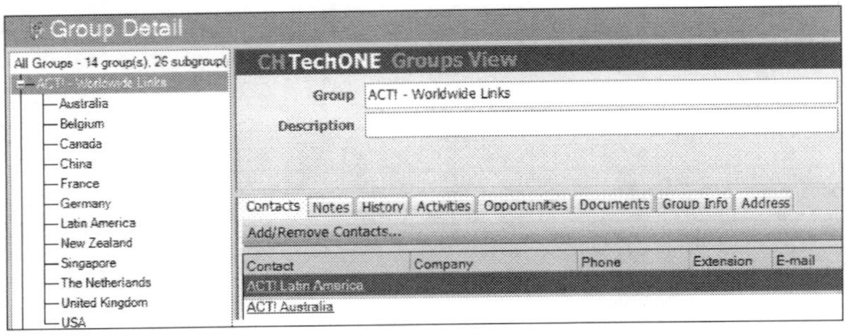

Figure 1-41 Group Detail view

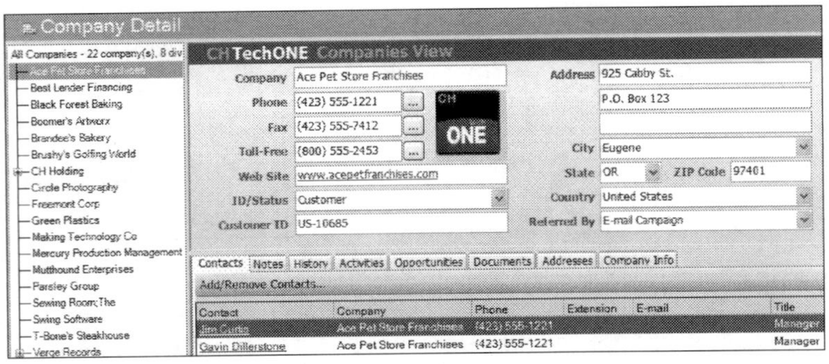

Figure 1-42 Company Detail view

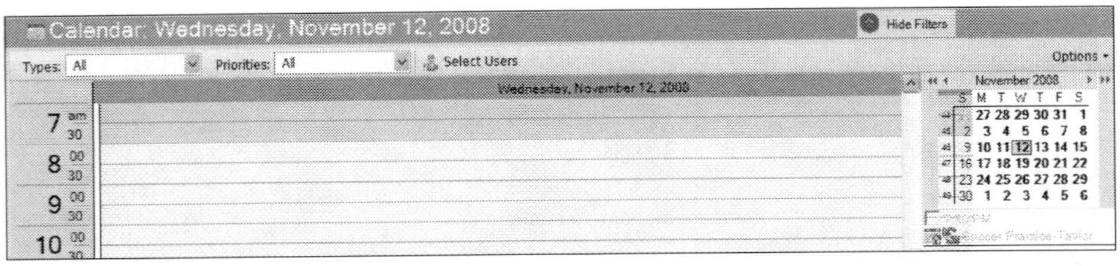

Figure 1-43 Calendar view

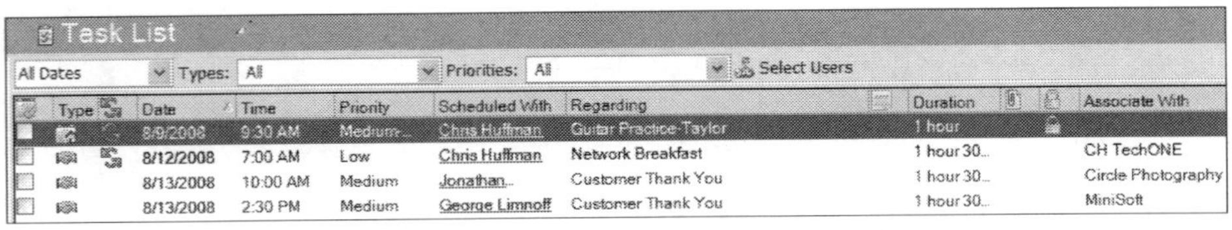

Figure 1-44 Task List view

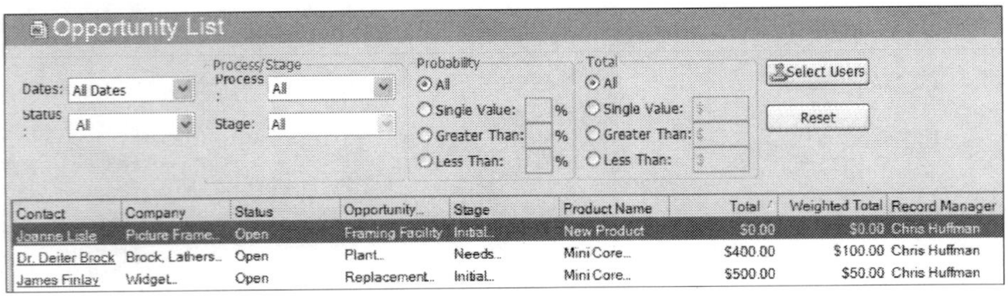

Figure 1-45 Opportunity List view

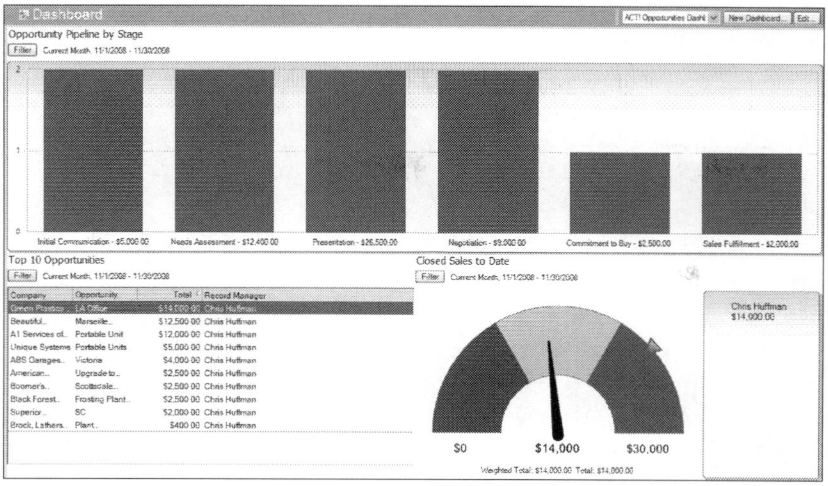

Figure 1-46 Dashboard view

Resizing The Top And Bottom Sections Of Detail Views

The **DETAIL** views have two sections which are sometimes referred to as primary and secondary sections. These sections can be resized as needed. The primary section is at the top of the view and contains basic information like the name and address for the contact, company or group. The top section of a detail view contains fields that you will probably enter a lot of information in because they are the fields that are used for most contacts when they are added to the database. The secondary section is at the bottom of the window and displays the tabs.

The information on each tab is for the contact, company or group displayed at the top of the window. As you scroll through the records, the data in both sections will change. This is known as **RELATIONAL DATA** because the data on the tabs is related to the contact, company or group displayed at the top of the window. You may need to make the bottom half (the Tabs section) longer or shorter. If this is the case, follow the steps below.

1. Place the mouse pointer on the bar illustrated in Figure 1-47.

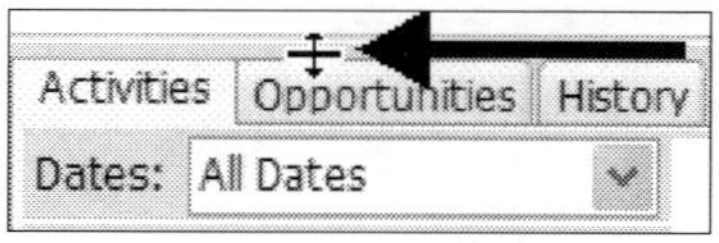

Figure 1-47 Mouse pointer in position to resize a section of the detail view

2. Press and hold down the left mouse button, then drag the bar up or down as needed.

The Detail View Tabs

As shown earlier in Figure 1-18, there are 11 tabs on the Contact Detail view: Activities, Opportunities, History, Notes, Documents, Groups/Companies, Secondary Contacts, Personal Info, Contact Access, Latest Activities and User Fields.

The fields on each of these tabs allow you to enter more information for each contact. Click on each of these tabs now to become familiar with the types of data that can be entered for a contact.

The company and group detail views have some of the same tabs as the contact view, plus tabs that the contact detail view does not have. Table 1-5 illustrates which detail view has which tabs.

Table 1-6 explains the type of information on each tab that comes with ACT!. Some tabs have been renamed in ACT! 2009. The old name is in parentheses. The lesson that the tab is covered in, is in brackets.

Tab	Contacts	Company	Group
Activities	X	X	X
Opportunities	X	X	X
History	X	X	X
Notes	X	X	X
Documents	X	X	X
Groups/Companies	X		
Secondary Contacts	X		
Personal Info	X		
Contact Access	X		
Latest Activities	X		
User Fields	X		
Billing and Shipping		X	
Company Profile		X	
Company Access		X	
Divisions		X	
Contacts		X	X
Group Address			X
Group Access			X
Subgroups			X

Table 1-5 Detail view tabs

Tab	Type Of Information
Activities	Scheduled activities. [Lesson 8] (3)
Billing and Shipping	Billing and shipping addresses for the company. (Addresses) [Lesson 4]
Company Access	Contains information about the person that created and last edited the company record. (Company Info) [Lesson 4]
Company Profile	Tracks the region, industry, revenue, SIC Code and more for each company. [Lesson 4]
Contact Access	Contains information about the person that created and last edited the contact record. (Contact Info) [Lesson 2] (4)
Contacts	List of contacts in the company or group. [Lesson 2]
Divisions	Lists the divisions that are associated to the company. [Lesson 4]
Documents	Lists files that have been attached to the record currently displayed. [Lesson 12] (3)
Group Access	Contains information about the person that created and edited the group record. (Group Info) [Lesson 5] (4)
Group Address	Address for the group. [Lesson 5]
Groups/Companies	Groups that the contact belongs to. This tab is only available in the Contact Detail view. [Lesson 4]
History	Displays completed and deleted activities, as well as, changes to other types of records. [Lesson 12] (3)
Latest Activities	ACT! automatically tracks the date that the last email, call, meeting and letter sent took place for each contact. The last date that the contact record was edited and by who is also tracked. [Lesson 2]
Notes	Notes that have been created for a contact. [Lesson 12] (3)
Opportunities	Open and closed sales. [Lesson 10] (3)
Personal Info	Home address information and alternate phone numbers for the contact. (Home Address) [Lesson 2]
Secondary Contacts	Names of people associated with the contact. [Lesson 12]
Subgroups	Shows a list of the subgroups for the group. [Lesson 5]
User Fields	You can customize all of the fields on this tab, so that you can enter any information that does not fit in any other field in the database. [Lesson 2]

Table 1-6 Information stored on tabs explained

(3) Depending on the view, the data displayed on this tab is for a contact, company, group or activity. In some instances, the data on this tab displays data from multiple detail views.

(4) Stores the Public/Private status of the contact, company or group. **PUBLIC** status means that anyone that opens the database can view the record. This is the default status. **PRIVATE** status means that only the person that created the record can view it.

CREATING AND EDITING CONTACT RECORDS

In this lesson you will learn about contact records including the following:

- ☑ Adding and deleting contact records
- ☑ Enter information on the Notes, Documents and Personal Info tabs
- ☑ Editing contact information
- ☑ Using the Date field calendar
- ☑ Attaching files on the Documents tab
- ☑ Duplicating contact information
- ☑ Using the Undo command

LESSON 2

What Is A Contact?

A contact in ACT! is any person or group of people that you need to have up to date information on, at your finger tips. When many people hear the word **CONTACT**, they immediately think of a business associate contact. It is true that many people use ACT! strictly for managing business contacts, but you can have friends, family members, prospects and vendors, as well as, business contacts in the same database. As you will see, ACT! handles much more than names and addresses.

If you are brand new to ACT!, this lesson and the next one are probably the most important ones for you to fully understand because creating, editing and looking up contacts are the tasks that you will spend most of your time doing. The key thing to remember when entering data is to be consistent. This will make finding the contacts that you need easier.

Contact Toolbar

The buttons on the toolbar shown in Figure 2-1 provide quick access to some of the most used options for contacts. Table 2-1 explains the buttons on the toolbar. The toolbar shown is for the Contact List and Contact Detail views. Each type of view (contact, company and group) has its own toolbar. For example, the Contact List and Contact Detail views have the same toolbar. You will see that not all buttons are enabled for both views.

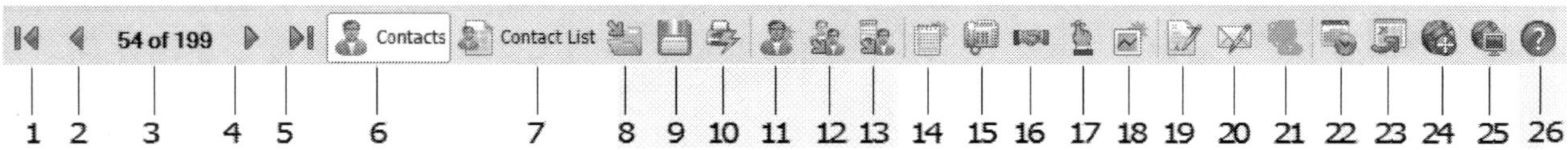

Figure 2-1 Contact toolbar

Button	Description
1	Displays the first record. (1)
2	Displays the previous record. (1)
3	The **RECORD COUNTER** displays the record number (Contacts are displayed in alphabetical order) of the contact that is currently displayed and how many records there are in total. **54 OF 199** means that you are currently viewing record 54 and that there are 199 records. (1)
4	Displays the next record. (1)
5	Displays the last record. (1)
6	Opens the Contact Detail view.
7	Opens the Contact List view.
8	Opens a database.
9	Saves the record. (2)
10	Opens the Print dialog box.
11	Creates a new contact record.
12	Duplicates the current contact record.
13	Is used to update contact fields that are linked to company fields. (2)
14	Creates a note. (3)
15	Schedules a telephone call activity. (3)
16	Schedules a meeting activity. (3)
17	Schedules a To-Do activity. (3)
18	Create a new opportunity. (3)
19	Opens the word processor.
20	Compose and send an email.
21	Call the contact on the phone through the Dialer application.
22	Copies calendar information between the ACT! and Outlook calendars.
23	Export (send) the data to an Excel spreadsheet. This option is only available from the Contact List view.

Table 2-1 Contact toolbar buttons explained

Button	Description
24	Opens Internet Explorer to Map Quest's web site with the contacts address information filled in. This is helpful if you need directions or need to view a map.
25	Checks for software updates.
26	Opens the Help system.

Table 2-1 Contact toolbar buttons explained (Continued)

(1) This option is either for the database or current lookup, which is a subset of records in the database. You will learn about lookups in Lesson 3.
(2) This option is only available from the Contact Detail view.
(3) This option is for the current contact on the Detail view. It can be used with multiple contacts on the list view, if the contacts are selected or tagged.

If you cannot remember the name of a button on the toolbar, hold the mouse pointer over the button. You will see the name of the button, as illustrated in Figure 2-2. This is known as a **TOOL TIP**.

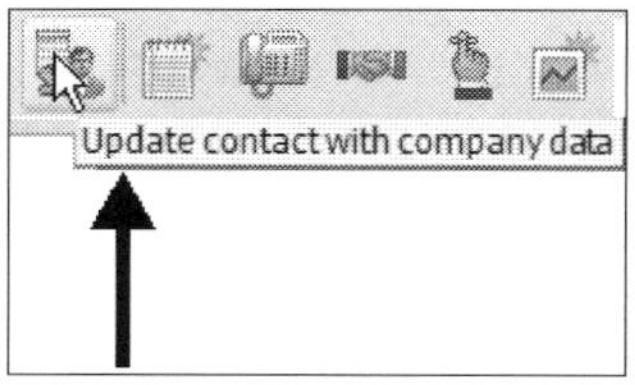

Figure 2-2 Tool tip illustrated

Difference Between The Enter And Tab Keys

You can use both of these keys to move from field to field when adding or editing data. The **TAB** key is used to move from field to field on the layout. The Tab key stops at every field by default. The **ENTER** key is used to move from field to field also. The difference is that the Enter key does not stop at every field. It stops at the most used fields. The order that these keys move in can be changed. You will learn how to modify the order that these keys move in, in Lesson 18.

In Lesson 1 you made a copy of the demo database to use with this book. A copy of the database does not make your My Record the default My Record. This means that when you open the My_ACT2009Demo database, the default My Record will be the creator of the original database, which is Chris Huffman. Do not change the owner to yourself. The exercises in this book are based on Chris Huffman being the default My Record owner.

Exercise 2.1: Creating A New Contact Record

You do not have to enter information in all of the fields, but you should enter enough information to make the contact record meaningful. You will learn how to enter data on several of the tabs on the Contact Detail view in this exercise.

The **ACTIVITIES TAB** is covered in Lesson 8. The **OPPORTUNITIES TAB** is covered in Lesson 10.

1. Click the **NEW CONTACT** button on the toolbar. You will see a blank record. Notice that the record counter has been incremented by one. There should now be 200 records in the database.

You can also press the **INSERT** key to add a new contact or select Contacts ⇒ New Contact.

2. Type `Sarah Baker` in the Contact field, then press Enter.

Notice that the contacts first name has automatically been filled in the Salutation field. That is because you selected the option on the Preferences dialog box, to automatically fill in the salutation field with the contacts first name.

3. Type `Capri Book Company` in the Company field.

   The button at the end of the Contact field on the Contact Detail view opens the dialog box shown in Figure 2-3. This button is called an **ELLIPSIS** button in ACT!. In other software, this is called the Browse button, which provides the same functionality.

   By default, ACT! automatically splits a contact name into three fields. Initially, the options on this dialog box display what ACT! thinks the first, middle and last name are, based on the preferences selected on the Contact Name dialog box.

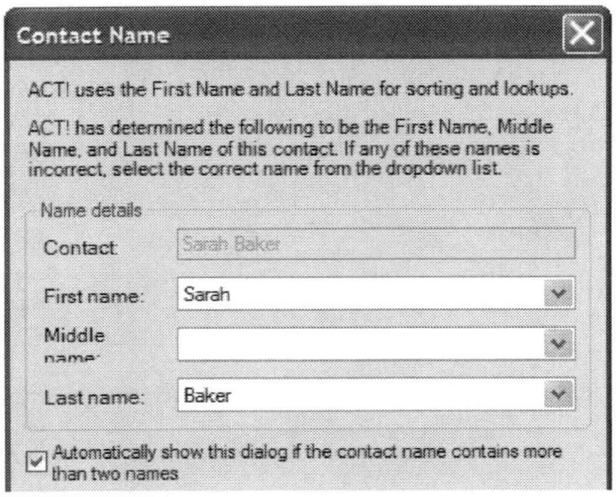

Figure 2-3 Contact Name dialog box

If a name has not been separated correctly, open the drop-down list for the name that is not correct and select the correct one. This may happen when someone's first or last name is two names like Johnnie Mae Westbrook. In this example, the contacts first name is Johnnie Mae. By default, ACT! will interpret it as shown in Figure 2-4. These separation options are what enables contacts to be sorted or used in a lookup by first or last name, even though the first and last name are in the same field.

By default, ACT! has been set up to not use Mr., Mrs., Ms., Esq., MD, PhD and Dr. as part of the first, middle or last name. I entered my name with "Dr" in front of it, then opened the dialog box and saw that ACT! separated my name correctly, as shown in Figure 2-5. You can change these options as needed. You will learn how to change them in Lesson 13.

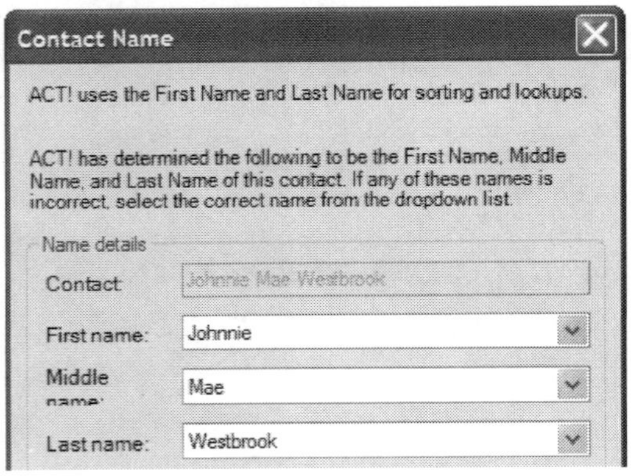

Figure 2-4 Contact with two first names

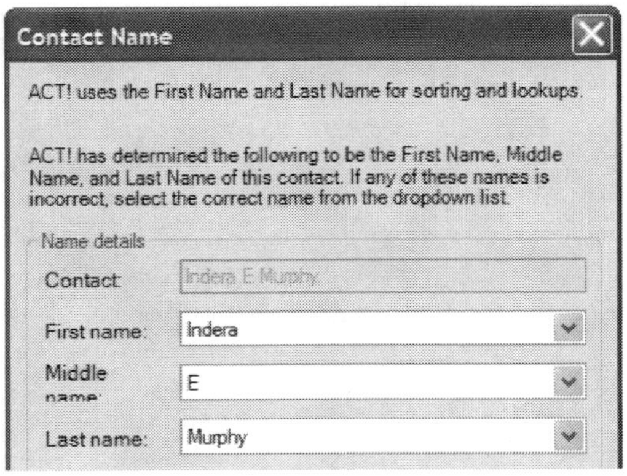

Figure 2-5 Contact name separated correctly

4. Open the Title field drop-down list.

   Scroll down the list and select the Sales Manager title, as illustrated in Figure 2-6.

   The **EDIT LIST VALUES** option is used to add, edit or delete the values in the drop-down list.

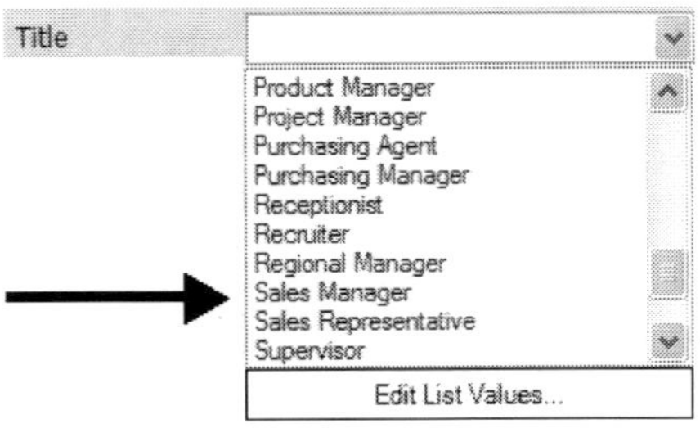

Figure 2-6 Title drop-down list values

5. Type `pur` in the Department field, then press Enter. Notice that the "Purchasing" department has been filled in automatically.

6. Type `765 417 5330` in the Phone field. (Do not put spaces between the numbers. I typed it that way to make it easier for you to read.) Notice that the phone number was automatically formatted.

Phone Number Formatting

Like the salutation field, the phone number fields also have default formatting. The **ELLIPSIS** button at the end of the Phone and Mobile fields will open the dialog box shown in Figure 2-7. The options shown are used to change how the phone number will be formatted. The default phone number format is for the US. If you enter a phone number for a different country and do not know the correct format for the country, open the Country field drop-down list shown in Figure 2-7 and select the country. After you click OK on the Enter Phone Number dialog box, the phone number will be formatted for the country that you selected.

The **EDIT FORMATS** button on the Enter Phone Number dialog box opens the dialog box shown in Figure 2-8. You can create your own phone number format or select one of the other formats shown in Figure 2-8 to be the new default format.

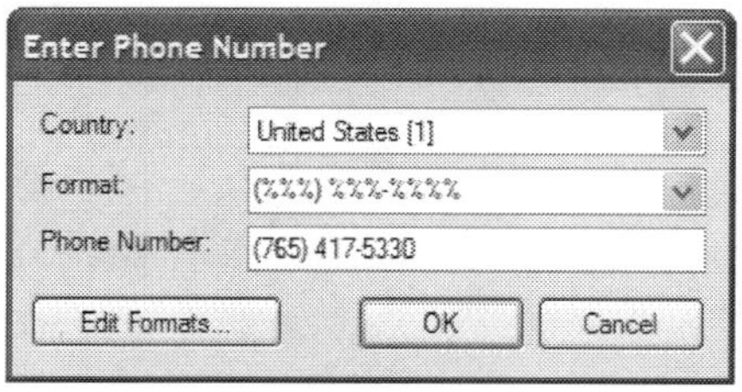

Figure 2-7 Enter Phone Number dialog box

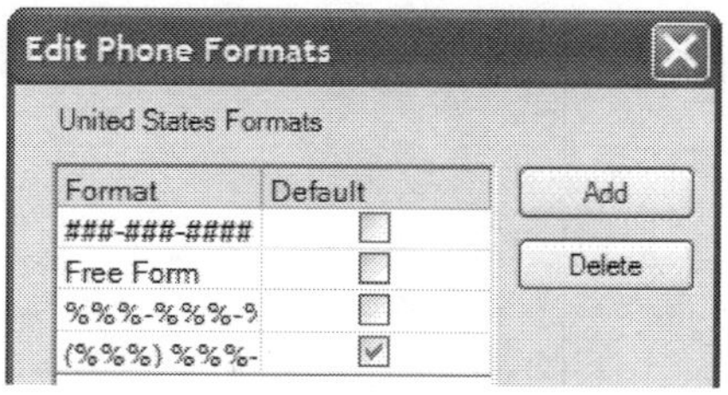

Figure 2-8 Edit Phone Formats dialog box

Using Country Codes

The **COUNTRY CODE** is the prefix that you have to enter before you dial the area code. The Country Code for the United States is 1, as shown above in Figure 2-7 in brackets. Being able to look up the country code in the Country drop-down list is helpful if you have contacts in other countries and do not know the country code.

7. Enter the information in Table 2-2 in the appropriate fields on the Contact Detail view.
   The top portion of your contact record should look like the one shown in Figure 2-9.
   This is the contact record that you will use to enter data on various tabs in the remainder of this exercise.

Field	Type This
Address 1	123 Main St
City	Los Angeles
State	CA
Zip	90277
Country	USA
ID/Status	Supplier

Table 2-2 Contact information

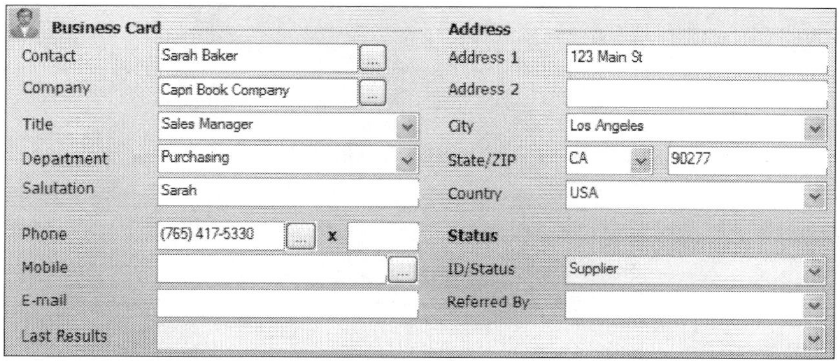

Figure 2-9 Information for a new contact

As shown above in Figure 2-9, there are two address fields. ACT! actually has three address fields. This view only displays two of them. All three fields are for one address, not three different addresses. Often, the physical street address goes in the Address 1 field and the other two address fields are used to enter the floor, suite or room number, for example.

Some company addresses also include a building name. These are examples of the type of address information that could be entered in the second and third address fields. If a contact has more than one company address, like a street address and a PO Box, you could use fields on the User Fields tab as long as the layout for that tab is modified to reflect what the fields are being used for.

The Notes Tab

The data on this tab is a log of each note that you or another user of the database created about the contact, company or group. The entries on this tab are created automatically each time a note is created. An unlimited number of notes can be created for each contact, company or group. Table 2-3 explains the buttons on the Insert Note dialog box toolbar shown in Figure 2-10.

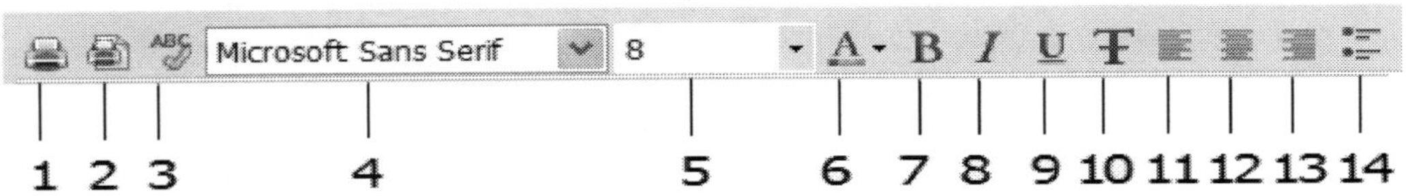

Figure 2-10 Insert Note dialog box toolbar

Button	Description
1	Prints the note.
2	Previews the note to show how it will look when it is printed.
3	Spell checks the note.
4	Changes the font for the body of the note.
5	Changes the font size for the body of the note.
6	Changes the font color for the body of the note.
7	Makes the selected text in the note bold.
8	Makes the selected text in the note italic.
9	Underlines the selected in the note text.
10	Draws a line through the selected text. This is usually done to indicate text that you want to delete.
11	Left aligns the text in the body of the note. This is the default alignment for text.
12	Centers the text in the body of the note.
13	Right aligns the text in the body of the note.
14	Creates a bulleted list in the body of the note.

Table 2-3 Insert Note dialog box toolbar buttons explained

1. On the **NOTES** tab, click the **INSERT NEW NOTE** button illustrated in Figure 2-11. Notice that the Date and Time fields are filled in automatically on the Insert Note dialog box. If you had created a My Record in this database, your name would be in the **RECORD MANAGER** field.

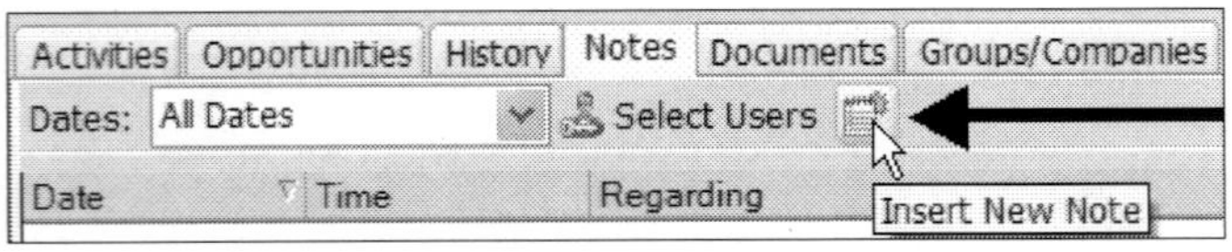

Figure 2-11 Insert New Note button illustrated

2. In the **REGARDING** field at the bottom of the dialog box type `This is my first note. It has an attachment and is associated to 3 contacts at Liberty.`

The **CONTACT** button on the Insert Note dialog box opens the dialog box shown in Figure 2-12.

If you need to attach the same note to other contacts, select the other contacts on this dialog box.

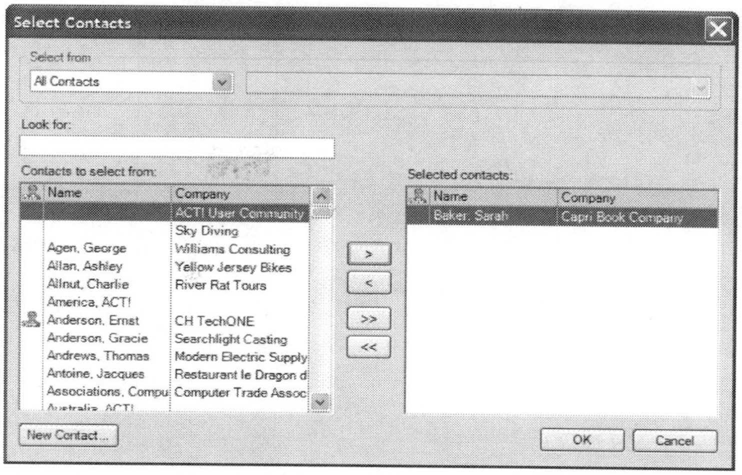

Figure 2-12 Select Contacts dialog box

> **Sorting Contact Records On The Select Contacts Dialog Box**
>
> If you click on the Name or Company columns in the **CONTACTS TO SELECT FROM** list or the **SELECTED CONTACTS** list, you can sort the contacts in ascending or descending order.

New Contact Dialog Box

Clicking the **NEW CONTACT** button shown above in Figure 2-12, opens the dialog box shown in Figure 2-13. This dialog box is used to create a new contact record.

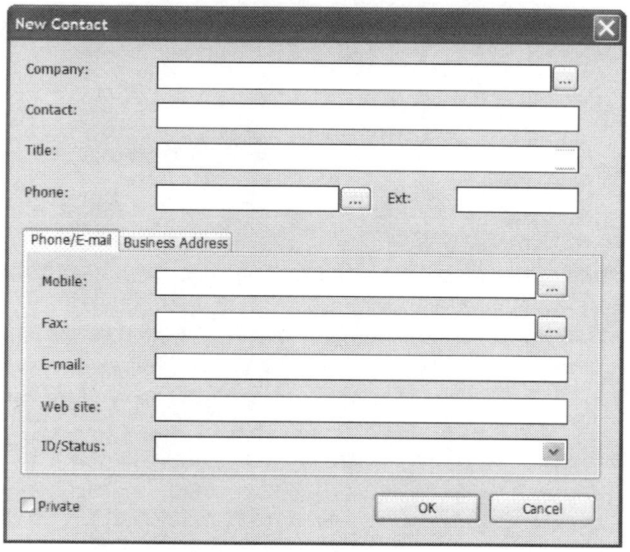

Figure 2-13 New Contact dialog box

Select Group/Company Dialog Box

The ellipsis button at the end of the **GROUP/COMPANY** field on the Insert Note dialog box will open the dialog box shown in Figure 2-14.

The options on this dialog box are used to share the note with everyone in a group or company.

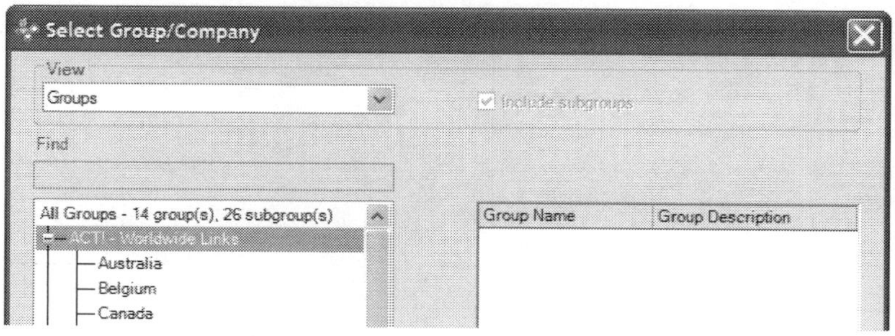

Figure 2-14 Select Group/Company dialog box

By default when you click the button at the end of the Group/Company field, you will see a message about showing public notes. You will learn about companies in Lesson 4 and groups in Lesson 5.

3. Click the Contact button on the Insert Note dialog box.

4. Select the three contacts at Liberty Savings & Loan, as shown in Figure 2-15, by clicking on the first contact at the company, then press and hold down the Shift key and click on the last contact at Liberty.

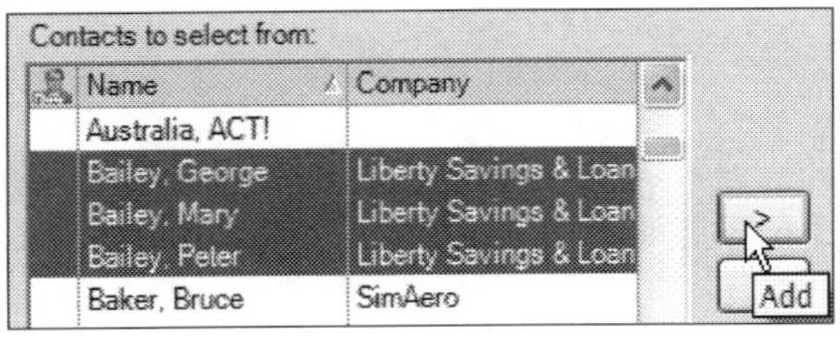

Figure 2-15 Contacts selected to add the note to

5. Click the **ADD** button shown above in Figure 2-15.

   There should be four names in the **SELECTED CONTACTS** list on the Select Contacts dialog box, as shown in Figure 2-16.

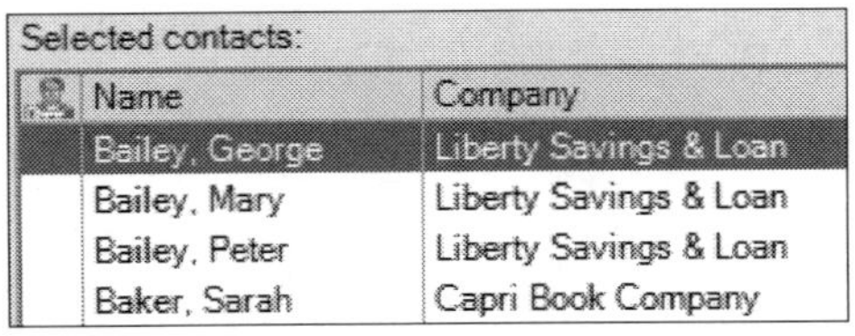

Figure 2-16 Contacts that will have the note attached

6. Click OK to close the dialog box.

How To Attach A File To A Contact Record

The **ATTACH** button on the Insert Note dialog box provides two ways to attach a file to a note, as shown in Figure 2-17.

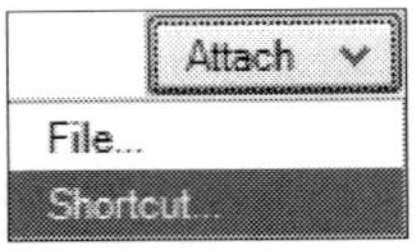

Figure 2-17 Attach button options

① Selecting the **FILE** option stores a copy of the file with the note. Changes can be made to the copy of the file that is attached to the record. These changes will not be made in the original file. The opposite is also true. Changes made to the original file will not be available in the copy of the document that is attached to a record in an ACT! database. Select this option if you know for sure that you will not need to see any changes that may be made to the original document. This option also increases the size of the database.

② The **SHORTCUT** option creates a link to a file. The link is not dynamic, which means that if the file is moved to another folder, renamed or deleted, the shortcut will no longer work.

If the attached file needs to be opened by other users of the database and the shortcut attachment option is selected, the file needs to be in a location (a folder) that other users have access to. I don't know how the computers in your office are networked, but I doubt that the person down the hall from you has access to the hard drive on your computer. If you find out that they do, you need to call your IT department immediately and have them change the status of your hard drive to not be shared <smile>.

1. Click the **ATTACH** button on the Insert Note dialog box, then select the File option.

2. Double-click on the **L2 ATTACH** file in your folder. The Insert Note dialog box should look like the one shown in Figure 2-18. You will have a different date and time.

   Checking the **PRIVATE** option will prevent other people that use the database from viewing the note.

   You will be the only person that can see the note.

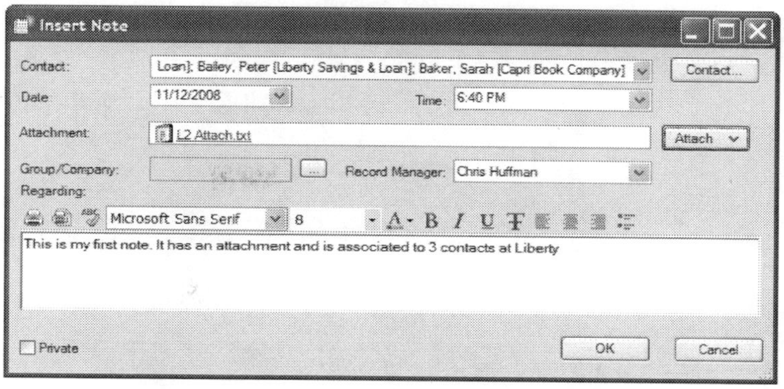

Figure 2-18 Insert Note dialog box

3. Click OK to close the Insert Note dialog box.

4. Click OK on the **SPELL CHECK STATUS** dialog box if you enabled the automatic spell checker. If you wanted to spell check the note manually, click the **SPELL CHECK** button on the Insert Note dialog box toolbar. The entry on the Notes tab should look like the one shown in Figure 2-19.

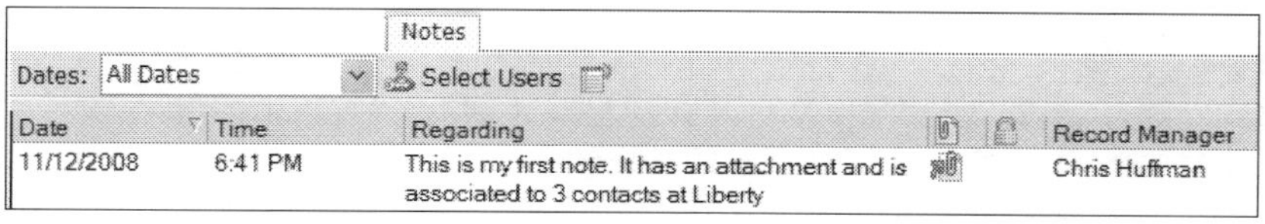

Figure 2-19 Information added to the Notes tab

A file that is attached to a note does not appear on the Documents tab.

Tips For Viewing And Deleting Attachments On The Notes Tab

① Notes are displayed with the most recent one at the top of the list.
② To view an attachment, double-click on the note that has the attachment, then click on the **ATTACHMENT** link on the Edit Note a dialog box.
③ To delete an attachment from a note, double-click on the note. Click the Attach button, then select **FILE**. You will see the message shown in Figure 2-20. Click Yes and the attachment will be deleted.

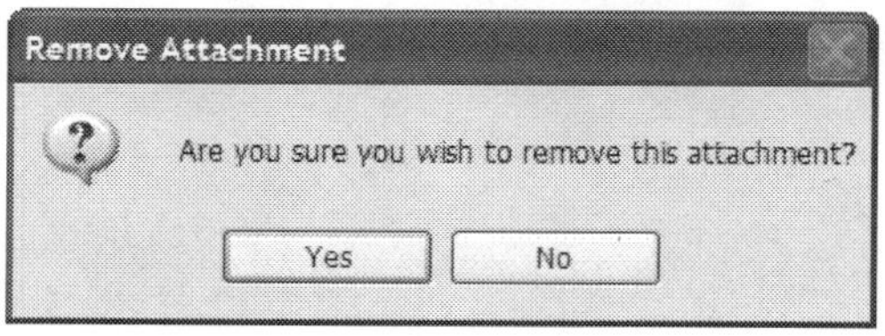

Figure 2-20 Remove Attachment message

Attaching Files On The Documents Tab

Earlier you attached a document to a note. The Documents tab displays the documents that are associated with the current contact. The documents on this tab cannot be linked to another contact from this tab. There is an option on the Documents tab that is also used to attach a document to the current contact. When you attach a document to a contact on this tab, a copy of the document is placed in the databases Attachments folder. You can edit the documents, as well as, view, email and print them.

1. On the **DOCUMENTS** tab, click the **ADD DOCUMENT** button, then select the File option.

2. Double-click on the **L2 DOCUMENTS TAB** file in your folder. You will see a reference to the document, as shown in Figure 2-21.

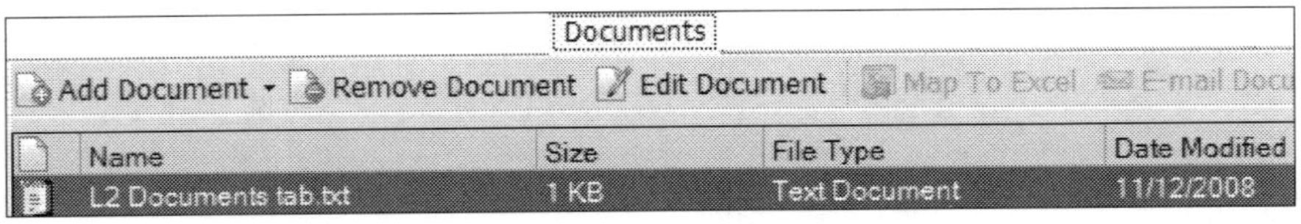

Figure 2-21 File added to the Documents tab

> **Tips For Viewing And Deleting Attachments On The Documents Tab**
>
> ① To view an attachment on the Documents tab, double-click on the attachment.
> ② To delete an attachment from the Documents tab, right-click on it and select **REMOVE DOCUMENT**.

> When you attach a file in ACT!, a copy of the file is placed in the Attachments folder of the database. The original copy of the file is still where is was before you attached it. If you make changes to the original file (the one outside of ACT!), you will not see the changes when you open the attachment in ACT!. In Lesson 12 you will learn how to edit attached documents. You have the three options discussed below to manage attachments:
>
> ① You can reattach the original file to the note if the original file was changed and you need the changes attached to the note.
> ② You can copy the original file that you changed, to the Attachments folder, as long as the original file still has the same file name.
> ③ You can make the changes to the copy in the Attachments folder.

Entering Information On The Personal Info Tab

> In ACT! 2008 and earlier, this was called the **HOME ADDRESS** tab.

In addition to the fields for the contacts home address, the following fields are also available on this tab:

① The **PERSONAL E-MAIL** field should not be used for the business e-mail address, especially if you plan to use the Mail Merge wizard to create an email mail merge. The wizard does not use this field.
② The **MESSENGER ID** field is used to store the contacts Instant Messenger ID or screen name.

> **Editing Web Site And E-mail Fields**
>
> These fields can be edited differently then other fields. You can delete the contents of the field and re-type it or you can right-click in the field and select **EDIT WEB SITE**, as shown in Figure 2-22 or **EDIT E-MAIL**. If selected, these options highlight the information in the field so that you do not have to delete it before you start typing in the field.

Figure 2-22 Edit Web Site field shortcut menu

1. On the **PERSONAL INFO** tab, type `1899 Payton Place Village Drive` in the Address 1 field.

2. Type `781 766 1308` in the Home Phone field.

3. Add the information in Table 2-4 to the appropriate fields.

Field	Type This
City	Sacramento
State	CA
Zip	99990

Table 2-4 Home Address information

Using The Date Field Calendar

Date fields, like the Birthday field, will have a calendar like the one shown in Figure 2-23. You can use the calendar to select the date or you can type the date in the field.

Find the month and year in the calendar, then click on the day that you need by using the options that are explained below.

The **TODAY** button will add the current date to the field.

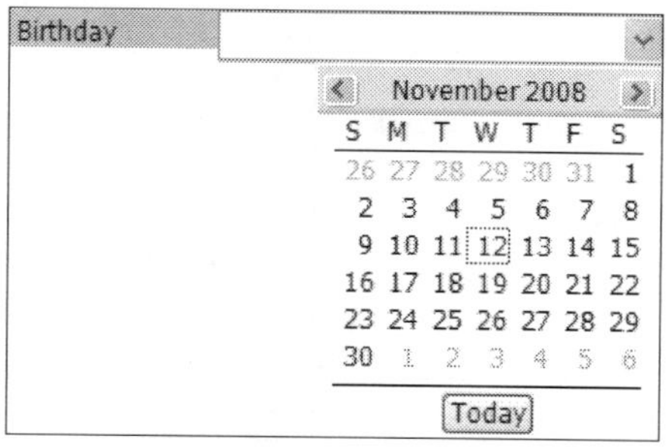

Figure 2-23 Date Field Calendar

Clicking the **LEFT ARROW** button at the top of the calendar will display previous months. Clicking the **RIGHT ARROW** button will display future months.

What I like about date fields is that you do not have to type a four digit year or type a zero as the first digit of a month or day. You can type 6/2/09 and ACT! will convert it to the date shown in Figure 2-24.

Figure 2-24 Date field converted

The **BIRTHDAY** field does not require you to enter the year the contact was born. Entering the day and month is sufficient. The current year will be filled in automatically if you do not enter it. In Lesson 3 you will learn about this and other **ANNUAL EVENT** fields and how to use them as a lookup field.

4. Click on the arrow at the end of the Birthday field, then select your next birthday on the calendar.

   The information on the Personal Info tab should look similar to the information shown in Figure 2-25.

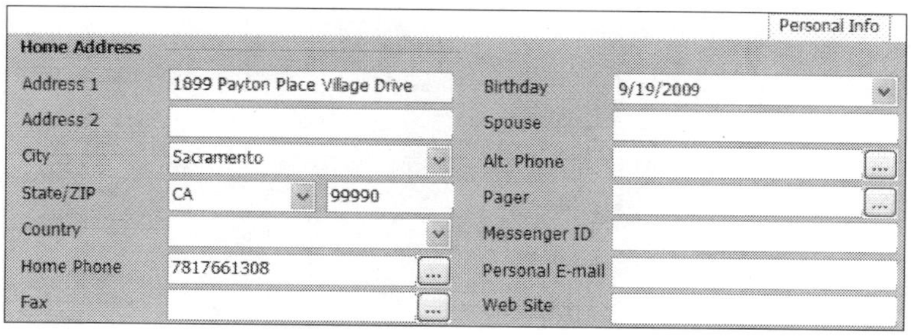

Figure 2-25 Personal Info tab fields

Contact Access Tab

> In ACT! 2008 and earlier, this was called the **CONTACT INFO** tab.

The fields shown in Figure 2-26 are filled in and updated by ACT! automatically. The values cannot be changed.

The **RECORD MANAGER** field lists the current owner of the contact record.

Figure 2-26 Contact Access tab fields

The **CREATE DATE** field stores the date that the record was created.

The **RECORD CREATOR** field stores the name of the user that created the contact record.

The **ACCESS LEVEL** options are used to make the contact record **PUBLIC** (anyone with rights to the database can view it) or **PRIVATE** (only the Record Manager can view it).

> I do not know why some of the fields have drop-down lists because these fields are updated automatically when a change in the status in any of the categories has been updated.

Latest Activities Tab

The fields shown in Figure 2-27 store the last time that a user of the database was in touch with the contact.

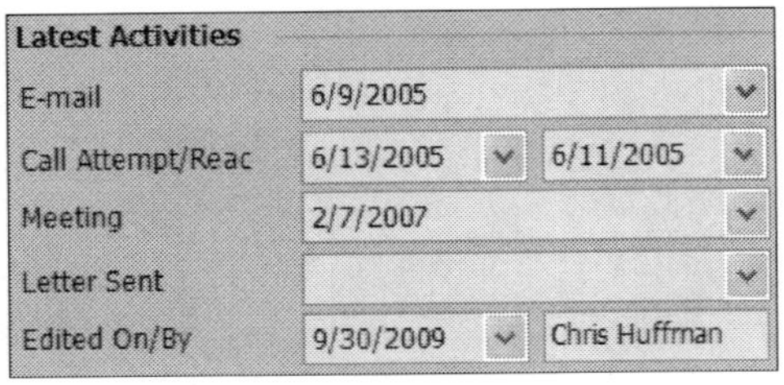

Figure 2-27 Latest Activities tab fields

User Fields Tab

The fields on the User Fields tab shown in Figure 2-28 are free form, which allows you to enter data that does not fit into any of the fields that currently exist in the database. Later in the book you will learn how to change the labels of these fields to something meaningful for the data that you enter on this tab.

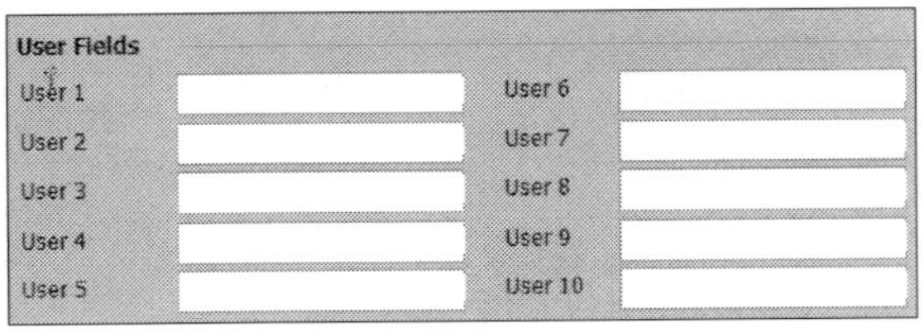

Figure 2-28 User Fields tab fields

While the fields on the User Fields tab seem like a good idea to use, they can be dangerous if more than one person is using the database. That is because by default, any user that has rights to modify the layout, add, edit or delete information, can do just that.

For example, one user may decide to use the User 2 field to store an alternate email address for the contact. Another user may use the User 2 field to store the date that they mailed the contact a sample product. If this happens, one of these types of data will have to be moved to a different field. This may have to be done manually, record by record, which is probably not something that you want to do.

Saving Data

If any of the fields on the view that you are using have the **GENERATE HISTORY** option enabled, a history record will be created and will appear on the History tab when the record is saved. You will learn about the History tab in Lesson 12. There are two ways to save the data that you enter, as discussed below.

① Move to another record.
② Click the Save button on the toolbar.

Exercise 2.2: Duplicating Contact Information

In Exercise 2.1 you created a new contact record for a company that was not already in the database. In this exercise you will create a new contact record based on information from an existing contact record. This is known as duplicating a contact. This will save you time because you do not have to retype the company information. Duplicating a contact record that has the company information that you need, duplicates data in some of the fields in the top half of the Contact Detail view. There are two ways that you can duplicate records, as discussed below:

① You can duplicate the primary fields, which are the company, phone, fax, address, city, state, zip code, country and web site fields. These are the primary fields that ACT! sets up as the default. You can make other fields primary fields as needed.
② All of the fields. If this option is selected, the only fields not duplicated are the contact name and e-mail address fields.

> Opportunity fields cannot be used as primary contact fields.

Creating A New Contact Based On The Primary Fields

1. Display record 62. The contact name is Jonathan Jenkins.

2. Click the **DUPLICATE CONTACT** button on the toolbar.

   You should see the dialog box shown in Figure 2-29.

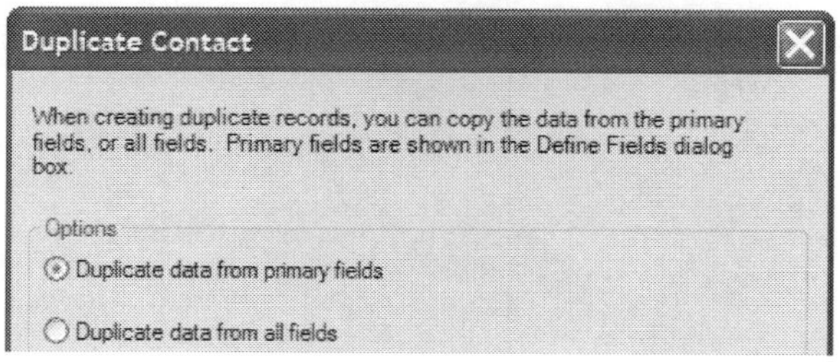

Figure 2-29 Duplicate Contact dialog box

3. Select the option **DUPLICATE DATA FROM PRIMARY FIELDS**, if it is not already selected, then click OK. You should see a new record with the primary fields filled in.

> **Other Ways To Open The Duplicate Contact Dialog Box**
>
> ① Right-click on a blank space on the Contact Detail view and select **DUPLICATE CONTACT**.
> ② Contacts ⇒ Duplicate Contact.

4. Add the information in Table 2-5 to the new contact record. The top half of the contact record should look like the one shown in Figure 2-30. Keep the record visible to complete the next exercise.

Field	Type This
Contact	Dan Day
Title	Analyst
Department	Engineering

Table 2-5 Duplicate contact information

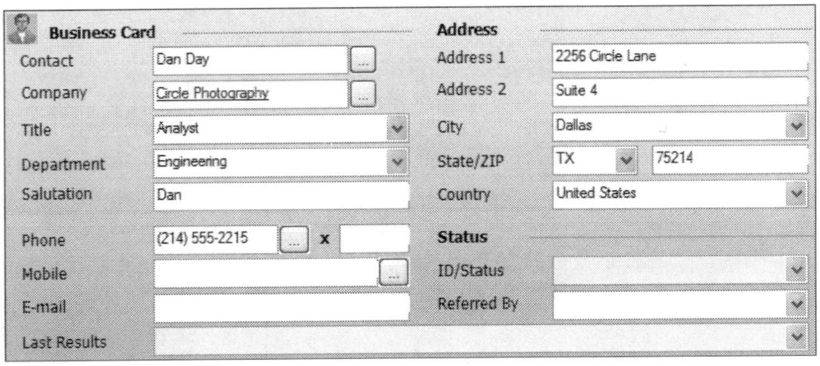

Figure 2-30 Contact information

Exercise 2.3: Using The Undo Command

This command can be useful when you need to reverse your last entry in a field. The command will only work if the cursor has not been moved out of the field that you need to edit. The record for Dan Day should still be on the screen.

1. Change the Zip Code to `10040`. Do not press the Enter or Tab key.

2. Edit ⇒ Undo. The Zip Code 75214 should have been restored.

3. Change the Zip Code to `10053`, then press Enter.

4. Open the Edit menu.

   Notice that the **UNDO** option is not available, as illustrated in Figure 2-31.

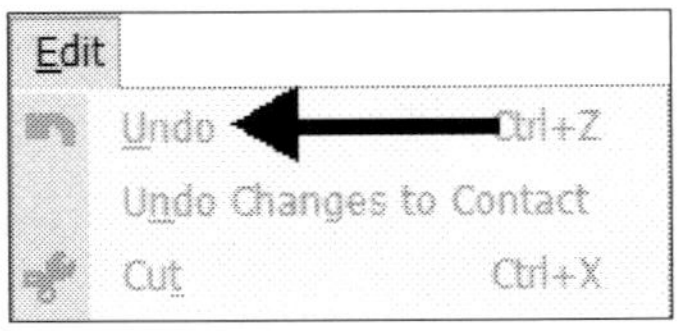

Figure 2-31 Edit menu Undo option

The two reasons that this option is not available is because after another record is displayed or another option is selected, the record is automatically saved.

5. Press the **ESC** key to close the menu.

> The **UNDO CHANGES TO CONTACT** option shown above in Figure 2-31 will delete the record created by the Duplicate Contact command.

FINDING CONTACTS IN THE DATABASE

In this lesson you will learn how to use the following search techniques:

- ☑ Lookup command
- ☑ Keyword Search lookups
- ☑ Multiple field lookups
- ☑ Narrow lookup option
- ☑ Add to lookup option
- ☑ Annual Events lookup

You will also learn the following:

- ☑ How to modify more than one record at the same time
- ☑ How to sort records
- ☑ How to delete records

LESSON 3

The Lookup Command

Having a database with hundreds or thousands of contacts is great. Being able to find the contacts that you need to access quickly, is a core reason of putting contact information into a database. ACT! comes with several lookup options to find contacts. Depending on the contacts that you need to find, one lookup option is probably a better solution then the other lookup options. Many of the lookup options are covered in this lesson. Some are specifically for contacts and others can be used to look up other types of records.

The Lookup command is used to find a record or records based on criteria that you select. Other software packages use the term **QUERY** when discussing finding specific records. You can find all contacts in one state or all contacts that have the same title. You can use the Lookup command to find contacts by Company, First Name, Last Name, Phone Number, City, State, Zip Code or ID/Status. Later you will learn how to find contacts using other fields. The biggest limitation to lookups is that the criteria cannot be saved. After you complete the lookup exercises, you will better understand why it is so important to enter data correctly and to enter as much data as possible.

Lookup Contacts Dialog Box Options

This dialog box provides several options to help you find the records that you need. The options are explained below.

The options shown in Figure 3-1 are used to select how to find the records. These options are used to include or exclude records.

The options shown in Figure 3-2 are used to select the type of records to search, to find the contacts that you are looking for.

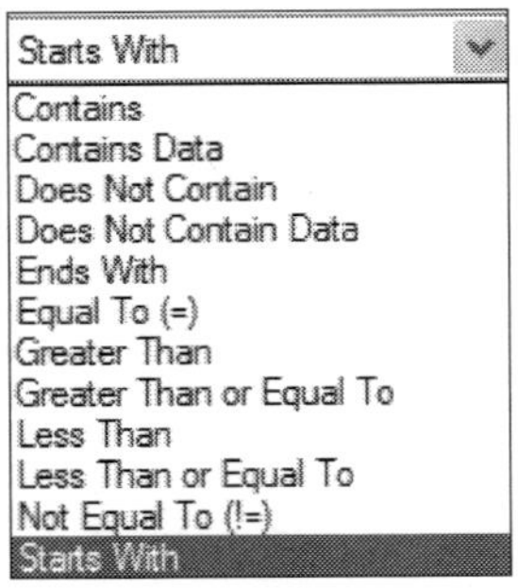

Figure 3-1 Search criteria options

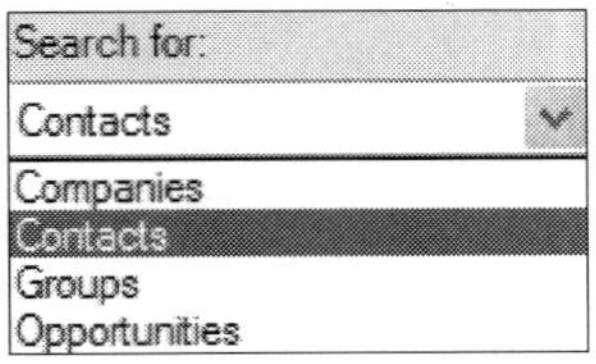

Figure 3-2 Record type search options

Current Lookup Options

The options shown in Figure 3-3 are used to determine what type of lookup you want to create. The options are explained in Table 3-1.

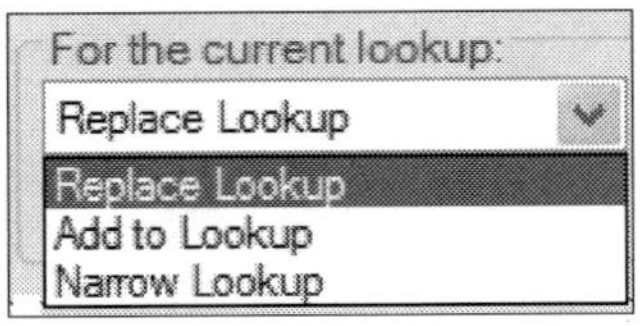

Figure 3-3 Lookup options

Option	Description
Replace Lookup	This is the default option. It creates a new lookup.
Add to Lookup	This option will add the contacts from the lookup that you are creating now, to the previous lookup that you created.
Narrow Lookup	This option searches the records from the previous lookup to exclude (remove) records from it, based on the criteria that you select in the current lookup.

Table 3-1 For the current lookup drop-down list field options explained

Exercise 3.1: Using The Lookup Command

1. Lookup ⇒ State.

2. Open the drop-down list on the right and select NY or type `NY` in the field.

3. Click on the words **SHOW MORE OPTIONS** on the dialog box. You should have the options shown in Figure 3-4.

   Click OK.

   You should see that record 2 of 20 is displayed.

   Notice the field in Figure 3-4 with the tool tip. I will refer to that field as the Search field.

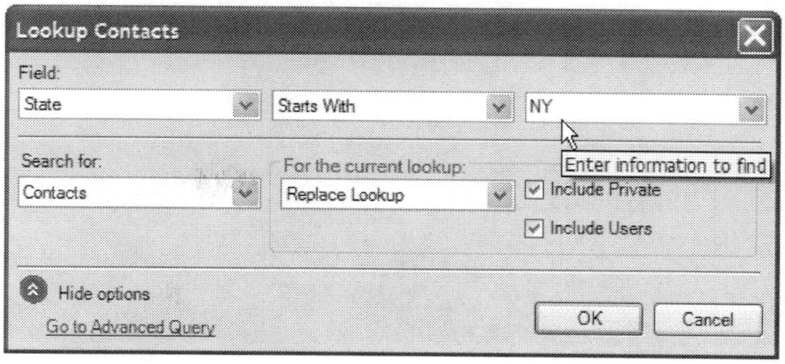

Figure 3-4 Lookup Contacts dialog box

If checked, the **INCLUDE PRIVATE** option is used to search your private records.
If checked, the **INCLUDE USERS** option is used to retrieve other database users "My Records", if they meet the search criteria.

The result of a lookup will only display records that match the criteria that you select. Notice that the view changed to the Contact List view. If you click the Contacts button on the toolbar, you will be able to see more information for each of the contacts that were retrieved by the lookup.

Notice that the information on the Status bar in the lower left corner of the window displays **LOOKUP: STATE**. This lets you know what field was selected for the current lookup.

4. Lookup ⇒ All Contacts. All of the contacts will be displayed.

5. Click the Contacts button on the toolbar.

Contact Detail View Lookup Shortcut

Using the lookup options on the menu is probably how most people create a lookup, but there is another way. Right-click in the field that you want to use as the lookup field and select **LOOKUP [FIELD NAME]**, as illustrated in Figure 3-5. The Lookup Contacts dialog box shown above in Figure 3-4 will open.

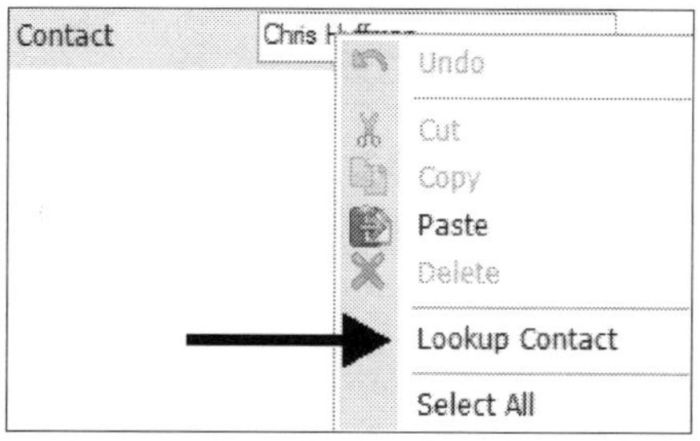

Figure 3-5 Contact field shortcut menu

Exercise 3.2: Using Keyword Search Lookups

Keyword search lookups are used to find records based on information in any field. You can perform a keyword search for a word or phrase in any field, including fields on the tabs. This is different from the lookup that you created in the previous exercise. The lookup that you created in the previous exercise searched for records that **START WITH** the value that you typed in or selected. Keyword searches are different. They retrieve records that have the value any place in a field.

This is very helpful when you remember a word or phrase, but do not remember what field it is in. Depending on how many tables you select to search in, the keyword search could take a while because all of the fields are searched, including fields on the System tabs, which each have their own table in the database. [See Lesson 18, Tabs Overview]

Finding Contacts In The Database

1. Lookup ⇒ Keyword Search. You should see the Keyword Search dialog box.
2. Type `Sales` in the **SEARCH FOR** field.
3. Select the **CONTACTS** Record type option if it is not already selected, then clear the **OPPORTUNITIES** option.

   You should have the options selected that are shown in Figure 3-6.

   These options will search for the word "Sales" in all contact, activity, history and notes fields.

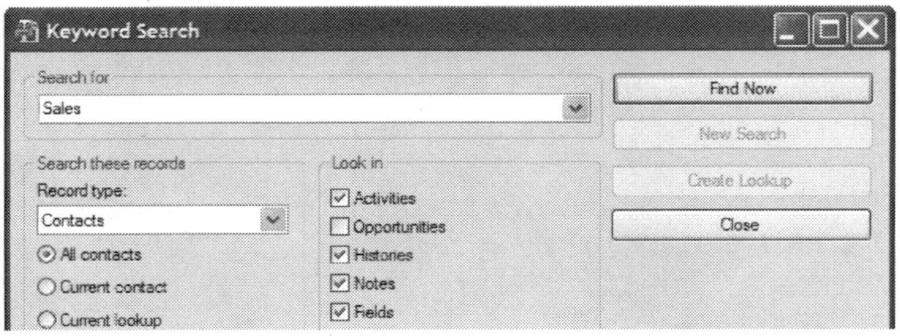

Figure 3-6 Keyword Search criteria

4. Click the **FIND NOW** button. The records shown at the bottom of the dialog box match the criteria that you selected.

You should see that the keyword search criteria "Sales" was found 783 times. Currently, there are not 783 records in the database. This is not the number of records that have the search criteria. It is the number of fields that have the word "Sales" in it. This means several records have the word "Sales" in more than one field.

Viewing The Keyword Search Results

When you view records retrieved from the search, the Keyword Search dialog box stays open. This allows you to go back to it to select other records to view in detail. You can also change the search options and perform another search. There are several options that you can select from, to view the results in the Contact Detail view, as discussed below.

① You can scroll through the list of records at the bottom of the Keyword Search dialog box. You may recognize the record(s) that you are looking for.
② If you right-click on a single record at the bottom of the dialog box and select **GO TO RECORD**, as illustrated in Figure 3-7, the detail record will open.
③ You can select more than one record to view by clicking on one record, then pressing and holding down the **CTRL** key and clicking on the other records that you want to view, as shown in Figure 3-8. Once the records are selected, right-click and select **LOOKUP SELECTED RECORDS**.
④ Click the **CREATE LOOKUP** button at the top of the Keyword Search dialog box. This option will create a lookup to display every record with the Record Type that you selected on the Keyword Search dialog box.

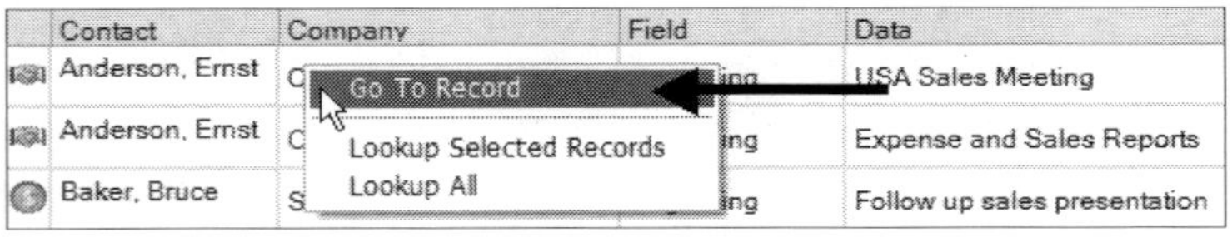

Figure 3-7 Keyword Search shortcut menu options

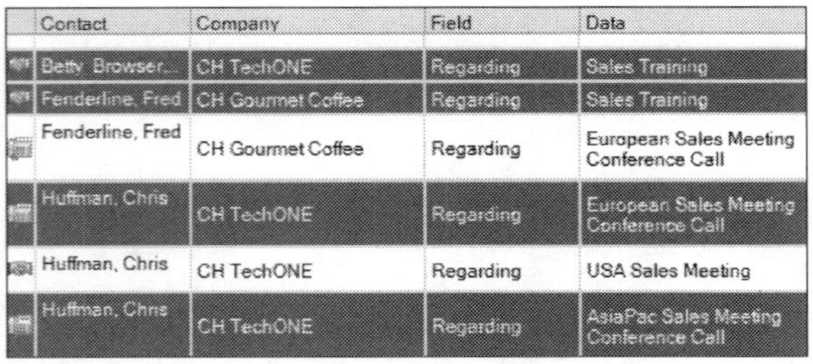

Figure 3-8 Records selected to view

Keyword Search Viewing Tips

① Selecting the **LOOKUP ALL** option on the shortcut menu shown earlier in Figure 3-7 is the same as clicking the Create Lookup button.
② Double-clicking on a record in the bottom half of the Keyword Search dialog box is the same as right-clicking on a record and selecting Go To Record.
③ To select adjacent records, click on the first one, then press and hold down the **SHIFT** key and click on the last record that you want to view.

5. Select the first 10 records on the Keyword Search dialog box, then right-click on any of the highlighted records and select **LOOKUP SELECTED RECORDS**.

Notice that the Keyword Search dialog box is minimized in the lower left corner of the screen. The reason that there are only five contact records is because some of these contact records have more than one field that has the word "Sales" in it.

6. Close the Keyword Search dialog box. Lookup ⇒ All Contacts, when you are finished viewing the contact records.

Exercise 3.3: How To Create A Lookup Using Multiple Fields

In Exercise 3.1 you learned how to perform a lookup using one field. In this exercise you will learn how to look up records using more than one field. If you wanted to email managers that are in Boise, you would have to search two fields. You would have to search the City field for "Boise" and you would have to search the Title field for "Manager".

If you open the Lookup menu you will see the City field. You will not see the Title field. It appears that you cannot search the Title field. The **OTHER FIELDS** option on the Lookup menu contains the fields that are not listed on the Lookup menu. You can also right-click in the Title field on the view and select the lookup option from the shortcut menu, as shown earlier in Figure 3-5.

1. Lookup ⇒ City.

2. Type `Boise` in the Search field, then press Enter. There are three contacts in Boise. Notice that only two contacts have the Manager title.

Using The Narrow Lookup Option

Until now, when you performed a lookup the Replace Lookup option was used. The Replace option tells ACT! to remove the records from the previous lookup and start over.

The **NARROW LOOKUP** option is used to reduce the number of contacts that are the result of the previous lookup. In this exercise, the previous lookup selected all contacts in Boise. Now you want to find the managers in Boise. If you selected the Replace lookup option you would get all managers, no matter what city they are in. This is not what you want in this exercise. The Narrow Lookup option will only search the records that were retrieved from the previous lookup.

1. Lookup ⇒ Other Fields. Open the Field drop-down list and select Title.

The **OTHER FIELDS** option does not provide any additional fields to search on, that are not already in the Field drop-down list. If the field that you want to search on, is not on the Lookup menu, you can select any field to open the Lookup Contacts dialog box and select the field that you need from the **FIELD** drop-down list.

2. Open the Search drop-down list and select Manager.

3. Select the **NARROW LOOKUP** option.

    The Lookup Contacts dialog box should have the options shown in Figure 3-9.

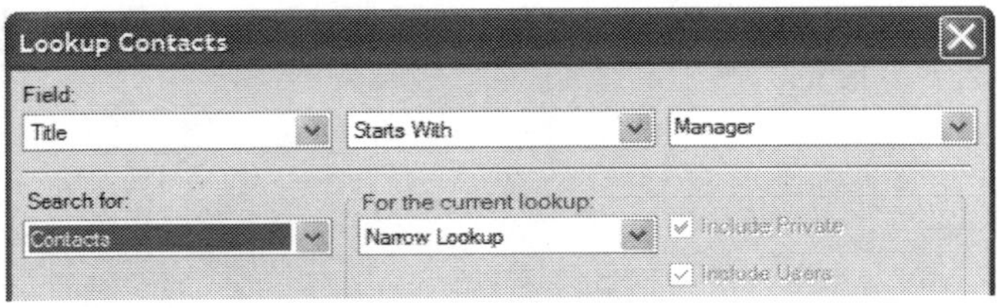

Figure 3-9 Options to search for a specific job title

4. Click OK. You should now have two records in the lookup. This means that one of the three original contact records retrieved does not have "Manager" in the Title field.

This may seem like a lot of work to remove one record. If the database retrieved thousands of records that met your initial lookup criteria, being able to perform another lookup to remove 1,000 records from the search automatically, makes this a good feature to use.

Exercise 3.4: Using The Add To Lookup Option

If you wanted to find contacts that lived in Texas or were sales reps, using the Replace lookup or Narrow lookup options would not give you the results that you are looking for. The **ADD TO LOOKUP** option allows you to combine the results from different lookups. The records from the various lookups do not have to be related. This is the type of lookup that you will learn how to create in this exercise.

1. Lookup ⇒ State. Type `TX` in the Search field.

2. Make sure that the **REPLACE LOOKUP** option is selected. Click OK. 14 records should have been retrieved.

3. Lookup ⇒ Other Fields. Select Title from the Field drop-down list.

4. Select Sales Representative from the Search drop-down list.

When performing lookups, you should select an item from the Search drop-down list as much as possible, even though the Search field will allow you to type in an entry. If you type in an entry and the entry that you type in is not used on any record, you will not retrieve the records that you expect.

5. Select the **ADD TO LOOKUP** option. Click OK. There should be 20 records displayed. All of the records in the lookup either have "TX" in the State field or "Sales Representative" in the Title field. If someone typed Texas in the State field on contact records, those records would not be retrieved in this search.

Finding Contact Records That Are Missing Information

In Exercise 3.3, the goal was to find contacts that meet specific criteria to send an email to. In order to send the contacts an email, they need to have an email address. You can use the Lookup command to find contacts that do or do not have an email address. Searching for records that do not have data in certain fields is a good way to keep records from having data missing.

Exercise 3.5: Find Contacts Without An Email Address

In this exercise you will find all contacts that do not have an email address.

1. Lookup ⇒ E-mail Address.

    Select the **DOES NOT CONTAIN DATA** option illustrated in Figure 3-10.

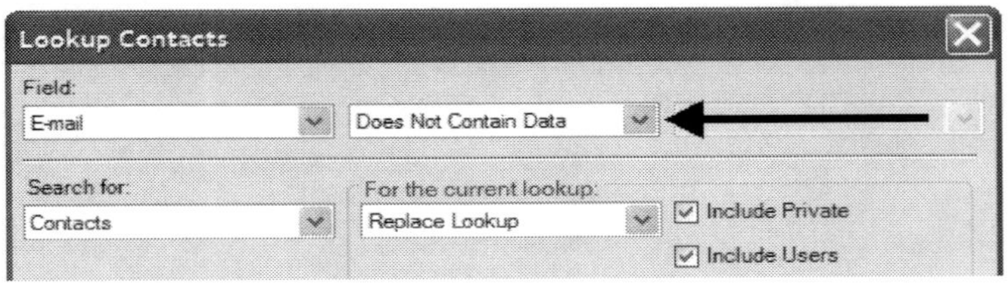

Figure 3-10 Options to find all contacts without an email address

2. Click OK. 110 contacts should be in the Contact List view. To verify that the records do not have an email address, click the Contacts button. View a few records and look at the E-mail field. You will see that the field is empty.

The reason that I had you view the records on the Contact Detail view is because the E-mail field is not displayed by default on the Contact List view. You will learn how to modify a layout to display the fields that you need.

Exercise 3.6: Finding Contacts That You Added To The Database

One way to help keep data accurate and consistent is to review it. Everyone that uses the database should do this periodically. The frequency that data is checked and verified depends on how many records are added and how often data is modified.

In this exercise you will create a lookup that finds all contacts that you added to the database in the last month. The fields that you need are the Record Creator and Create Date fields on the Contact Access tab. [See Lesson 2, Contact Access tab] In Lesson 16 you will create a report to print this data.

1. Lookup ⇒ Other Fields.

   Select the options shown in Figure 3-11.

   You have to type in the Record Creators name. Click OK.

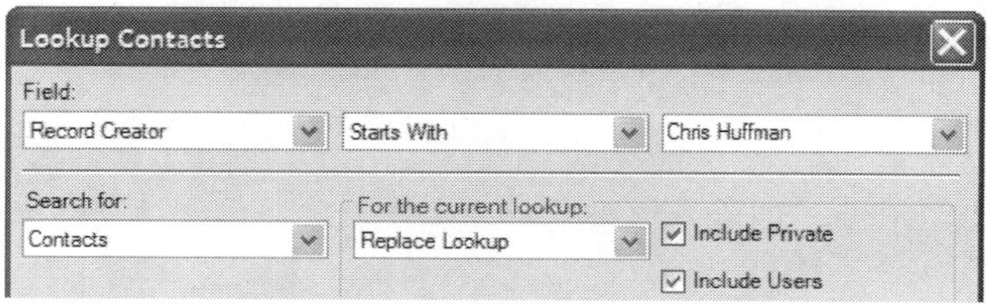

Figure 3-11 Record Creator field lookup criteria

2. Lookup ⇒ Other Fields.

   Select the options shown in Figure 3-12.

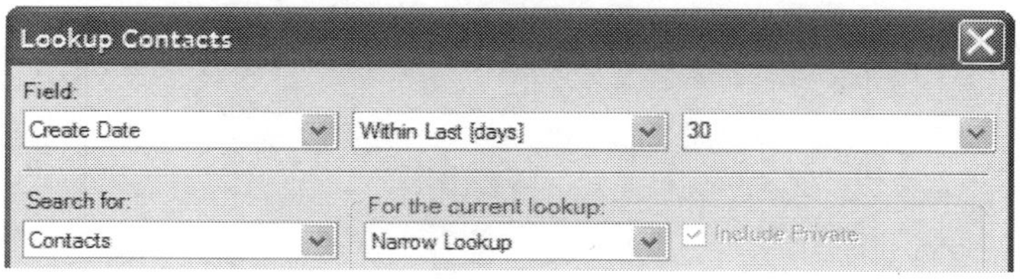

Figure 3-12 Create Date field lookup criteria

3. Click OK. You should see the two records shown in Figure 3-13. These records should look familiar because you created them earlier.

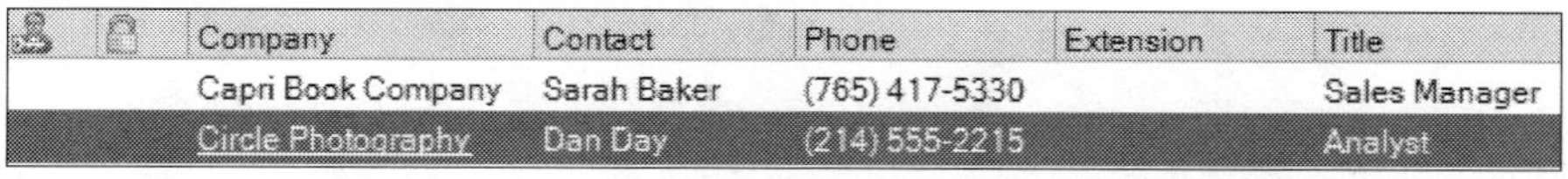

Company	Contact	Phone	Extension	Title
Capri Book Company	Sarah Baker	(765) 417-5330		Sales Manager
Circle Photography	Dan Day	(214) 555-2215		Analyst

Figure 3-13 Contacts that you added to the database in the last 30 days

Annual Events Lookup

Annual events is another type of lookup. Examples of annual events are anniversaries, birthdays and yearly salary reviews. By default, annual events do not appear on calendars, but they can be added to a calendar. [See Lesson 13, Annual Events] Creating a lookup is one way to be able to view annual events.

> Annual event fields only search the month and day portion of the date field, because they are tracked from year to year.

Exercise 3.7: Lookup Annual Events

In this exercise you will create a lookup to find all contacts with a birthday between January 1, 2007 and March 31, 2007.

1. Lookup ⇒ Annual Events.

   The options in the **SEARCH FOR** drop-down list shown in Figure 3-14 display all of the types of annual events that are currently being used in the database.

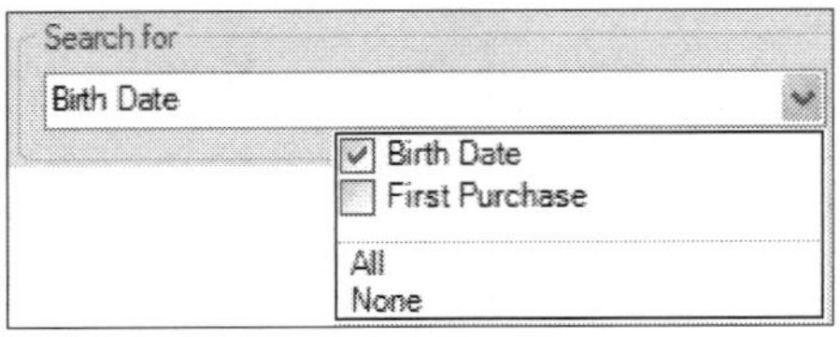

Figure 3-14 Annual event types

2. Accept the Birth Date search option, then select the **DATE RANGE** option.
3. Open the first date drop-down list field and select January 1, 2007, as shown in Figure 3-15. Open the second date drop-down list field and select March 31, 2007. You should have the options selected that are shown in Figure 3-16.

Figure 3-15 Date field calendar

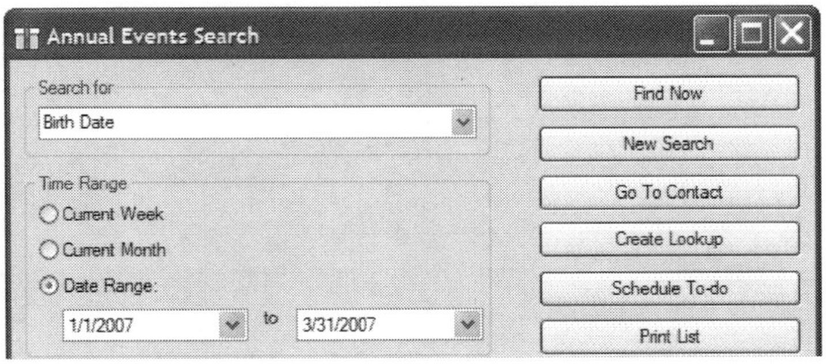

Figure 3-16 Birth Date annual event search options

4. Click the **FIND NOW** button. You will see the 10 contacts that have a birthday in the date range that you selected.
5. Close the Annual Events Search dialog box and display all of the contacts.

If you click the **SCHEDULE TO-DO** button, you can create an activity for the contact that is selected at the bottom of the Annual Events Search dialog box. The contacts name will appear on the Schedule Activities dialog box. This option will not recognize more than one selected contact.

Annual Events Search Viewing Tips

The records shown at the bottom of the Annual Events Search dialog box match the criteria. The options discussed below are how you can view the results.

① You can search for more than one annual event at the same time. As shown earlier in Figure 3-14, you can check more than one annual event type or you can select the **ALL** option to lookup all of the annual event types that you have created.
② If you right-click on a single record at the bottom of the Annual Events Search dialog box and select **GO TO CONTACT**, the record will be displayed.
③ Click the **CREATE LOOKUP** button. This button will create a lookup to display every record that is displayed at the bottom of the Annual Events Search dialog box.
④ Double-clicking on a record is the same as right-clicking and selecting **GO TO CONTACT**.

ACT! Annual Events Report

The **PRINT LIST** button on the Annual Events Search dialog box prints the report shown in Figure 3-17.

ACT! Annual Events

Contact	Company	Phone	Birth Date
Emily Dunn	Boomer's Artworx	(602) 555-4874	3/11/1959
Allison Mikola	CH TechONE	(212) 555-2485	1/13/1968
Melissa Pearce	CH TechONE	(212) 555-2485	3/15/1965
Jonathan Sommer	CH TechONE	(212) 555-2485	2/5/1973
Morty Manicotti	Corleone's Pasta Company	(480) 555-4512	3/17/1967
Todd Hornsby	Harbor Lights Restaurant	(757) 555-1221	3/15/1970
Alexander O'Brien	Manxsys Financial	(206) 555-4247	1/7/2003
Gracie Anderson	Searchlight Casting	(480) 555-3764	1/4/1968
Brandon Sloan	Sierra's Cafe	(562) 555-2142	1/7/1968
William Rosemann	Williams Consulting	(03) 680 4 445	1/21/1982

Figure 3-17 ACT! Annual Events report

Contact Activity Lookup

This type of lookup is used to find contacts whose records were or were not updated since a certain date. The lookup searches on any or all of the following tabs: Notes, History, Activities, Opportunities and Contact Access. This lookup is useful if you have a lot of contacts that you need to keep up with on a regular basis. It is also a good way to make sure that the data is accurate and that none of your contacts are being neglected or have fallen off of your radar, as they say.

Exercise 3.8: Find Contacts That Have Not Been Updated

In this exercise you will search for contacts that have not had the notes, opportunities or activities updated since February 1, 2007.

1. Lookup ⇒ Contact Activity.

2. Change the **SINCE DATE** to 2/1/2007.

I am not sure why, but the value in the **SINCE DATE** field is saved in ACT!. This means that the next time that you open this dialog box, the date that you selected the last time that you used the dialog box will automatically be in this field.

3. Clear the following options: Contact fields and Histories.

   You should have the options selected that are shown in Figure 3-18.

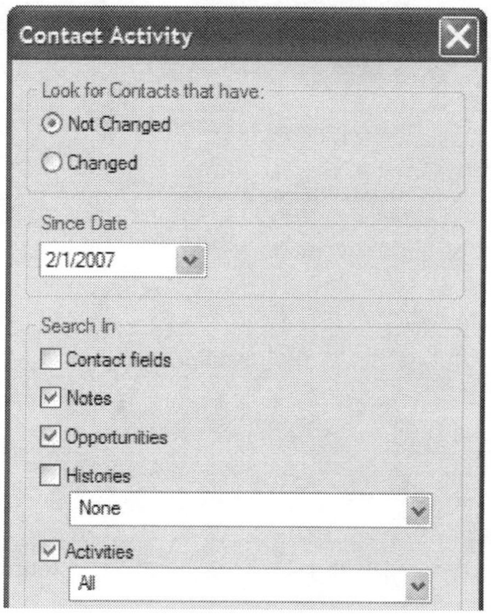

Figure 3-18 Contact Activity options

> The Histories and Activities options let you select specific categories to search for, as shown in Figure 3-19.

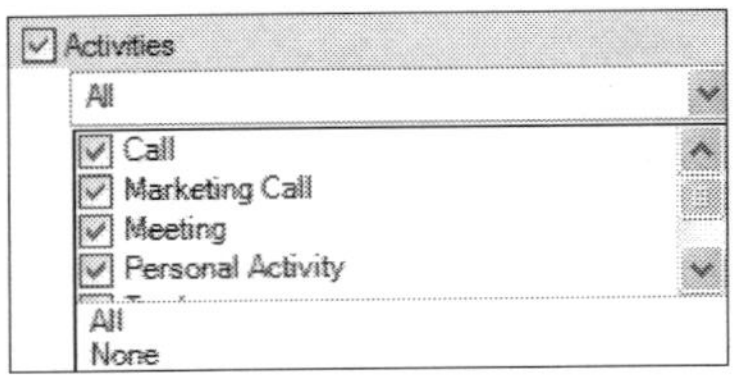

Figure 3-19 Activity options

4. Click OK. There should be 30 records on the Contact List view. This would be the list that you would work from, because the contact records have not been updated in a long time.

> **Contact Activity Lookup Tips**
>
> ① Lookups are not case sensitive. Typing "Marketing" and "marketing" will return the same results.
> ② **LOOKUP ⇒ PREVIOUS** displays the last nine searches that you ran, as shown in Figure 3-20. You can select the search that you want to run again. When you reopen ACT!, these searches will not be available because they are not saved.
> ③ Right-click in a field in the top half of the Contact Detail view and select Lookup (Field Name) to open the Lookup dialog box.
> ④ When only one record meets the lookup criteria, it is displayed in the Contact Detail view. You do not have to display all contacts before creating a lookup.

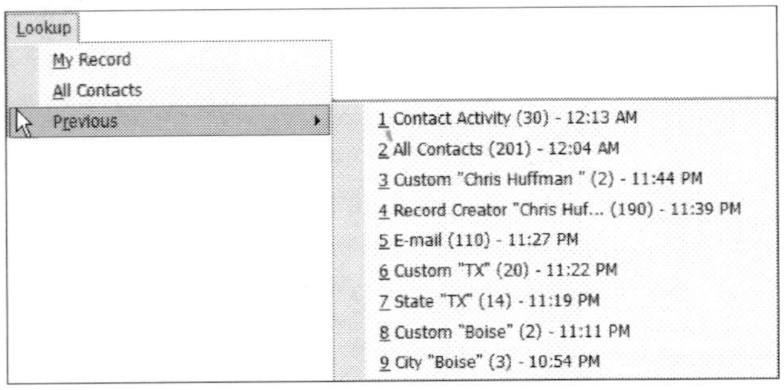

Figure 3-20 Previous searches

Modifying Several Records At The Same Time

You may have the need to change the data in the same field(s) on several records. You could make the changes one record at a time or you could create a lookup to retrieve all of the records that you need to change and change all of them at the same time.

> If you do not create a lookup first, the changes will be made to every record in the database.

If you have several company contacts at the same address and the company moves, you could look up the address that you need to change and change all of the records at the same time, if the address fields are not linked. You can also change data on the User Fields, Personal Info and Secondary Contacts tabs this way.

The **REPLACE FIELD** command is used to change the data in a field for multiple records at the same time.

Exercise 3.9: How To Modify Several Records At The Same Time

In this exercise you will change the value in the Last Results field and add a note to a user defined field for all contacts in NY. The tasks that you will learn in this exercise are helpful for updating several records at the same time, as well as, keeping the data consistent and accurate.

It is a good idea to make a back up copy of the database before modifying several records at the same time. This is known as a **GLOBAL** change. This type of change cannot be undone. You do not have to create a back up copy now because this is a practice database.

Change The Last Results Field

1. Create a lookup to find all records in the State of NY. The lookup should find 20 records.

2. Edit ⇒ Replace Field. You will see the Replace Data dialog box.

3. Open the Replace Contents of drop-down list and select the **LAST RESULTS** field.

4. Open the Value drop-down list and select **DISCUSSED OPPORTUNITIES**, as shown in Figure 3-21.

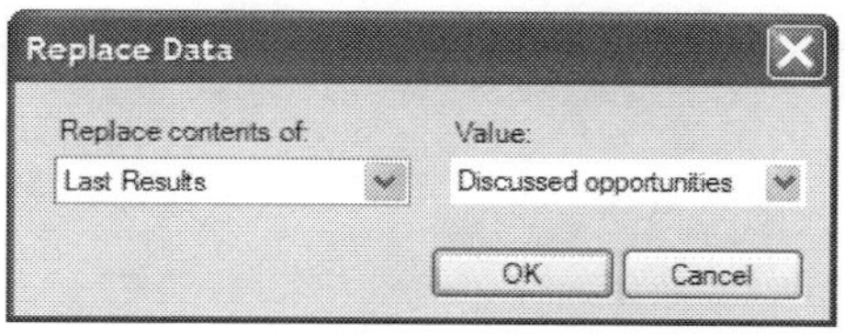

Figure 3-21 Replace data options for the Last Results field

5. Click OK. When you see the Replace/Swap/Copy message that lets you know that all records in the current lookup will be modified, click Yes to modify the records.

Change The Value In A User Defined Field

In this part of the exercise you will use the Replace Field command to change the value in a user defined field. User defined fields are free form fields that are used to enter data that there is no existing field for.

1. Edit ⇒ Replace Field.

2. Select the User 10 field from the first drop-down list, then type `Should this record be private?` in the **VALUE** field, as shown in Figure 3-22.

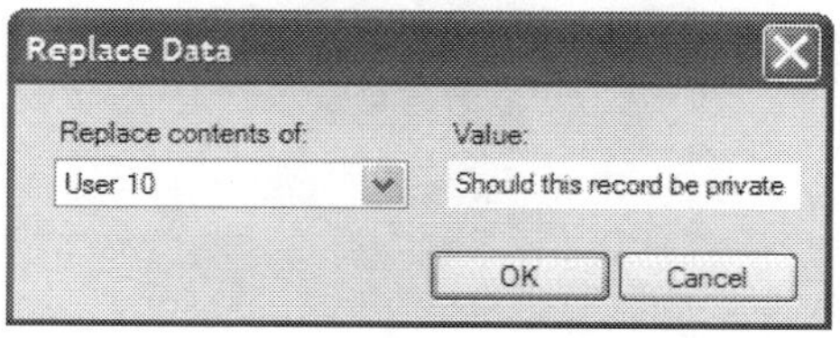

Figure 3-22 Replace data options for the User 10 field

3. Click OK, then click Yes to modify the records.

Observe the following information about the 20 records in the lookup by clicking the Contacts button.

① The **LAST RESULTS** field on the Contact Detail view has been set to Discussed Opportunities. (1)
② The **EDIT ON** field on the Latest Activities tab has today's date. (1)
③ The **USER 10** field on the User Fields tab has the text that you typed in the Value field shown above in Figure 3-22.

(1) In ACT! 2008 and earlier, this field was on the Contact Info tab, which is now the Contact Access tab.

Exercise 3.10: How To Delete Data From Several Records At The Same Time

Just like you can add or change data in a field for multiple records, you can also delete data from a field for multiple records at the same time. You will learn how in this exercise.

1. With the 20 NY records still in the lookup, Edit ⇒ Replace Field.

2. Select the User 10 field from the first drop-down list and leave the Value field empty. Leaving the Value field empty will overwrite the data in the field with blanks, which produces the same effect as deleting data in the field.

3. Click OK, then click Yes. You can view the information on the User Fields tab. You will see that the User 10 field for the 20 records is now blank.

4. Lookup ⇒ All Contacts.

Using The Contact List View

Until now, you have been using the Contact Detail view to look at records which only displays one record at a time. The Contact List view resembles a spreadsheet and displays all of the contacts that you have the right to see. Options not covered on the Contact List view in this lesson are covered in Lesson 12. [See Lesson 12, Tagging Contacts]

The first two columns on the Contact List view shown in Figure 3-23, are used to visually bring things to your attention.

The first column will have a key icon in it if the contact record is a user of the database.

The second column will display a lock icon if the record was marked private by the current user (you).

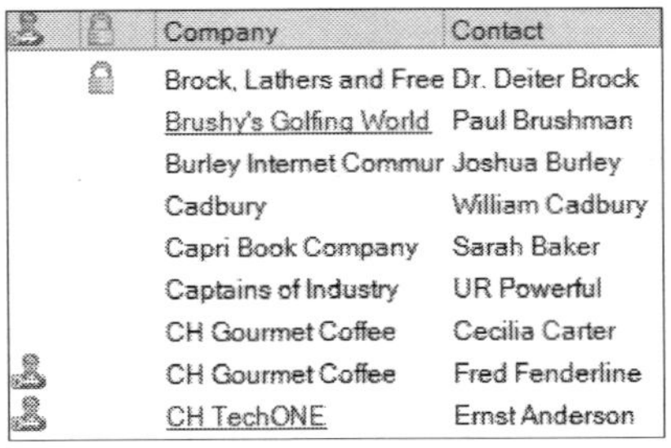

Figure 3-23 Contact List view

Sorting By Columns In The Contact List View

You can sort the records in the Contact List view by clicking on the column heading that you want to sort on. The default sort order is based on the Company field.

1. On the Contact List view, click on the Contact column heading. Notice that the records are now sorted by the contacts last name, even though the first and last names are in the same column. The Last name field is the field that the Contact column actually sorts on.

You should see a triangle in the Contact column heading. If the triangle points up like this ▲, the records are sorted in ascending (A to Z or 1 to 10) order. If the triangle points down like this ▼, the records are sorted in descending order (Z to A or 10 to 1).

> If your database has hundreds or thousands of records, you may not want to scroll down the list even though the records are currently sorted to find the contact that you need. If that is the case, the steps below will show you how to find to a specific record in the list without scrolling.

2. Click on the column heading, not the arrow on the column heading, of the field that has the value that you want to look for.

3. Type the first few letters of what you are looking for. In this example, type `York`, because that is a contacts last name.

You will see the first contact in the list that matches what you typed in, is highlighted. Also notice that the letters that you typed in are in the **LOOK FOR** field even though you did not click in the field before you typed in the information.

The more letters that you type, the closer ACT! will be able to find the record that you are looking for. This works for all columns, as long as the list is sorted on that column before you start typing in the search criteria.

How To View Detail Information From The Contact List View

If you want to view all of the data for a contact from the Contact List view, double-click on the contact that you want to view. If you click on a field that is hyperlinked (blue), like the company or web site fields, you will open the Company Detail record or the web site.

How To Select And View Specific Records

If you have a database with thousands of records, you will probably not want to see all of the records in the Contact List view. You can select (highlight) any of the records and only view the records that you select.

1. Click the Contact List button. Click on the Company column heading. The records should be in alphabetical order by company. If not, click on the Company column heading again.

2. Click on the first record with the company name A1 Services. Press and hold down the Shift key, then click on the last record with the same company name.

3. Press and hold down the CTRL key, then select all of the Beautiful Friendship company records.

   The Contact List view should look like the one shown in Figure 3-24.

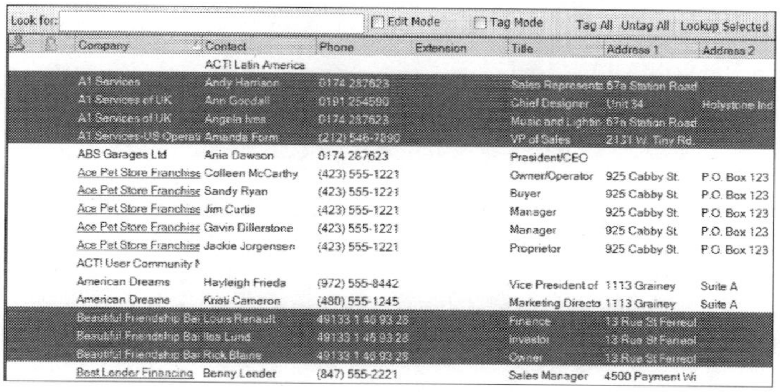

Figure 3-24 Contact List view with records selected

4. Right-click in the Contact List view on a highlighted record and select the option, **LOOK UP SELECTED CONTACTS** on the shortcut menu, as illustrated in Figure 3-25.

   In the Contact List view you should now only see the seven records that you selected.

Figure 3-25 Contact List view shortcut menu

You can also click the **LOOK UP SELECTED CONTACTS** button on the Contact List toolbar.

Exercise 3.11: Sorting Records

Earlier, you learned how to sort records in the Contact List view by clicking on a column heading. That is how to sort on a single column. If you want to sort on more than one column or sort on a column that is not displayed on the Contact List view, you have to use the Sort dialog box. Follow the steps below to sort records in the Contact views.

1. Lookup ⇒ All Contacts.

2. Edit ⇒ Sort. You should see the Sort dialog box.

3. Open the **SORT BY** drop-down list. You will see all of the fields on the current layout. Select the State field, then select the **ASCENDING** sort order option.

4. Open the **AND THEN BY** drop-down list and select the Referred By field, which is not displayed on the Contact List view, then select the Descending sort order option.

5. You should have the options selected that are shown in Figure 3-26.

   Click OK.

   The records are now sorted by the State and Referred By fields.

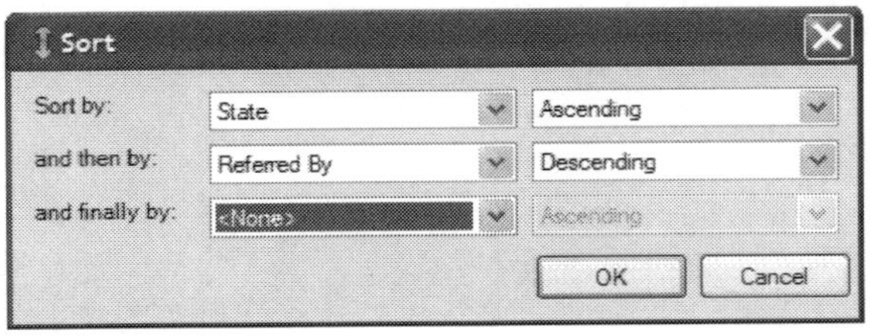

Figure 3-26 Sort dialog box options

Exercise 3.12: How To Delete Contacts From The Database

If you no longer need to keep information on a particular contact or secondary contact, you can delete the record. Once you delete a record, it is gone forever unless you restore it from a back up copy of the database. The contact record is deleted from all companies that it is associated or linked to. The contact is also deleted from any group that it is a member of. When deleting a contact you have the following two options:

① Delete the current contact.
② Delete all of the contacts in the current lookup.

When you delete a contact, the Notes and History records for the contact are also deleted. The programmer in me knows that just deleting records from a database is usually not the best solution. A better solution would be to export the records that you do not need to another database. You can name this database anything that you like. This second database is sometimes referred to as a **HISTORY** or **ARCHIVE DATABASE**, meaning that it does not contain any current or active records. Once you export the records from the live database to the second database, you can delete them from the live database.

How To Delete One Record

1. Right-click on the record for William Cadbury that does not have a company name and select **DELETE CONTACT**, as shown in Figure 3-27.

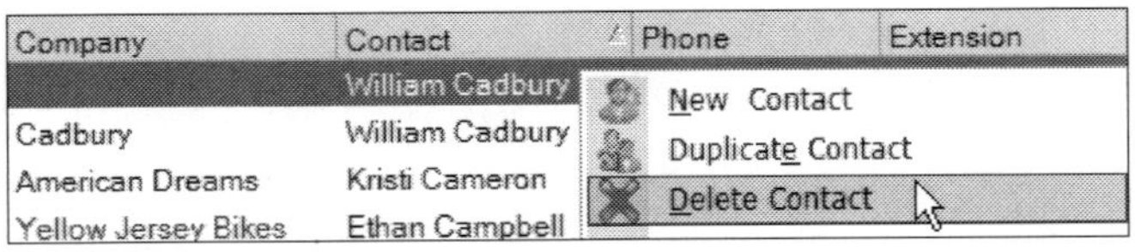

Figure 3-27 Contact List view shortcut menu options

2. Click the Delete Contact button shown in Figure 3-28, then click Yes to confirm that you want to delete the record.

Figure 3-28 Delete contact confirmation dialog box

How To Delete Multiple Records At The Same Time

If you need to delete several records, create a lookup to find the records that you want to delete.

1. Lookup ⇒ Company. Type `A1` in the Search field.
2. Press Enter or click OK. Four records should be displayed.
3. Contacts ⇒ Delete Contact.
4. Click the **DELETE LOOKUP** button shown above in Figure 3-28.
5. Click Yes to confirm that you want to delete the records.
6. In a few seconds, you will see a message that tells you that no more records match the lookup criteria. Click OK. There should be 196 records in the database.

View The My Record

Now that you have edited and deleted records, you can check the History tab to see the entries for the changes that you made to the database.

1. Lookup ⇒ My Record.
2. On the History tab, the first six entries should be for the records that you deleted or changed, as shown in Figure 3-29.

   The **REGARDING & DETAILS** column is used to let you know what the change to the record is.

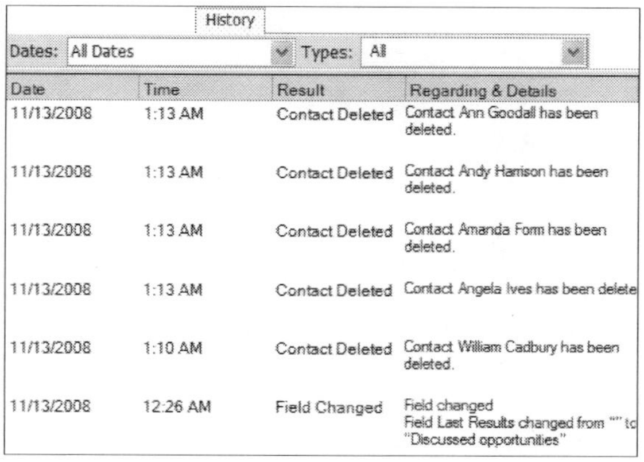

Figure 3-29 History log of deleted and changed records

3. Lookup ⇒ All Contacts.

CREATING COMPANY AND DIVISION RECORDS

In this lesson you will learn about the following company and division record options:

- ☑ Using the Companies tree
- ☑ Creating company and division records
- ☑ Associating and linking contacts to companies
- ☑ Duplicating company and division records
- ☑ Using the Company Lookup command

LESSON 4

Company And Division Records Overview

Company records allow contacts associated with a company to be managed easier. If a company has a lot of contacts, it may be easier to manage the contacts if divisions were created for the company. Brick and mortar companies have divisions, departments and business units. Companies in ACT! can have them also. You can create companies and divisions that best meet your needs. It is also possible that you may not need any companies or divisions. Figure 4-1 shows the Company Detail view.

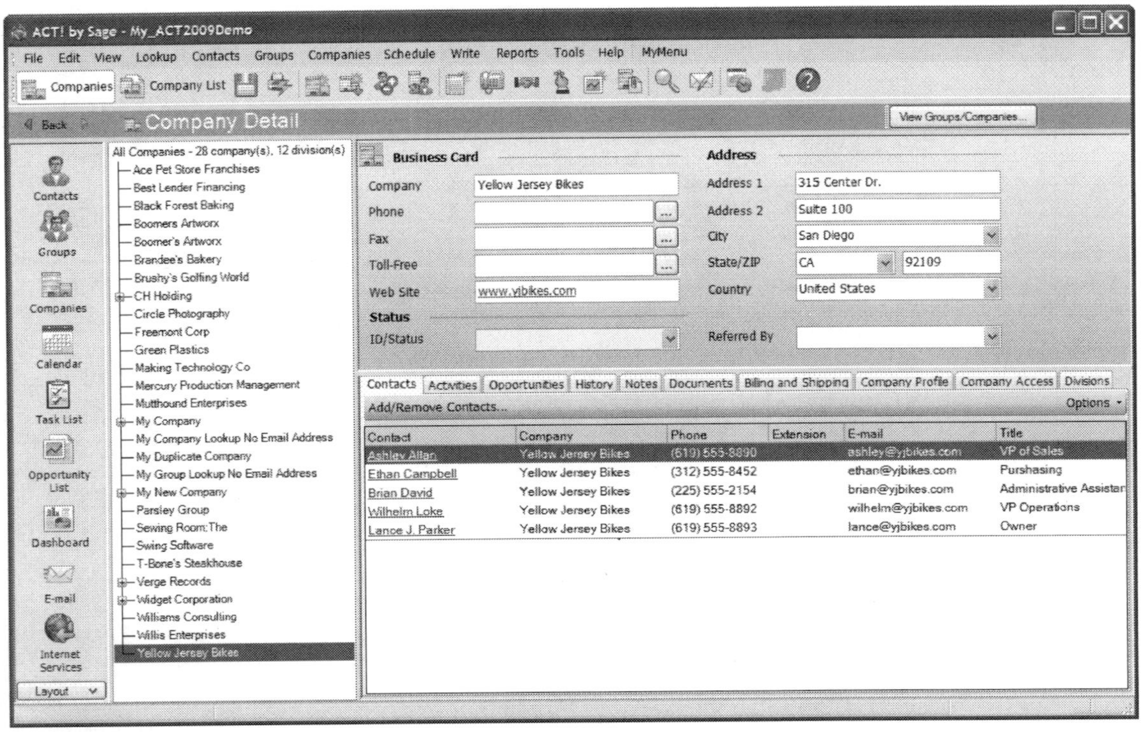

Figure 4-1 Company Detail view

The **COMPANY** record type allows you to keep track of contacts in the same company. In a way, a company record is similar to a group. This may be why the groups and companies are on the same tab on the Contact Detail view. You can see all of the companies and groups except dynamic groups that a contact is a member of. It would be nice if there was a way to know if the entries on this tab are a company or group. Contacts can be associated with more than one company.

An example of when you would associate a contact to more than one company would be if one consultant (a contact) did work for multiple companies that are in your database. You can create activities, notes and opportunities, as well as, attach documents to a company record. In ACT!, any of the following are acceptable ways to categorize contacts in a company. These categories would be divisions that you create. I am sure that you can come up with several others.

① By department.
② By title.
③ By contacts home state.

Keep in mind that company records in ACT! do not have the same limitations as brick and mortar companies. Company records in ACT! function more like folders, meaning that the contact records associated to a company, do not have to have anything related. While the company records displayed in the Companies tree have the name of a company, you can create a company record with any name that you want. You could create a company record that has your first name as the company name.

In addition to being able to create 15 levels of divisions per company record, you can also create **SUBDIVISIONS**. Subdivisions are used to further divide the contacts into categories per company that are easier to manage.

An example of when it would be appropriate to create subdivisions would be for a company that has 1,000 sales reps. I would create a division called "Sales Reps". I would then create subdivisions for each of the product lines the company has like telephones, digital cameras, camcorders and televisions. I would add the sales reps to the appropriate subdivision(s) based on the product line(s) that the sales rep sells. As you can see, divisions and subdivisions can be used to organize contacts in the way that works best for you. A contact that is in a division does not have to also be part of the company. This means that you can add a contact to a division without being required to associate it to the company. Divisions are independent of the company that they are created under.

Differences Between Companies And Groups

In this lesson you will learn how to create company records. In the next lesson you will learn how to create group records. On the surface they may appear to be the same and have the same functionality, but there are some differences.

Company records have more functionality than group records. For example, company records have more fields that can be used to automatically fill in fields on a contact record. The opposite is also true. Fields on a contact record can be used to fill in fields on a company record.

Creating a group is like saving a lookup because the records do not have to have the same data in a specific field. When you view contacts from the Company Detail view you can see the notes, activities and opportunities for all of the contacts in the company on the same tab. The same is true if contact records are viewed from the Group Detail view.

Company Toolbar

Many of the buttons on the company toolbar are the same as the contact and group toolbars.
Figure 4-2 shows the Company toolbar. Table 4-1 explains the buttons on the toolbar.

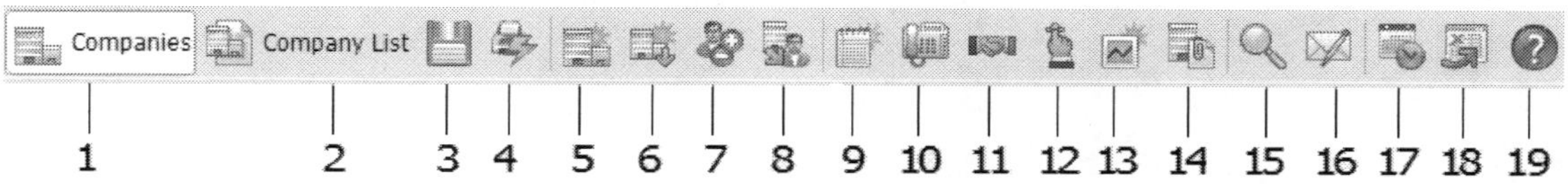

Figure 4-2 Company toolbar

Button	Description
1	Opens the Company Detail view.
2	Opens the Company List view.
3	Saves the record. (1) (2)
4	Opens the Print dialog box.
5	Creates a new company record.
6	Creates a new division record.
7	Add or remove a contact. (2)
8	Updates the linked contacts for the selected company.
9	Creates a note. (2)
10	Schedules a telephone call activity. (2)
11	Schedules a meeting activity. (2)
12	Schedules a To-Do activity. (2)
13	Creates a new opportunity. (1) (2)
14	Attach a file. (2)
15	Displays the members of the company that is selected. (2)
16	Compose and send an email.
17	Copies calendar information between the ACT! and Outlook calendars.
18	Exports the company list to Excel. This option is only available from the Company List view.
19	Opens the Help system.

Table 4-1 Company toolbar buttons explained

(1) This option is only available from the Company Detail view.
(2) This option applies to companies and divisions.

The Companies Tree

The Companies tree is on the left side of the Company Detail view. At the top of the Companies tree, the number of companies and divisions in the database are displayed. This tree displays all of the companies, divisions and subdivisions in the database, as illustrated in Figure 4-3.

A plus sign in front of an entry in the tree means that there is at least one company or division below it.

If you click on an entry in the tree, you will see the detail information for it on the right side of the window. The companies and divisions at this level are recognized as divisions.

Company records in the Companies tree may or may not contain the same companies that you see in the Contacts view. For example, in the Contact List view you will see the following companies, Cadbury, County Tennis Supplies and Liberty. If you look in the Companies tree, you will not see an entry for these companies. It is not a requirement that every company have a company record.

You can use the tree to complete several tasks including moving, creating and deleting a company. Any task that you can do for a company, you can also do for a division or subdivision.

Like other features in ACT!, the Companies tree has a shortcut menu, as shown in Figure 4-4.

Figure 4-3 Companies tree

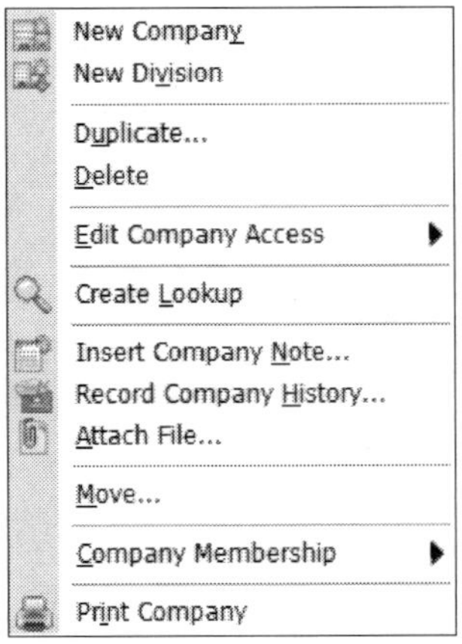

Figure 4-4 Companies tree shortcut menu

Exercise 4.1: Create New Contact Records

To complete some of the company exercises, you need to add more contact records to the database.

1. Create contact records for the following names. You only have to enter the name in each record. John Doe, Jennifer Doe, Charles Smith, Mary Wood and Bill Grant.

2. Create contact records for the following names: Laura Smith and Tom Wood. Type `Lookup` in the Company field for these two records. They will be used later in this lesson to lookup contacts and link them to a company.

Exercise 4.2: Create A Company Record

1. Click the **COMPANIES** button on the Navigation bar.

2. Click the **NEW COMPANY** button on the toolbar, then create records for the two companies in Table 4-2.

   The first record should look like the one shown in Figure 4-5.

Field	Company #1	Company #2
Company	My Company	My Other Company
Address 1	123 Main St	456 South St
City	Hitsville	Hollywood
State	CA	CA

Table 4-2 Company record data

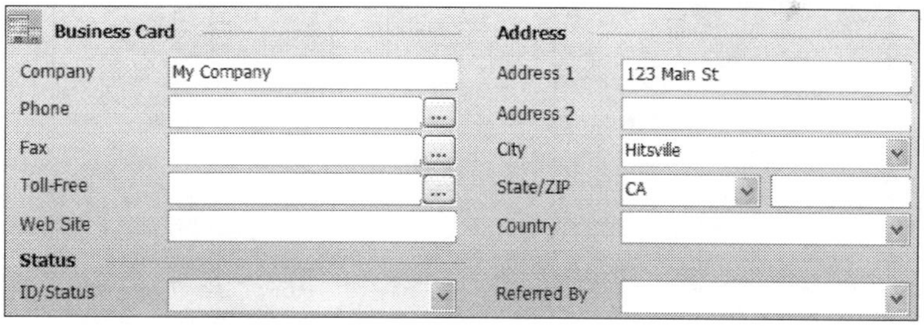

Figure 4-5 New company record

ACT! tries to prevent you from creating duplicate records. If you enter a company name that already exists as a company record in the database, you will see the warning message shown in Figure 4-6 when you try to go to another company record.

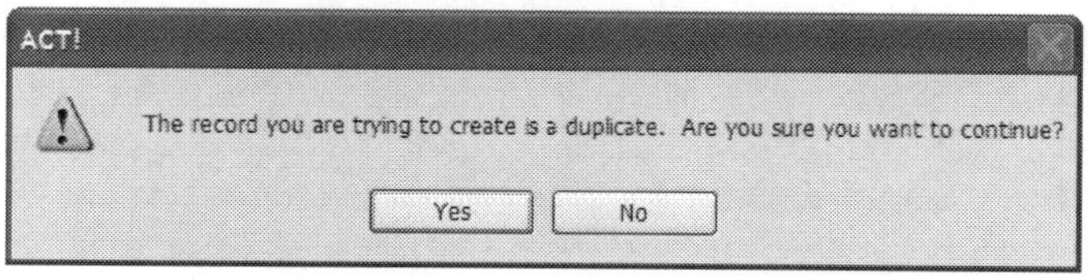

Figure 4-6 Duplicate company warning message

If you recall, in Lesson 1 you changed how ACT! checks for duplicate companies.
If you click Yes, the company record that you just created will be added to the database.
If you click No, you will have to change the company name to save the record.

Exercise 4.3: Create Divisions For A Company

Creating a division uses the same screen as the one for creating a company record.

1. Display the company (or division) record that you want to create a division for. For this exercise click on the company, My Company in the Companies tree.

2. Click the **NEW DIVISION** button on the toolbar.

3. Type the division name in the Company field. For this exercise type `Finance` in the Company field.

4. If you click on the company in the Company tree you will see the division.

   You will also see the **HIERARCHY** of the company and its divisions on the Divisions tab, as illustrated at the bottom of Figure 4-7.

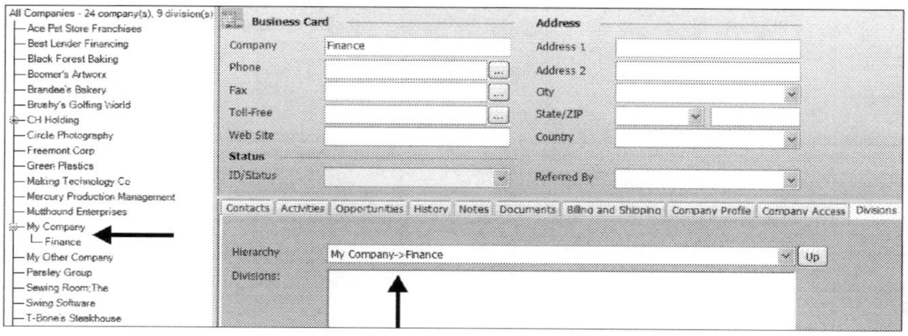

Figure 4-7 Division associated to a company

5. Create the divisions in Table 4-3 under the correct company.

Division	Company
Technology Division	My Company
Marketing	My Other Company
Sales Division	My Other Company

Table 4-3 Divisions to create

Associating Contacts To Companies And Divisions

Contacts can exist in an ACT! database without being linked or associated to a company. Companies can be in the database without having contacts linked to them. There is no requirement that contacts and companies be linked or associated, so do not be alarmed if you have contact records that are not linked to company records or vice versa. Although, I am not sure why someone would create a company and not associate any contacts to it, but it is acceptable in ACT!. There are two ways to associate contacts to companies as discussed below.

① **Manually** This method entails creating the link between a contact and a company. ACT! refers to this type of link as a **STATIC** link. That is because the link will remain intact until you manually change it.

② **Automatically** This method entails creating a query that selects the contact records that will be linked to a company. ACT! refers to this type of a link as a **DYNAMIC** link. This is because the contacts associated to a company will change automatically, depending on whether or not the data in the contact record meets the criteria in the query. A contact record can meet the criteria in the query this week and not meet the criteria next week, if the data in any of the contact record fields that the query uses, changes. You will learn how to create queries in Lesson 11.

Exercise 4.4: Associate A Contact To A Company Record

There are several ways to associate contacts to a company record. In this exercise you will learn different ways to accomplish this task. Contact records can be associated to companies from the contact record. The opposite is also true. Contact records can be associated to companies from the company record.

1. Open the company record for My Other Company in the Company Detail view. On the Divisions tab, you should see the two divisions that you created for the company.

2. Click the Add/Remove Contacts to Company button on the toolbar.

3. Click the **CONTACTS** button on the dialog box, then type `Doe` in the Look for field.

4. Select the contact record for John Doe, then click the Add button.

5. Click OK.

   The contact should be in the **STATIC MEMBERS** section of the dialog box, as shown in Figure 4-8.

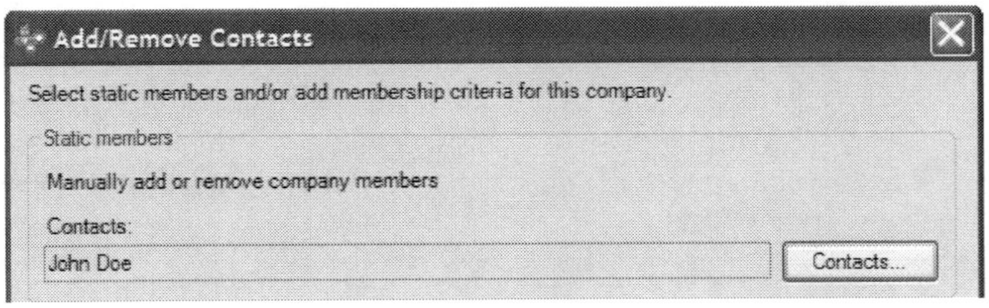

Figure 4-8 Add/Remove Contacts dialog box

6. Click OK. You will see the contact on the Contacts tab on the Company Detail record.

> **More Ways To Open The Add/Remove Contacts Dialog Box From A Company View**
>
> ① Companies ⇒ Company Membership ⇒ Add/Remove Contacts.
> ② Right-click on the company name in the Companies tree or Company column (in the Company List view) and select Company Membership ⇒ Add/Remove Contacts.
> ③ On the Contacts tab, click the Add/Remove Contacts button.
> ④ On the Contacts tab, in the Contact List section, right-click and select Company Membership ⇒ Add/Remove Contacts, on the shortcut menu.

> **How To Open The Add Contacts To Group/Company Dialog Box From A Contact View**
>
> The options on this dialog box also allow you to add contacts to companies.
>
> ① Companies ⇒ Company Membership ⇒ Add Selected to Company. You will see the dialog box shown in Figure 4-9.
> ② On the Contact List view, right-click and select Add Contacts to Company from the shortcut menu. You will see the dialog box shown in Figure 4-9.
> ③ On the Groups/Companies tab, select Companies and Divisions from the **SHOW MEMBERSHIP FOR** drop-down list field, then click the Add Contact to Company button, illustrated in Figure 4-10.

The entries in the **COMPANY MEMBERSHIP** list are companies, divisions and subdivisions that the contact is a member of.

I find this dialog box helpful because you can add and remove companies and divisions for the contact at the same time.

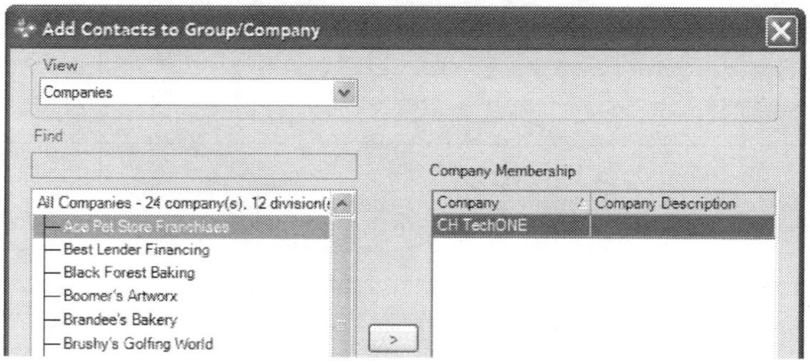

Figure 4-9 Add Contacts to Group/Companies dialog box

Figure 4-10 Company options on the Groups/Companies tab on the Contact Detail view

Exercise 4.5: Create A Company Record From A Contact Record

Earlier you created a company record from scratch. Creating a company record from a contact record that has the address information for the company will keep you from having to type the same information in again. You can create a company record from a contact record by following the steps below.

1. Select the contact that has the information for the company record that you want to create. In this exercise select the contact Jane Bellamy of Boomers Artworx.

2. Companies ⇒ Create Company from Contact.

The Company Detail view will open and the company name and address fields will automatically be filled in. If you needed to make any changes to the information for the new company record, you could. Notice in the Companies tree that the company name is similar to another company. The difference is the apostrophe in the other company name.

Exercise 4.6: Create A Contact Record From A Company Record

Creating a contact record from a company record that has the address information will keep you from having to type in the same information again. You can create a contact record from a company record by following the steps below.

1. Select the company in the Companies tree that has the information for the contact record that you want to create. In this exercise select the company Circle Photography.

2. Companies ⇒ Create Contact from Company. The Contact Detail view will open and the company name and address fields will automatically be filled in.

3. Type `Test Record` in the Contact field, then display another record.

Refreshing Linked Data In Contact Records

It is possible that you may not be viewing the most current data that is in the database. This happens when there are several people adding and editing records in the database. To make sure that you are viewing the most current data, refresh the data of the contact record that is displayed in the Contact Detail view.

Contacts ⇒ Update Linked Contact, will refresh the data. If this option is not available on the menu, it means that the contact is not linked to a company record.

Linking Company And Contact Records

If you scroll through the contact records you will see that some company names are blue and underlined and others are not. The company names that are blue and underlined are hyperlinked. You can click on this link to open the company, division or subdivision record.

Fields on the contact record that are linked will automatically be updated when the corresponding field in the company record is updated. This means that if the company name field on the company record changes from DEF Company to HIJ Company, any contact records that are linked to the DEF company on the company name field will automatically be updated if the **AUTOMATICALLY LINK NEW CONTACTS TO THEIR COMPANY RECORD** option is checked, as shown in Figure 4-11.

Tools ⇒ Preferences ⇒ Startup tab ⇒ Company Preferences button, will open the Company Preferences dialog box shown in Figure 4-11.

The ellipsis button at the end of the Company field on a contact record that is not already linked, opens the dialog box shown in Figure 4-12. If the contacts company name already exists in the database, you can link the contact to the company by selecting the company name on the dialog box.

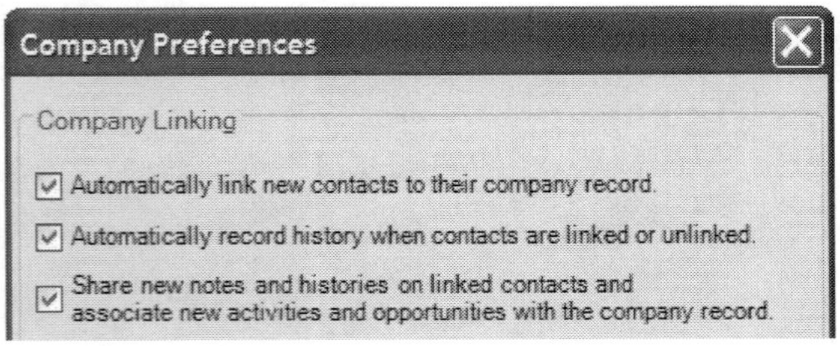

Figure 4-11 Company Preferences dialog box

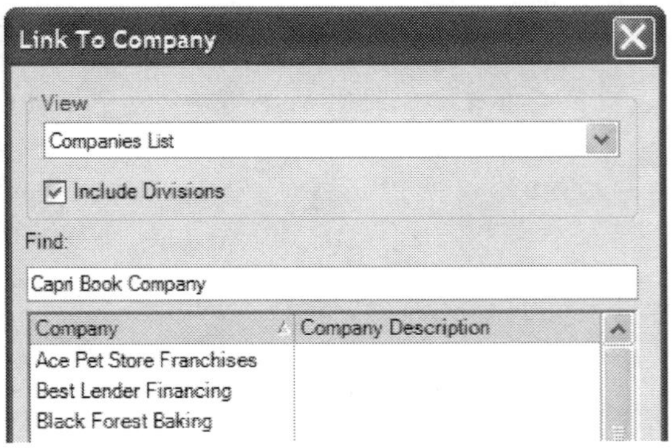

Figure 4-12 Link To Company dialog box

Associate vs Linking

On the surface, these terms sound like they perform the same function. Understanding the difference is important if you have the need to make some contacts private. In ACT!, associating and linking have different functionality as discussed below. I find it somewhat deceiving how the "Private" option works.

In "My world", when you mark a contact as private, whether or not the contact is "linked" to a company, any information that you enter on any of the tabs for the contact is also marked as private by default. The exception would be if you manually override the private option for a specific piece of information. If a history record is created when information about the contact is added, changed or deleted, the history record would also be automatically marked as private. Well, I started this paragraph off by saying in "My world".

The scenario that I just described is **NOT** how the private option works in ACT! if the contact record is marked as private and "linked" to a company record. When a note or history record is created for a contact that is linked to a company record, they are visible (available for other users to see) from the company record by default. If this is not what you want to happen, mark the note as private on the Insert Note dialog box.

Depending on a users rights, they may not be able to see all of the contact information that is displayed under the company record. Users that have rights to the contact record will be able to view the activity and opportunity records that are displayed under the company record.

Contacts can be associated to multiple companies and divisions, but can only be linked to one company.

Linking Issues

Overall, linking contacts to companies is a good feature to have and use. Depending on how sensitive some of the contact data is, you may not want it to be shared. Some contact data is automatically shared. I think that it is important that you understand how linking works.

By default, contact notes, history, activity and opportunity records are displayed under the company record(s) that they are linked to. I thought that if the link between a contact and company was removed, that the contacts history, activity and opportunity records would also be removed from the company record, but that is not the case.

I can understand why they are not automatically removed because the primary purpose of company records is to build a profile of the company, which includes the interactions with all of the contacts associated or linked with the company. I just wanted to let you know that the contacts linked data is not automatically removed from the company record when the contact record is unlinked.

Solutions

There are ways to prevent notes and history records that you want to remain private, from being displayed under the company record.

① As you already learned, when you create a note you can mark it as **PRIVATE**.

② If you know that you do not want any contact note and history records to be displayed under company records, clear the **SHARE NEW NOTES AND HISTORIES ON LINKED CONTACTS. . .** option shown earlier in Figure 4-11. With this option cleared (not checked), you can share a specific note if you have the need to do so.

Associating Companies And Groups

You can associate companies and groups to the following types of records: Activity, history, notes and opportunity with relative ease, as you will learn throughout this book. Each of the dialog boxes listed below have an **ASSOCIATE WITH** or **GROUP/COMPANY** field. Click the ellipsis button at the end of either of these fields and select the companies and groups that you want to associate to the record.

① Schedule Activities [See Lesson 8, Figure 8-1]
② Record History [See Lesson 12, Figure 12-24]
③ Insert Note [See Lesson 2, Figure 2-18]
④ Opportunity [See Lesson 10, Figure 10-16]

Exercise 4.7: Creating Manual Links Between Contacts And Companies

In this exercise you will learn several ways to link contact and company records.

Manually Link A New Contact With A Company

In this part of the exercise you will create the contact record and then link it to a company.

1. Open a new contact record and enter the name `Jane Doe`.

2. Click the ellipsis button next to the Company field, then select the company, My Company and click OK. You will see that the company name is a link on the Contact Detail view.

3. Click the Save button. If you click on the company link, you will see the company record on the Company Detail view.

Manually Link An Existing Contact With A Company

In this part of the exercise you will learn how to link an existing contact to a company.

1. Right-click in the Contact field in the Contact Detail view and select **LOOKUP CONTACT**.

2. Type `Charles Smith` in the Contact field, then press Enter.

3. Click the ellipsis button next to the Company field. Select the company, My Company, then click OK.

> You can link or associate a contact to a division or subdivision the same way that you link a contact to a company. In both parts of Exercise 4.7, instead of selecting the company, select the division or subdivision.

Exercise 4.8: Link Multiple Contact Records To A Company Record

This type of linking is another example of the static link option that you learned about earlier.

1. Create a lookup that retrieves records that have **LOOKUP** in the Company field.

2. Select (highlight) both records in the Contact List view, then Companies ⇒ Link to Company.

3. Select the company, My Other Company, then click OK.

4. Click Yes when prompted to replace the company link. Click OK when prompted that no more records match the search criteria.

This message is letting you know that the company name will be replaced, which is what you want. This is one way that you can change the company that several contacts are linked to, at the same time.

If you look at the My Other Company record on the Company Detail view, you will see that both contacts (Laura Smith and Tom Wood) have the new company name. Their old company name was "Lookup".

Exercise 4.9: Understanding The Power Of Linking

In the previous exercise you linked two contact records to a company record. Figure 4-13 shows the company and contacts associated with it. Notice that the Company field for John Doe is blank. This is how you can visually tell which contacts are linked to a company and which ones are associated to a company. In this exercise you will rename the company and observe the changes.

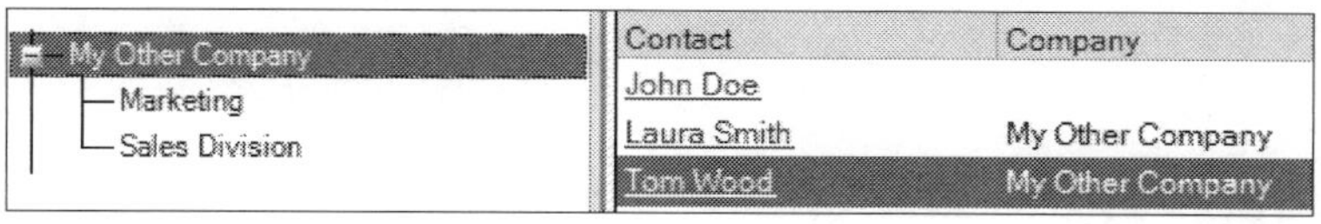

Figure 4-13 Contacts linked and associated to the same company

1. Open the My Other Company record in the Company Detail view.
2. Change the Company name to `My New Company`.
3. View ⇒ Refresh. This will update the company name throughout the database.

Linking And Unlinking Contact And Company Fields

You have learned that you could link the company name field on the contact record to the company name field in the company record. This is also true for other fields on the contact record.

An important concept to remember about linking fields is that the fields that you want to link should be the same data type or a compatible data type. Otherwise, you will have trouble linking the fields. For example, you should not try to link a date field to an email field.

> If you created a linked company record field it is applied to all company records, not just a particular record. The same is true if you unlink a company record field.

Viewing Linked Fields

Companies ⇒ View Linked Fields, will display how company fields are linked to contact fields, as shown in Figure 4-14.

The **DEFINE FIELDS** button opens a dialog box that allows you to create, edit or delete fields. You will learn more about this option in the next exercise.

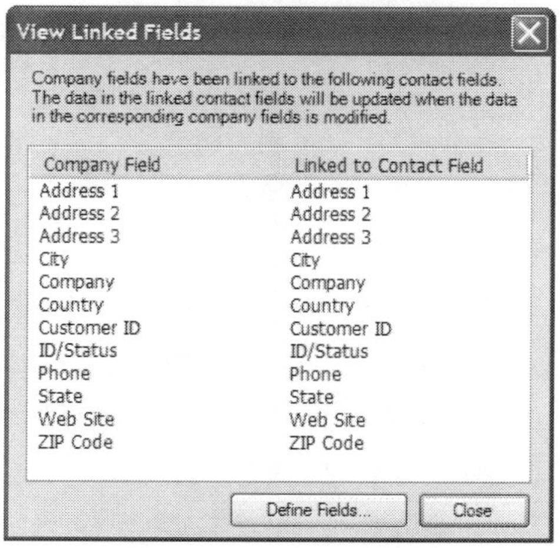

Figure 4-14 View Linked Fields dialog box

Exercise 4.10: Create A Linked Billing Address Field

In this exercise you will modify the Billing Address 1 field in the company record so that it is linked to the contact User 5 field. This is not a link that you would create in a live database because it really does not make a lot of sense. The fields that are normally linked between contact and company records are already linked in this database, as shown above in Figure 4-14. Therefore, I had to select fields that were not already linked, to demonstrate how to use the linking feature.

1. Tools ⇒ Define Fields.

   Notice that the database is locked, as illustrated in Figure 4-15.

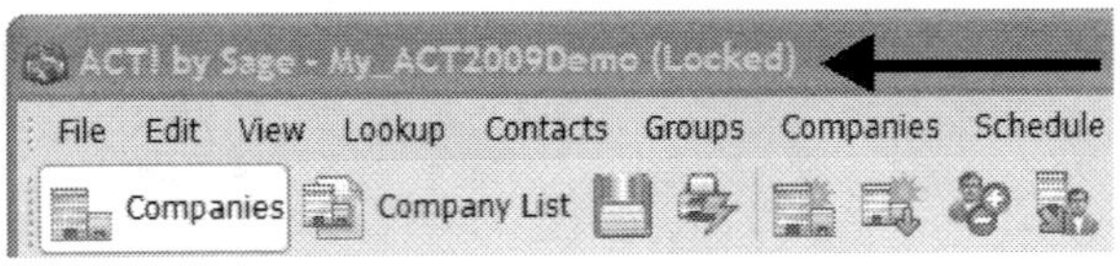

Figure 4-15 Locked database notification illustrated

2. Open the **VIEW FIELDS FOR** drop-down list and select Companies, if it is not already selected.

3. Click on the Billing Address 1 field.

   Click the **EDIT FIELD** link, illustrated in Figure 4-16, then click Next.

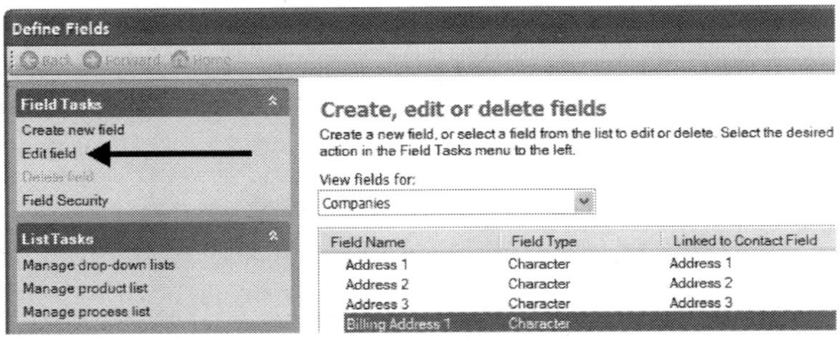

Figure 4-16 Edit Field link illustrated

4. On the Customize field behavior screen, check the **LINK TO CONTACT FIELD** option, then open the drop-down list. Notice that some fields are not enabled. You cannot select these fields to link to, because they have already been linked to a field.

5. Scroll down the list and select the User 5 field, then click Finish.

   In Figure 4-17, you will see that the Billing Address 1 field is linked to the User 5 contact field.

Field Name	Field Type	Linked to Contact Field
Address 1	Character	Address 1
Address 2	Character	Address 2
Address 3	Character	Address 3
Billing Address 1	Character	User 5

Figure 4-17 Billing Address 1 field linked to the User 5 contact field

6. Click Close.

Billing And Shipping Tab

In ACT! 2008 and earlier, this was called the **ADDRESSES** tab.

The fields shown in Figure 4-18 are used to store the billing and shipping address of the company, division or subdivision.

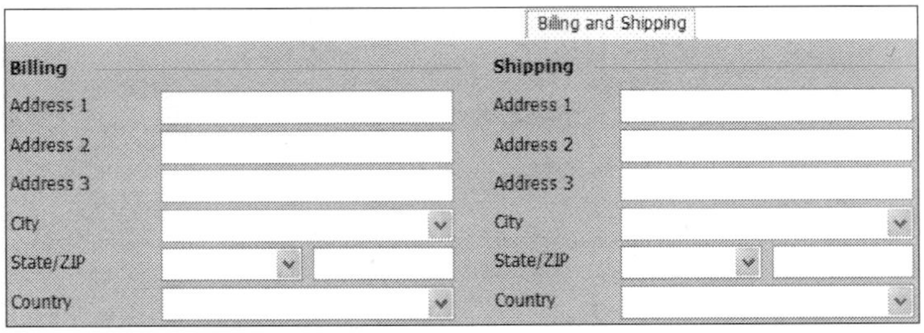

Figure 4-18 Billing and Shipping tab fields

Updating Contact Address Fields From The Linked Company Record

If a company moves, you would update the address fields on the company record. The next step is to update the contact records that are linked to the company record so that they display the updated address information. Before changing the company record, it is a good idea to view the linked contacts to make sure that they have the address that you are about to change. Companies can have several locations which means that there would be different addresses for the same company. You could create divisions under the company or create a different company record for each location. The steps below will show you how to change the address on the company record and update the linked contact records. For now you can read the steps. In the next exercise you will be able to practice this technique.

1. Open the company record and change the information in the linked field, then save the changes.
2. Click the **UPDATES THE LINKED CONTACTS FOR THE CURRENT COMPANY** button on the toolbar.
3. Click **YES** when you see the message shown in Figure 4-19.

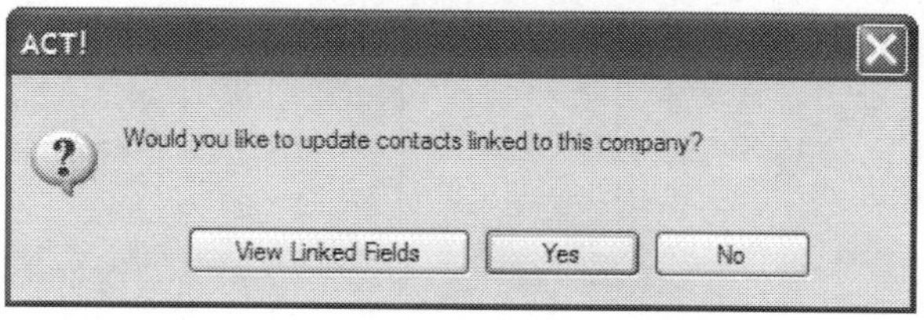

Figure 4-19 Update linked contacts message

Exercise 4.11: Test The Linked Field That You Created

To test the linked field, you will enter data in the Company Billing Address 1 field and observe how the linked contact records are updated.

1. Select the company My New Company, then click on the Billing and Shipping tab.
2. Type `Test field link` in the Address 1 Billing field.
3. Click the Updates the linked contacts for the current company button on the toolbar. Click Yes when you see the message shown above in Figure 4-19. The contact records will now be updated.

> If you click the Save button after making this type of change, you will also see the dialog box shown above in Figure 4-19.

4. On the Contacts tab, click on one of the records that has the company name, My New Company.
5. On the User Fields tab of the contact record, you should see the text that you entered in the Billing Address 1 field in the User 5 field, as shown in Figure 4-20.

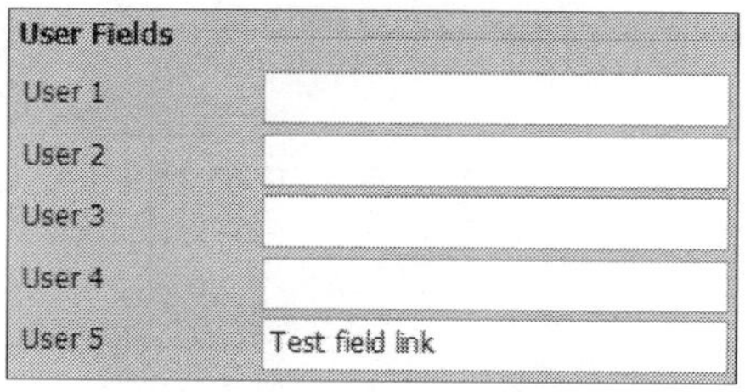

Figure 4-20 User 5 field updated

User Fields Tab

In the exercise that you just completed, you added data to a user field. If this were a live database you would rename the user field and update the layout. If you do not do this, other people that use the database will not know what type of data should be entered in the field.

Company Profile Tab

The fields shown in Figure 4-21 track the region, industry, revenue, SIC Code and more for each company, division and subdivision.

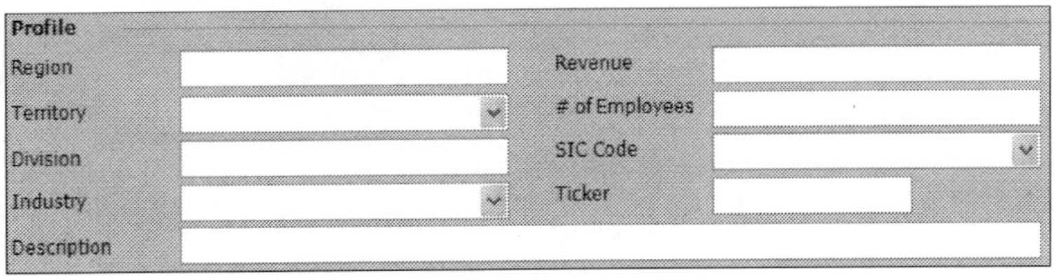

Figure 4-21 Company Profile tab fields

Company Access Tab

In ACT! 2008 and earlier, this was called the **COMPANY INFO** tab.

The fields shown in Figure 4-22, except for the Access Level options are updated by ACT! automatically. These fields store when the company record was created, by who and when it was last changed.

The **RECORD MANAGER** field can be manually changed to another user.

The **EDITED ON/BY** field contains when and who last updated the record.

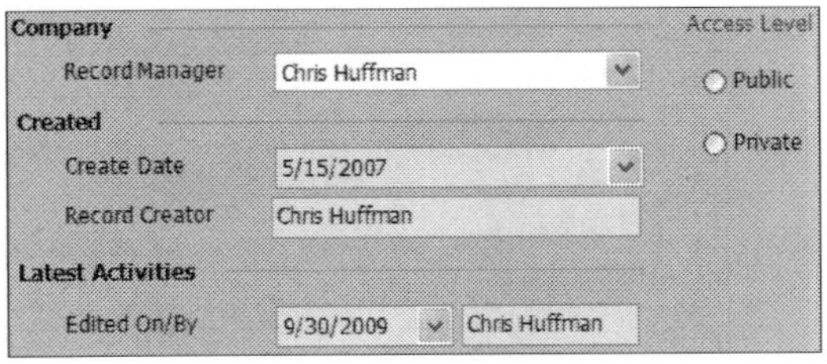

Figure 4-22 Company Access tab fields

Unlink A Company Record Field

If you have a company record field that is linked, but no longer need it to be linked, follow the steps below. You do not have to complete these steps now.

1. Tools ⇒ Define Fields.
2. Select the field that you want to unlink, then click the **EDIT FIELD** link.
3. Click Next, then clear the **LINK TO CONTACT FIELD** option shown in Figure 4-23.

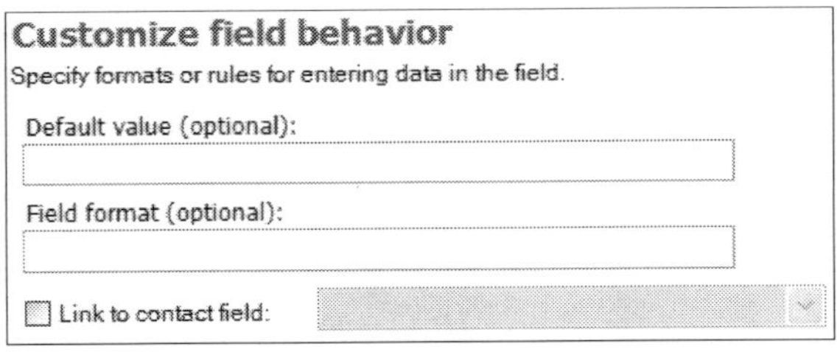

Figure 4-23 Customize field behavior options

4. Click Finish, then click Close.

Previously linked contact record fields that have data will keep the data even though the field is no longer linked to a company record field. Keep in mind that contact records can link to company records, which would update the company record when a contact record is changed.

Adding Contacts To Divisions

There are several ways to add contacts as discussed below. It would be easier if we could use drop and drag to add or move a contact record from one company or division to another one.

① Right-click on the division in the Companies tree and select **COMPANY MEMBERSHIP ⇒ ADD REMOVE/CONTACTS**. You will see the Add/Remove Contacts dialog box.
② Right-click on the contact on the Company Detail view and select **COMPANY MEMBERSHIP ⇒ ADD REMOVE CONTACTS**. You will see the Add/Remove Contacts dialog box.
③ Right-click on the contact on the Company Detail view and select **COMPANY MEMBERSHIP ⇒ ADD SELECTED TO COMPANY**. You will see the Add Contacts to Group/Company dialog box.

Exercise 4.12: Using The Companies Tree To Move A Division

You can drag divisions from one company to another. You can also drag a company to another company and make it a division.

1. In the Companies tree, expand the two companies that you created earlier in this lesson by clicking on the plus sign in front of them.

2. Drag the Finance division from the first company to the second company.

   Click Yes when prompted if you are sure that you want to move the company to a new location.

   The Companies tree should look like the one shown in Figure 4-24.

Figure 4-24 Division moved from one company to another

3. Use the Companies tree to move the contacts in Table 4-4 to the appropriate division.

Contact	Move From	Move To
Tom Wood	My New Company	Marketing
Laura Smith	My New Company	Sales Division
Jane Doe	My Company	Finance
Charles Smith	My Company	Sales Division

Table 4-4 Contacts to move

Exercise 4.13: Duplicating Company And Division Records

You can duplicate a company that has divisions, but the divisions are not duplicated. This is known as **DUPLICATING** a company. The process is similar to duplicating contacts.

1. In the Company Detail view, right-click on the company, My New Company and select Duplicate.

2. On the dialog box shown in Figure 4-25, select the option **DUPLICATE DATA FROM ALL FIELDS**, then click OK.

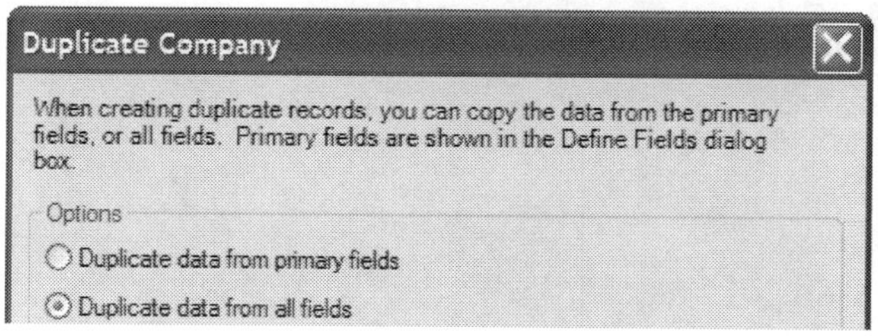

Figure 4-25 Duplicate Company dialog box

3. You will see a company record that looks like the one that you duplicated. Type `My Duplicate Company` in the Company field.

4. View ⇒ Refresh. Click on the new company in the tree.

Notice that there are no divisions and that the contact John Doe is a member. That is because this contact is not linked to the company, My New Company. If you click on the company record, My New Company, you will see the two other contacts shown earlier in Figure 4-13 because they are linked to the company.

Looking Up Companies

Looking up companies is similar to looking up contacts. Lookup ⇒ Companies, will display the Lookup Companies dialog box, which is similar to the dialog box that you use to look up contacts. The differences are discussed below.

① The Title bar on the dialog box has "Lookup Companies" instead of "Lookup Contacts".

② The fields in the first drop-down list are company related fields.

Exercise 4.14: Finding Companies

It is really important to make sure that the company data is as accurate as possible. Often, when adding a new company, you may not know or have all of the information that you want to enter for the company. From time to time it is a good idea to either look up records that do not have data in certain fields or create reports that show records that are missing data. If your company does a variety of promotional campaigns, it may be important to track how each contact was obtained. You could use the Referred By field to store this information. In this exercise you will find companies where the Referred By field is empty.

1. Lookup ⇒ Companies ⇒ Other Fields.
2. Open the Field drop-down list and select Referred By.
3. Open the second drop-down list and select the option **DOES NOT CONTAIN DATA**, as shown in Figure 4-26, then click OK.

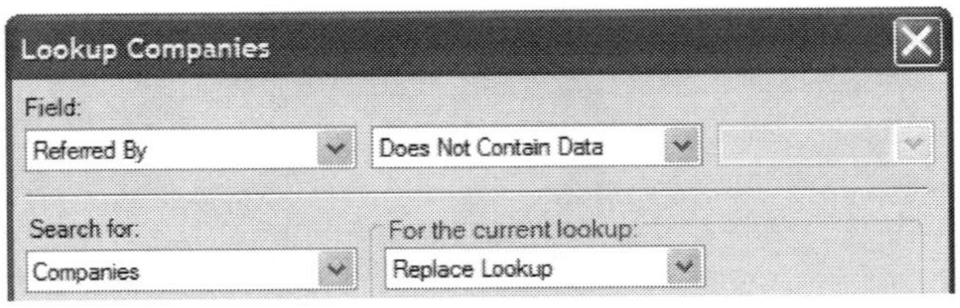

Figure 4-26 Lookup Companies dialog box

The companies and divisions that you see in the Company List do not have the Referred By field filled in. Someone should try to fill in this information.

Create A Company Note And Attachment

Creating a note for a company is the same process as creating a note for a contact. Creating a note for a company uses the same Insert Note dialog box that is used for creating notes for contacts. Creating a note with an attachment is also the same process as attaching a file to a contact record. Right-click on the company that you want to create a note for and select **INSERT COMPANY NOTE**. The company name will automatically be filled in the Group/Company field on the Insert Note dialog box.

Viewing Company Notes

Over time, the number of notes for companies can grow. If contacts are associated with a company, the Notes tab on the Company Detail view will have even more notes for you to sift through. As shown in Figure 4-27, the Notes tab on the Company Detail view has the **SHOW FOR** drop-down list filter.

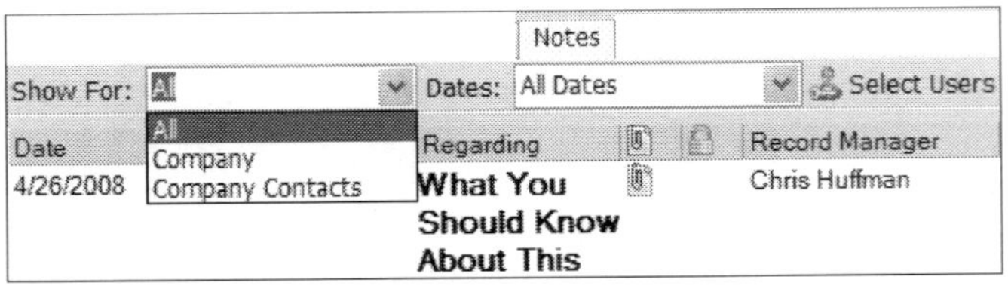

Figure 4-27 Notes tab on the Company Detail view

ALL will display both company and company contact notes.
COMPANY only displays notes that are created from a company record.

COMPANY CONTACTS only displays notes that were created for a contact in the company.
The difference between the Company and Company Contacts options are the level that the notes are created at.

Moving Companies And Divisions

Earlier in this lesson you learned that in the Companies tree you can drag companies and divisions to new locations. If you do not like to drag them, you can use the **MOVE** option on the shortcut menu shown earlier in Figure 4-4. You can complete this task from either company view. The steps below explain the process.

1. Right-click on the company or division that you want to move and select **MOVE**.

2. Select one of the options discussed below.

   ① On the dialog box shown in Figure 4-28, select the **PROMOTE DIVISION TO COMPANY** option to make the division that you selected a company.
   ② Select the **CHANGE TO BE DIVISION OF** option if you want the company or division that you selected to be a division of another company.

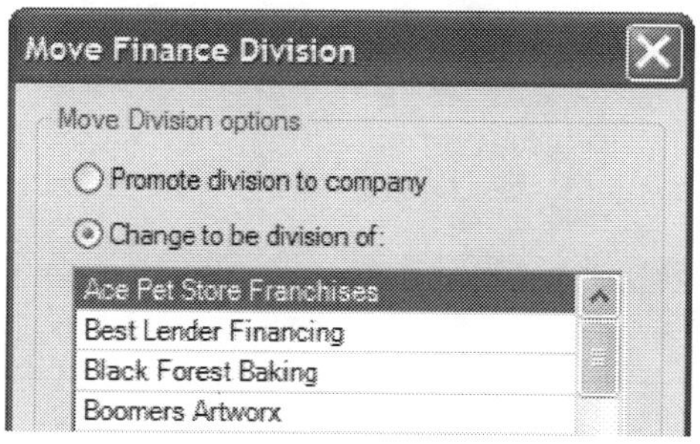

Figure 4-28 Move Division dialog box

3. Select the company that you want to move it to on the Move Division dialog box, then click OK.

> **Deleting A Company Record**
>
> If you need to delete a company record, any division records under it will be promoted to a company record, unless you delete the division record(s) first. You will not receive a warning that the company record that you are deleting has division record(s).

Removing Links Between Contact And Company Records

If a contact record is linked on the Company (name) field, it cannot be changed until you remove the link. You already learned that contact notes and history records that appear under the company record are not automatically removed. Removing the link between the contact and company is how the contact notes and history records remain under the company record. When you have the need to remove links, you can follow the steps below.

1. Open the contact record (in the Contact Detail view) that you want to remove to company link from.

2. Click the ellipsis button at the end of the Company field. You will see the message shown in Figure 4-29.

   The **UNLINK FROM COMPANY** option will remove the link between the contact and company records.

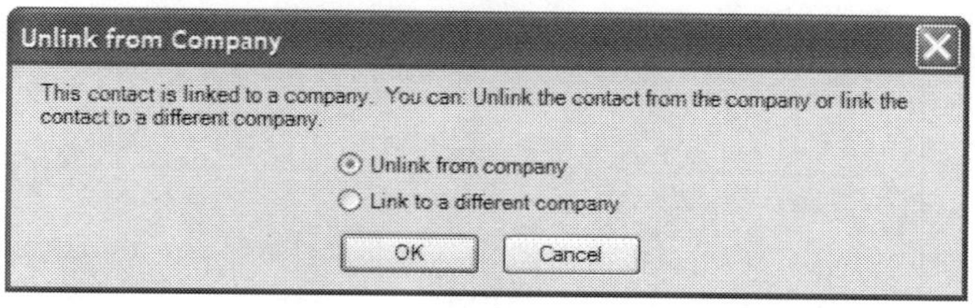

Figure 4-29 Unlink from Company dialog box

The **LINK TO A DIFFERENT COMPANY** option shown above in Figure 4-29, is used to link the contact to a different company. This would be helpful if the contact needs to be moved to a different company.

Selecting this option opens the dialog box shown in Figure 4-30, which is used to select the company. The company or division that you want to move the contact to, must already have a record in the database.

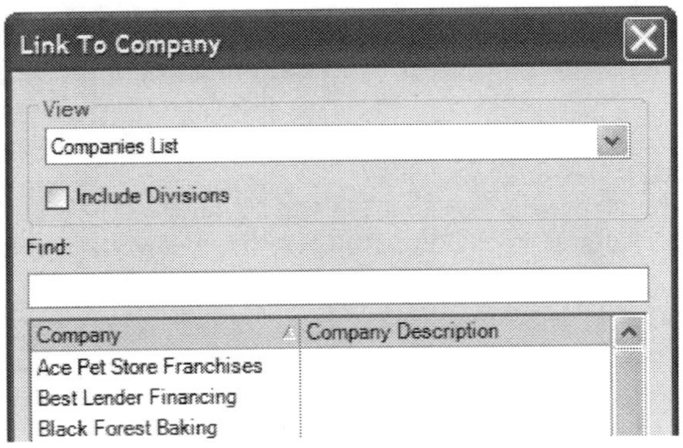

Figure 4-30 Link To Company dialog box

3. Click OK on the Unlink from Company dialog box. The link will be removed from the Company name field.

Using The Company List View

While the Company Detail view is probably the company view that you will use most often, the Company List view provides the same functionality. The Company List view shown in Figure 4-31 has the same shortcut menu options as the Companies tree shown earlier in Figure 4-3. Actually, the shortcut menu in the Company List view has more options. Like the Contact List view, you can sort on the column headings in the Company List view. If there are a lot of companies in the list you may have a need to filter them.

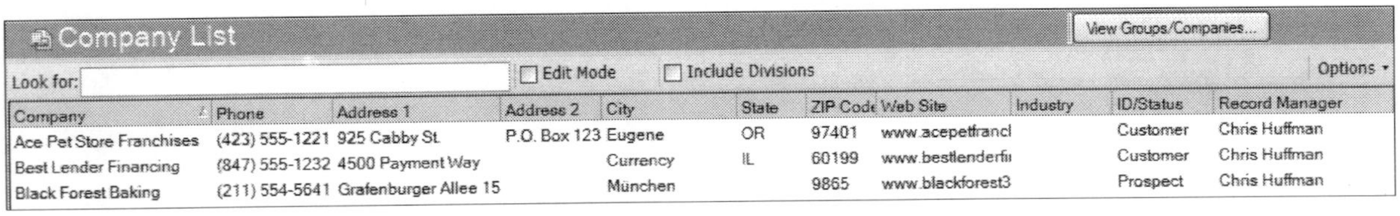

Figure 4-31 Company List view

The **EDIT MODE** option is used to modify records in the Contact List view.

The **INCLUDE DIVISIONS** option will display all of the division and subdivisions in the database. The problem is that the default options on the Company List view do not provide a visual way to know which record is a company, division or subdivision or which company a division or subdivision record belongs to.

If you customize the view and add the **HAS DIVISIONS**, **DIVISION** and **HIERARCHY LEVEL** fields to the view, you will be able to tell a division from a company, but not which company a division belongs to, as shown in Figure 4-32.

Hierarchy Level 0 is a company record.

Hierarchy Level 1 is a company or division record.

Hierarchy Level 2 is a division record.

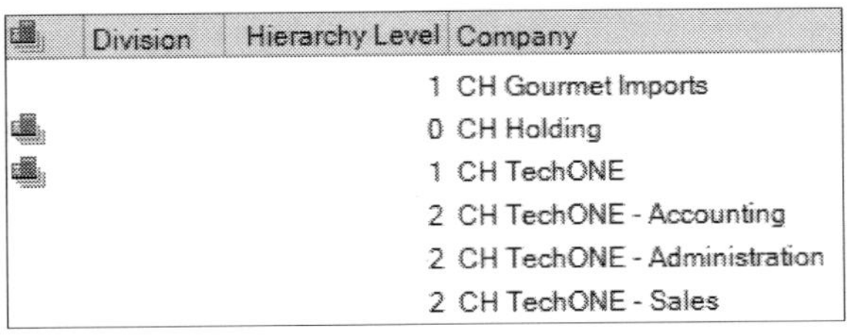

Figure 4-32 Company List view with division fields

Create A New Division

To create a new division from the Company List view, right-click on the company that you want to create the division for and select **NEW DIVISION**.

GROUPING CONTACTS

In this lesson you will learn about the following group and subgroup record options:

- ☑ Using the Groups tree
- ☑ Creating groups
- ☑ Adding contacts to a group or subgroup
- ☑ Managing group notes and attachments
- ☑ Saving the result of a lookup as a group or company
- ☑ Creating subgroups
- ☑ Converting a group to a company
- ☑ Using the Convert Groups to Companies Wizard

LESSON 5

Groups Overview

Grouping records is another way for you to be able to categorize and find contacts. You have learned how to use the lookup command to find contacts. The limitation to using the lookup command is that all of the contact records that you want to find have to have the same information in the same field. You could think of the group option as a free form way to classify or categorize contacts, because the contacts that you add to a group do not have to have any data in common. Like company records, group records can have 15 levels. You can create as many groups as you need.

If you wanted to group certain contacts together because they are all involved in the same project, you could create a group. You can add a contact to as many groups as needed. Grouping contacts helps you find and organize them quickly. The main benefit to creating groups over creating lookups, is that the group information is saved. Figure 5-1 shows the Group Detail view.

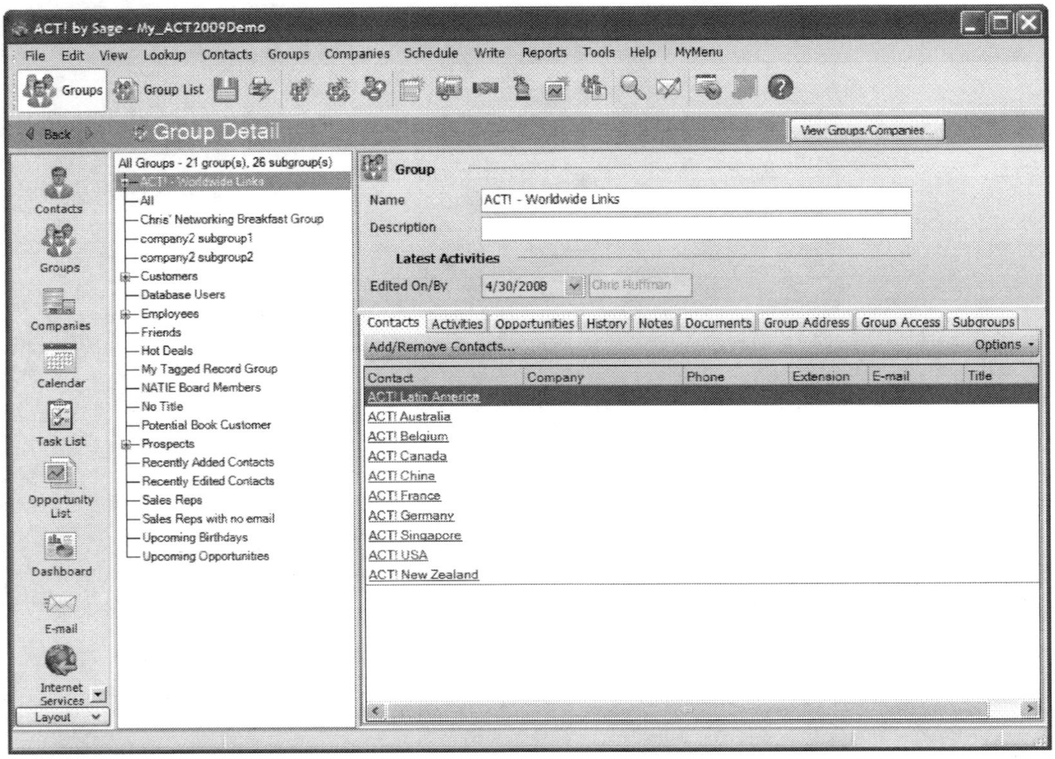

Figure 5-1 Group Detail view

The top right section of the Group Detail view displays the group name and description of the group that is selected in the tree. The bottom right section displays different information depending on which tab is selected. For example, the Group Access tab shows information about when the group was created, whether or not the group is private and who created it. The names on the Contacts tab are the contacts or companies that are in the group.

Groups Toolbar

Figure 5-2 shows the Groups toolbar. Table 5-1 explains the buttons on the toolbar.

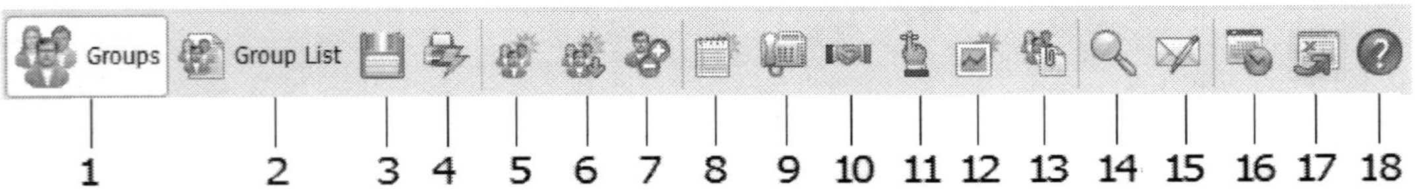

Figure 5-2 Groups toolbar

Button	Description
1	Opens the Group Detail view.
2	Opens the Group List view.
3	Saves the record. (1)
4	Opens the Print dialog box.
5	Creates a new group record.
6	Creates a new subgroup record.
7	Add or remove a contact. (2)
8	Creates a note. (2)
9	Schedules a telephone call activity. (2)
10	Schedules a meeting activity. (2)
11	Schedules a To-Do activity. (2)
12	Creates a new opportunity. (1) (2)
13	Attach a file. (2)
14	Displays the members. (2)
15	Compose and send an email.
16	Copies calendar information between the ACT! and Outlook calendars.
17	Exports the group list to Excel. Subgroup lists cannot be exported. This option is only available from the Group List view.
18	Opens the Help system.

Table 5-1 Groups toolbar buttons explained

(1) This option is only available from the Group Detail view.
(2) This option applies to groups and subgroups.

Good Groups And Not So Good Groups

These are the types of groups that you can create. An example of a not so good group would be a group that contained contacts in the same state. This is not a good use of a group because you can create a lookup by state to accomplish this.

An example of a good group would be a group that contained contacts that attended an insurance seminar that you were a guest speaker at. This is a good group because there is no existing field that you could create a lookup on to find these contacts. You could create an activity for the contacts in the group. It would appear on the Activities tab for the group.

The Groups Tree

The Groups tree is on the left side of the Group Detail view. At the top of the Groups tree, the number of groups and subgroups in the database are displayed, as shown above in Figure 5-1. If you click on a group in the tree, you will see the subgroups on the Subgroups tab.

A plus sign in front of a group means that there is at least one subgroup below it. The Employees group shown in Figure 5-3 has two subgroups, International Employees and USA Employees. The International Employees group has two subgroups, AsiaPac Employees and European Employees.

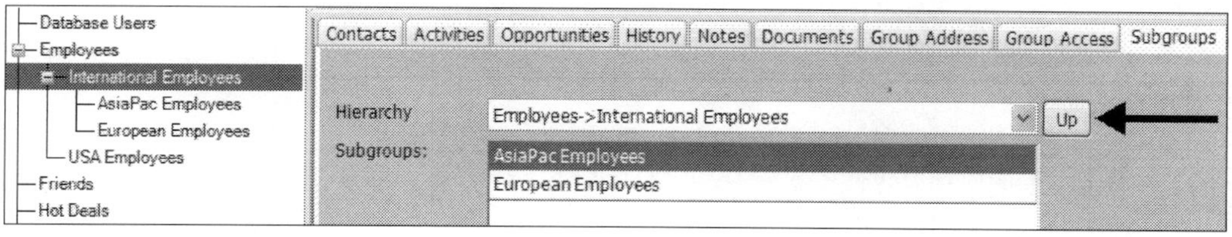

Figure 5-3 Groups and Subgroups on the Subgroups tab

The **UP** button illustrated above in Figure 5-3 is enabled if the group or subgroup that is selected is part of a larger group. Clicking this button will move up the hierarchy, one level at a time. This button is also on the Company Detail view. If you double-click on any subgroup shown, the detail record for the subgroup will be displayed.

View Groups/Companies Button

This button is available on the Contacts, Groups and Company Detail views. It will open the dialog box shown in Figure 5-4. It provides a quick way to view the public groups, subgroups, companies and divisions that are in the database.

Select the option in the **VIEW** drop-down list for the type of records (group or company) that you want to see. The corresponding records will be displayed at the bottom of the dialog box.

If you click OK, the records displayed are from the view that you selected.

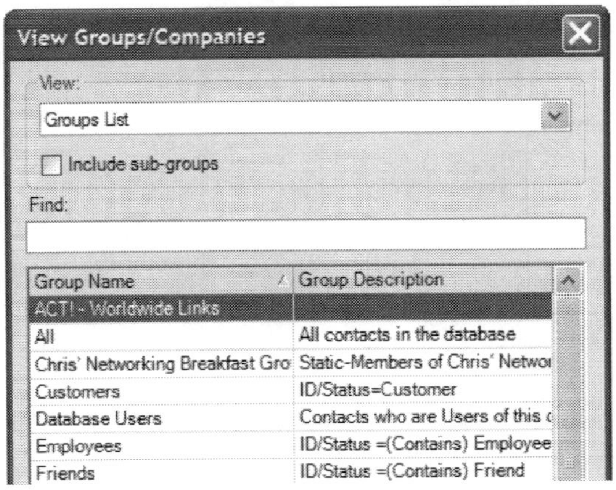

Figure 5-4 View Groups/Companies dialog box

Exercise 5.1: How To Create A Group

1. Click the **GROUPS** button in the Navigation bar.
2. Click the **NEW GROUP** button on the toolbar. You should see a new group record at the top on the right of the window.

You can also right-click on a blank space in the Groups tree and select **NEW GROUP.**

3. Type `Potential Customer` in the Group field.
4. Press the Tab key, then type `This group contains contacts that are interested in the next version of the book` in the Description field.

The Description field can have up to 128 characters.

5. Click Save.

   The group record should look like the one shown in Figure 5-5.

   Notice that the **HIERARCHY** field was filled in automatically and that the group appears on the left side of the window.

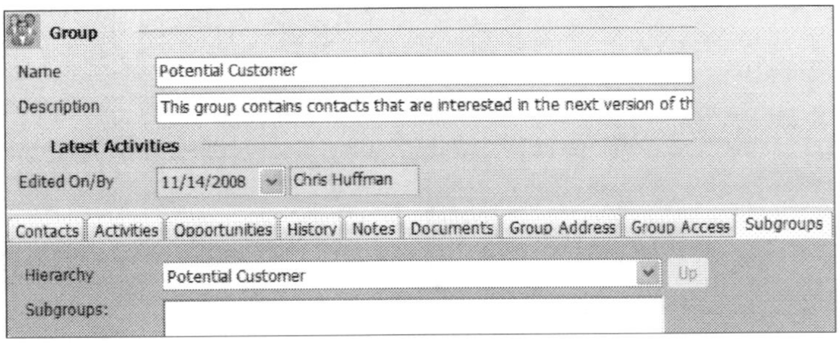

Figure 5-5 New group record created

Adding Contacts To A Group

There are several ways that you can add contacts to a group (or subgroup), as discussed below:

① You can scroll through the entire list of contacts in the Contact List view and select the contacts that you want, one by one and add them to a group. This is known as a **STATIC** group. The contacts stay in the group until you remove them.
② If possible, you can use the lookup command to find at least some of the contact records that you want to add to a group.
③ Select an existing group and add contacts from the existing group to the new group.
④ Contacts can automatically be added to a group if they meet the criteria of the query. This is known as a **DYNAMIC** group because contacts are added and removed based on whether or not they meet the criteria. There is no intervention on your part after creating the query. This type of group is updated each time the Groups/Companies tab on the Contact Detail or Group Detail view is displayed.
An example is a group for contacts that have the Sales Rep title. Contacts added to the database that have this title would automatically be added to the group. Any contact in the group whose title changes from Sales Rep would automatically be removed from the group. You will learn how to create this type of group in Lesson 11.

The benefit of using the last three options discussed above to add contacts to a group is that you do not have to scroll through all of the records in the database to select contacts to add to a group.

When you add a contact that has a note to a group, the contacts notes are displayed on the Groups Notes tab, unless the note is marked private. The owner of the private note will see the note on the Groups Notes tab, but other database users will not.

Exercise 5.2: How To Add Contacts One By One To A Group

The contacts that you will add to the group in this exercise are static.

1. Select the group that you want to add contacts to. In this exercise select the Potential Customer group.

2. Click the **ADD/REMOVE CONTACTS TO GROUP** button on the toolbar or the **ADD/REMOVE CONTACTS** button in the tab section of the window. You will see the Add/Remove Contacts dialog box.

3. Click the Contacts button.

4. Click on the contact Ashley Allan, then press and hold down the **CTRL** key and click on the following names: Bruce Baker, Sarah Baker and Kirby York.

5. Click the **ADD** button.

   The four contacts that you selected should be visible in the **SELECTED CONTACTS** list, as shown in Figure 5-6.

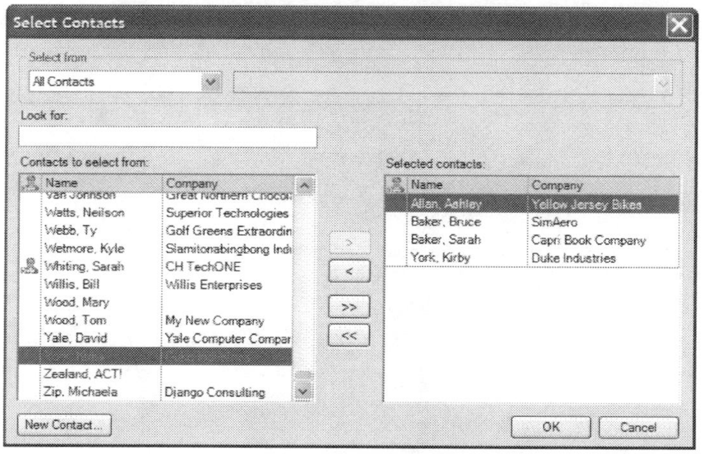

Figure 5-6 Contacts selected to be added to the group

The options in the **SELECT FROM** drop-down list and the (Group names) drop-down list to the right of it, are used to narrow or widen the number of names that appear in the **CONTACTS TO SELECT FROM** list. If you select the **GROUPS** option from the first drop-down list and the Hot Opportunities group from the second drop-down list you will see the contacts shown on the left of Figure 5-7.

If the database has a lot of names and you do not want to scroll through the list, you can type the name that you want to add to the group in the **LOOK FOR** field.

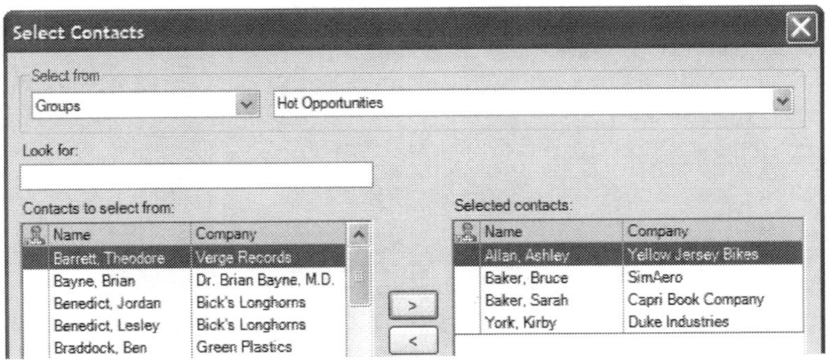

Figure 5-7 Contacts from an existing group

If you scroll through the list of names on the left, you will see that the names that you added to the group are grayed out. This lets you know that the contact is already a member of the current group or has been selected to be a member of the current group.

6. Click OK. You should see the contacts in the **STATIC MEMBERS** section of the Add/Remove Contacts dialog box.

7. Click OK. The contacts will now be added to the Potential Customer group. You will see the contacts at the bottom of the Contacts tab, as shown in Figure 5-8.

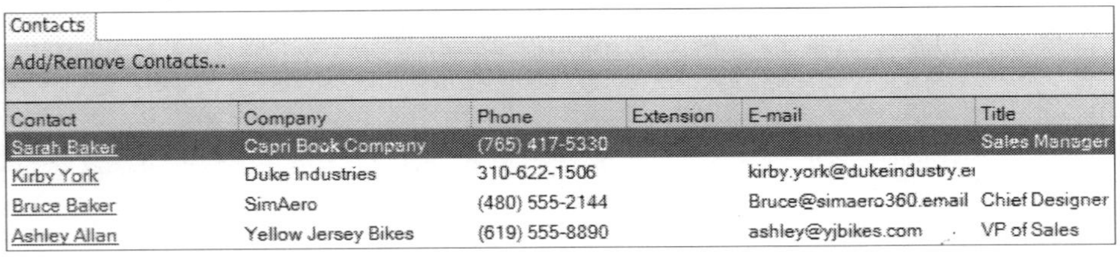

Figure 5-8 Contacts added to the group

To add a contact to a group, you can right-click on a contact record on either contact view and select **ADD CONTACT TO GROUP.**

Looking Up Groups

Looking up groups is similar to looking up companies. Lookup ⇒ Groups ⇒ Select an option, will display the same dialog box that you used in Lesson 3 to look up contacts. The differences on the Lookup dialog box are the same as the differences between contacts and companies. [See Lesson 4, Looking Up Companies]

Exercise 5.3: Finding Group Records

You have already learned how to find (look up) all of the contacts that were associated with a company. Looking up contacts that are in the same group is basically the same process. In this exercise you will create a look up for groups that do not have data in the Address 1 field.

1. Lookup ⇒ Groups ⇒ Other Fields.

2. Open the Field drop-down list and select the Address 1 field.

3. Open the next drop-down list and select the **DOES NOT CONTAIN DATA** option, as shown in Figure 5-9, then click OK.

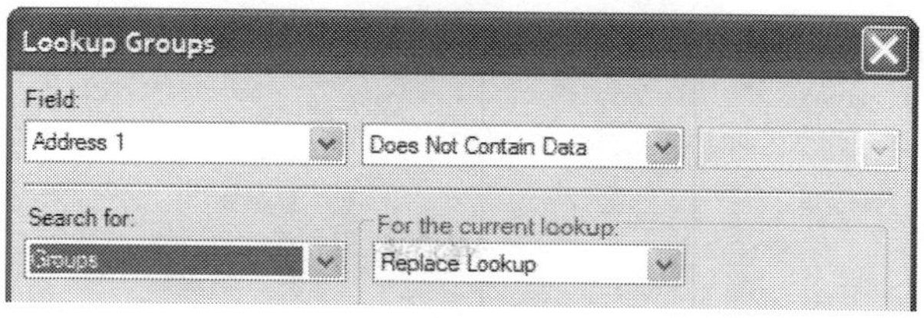

Figure 5-9 Lookup Groups dialog box

You will see the groups that do not have any information in the Address 1 field. If you double-click on any group in the Group List view and then click on the Group Address tab, you will see that the Address 1 field is empty.

Exercise 5.4: How To Rename A Group

The steps below will show you how to rename a group. To rename a subgroup, select the subgroup in step 1 instead of a group.

1. Click on the group that you want to rename in the Groups tree. In this exercise click on the Potential Customer group.

2. Type in the new group name. Type the word `Book` after the word **POTENTIAL** in the Name field on the right.

3. Click the Save button. The group will be renamed and the new name is displayed on the Groups tree.

> The reason that I click the Save button is because it refreshes the view. If you clicked on another group or subgroup in the tree and then come back to the group that you changed, you would see that the group was renamed.

Exercise 5.5: Add Contacts To An Existing Group

In this exercise you will find contacts in Arizona and add them to the Potential Book Customer group. To add contacts to a subgroup, select the subgroup in step 3 instead of a group.

Create The Lookup And Add The Contacts To The Group

1. Create a lookup to find all contacts in Arizona. There should be 18 records in the Contact List view.

2. Select (highlight) all of the records, then right-click on the highlighted records and select **ADD CONTACTS TO GROUP**, as illustrated in Figure 5-10.

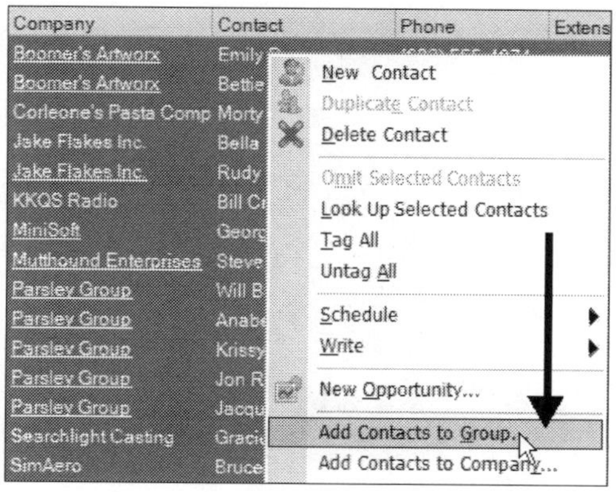

Figure 5-10 Option to add the contacts to a group illustrated

> If you do not want to right-click on the records, you can use Groups ⇒ Group Membership ⇒ Add Selected to Group.

3. Click on the Potential Book Customer group shown in Figure 5-11, then click OK.

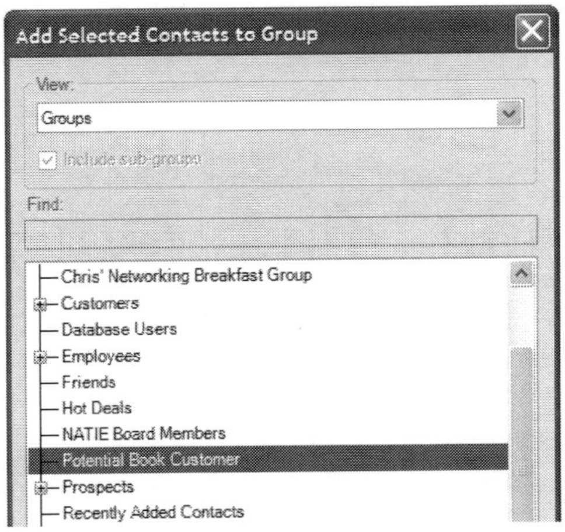

Figure 5-11 Group selected to add the contacts to

View The Contacts In The Group

1. Click the Groups button on the Navigation bar, then click on the Potential Book Customer group in the Groups tree.

2. On the Contacts tab, you should see the 18 contacts that you just added, plus the contacts that you added in a prior exercise. Click the Save button.

Exercise 5.6: Use The Lookup Command To Add Contacts To A Group

You can use this option when you have several records that have something in common that you want to add to the same group or subgroup. In this exercise you will create a lookup to find all contacts that have the Sales Representative title. After that, you will create a group and add the contacts to a group.

1. Create a lookup that finds all contacts that have Sales Representative as the title. Five records should have been retrieved.

2. Groups ⇒ New Group.

3. Type `Sales Reps` in the Name field, then type `This group contains all of the sales reps.` in the Description field.

4. Click the Add/Remove Contacts button below the tabs, then click the Contacts button.

5. Select the **CURRENT LOOKUP** option from the first drop-down list.

   You should only see the contacts from the lookup that you created, in the list of names on the left side of the dialog box, as shown in Figure 5-12.

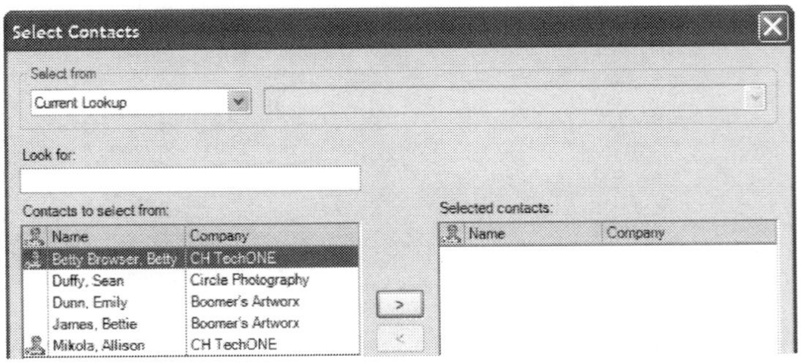

Figure 5-12 Contacts from the current look up

6. Click the **ADD ALL>>** button. All of the contacts should be in the **SELECTED CONTACTS** list on the right side of the dialog box. Click OK twice to close both dialog boxes.

7. In the Group Detail view click on the Sales Reps group in the Groups tree, if it is not already selected. On the Contacts tab you will see the five contacts that are in the group.

How To View The Groups That A Contact Is A Member Of

1. Click on the link for Emily Dunn.

2. On the Groups/Companies tab in the Contact Detail view, open the **SHOW MEMBERSHIP FOR** drop-down list and select Groups and Subgroups. You will see that this contact is a member of the Sales Rep group that you just created and the Potential Book Customer group that you created earlier in this lesson.

Exercise 5.7: How To Manage Group Notes And Attachments

The Notes tab on the Group Detail view is used to view notes for the group, just like you can view notes for a contact. If you create a note for the group, you only have to type it in once and it will be associated with all contacts in the group. You can also assign a contacts note to a group. There are several ways to create a note for a group.

All of the group management of notes and attachments discussed in this exercise also apply to creating, editing and maintaining company notes and attachments.

How To Create A Group Note And Attach A File To The Group Note

In addition to adding a note to a group, you can attach files like charts, spreadsheets or sales literature to a group. Doing this allows you to keep all of the attachments for the group in one place.

1. Click the Groups button, then click on the Potential Book Customer group.

2. On the Notes tab, click the **INSERT NEW NOTE** button. You should see the Potential Book Customer group name in the Group/Company field on the Insert Note dialog box.

3. Type `These contacts have requested a book catalog.` in the **REGARDING** field.

4. Select the text that you just typed and change the font to Comic Sans MS, then change the font size to 12.

5. Change the color to red. The color option is to the right of the Font size drop-down list. Leave the dialog box open to complete the next part of the exercise.

How To Attach A File To A Group

In Lesson 2 you attached a file to a contact record. Attaching a file to a group record is the same process.

1. Click the **ATTACH** button, then select File.

2. Double-click on the L2 Attach file in your folder.

   The note should look like the one shown in Figure 5-13.

   Click OK.

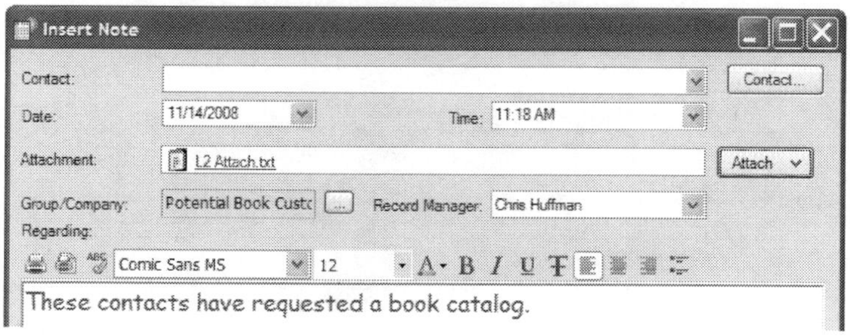

Figure 5-13 Group note

View The Group Notes And Attachments

1. On the Notes tab, open the **SHOW FOR** drop-down list and select Group. The entry should be the one for the note shown above in Figure 5-13.

2. Click on the Attachment icon for the note. The attached file will open. Close the attached file.

Exercise 5.8: Assign A Contact Note To A Group And Individual Contacts

In this exercise you will complete the following tasks:

① Create two notes for a contact that is in a group.
② Associate one of the notes to contacts in the group that the contact in the task above, is a member of.
③ Associate one of the notes to one contact that is not in the group.
④ Associate the second note to a group that the contact in the first task above is not a member of.

Add The Contact To Another Group

1. Click on the Potential Book Customer group on the Group Detail view.

2. On the Contacts tab, right-click on the contact Sarah Baker and select Group Membership ⇒ Add Selected to Group.

3. Scroll down the list of groups on the left and select the Prospects - Hot Opportunities group, then click the Add button.

   The contact should be a member of the two groups shown in the Group Membership list in Figure 5-14.

   Click OK.

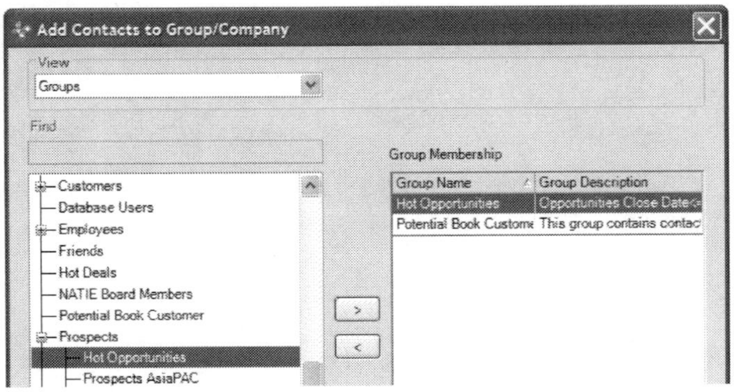

Figure 5-14 Add Contacts to Groups/Company dialog box

Create The Notes

In this part of the exercise you will create the notes for Sarah Baker.

1. Open the Contact Detail view for the contact Sarah Baker. (**Hint:** If you are in the Group Detail view, click on the contacts name on the Contacts tab).

2. Click on the Notes tab in the Contact Detail view, then create the notes in Table 5-2.

Note	Regarding Field	Formatting
1	`This is the first contact note for S. Baker. It will be applied to individual contacts in 2 groups and 1 contact that is not in a group.`	Change the font size to 10. Change the text color to green and bold.
2	`This is the second contact note for S. Baker. It will be applied to the group via the Insert Note dialog box.`	Change the color of the text to purple, bold and italic. Complete steps 3 and 4 below, before closing this note.

Table 5-2 Notes to create for Sarah Baker

3. Click the button at the end of the Group/Company field on the Insert Note dialog box.

   Click OK to share the note, as indicated in Figure 5-15.

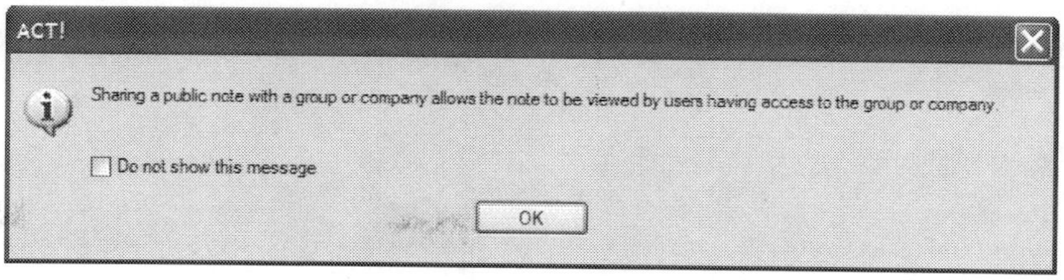

Figure 5-15 Sharing a public note message

4. Select the Potential Book Customer group to add to the note. You should have the options shown in Figure 5-16.

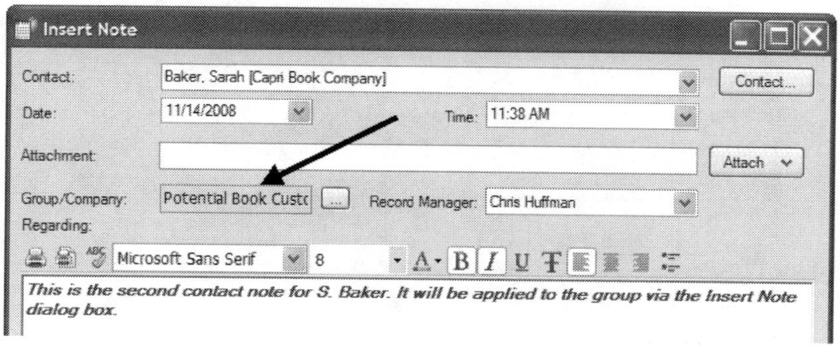

Figure 5-16 Note associated to a group

Associate The Notes

In this part of the exercise you will associate the two notes that you just created to other contacts.

1. Locate the first note that you created in Table 5-2 above for Sarah Baker in either the Contact Detail or Group Detail view, then double-click on the note.

2. Click the **CONTACT** button on the Edit Note dialog box and add the contact George Bailey to the Selected contacts list.

3. Open the **SELECT FROM** drop-down list on the Select Contacts dialog box and select Groups, then select the Sales Reps group from the next drop-down list. You will see the contacts for the group at the bottom of the dialog box.

4. Add Bettie James to the contact list.

5. Select the Prospects group from the second drop-down list at the top of the dialog box.

6. Add the contacts Mary Bailey and Kirby York.

   You should have the contacts selected that are shown in Figure 5-17.

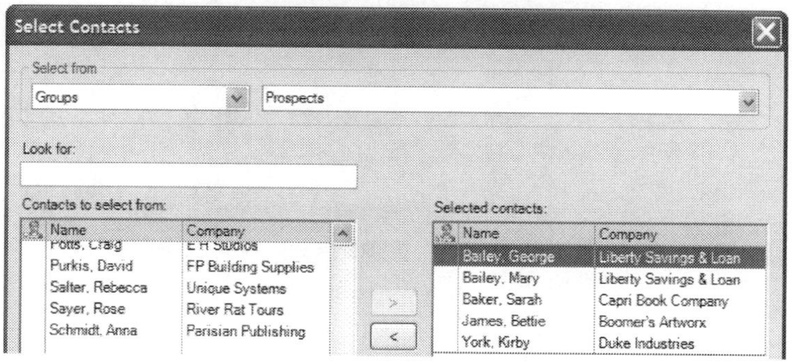

Figure 5-17 Group contacts selected

7. Click OK twice to close both dialog boxes.

   When you see the dialog box shown in Figure 5-18 select the first option, then click OK.

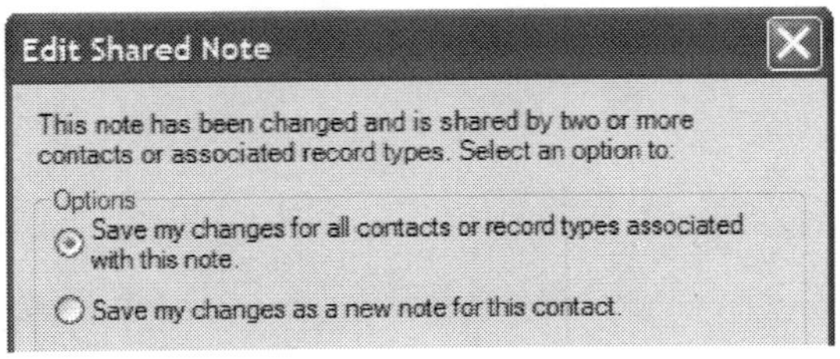

Figure 5-18 Edit shared note options

Editing A Shared Note

After creating a note, you may need to update the information in the note. When you modify a note that is shared with groups or contacts, you will see the dialog box shown above in Figure 5-18. Select the option for how you want the changes to the note to be applied.

View The Notes

1. Create a lookup by last name. Search for Bailey. You will see three contacts.

2. Switch to the Contact Detail view. George and Mary Bailey will have the first note in Table 5-2 above (in green). Peter Bailey does not. This is correct.

3. Switch to the Group Detail view. The note with green text should also be available in the Prospects group. If you do not see the note, select **GROUP CONTACTS** in the Show for drop-down list.

4. View the Potential Book Customer group notes. You will see the second note that you created in Table 5-2 above. You will also see the first note because it was created by Chris Huffman (aka you) who is a member of the Potential Book Customer group.

Show For Drop-Down List Options

The options in the **SHOW FOR** drop-down list shown in Figure 5-19 are available on the Notes, History, Activities and Opportunities tabs in the Group Detail view.
The options are used to filter the records that are displayed on the tab. [See Lesson 4, Viewing Company Notes]

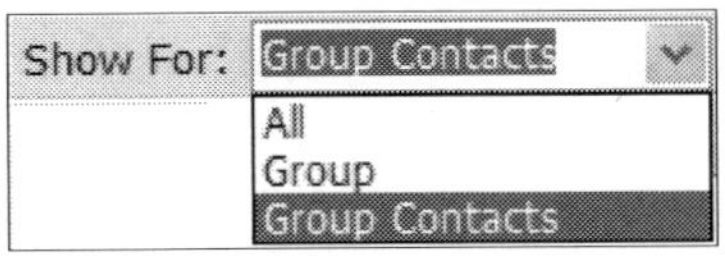

Figure 5-19 Show For drop-down list options

By default, group level notes cannot be viewed on the Notes tab in the Contact Detail view.
To know if there is a group note for the contact, click on the Groups/Companies tab on the Contact Detail view. Double-click on the group, then click on the Notes tab in the Group Detail view.

If the note is long, you will not see all of it on the Notes tab. If you look to the far right of the window, you should see a shaded area. This is the Preview area.

If you click on a note, you will see the entire note on the right side in the preview area. You can resize the Preview area by placing the mouse pointer in the position illustrated in Figure 5-20, then drag the mouse pointer in the direction that you want to resize the window to.

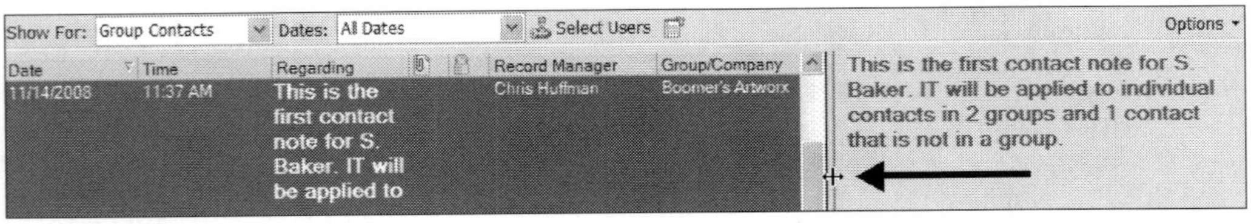

Figure 5-20 Preview area illustrated

If you do not want to have the Preview area visible, you can hide it by clicking on the Options button and clearing the **SHOW PREVIEW** option, shown in Figure 5-21. You can do this on any Notes tab.

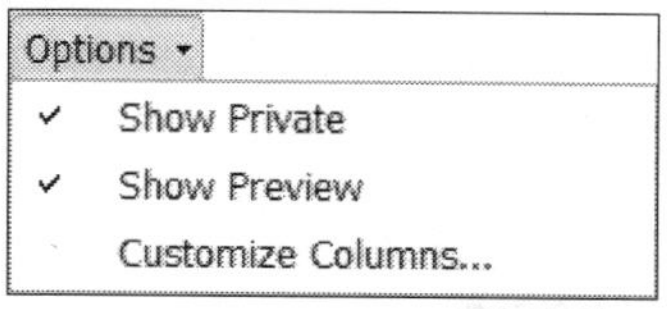

Figure 5-21 Options button drop-down list

Exercise 5.9: How To Save The Result Of A Lookup As A Group Or Company

If you create a lookup that you will need to use over and over, you can save it as a Group or Company by following the steps below. The number of records in this type of group or company can change. If the value in the field(s) that the lookup is using changes and now meets the criteria, the contact record will automatically be added to the group or company. If the value in a contact record field changes and no longer meets the lookup criteria, the record will automatically be removed from the group or company.

In this exercise you will save the results of the lookup as a group and a company. On your own, you do not have to save the same lookup results both ways. Select the option that works best for you.

1. Create an Email Address lookup for contacts that do not have an email address. 114 records should be retrieved.

2. Lookup ⇒ Groups ⇒ Save Lookup as Group.

3. Type `My Group Lookup No Email Address` as the group name, then View ⇒ Refresh, or press the F5 key.

4. Lookup ⇒ Companies ⇒ Save Lookup as Company.

5. Type `My Company Lookup No Email Address` as the company name, then View ⇒ Refresh.

If you view the records under the company and group that you just created, you will see that both have the same records. Normally, you would not save the same records to a group and company. It is done here for illustration purposes so that you can learn both methods of saving the result of a lookup.

Subgroups

A subgroup is usually a subset of the contacts in the group. In the previous exercise you created a group that contains contacts that do not have an email address. If you wanted to further categorize the contacts in the group by company, title, state, status or just about anything that you can think of, you can create a subgroup. Subgroups can be 15 levels deep, meaning subgroups can have subgroups. Subgroups are similar to divisions that companies have.

Exercise 5.10: Creating Subgroups

In this exercise you will create two subgroups for the My Group Lookup No Email Address group: One for sales reps and one for title.

1. In the Group Detail view, right-click on the My Group Lookup No Email Address group in the Groups tree and select **NEW SUBGROUP**.

2. Type `Sales Reps with no email` in the Name field.

3. In the Description field, type
   `This subgroup contains sales reps that do not have an email address.`

4. Click on the My Group Lookup No Email Address group in the Groups tree. You should see the subgroup.

5. Create another subgroup under the My Group Lookup No Email Address group. Use `No Title` as the subgroup name.

6. In the Description field, type
   `These contacts do not have a title.`

   You should have the subgroups shown in Figure 5-22.

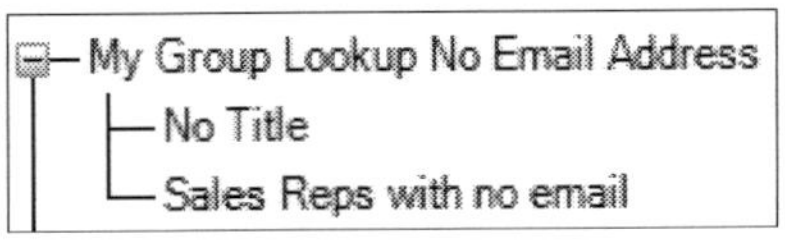

Figure 5-22 Subgroups

Exercise 5.11: Moving (Copying) Contact Records Between Groups And Subgroups

After the subgroups are created, it is a good idea to move the appropriate records from the group to a subgroup, if applicable. In this exercise you will move contacts that have the Sales Rep title to the corresponding subgroup and contacts that do not have a title to a different subgroup. There are two ways to move contact records between groups and subgroups, as discussed below:

① Move the contacts manually.
② Use a query. You will learn how to do this in Lesson 11.

Keep in mind that the contact records are not physically removed from the group and placed in the subgroup. The contact records are copied. This means that contact records at the group level can also be in a subgroup.

There are three ways to avoid this if you think that it will drive you crazy to see the same contacts in the group and subgroup. This is one of the items on my wish list that I would like to see improved. I think it would be easier if we could move contacts between groups and subgroups.

① Do not create any subgroups. Only create groups.
② Use the Add/Remove Contacts dialog box to remove the contacts from the group after they are added to a subgroup.
③ Do not add records to a group that you really only want to see in a subgroup.

Moving Records Manually

1. Click on the My Group Lookup No Email Address group, then click on the Contacts tab.

2. Sort the contacts by the Title field. The contacts that do not have a title should be at the top of the list.

3. Click in the row of the first contact without a title. Press and hold down the Shift key, then click in the row of the last contact record that does not have a title.

4. Groups ⇒ Group Membership ⇒ Add Selected to Group.

> Right-clicking on the highlighted records opened a shortcut menu, but did not keep all of the records selected.

5. Scroll down the list and select the **NO TITLE** subgroup, illustrated in Figure 5-23, then click OK.

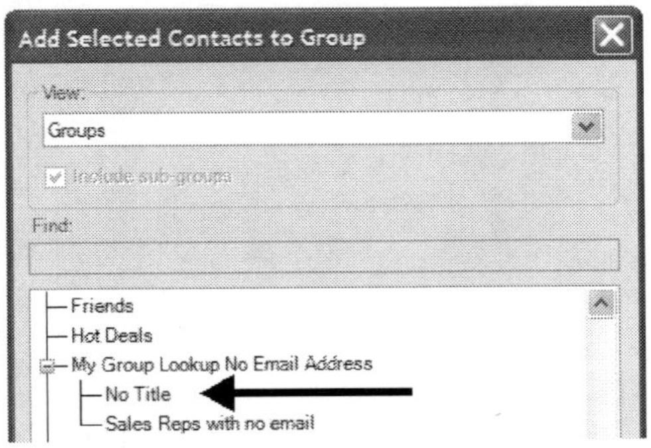

Figure 5-23 Subgroup illustrated

6. On the Contacts tab, select all of the contacts that have the Sales Representative title in the My Group Lookup No Email Address group and add them to Sales Reps with no email subgroup. (**Hint:** Sort the contacts on the Title field.)

7. If you click on the Sales Reps with no email subgroup you will see the contacts that you added, as shown in Figure 5-24.

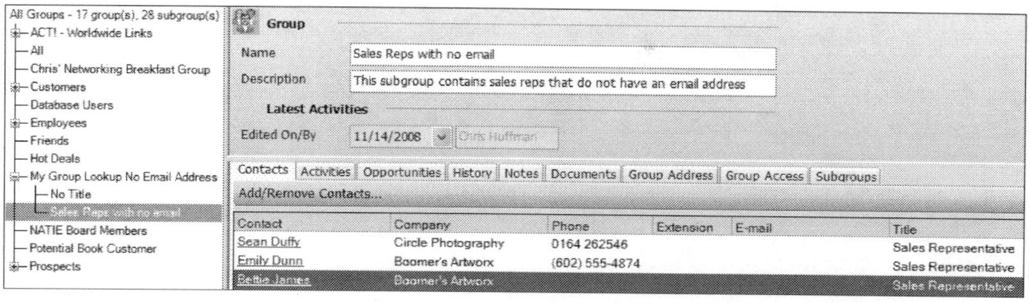

Figure 5-24 Contacts in a subgroup

Deleting Groups Or Subgroups

You may have a need to delete a group or a subgroup. When you delete a group or subgroup, the contacts in the group or subgroup, their notes and attachments are not deleted. The groups notes, history records and attachments are deleted.

Subgroups of the group that will be deleted are not deleted. The subgroup is automatically promoted to a group. If you need to delete a group or subgroup, you can follow the steps below. For now, you can read this section because you do not need to delete a group or subgroup.

How To Delete A Group

1. Right-click on the group in the Group Detail or Group List view and select Delete.

2. Click Yes when prompted to delete the current group.

How To Delete A Subgroup

1. Right-click on the subgroup in the Group Detail or Group List view and select Delete.

2. Click Yes when prompted to permanently delete the current subgroup.

Removing Contacts From Companies Or Groups

There may be times when you need to remove contacts from a company, division, group or subgroup. An example would be if the contact leaves the company. If this is the case, you can follow the steps below to remove contacts that are not linked to a company, division or group record.

1. Right-click on the company, division, group or subgroup that has contacts that you want to remove in the tree, then select the appropriate option below.

   ① Company Membership ⇒ Add/Remove Contacts.
   ② Group Membership ⇒ Add/Remove Contacts.

2. Click the Contacts button on the Add/Remove Contacts dialog box.

3. Select the names that you want to remove in the **SELECTED CONTACTS** list, then click the Remove button.

4. Once you have removed the contact records, click OK twice to close both dialog boxes.

Converting A Group To A Company

Groups and subgroups can be converted to a company. If the group or subgroup that you convert has subgroups, the subgroups are not converted by default. They move up the hierarchy and quite possibly become a group. Contacts that are in the group or subgroup that is being converted, become members of the company.

One reason that you may convert a group to a company is because you need to use a feature (for the contact records that are currently in a group) that only a company record has. In the next exercise you will convert the My Group Lookup No Email group to a company.

Once you convert a group to a company, it cannot be converted back.

Exercise 5.12: Using The Convert Groups To Companies Wizard

1. In the Group Detail view, right-click on the My Group Lookup No Email Address group and select **CONVERT TO COMPANY**.

2. Click Next on the first screen of the wizard. You will see the screen shown in Figure 5-25.

   The **SELECT GROUPS** screen is used to select the group(s) that will be converted to a company.

   Because you selected the group before opening the wizard, the group is already selected and in the **SELECTED GROUPS** list on the right. This means that the group is ready to be converted to a company.

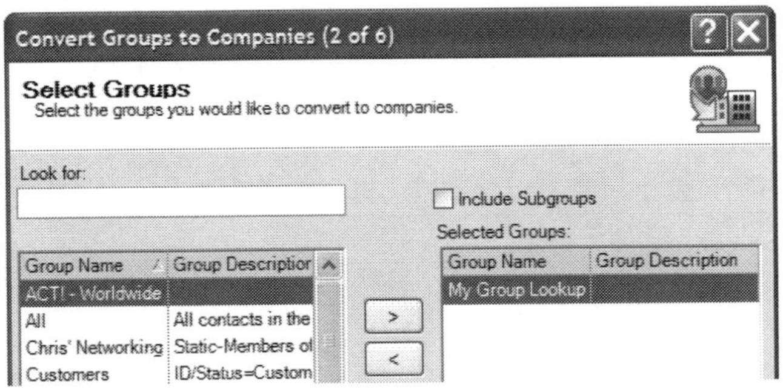

Figure 5-25 Select Groups screen

   If the group has subgroups that you also want to convert, check the **INCLUDE SUBGROUPS** option. If the group has more than one subgroup, the wizard does not allow you to select a specific subgroup to convert. You can convert the subgroups separately if you do not select the group first.

Groups ⇒ Convert To Company, will also open the wizard shown above in Figure 5-25.

3. Click Next.

   The **MAP FIELDS** screen shown in Figure 5-26 is used to select the field in the company record that data from a field in the group record will be moved to.

   If you need to select a different company field, click in the company field that needs to be changed and select the field that you need from the drop-down list, as shown on the right in Figure 5-26.

   If you modified the group view by adding fields to it, you will not see a corresponding field in the list of company fields. You will have to add a field to the company table first.

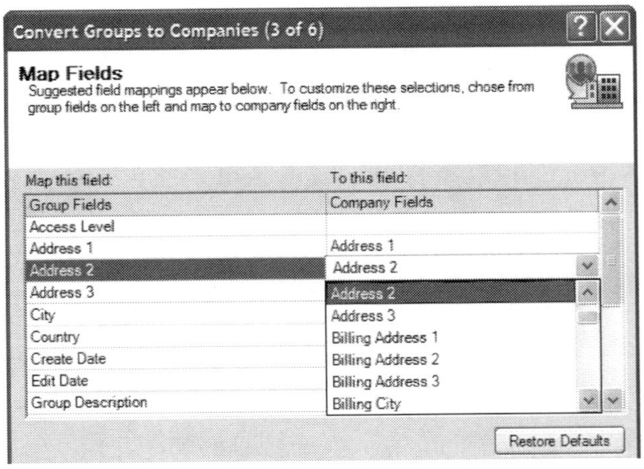

Figure 5-26 Map Fields screen

4. The fields are mapped correctly. Click Next on the Map Fields screen.

   The screen shown in Figure 5-27 displays the group(s) that will be converted.

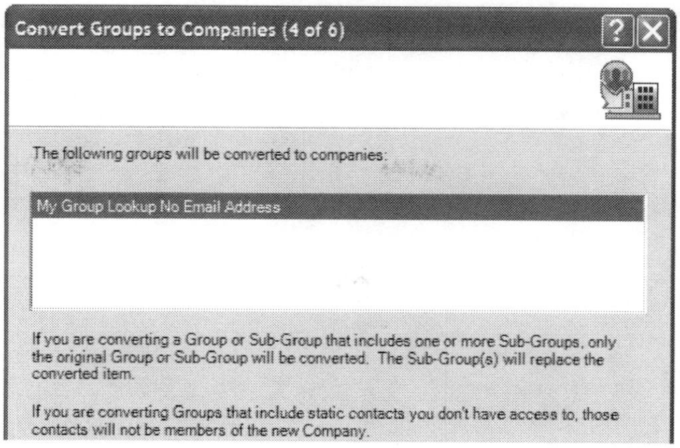

Figure 5-27 Groups to be converted screen

5. Click Next on the screen shown above in Figure 5-27. The Convert Groups to Companies screen informs you when the group has been converted.

6. Click Next after the group has been converted. Click Finish on the last screen of the wizard.

The group record has been removed. If you look in the Company Detail view you will see the My Company Lookup No Email Address company. If you need to change the company name you can.

Group Address Tab

The fields shown in Figure 5-28 are used to enter an address for the group.

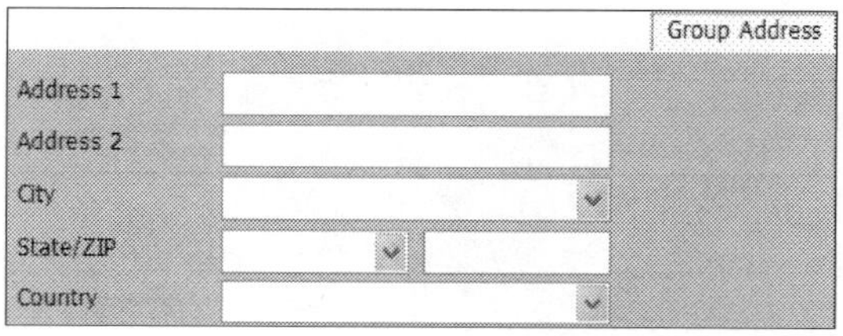

Figure 5-28 Group Address tab fields

Group Access Tab

In ACT! 2008 and earlier, this was called the **GROUP INFO** tab.

The fields shown in Figure 5-29 are filled in and updated by ACT! automatically. They cannot be changed. The fields are explained in Lesson 2. [See Lesson 2, Contact Access Tab]

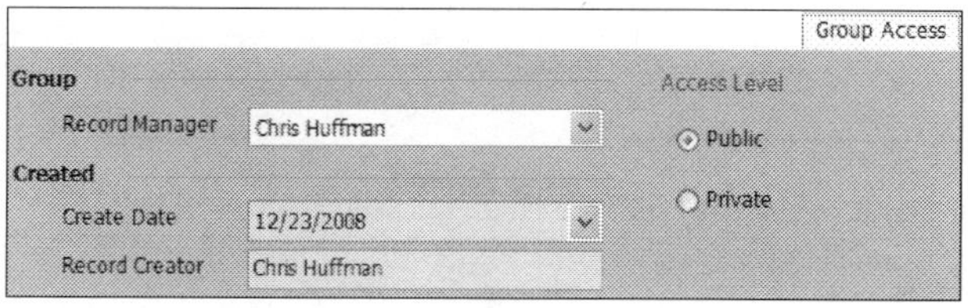

Figure 5-29 Group Access tab fields

Group List View

This view provides an easy way to see groups and subgroups, as shown in Figure 5-30.

The icon in the first column indicates that the group has subgroups, which is a benefit over the Company List view. If you do not want to see the subgroups, clear the **INCLUDE SUBGROUPS** option.

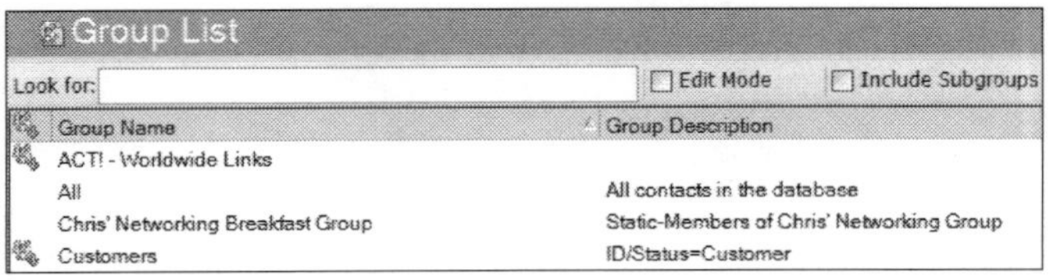

Figure 5-30 Group List view

USING THE ACT! WORD PROCESSOR

In this lesson you will learn the following word processing features:

- ☑ Creating, editing and formatting a document
- ☑ Creating bulleted lists
- ☑ Creating and changing tab stops
- ☑ Creating tables
- ☑ Header and Footer options
- ☑ Using Spell Check, Find and Replace
- ☑ How to add graphics to a document

If you do not plan to use the word processor that comes with ACT!, you can skip this lesson.

LESSON 6

ACT! Word Processor Overview

There is a word processing program included with ACT!. It should handle the majority of your needs. You can create letters, use existing templates and create new templates. You can also use the word processor to perform mail merges. This lesson does not go into detail on every word processing feature. The focus of this lesson is to demonstrate some of the word processors capabilities and options that you may use to complete tasks in ACT!.

Opening The Word Processor

If you have used another Windows based word processor, you will be very comfortable using this one.

1. Write ⇒ New Document.

   You should see the window shown in Figure 6-1.

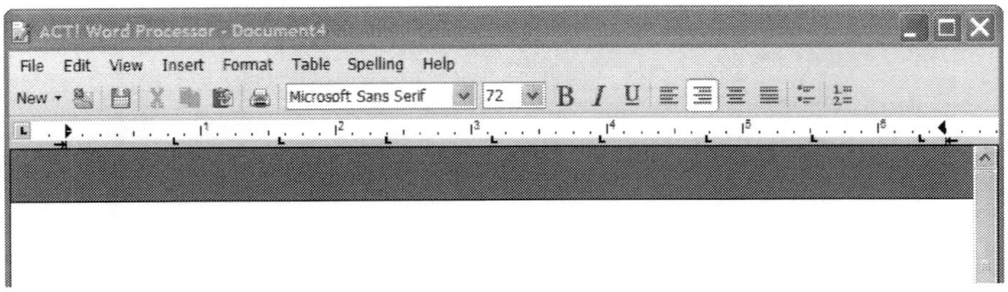

Figure 6-1 ACT! Word Processor window

Word Processing Toolbar

Figure 6-2 shows the word processing toolbar. Table 6-1 explains the buttons on the toolbar.

Figure 6-2 Word processing toolbar

Button	Description
1	Opens a new document or template.
2	Opens an existing document.
3	Saves the active document.
4	Deletes the selected text.
5	Copies the selected text to the clipboard.
6	Copies the selected text in the clipboard to a document.
7	Prints the active document.
8	Select a font.
9	Select a font size.
10	Makes the selected text bold.
11	Makes the selected text italic.
12	Underlines the selected text.
13	Aligns the text on the left side of the paragraph. This is the default alignment.
14	Aligns the text on the right side of the paragraph.
15	Centers the text between the margins.
16	Stretches the text between the left and right margins.
17	Creates a bulleted list.
18	Creates a numbered list.

Table 6-1 Word processing toolbar options explained

Word Processing Status Bar

The Status Bar provides the information shown in Figure 6-3. Table 6-2 explains the options.

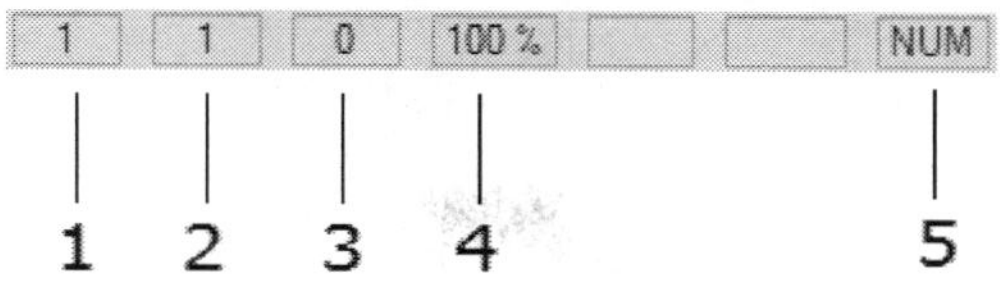

Figure 6-3 Word processing status bar

Button	Description
1	Shows which page in the document the insertion point is on.
2	Shows which line on the page the insertion point is on.
3	Shows how many spaces from the first character in the line, the insertion point is.
4	Shows the current zoom percent. View ⇒ Zoom, as shown in Figure 6-4, displays the zoom percent options that you can select. The larger the percent, the larger the document text is displayed in the word processing window.
5	Informs you that the Num Lock key on your keyboard is on if you see the letters **NUM**.

Table 6-2 Word processing status bar options explained

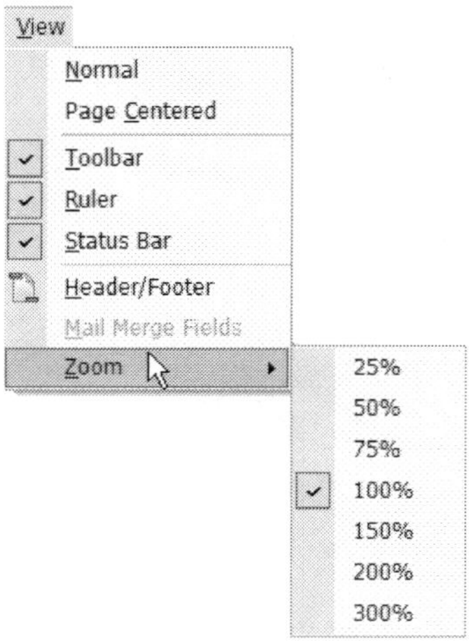

Figure 6-4 Zoom options

The Ruler

The ruler can be used to change the paragraph margins. You can also modify the Tab stops on the ruler. Figure 6-5 shows the left margin, ruler and tab stops.

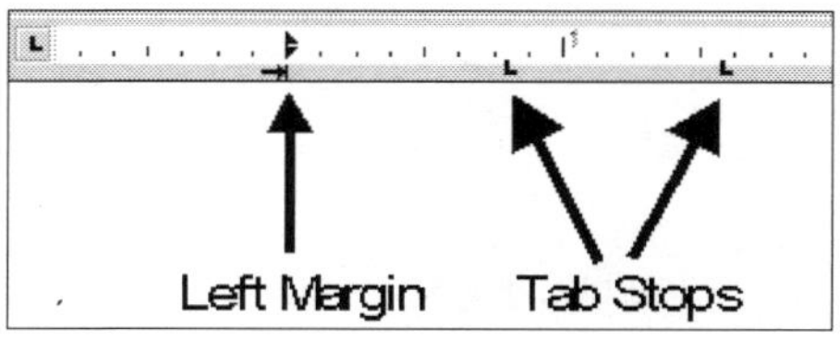

Figure 6-5 Ruler with margin marker and tab stops illustrated

Using The Ruler To Change Paragraph Margins

If you need to change the margins of a paragraph you can change them on the ruler. To change a margin, click in the paragraph that you want to change the margin of, then drag the left or right margin marker on the ruler to where you want the new margin.

Using The Ruler To Change Tab Stops

If you need to change the Tab Stops you can change them on the ruler.

To change a tab stop, click on the tab stop that you want to change, then drag the tab stop on the ruler to the new location.

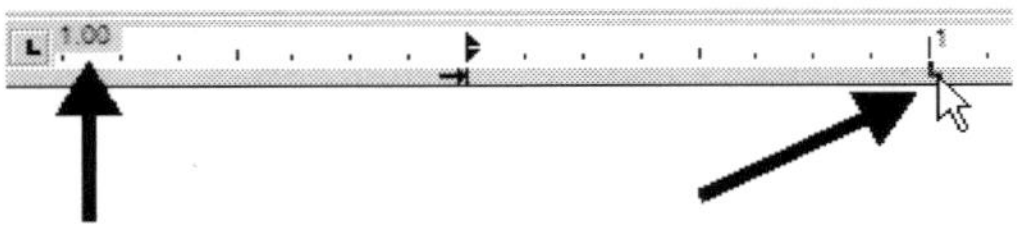

Figure 6-6 First tab stop moved to the one inch mark on the ruler

In the left corner of the ruler you will see the actual number in inches of where the tab stop is. If you want to delete a tab stop, drag it off of the ruler. Figure 6-6 above shows that the first tab stop has been moved to the one inch mark.

Exercise 6.1: Document Editing Techniques

In this exercise you will learn several techniques that are commonly used to edit documents. You may have the need to edit a document to enhance it or to use it for a different task, then it was originally created for.

1. Click the Open an existing document button. Navigate to your folder.

2. Open the Files of type drop-down list and select the **RICH TEXT FORMAT (*.RTF)** option, highlighted in Figure 6-7.

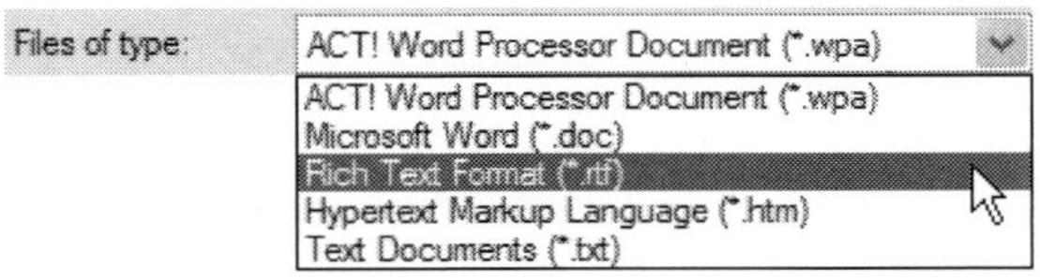

Figure 6-7 Files of type drop-down list options

3. Double-click on the New Classes Letter file. Save the document as `Word Processing Practice`.

4. Click on the line above the word Dear. Insert ⇒ Date. You should see the dialog box shown in Figure 6-8.

   If you want the date to change every time that you open the document, select the **ALWAYS UPDATE IN DOCUMENT** option.

   If you do not want the date to change every time that you open the document, select the **NEVER UPDATE IN DOCUMENT** option.

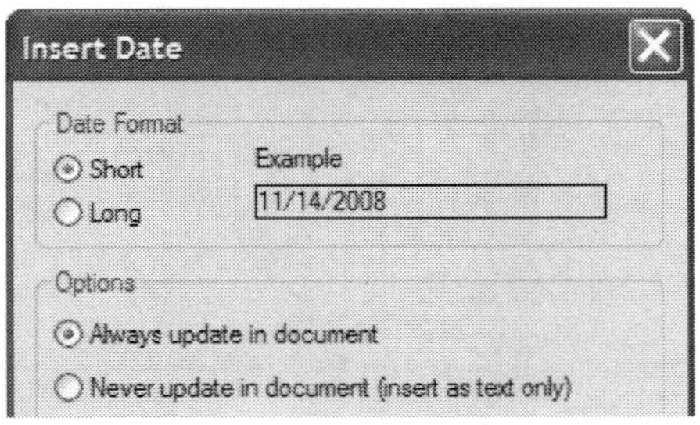

Figure 6-8 Insert Date dialog box

5. Select the Never update in document option and click OK, then press Enter.

Copying Text

If you need the same text in more than one place in the document, you can copy it.

1. Select the first sentence in the third paragraph, as shown in Figure 6-9.

Dear,

As owner of Capri Company, I want to express my sincere appreciation for the business you have brought us over the years. In response to numerous requests from our customers, the staff at Capri Company has decided to begin offering computer classes here at our new, larger location.

Our higly skilled training team is looking forward to sharing their knowledge with you! We will soon be offering the following classes on the dates listed below:

So come on in and see what we have to offer. Be on the lookout for git certificates that we will be mailing soon that can be applied to any of our classes.

I am looking forward to seeing you soon!

Sincerely,

Your name goes here

Figure 6-9 Text highlighted to be copied

2. Click the Copy button on the toolbar or press the **CTRL** + **C** keys.

3. Place the cursor on a blank line after the word **SINCERELY**, then click the Paste button or press the **CTRL** + **V** keys. You should see a copy of the text.

Moving Text

If you need to move text from one part of the document to another, follow the steps below.

1. Select the second paragraph, then right-click on the highlighted text. You should see the shortcut menu shown in Figure 6-10.

   Select Cut.

   The options on the shortcut menu work the same way as the corresponding buttons on the toolbar.

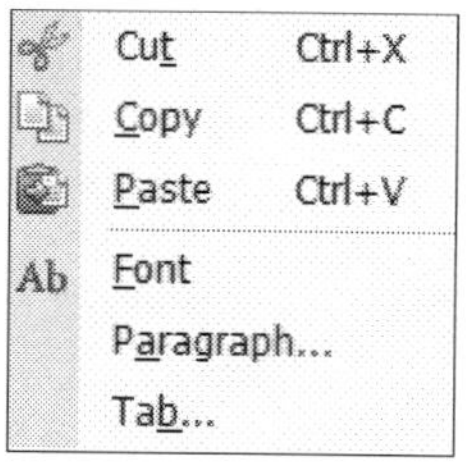

Figure 6-10 Shortcut menu

2. Right-click on the line below the words "Your name goes here", in the letter shown earlier in Figure 6-9, then select Paste.

Using The Replace Command

This command is used to search for text in a document and replace it with different text. You should place the insertion point at the beginning of the document before you use this command so that the entire document will be searched. The default search process is to start the search where the insertion point is in the document.

1. Click in front of the date at the top of the letter. Edit ⇒ Replace. You should see the Replace dialog box.

2. Type `Capri` in the **FIND WHAT** field, then press the Tab key and type `Capri Book` in the **REPLACE WITH** field, as shown in Figure 6-11.

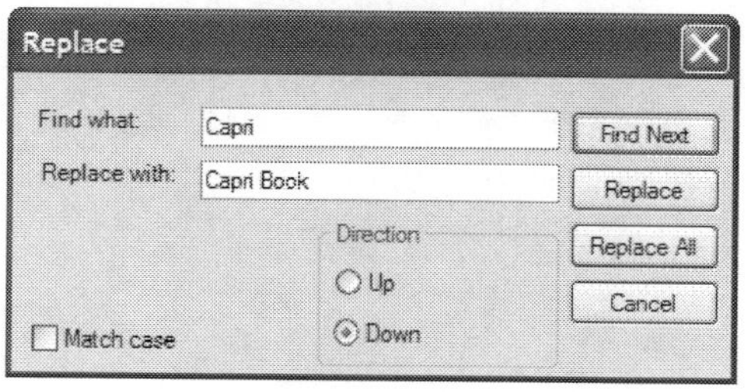

Figure 6-11 Replace dialog box

3. Click the Replace All button, then click OK.

4. Click the Cancel button to close the Replace dialog box. Every place that the word "Capri" is in the document, it will now have "Capri Book".

5. Save the changes.

Exercise 6.2: Formatting A Document

There are three types of formatting that you can apply to a document as discussed below. Character and paragraph formatting work in a similar way.

① **Character** formats the selected text.
② **Paragraph** formats the entire paragraph.
③ **Page** formats the entire document.

> You can right-click in a paragraph to add font, paragraph and tab formatting as shown earlier in Figure 6-10.

Character Formatting

You can change the default font and font size options, as well as, add color to the text.

1. Select the first line in the first paragraph.

2. Open the **FONT LIST** drop-down list and select Arial.

3. Change the font size to 16, then click the Italic button.

Paragraph Formatting

1. Select the second paragraph. Format ⇒ Font.

2. Open the Text drop-down list at the bottom of the dialog box and select the color Red, then click OK. Click the Bold button.

3. Select the first paragraph. Click the Align Center button on the toolbar. Each line in the paragraph should now be centered.

4. With the text still selected, right-click and select Paragraph.

Paragraph Dialog Box

In addition to the paragraph formatting options that you just learned about, paragraph formatting also includes alignment, indenting and line spacing. Figure 6-12 shows these paragraph formatting options. Figure 6-13 shows the Frame and Page Break paragraph formatting options.

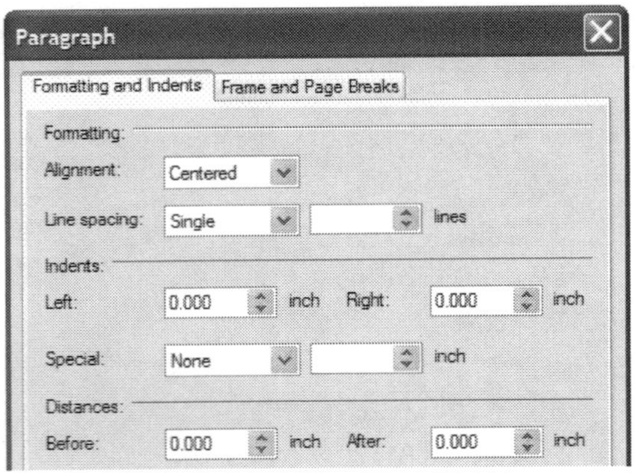

Figure 6-12 Paragraph dialog box

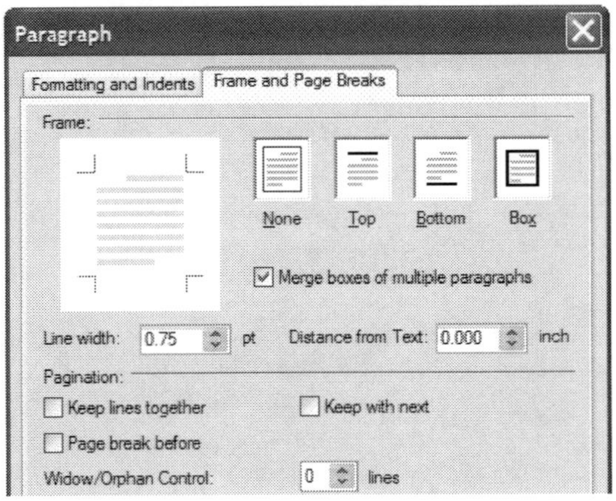

Figure 6-13 Frame and Page Breaks options

5. Open the **LINE SPACING** drop-down list and select Double, then click OK. The first paragraph should be double spaced.

Indenting Text

This option is used to change the left and right margins of a paragraph. The options in the **INDENTS** section of the Paragraph dialog box are used to change the indentation. To change the margins for a paragraph, click in the paragraph that you want to change, then select the left and right options.

1. Click in the second paragraph, then open the Paragraph dialog box.

2. Change the Left indent option to `4.000`, then click OK.

   The second paragraph should look like the one shown near the bottom of Figure 6-14.

   Notice that no other paragraph has changed.

> *As owner of Capri Book Company, I want to express my sincere appreciation for* the business you have brought us over the years. In response to numerous requests from our customers, the staff at Capri Book Company has decided to begin offering computer classes here at our new, larger location.
>
> **So come on in and see what we have to offer. Be on the lookout for git certificates that we will be mailing soon that can be applied to any of our classes.**
>
> I am looking forward to seeing you soon!

Figure 6-14 Text indented

Using Bullets

Bullets are often used to make lines of text stand out in a document. They are also used to create lists.

Two Ways To Create A Bulleted List

① Position the cursor in the document at the place where you want the first bullet. Click the **BULLETED LIST** button on the toolbar. Start typing the items for the list. Press the Enter key after typing each item. When you type the next item a bullet will appear. After you type the last item in the list do not press the Enter key, press the down arrow key instead.

② Type the list of items first, then select all of the items and click the Bulleted List button.

> To remove the bullets, select the bulleted list in the document, then click the Bulleted List button on the toolbar.

Exercise 6.3: How To Create A Bulleted List

1. Move the cursor to the line above **I AM LOOKING FORWARD TO SEEING YOU SOON** and press Enter. Type `Introduction To Multimedia`, then press Enter.

2. Type `Introduction To Web Page Creation`, then press Enter. Type `Introduction To Networking`, then press Enter.

3. Select the three lines that you just typed, then click the Bulleted List button.

   Your bulleted list should look like the one shown in Figure 6-15.

> • Introduction To Multimedia
> • Introduction To Web Page Creation
> • Introduction To Networking
>
> I am looking forward to seeing you soon!

Figure 6-15 Bulleted list added to the document

Exercise 6.4: Changing Tab Stops With The Tabs Dialog Box

Earlier in this lesson you learned how to change tab stops on the ruler. If you need more tab stop functionality, you can use the Tabs dialog box. By default, the tab stops are at every half an inch. In this exercise you will learn how to use the Tabs dialog box to modify the tab stops so that they are only at every inch. You will also learn how to create a new tab stop.

1. Format ⇒ Tab.

2. The 0.50 tab stop should be selected, as shown in Figure 6-16.

   Click the Clear button.

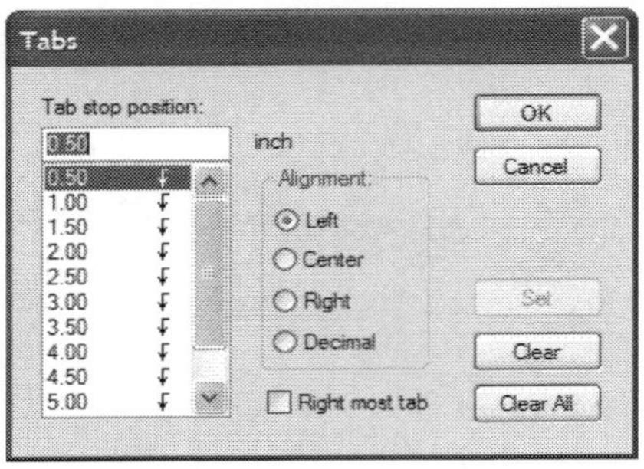

Figure 6-16 Tabs dialog box

3. Click on the 1.50 tab stop and clear it. Leave the dialog box open.

How To Create A Tab Stop

1. Type the location of the tab stop that you want to create in the **TAB STOP POSITION** field. In this exercise type `1.25` in the field.

2. Select the **RIGHT** alignment option.

3. Click the **SET** button.

   You should have the tab stops shown in Figure 6-17.

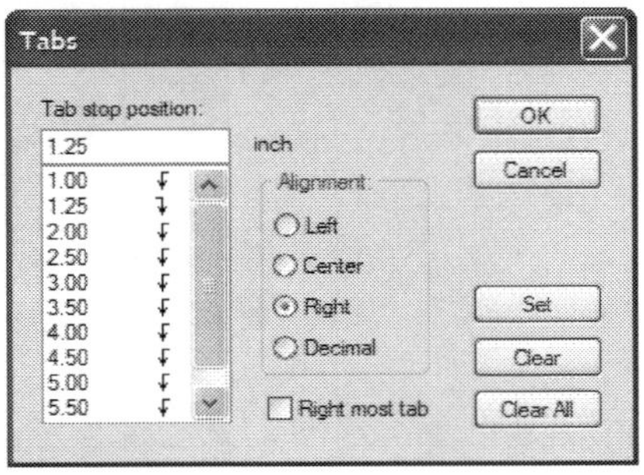

Figure 6-17 Modified tab stops

4. Click OK. If you press the Tab key you will see that the cursor only stops at the places shown above in Figure 6-17.

5. Save the changes and close the document.

Exercise 6.5: Creating Tables

Tables are used to add rows and columns like a spreadsheet to a word processing document. In this exercise you will create a table that contains data for upcoming classes.

1. Open the New Classes Letter and save it as `New Classes Letter (with table)`.

2. Place the cursor on the blank line after the second paragraph, then press Enter.

3. Table ⇒ Insert ⇒ Table.

4. Change the **NUMBER OF COLUMNS** field to 3, by clicking on the up arrow at the end of the field.

   Change the **NUMBER OF ROWS** field to 4.

   You should have the options shown in Figure 6-18.

   Click OK.

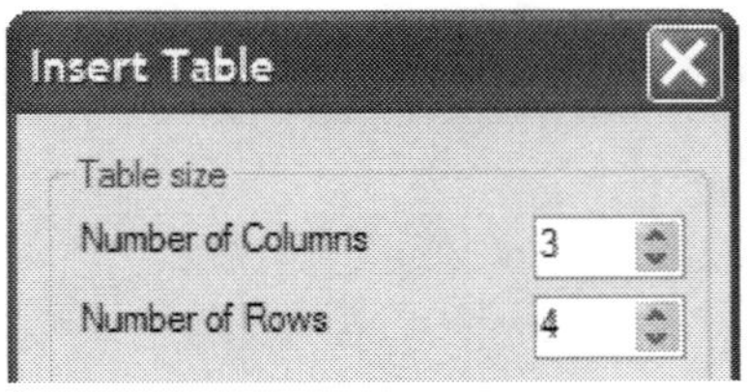

Figure 6-18 Table options

I am not sure why, but sometimes a table will not display all of the gridlines, as illustrated in Figure 6-19.

Class	Price	Next Class Starts
Works	$295	February 10
Word	$495	February 12
Access	$1,295	February 10

Missing gridline

Figure 6-19 Table without all of the gridlines visible

5. Add all of the data in Table 6-3 to the table in your document.

Class	Price	Next Class Starts
Works	$295	February 10
Word	$495	February 12
Access	$1,295	February 10

Table 6-3 Data to add to the table

To move from one column to the next, press the Tab key or press the arrow key that points in the direction that you want to move.

Modify The Table Properties

1. Select all of the text in the table. Table ⇒ Table Properties.

2. Click on the **GRID** option shown in Figure 6-20, then click OK.

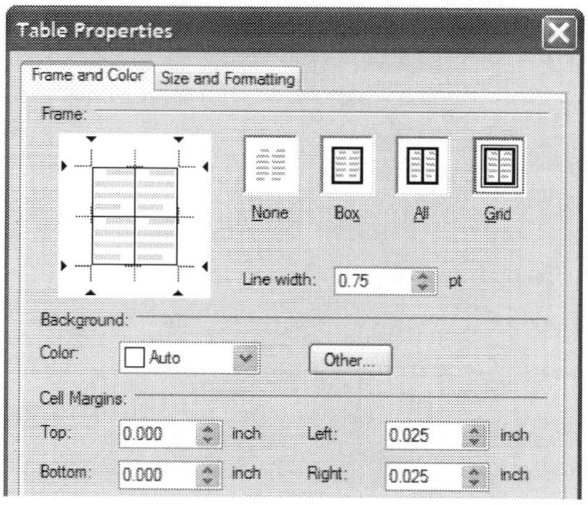

Figure 6-20 Frame and Color table options

If you want to force the entire table to display and print on the same page, clear the **ALLOW ROW TO BREAK ACROSS PAGES** option shown in Figure 6-21, then click OK.

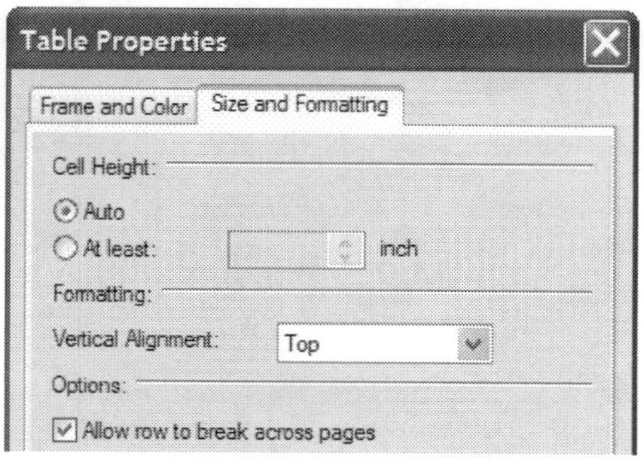

Figure 6-21 Size and formatting table options

3. Select the first row in the table, then click the Bold button.

4. With the first row still selected, open the Table Properties dialog box and change the **BACKGROUND COLOR** to yellow, then click OK.

5. Make each column smaller so that your table looks like the one shown in Figure 6-22.

   Save the changes and leave the document open.

Class	Price	Next Class Starts
Works	$295	February 10
Word	$495	February 12
Access	$1,295	February 10

Figure 6-22 Modified table

I find changing the column size some what difficult. If you start adjusting the columns from left to right, meaning change the size of the first column first, the table does not stay aligned on the left.

Adding Rows And Columns To A Table

In addition to right-clicking in a cell in the table and then selecting one of the **INSERT** options on the shortcut menu shown in Figure 6-23, the last four options shown on the submenu in Figure 6-24 are used to add rows and columns. Table ⇒ Insert, will also open the menu shown in Figure 6-24.

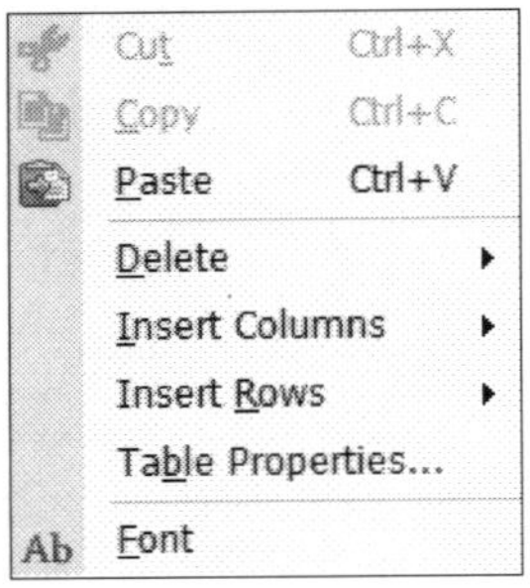

Figure 6-23 Table cell shortcut menu

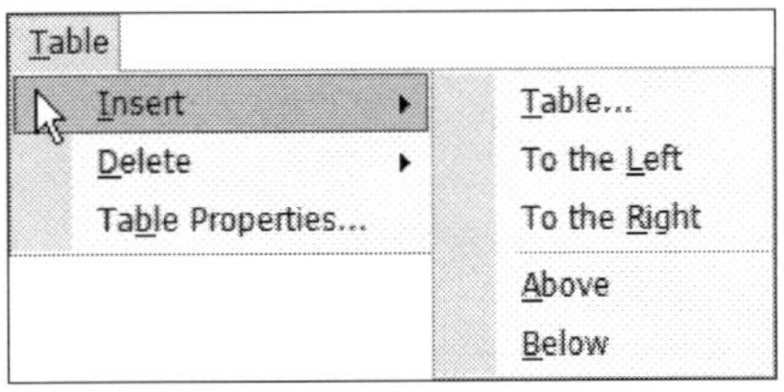

Figure 6-24 Table Insert (Row & Column) menu options

Header And Footer Settings

The header and footer sections of a document have their own margins. You can select how far from the page border they will start.

Format ⇒ Header/Footer Settings.

You should see the dialog box shown in Figure 6-25.

These options are used to change the margins for the header and footer sections of a document.

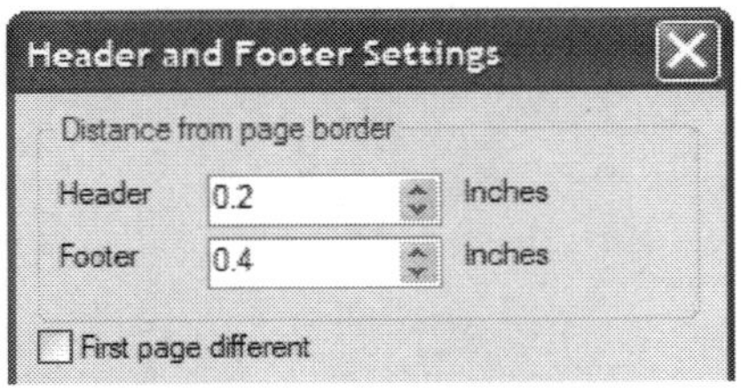

Figure 6-25 Header and Footer Settings dialog box

If checked, the **FIRST PAGE DIFFERENT** option allows different information to be added to the header and footer section on the first page of the document. An example of how this option works is the first page of every lesson in this book. The first page does not have any text in the header.

Exercise 6.6: Using Headers And Footers

Headers and footers are used to print information that you want to appear on every page, or almost every page of the document. Headers print at the top of the page and footers print at the bottom of the page. Items commonly placed in headers and footers include page numbers or the document name. Anything that you can put in the main portion of a document you can put in the header or footer, including clip art.

1. Open the New Classes Letter document. View ⇒ Header/Footer. Scroll to the bottom of the first page. You should see a dotted box. That is the footer section.

2. Tab over to the three inch mark in the footer section. Type `Page`, then press the space bar.

3. Insert ⇒ Page Number. The footer should look like the one shown in Figure 6-26. Save the changes.

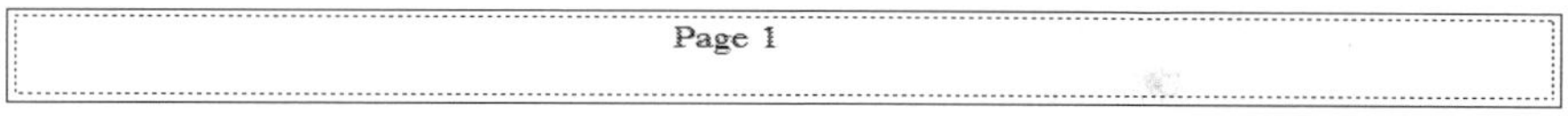

Figure 6-26 Page number added to the footer

Exercise 6.7: Page Formatting

You can change the page margins to fit the needs of the document. Unlike using the Indent option to set margins, the page margins that you set are for the entire document. There are two ways to set page margins, as discussed below:

① Use the ruler which you learned about earlier in this lesson.
② Use the Page Setup dialog box.

1. Open the New Classes Letter document, if it is not already open. File ⇒ Page Setup.

2. Change the left and right margins to `1.5` inches, as shown in Figure 6-27, then click OK.

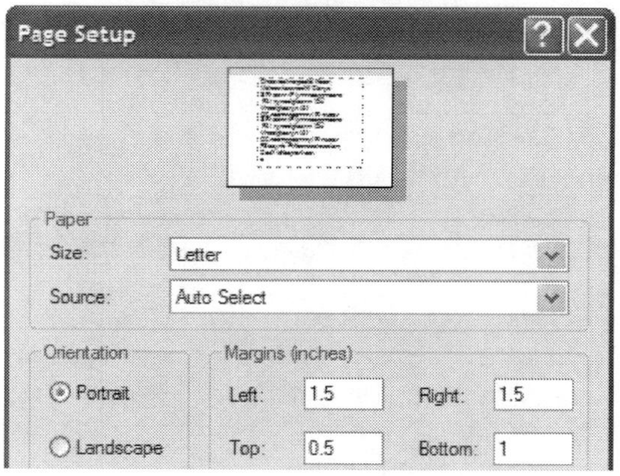

Figure 6-27 Page Setup dialog box

Exercise 6.8: Using The Spell Checker

You can check the spelling for an entire document or a portion of the document. To spell check a portion of the document, highlight the portion that you want to check before starting the spell checker.

1. Place the cursor above the word Dear at the top of the letter.

2. Spelling ⇒ Check Document.

   You will see the dialog box shown in Figure 6-28.

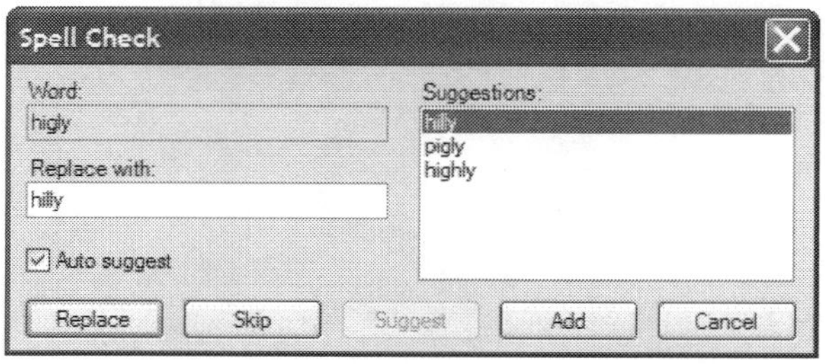

Figure 6-28 Spell Check dialog box

3. The word **HIGHLY** in the Suggestions list is the word that you want. Click on it now, then click the Replace button.

If the word that you need to use is not in the Suggestions list, you can type the word in the **REPLACE WITH** field.
If the word is spelled correctly, you may want to add it to a custom dictionary.
If you do not want to change the word, click the **SKIP** button.

You should now see the message shown in Figure 6-29.

This message lets you know how many words were checked and how many questionable (misspelled) words were found.

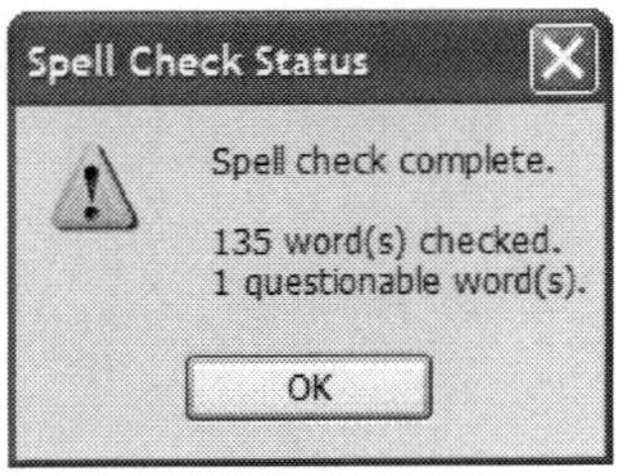

Figure 6-29 Spell Check Status message

4. Click OK.

Saving Documents

When you create a new document and are ready to save it, click the Save button. You will then be prompted to type in a file name. To save an existing document with the same name, click the Save button.

If you want to save an existing document with a new name, File ⇒ Save As. Type in the new name for the document. Saving an existing document with a new name will leave the original document unchanged.

Printing Documents

Once you have created, edited and spell checked a document, you may want to print it. If you only need to print a portion of a document or need to print more than one copy, you can select the options on the Print dialog box.

1. File ⇒ Print. You will see the Print dialog box. Click the Cancel button.

2. File ⇒ Exit. Do not save the changes.

To print more than one copy of the document, change the value in the **NUMBER OF COPIES** field shown in Figure 6-30 to the number of copies that you want to print.

If you need to print more than one copy of a document that has more than one page, check the **COLLATE** option after selecting the number of copies.

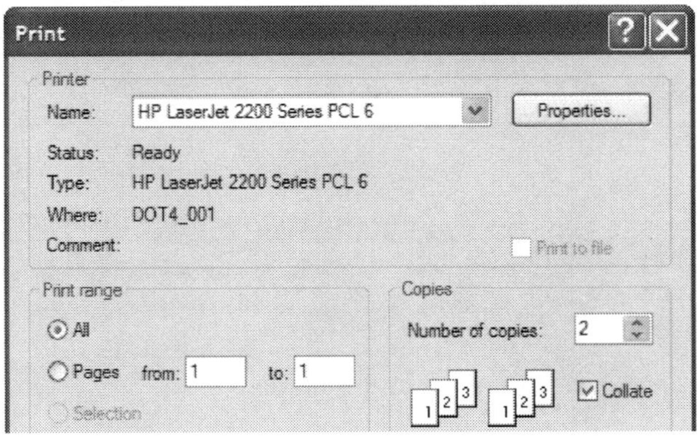

Figure 6-30 Print dialog box

Printing Specific Pages Of A Document

To print a specific page or a range of pages, select the **PAGES** option.

If you only want to print one page of a document that has more than one page, type the page number that you want to print in the **FROM** and **TO** fields.

If you want to print a range of pages, like pages 2, 3, 4 and 5, you would type 2 in the **FROM** field and 5 in the **TO** field.

Adding Graphics To Documents

If you need to add graphics to a word processing document, follow the steps below.

1. Open the document that you want to add the graphic to, then click on the location in the document where you want to add the graphic.

2. Insert ⇒ Image, as shown in Figure 6-31, then select one of the options explained below.

   The **FIXED POSITION** option causes the text to be wrapped around the image.

   The **CHARACTER POSITION** option causes the image to move when the text around it moves.

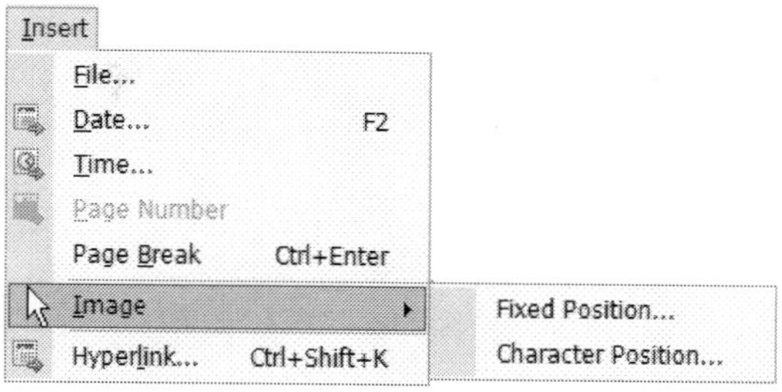

Figure 6-31 Insert image options

3. Select the image that you want to add to the document.

WORD PROCESSING TEMPLATES

In this lesson you will learn about the following word processing template features:

- ☑ Modifying existing templates
- ☑ Mail merge
- ☑ Creating a template
- ☑ Using the Setup Assistant Wizard to set up Microsoft Word

LESSON 7

Templates Overview

Templates are a special type of document that can contain text and fields that you want to merge together to create a new document. Examples of templates are a fax cover page or a form letter. More than likely you have received several of these form letters. Some refer to this type of letter as "junk mail". You can also have fields in a template that will retrieve data from an ACT! database and merge the data into a template.

The difference between a template and a document is that you can use the template over and over. Templates do not save the data in the fields. The document saves the content from the template and the data from fields.

You can customize a template as much or as little as you need. The majority of a letter template is the same for each person that it is sent to. The customizations could include the customers name, address and amount of their last order. If you know that you will have the need to create form letters, make sure that the fields that you need in the database are being filled in. You may find that you need to collect additional information. If so, you can use the fields on the User Fields tab or create your own fields.

ACT! comes with templates that you can use as they are, or you can modify them. It is best to save the templates that come with ACT! with another file name, if you need to modify them. That way, you will still have the original template should something not work as expected. You can also create your own templates. You can add a template that you create to the Write menu, just like you added a look up that you created to the Lookup menu.

Exercise 7.1: How To Modify An Existing Template

If there is an existing template that meets most of your needs, it is easier to use that one and modify it as needed. In this exercise you will modify the Fax Cover Page template to include the senders email address.

1. Write ⇒ Edit Template.
2. Double-click on the file **FAX COVER PAGE.TPL**, illustrated in Figure 7-1.

   You should see the Fax Cover Page template, as shown in Figure 7-2.

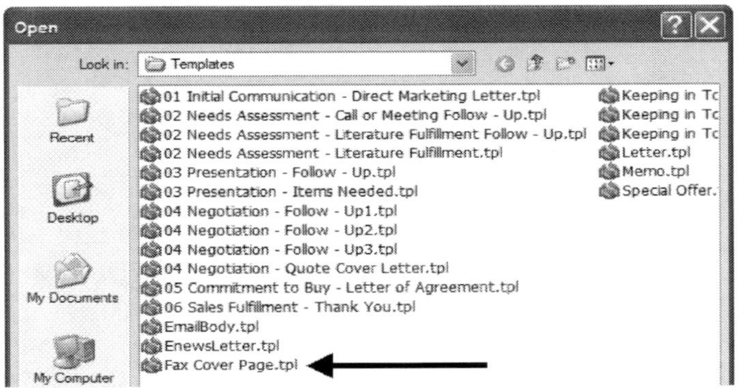

Figure 7-1 ACT! templates

The options on the right side of the window are used to add fields from the database to the template. You can add fields from the Contact record and the My Record.

Notice that the fields in the second column of the template have the word **MY** in the field name, as shown in Figure 7-2.

This lets you know that these fields are from the My Record.

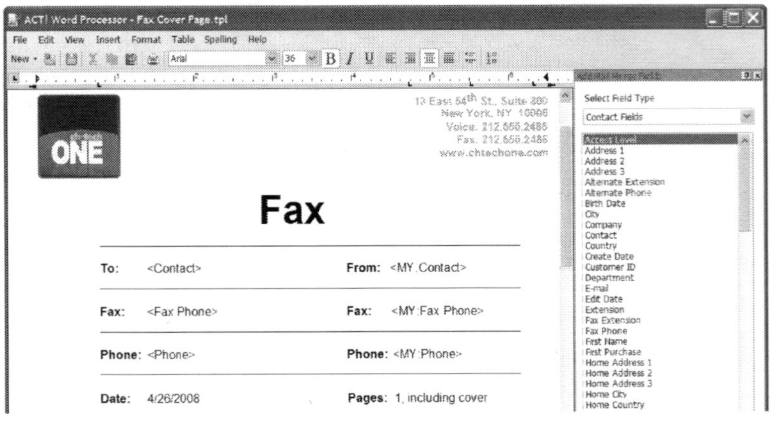

Figure 7-2 Fax cover page template

Adding A Field To The Template

1. Click after the word **SUBJECT**, then press the Enter key twice.
2. Type `E-mail:`, then press the space bar once.
3. Click the Bold button. This will turn the bold option off for the field that you will add next.
4. Open the **SELECT FIELD TYPE** drop-down list and select the My Record Fields option.
5. Double-click on the E-mail field.

   The template should look like the one shown in Figure 7-3.

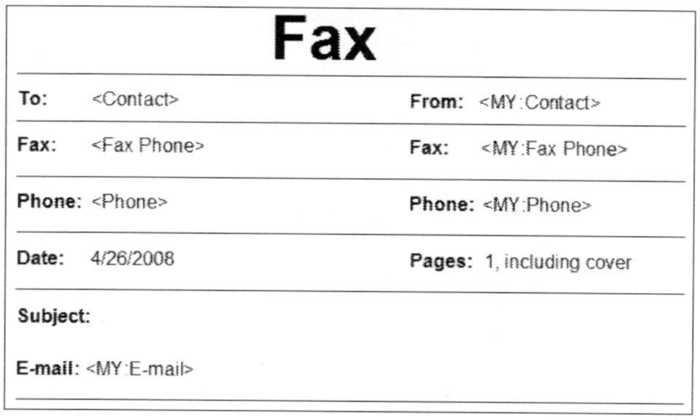

Figure 7-3 Fax Cover Page with a new field added

Saving Templates

Templates are saved the same way that you save any other word processing document. The only difference is that you have to change the Save As Type field to **ACT! WORD PROCESSOR TEMPLATE (*.TPL)**. The default location to save templates in, is the Templates folder.

1. File ⇒ Save As.
2. Type `New Fax Cover Page` in the File name field.
3. Select ACT! Word Processor Template (*.tpl) as the **SAVE AS TYPE**, if it is not already selected.

If you know that you will not use the Fax Cover Page template that comes with ACT!, you can save a fax cover page template that you create or modify with the same name as the one that comes with ACT!, as illustrated earlier in Figure 7-1. The one you save will open when you select the Fax Cover Page option on the Write menu. If you want to do this, it may be a good idea to save the original one with a different file name in case you need it in the future.

4. Click Save. File ⇒ Exit.

Exercise 7.2: Mail Merge

Mail merge is used to take data from fields like names and addresses and put the data into a document to make it personalized. During the merge process, a copy of the template is created for each contact in the database that meets the criteria. This tool is often used to customize a form letter. Creating a mail merge is a two step process as discussed below.

① Look up the contacts that you want to use in the mail merge.
② Merge the contact fields with a template.

> What may not be obvious is that you can use the same mail merge template for letter and email mail merge tasks.

Create The Merge

Before creating the merge you should look up the contacts that you want to use in the merge.

1. Create a lookup to find the contacts in the company CH TechONE. There should be nine contacts.

2. Write ⇒ Mail Merge. You will see the first screen of the Mail Merge Wizard. Usually, the first screen of a wizard does not provide any useful information, so it is ok to check the option to hide the first screen in the future.

3. Click Next. Select the Word processor option if it is not already selected, as shown in Figure 7-4, then click Next.

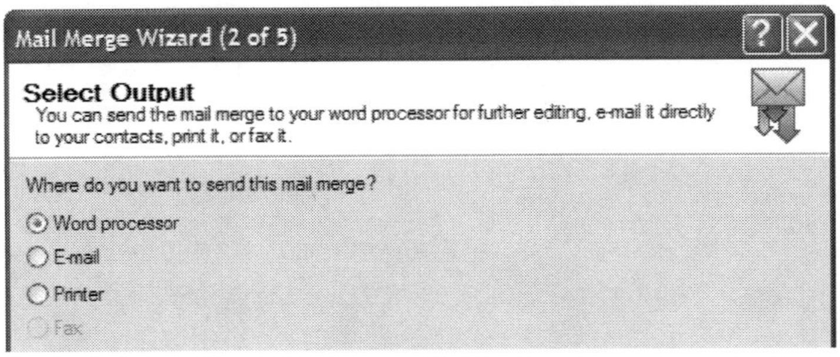

Figure 7-4 Select Output wizard screen

4. Click the Browse button and double-click on the 01 Initial Communication file in the Templates folder. The Templates folder is under your database folder. The path is shown in Figure 7-5. You should see the template name in the field shown in Figure 7-6.

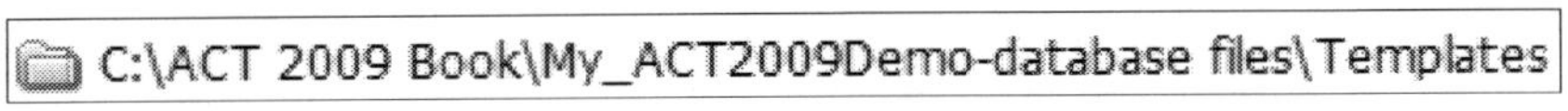

Figure 7-5 Path to the Templates folder

By default, the last template used in the Mail Merge wizard will be displayed in the field the next time the Mail Merge wizard is run.

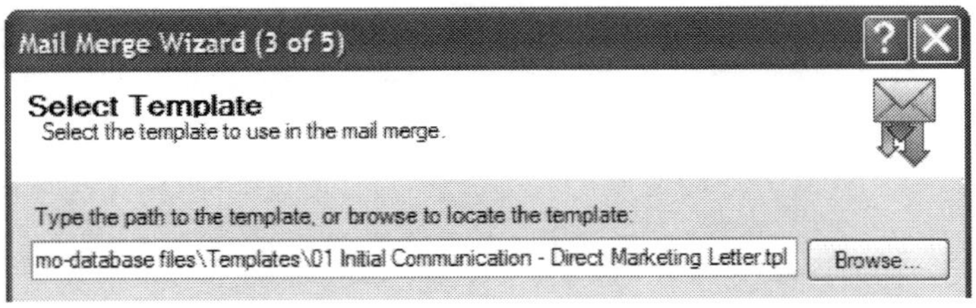

Figure 7-6 Select Template wizard screen

5. Click Next.

   The options on the screen shown in Figure 7-7 are used to select the contacts that will be used in the mail merge.

   The **CURRENT LOOKUP** option will use the contacts from the lookup as the data source for the mail merge.

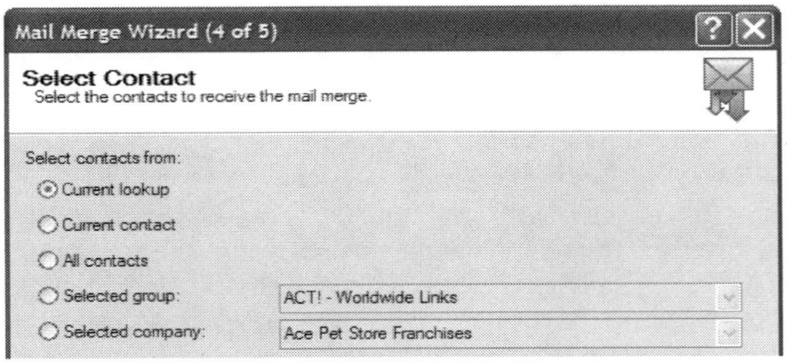

Figure 7-7 Select Contact wizard screen

The **CURRENT CONTACT** option will only create the mail merge for the contact that is visible or the contact that is selected (highlighted) if the current view is a list view.

The **ALL CONTACTS** option will create a merge letter for every contact in the database.

The **SELECTED GROUP** option is used to select a group to send the mail merge document to, as shown in Figure 7-8.

A mail merge document will be created for all of the contacts that are associated with the group.

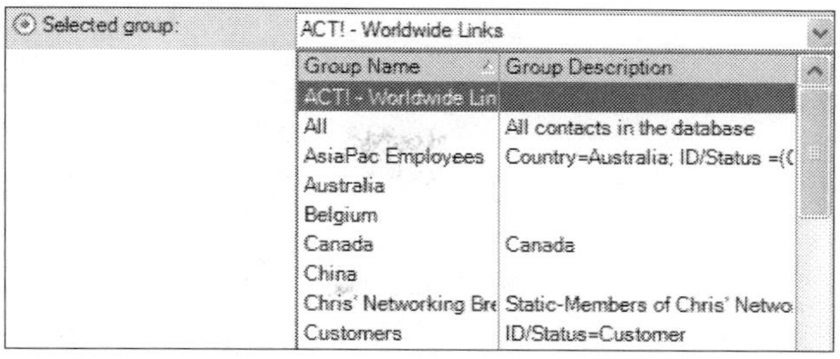

Figure 7-8 Selected group options

The **SELECTED COMPANY** option is used to select a company to send the mail merge document to. A mail merge document will be created for all of the contacts that are associated with the company.

6. Select the Current Lookup option, then click Next.

   The last screen in the wizard displays the options that you selected for the mail merge, as shown in Figure 7-9.

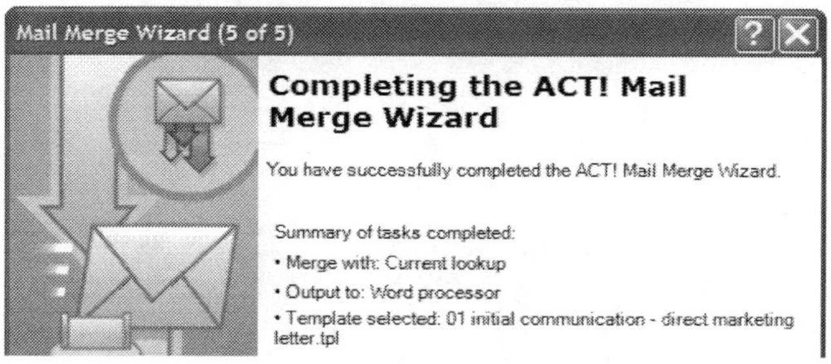

Figure 7-9 Last mail merge wizard screen

7. Click Finish. You will see the letter shown in Figure 7-10.

   If you count the number of letters in the document, you will see eight letters.

   You may be asking why there are only eight letters instead of nine, which is the number of contacts in the lookup.

   The reason is because one of the contacts in the lookup is the My Record. ACT! figures that you do not want to send a letter to yourself.

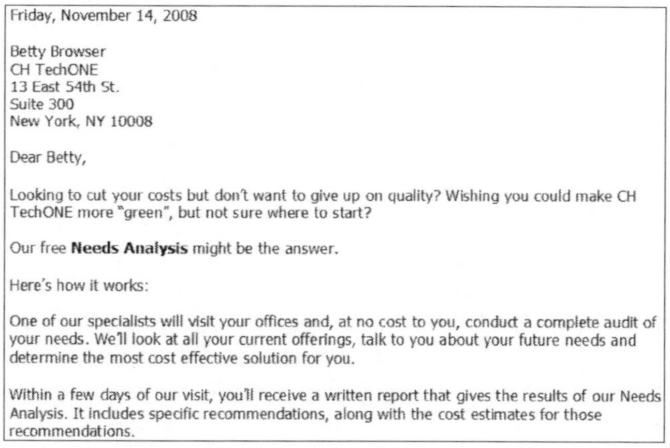

Friday, November 14, 2008

Betty Browser
CH TechONE
13 East 54th St.
Suite 300
New York, NY 10008

Dear Betty,

Looking to cut your costs but don't want to give up on quality? Wishing you could make CH TechONE more "green", but not sure where to start?

Our free **Needs Analysis** might be the answer.

Here's how it works:

One of our specialists will visit your offices and, at no cost to you, conduct a complete audit of your needs. We'll look at all your current offerings, talk to you about your future needs and determine the most cost effective solution for you.

Within a few days of our visit, you'll receive a written report that gives the results of our Needs Analysis. It includes specific recommendations, along with the cost estimates for those recommendations.

Figure 7-10 Mail merge letter

8. File ⇒ Exit. Navigate to your folder, if necessary. Type `Mail Merge` as the file name, then press Enter.

Email Mail Merge Options

Figure 7-11 shows the additional email mail merge options.

The email options are for external email software, like Internet email.

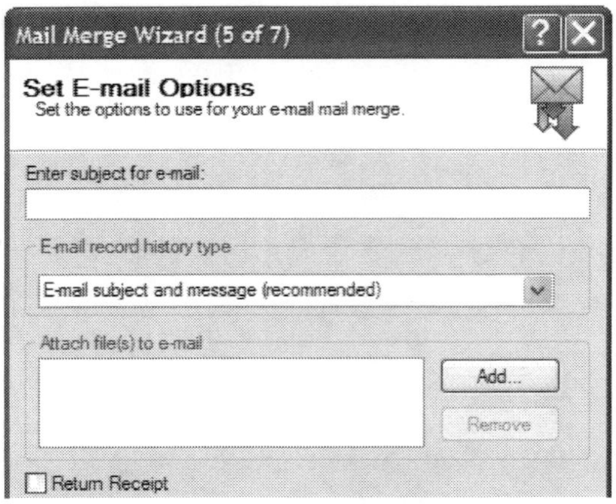

Figure 7-11 E-mail mail merge options

Printer Mail Merge Options

Figure 7-12 shows the record history options for a printer mail merge.

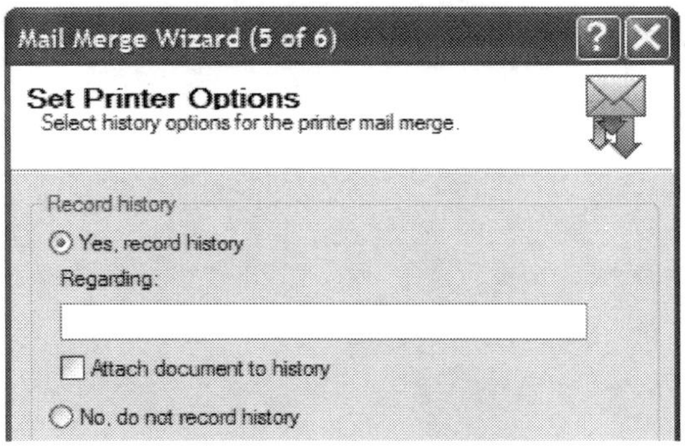

Figure 7-12 Printer mail merge options

Exercise 7.3: How To Create A New Template

When creating a mail merge the template must have all of the information, including the body of the letter, before you start the merge process. Some of the templates that come with ACT! are empty (ie. EmailBody, Letter and Memo). They are a good starting point for you to create your own template when none of the templates that come with ACT! are close to what you need. In this exercise you will learn how to create a template from scratch.

Add The Merge Fields

1. Write ⇒ New Letter/E-mail Template.

2. Click in the body of the document, then Insert ⇒ Date.

   Select the options shown in Figure 7-13, then click OK.

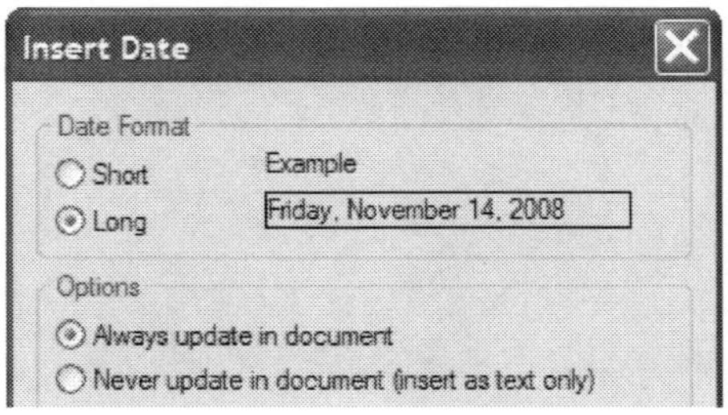

Figure 7-13 Insert Date dialog box

3. Press the Enter key five times. Make sure that the Field type **CONTACT FIELDS** is selected, then double-click on the Contact field in the list box.

4. Press Enter, then add the fields shown in Figure 7-14.

Friday, November 14, 2008

<Contact>
<Title>
<Company>
<Address 1>
<Address 2>
<City>, <State> <ZIP Code>

Figure 7-14 Fields for the template

5. Place the cursor between the City and State fields (between the > < brackets). The easiest way to do this is to use the arrow keys to move the cursor. Type a comma, then press the space bar.

6. Add a space between the State and Zip Code fields. Put the cursor after the Zip Code field, then press the Enter key three times.

7. Type `Dear`, then press the space bar.

8. Insert the Salutation field, then type a comma.

Add The Body Of The Letter

1. Press the Enter key three times, then type `You were referred to us by.`

2. Press the space bar, then add the Referred By field.

3. Type a comma, then press the space bar.

> Before you would run this merge, you should create a lookup for the contacts that you want to use in the merge to make sure that the Referred By field is not empty. If the field is empty you need to fill it in, otherwise there will be a blank space in the letter where the field is. The other option is to remove the record from the merge.

4. Type `as the person that is in charge of buying computer equipment.`

5. Press the Enter key twice, then type `Enclosed please find our latest catalog.`

6. Press the Enter key four times, then type `Sincerely,`. Press the Enter key four times.

7. Open the Field Type drop-down list and select the My Record Fields option.

8. Add the Contact field.

9. Highlight the entire letter and change the font to Arial and the font size to 10.

   The letter should look like the one shown in Figure 7-15.

Friday, November 14, 2008

<Contact>
<Title>
<Company>
<Address 1>
<Address 2>
<City>, <State> <ZIP Code>

Dear <Salutation>,

You were referred to us by <Referred By>, as the person that is in charge of buying computer equipment.

Enclosed please find our latest catalog.

Sincerely,

<MY:Contact>

Figure 7-15 Mail merge template

10. Save the template in your folder. Type `My Sales Letter Template` as the file name.

11. File ⇒ Exit. The nine contacts should still be on the screen.

Run The Mail Merge

Now that the mail merge template has been created you can run the merge.

1. Write ⇒ Mail Merge. Click Next on the first and second wizard screens.

2. Select the My Sales Letter Template file on the third wizard screen, then click Next.

3. Select the Current Lookup option. Click Next, then click Finish.

   You will see the letter shown in Figure 7-16 for each of the contacts except the My Record.

   Notice that there is no name after the word "By" on the first line of the letter. This is because the Referred By field on the contact record is empty.

Friday, November 14, 2008

Ernst Anderson
Vice President of US Operations
CH TechONE
13 East 54th St
Suite 300
New York, NY 10008

Dear Ernst,

You were referred to us by , as the person that is in charge of buying computer equipment.

Enclosed please find our latest catalog.

Sincerely,

Chris Huffman

Figure 7-16 Mail merge letter

4. Save the mail merge document in your folder. Type `Sales Letter Mail Merge` as the file name.

5. Close the word processor. Lookup ⇒ All Contacts.

Create History Dialog Box

After you print the letters you will see the dialog box shown in Figure 7-17.

The **REGARDING** field will be filled in automatically for some tasks. If not, you can type something descriptive in the field.

If checked, the **ATTACH DOCUMENT TO HISTORY** option will save a copy of the document with the history record.

A history record like the one shown in Figure 7-18 will be created for each contact associated to the task.

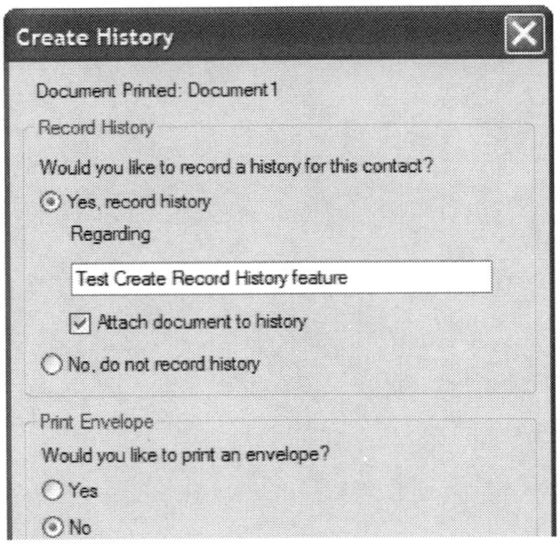

Figure 7-17 Create History dialog box

Date	Time	Result	Regarding & Details			Record Manager
12/16/2008	3:06 PM	Letter Sent	Test Create Record History feature			Chris Huffman

Figure 7-18 History record

Using The Setup Assistant Wizard To Set Up Microsoft Word

In the previous exercise you created a mail merge using the word processor that comes with ACT!. If you normally use Microsoft Word or want to start using it with ACT!, for mail merges and other types of word processing documents, you can. One of the options on the Setup Assistant wizard is to set up Microsoft Word to work with ACT!. You do not have to complete these steps now.

> If you are using the ACT! 2009 Premium for Web edition, I have read that you cannot use Microsoft Word as your word processor.

1. Help ⇒ Setup Assistant. Click Next on the first screen.

2. Click Next until you get to screen 8.

3. Select Microsoft Word, as illustrated in Figure 7-19.

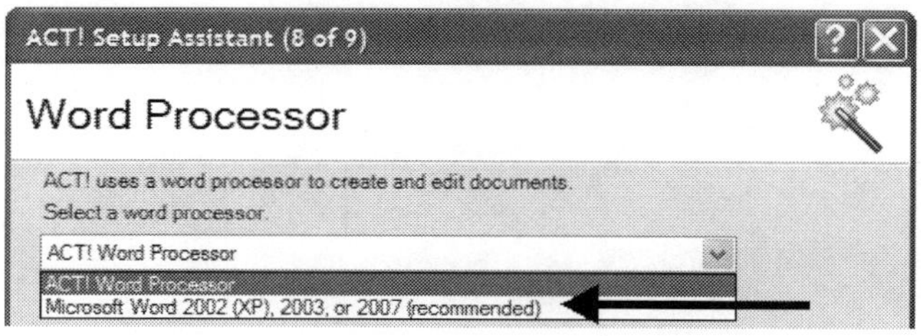

Figure 7-19 Word processor options

4. Click Next, then click Finish.

The ACT! Menu In Word And Excel

A menu for ACT! is installed in Word and Excel even if you will not use these software packages with ACT!.

Figure 7-20 shows the ACT! menu in Word. Table 7-1 explains the menu options.
Figure 7-21 shows the ACT! menu in Excel. Table 7-2 explains the menu options.

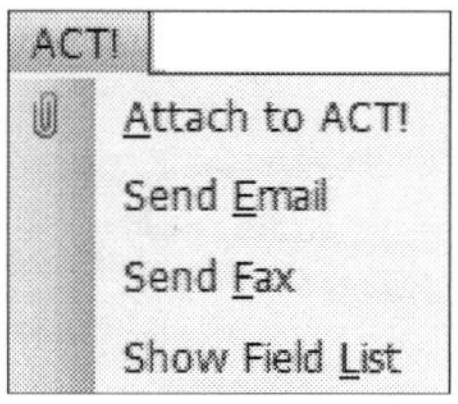

Figure 7-20 ACT! menu in Word

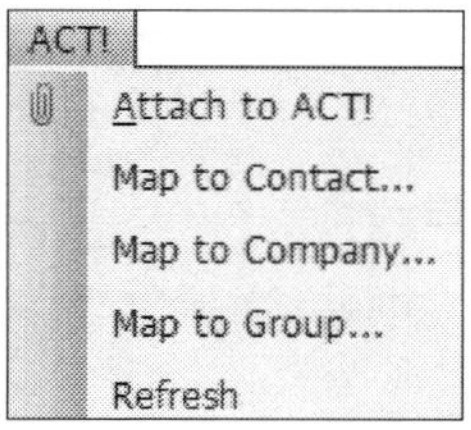

Figure 7-21 ACT! menu in Excel

Menu Option	Description
Attach to ACT!	Saves a copy of the document in the Attachments folder. If the document has already been saved in a folder other then the Attachments folder before selecting this option, you will see a message asking if you want to use the copy of the document that is in the Supplemental Attachments folder. (1)
Send Email	Places the current document in the body of the email message or as an attachment, so that it will be included in the email.
Send Fax	Faxes the current document to the contact(s) that you select. You have to have the fax software installed to use this option.
Show Field List	Displays the **SHOW MAIL MERGE FIELDS** dialog box so that you can select fields from the ACT! database to use in your mail merge document.

Table 7-1 ACT! menu options in Word explained

Menu Option	Description
Attach to ACT!	Saves a copy of the document in the Attachments folder. If the document has already been saved in a folder other then the Attachments folder before selecting this option, you will see a message asking if you want to use the copy of the document that is in the Supplemental Attachments folder. (1)
Map to Contact	Opens the Map Contact Fields dialog box shown in Figure 7-22, which is used to select the contact field(s) that you want to map to.
Map to Company	Opens the Map Company Fields dialog box, which is used to select the company field(s) that you want to map to.
Map to Group	Opens the Map Group Fields dialog box, which is used to select the group field(s) that you want to map to.
Refresh	I posted a question in the forum to find out the purpose of this option, but did not get a response.

Table 7-2 ACT! menu options in Excel explained

(1) This menu option opens the Select Contacts dialog box, which is used to select the contact(s) for the task that you are working on.

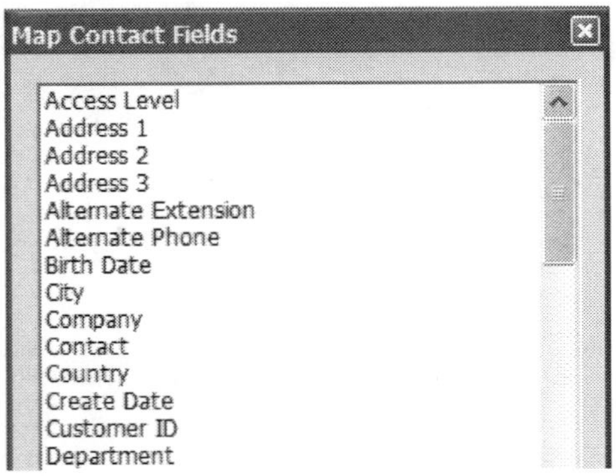

Figure 7-22 Map Contact Fields dialog box

Normal.dot Potential Problem In Microsoft Word 2003

If you see a message when you close Word that says "Changes have been made that effect the global template, Normal.dot. Do you want to save these changes?", there are three options in Microsoft Word that you can use to try and fix the problem, if you are sure that the hard drive does not have a virus.

① Turn off the option in Word that prompts to save changes to Normal.dot.
Tools ⇒ Options ⇒ Save tab.
② Remove the ACT! menu from the menu bar in Word.
③ Run the **DETECT AND REPAIR** option on the Help menu in Word.

SCHEDULING ACTIVITIES

In this lesson you will learn the following scheduling activity features:

- ☑ Timeless activities
- ☑ Scheduling a To-Do
- ☑ Scheduling the same activity for multiple contacts
- ☑ Sending email to activity contacts
- ☑ Scheduling activities for other users
- ☑ Using the alarm
- ☑ Rescheduling an activity
- ☑ Handling activity conflicts
- ☑ Group activities
- ☑ Creating and deleting recurring activities
- ☑ Scheduling random activities
- ☑ Filter and sort activities
- ☑ Creating and editing an Activity Series

LESSON 8

Activities Overview

Activities are more formal than notes. I think of activities as a really large, well thought out and detailed to-do list for your contacts. Activities let you keep up with your contacts. You can enter as much or as little information for each activity that you create. While it is tempting to only enter a little information, you may not remember everything that you know now, when the time comes to complete the task that an activity is for.

There are different types of activities that you can schedule. Some activities that you will schedule with contacts are business related and others are personal. The default activity types that you can schedule with contacts are meetings, telephone calls and to-do's. Each of these activities are basically created the same way. Activities are reminders of tasks that you need to complete. You can also create your own activity types.

It is a good idea to display the contact that you want to schedule the activity with before you open the Schedule Activity dialog box. This is not a requirement because there is an option on the dialog box to select the contact(s). If you want to schedule the same activity for more than one contact, select the group or create a lookup that will display the contacts that you want to schedule the activity for. You can also create the same activity for people that are not part of the same group or lookup at the same time. In addition to being able to view activities on the Activities tab on detail views, you can also view them on the calendar and Task List.

Figure 8-1 shows the Schedule Activity dialog box. Table 8-1 explains the options on the Schedule Activity dialog box.

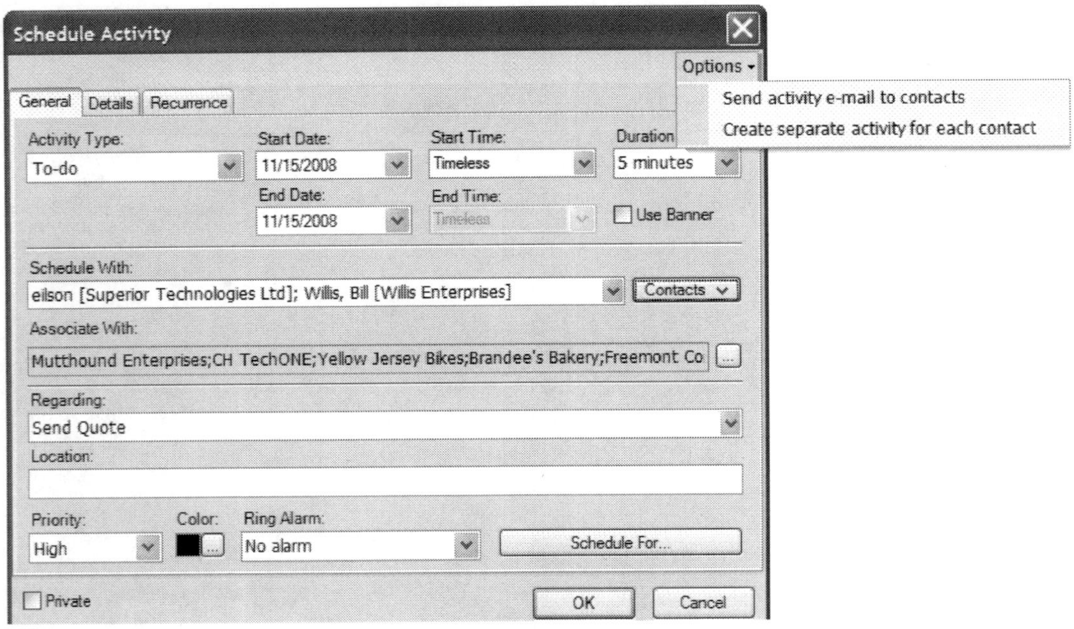

Figure 8-1 To-Do Activity options

The **SEND ACTIVITY E-MAIL TO CONTACTS** option shown in the upper right corner of Figure 8-1 above, will display a message in the banner at the top of the Schedule Activity dialog box stating that contacts will receive an email notification of the activity and users will receive an invitation. Once the activity is set up, the appropriate emails and invitations will be sent automatically.

The **CREATE SEPARATE ACTIVITY FOR EACH CONTACT** option will create an activity for each contact listed in the Schedule With field.

Option	Description
Activity Type	Select or change the type of activity that you are creating or editing. This field will initially be filled in based on the option that you select to open this dialog box. For example, if you click the Schedule Meeting button, "Meeting" will be the value displayed in this field when the dialog box is first opened, but you can change it.
Start Date	The date that the activity should start. The default value is today's date.
Start Time	The time that the activity should start. The default value is **TIMELESS**.
End Date/Time	This field will change automatically when the duration is selected.
Duration	Select the length of time needed to complete the activity.
Use Banner	Displays a banner on the daily calendar if the duration of the activity meets the requirement of the **SHOW FULL DAY** banner calendar preferences option. The banner is also displayed at the top of the Schedule Activity dialog box, as illustrated in Figure 8-2.
Schedule With	By default, this field contains the contact that was displayed before the dialog box was opened. Other contacts can be added.
Contacts	The options on this button are used to select contacts for the activity. (1)
Associate With	Select the groups, subgroups, companies and divisions that need to be included on the activity.
Regarding	Is used to provide a description of the activity. The options that will be displayed in the drop-down list depend on the activity type that is selected. (2)
Location	A free form field that is used to enter where the activity will take place.
Priority	Select how important the activity is. Setting a priority is optional.
Color	Select the color for the priority. (3)
Ring Alarm	If a time is selected from this drop-down list, your computer will beep the number of minutes selected, before the activity is scheduled to start.
Schedule For Button	Select a user in the database to assign the activity to. Activities can be scheduled for more than one user. (4)
Private	If the **PRIVATE** option shown earlier at the bottom of Figure 8-1 is selected on any tab on the Schedule Activity dialog box, other users of the database will not be able to view the activity.

Table 8-1 Schedule Activity dialog box options explained

(1) This button opens the menu shown in Figure 8-3.
The **SELECT CONTACTS** option is used to select the contact(s) that the activity is for.
The **NEW CONTACT** option is used to create a new contact, which you can add to the activity.
The **MY RECORD** option is used to add yourself to the activity. If you need to use this option, select it first, then add the other contacts. This option will remove contacts that are already in the Schedule With field, including the original contact that was there.

(2) Figure 8-4 shows the Regarding field drop-down list options for the Meeting activity type. Figure 8-5 shows the Regarding field drop-down list options for the To-Do activity type. If none of the options in the drop-down list fit your needs, you can type in a new description, which can be up to 256 characters.
If you know that you will do a lot of searches or use this field as criteria for a query or report, you should customize it so that only options from the drop-down list can be selected.

(3) By default, each priority level is a different color. If you want to change the color, click the button next to the option. You will see the dialog box shown in Figure 8-6. Keep in mind that the color is associated to a priority level and not the specific activity. If you change the color, the color that you select will automatically be applied to all activities with the same priority, going forward.

(4) Click the **SCHEDULE FOR** button when you need to schedule the activity for another user of the database. In order to schedule an activity for another user, you must have rights to do so. If you have rights to schedule activities for other users and click this button, you will see the dialog box shown in Figure 8-7. Select the person that you want to schedule the activity for. The activity will display on the users calendar and Task List. Don't be surprised when the user (probably a co-worker) does not thank you for giving them more work <smile>.

You can view partial activity entries in the banner section.

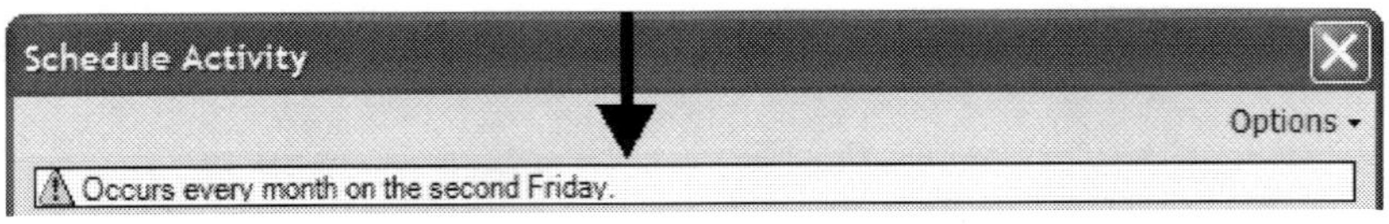

Figure 8-2 Banner section illustrated

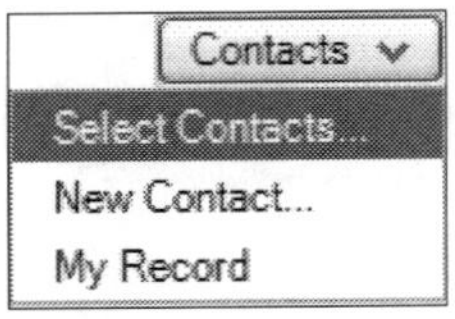

Figure 8-3 Contacts button options

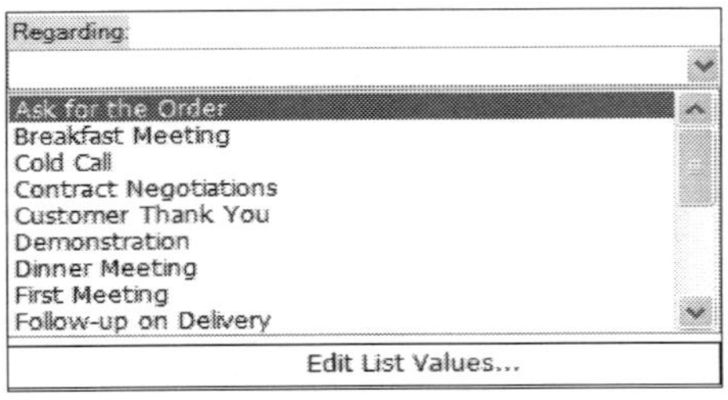

Figure 8-4 Meeting options

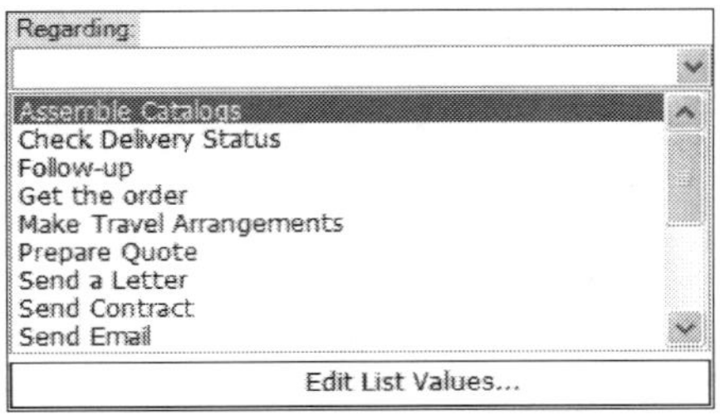

Figure 8-5 To-Do options

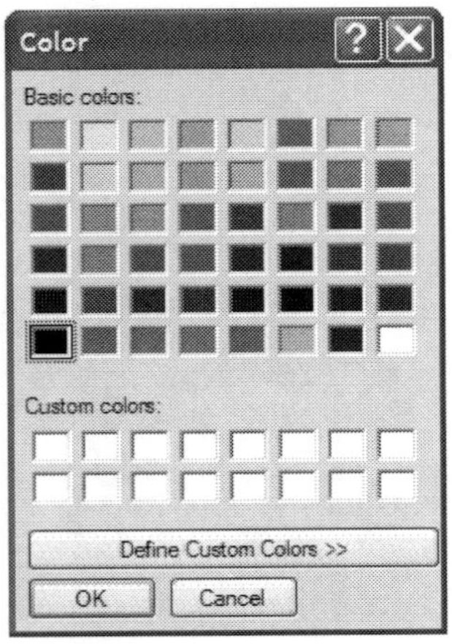

Figure 8-6 Color dialog box

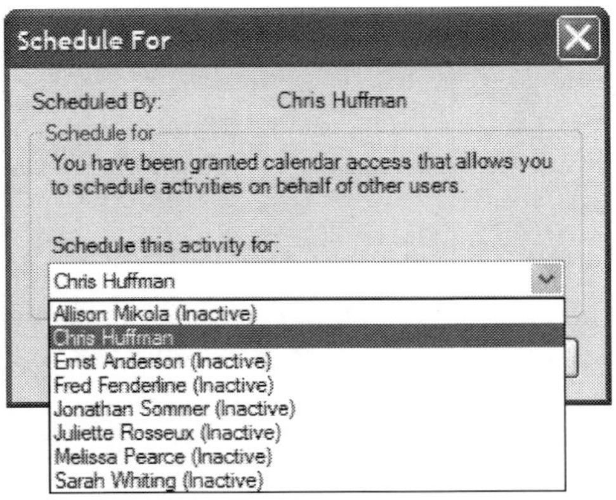

Figure 8-7 Schedule For dialog box

You will only see users that you have the rights to schedule activities for in the drop-down list on the Schedule For dialog box, shown above in Figure 8-7. In Lesson 17 you will learn how to grant calendar access, which in addition to being able to view entries on another users calendar, also allows you to create activities and assign them to other users.

Activity Types

There are six default types of activities that you can create, as explained in Table 8-2.

Activity	Is Used To Schedule . . .
Call	A telephone call.
Meeting	A meeting.
To-Do	A task that needs to be completed.
Marketing Call	A telephone call. You could use this option for cold call telephone sales.
Personal Activity	A non business related task. (5)
Vacation	Vacation time. (5)

Table 8-2 Activity types explained

(5) There is no button on the toolbar for this activity type. Schedule ⇒ Other, as shown in Figure 8-8 displays the entry point for these activity types. If you do not want to use the menu options to access these activity types, you can click on any of the schedule activity icons on the toolbar to open the Schedule Activity dialog box and then select the activity type from the drop-down list. In Lesson 13, you will learn how to create new activity types.

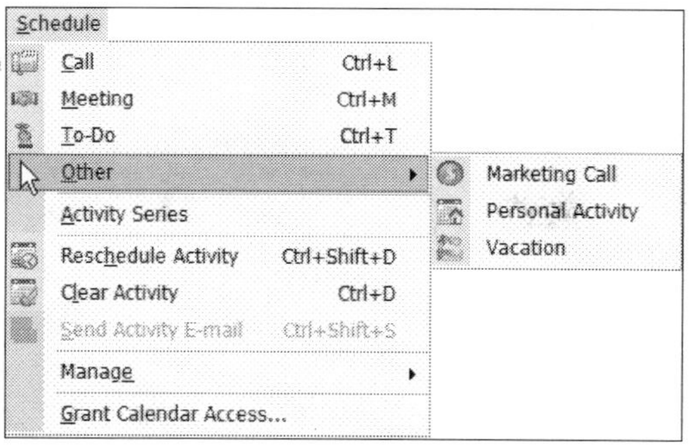

Figure 8-8 Schedule menu options

Timeless Activities

This type of activity is one that does not have a time associated with it. Many types of To-Do activities, like sending an email or fax can be timeless. When you create a To-Do activity, you will see that the default start time displayed is **TIMELESS**. You can change the start time to a specific time if you need to. You can select the timeless option as the default for any type of activity on the Preferences dialog box.

Public Or Private Activities

This option is only useful if more than one person uses the database. If the contact record is marked as private, the activities for the contact are marked as private by default. You can make activities private, even if the contact is not. The symbol illustrated in Figure 8-9 on the Activities tab, denotes that the activity is private.

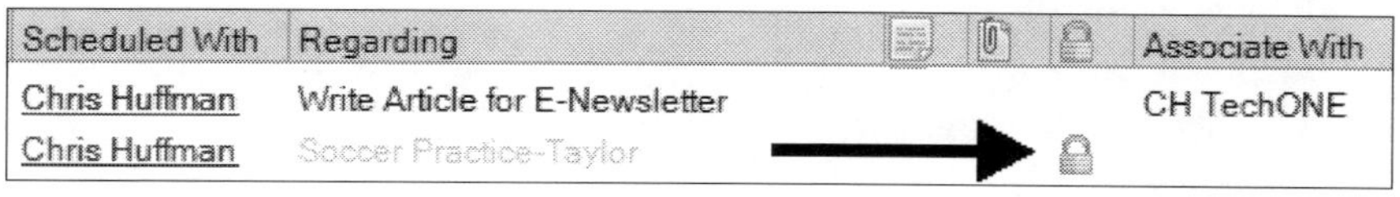

Figure 8-9 Private activity illustrated

Keep the following in mind when deciding whether or not to make an activity private.

① Private activities will partially appear on other users calendars when your name is part of the filter that they use. The actual contents of the activity does not appear, but the word **PRIVATE** appears next to your name.
② When you clear a private activity, it is still marked as private when it is moved to the History tab.
③ Private activities are not displayed in other users Task List.

Exercise 8.1: How To Schedule A To-Do Activity

In this exercise you will create a To-Do activity.

1. Look up the contacts that have "Customer" in the **ID/STATUS** field.
2. The highlighted record should be for Colleen McCarthy. Click the Contacts button.
3. On the Activities tab of the Contact Detail view, click the **SCHEDULE TO-DO** button on the toolbar. You will see the Schedule Activity dialog box.
4. Open the **REGARDING** drop-down list and select Send Quote.
5. Change the **PRIORITY** to High. Leave the dialog box open to complete the next part of this exercise.

Selecting Who To Schedule The Activity With

You cannot schedule an activity without associating it to a contact in the database. If the contact that you want to schedule the activity with is not in the database you have to add the contact to the database and then associate it to the activity.

1. The **SCHEDULE WITH** drop-down list should look like the one shown in Figure 8-10.
   For now, leave the current contact selected.

   If you click on the Name or Company column heading in the drop-down list, you can change the sort order.

   Clicking the **MY RECORD** button at the bottom of the drop-down list will add the My Record as the person that you want to schedule the activity with.

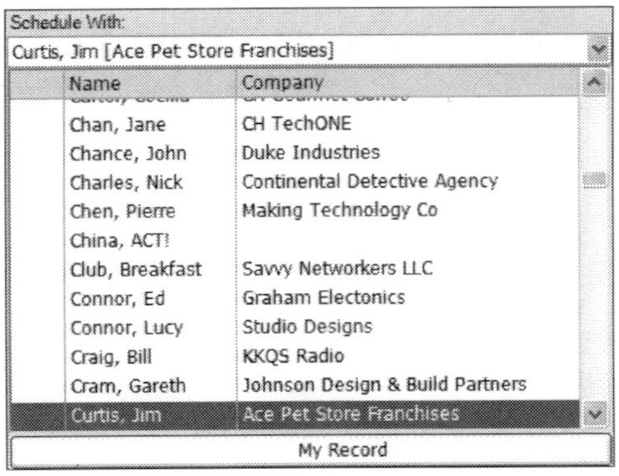

Figure 8-10 Schedule With drop-down list

How To Schedule An Activity For A New Contact

As mentioned earlier, you can schedule the activity for more than one contact. If a contact that you want to schedule the activity with is not in the database, you can create a new contact by clicking on the Contacts button on the Schedule Activity dialog box and selecting New Contact as shown earlier in Figure 8-3. Selecting this option will open the New Contact dialog box.

How To Add A New Contact To An Activity From The Schedule Activity Dialog Box

In this part of the exercise you will create a new contact for the activity.

1. Click the Contacts button on the Schedule Activity dialog box, then select New Contact. You should see the New Contact dialog box.

2. Enter the information in Table 8-3, for the new contact, then click OK.

   The address fields are on the Business Address tab.

   You will see the new contact listed in the Schedule With field on the Schedule Activity dialog box.

Field	Type This
Company	Spice Plus
Contact	Jennifer Milton
Address	456 Treasury St
City	Astoria
State	PA
Zip	10210

Table 8-3 Information for the new contact

How To Select Multiple Contacts

1. Click the **CONTACTS** button on the Schedule Activity dialog box, then select the option Select Contacts. You will see the Select Contacts dialog box.

Notice that you can add a new contact from this dialog box also.

You can assign the activity to all contacts, contacts in the current lookup, a group or company. You can also assign the activity on a contact by contact basis by selecting names from the list.

2. Open the **SELECT FROM** drop-down list and select Current Lookup. You will see the names that are from the ID/Status = Customer lookup that you created earlier in this exercise.

3. Click the **ADD ALL>>** button. You will see all of the contacts from the current lookup in the Scheduled Contacts list.

> If you wanted to assign this activity to other contacts, you could add them now. ACT! will not add names to the Selected contacts list if they have already been selected to be added to the activity.

4. Select the **GROUPS** option from the drop-down list, then open the drop-down list across from the Select From drop-down list and select the Sales Reps group.

5. Select the first three names from the Sales Reps group by holding down the **CTRL** key and clicking on each name, then click the **ADD>** button. Click OK.

6. Click the Options button in the upper right corner of the Schedule Activity dialog box and select the option, **CREATE SEPARATE ACTIVITY FOR EACH CONTACT**. This will create an entry on the Activities tab of each contact record.

7. Check the **USE BANNER** option. (**Hint**: It is below the Duration field.)

   You should have the options selected that are shown in Figure 8-11.

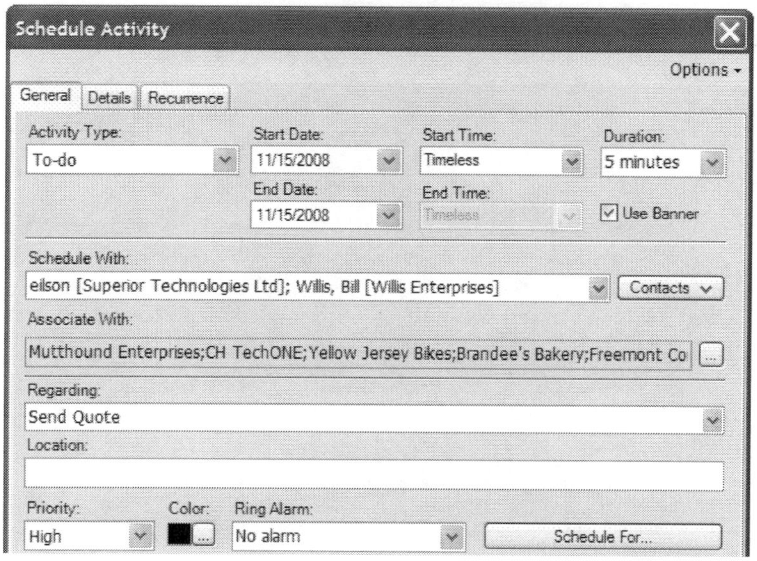

Figure 8-11 General tab activity options

> **Activity Linking Issue**
>
> When an activity is cleared from a contact that is linked to a company record, the history record that is created for the activity can be viewed from the contact record by default. To prevent this from happening, clear the **ASSOCIATE WITH** field, shown above in Figure 8-11.

Viewing An Activity With Multiple Contacts

If the same activity is assigned to more than one contact, you will not see all of the contact names in the **SCHEDULED WITH** column on the Activities tab. You will see a plus sign at the beginning of the list of names, as illustrated in Figure 8-12. If you click on this link, all of the contacts associated with the activity will be displayed in the Contact List view.

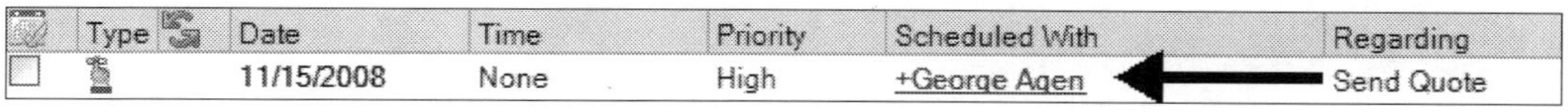

Figure 8-12 Multiple contacts for an activity illustrated

Why I Think It's Best To Schedule Phone Calls Individually

Looking at the activity illustrated above in Figure 8-12, you will not know how many people need to be called, if this was a telephone call activity. You would have to open the Schedule Activity dialog box to see the contact names, which adds an extra step to the process. If you call some of the contacts but cannot reach other contacts, it will be difficult to know which contacts you still have to call.

If you do not call all of the contacts, but mark the task as being complete, you may not remember that you still need to call other contacts that are listed on the activity because the activity will no longer appear on the Activities tab or Task List. This is the other reason why I think it is best to schedule phone calls individually. If you want to automatically have activities assigned to multiple contacts scheduled individually, select the option on the Scheduling Preferences dialog box. [See the Modifying Scheduling Preferences section later in this lesson]

Details Tab Options

The options on this tab are used to add comments, as well as, add an attachment to the activity. The Details tab is used to enter more text than the Regarding field on the General tab can store.

1. On the Details tab, type `This is a To-Do activity`, as shown in Figure 8-13.

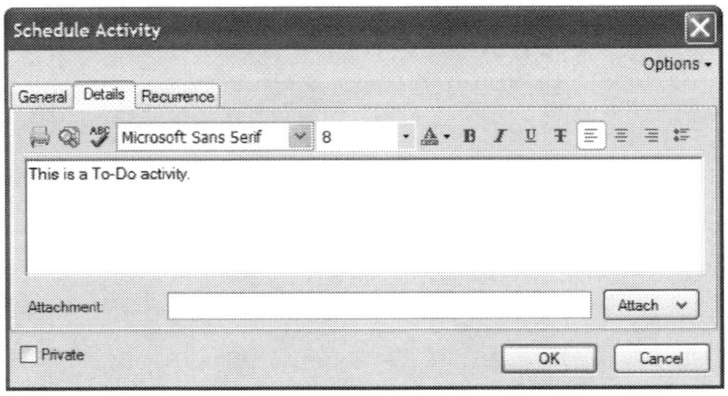

Figure 8-13 Details tab options

Recurrence Tab Options

The options on this tab are used to select the frequency of the activity, as well as, the start and end date for a recurring activity.

1. No options need to be selected on this tab. Click OK.

Send Activity E-Mail To Contacts Option

If you select this option and have email software configured to work with ACT!, once you click OK on the Schedule Activity dialog box, the email will be generated.

Your email software will open and you will see an email similar to the one shown in Figure 8-14.

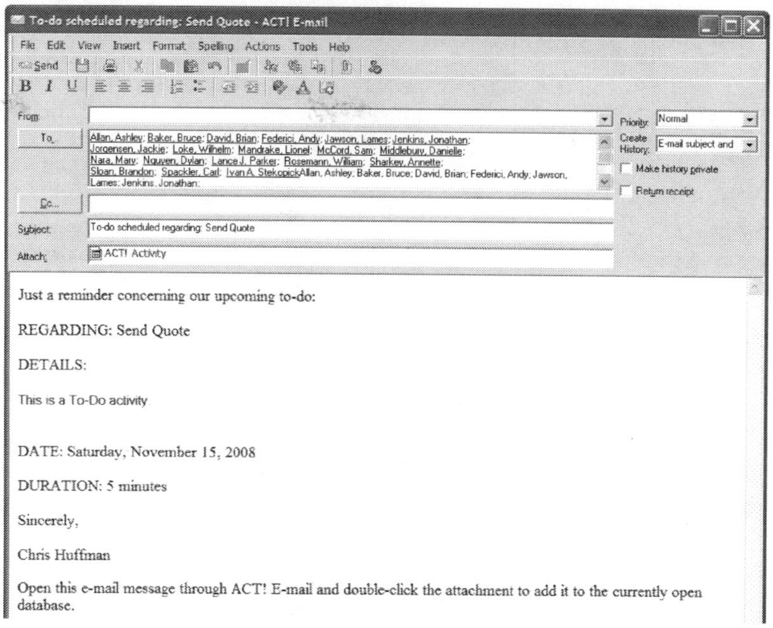

Figure 8-14 Activity e-mail that will be sent to the contacts

View The Activity

1. On the Activities tab, scroll through the records. You will see the To-Do activity that you created, as illustrated in Figure 8-15.

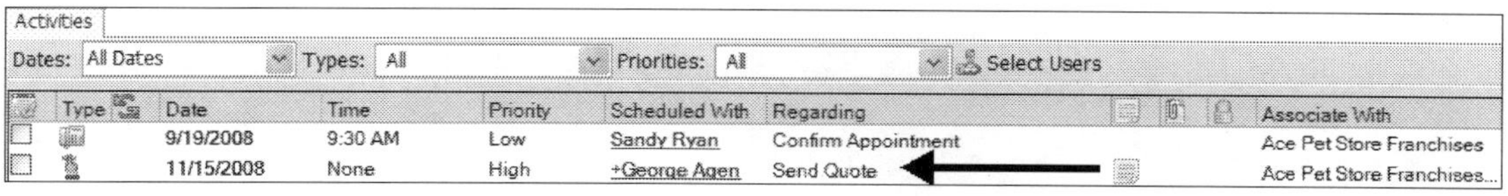

Figure 8-15 To-Do activity illustrated in the Contact Detail view

You may be asking yourself, what if I schedule an activity for a future date? How will I remember it? On the Task List view, you can view all of the activities that are scheduled in the future.

Exercise 8.2: Scheduling Activities For Other Users

The **SCHEDULE FOR** button at the bottom of the General tab on the Schedule Activity dialog box is used to create an activity for another user of the database. For example, if you wanted a sales manager in your company to send a thank you note to all of your suppliers, you could schedule the activity for the sales manager. Won't the sales manager be thrilled!

How To Schedule A Call

This activity type is used to create a reminder to call a contact. In this exercise you will schedule a phone call activity for another user of the database.

1. Look up the contact George Agen.

2. Click the **SCHEDULE CALL** button.

3. Change the Priority to Medium, then select the Regarding option, Confirm Appointment.

4. Click the **SCHEDULE FOR** button. Open the drop-down list and select Allison Mikola, then click OK.

5. You will see the banner shown in Figure 8-16 at the top of the Schedule Activity dialog box.

   Click OK.

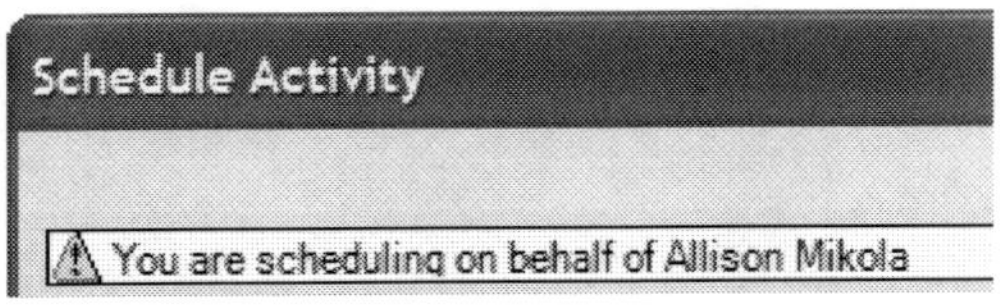

Figure 8-16 Activity banner

Exercise 8.3: Using The Alarm

This feature is designed to remind you of a scheduled activity. ACT! has to be open in order for the alarm to notify you of an activity. If ACT! is open, the Alarms dialog box will pop up. If ACT! is open, but minimized, the ACT! button on the Windows Taskbar will flash. Your computer will beep if you have the Ring Alarm option enabled. If you only select the Set Alarm option, you will only be notified at the time that activity starts, not before.

The alarm also has a snooze option, which you can use to be reminded of an activity. It works like the snooze button on an alarm clock, by notifying you in advance of the activity. You can reset the alarm to go off again at a later time. You can also clear the alarm to turn it off completely. Turning off the alarm does not clear the activity.

The snooze option is useful if you need time before the activity to prepare for it. If you want a snooze time that is not in the Ring Alarm field drop-down list, you can type it in. For example, you can enter any of the following times in the field: 46 minutes, 46 hours or 46 days.

1. Lookup the contact Jim Curtis.

2. Click the **SCHEDULE CALL** button.

3. Open the Start Time drop-down list. Scroll down the list and click in the time slot that is to the nearest, next half hour. (If it is currently 8:20 PM, select 8:30 PM. If it is 4:35 PM, select 5 PM.)

4. Change the Priority to Medium, then select the Regarding option, Confirm Appointment.

5. Open the **RING ALARM** drop-down list and select 5 minutes. This means that you will be notified five minutes before this activity starts.

6. You should have the options selected that are shown in Figure 8-17.

   You will see a different date and time. Click OK. You should now see an entry for this activity on the contact record for Jim Curtis.

   When the Alarms dialog box appears, as shown in Figure 8-18, come back to the section below: Alarm Notification Options.

   For now, continue going through the book by going to Exercise 8.5: Handling Activity Conflicts.

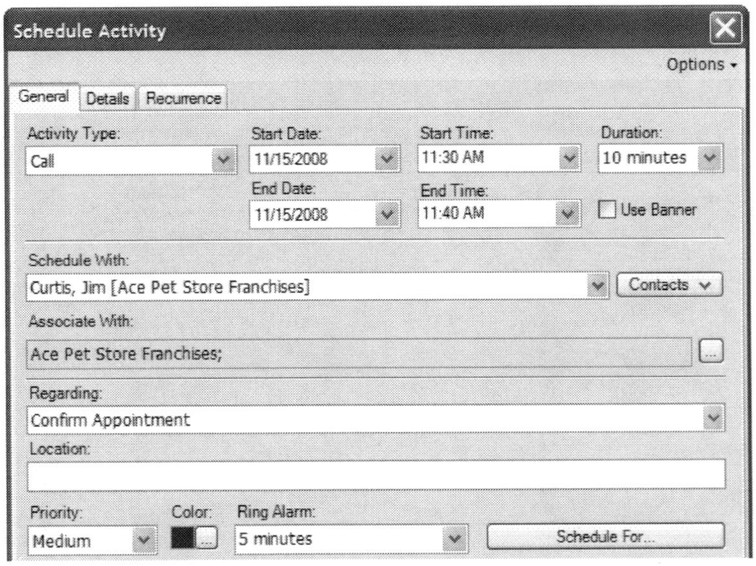

Figure 8-17 Telephone call options

Alarm Notification Options

You should now see the dialog box shown in Figure 8-18. The alarm options discussed below are available.

Select All Is used to set the same option for all of the activities that are displayed on the Alarms dialog box.

Snooze Is used to reset the snooze time on the dialog box shown in Figure 8-20.

Clear Alarm Turns the alarm off for the rest of the day. The activity will still stay on your calendar.

Clear Activity Opens the Clear Activity dialog box so that you can mark the activity as being complete.

Reschedule Opens the Schedule Activity dialog box, which allows you to select a different date or time for the activity.

Go To Takes you to the contact record that the alarm is for.

Show Details Displays the Activity Details section, shown in Figure 8-19. It is at the bottom of the Alarms dialog box. When the details are displayed, Show Details will change to **HIDE DETAILS**.

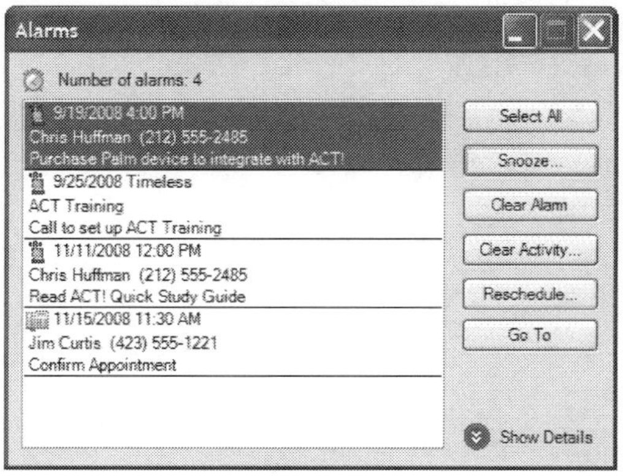

Figure 8-18 Alarms dialog box

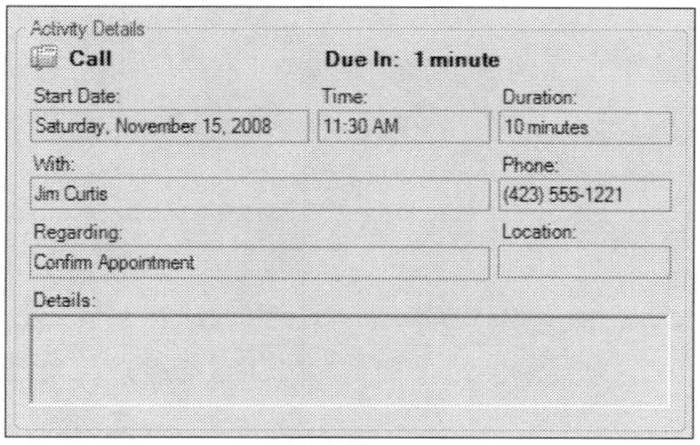

Figure 8-19 Activity details

Setting The Snooze Alarm

1. Click the Snooze button.

   You should see the dialog box shown in Figure 8-20.

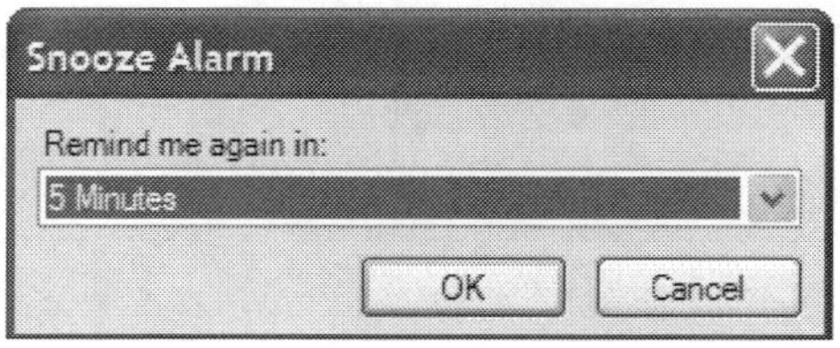

Figure 8-20 Snooze Alarm dialog box

2. Select the **10 MINUTES** option, then click OK. 10 minutes from now you will be notified again of the meeting that you have scheduled.

When the alarm notifies you again, come back and complete Exercise 8.4: Rescheduling An Activity. For now, continue going through the book, where you left off.

Exercise 8.4: Rescheduling An Activity

Rescheduling allows you to change when an activity will take place.

1. On the Alarms dialog box, click on the activity for Jim Curtis.

2. Click the **RESCHEDULE** button. You will see the Schedule Activity dialog box for the activity. If you were doing this for real, you would select a new date or time on the Schedule Activity dialog box.

3. For now, click the Cancel button.

4. Click the **CLEAR ALARM** button on the Alarms dialog box, then close the dialog box. Look up the contact Jim Curtis.

5. Double-click on the activity. Change the **RING ALARM** option to **NO ALARM**, then click OK.

Exercise 8.5: Handling Activity Conflicts

ACT! will warn you of activity conflicts and to try to keep you from scheduling two activities at the same time. If this occurs, you will be notified when you are creating an activity that conflicts with an existing activity. You will have the option to reschedule the time and/or date of the new activity.

In this exercise you will schedule a meeting activity for a time when an activity already exists.

1. Look up the contact Rick Blaine.

2. Click the **SCHEDULE MEETING** button.

3. Change the Start date to 9/18/2008. You can do this by typing the date in the field or by using the calendar attached to the field. Change the Start time to 2:30 PM. (Yes, I know that this is a date in the past, but bear with me.)

4. Select the **PRESENTATION** Regarding option.

   You should have the options shown in Figure 8-21.

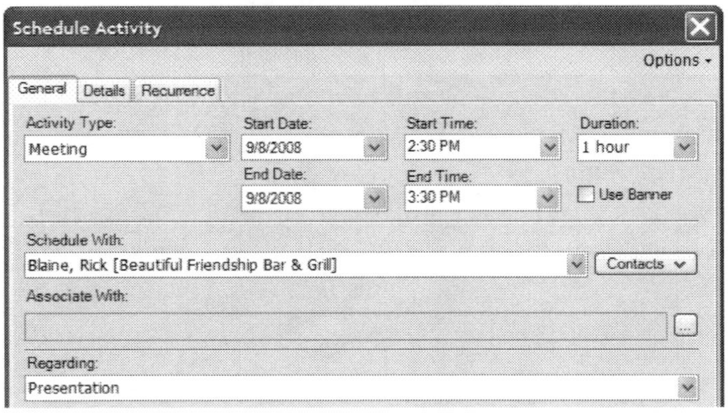

Figure 8-21 Meeting options selected

5. Click OK.

   You should see the message shown in Figure 8-22.

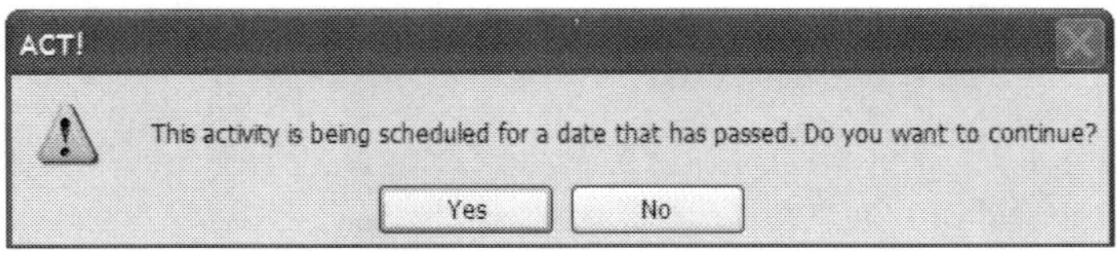

Figure 8-22 Activity warning message

Normally, you would not see this dialog box because you would not be trying to schedule an activity for a date in the past, unless you typed in a date in the past by mistake. It is being done here on purpose to demonstrate how to handle activity conflicts.

6. Click Yes to continue. You will see the dialog box shown in Figure 8-23.

   This dialog box is telling you that the activity that you are trying to schedule is conflicting with an existing activity. Figure 8-23 shows that an activity has already been scheduled with the contact on 9/8/2008 starting at 8 AM. Therefore, it is probably a good idea to reschedule this activity for another date or time.

   If you still want to schedule this activity, click the **ACCEPT** button. If you want to change the date or time of the activity, click the **RESCHEDULE** button.

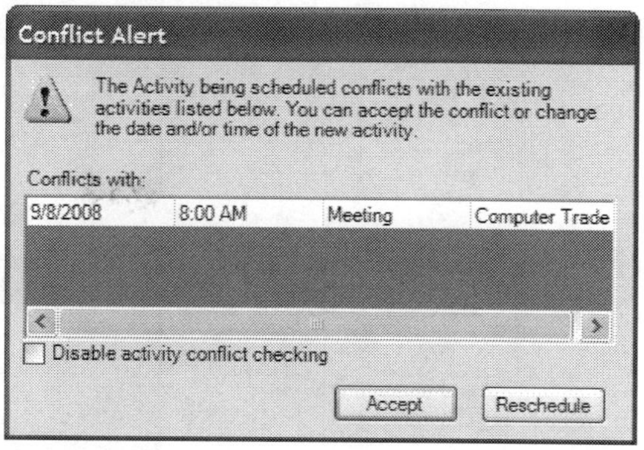

Figure 8-23 Conflict Alert dialog box

How To Reschedule A Conflicting Activity

1. Click the **RESCHEDULE** button.
2. Change the Start date to `11/6/08`, then click OK. This date and time does not conflict with other activities.
3. Click Yes when prompted that the activity has been scheduled for a date in the past.

Exercise 8.6: Group Activities

You can schedule an activity with a group. Doing this means that each contact in the group will be associated to the group activity. The group activity will appear on the Activities tab of each contact in the group.

In this exercise you will create a group activity for the Sales Reps group. The majority of the steps to create a group activity are the same as creating an activity for one contact.

1. Open the Group Detail view, then click on the Sales Reps group.
2. Click the Schedule Meeting button on the toolbar.
3. Change the Start Date to tomorrow.

Notice that the group name is in the Associate With field on the Schedule Activity dialog box. You can also add individual contacts and other groups to the activity.

4. Click the Contacts button and select the Select Contacts option.
5. Open the Select From drop-down list and select Groups.
6. Open the next drop-down list and select the group, Sales Reps with no email. Add the three contacts in the group to the list, then click OK.
7. Select the **FOLLOW-UP ON PRESENTATION** Regarding option, then click OK.

Recurring Activities

Recurring activities are activities that are repeated on a consistent frequency. The four types of recurring activities that can be created are discussed below. The recurring options look somewhat similar, but the fields perform differently. To make sure that you have selected the correct options, read the information in the banner at the top of the dialog box. It briefly explains what the options that you selected represent.

The **EVERY** field determines how many days, weeks, months or years are between each occurrence of the activity.

The **STARTS** field is the date that you want the first occurrence of the recurring activity to begin.

The **ENDS** field is the date that you want the last occurrence of the activity to happen.

There are two ways that recurring activities can be scheduled, as discussed below:

① Activities that occur on a regular basis, like monthly staff meetings.
② Activities that occur randomly, like processing payroll every other Friday.

Recurring Activity Types Explained

① **Daily** Select this option if the interval for the recurring activity is in days.

For example, the options shown in Figure 8-24 are for an activity that will happen every five days.

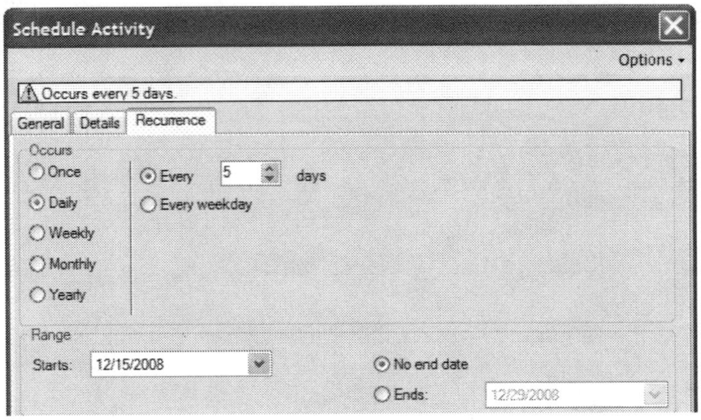

Figure 8-24 Daily recurring activity type options

② **Weekly** Select this option for activities that you want to occur weekly.

The options shown in Figure 8-25 are for a weekly meeting that will take place every Thursday and Friday, indefinitely.

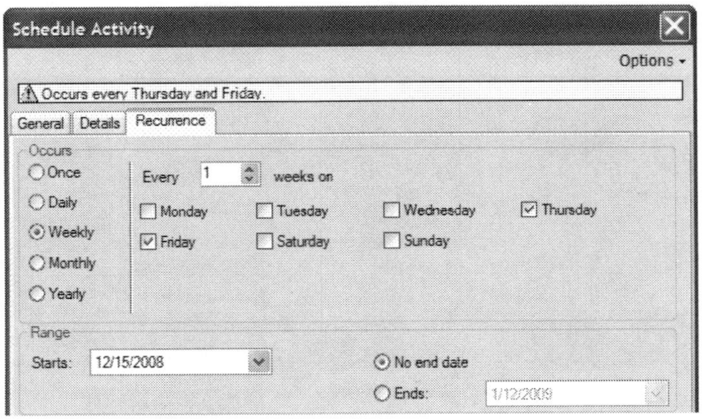

Figure 8-25 Weekly recurring activity type options

③ **Monthly** Select this option for activities that you want to occur monthly.

The options shown in Figure 8-26 will create a monthly activity that takes place on the second Tuesday of every month.

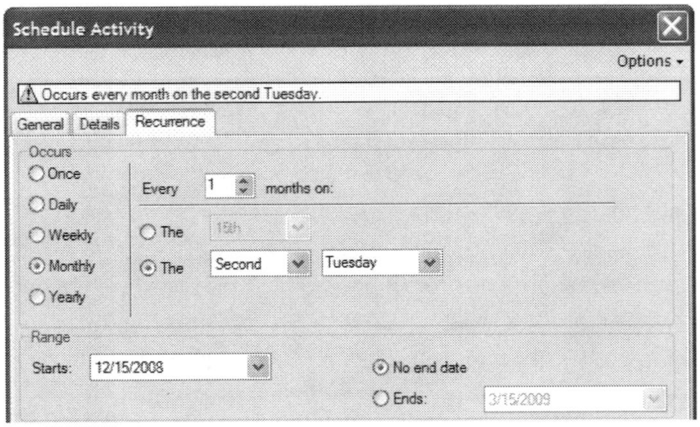

Figure 8-26 Monthly recurring activity type options

④ **Yearly** Select this option for activities that you want to occur yearly.

The options shown in Figure 8-27 will create a yearly activity that takes place on the last Tuesday of March.

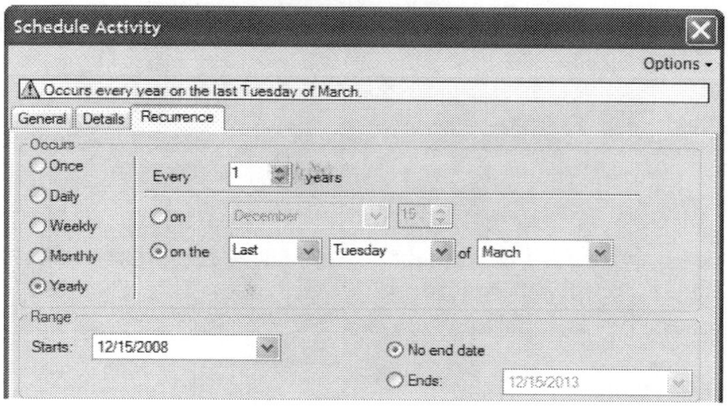

Figure 8-27 Yearly recurring activity type options

Exercise 8.7: How To Schedule Recurring Activities

If you know that you will need to have monthly meetings, you can schedule the meeting once and have ACT! automatically schedule the rest of the monthly meetings for the time period that you specify.

1. Look up the contact Rick Blaine, then click the Schedule Meeting button.

2. Select the options in Table 8-4 for the meeting activity.

Option	Change To
Start Date	The 15th of next month
Start Time	3 PM
Duration	2 hours
Regarding	Contract Negotiations

Table 8-4 Meeting activity options

3. On the **RECURRENCE** tab, select the Monthly option, then change the first **THE** option to the 15th, if it is not already.

4. Select the **ENDS** option and type in the date a year from today.

   You should have options selected that are similar to the ones shown in Figure 8-28.

   The options that you selected will schedule a meeting the 15th of each month for the next year.

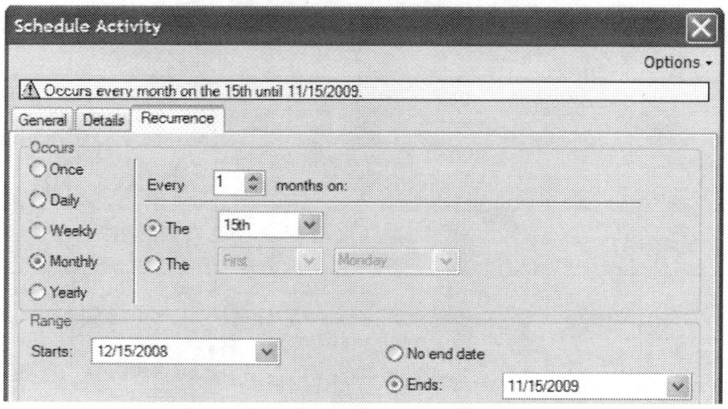

Figure 8-28 Recurrence tab options

5. Click OK. If there is a conflict, reschedule the activity and change the Start date on the Schedule Activity dialog box to the 16th.

   On the Activities tab for Rick Blaine, you will see a recurring meeting that starts on the 15th of next month, as shown in Figure 8-29.

   The recurring activity symbol is illustrated.

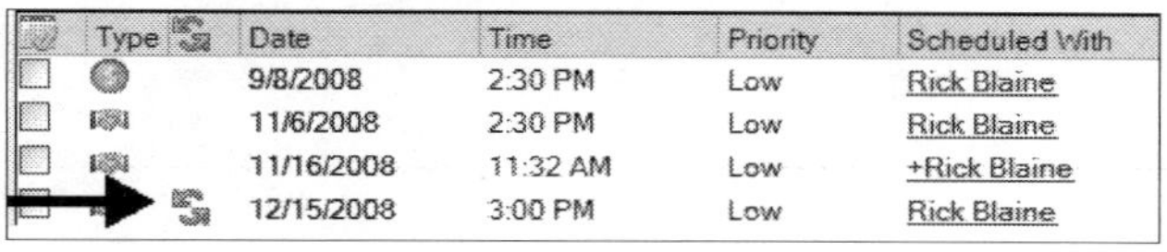

Figure 8-29 Recurring meeting illustrated

> Only the next occurrence of recurring activities will appear on the Activities tab and Task List. All of the occurrences of a recurring activity will appear on your calendar. This means that you will see each occurrence of a weekly meeting on a calendar, but you will only see the next occurrence of the weekly meeting on the Activities tab.

Exercise 8.8: How To Schedule Random Activities

Scheduling random activities allows you to schedule a conference call on the last day of the month. If you select the 31st, ACT! will schedule the recurring activity on the last day of the month, no matter what the actual last date of the month is.

1. Look up the My Record.
2. Click the **SCHEDULE CALL** button, then select the options in Table 8-5.

Option	Change To
Start Time	5 PM
Duration	15 minutes
Regarding	Discuss legal points
Priority	High

Table 8-5 Schedule call activity options

3. On the Recurrence tab, select the Monthly option. Open the first drop-down list and select the 31st. If you wanted the activity to end, you would enter a date in the **ENDS** field. You should have similar options to those shown in Figure 8-30. Click OK.

On the Activities tab of the My Record (Chris Huffman), you should see a phone call scheduled for the last day of the current month.

If the current month does not have 31 days, the activity will appear on the last day of the month. This may or may not be a workday.

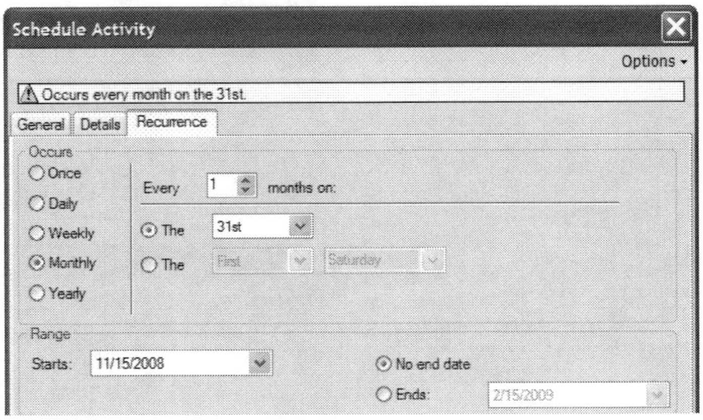

Figure 8-30 Monthly recurrence tab settings

Scheduling An Activity For The Last Workday Of The Month

In the previous exercise you created a random recurring activity that would automatically be scheduled for the last calendar day of the month.

If you need to schedule a monthly activity for the last workday of the month, select the monthly options illustrated in Figure 8-31.

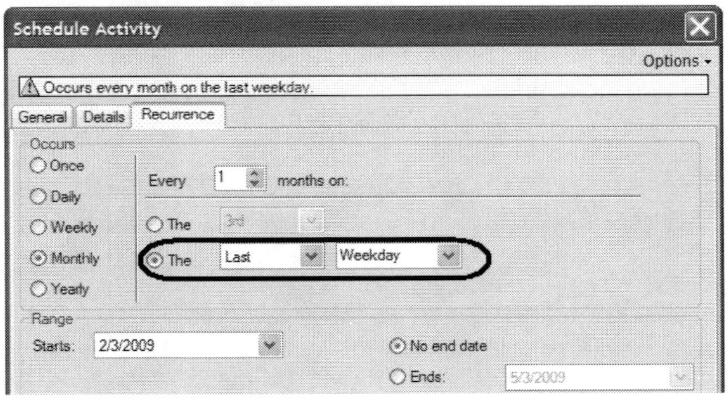

Figure 8-31 Options for a last workday of the month activity

Other Ways To Open The Schedule Activity Dialog Box

The majority of the activities that you created in this lesson used a button on the toolbar to open the Schedule Activity dialog box. There are other ways to open the Schedule Activity dialog box as discussed below.

① Double-click on a time slot on the calendar. This is helpful because it can help prevent you from trying to schedule conflicting activities.
② Open the Schedule menu.
③ On the Activities tab of a detail view, right-click in the list of activities and select Schedule ⇒ Meeting, as shown in Figure 8-32.

Figure 8-32 Activities tab shortcut menu

Deleting Recurring Activities

If you have scheduled a recurring activity and either no longer need the remaining activities or need to clear (delete) a recurring activity for a specific date, you can.

Exercise 8.9: How To Clear All Future Recurring Activities

In this exercise you will learn how to delete all of the remaining occurrences of an activity.

1. If the My Record is not displayed, display it now.
2. On the Activities tab, right-click on the monthly activity that you just created. Select the **ERASE ACTIVITY** option.
3. You will see the dialog box shown in Figure 8-33 letting you know that this is a recurring activity.

   Select the **DELETE ALL OCCURRENCES** option, then click OK.

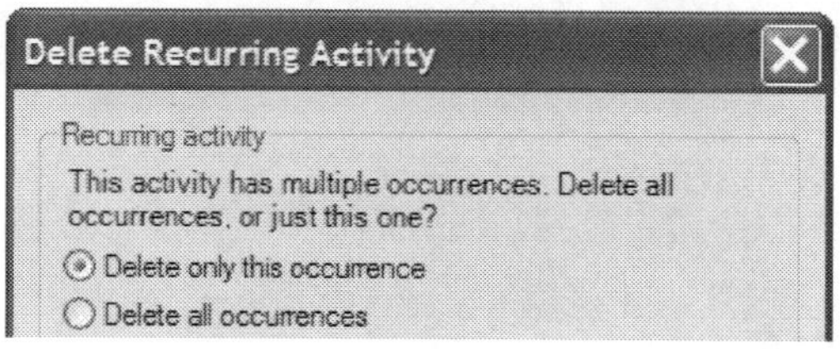

Figure 8-33 Delete Recurring Activity dialog box

Exercise 8.10: How To Clear A Single Recurring Activity

In this exercise you will learn how to clear one occurrence of the remaining occurrences of an activity.

1. Look up the contact Rick Blaine.
2. Right-click on the presentation activity on 11/6/2008 that you created earlier in this lesson and select **CLEAR ACTIVITY**.

3. Select the **ERASE** option on the Clear Activity dialog box, as illustrated in Figure 8-34, then click OK. The activity has been deleted.

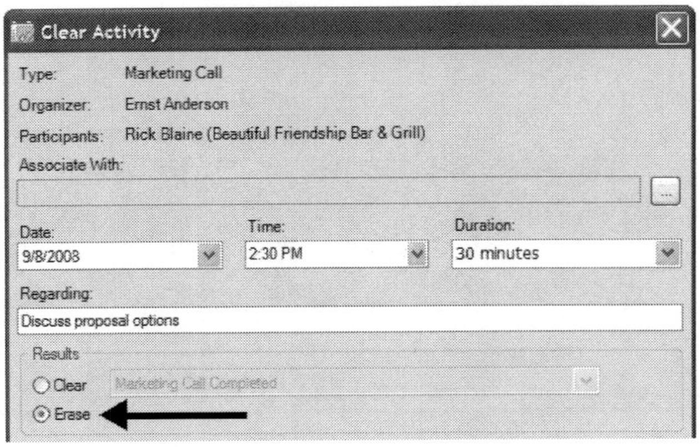

Figure 8-34 Clear Activity dialog box

Modifying An Activity

In this part of the exercise you will modify the priority of an activity.

1. Double-click on the 11/6/08 activity for Rick Blaine.
2. Change the Priority to Medium-High, then click OK.
3. Click Yes when prompted that the date has passed.

Clearing Activities

It is good practice to clear activities once you complete them. When you clear an activity, a record is automatically created on the History tab of the contact that the activity belongs to. This way, if you need to know whether or not an activity was completed or ever existed, you will be able to easily tell.

Other Reasons To Clear Activities

① Some reports are based on history records that are created when an activity is cleared. Without history records, the reports will not produce the correct output.
② Allows you to schedule follow up activities.
③ You will not be reminded of the activity.
④ Fields on the Latest Activities tab are updated.

How To Clear Activities

You have already learned how to clear recurring activities from the Activities tab. Clearing other types of activities is basically the same process. You can right-click on an activity anyplace except the History tab. The other ways to clear an activity are discussed below:

① On the Task List, click in the check box illustrated in Figure 8-35.
② On any Calendar view, click in the check box illustrated in Figure 8-36.
③ Select the activity on the Activities tab that you want to clear, then Schedule ⇒ Clear Activity.

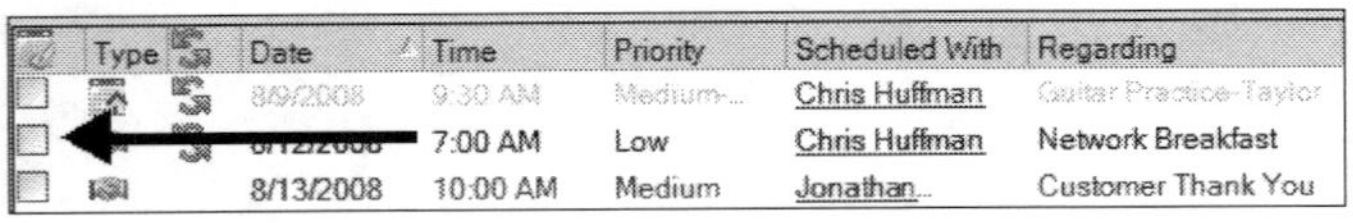

Figure 8-35 Task List option to clear an activity

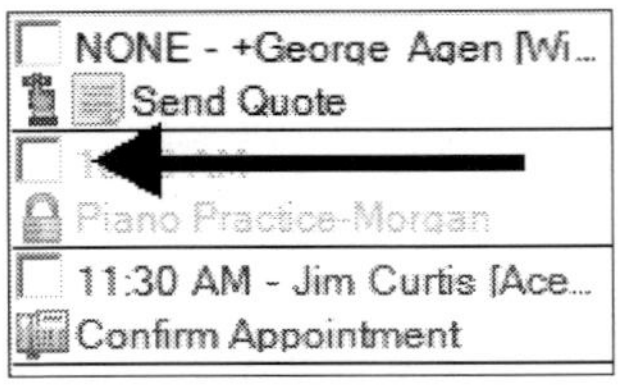

Figure 8-36 Calendar view option to clear an activity

Exercise 8.11: Clear An Activity For A Contact

When you clear an activity you can leave the options the way that they are or you can add or change information about the activity as needed. You should make changes that will help you remember more about the activity in the future.

1. Right-click on the 11/6/08 activity for Rick Blaine, then select **CLEAR ACTIVITY**.
2. Click the **FOLLOW-UP** button. The follow-up option is used to schedule another activity for the contact. (Amazingly, this is called a follow up activity.) This is the equivalent of creating a paper trail.
3. Open the **REGARDING** drop-down list and select the Follow-up on Presentation option, then click OK.
4. Select the **MEETING NOT HELD** results option.
5. Check the **ADD DETAILS TO HISTORY** option, if it is not already checked.

   You should have the options shown in Figure 8-37.

   Click OK.

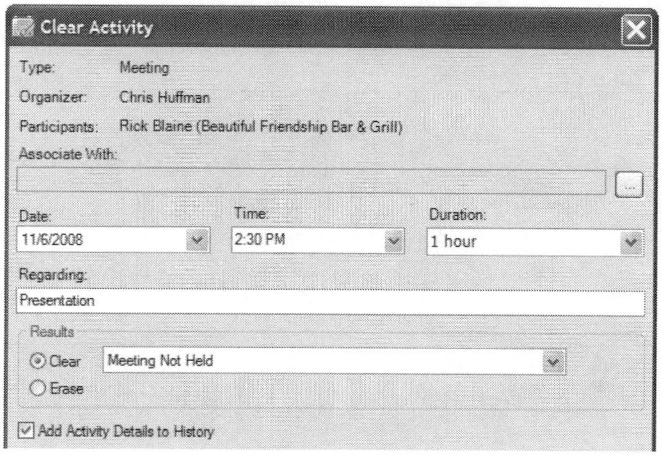

Figure 8-37 Clear Activity options

The activity for 4/6/08 is no longer on the Activities tab. You should see a new activity with today's date that has "Follow-up on Presentation" in the Regarding field. On the History tab, you will see an entry for the meeting not held activity.

How To Clear More Than One Activity At The Same Time

You can clear more than one activity on the Activities tab or the Task List at the same time by selecting the activities that you want to clear, then right-click on them and select **CLEAR MULTIPLE ACTIVITIES**, as illustrated in Figure 8-38.

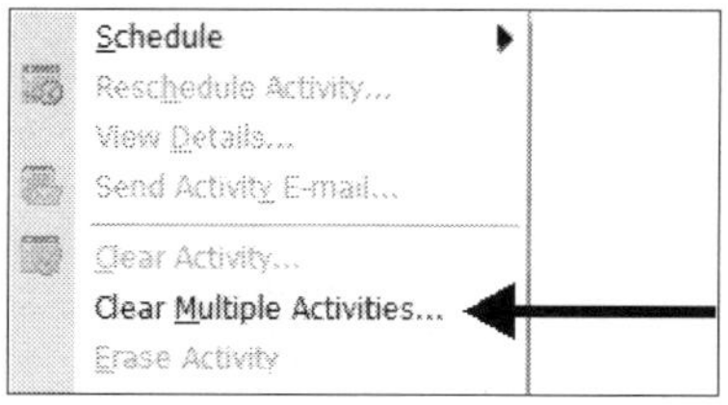

Figure 8-38 Task List multi select shortcut menu

Exercise 8.12: Clear An Activity For A Group

The steps below will show you how to clear a group activity. In this exercise you will clear the group activity that you created earlier in this lesson. Clearing a group activity is the same process as clearing an activity for a contact.

1. Click the Groups button, then click on the Activities tab.

2. You should see a Follow-up activity with tomorrows date. It may be a date in the past if you completed Exercise 8.6 before today. Right-click on the activity and select **CLEAR ACTIVITY**.

3. Click OK on the Clear Activity dialog box because none of the information for the activity needs to be changed.

Exercise 8.13: How To Filter Activities

You may only want to see certain types of activities or activities in a certain date range. Filtering allows you to accomplish both of these tasks. In this exercise you will learn how to filter activities.

1. Look up the My Record. On the Activities tab, open the **TYPES** drop-down list and clear the Vacation option. If there are vacation activities, you will not see them now.

2. Right-click in the Activities tab and select Filter Activities.

3. You should see the Filter Activities dialog box. Open the Dates drop-down list and select **TODAY AND FUTURE**.

4. Open the Types drop-down list and clear the Personal Activity option.

   You should have the options selected that are shown in Figure 8-39.

   Click OK.

   There should be less activities displayed.

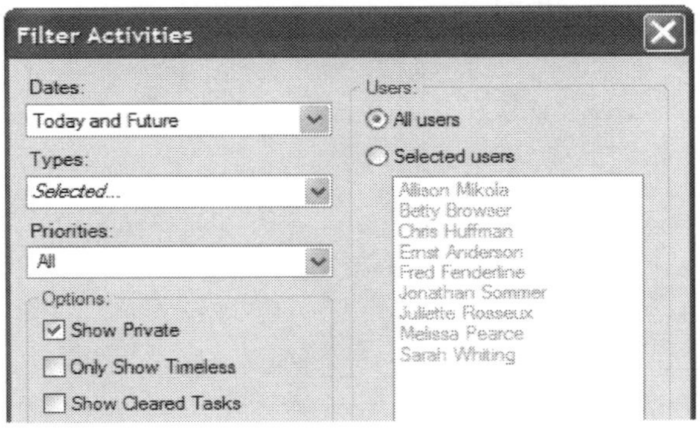

Figure 8-39 Filter Activities dialog box

> **Sorting Activities**
>
> You can sort the activities on the Activities tab in ascending or descending order by clicking on the column heading of the field that you want to sort on.

Exercise 8.14: How To Delete An Activity

If you have an activity that you do not need anymore or will not complete, you can delete it. If you delete an activity, it is not automatically recorded on the History tab, but it is removed from your schedule.

1. Look up the contact Rick Blaine. Display all of the activities by changing the **DATES** option to All Dates. Change the **TYPES** option to All.

2. Click on the activity that has today's date or the most recent date if you completed the prior exercises in this lesson before today.

3. Press the Delete key.

4. Select the Erase option on the Clear Activity dialog box, then click OK.

5. Select the option to delete all occurrences if prompted, then click OK.

Modifying Scheduling Preferences

In this lesson you have created a variety of activities. ACT! has scheduling options that you can modify as needed, by following the steps below.

1. Tools ⇒ Preferences ⇒ Calendar & Scheduling tab. Click the Scheduling Preferences button.

2. Select the activity type that you want to change, then select or change the options as needed. Each activity type can have different options.

   Figure 8-40 shows the activity options that can be modified.

   The **AUTOMATICALLY ROLL OVER TO TODAY** option moves activities that have not been completed to the next day. This can be used to ensure that activities do not fall through the cracks, as they say. This option is only applied to activities that have a single user.

   If you create a lot of activities that need to be assigned to multiple contacts and want each contact to have an activity record created automatically, check the option **CREATE SEPARATE ACTIVITIES WHEN SCHEDULING WITH MULTIPLE CONTACTS**.

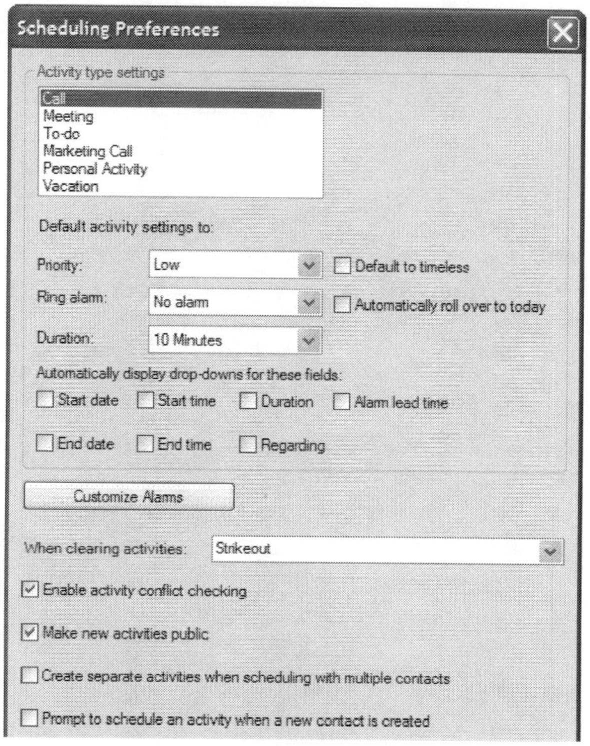

Figure 8-40 Scheduling Preferences dialog box

> If you want to set or remove the same option(s) for all of the activity types, select all of the activity types in the **ACTIVITY TYPE SETTINGS** list and then make the changes to all of them at the same time.

Alarm Preferences

1. Click the **CUSTOMIZE ALARMS** button on the Scheduling Preferences dialog box.

   The options shown in Figure 8-41 are used to customize the sound that the alarm will make.

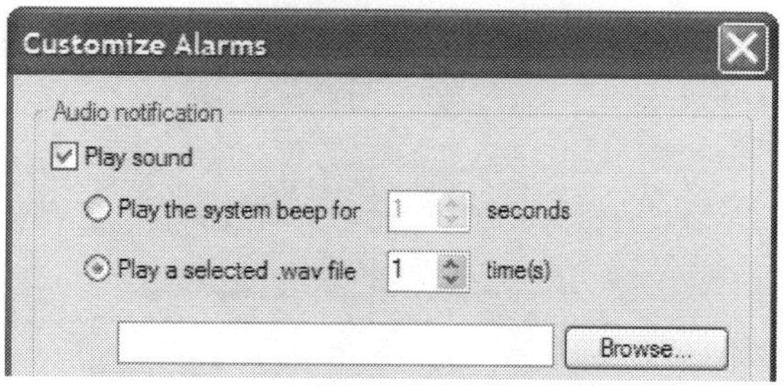

Figure 8-41 Customize Alarms dialog box

2. Close all open dialog boxes.

Activity Series

ACT! comes with two activity series that you can use. You can also create your own activity series. Activity series remind me of a project plan or mini to-do list that has all of the tasks that you need to do, to complete a project. An activity series is used to schedule pre-defined activities with contacts. An activity series saves you time because you do not have to remember all of the tasks or create a series of activities manually for each contact. Like other features in ACT!, the activity series can be public or private.

The key to understanding how an activity series works is understanding the concept of the **ANCHOR DATE**. The anchor date is the date the activities in the series use as a starting point. It is the date that all activities in the series are based from. You can schedule activities, days, weeks or months before or after the anchor date. If you are trying to figure out when you would have the need to schedule an activity before the anchor date, hopefully, the following scenario will help.

If you are planning to have a product launch, a lot of activities need to be completed weeks and months before the product is actually launched. Some of the tasks that need to be completed prior to the launch include the following: Inviting the media, finding and booking a location for the launch, creating and inviting potential customers, creating and executing an advertising campaign and hiring a caterer. These activities would have a date prior to the anchor date. In this scenario, the anchor date would be the date of the product launch.

The **ACTIVITY SERIES TEMPLATE CREATION WIZARD** can be accessed from any view. It is used to create a list of activities to complete. You can create as many activity series as you need. Having a list makes it easier to remember what the next task is that needs to be completed.

Another example of an activity series would be the tasks that have to be completed when you obtain a new customer. The following items could be the activities that need to be completed for new customers.

① Verify the contact information. (Send email)
② Send the customer a welcome kit. (Send literature)
③ Call the customer five days after the welcome kit is sent out. (Confirm shipment)
④ Set up another opportunity for the customer. (Send quote)

Exercise 8.15: Create An Activity Series

In this exercise you will create an activity series that will be used as the guidelines for changing a prospect to a customer. The series will include the four activities discussed above.

1. Schedule ⇒ Manage ⇒ Activity Series Templates.

   You will see the dialog box shown in Figure 8-42. Select the first option, then click Next.

Figure 8-42 Activity Series Template Creation Wizard screen

> Select the **EDIT AN EXISTING ACTIVITY SERIES** option, on the first wizard screen shown in Figure 8-43, when you want to view the existing activities. You would also select this option if you need to edit an activity series.

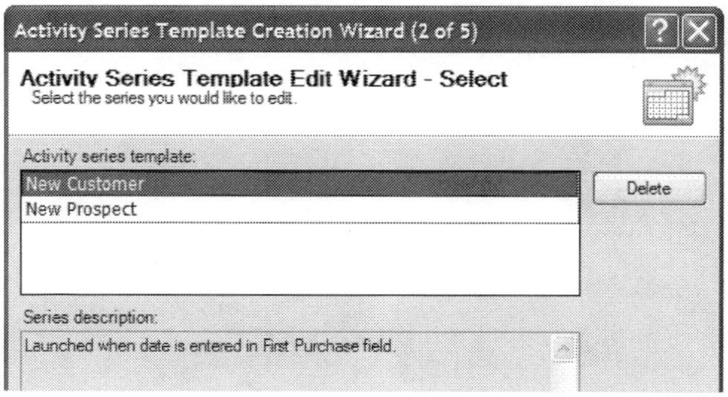

Figure 8-43 Existing activity series

2. Type `My Activity Series` in the Name field.

   Type `New Customers Welcome Kit` in the Description field, as shown in Figure 8-44, then click Next.

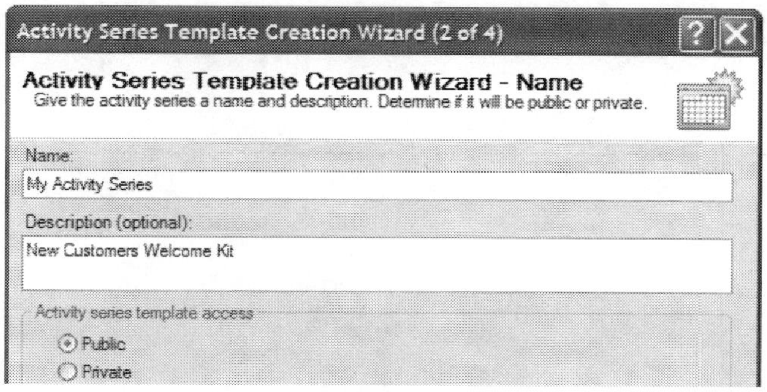

Figure 8-44 Activity Series Name screen

3. Click the Add button on the third wizard screen. Open the Activity Type drop-down list and select To-Do. Select the **SEND EMAIL** Regarding option. You should have the options shown in Figure 8-45.

   The **STARTS** field is how many days, weeks or month's from the Series Anchor date that you want the activity to begin.

   The options in the next drop-down list are used to select the interval (days, weeks or months) that the activity needs to be completed.

   The third drop-down list is used to select whether the activity should start **BEFORE** or **AFTER** the Anchor date.

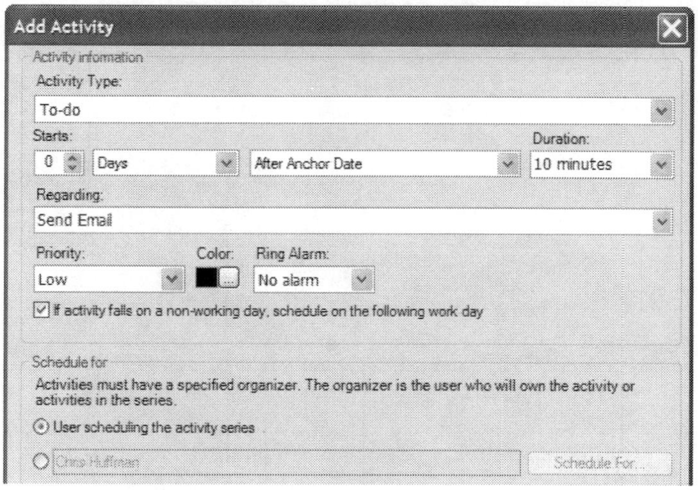

Figure 8-45 Add Activity dialog box

4. Click OK. You should see the activity that you just created on the third wizard screen.

5. Create the activities in Table 8-6.

Field	Activity #1	Activity #2	Activity #3
Activity Type	To-Do	Call	Marketing Call
Starts	1	6	8
Regarding	Send Literature	Confirm Shipment	Follow up per email
Priority	High	Medium High	Medium

Table 8-6 Activities for the series

6. When you are finished, the Activity Series screen should look like the one shown in Figure 8-46.

   If necessary, you can resize the columns on this screen just like you can on the tabs on the Contact Detail view.

   Click Next.

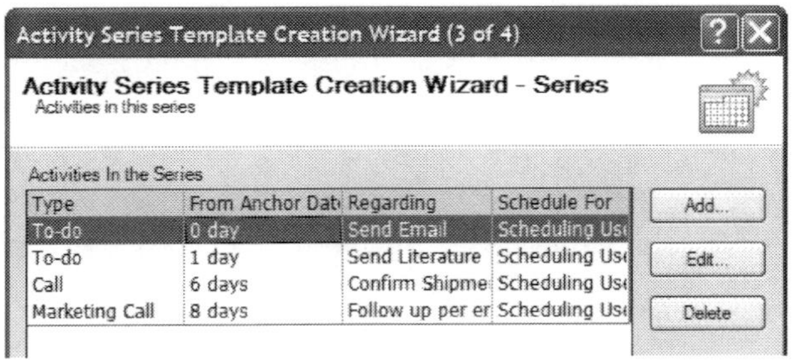

Figure 8-46 Activities in the series

7. The option **YES, SCHEDULE NOW** should be selected, as shown in Figure 8-47.

   Click Finish.

   You will see the Schedule Activity Series dialog box.

Figure 8-47 Activity Series Finish screen

Assign The Activity Series To Contacts

You can assign the activities in the series to one or more contacts as soon as you create the activity series, by following the steps below.

1. Click the Contacts button on the Schedule Activity Series dialog box and select the first option.
2. Assign the activities to all of the contacts in the Sales Reps with no email address group, then click OK.
3. Change the **SERIES ANCHOR DATE** to next Monday.
4. You should have the options shown in Figure 8-48.

   The only difference should be the date.

   Click the Schedule button.

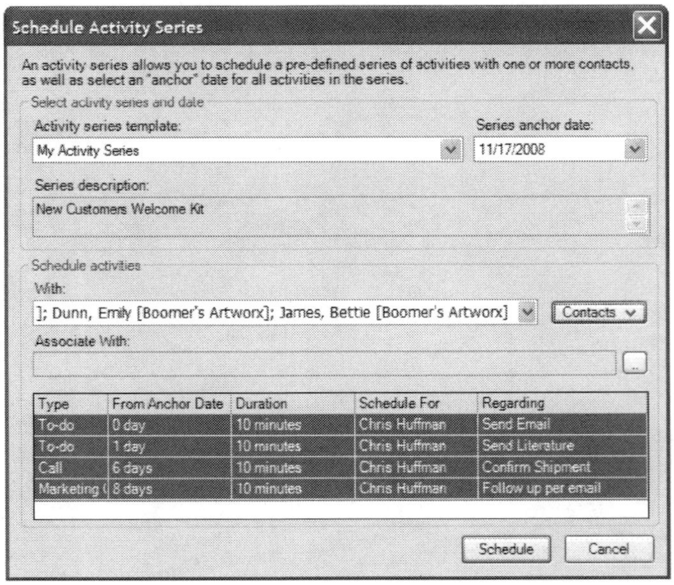

Figure 8-48 Schedule Activities Series dialog box

5. Look up the contact Emily Dunn, then click on the Activities tab. You should see the four activities from the series, as illustrated in Figure 8-49.

   Notice that they are in date order.

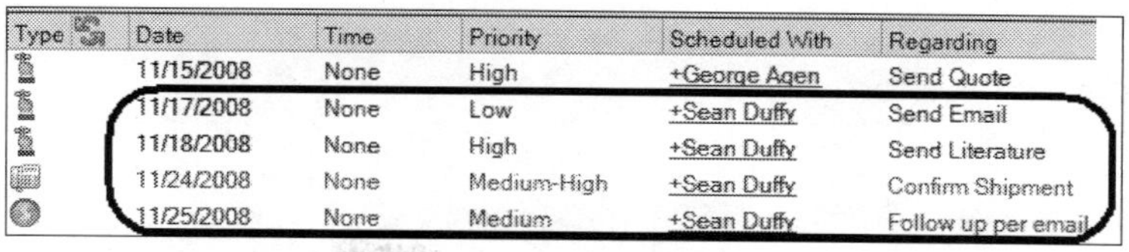

Figure 8-49 Activities from the series

Exercise 8.16: How To Edit An Activity Series

In this exercise you will modify the activity series that you just created. You will also assign users to tasks in the activity series.

1. Schedule ⇒ Manage ⇒ Activity Series Templates. Select the **EDIT AN EXISTING ACTIVITY SERIES** option, then click Next.

2. Select the activity series that you created, then click Next.

3. Add the following to the Description field. - `(Select the anchor date to equal the date that you will send the literature)`, as shown in Figure 8-50, then click Next.

   The reason that I include information about the anchor date in the Activity Series description is so that I will know which activity is the one driving the series. Doing this is optional.

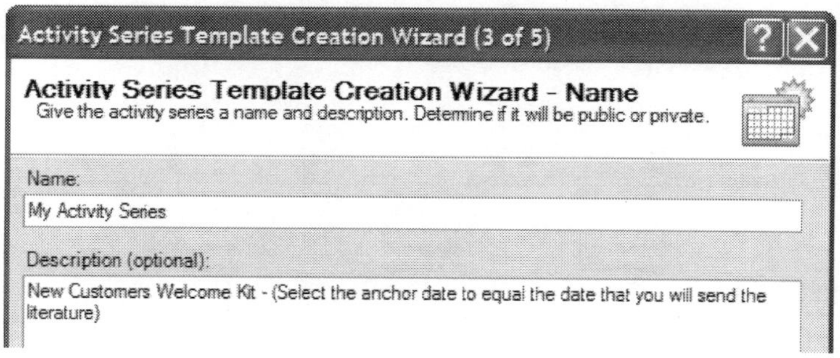

Figure 8-50 Modified activity series description

4. Select the Send Literature activity, then click the Edit button.

5. Click the last option in the **SCHEDULE FOR** section.

6. Click the **SCHEDULE FOR** button. Open the drop-down list on the Schedule For dialog box and select Allison.

7. Click OK twice to return to the Activity Series wizard screen.

8. Repeat the steps above to assign a user to the activities in Table 8-7.

Activity	Assign To
Confirm Shipment	Ernst
Follow up per email	Jonathan

Table 8-7 Activities to assign to users

9. Change the Starts field of the Send Email activity to 2, then select **BEFORE ANCHOR DATE** from the drop-down list, as illustrated in Figure 8-51.

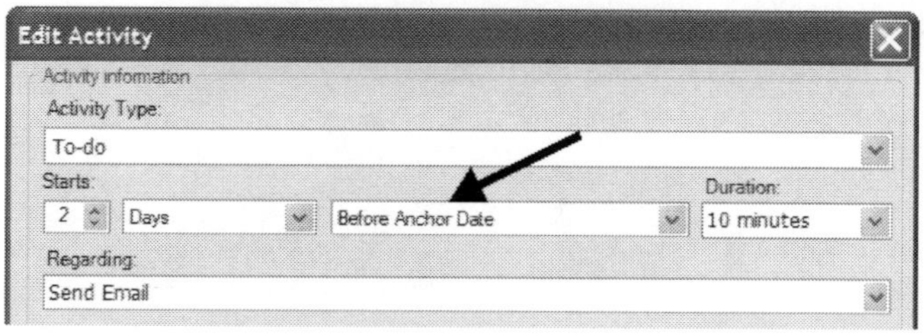

Figure 8-51 Anchor Date modified

When you are finished, the **SCHEDULE FOR** column on the wizard screen should look like the one shown in Figure 8-52.

Notice that the first To-Do activity has **-2 DAYS** in the From Anchor Date column. That is because you selected the Before Anchor Date option, which means that this activity should be started two days before the anchor date.

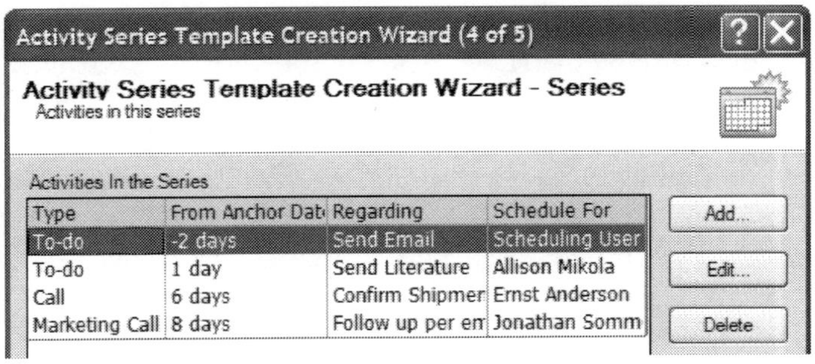

Figure 8-52 Modified activity series

10. Click Next. Select No, Schedule later, then click Finish.

RUNNING REPORTS

In this lesson you will learn the following about running reports:

- ☑ Selecting report criteria
- ☑ Custom date ranges
- ☑ Printing calendars, address books, labels and envelopes
- ☑ Using the Quick Print options

LESSON 9

Reports Overview

ACT! comes with several reports already created that you can use. They are on the Reports menu. In this lesson you will learn how to run some of the reports on the Reports menu. The reports that you run can be printed and saved. Reports are probably a key feature in ACT! because we are a report driven society. For many, reports are the only reason they enter contact information in ACT!. Once you have been using ACT! for a while you will probably see that you are running the same reports on a regular basis. Take some time once you have run reports for about a month and carefully look at the data. Are there columns on the report that do not have any data or very little data? Is the report providing the level of detail that you need? If not, you may need to modify the report and/or enter more data.

The label and envelope options are on the Print dialog box, which is accessed from the File menu. The calendars and address book print options are with the labels and envelopes. Some people think that it is strange that these options are not on the Reports menu, but if you think about it, they are not reports in the true sense of the word.

The Reports menu shown in Figure 9-1 is how you access most of the reports.

Notice the **OTHER REPORTS** options (For example, Other Contact Reports and Other Group Reports). The wording gives the impression that these options would display more reports.

As a programmer, I was not misled by this wording because these options do not have a right arrow like the Group, Company and Opportunity Reports menu options have. A programming standard when a menu option will open a submenu is to put a triangle next to the option.

If you look closely, you will see that the "Other Reports" menu options have three periods (called an ellipsis) after them. This is another programming standard. This is used to signify that selecting the option will open a dialog box.

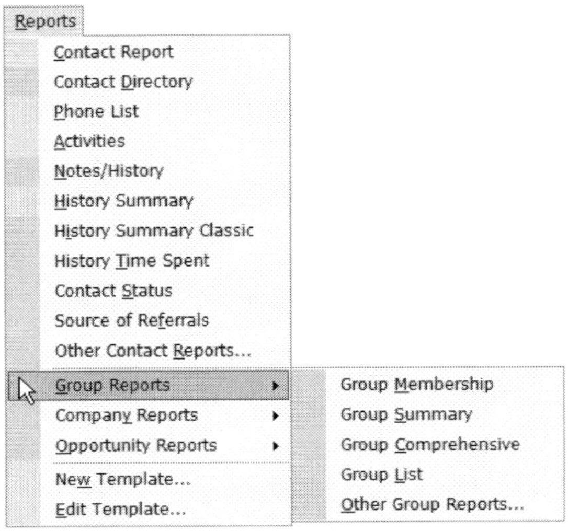

Figure 9-1 Reports menu

When you select any of the "Other Reports" options, you will see the **SELECT REPORT** dialog box which has all of the reports that came with ACT!. If you modify reports or create new ones and other people will use the reports, you could save them in this folder or add them to a menu so that other people can access them. OK, the programming lesson for today is over!

Define Filters Dialog Box

The Define Filters dialog box should reduce any anxiety that you may have about selecting options to run various reports, because it is used to select the criteria for each report. Options that are not available for a report are not enabled. You have to create the lookup or run a saved query before selecting a report to run if you do not want to be limited by the options on the Define Filters dialog box. If you know that a certain report needs a lookup or query, you should create it and save it. It would be a nice feature to be able to select a saved lookup or query from this dialog box.

Activity, Notes, History And Opportunity Reports

The default date range option for these reports is **CURRENT MONTH**. If left unchanged, this may produce unexpected results by not displaying all of the data that you would expect to see. For example, you create a lookup or run a query that retrieves contact records that have a create date in 2007.

If you leave the default date range of the current month selected, the report will not display any activity, note, history or opportunity data for 2007. Only data for the current month will be displayed on the report. More than likely, you would be expecting to see data for these types of records from 2007.

Tips For Running Reports In This Lesson

① Unless stated otherwise, make sure that the **SEND THE REPORT OUTPUT TO** option on the General tab of the Define Filters dialog box is set to Preview for the report exercises, unless you want to print the report. The remaining report output options are explained in Table 9-1.
② Make sure that the **EXCLUDE 'MY RECORD'** option is checked on the General tab of the Define Filters dialog box. Selecting this option will keep the My Record from printing.
③ Save any report that you want to keep in your folder.
④ Close the report when you are finished viewing it.

File Type	Select This File Type If The Report . . .
Rich-Text	Needs to be edited in a word processor.
HTML	Will be posted on the Internet.
PDF	Needs to be distributed to someone that does not have ACT!. Either the full version of Adobe Acrobat or the free Adobe Reader is needed to view a PDF file.
Text	Needs to be in plain text format. Non text objects like image files are not saved in this format.
Printer	Needs to be printed on paper.
Email	Needs to be sent via email.

Table 9-1 Report output file types explained

Exercise 9.1: The Contact Report

This report will print a profile for each contact that is selected. You can filter the report to include or not include the notes, history, opportunities and activity information.

1. Reports ⇒ Contact Report.

2. On the General tab, select the **ALL CONTACTS** option.

   You should have the options selected that are shown in Figure 9-2.

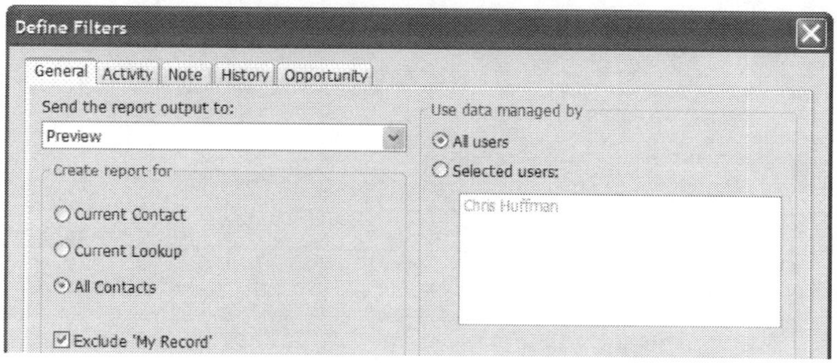

Figure 9-2 General tab options for the Contact report

If you created a look up for the records that you want to appear on the report prior to opening the report, select the **CURRENT LOOKUP** option. If you only want the report to use the contact record that you have open, select the **CURRENT CONTACT** option.

3. On the Activity tab, clear the **MEETINGS** option. Clearing this option will keep the meeting activities from printing on the report.

4. Open the **DATE RANGE** drop-down list and select Past.

The **PAST** date range option will only print activities that have a date in the past. The **CUSTOM** button is used to select a specific date range for the activities that you want to include on the report.

5. Clear the **INCLUDE CLEARED ACTIVITIES** option.

   You should have the options selected that are shown in Figure 9-3.

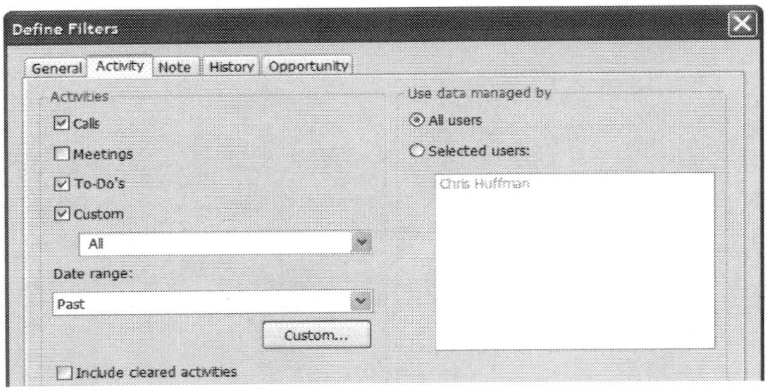

Figure 9-3 Activity options for the Contact report

6. On the Note tab, clear the Notes option.
7. On the History tab, clear the Email and Attachments options, then select the **ALL** date range option.
8. On the Opportunity tab, clear the Closed-Won, Closed Lost and Inactive options.
9. Change the Date Range to All, then click OK. The report will open in its own window. In the lower left corner of the Print Preview window you will see the report pages being created.

Report Print Preview Toolbar

Like many other windows in ACT!, the Print Preview window has a toolbar, as shown in Figure 9-4. Table 9-2 explains the buttons on the toolbar.

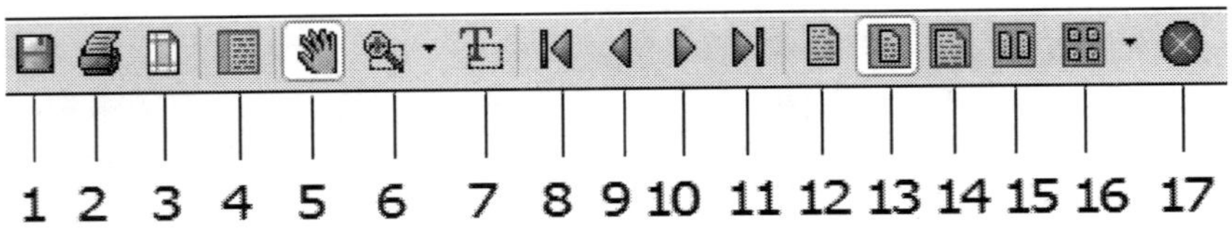

Figure 9-4 Print Preview toolbar

Button	Description
1	Saves the report.
2	Prints the report.
3	Change the paper size, margins and orientation of the report.
4	The Show Navigation Bar button displays the report pages in the thumbnail view, as shown in Figure 9-5.
5	The Hand Tool button is used to move the report page around in the window.
6	The Zoom In Tool button is used to change the magnification of the report displayed on the screen.
7	The Select Text button is used to select text in the report that you want to copy to another document.
8	Displays the first page of the report.
9	Displays the prior page of the report.
10	Displays the next page of the report.
11	Displays the last page of the report.
12	The Actual Size button is used to enlarge the report on the screen.
13	The Full Page button is used to display an entire page of the report, whether or not it is readable.

Table 9-2 Print Preview toolbar buttons explained

Button	Description
14	The Page Width button is used to resize the report so that it is the size of the Print Preview window.
15	The Two Pages button is used to display two pages of the report in the window at the same time, as shown in Figure 9-6.
16	The Four Pages button is used to display four pages of the report in the window at the same time. (1)
17	Cancels the print preview process from generating the entire report.

Table 9-2 Print Preview toolbar buttons explained (Continued)

Viewing Other Pages In A Report

Most reports have more than one page. If you want to move around the report quickly, the easiest way to do that is to click the **SHOW NAVIGATION BAR** button on the toolbar.

This will let you view a thumbnail of each page of the report, as shown in Figure 9-5. This option is useful if the report is large. You can scroll down the thumbnails and click on the page that you want to see.

Scrolling down the thumbnails and clicking on page 32 is faster then clicking the Next Page ▶ button 31 times if the current page is the first page of the report.

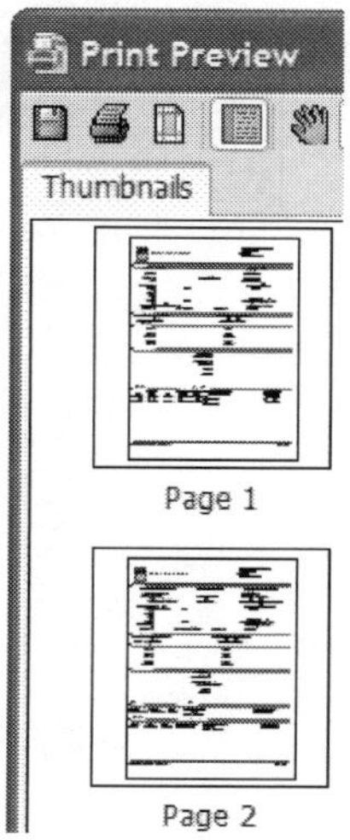

Figure 9-5 Report thumbnail option

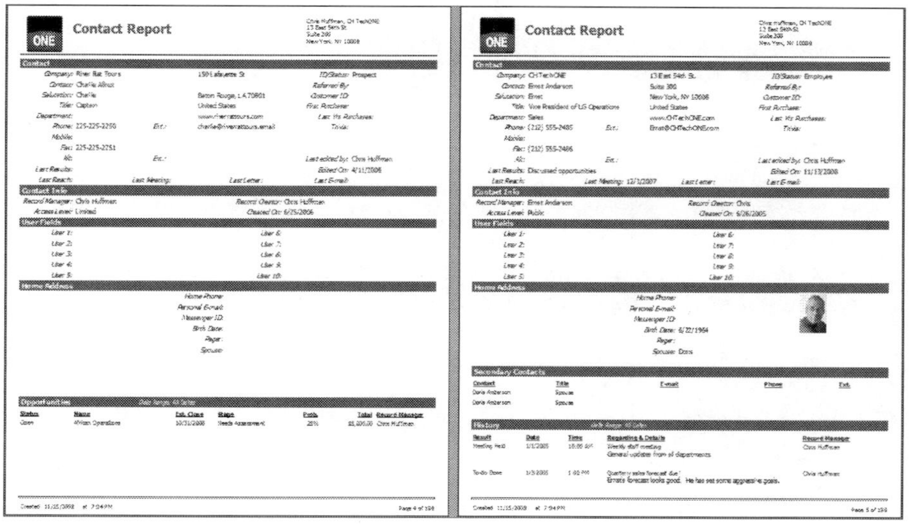

Figure 9-6 Two pages of the report visible at the same time

(1) Clicking on the arrow at the end of the **FOUR PAGES** button displays the grid shown in Figure 9-7. This is used to select how many pages to display in the window.

When you want to display a specific number of pages from the report, click in the first square in the upper left corner of the grid, then drag the mouse to the right and then down until you see the number of rows and columns that you need. In the example shown, 12 pages of the report will be displayed on the screen.

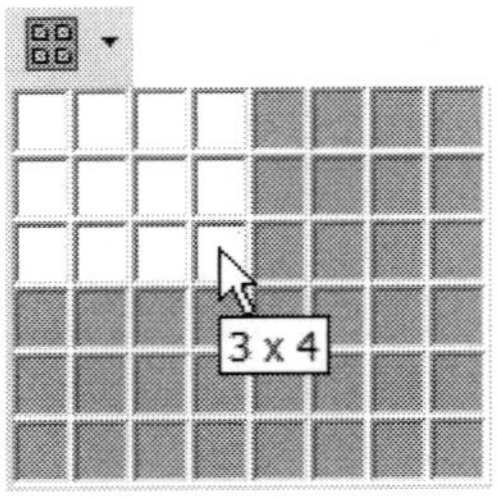

Figure 9-7 Four Pages button options

Preview The Report

1. Click the **ZOOM IN TOOL** button, then click on the report three times.

   The report should look like the one shown in Figure 9-8.

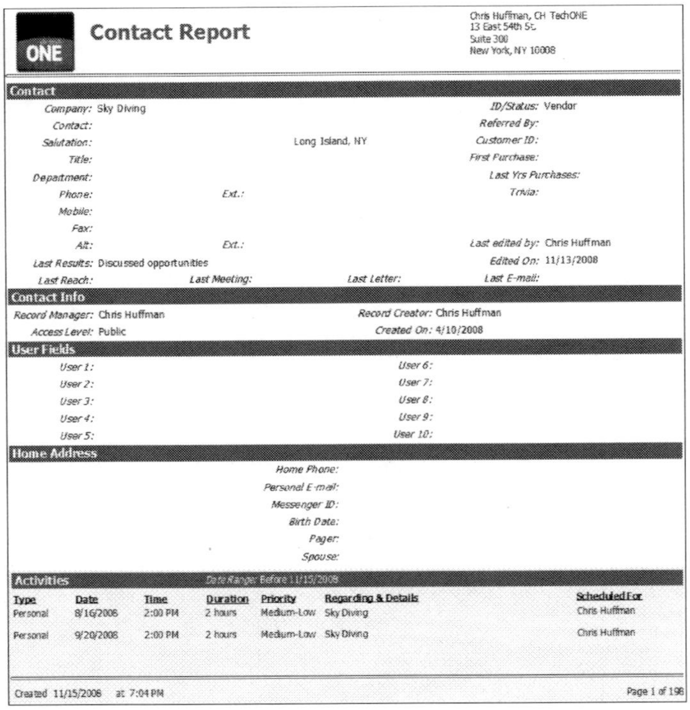

Figure 9-8 Contact report

Save The Report

2. Click the **FILE SAVE** button on the Print Preview window toolbar. You should see the folder that you created. For now, you can accept the default file name, then click the Save button.

Exercise 9.2: The Contact Directory Report

This report is similar to the contact report in the previous exercise. The difference is that the information on the Activities, Notes, History and Opportunities tabs will not print on the Contact Directory report. This report prints the contact address information.

1. Reports ⇒ Contact Directory.

2. Select the All Contacts option, then click OK.

   The report should look like the one shown in Figure 9-9.

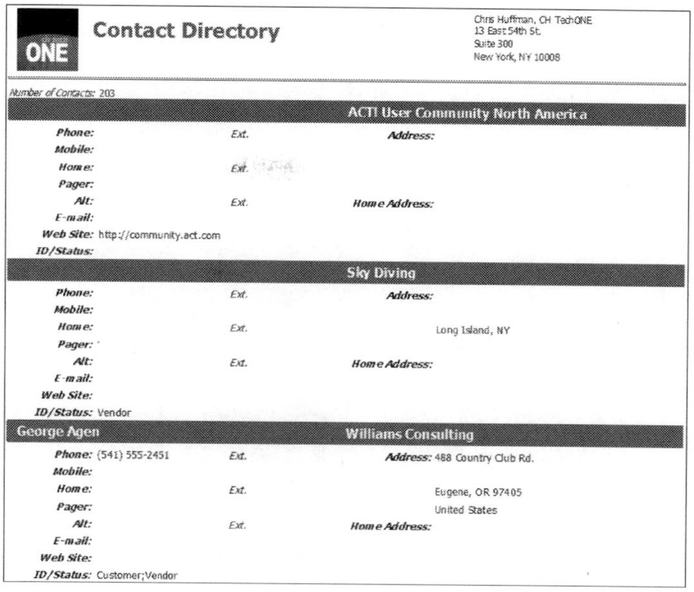

Figure 9-9 Contact Directory report

Exercise 9.3: The Phone List Report

This report will print the company, contact, phone, mobile phone and extension fields. Earlier in this lesson you learned that if you wanted to only print records based on the result of a lookup or contacts in a specific group, you have to create the lookup or select the group before you run the report. In this exercise you will create a lookup before running the report.

1. Create a lookup to find all contacts in the state of Washington. You should have six records displayed.
2. Reports ⇒ Phone List.
3. Select the Current lookup option if it is not already selected, then click OK.

   The report should look like the one shown in Figure 9-10.

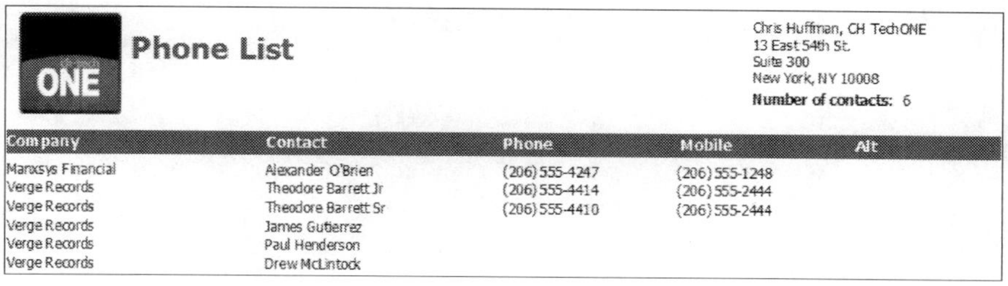

Company	Contact	Phone	Mobile	Alt
Marxsys Financial	Alexander O'Brien	(206) 555-4247	(206) 555-1248	
Verge Records	Theodore Barrett Jr	(206) 555-4414	(206) 555-2444	
Verge Records	Theodore Barrett Sr	(206) 555-4410	(206) 555-2444	
Verge Records	James Gutierrez			
Verge Records	Paul Henderson			
Verge Records	Drew McLintock			

Figure 9-10 Phone List report

Exercise 9.4: The Activities Report

This report will print the activities that are scheduled and completed with contacts. The default option is to print the report for all users in the database.

1. Reports ⇒ Activities.
2. On the General tab, select the All Contacts option.
3. On the Activity tab, clear the To-Do's and Include Cleared Activities options.

How To Create A Custom Date Range

Often, you may have the need to print a report to include information for a few weeks or a few months. To do this you need to create a custom date range.

1. On the Activity tab, click the **CUSTOM** button. You will see the Select Date Range dialog box.
2. Click the **<** arrow on the **FROM** calendar until you see September 2008, then click on the 19th.
3. Type `11/20/2008` in the **TO** field, then press the Tab key.

   You should have the options shown in Figure 9-11.

   Click OK.

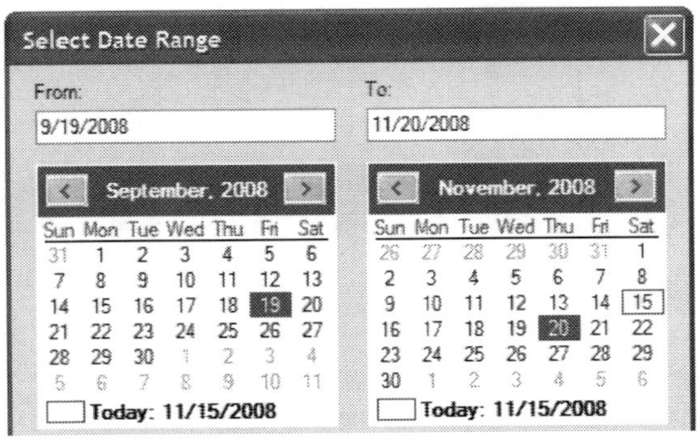

Figure 9-11 Date range options selected

4. You should have the options selected on the Activity tab that are shown in Figure 9-12. Click OK. The report should look like the one shown in Figure 9-13.

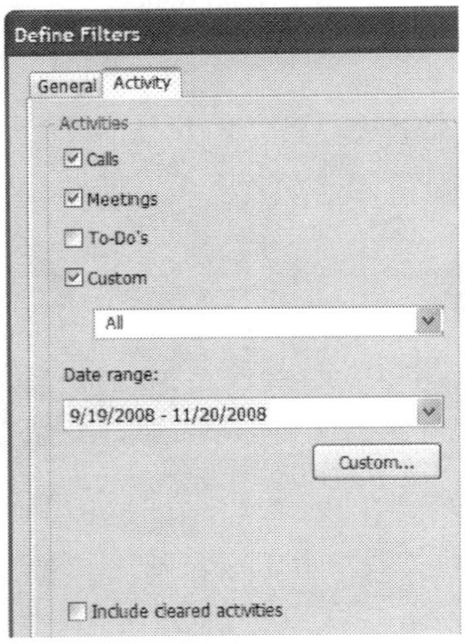

Figure 9-12 Activity tab options

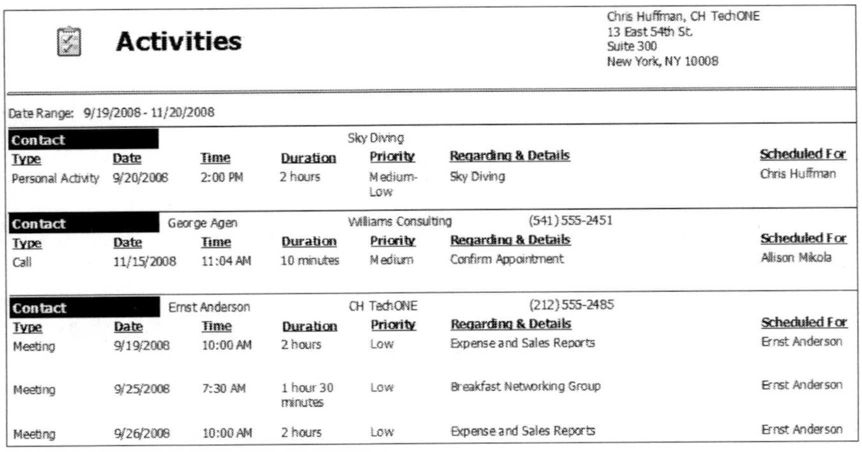

Figure 9-13 Activities report

Exercise 9.5: The Group Membership Report

This report will print the contacts in each group. This enables you to see which contacts are in what group. This would be a report that you may want to create a lookup or saved query for. The contacts name, company, title, phone and email fields are printed on the report.

1. Select the Sales Reps group in the Groups tree.
2. Reports ⇒ Group Reports ⇒ Group Membership.

3. Select the **CURRENT GROUP** option shown in Figure 9-14.

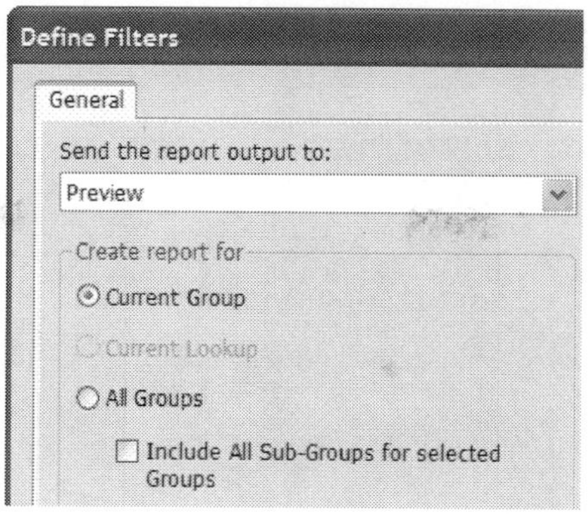

Figure 9-14 Group Membership report filter options

4. Click OK. The report should look like the one shown in Figure 9-15.

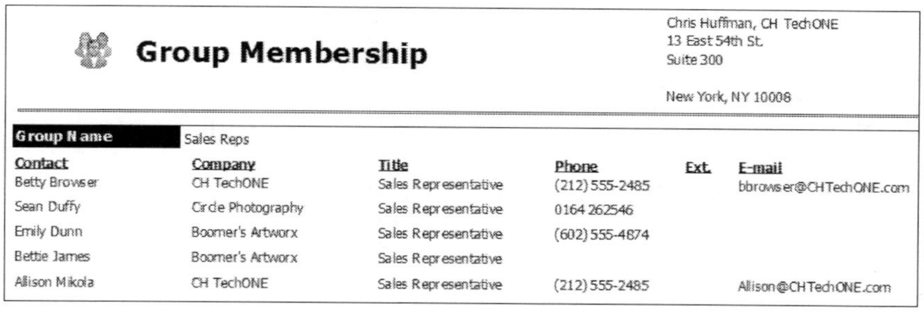

Group Membership

Chris Huffman, CH TechONE
13 East 54th St.
Suite 300
New York, NY 10008

Group Name	Sales Reps				
Contact	**Company**	**Title**	**Phone**	**Ext.**	**E-mail**
Betty Browser	CH TechONE	Sales Representative	(212) 555-2485		bbrowser@CHTechONE.com
Sean Duffy	Circle Photography	Sales Representative	0164 262546		
Emily Dunn	Boomer's Artworx	Sales Representative	(602) 555-4874		
Bettie James	Boomer's Artworx	Sales Representative			
Allison Mikola	CH TechONE	Sales Representative	(212) 555-2485		Allison@CHTechONE.com

Figure 9-15 Group Membership report for one group

5. If you run the report again and select **ALL GROUPS**, page two of the report will look like the one shown in Figure 9-16.

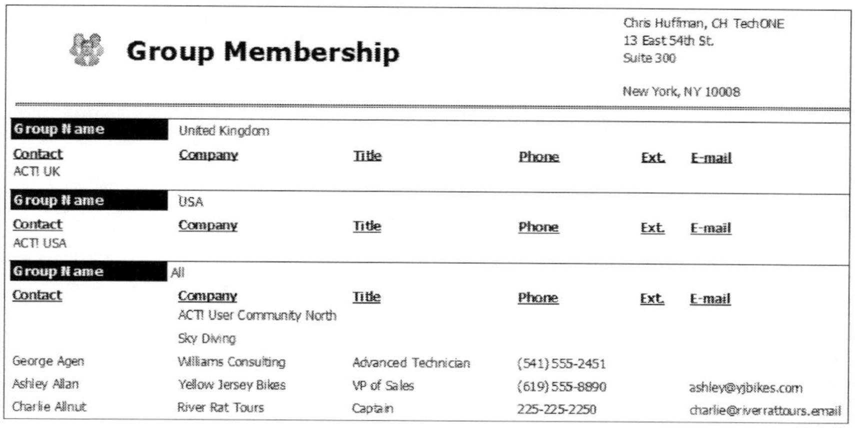

Group Membership

Chris Huffman, CH TechONE
13 East 54th St.
Suite 300
New York, NY 10008

Group Name	United Kingdom				
Contact	**Company**	**Title**	**Phone**	**Ext.**	**E-mail**
ACT! UK					
Group Name	USA				
Contact	**Company**	**Title**	**Phone**	**Ext.**	**E-mail**
ACT! USA					
Group Name	All				
Contact	**Company**	**Title**	**Phone**	**Ext.**	**E-mail**
	ACT! User Community North				
	Sky Diving				
George Agen	Williams Consulting	Advanced Technician	(541) 555-2451		
Ashley Allan	Yellow Jersey Bikes	VP of Sales	(619) 555-8890		ashley@yjbikes.com
Charlie Allnut	River Rat Tours	Captain	225-225-2250		charlie@riverrattours.email

Figure 9-16 Group Membership report for all groups

In prior versions of ACT!, the Group Membership report would print contacts that were not in any group, at the beginning of the report, as shown in Figure 9-17. Fortunately, this has been fixed.

Group Membership

Chris Huffman, CH Gourmet Gifts
13 East 54th St.
New York, NY 10008

Ivan A. Stekopick	Swing Software	Vice President	(011) 465-52		IStekopick@swinfsoft27.spb.ru
Rae Stevens	Hare's Tavern Corporate	CEO	(02) 861 2		RaeStevens@harestavern.com
Tina Stewart	Wiseman Paper Products	Owner	0191 987389		
Mike Underwood	T-Bone's Steakhouse	Owner	(541) 555-2422		
Neilson Watts	Superior Technologies Ltd	Administrative Assistant	0164 222223		
Bill Willis	Willis Enterprises	Owner	(480) 555-1232		
Group Name	Customers-AsiaPac				
Contact	**Company**	**Title**	**Phone**	**Ext.**	**E-mail**
Paul Brushman	Brushy's Golfing World	Chief Golf Sales Manager	(455) 555-2221		ginger@neyfamily.net
Ed Connor	Graham Electonics	Public Relations Manager	0198 356712		
Vivian Grace	International Safari	Buyer			
Chris Mears	Mutthound Enterprises	Vice President	01789 656556		
William Rosemann	Williams Consulting	Senior Technician	(03) 680 4		WRose@williamsconsulting5.com
Rae Stevens	Hare's Tavern Corporate	CEO	(02) 861 2		RaeStevens@harestavern.com

Figure 9-17 Group Membership report in a prior version of ACT!

Exercise 9.6: The Company Comprehensive Report

This report will display the following data for a company: Contacts, notes, history, activities and opportunities. This report can be used to produce a company profile. You can select options including a date range for each type of data. For example, you can select the All date range for history records and the last year date range, for notes. The good thing is that the date range that you select for each type of data, prints at the beginning of that section of the report. The Company Summary report, which is similar, does not print contacts or notes.

1. Create a lookup to find the company Ace Pet Store Franchises.
2. Reports ⇒ Company Reports ⇒ Company Comprehensive.
3. On the General tab, select the Current lookup option.
4. On the Activity tab, create a date range for all of 2008.
5. On the Note tab, select the date range All.
6. On the History tab, select the date range 1/1/2005 to 12/31/2008.
7. On the Opportunity tab, create a date range for 1/1/2008 to 12/31/2009, then click OK.

Figure 9-18 shows the first page of the report. Make sure that your date ranges match those shown in the figures. Figure 9-19 shows the activities on page 4. Figure 9-20 shows the opportunities.

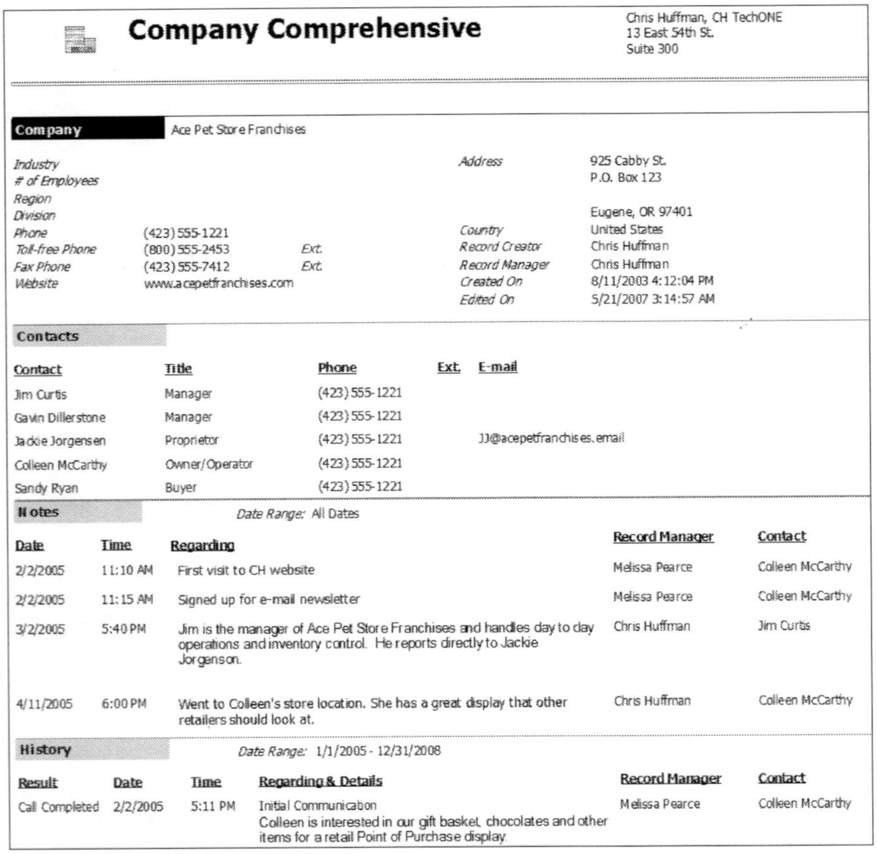

Company Comprehensive

Chris Huffman, CH TechONE
13 East 54th St.
Suite 300

Company Ace Pet Store Franchises

Industry			*Address*	925 Cabby St.
# of Employees				P.O. Box 123
Region				
Division				Eugene, OR 97401
Phone	(423) 555-1221		*Country*	United States
Toll-free Phone	(800) 555-2453	*Ext.*	*Record Creator*	Chris Huffman
Fax Phone	(423) 555-7412	*Ext.*	*Record Manager*	Chris Huffman
Website	www.acepetfranchises.com		*Created On*	8/11/2003 4:12:04 PM
			Edited On	5/21/2007 3:14:57 AM

Contacts

Contact	Title	Phone	Ext.	E-mail
Jim Curtis	Manager	(423) 555-1221		
Gavin Dillerstone	Manager	(423) 555-1221		
Jackie Jorgensen	Proprietor	(423) 555-1221		JJ@acepetfranchises.email
Colleen McCarthy	Owner/Operator	(423) 555-1221		
Sandy Ryan	Buyer	(423) 555-1221		

Notes *Date Range:* All Dates

Date	Time	Regarding	Record Manager	Contact
2/2/2005	11:10 AM	First visit to CH website	Melissa Pearce	Colleen McCarthy
2/2/2005	11:15 AM	Signed up for e-mail newsletter	Melissa Pearce	Colleen McCarthy
3/2/2005	5:40 PM	Jim is the manager of Ace Pet Store Franchises and handles day to day operations and inventory control. He reports directly to Jackie Jorgenson.	Chris Huffman	Jim Curtis
4/11/2005	6:00 PM	Went to Colleen's store location. She has a great display that other retailers should look at.	Chris Huffman	Colleen McCarthy

History *Date Range:* 1/1/2005 - 12/31/2008

Result	Date	Time	Regarding & Details	Record Manager	Contact
Call Completed	2/2/2005	5:11 PM	Initial Communication Colleen is interested in our gift basket, chocolates and other items for a retail Point of Purchase display.	Melissa Pearce	Colleen McCarthy

Figure 9-18 First page of the Company Comprehensive report

Activities *Date Range:* 1/1/2008 - 12/31/2008

Type	Date	Time	Priority	Scheduled With	Regarding & Details	Scheduled For
Meeting	5/16/2008	10:00 AM	Low	Gavin Dillerstone	Presentation	Chris Huffman
Meeting	5/28/2008	8:00 AM	Low	Gavin Dillerstone	Customer Thank You	Chris Huffman

Figure 9-19 Activities section of the Company Comprehensive report

Opportunities *Date Range:* 1/1/2008 - 12/31/2009

Status	Name	Est. Close	Stage	Prob.	Total	Record Manager	Contact
Open	Corporate Office	12/19/2008	Needs Assessment	25%	$4,500.00	Chris Huffman	Gavin Dillerstone
Open	Upgrade for Oregon	1/30/2009	Initial Communication	10%	$600.00	Ernst Anderson	Gavin Dillerstone

Figure 9-20 Opportunities section of the Company Comprehensive report

Other Reports

The reports that you have run so far in this lesson are just the beginning. Below are three more reports that you many find useful.

Source Of Referrals Report

This report is based on the value in the Referred By field. The report includes the total number of referrals, as illustrated in Figure 9-21.

Source of Referrals

Chris Huffman, CH TechONE
13 East 54th St.
Suite 300

New York, NY 10008

Referred By *Total Referrals:* 177

Company	Contact	Title	Phone
Interactive Gifts	Chris Fierros	VP of Sales	(212) 555-3448
Continental Detective Agency	John Guild	Chief Investigator	406-202-4400
Black Forest Baking	Kristi Elmendorf	Manager	012-555-54

Figure 9-21 Source of Referrals report

History/Time Spent Report

This report provides detail information on the tasks and time that you spent with each contact, as shown in Figure 9-22.

History/Time Spent

Chris Huffman, CH TechONE
13 East 54th St.
Suite 300
New York, NY 10008

Date Range: 12/15/2007 - 12/15/2008

Contact

Result	Date	Time	Duration	Regarding & Details
Field Changed	11/13/2008	12:26 AM	0 minutes	Field changed Field Last Results changed from "" to "Discussed opportunities"

Total time Timeless

Contact Ashley Allan

Result	Date	Time	Duration	Regarding & Details
Call Completed	6/11/2008	3:00 PM	0 minutes	Conference Call for group presentation Conference Call Details: Call In number: 1800-555-5555 Participant Code: 234-2342-33234

Total time Timeless

Contact Ernst Anderson

Result	Date	Time	Duration	Regarding & Details
Meeting Held	7/25/2008	10:39 PM	2 hours	Expense and Sales Reports
Meeting Held	8/8/2008	8:00 AM	1 hour 30	USA Sales Meeting
Meeting Held	4/4/2008	10:00 AM	2 hours	Expense and Sales Reports

Figure 9-22 History/Time Spent report

Notes/History Report

This report prints the notes and history records for the contacts that you select, as shown in Figure 9-23.

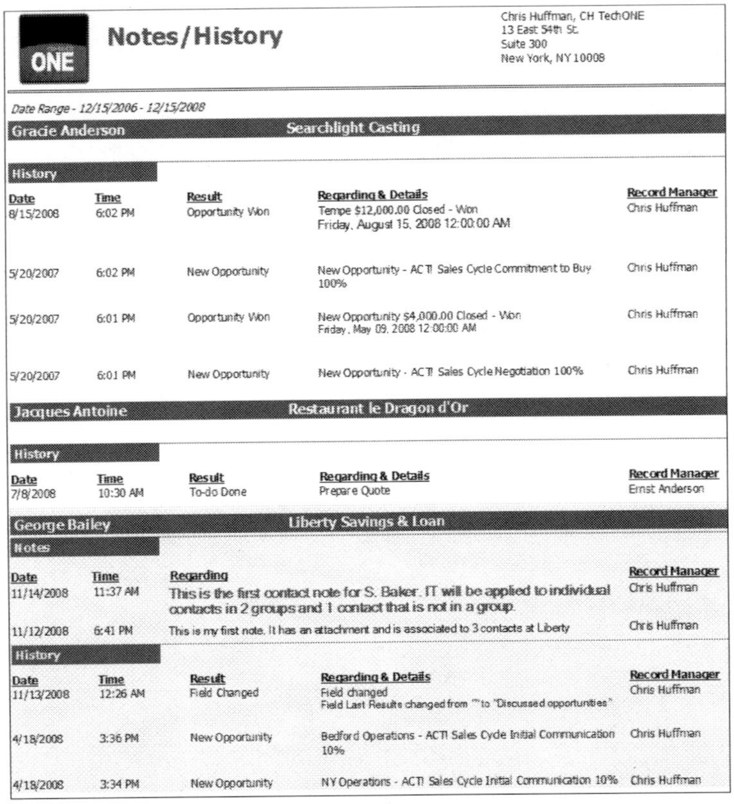
ONE **Notes/History**

Chris Huffman, CH TechONE
13 East 54th St.
Suite 300
New York, NY 10008

Date Range - 12/15/2006 - 12/15/2008

Gracie Anderson — **Searchlight Casting**

History

Date	Time	Result	Regarding & Details	Record Manager
8/15/2008	6:02 PM	Opportunity Won	Tempe $12,000.00 Closed - Won Friday, August 15, 2008 12:00:00 AM	Chris Huffman
5/20/2007	6:02 PM	New Opportunity	New Opportunity - ACT! Sales Cycle Commitment to Buy 100%	Chris Huffman
5/20/2007	6:01 PM	Opportunity Won	New Opportunity $4,000.00 Closed - Won Friday, May 09, 2008 12:00:00 AM	Chris Huffman
5/20/2007	6:01 PM	New Opportunity	New Opportunity - ACT! Sales Cycle Negotiation 100%	Chris Huffman

Jacques Antoine — **Restaurant le Dragon d'Or**

History

Date	Time	Result	Regarding & Details	Record Manager
7/8/2008	10:30 AM	To-do Done	Prepare Quote	Ernst Anderson

George Bailey — **Liberty Savings & Loan**

Notes

Date	Time	Regarding	Record Manager
11/14/2008	11:37 AM	This is the first contact note for S. Baker. IT will be applied to individual contacts in 2 groups and 1 contact that is not in a group.	Chris Huffman
11/12/2008	6:41 PM	This is my first note. It has an attachment and is associated to 3 contacts at Liberty	Chris Huffman

History

Date	Time	Result	Regarding & Details	Record Manager
11/13/2008	12:26 AM	Field Changed	Field changed Field Last Results changed from "" to "Discussed opportunities"	Chris Huffman
4/18/2008	3:36 PM	New Opportunity	Bedford Operations - ACT! Sales Cycle Initial Communication 10%	Chris Huffman
4/18/2008	3:34 PM	New Opportunity	NY Operations - ACT! Sales Cycle Initial Communication 10%	Chris Huffman

Figure 9-23 Notes/History report

Printing In ACT!

So far in this lesson you have learned how to print reports that come with ACT!. Reports are not the only thing that can be printed from ACT!. The remaining exercises in this lesson show you how to print labels, envelopes, an address book and how to use the Quick Print options on the File menu.

Exercise 9.7: How To Print Labels

There are several label templates that you can select from. There is also a template that you can use to create a custom label template.

> If you do not use Avery brand labels, you may be able to find the Avery label size equivalent of your labels on your box of labels.

1. File ⇒ Print.
2. Select the **LABELS** Printout type, then select the Avery (label size) Paper type.
3. Click the Print button.

4. Select the appropriate **CREATE REPORT FOR** option on the Define Filters dialog box, then click OK.

   The labels should look similar to the ones shown in Figure 9-24.

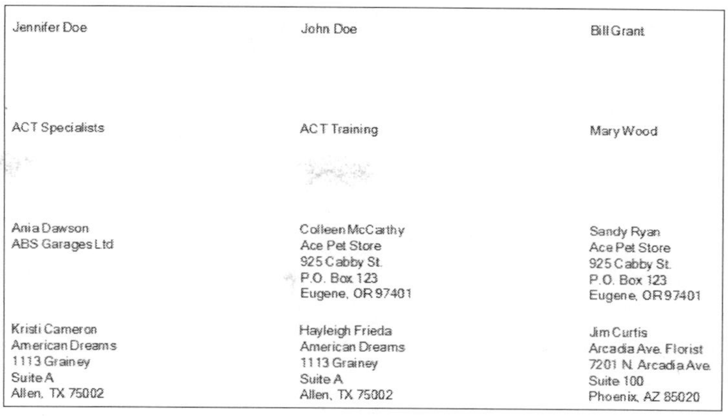

Figure 9-24 Labels

Selecting Where To Start Printing Labels

Unless you print the same number of names and addresses that the sheet of labels has, you will always have sheets of partially used labels. You can select where the labels should start to print on the sheet. The options on the **POSITION** tab (File ⇒ Print ⇒ Select the label size, then click the Print button) on the Define Filters dialog box shown in Figure 9-25 are used to select the Row and Column that the labels should start printing on. If you need to start printing labels on the first row, third column, you would select the options shown in Figure 9-25.

It would be nice if the layout of the sheet of labels was displayed on the dialog box so that you could make sure that you selected the correct row and column before you previewed the labels. If you selected the options shown in Figure 9-25 and previewed the labels, they would look like the ones shown in Figure 9-26.

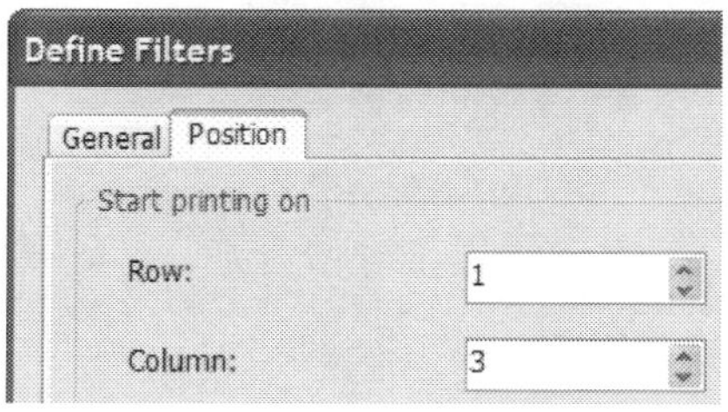

Figure 9-25 Position tab options

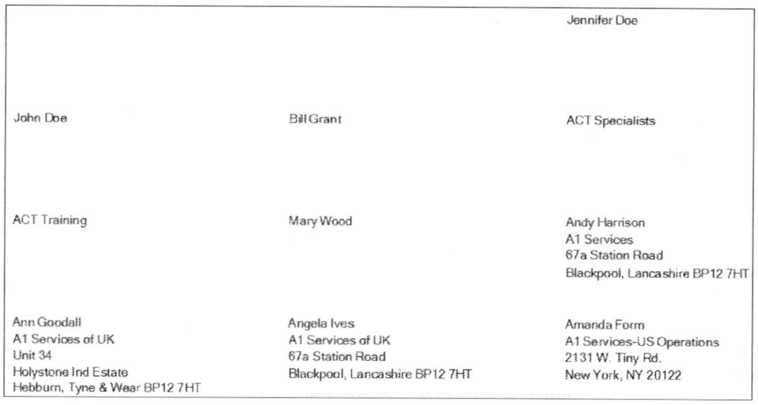

Figure 9-26 Labels with Position tab options changed

Exercise 9.8: How To Print Envelopes

In this exercise you will learn how to print envelopes using an envelope template.

1. File ⇒ Print.

2. Select the **ENVELOPES** Printout type, then select the envelope size in the Paper type list shown in Figure 9-27.

   The options in the **PAPER TYPE** section are the envelope sizes.

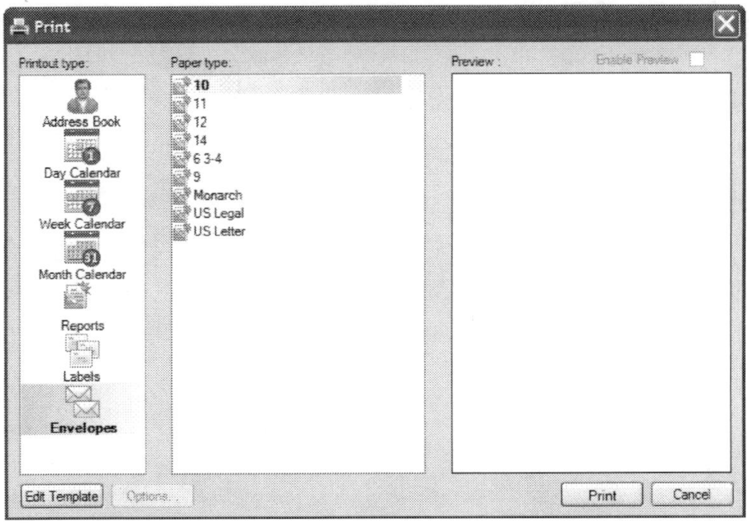

Figure 9-27 Envelope options

3. Click the Print button.

4. Select the appropriate **CREATE REPORT FOR** option, then click OK. The envelope should look like the one shown in Figure 9-28.

   Notice that the return address information has been filled in.

   You may have a different addressee on the envelope, depending on which record was displayed before you started this exercise.

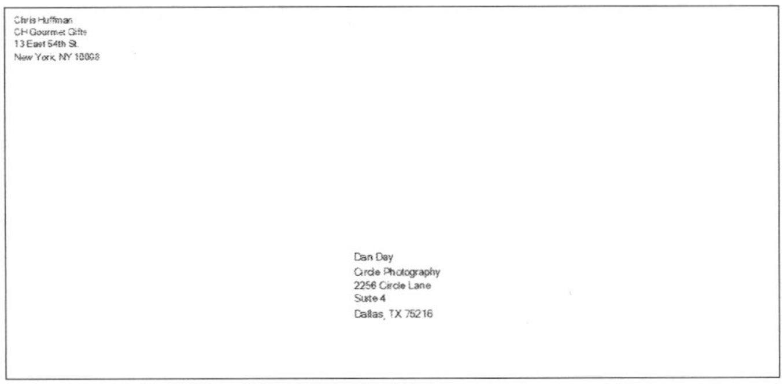

Figure 9-28 Envelope in print preview

5. Close the Print Preview window.

Exercise 9.9: How To Create And Print An Address Book

Printing an address book is useful if you need to have contact information from the database when you do not have access to a computer. You can select up to three additional fields to print in the address book. If you use a Day Timer or Day Runner, you can print the contacts in these address book formats. There are several print options that you can select from.

1. File ⇒ Print. Select the **ADDRESS BOOK** Printout type, then check the **ENABLE PREVIEW** option.

2. Select the Day-Timer Folio (2 Col) Paper type option.

   The preview should look like the one on the right side of Figure 9-29.

   The preview may take a few seconds to display.

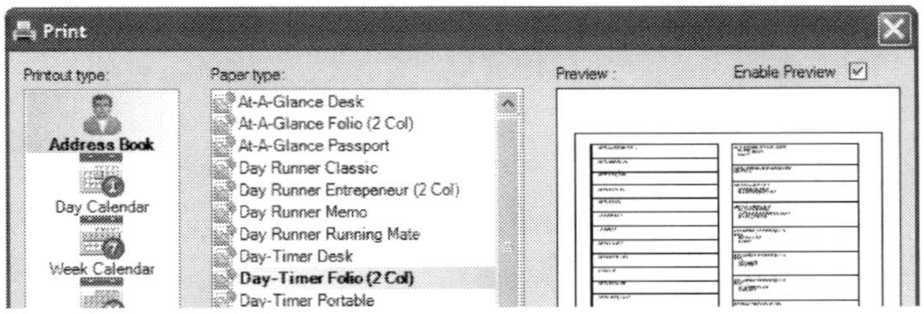

Figure 9-29 Print dialog box

3. Click the **OPTIONS** button, then clear the Alternate Address and Secondary Contacts options, if they are checked.

4. Select the Primary Address, Phone Numbers and E-mail Address options if they are not already selected.

5. Check the **LETTER AT THE TOP OF EACH PAGE** option in the Print Settings section.

6. Open the first **ADDITIONAL FIELDS** drop-down list and select Fax Phone.

7. Change the Sort Order to **CONTACT LAST NAME**, then select the All Contacts **CREATE PRINTOUT FOR** option.

8. Change the Font size to 10. You should have the options shown in Figure 9-30.

   Click OK.

   If you create a field it will not be listed in the **PRINT** section of the Options dialog box. You have to select a field that you create from one of the three **ADDITIONAL FIELDS** drop-down lists.

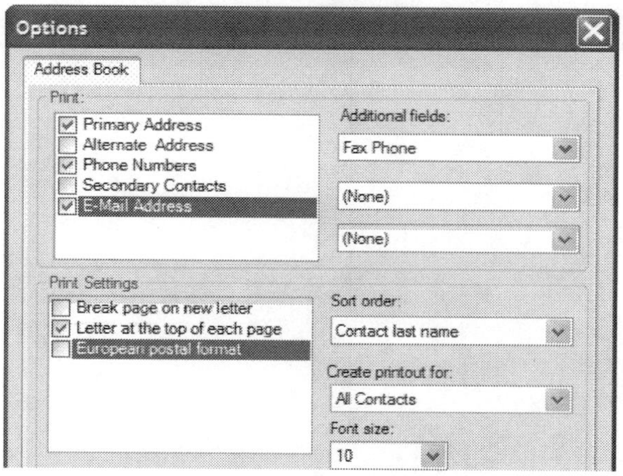

Figure 9-30 Address Book options

9. If you want to print the address book, click the Print button on the Print dialog box.

How To View The Address Book Without Printing It

If you want to see what the address book will look like without printing it and have the full version of Adobe Acrobat installed, select the Adobe PDF option on the Print dialog box, as illustrated in Figure 9-31.

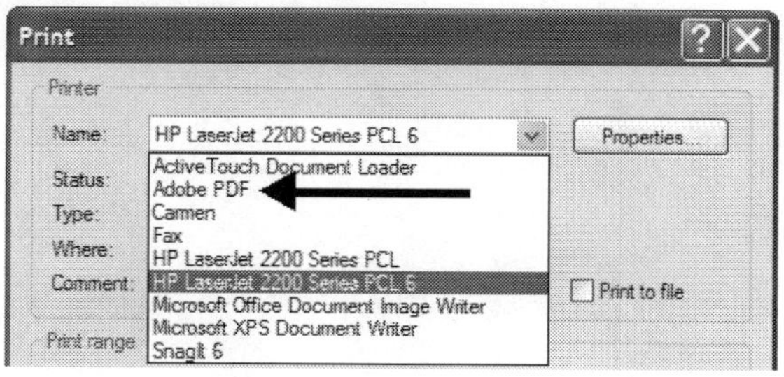

Figure 9-31 Print dialog box options

If you have another software package installed that creates PDF files, select it from the drop-down list.

This will let you create a PDF version of the address book shown in Figure 9-32. Otherwise, click the Cancel button.

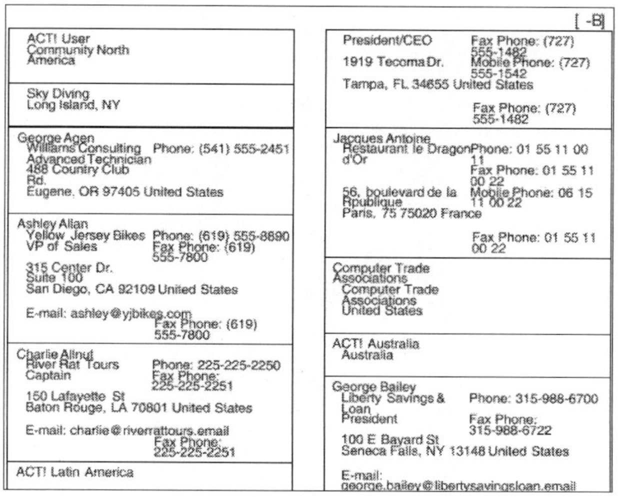

Figure 9-32 Printed address book

Exercise 9.10: Using The Quick Print Options

The **QUICK PRINT CURRENT WINDOW** and **QUICK PRINT SELECTED** options are useful if you just want to print what is on the screen. If you are going to print the data on a tab, it is probably a good idea to resize the columns so that the data is not cut off. The Quick Print options print data exactly as it appears. It is not perfect, but it may handle your basic printing needs. The steps below show you how to print the data in the current window.

1. Look up the My Record.

2. Make sure the Contact Detail view is open, then click on the Activities tab.

3. File ⇒ Quick Print Current Window. You will see the Print dialog box. If you click the Properties button you can change the printing options as needed.

If you printed the data on the Activities tab that is visible, it would look similar to the data shown in Figure 9-33.

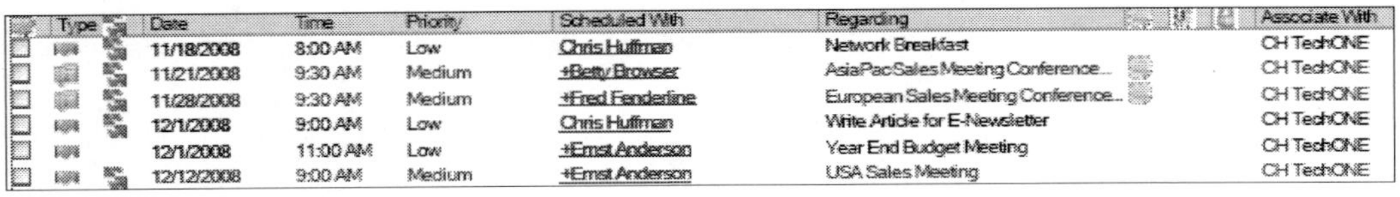

Type	Date	Time	Priority	Scheduled With	Regarding	Associate With
	11/18/2008	8:00 AM	Low	Chris Huffman	Network Breakfast	CH TechONE
	11/21/2008	9:30 AM	Medium	+Betty Browser	AsiaPacSales Meeting Conference...	CH TechONE
	11/28/2008	9:30 AM	Medium	+Fred Fenderline	European Sales Meeting Conference...	CH TechONE
	12/1/2008	9:00 AM	Low	Chris Huffman	Write Article for E-Newsletter	CH TechONE
	12/1/2008	11:00 AM	Low	+Ernst Anderson	Year End Budget Meeting	CH TechONE
	12/12/2008	9:00 AM	Medium	+Ernst Anderson	USA Sales Meeting	CH TechONE

Figure 9-33 Quick print of the current tab

If you displayed the monthly calendar and used the Quick Print option to print the calendar, it would look like the one shown in Figure 9-34.

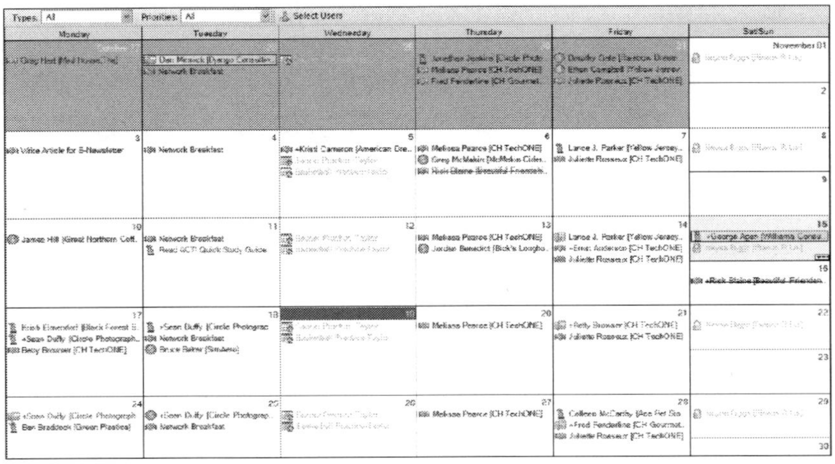

Figure 9-34 Quick print of a monthly calendar

OPPORTUNITIES

In this lesson you will learn the following tasks that will show you how to create and manage opportunities.

- ☑ Schedule a follow up activity for an opportunity
- ☑ How to edit the Product List
- ☑ How to view an opportunity
- ☑ How to associate an opportunity to a company
- ☑ Lookup opportunity options
- ☑ Export opportunities to Excel
- ☑ Creating quotes
- ☑ Change the status of an opportunity
- ☑ Opportunity reports
- ☑ Create opportunity graphs and pipelines
- ☑ Customize products and processes
- ☑ Creating process lists and stages
- ☑ Importing and exporting stages
- ☑ Importing and exporting products

LESSON 10

What Is An Opportunity?

An opportunity is a sale in progress, meaning there is some likelihood that the contact may make a purchase. Opportunities automate the sales process. You can run reports that will show what stage opportunities are in and which opportunities you have the best chance of turning into a sale. Each opportunity can only be associated to one contact, but a contact can have more than one opportunity. You can view the opportunity and check on the status. Like activities, opportunities create history records when they are created or when certain fields like the Status or Close Date is changed.

Tracking Potential Sales

ACT! provides a way to manage and track potential sales through opportunities. The tracking process is quite extensive. You can track the opportunities from the beginning, through each stage of the process. There are six stages that you can monitor in the Sales Cycle process that comes with ACT!. You can track opportunities by dollar amount, sales rep, status and more. You can also customize the opportunity process and products that come with ACT!. You can create your own opportunity processes and import processes that are created in another software package. Opportunities can be exported, which will allow you to analyze the data in different ways.

Opportunity List Toolbar

Figure 10-1 shows the Opportunity List toolbar.

Table 10-1 explains the buttons on the toolbar.

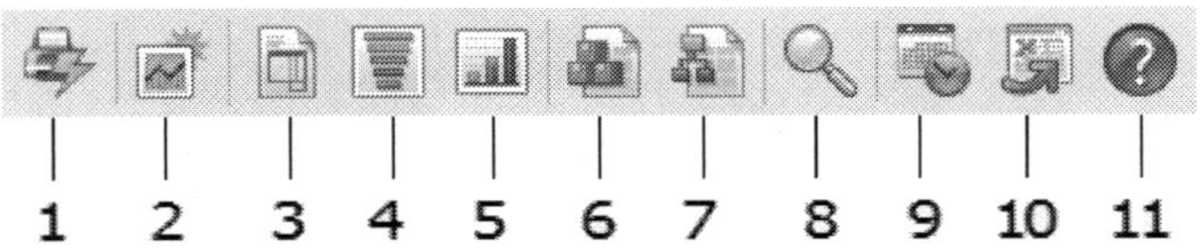

Figure 10-1 Opportunity List toolbar

Button	Description
1	Opens the Print dialog box.
2	Opens a new opportunity record.
3	Create a quote.
4	Create an opportunity pipeline.
5	Create an opportunity graph.
6	Opens the Manage Product List tool.
7	Opens the Manage Process List tool.
8	Look up contacts to view opportunities for.
9	Copies calendar information between the ACT! and Outlook calendars.
10	Export the opportunity to Excel.
11	Opens the Help system.

Table 10-1 Opportunity List toolbar buttons explained

Opportunity List View

You have the option of viewing all or some of the opportunities for contacts that you have access to. Like the Notes tab, you can filter opportunities. You can also print opportunities, as well as, customize the Opportunity List view, which you will learn how to do in Lesson 13.

1. Click the Opportunity List button on the Navigation bar. If you click on a contact name you will open the Contact Detail view for the contact.

Using The Opportunity List Filters

The filter options for the Opportunity List view are shown in Figure 10-2. They are helpful if there are a lot of opportunities displayed in the list view and you only need to see certain ones. Like other views, you can sort the data on the bottom half of the view by clicking on the column headings. The filter options are explained below.

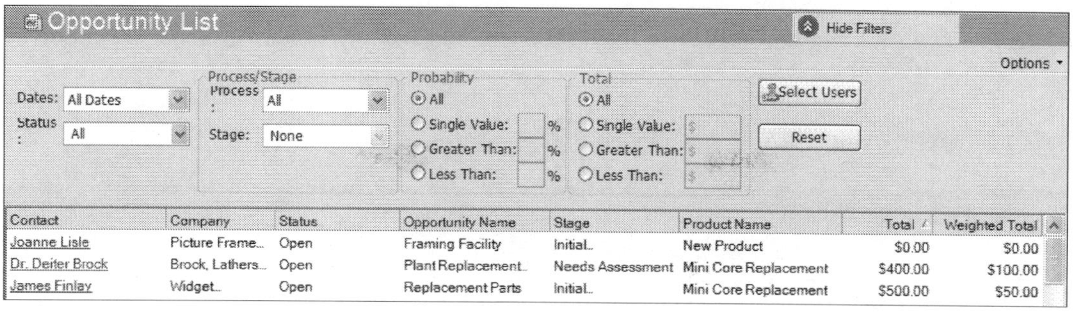

Figure 10-2 Opportunity List filters

① The **DATES** drop-down list options shown in Figure 10-3 are used to select the date range that you want to see opportunities for.

② The **STATUS** drop-down list options shown in Figure 10-4 are used to select the statuses that you want to see opportunities for.

③ The **PROCESS** drop-down list options shown in Figure 10-5 are used to select the process that the opportunities must have in order to be displayed.

④ The **STAGE** option is only available once a process has been selected. The options in the drop-down list shown in Figure 10-6 are specific to the process that is selected. The default stage is **ALL**.

⑤ The **PROBABILITY** options are used to select a single value and percent for opportunities that you want to see. If you only wanted to see opportunities that have a 91% or greater probability of closing (making the sale), you would select the options shown in Figure 10-7. The 90% shown in the **GREATER THAN** field will NOT return probabilities that are 90%, only probabilities that are greater. If you wanted to include 90%, you would have to enter 89% in the field.

⑥ The **TOTAL** options are used to select the total dollar amount that the opportunity must have to be displayed. If you only wanted to see opportunities that have a total amount less than $1,000, you would select the options shown in Figure 10-8.

⑦ The **SELECT USERS** button opens a dialog box that is used to select the users that you want to see opportunities for.

⑧ The **RESET** button will clear all of the filter options that you previously selected. I tend to click this button as soon as I open the Opportunity List view so that all of the opportunities are displayed before I apply any filters.

⑨ The **OPTIONS** button is used to select whether or not private opportunities should be displayed. You can also customize the columns in the Opportunities List by selecting the **CUSTOMIZE** option on this button.

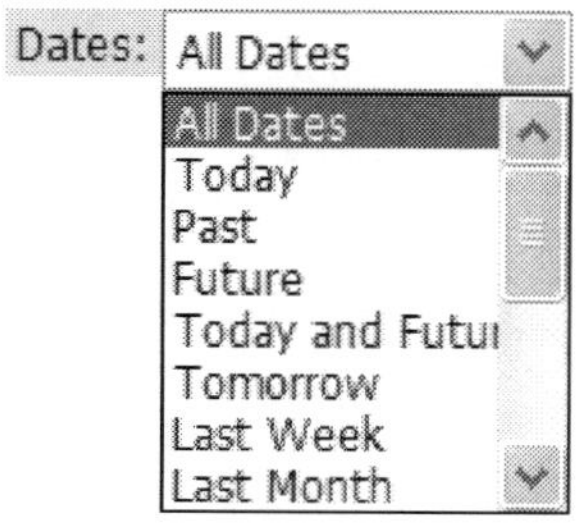

Figure 10-3 Date options

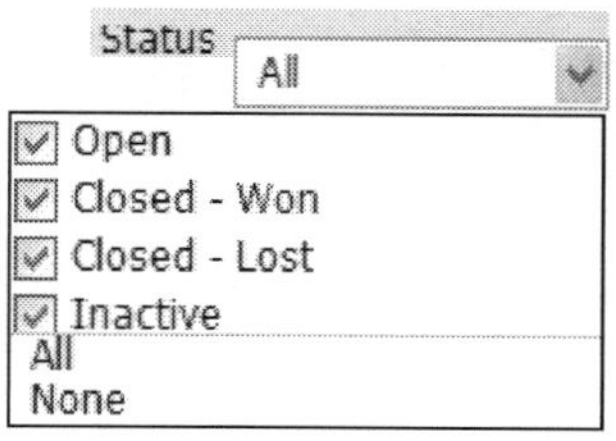

Figure 10-4 Status options

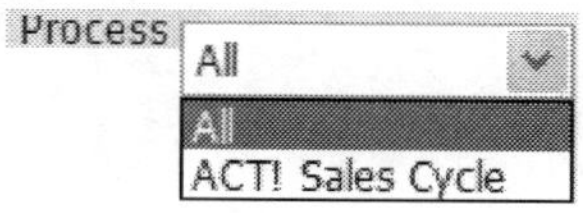

Figure 10-5 Process options

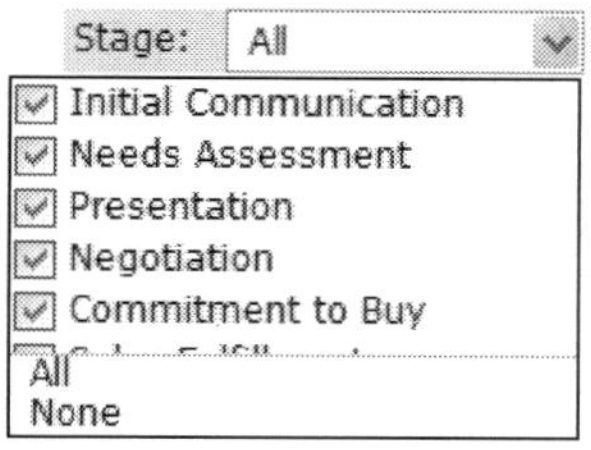

Figure 10-6 Stage options

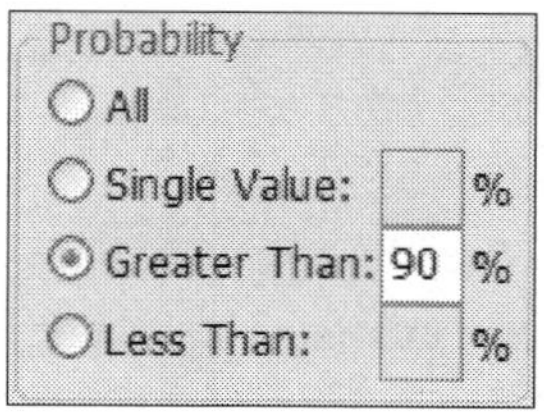

Figure 10-7 90% or greater probability options

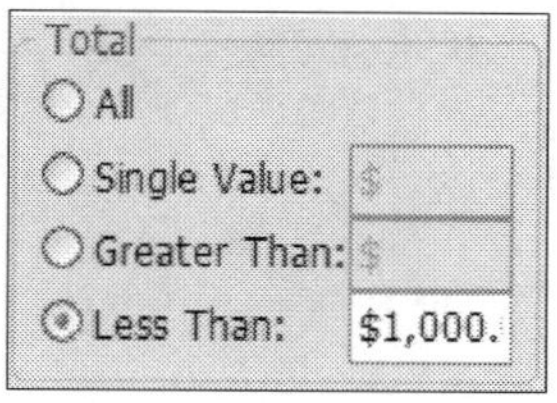

Figure 10-8 Total amount less than $1,000 options

> **Additional Ways To Filter Contacts On The Opportunity List View**
>
> ① Right-click and select **CREATE LOOKUP**.
> ② Click the **CREATE CONTACT LOOKUP** button on the toolbar.

> **Product Name Column Sorting**
>
> Unlike the other columns in the Opportunity List view, sorting on the Product Name column works differently because it allows multiple values to be stored in the field. The column is sorted by the first product or service in the field.

Status Bar Information

Figure 10-9 shows the information that is displayed in the Status bar. You will see the total number of opportunities, the weighted and grand total dollar amounts of the opportunities that are displayed.
The **WEIGHTED TOTAL** field is calculated based on the product total and the probability of closing the opportunity.

Figure 10-9 Opportunity status bar information

Opportunity List Shortcut Menu

The Opportunity List shortcut menu shown in Figure 10-10 provides a lot of help and information for the selected opportunity. The options on this shortcut menu may help keep you from having to open the Opportunity dialog box.

The **SHOW CONTACTS** option opens the dialog box shown in Figure 10-11. It provides additional information about the contact.

The **SHOW PRODUCTS** option opens the dialog box shown in Figure 10-12. It displays all of the products on the opportunity.

The **EDIT ESTIMATED CLOSE DATE** option opens the dialog box shown in Figure 10-13. It is used to change the closing date of the opportunity.

The **VIEW SUMMARY REPORT** option opens the dialog box shown in Figure 10-14. It displays the history records for the opportunity.

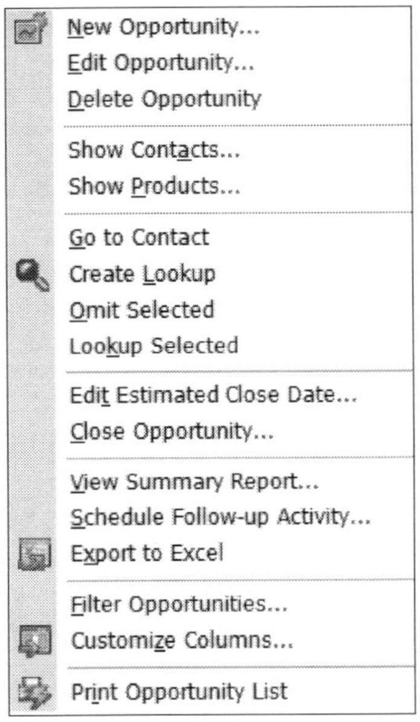

Figure 10-10 Opportunity List shortcut menu

The **FILTER OPPORTUNITIES** option opens the dialog box shown in Figure 10-15. It is another way to filter the opportunities. It contains the same options that are at the top of the Opportunity List view.

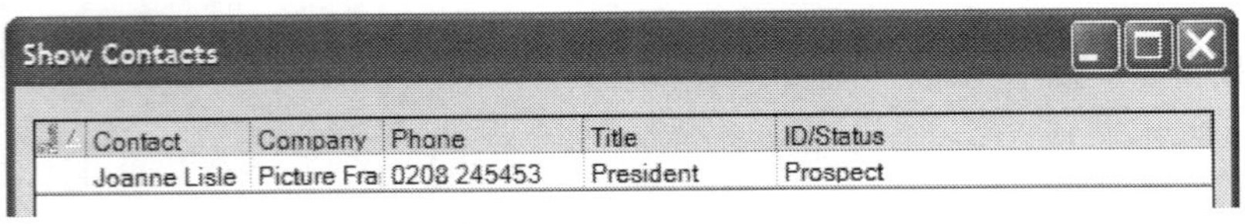

Figure 10-11 Show Contacts dialog box

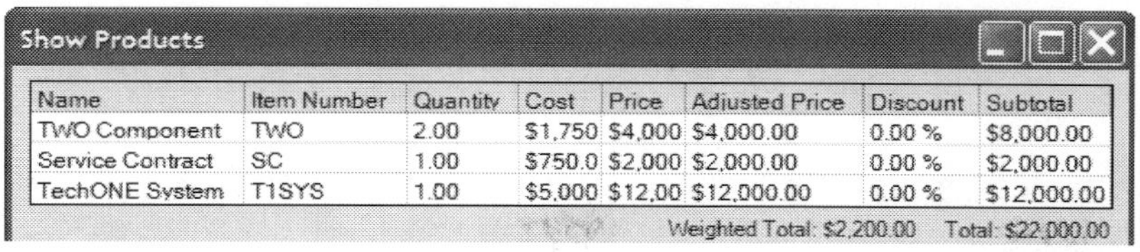

Figure 10-12 Show Products dialog box

When this dialog box is opened, the **NEW CLOSE DATE** field defaults to today's date.

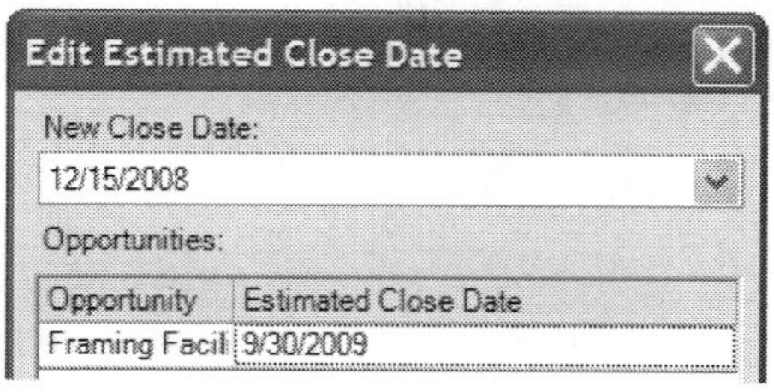

Figure 10-13 Edit Estimated Close Date dialog box

Figure 10-14 View Summary Report

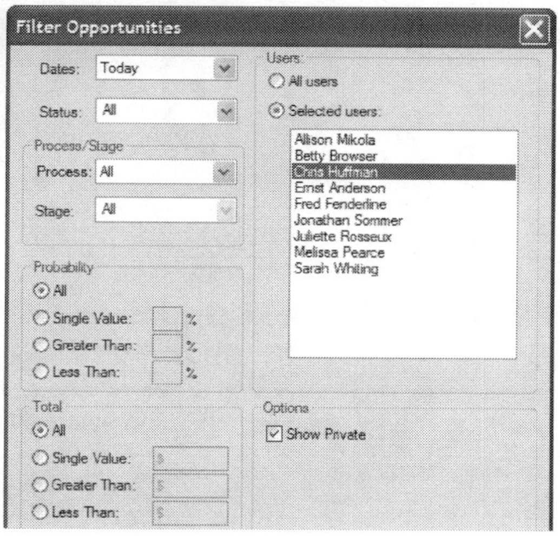

Figure 10-15 Filter Opportunities dialog box

The Opportunity Dialog Box

The Opportunity dialog box is used to create and edit sales orders.

There are four tabs on the dialog box shown in Figure 10-16.

The purpose of each of the tabs is explained below.

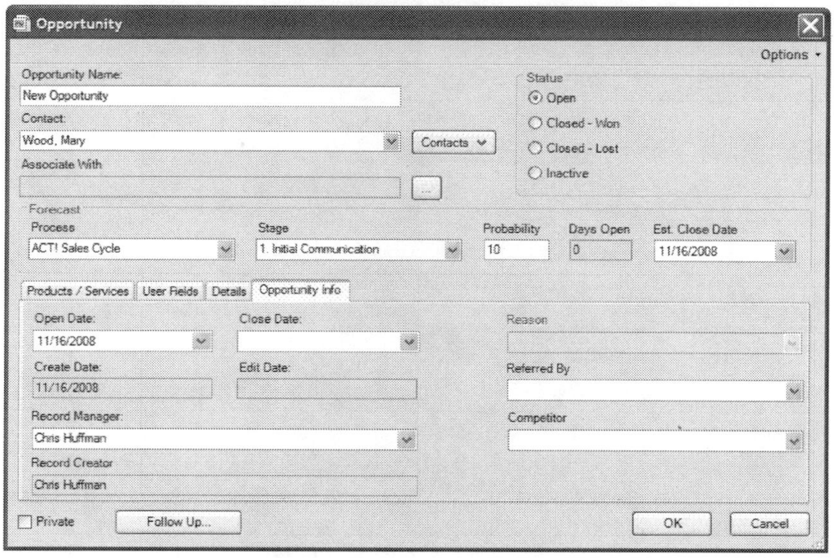

Figure 10-16 Opportunity dialog box

> Many people use a purchase order number or the contacts company name and a sequential number as the **OPPORTUNITY NAME**.

① **Products/Services** This is the first tab that you see when you open the Opportunity dialog box. It stores the basic information about the opportunity.
② **User Fields** Some of the eight fields on this tab, as shown in Figure 10-17, are similar to fields on the User Fields tab on the Contact Detail view. You can use the fields to store data that does not fit in any of the other fields on the Opportunity dialog box. They are free form because they have the character field type. You can rename these fields in the layout, but you cannot change the field type unless you are using a Premium edition of ACT!.
③ **Details** The fields on this tab are used to enter information about the opportunity that does not fit in any of the other fields.
④ **Opportunity Info** Some of the fields on this tab are similar to the fields on the Contact Access tab. Entering data on this tab is optional.

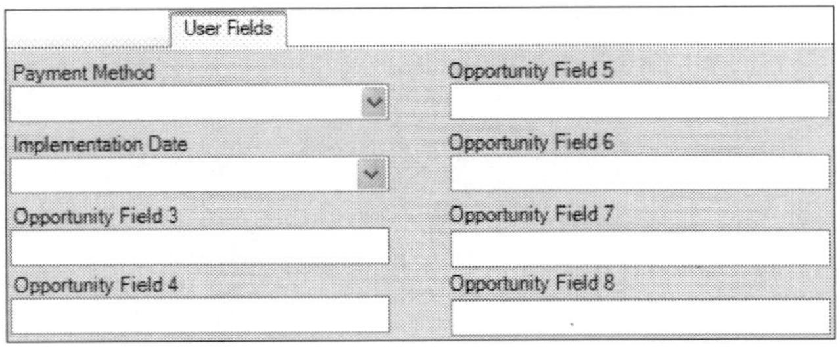

Figure 10-17 User Fields tab

Exercise 10.1: Create An Opportunity

If you have viewed the Opportunity Tracking tour in the Help system, you may think that creating an opportunity is complicated. You can view the tour or look at the examples, but the process probably won't "click" until you create a new opportunity, which is the best way to fully understand each component of an opportunity.

> Opportunities inherit the security that the contact has.

1. Open the contact record for Mary Wood in the Contact Detail view.

2. On the Opportunities tab, click the **NEW OPPORTUNITY** button, illustrated in Figure 10-18.

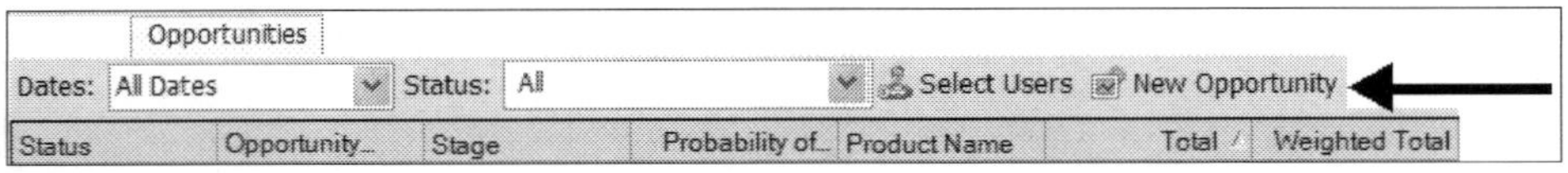

Figure 10-18 Opportunities tab options

3. Type `My first opportunity` in the Opportunity Name field.

Status Options

There are four status options as discussed below.

① **Open** This is the default status for a new opportunity. This status means that there is activity for the opportunity. Often, the activity is you hearing from the contact or you contacting them.
② **Closed - Won** Select this option when the opportunity results in a sale.
③ **Closed - Lost** Select this option if the opportunity did not result in a sale and there is currently no activity for the opportunity.
④ **Inactive** Select this option if there is currently no activity for the opportunity, but there is still a chance that a sale may happen.

What Is A Process List?

A Process List contains the tasks that need to be completed for a sale. If you or your company has a set of tasks for a sale or part of a sale, you should create a process list so that everyone that creates an opportunity will complete the same set of tasks for each opportunity that is created. A process list may remind you of an activity series.

For example, you or your company may have a process for new contacts like call the contact, send the contact a brochure and go see the contact. These three tasks would be a process list that you could create. You can also incorporate an existing process list.

Select The Process

The process shown earlier in Figure 10-5 comes with ACT!. Each process has its own list of stages. Later in this lesson you will learn how to create your own process list.

Select The Stage

The stage options are based on the process that is selected. The options shown in Figure 10-19 are the stages for the ACT! Sales Cycle process.

The stage indicates where the opportunity is in the sales process. This can be used to let you know which opportunities need your immediate attention.

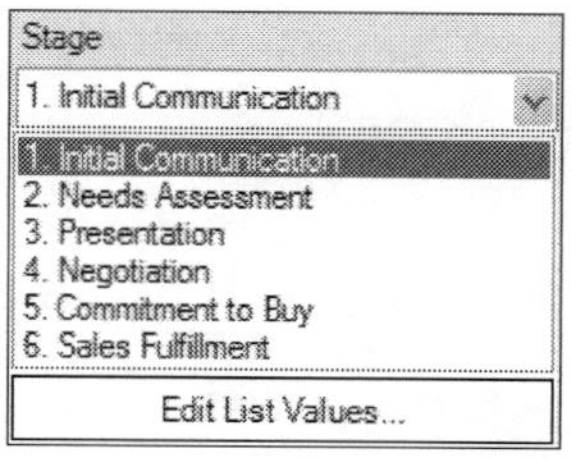

Figure 10-19 Stage options for the ACT! Sales Cycle process

4. Select the Needs Assessment stage.

Select The Probability

The probability is a percent. It signifies to what degree you think that the opportunity will result in a sale. Throughout the opportunity process, the probability can change.

5. Type `80` in the Probability field.

Enter The Estimated Close Date

This is the date that you would like to have the sale closed by. Like the Probability field, the value in this field can change during the course of the opportunity process.

6. Enter a date that is 30 days from today. The top half of the Opportunity dialog box should look like the one shown in Figure 10-20. The only difference should be the date in the Est. Close Date field.

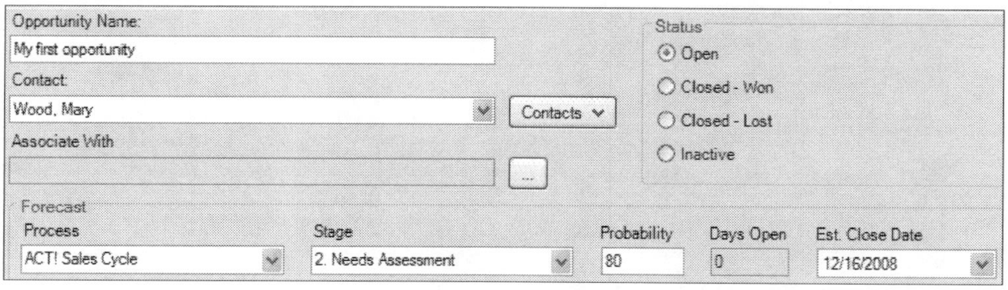

Figure 10-20 Options for a new opportunity

> The **ESTIMATED CLOSE DATE** is the field used in date range criteria for filters, lookups and reports for open and inactive opportunities. The **CLOSE DATE** field on the Opportunity Info tab is used in date range criteria for closed opportunities.

Products And Services

The fields that you just filled in are the basic fields for an opportunity. The options on the Products/Services tab are the items for the opportunity that the contact will hopefully purchase.

The **NAME** drop-down list shown in Figure 10-21 includes all of the products and services that the contact can purchase.

It is not advised, but you can also type a new product in. It will only be available for the current opportunity. The reason that you should add the product to the list is to help keep the products consistent for all opportunities.

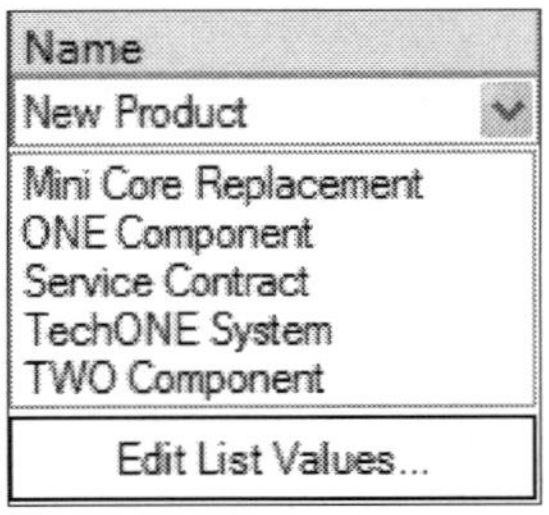

Figure 10-21 Name drop-down list items

Select The Products And Services For The Opportunity

1. Open the Name drop-down list and select the service, ONE Component.

It is not a requirement that products or services have an item number. Item numbers should be set up when the product is added to the list. If the information is incorrect in the Product List you can change it in the opportunity that you are working on. Changing it here would only apply the change to the opportunity that you have open. It is best to change the item number in the product list.

2. Press the Tab key twice, then type `2` in the Quantity field.

Price Considerations

The cost and price are automatically filled in because they are stored in the product list. If these values are not correct, you have two options to correct them as discussed below.

① Edit the fields on the Opportunity dialog box. This option only changes the values in the current opportunity.
② Edit the data in the product list. This option will change the price throughout the database.

Adjusted Price

Filling in this field is optional. It is used to give the contact a discount or price that is different then the default price for the product or service. If you change the price in this field, the discount percent is automatically recalculated.

3. Click the Add button, then add the Service Contract service.

4. Change the discount to `20%`.

   You should have the products shown in Figure 10-22.

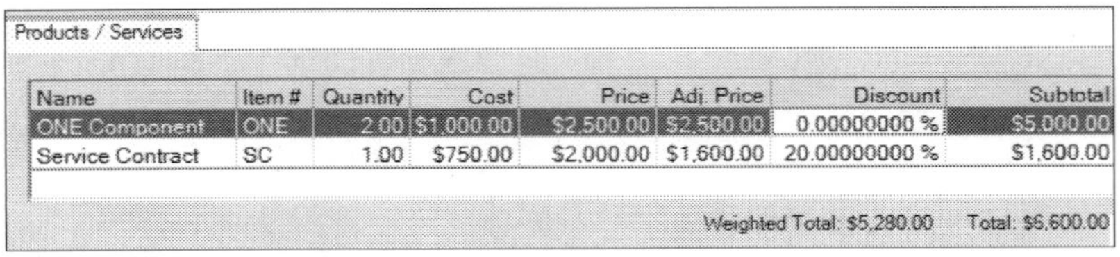

Figure 10-22 Products/Services added to the opportunity

Giving A Discount

As you just learned, you can discount each item on the opportunity. You can also give a discount off of the entire order. For example, "Spend $100, get $20 off". To set up this kind of discount you would type `Discount` in the Name field and the amount that you want to take off in the **PRICE** field, with a minus sign. The last row in Figure 10-23 shows what this type of discount would look like.

Name	Item #	Quantity	Cost	Price	Adj. Price	Discount	Subtotal
ONE Component	ON	2.00	$1,000.00	$2,500.00	$2,500.00	0.00000000 %	$5,000.00
Service Contract	SC	1.00	$750.00	$2,000.00	$1,600.00	20.00000000 %	$1,600.00
Discount		1.00	$0.00	($20.00)	($20.00)	0.00000000 %	($20.00)

Figure 10-23 Discount for the opportunity

The Details Tab

If there is information that does not fit in any of the other fields, you can enter it on the Details tab. This is like a notes or comments field.

1. On the Details tab, type `This is my first opportunity` in the field. Your Details tab should look like the one shown in Figure 10-24.

   Like the Regarding field on the Schedule Activities dialog box, you can format the information that you enter in this field.

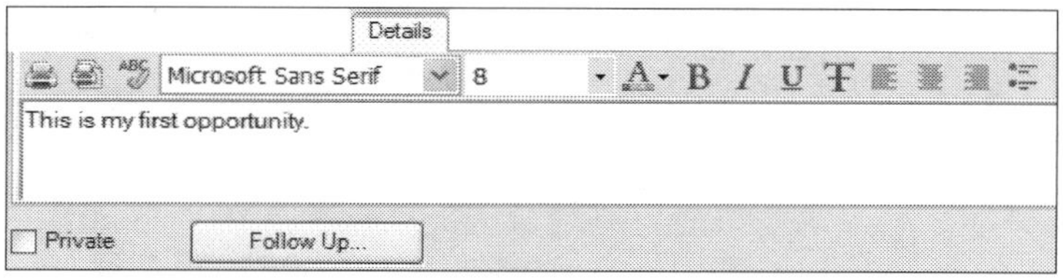

Figure 10-24 Details tab

The Opportunity Info Tab

Figure 10-25 shows the fields on this tab.

The field(s) that you may want to fill in when creating an opportunity are the Referred By and Competitor fields.

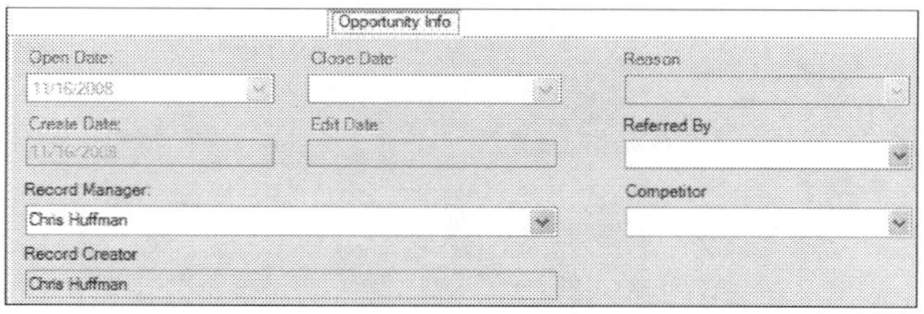

Figure 10-25 Opportunity Info tab

Exercise 10.2: Schedule A Follow Up Activity For The Opportunity

The default follow up opportunity activity is a phone call. The default Regarding information is the opportunity name.

If there is a stage, it is automatically included in the Regarding field, as illustrated in Figure 10-26.

Scheduling an activity for an opportunity is the same as scheduling other activities.

In this exercise you will schedule a phone call activity for tomorrow for the opportunity that you are creating.

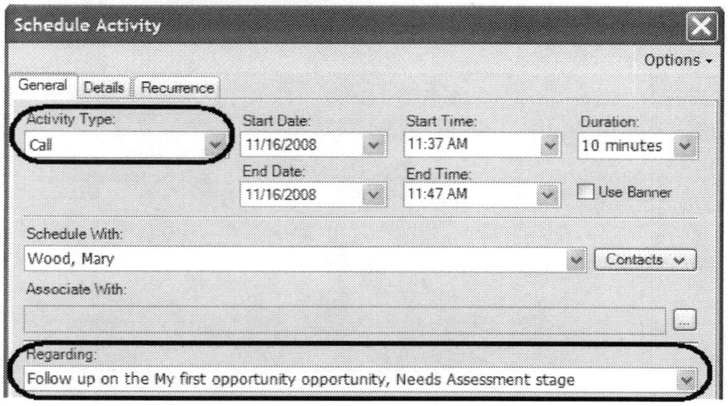

Figure 10-26 Opportunity follow up activity

1. Click the **FOLLOW UP** button.
2. Change the Start Date to tomorrow, then change the Start time to 2 PM.
3. Click OK twice to close the Scheduled Activity and Opportunity dialog boxes.

Exercise 10.3: Edit The Product List

In this exercise you will learn how to add a new product to the Product drop-down list.

1. Tools ⇒ Define Fields. Click on the **MANAGE PRODUCT LIST** link.

> **Other Ways To Open The Manage Product List Dialog Box**
>
> ① Click the Manage Product List button on the Opportunity List view toolbar.
> ② Contacts ⇒ Opportunities ⇒ Manage Product List.

2. Click the Add button, then type `ACT! Book` in the Name field.
3. Press the Tab key and type `BK-0001` in the Item Number field, then type `10` in the Cost field.
4. Type `39.95` in the Price field.

   The item should look like the one illustrated in Figure 10-27.

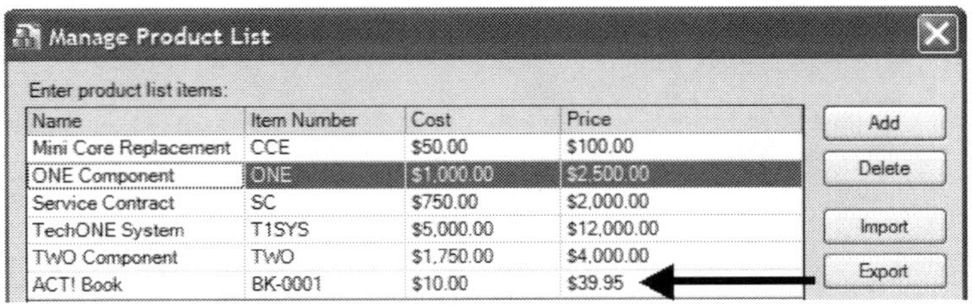

Name	Item Number	Cost	Price
Mini Core Replacement	CCE	$50.00	$100.00
ONE Component	ONE	$1,000.00	$2,500.00
Service Contract	SC	$750.00	$2,000.00
TechONE System	T1SYS	$5,000.00	$12,000.00
TWO Component	TWO	$1,750.00	$4,000.00
ACT! Book	BK-0001	$10.00	$39.95

Figure 10-27 New product illustrated

5. Click OK, then click Close on the Define Fields dialog box.

Exercise 10.4: How To Associate An Opportunity To A Company

In this exercise you will associate the opportunity that you created in Exercise 10.1 to a company.

1. Open the Dates drop-down list field on the Opportunity List view and select **FUTURE**.
2. Double-click on the opportunity for Mary Wood, then click the button at the end of the **ASSOCIATE WITH** field.
3. Open the View drop-down list and select Companies. Scroll down the list and select My New Company, then click the Add button.
4. Click OK. You will see the company in the Associate With field. Click OK to close the opportunity.

> **Opportunity Linking Issue**
>
> As you have learned in previous lessons, linked contacts that are marked as private can still have data from various tabs displayed under the company record that it is linked to. Opportunity records of linked contacts will not be visible from the company record, but opportunity history records will be visible from a company record. If you do not want the opportunity history records of private contacts visible, you have to clear the **AUTOMATICALLY RECORD HISTORY WHEN CONTACTS ARE LINKED OR UNLINKED** option on the Company Preferences dialog box. [See Lesson 4, Linking Company And Contact Records]

Exercise 10.5: Lookup Opportunities

The Lookup Opportunity options are similar to the opportunity filter options because they are used to narrow down the opportunities that will be displayed. By default, the opportunities that are displayed from the lookup are the ones for the current user (you). If you want to view opportunities for all users or specific users, you have to select the users. In this exercise you will perform three opportunity lookups.

Figure 10-28 shows the Opportunity lookup menu options. Most of the options shown were explained earlier in this lesson in the Using The Opportunity List Filters section. The other options are explained below.

The **NAME** option searches the Opportunity Name field for the name that you want to search for.

The **PRODUCT** option searches the Product Name field for the product that you want to search for.

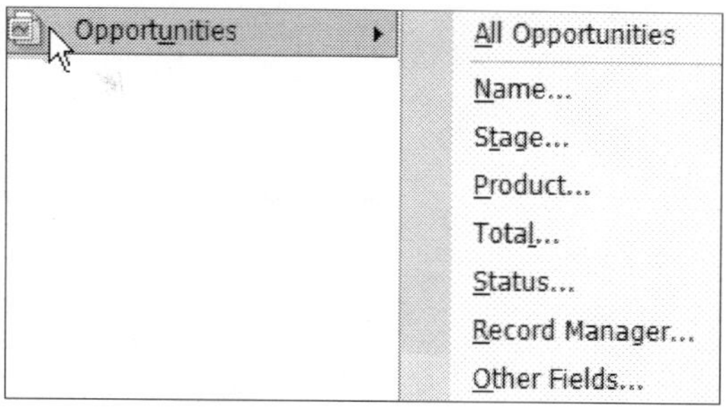

Figure 10-28 Opportunity lookup menu options

Lookup Opportunity #1

In this lookup exercise you will find opportunities for all users that are in the Initial Communication stage of the ACT! Sales Cycle process.

1. Lookup ⇒ Opportunities ⇒ Other Fields.
2. Select the **PROCESS** field to search on.
3. Type `ACT! Sales Cycle` in the Search for field.

   You should have the options shown in Figure 10-29.

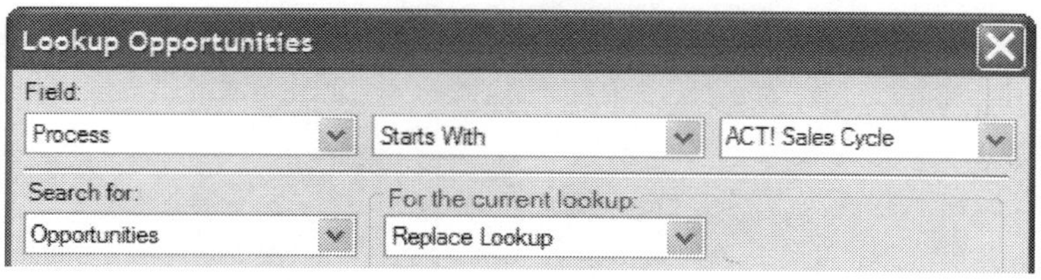

Figure 10-29 Lookup Opportunity options to find a process

4. Click OK. You will see fewer opportunities because all of the opportunities are not in the process that you selected in the lookup.
5. Lookup ⇒ Opportunities ⇒ Stage.
6. Type `Initial Communication` in the Search field.
7. Select the Narrow Lookup option shown in Figure 10-30.

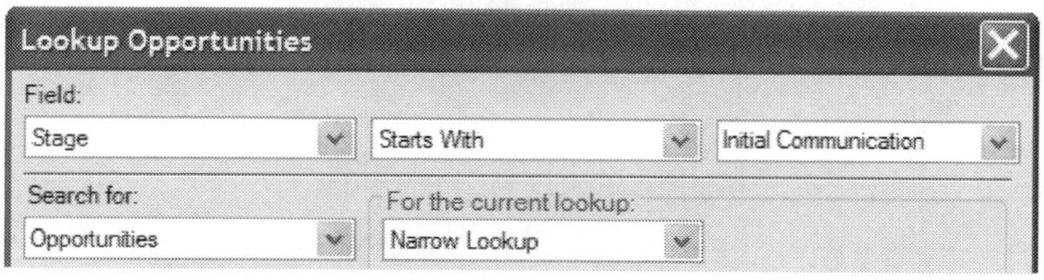

Figure 10-30 Lookup Opportunity options to limit the search to a specific stage

8. Click OK. You will see less opportunities.

Lookup Opportunity #2

In this lookup exercise you will find opportunities that have been open for more than 30 days. This requires two lookups: one to find opportunities with the number of days greater than 30 and one to narrow down the opportunities to only those that are open. When the lookup requires searching on more than one field, the efficient rule of thumb is to select the field that will eliminate the most records first. In databases with thousands of records, this will greatly speed up the search process. Being able to see a list of these opportunities will allow you to follow up to see what you can do to close the sale.

1. Lookup ⇒ Opportunities ⇒ Other Fields, then select the **DAYS OPEN** field to search on.

2. Select the **GREATER THAN** option, then type `30` in the field next to it.

   You should have the options selected that are shown in Figure 10-31.

   Click OK.

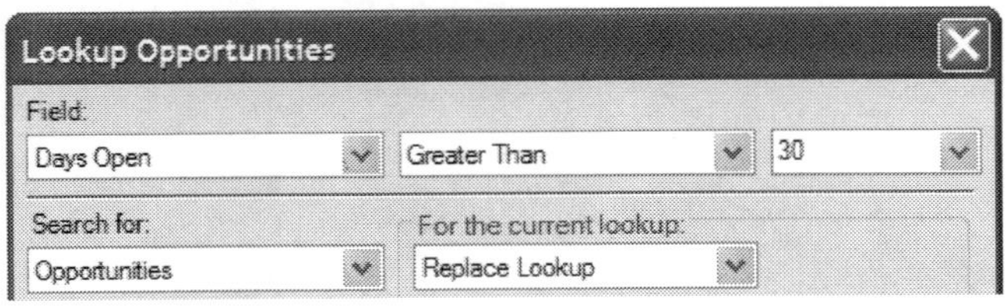

Figure 10-31 Lookup Opportunity options to find opportunities greater than 30 days

3. Lookup ⇒ Opportunities ⇒ Status. Type `Open` in the Search field.

4. Change the Current lookup option to Narrow Lookup, then click OK. You will see the opportunities that have been open for more than 30 days.

Lookup Opportunity #3

In this lookup exercise you will find opportunities that have a specific product.

1. Lookup ⇒ Opportunities ⇒ Product.

2. Type `Two Component` in the Search field, then click OK.

As you can see in Figure 10-32, in addition to opportunities that have the Two Component product, there are also opportunities with other products. That is because the other opportunities have the Two Component product listed, just not as the first product in the Product Name field.

Contact	Company	Status	Opportunity...	Stage	Product Name
Dan Minnick	Django...	Closed - Won	New...	Negotiation	TWO Component
Morty Manicotti	Corleone's...	Closed - Won	New...	Sales Fulfillment	TWO Component
Sean Duffy	Circle...	Closed - Won	New...	Needs...	TWO Component
Jordan Benedict	Bick's...	Open	East Texas...	Initial...	Service Contract...
Carl Spackler	Golf Greens...	Closed - Won	New...	Sales Fulfillment	TWO Component
Marion Morrison	Duke Industries	Open	Santa Monica...	Negotiation	TWO Component

Figure 10-32 Result of the lookup

How To Close An Opportunity

This is the part of the opportunity process that will probably make you happy. When a contact makes a purchase they become a customer and their opportunity needs to be closed. If a contact does not make a purchase for whatever reason, the opportunity should be closed indicating that. The steps below will show you how to close an opportunity.

1. Open the opportunity that you want to close by selecting one of the following options:

① Double-click on the opportunity in the Opportunity List view.

② Right-click on the opportunity (on the Opportunities tab of the Contact Detail view), then select Close Opportunity, as illustrated in Figure 10-33.

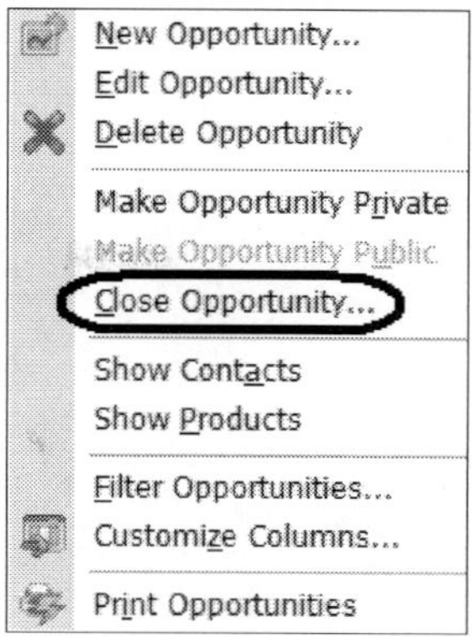

Figure 10-33 Opportunity shortcut menu

2. Select the appropriate closed status. [See Status Options earlier in this lesson]

3. Select or type in a **REASON** if applicable, on the Opportunity Info tab.

4. You can also add comments on the **DETAILS** tab shown earlier in Figure 10-24. Click OK.
   A history record similar to the one shown in Figure 10-34 will be created for the opportunity.

Date	Time	Result	Regarding & Details	Record Manager	Group/Company
8/15/2005	11:40 AM	Opportunity Lost	New Opportunity $1,440.00 Closed - Lost Monday, August 15, 2005 12:00:00 AM	Chris Huffman	

Figure 10-34 History record for a closed opportunity

Exercise 10.6: Export Opportunities To Excel

In this exercise you will export the opportunities to Excel. In Lesson 12 you will learn how to export contact data to Excel. Exporting the opportunity data will allow the data to be analyzed, as well as, create charts.

1. Click the **OPPORTUNITY LIST** button. Lookup all of the opportunities.

2. Click the Export To Excel button on the toolbar.

The opportunity records will be exported and Excel will open automatically. The Pivot chart should look like the one shown in Figure 10-35.

The Pivot Table Field List dialog box shown in Figure 10-35 displays all of the fields that were exported to Excel. You can drag any of those fields to the chart.

The Pivot sheet tab should look like the one shown in Figure 10-36.

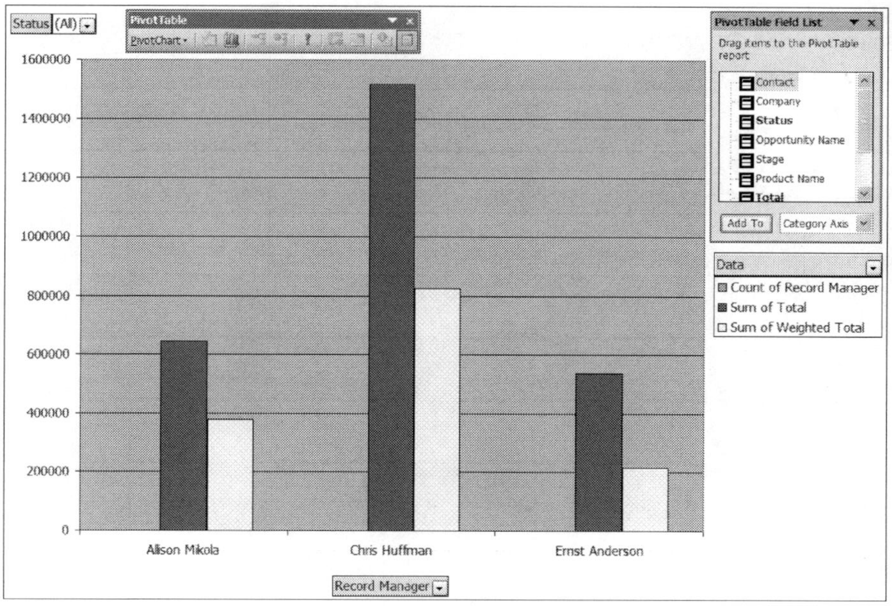

Figure 10-35 Opportunities Pivot chart

B	C	D	E
Status	(All)		
	Data		
Record Manager	Count of Record Manag	Sum of Total	Sum of Weighted Total
Allison Mikola	95	$643,600.00	$378,375.00
Chris Huffman	176	$1,516,480.00	$825,774.00
Ernst Anderson	89	$537,900.00	$215,670.00
Grand Total	360	$2,697,980.00	$1,419,819.00

Figure 10-36 Opportunities Pivot sheet tab

If you look at the bottom of the spreadsheet you will see three tabs. The first tab displays the data from the Opportunity List view.

The second tab on the spreadsheet displays a Pivot chart of the data.

The third tab displays the summary information that is displayed on the Pivot chart. If you change the options on this tab, the chart will automatically be updated to reflect the changes. You can select different options in the drop-down lists (Status, Record Manager and Data) to filter the data like you can on the Pivot chart. Doing this will cause the following to happen.

① The data will be recalculated on the Pivot Sheet tab.

② The Pivot chart will change.

3. Close Excel when you are finished viewing the data. You can save the spreadsheet in your folder if you want. It is not mandatory to save it because you will not need it to complete any other exercise.

Crash Course In Pivot Table Data

This is truly a crash course in Pivot table data. Hopefully it is enough for you to understand the basic functionality if you have not used this tool in Excel before. The Pivot Chart tab displays the summary opportunity data graphically. ACT! displays the data in detail.

In the upper left corner of the chart is the **STATUS** drop-down list. If you select a different status, the data will be recalculated based on the status that you select and the chart will change. At the bottom of the chart is the **RECORD MANAGER** drop-down list. When you select a user from the list, the opportunities that the user created will appear on the chart.

Figure 10-37 shows the Pivot chart with the Status changed to **CLOSED-WON**.

The **DATA** button is used to filter the following total fields: Count of Record Manager, Grand total (Sum of Total) and the Sum of Weighted Total.

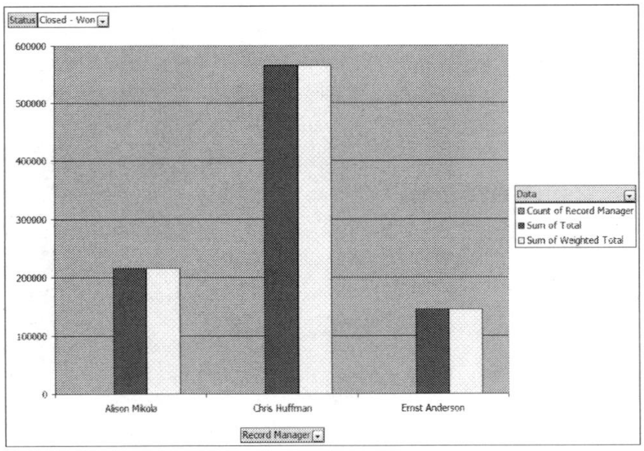

Figure 10-37 Status changed to Closed-Won

You can move the buttons around on the Opportunities Pivot tab, as shown in Figure 10-38.

Compare this to Figure 10-36 shown earlier.

B	C	D	E
Record Manager	(All)		
Status	Closed - Won		
	Data		
	Count of Record Manager	Sum of Total	Sum of Weighted Total
Total	116	$925,900.00	$925,900.00

Figure 10-38 Record Manager button moved on the Opportunities Pivot tab

If you move the Record Manager button before the Status button on the Opportunities Pivot tab and then view the chart, it will look like the one shown in Figure 10-39.

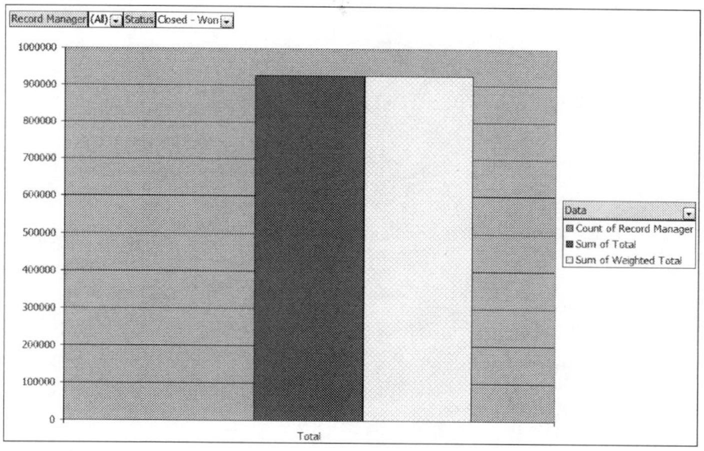

Figure 10-39 Pivot chart after the Record Manager button is moved

Generating Quotes

Often you may need to send the opportunity that you create to a contact when they request a quote. In order to generate a quote you have to have the 2002, 2003 or 2007 version of Microsoft Word and Excel installed.

Quote Preferences

There are preferences for quotes that you can set.

Tools ⇒ Preferences ⇒ General Tab ⇒ Quote Preferences button, will open the Quote Preferences dialog box.

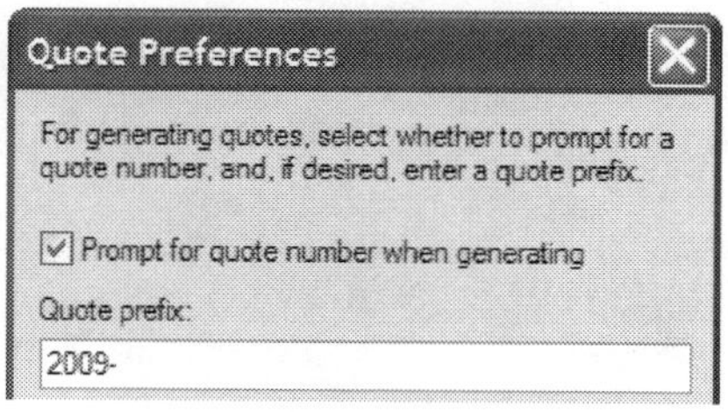

Figure 10-40 Quote Preferences dialog box

If the option **PROMPT FOR QUOTE NUMBER WHEN GENERATING** is checked, you can select a prefix for quote numbers, as shown above in Figure 10-40. Adding a quote prefix means that all quotes that you create will start with the same characters and numbers that you enter in the **QUOTE PREFIX** field. You can enter the prefix of your choice or leave it blank if you want to enter a free form quote prefix.

Exercise 10.7: Create A Quote

1. On the Opportunity List view, double-click on the quote that you created for Mary Wood.

2. On the Products/Services tab, click the **QUOTE** button. The document shown in Figure 10-41 will open in Microsoft Word. If you want to save the quote, save it in your folder.

Notice that the shipping and handling charges have not been filled in. You have to fill this in manually.

To modify this field, double-click in the section that has the products. The Excel spreadsheet shown in Figure 10-42 will appear. It has the formulas for the calculations.

The tax rate that you enter should be the tax rate for your state.

If you plan to use the quote document, you may want to customize it a little by adding fields or change the font.

This quote template is really two files, as discussed below.

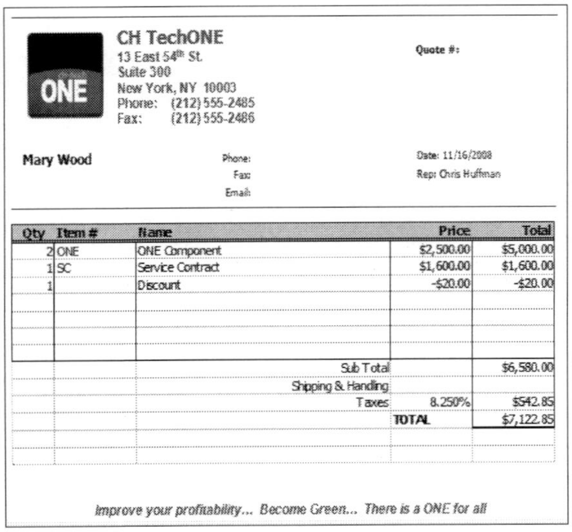

Figure 10-41 Quote

① The **QUOTE.ADT** file is the portion of the quote created as a Word template, which you can modify.

② The **QUOTE.XLT** file is the portion of the quote created in Excel, as shown in Figure 10-42. You should not modify the structure of this part of the quote template.

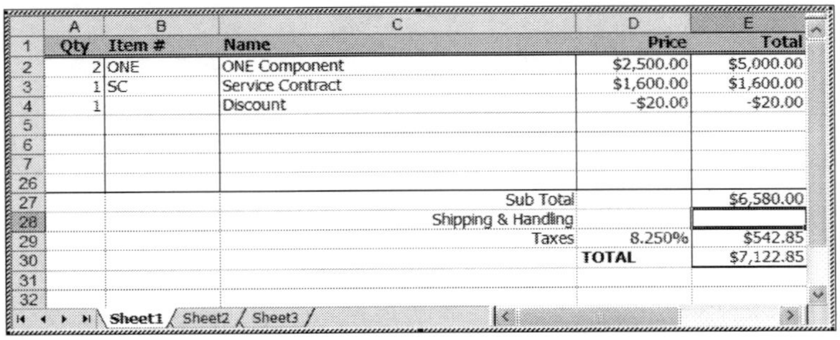

Figure 10-42 Spreadsheet in the Word document

Exercise 10.8: How To Change The Status Of An Opportunity

Earlier in this lesson you learned that an opportunity can have one of four statuses. When you need to change a status, follow the steps below.

1. On the Opportunity List, double-click on the opportunity that you want to change the status of.
   In this exercise select the opportunity for Mary Wood.

2. Select the status that you want. Select Closed-Won for this exercise.

3. On the Opportunity Info tab, type `Purchased service` in the Reason field, then click OK.

Viewing Opportunities From The Opportunities Tab

You have created opportunities, viewed them and learned how to filter them from the Opportunities List view. In addition to being able to view opportunities from the Opportunities List view, you can view opportunities from the Opportunities tab on detail views. Like other tabs that you have learned about, you can also customize the layout of the Opportunities tab.

As shown in Figure 10-43, some of the filter options that are available on the Opportunities List view are available on the Opportunities tab. If you need more filter options, right-click in the opportunities and select **FILTER OPPORTUNITIES**. You will see the dialog box shown in Figure 10-44. This dialog box is a scaled down version of the one that you saw earlier in Figure 10-15.

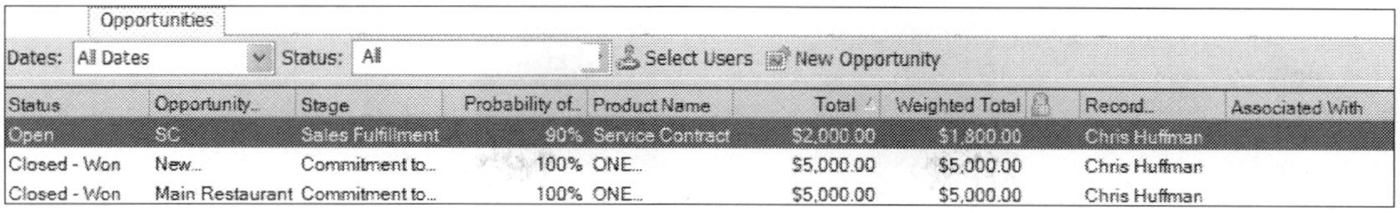

Figure 10-43 Opportunities tab

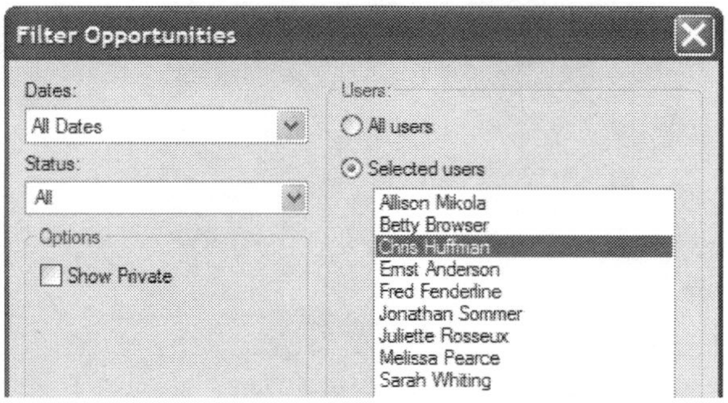

Figure 10-44 Filter Opportunities dialog box

Opportunity Reports

ACT! comes with reports that are specifically for opportunities. In addition to being able to preview and print the reports, there are five other output options that you can select from. You can save the reports and send them as an attachment in an email. You can also save them as a PDF file. The benefit of saving the report in PDF format is that anyone with the free Adobe Reader can view the report.

Report Options

After running some of the reports on the Opportunity Reports submenu, I noticed that the Define Filters dialog box for some opportunity reports have the options on the General tab that are usually on the Opportunity tab. The following reports are like this: Sales Analysis by Record Manager, Total By Status, Adjusted for Probability, Pipeline Report and Opportunities By Record Manager.

Exercise 10.9: Sales Analysis By Record Manager Report

This report will display any or all of the available status categories, as well as, the number and percent for each category selected. It also provides a Closed/Won analysis that provides the average and total amounts for the date range and employees that you select.

1. Reports ⇒ Opportunity Reports ⇒ Sales Analysis By Record Manager.

2. Select **PAST** as the Date Range, as shown in Figure 10-45.

   The filter options for this report are used to select opportunities based on the status and date range.

Figure 10-45 Sales Analysis By Record Manager report options

3. Click OK. Your report will look similar to the one shown in Figure 10-46.

   Your report will have more records because you are running the report after I did.

Sales Analysis by Record Manager

Date Range: Before 11/16/2008

Allison Mikola

Total		$142,500.00	**Closed/Won Analysis:**	
Total Number of Opportunities:		48	Avg. Sales Amount	$6,785.71
Status	**#**	**%**	Avg. Discount	0.00%
Open	15	31.00	Total Gross Margin	$83,000.00
Closed/Won	21	44.00	Avg. Gross Margin	$3,952.38
Closed/Lost	12	25.00	Avg. # Products per Sale	1.24
Inactive	0	0.00	Avg. Days Open	190.76

Figure 10-46 Sales Analysis By Record Manager report

Exercise 10.10: Opportunities Adjusted For Probability Report

This report will allow the reader to look for trends in the opportunities that they have and are currently working on. For each status that is selected, the opportunity records will be printed. The total order amount and weighted total amount per status is calculated and printed.

1. Reports ⇒ Opportunity Reports ⇒ Adjusted For Probability.
2. Select all of the opportunity status options, then select the **PAST** Date Range.
3. Click OK.

   Your report should look like the one shown in Figure 10-47.

Opportunities Adjusted for Probability

Date Range: Before 11/16/2008 **Weighted Total:** $798,360.00

Status Open **Total for Status:** $390,100.00 **Weighted Total for Status:** $126,060.00

Contact	Company	Name	Stage	Est. Close	Prob.	Weighted Total	Total	Record Manager
Nathan Cutting Britties	Duke Industries	Northern California Facility	Presentation	10/19/2008	40%	$4,800.00	$12,000.00	Allison Mikola
Sean Duffy	Circle Photography	Film Facilities	Initial Communication	8/29/2008	10%	$1,200.00	$12,000.00	Ernst Anderson
Jordan Benedict	Bick's Longhorns	West Texas	Needs Assessment	10/31/2008	25%	$6,000.00	$24,000.00	Chris Huffman
Jordan Benedict	Bick's Longhorns	East Texas Operations	Initial Communication	9/19/2008	10%	$2,200.00	$22,000.00	Chris Huffman
Lucy Connor	Studio Designs	Cheshire Warehouse	Presentation	8/29/2008	40%	$2,000.00	$5,000.00	Chris Huffman
Marion Morrison	Duke Industries	Office Upgrade	Negotiation	8/29/2008	65%	$7,800.00	$12,000.00	Allison Mikola
Marion Morrison	Duke Industries	Santa Monica Offices	Initial Communication	9/26/2008	10%	$250.00	$2,500.00	Allison Mikola
Jane Bellamy	Boomers Artworx	Headquarters	Initial Communication	10/30/2008	10%	$1,200.00	$12,000.00	Ernst Anderson
Charles Foster Kane	Rosebud Publications	Studio	Presentation	9/19/2008	40%	$4,800.00	$12,000.00	Chris Huffman

Figure 10-47 Opportunities Adjusted for Probability report

Opportunity Graphs And Pipelines

In addition to opportunity reports, ACT! has the ability to create graphs and pipelines for opportunity data. These options are accessed from the Opportunity List view. Both can be printed and saved in different file formats.

Exercise 10.11: Creating Graphs

The graphs for opportunities that you can create have several options that you can use to customize the graph, like the type of graph and date range.

Create A Bar Graph

In this part of the exercise you will create a bar graph for opportunities in 2008.

1. On the Opportunity List view, click the **OPPORTUNITY GRAPH** button.

2. On the General tab, select the options below. Your dialog box should have the options shown in Figure 10-48.

   - Display data for all users
   - Graph by month
   - Starting 1/1/2008
   - Ending 12/31/2008

   Depending on the data that is needed to create the graph, you may need to create a lookup first.

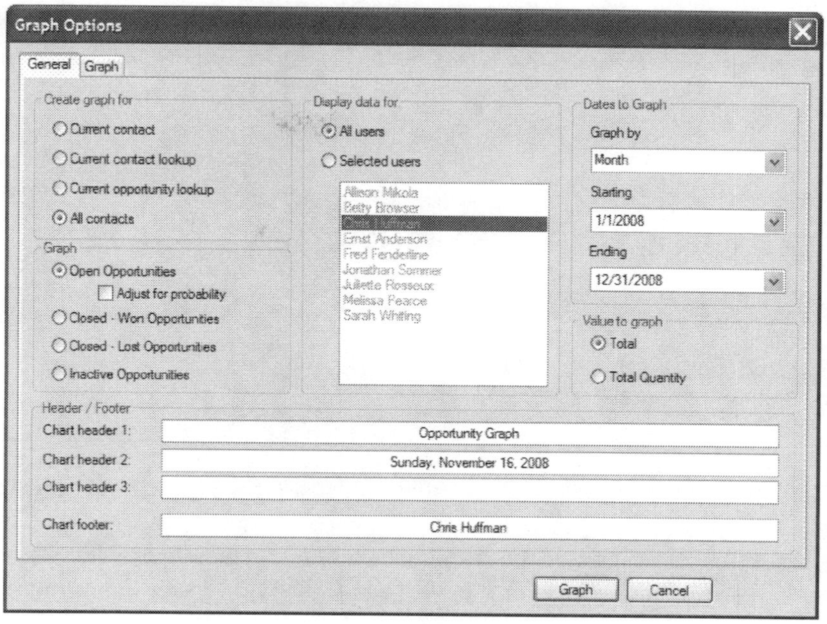

Figure 10-48 General tab (bar) graph options

3. On the Graph tab, select the following options.

   - Allow graph to scroll
   - Show horizontal grid lines
   - 3-D Style

4. Click the button at the end of the **COLOR GRAPH** option and select a different color.

   Your dialog box should have the options shown in Figure 10-49.

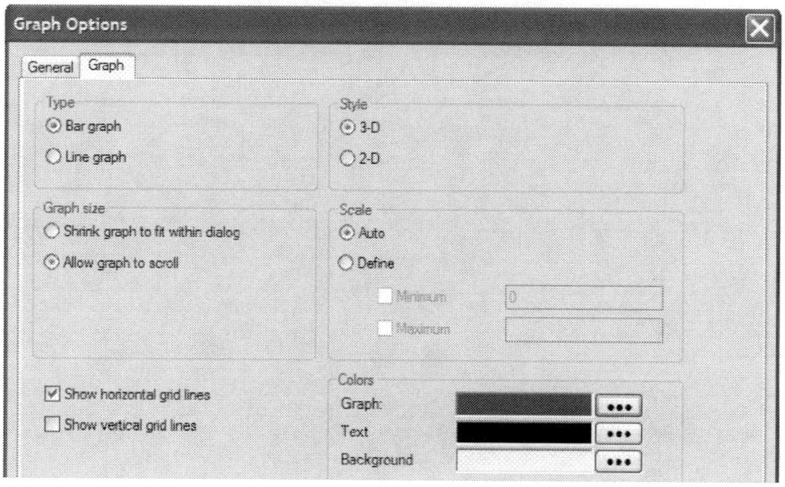

Figure 10-49 Graph tab options

5. Click the **GRAPH** button at the bottom of the dialog box.

The Graph button creates a graph based on the options that are selected. Your graph should look like the one shown in Figure 10-50. You may have to use the scroll bar below the graph to scroll to the right to see the charted data.

The **LOOKUP** button will open the Opportunity List view and display the opportunities that are depicted in the graph.

The **SAVE** button is used to save the graph in .BMP or .JPG graphic file format.

Save all of the graphs and pipelines that you create in this lesson in .JPG format.

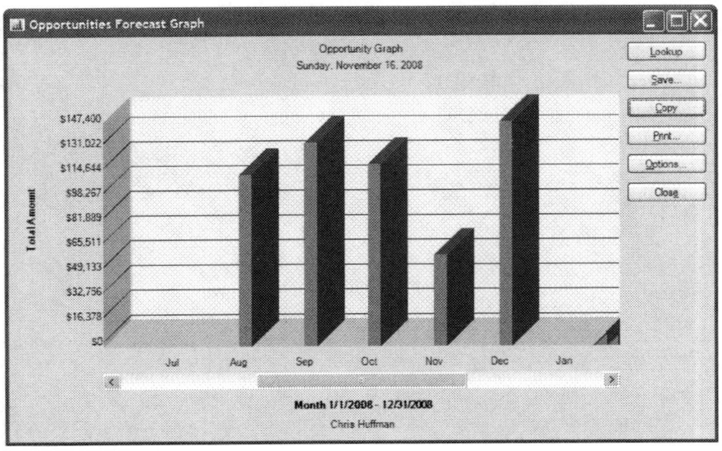

Figure 10-50 Bar graph

The **COPY** button sends a copy of the graph to the Clipboard in Windows. This allows you to paste a copy of the graph into a document like the ACT! Word Processor or a Power Point presentation.

The **PRINT** button will print the graph.

The **OPTIONS** button opens the Graph Options dialog box shown earlier in Figure 10-48, so that you can make changes and recreate the graph.

6. Save the graph in your folder as `Bar Graph`, as illustrated in Figure 10-51, then close the Opportunities Forecast Graph dialog box.

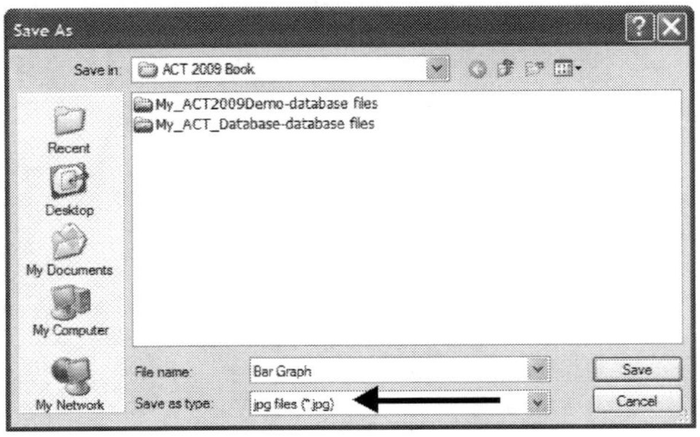

Figure 10-51 Save options for the graph

Create A Line Graph

In this part of the exercise you will create a line graph for opportunities in a specific date range.

1. On the Opportunity List view, click the Opportunity Graph button.

2. On the General tab, select the options below. Your dialog box should have the options shown in Figure 10-52.

   - Display data for all users
   - Graph by week
   - Starting 11/1/2008
   - Ending 12/31/2008
   - Chart header 1 `Opportunity Line Graph`

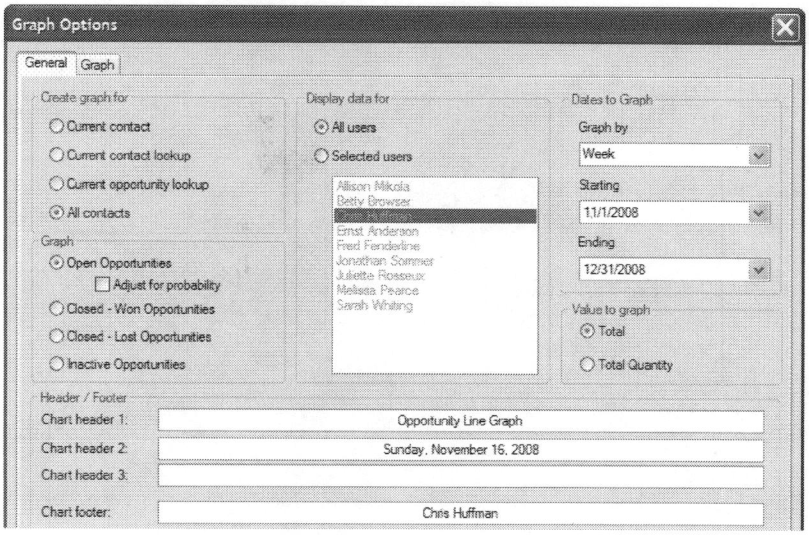

Figure 10-52 General tab (line) graph options

3. On the Graph tab, select the following options. Your dialog box should have the options shown in Figure 10-53.

   - Line graph
   - Allow graph to scroll
   - 3-D Style
   - Show vertical grid lines
   - Show horizontal grid lines

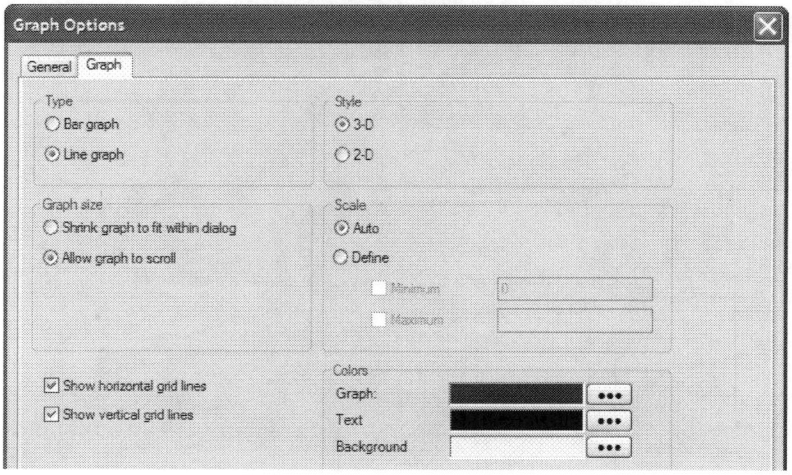

Figure 10-53 Graph tab options

4. Click the Graph button.

   Your graph should look like the one shown in Figure 10-54.

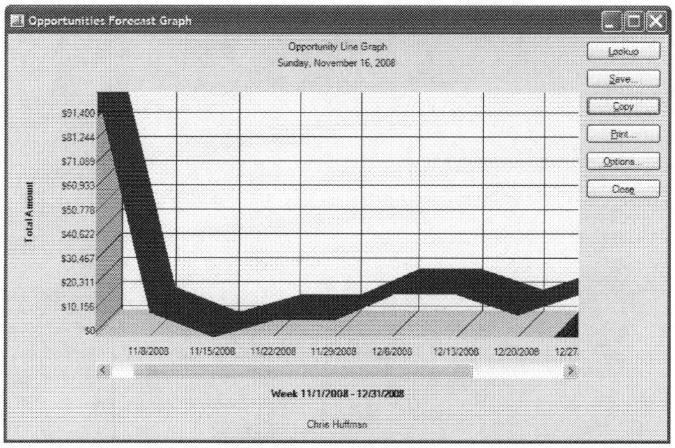

Figure 10-54 Line graph

5. Save the graph in your folder as `Line Graph`.

6. Close the Opportunities Forecast Graph dialog box.

Pipelines

Pipelines graphically display opportunities that have an "Open" status for a specific process at each stage. The options to create a pipeline graph are similar to the ones to create a bar or line graph.

Exercise 10.12: Create A Pipeline Graph

1. On the Opportunity List view, click the Opportunity Pipeline button.

2. Select the options below. Your dialog box should have the options shown in Figure 10-55.

   - All contacts
   - All users
   - Graph header 3
     `My First Pipeline`

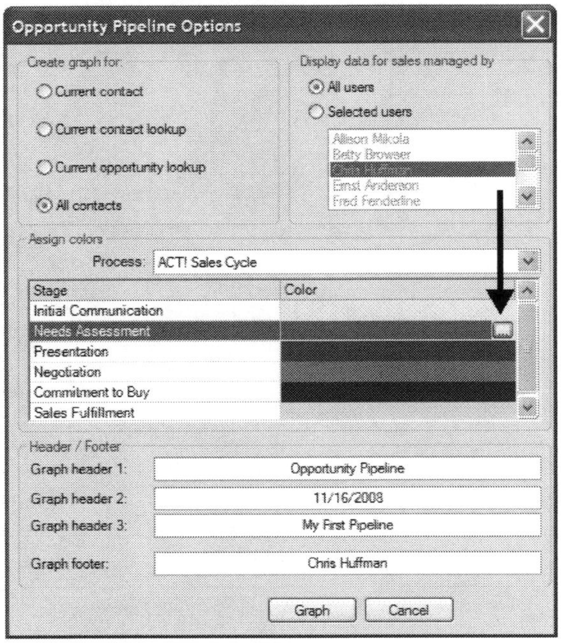

Figure 10-55 Opportunity Pipeline Options dialog box

> To change a color on the pipeline graph for a stage in the process, click the ellipsis button at the end of the stage in the **COLOR** column, as illustrated above in Figure 10-55.

3. Click the Graph button.

   You should see the pipeline graph shown in Figure 10-56.

   Save the pipeline graph in your folder as `Pipeline Graph`, then close the Opportunity Pipeline dialog box.

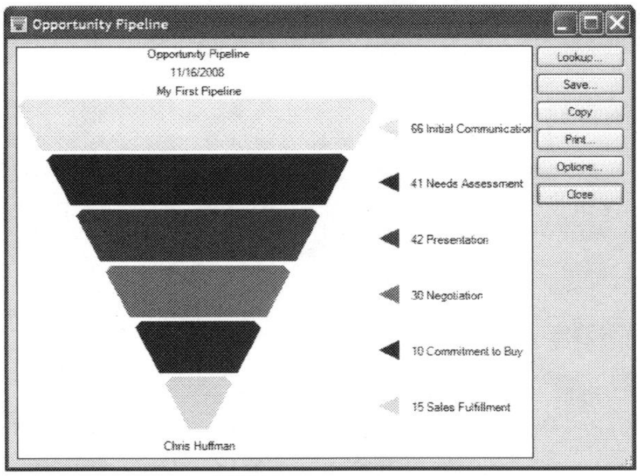

Figure 10-56 Pipeline graph

How To Create And Customize Product And Process Lists

Like the drop-down lists on the Contact Detail view, the Opportunity products and processes drop-down lists can be customized. Earlier in Exercise 10.3, you learned how to add a new product. The remaining exercises in this lesson will show you how to modify opportunity products and processes, as well as, how to import and export stages and products.

Exercise 10.13: Creating Process Lists And Stages

In this exercise you will create a process list and the stages for the process.

1. On the Opportunity List view, click the **MANAGE PROCESS LIST** button.
2. Click on the **CREATE NEW OPPORTUNITY PROCESS** link in the Process Tasks section.
3. Type `My first process` in the Opportunity Process field, then type `This process has 3 stages` in the Description field, as shown in Figure 10-57.

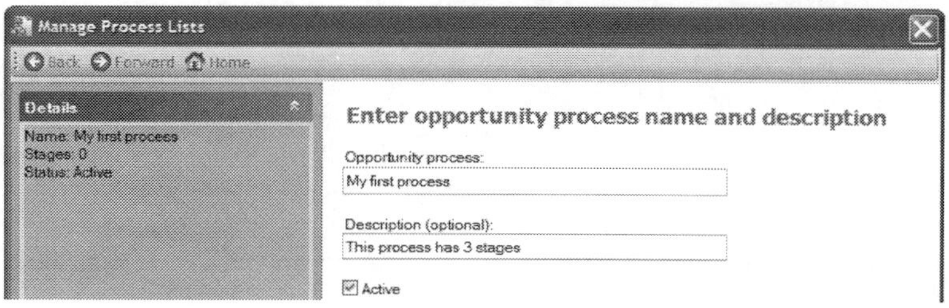

Figure 10-57 Manage Process Lists screen

4. Click Next. Click in the Name field and type `First Stage`.
5. Press the Tab key twice and type `80` in the Probability field.
6. Click the Add button, then add the two other stages shown in Figure 10-58.

   The **MOVE UP** and **MOVE DOWN** buttons are used to change the order of the stages.

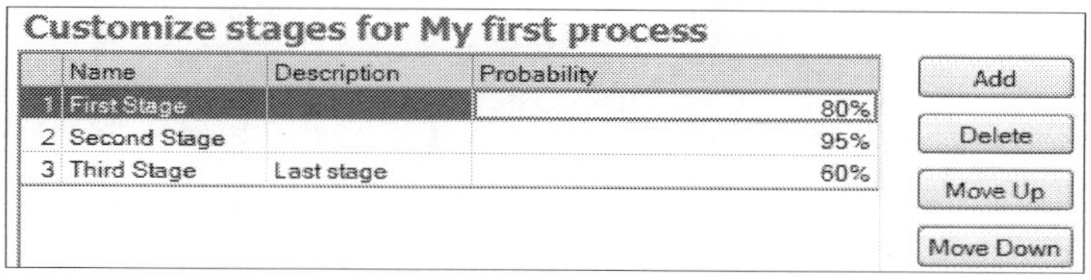

Figure 10-58 Stages for the process

7. Click Finish. You will see the process that you created. In the **PROCESS TASKS** section, notice that there are options to edit and delete processes. Leave the Manage Process Lists window open to complete the next exercise.

Exercise 10.14: Importing Stages

In the previous exercise you created an opportunity process. You also created three stages for the process. If you have a lot of stages for a process or prefer to create them in a spreadsheet, which would allow you to spell check them, you can import the spreadsheet with the stages into ACT!. In this exercise you will import three stages for the process that you created in the previous exercise. The **MANAGE PROCESS LISTS** window should already be open.

1. Select the **MY FIRST PROCESS** opportunity process, then click on the Edit Opportunity Process link.
2. Change the description to have six stages, then click Next.

3. Click the **IMPORT OPPORTUNITY STAGES** link. In your folder, double-click on the Import_Opportunity_Stages file.

   You will see the three new stages, as shown in Figure 10-59.

   If you needed to, you could rearrange the order of the stages.

Customize stages for My first process

	Name	Description	Probability
1	First Stage		80%
2	Second Stage		95%
3	Third Stage	Last stage	60%
4	Fourth Stage	Add to catalog ma	90%
5	Fifth Stage	Placed Order	95%
6	Sixth Stage	Order Shipped	95%

Figure 10-59 Imported stages

4. Click the Finish button. Leave the Manage Process Lists window open to complete the next exercise.

Exercise 10.15: Exporting Stages

You can export the opportunity stages to a **.CSV** file, which is a file format that you can open in Excel. The **MANAGE PROCESS LISTS** window should already be open.

1. Select the Opportunity Process for the stages that you want to export. In this exercise select the **ACT! SALES CYCLE** process, then click on the Edit Opportunity Process link.

2. Click Next. Click the Export Opportunity Stages link.

3. Type `My Export Stages` in the File name field, then press Enter.

4. If you open this file in Excel, it will look like the one shown in Figure 10-60.

   The reason column B is empty is because the stages that were exported do not have any descriptions. Close the Manage Process Lists dialog box.

	A	B	C
1	Initial Communication		10%
2	Needs Assessment		25%
3	Presentation		40%
4	Negotiation		65%
5	Commitment to Buy		80%
6	Sales Fulfillment		90%

Figure 10-60 Exported stages

How To Create A Product List In Excel

The steps below will show you how to create a product list in Excel.

1. Create four columns: Name, Item Number, Cost and Price. Typing in the column names is optional. If you type them in, make sure that you do not import the first row of the spreadsheet.
2. Enter the information for each product.
3. Change the Save as type to **CSV (COMMA DELIMITED) (*.CSV)**, as illustrated in Figure 10-61, then save the file.

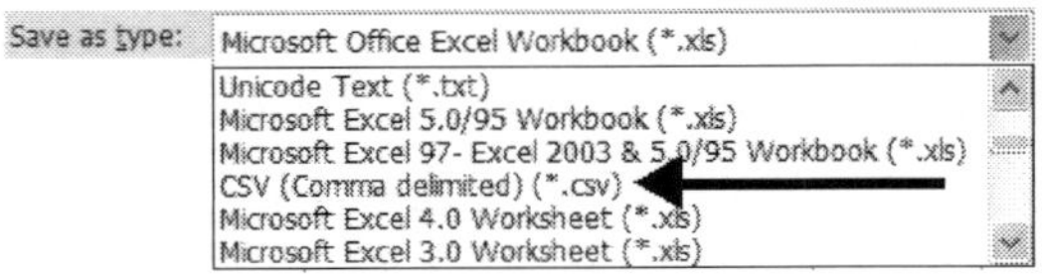

Figure 10-61 CSV file type illustrated

Exercise 10.16: Importing Products

If you need to add a lot of products to the database or have the products in an existing file, you can import them into the database. This means that you can create the product list in Excel and save it in .csv format. In this exercise you will learn how to import data.

1. On the Opportunity List view, click the **MANAGE PRODUCT LIST** button.

2. Click the **IMPORT** button, then click the **BROWSE** button on the Import Products dialog box.

3. Double-click on the Products_To_Import file. If you cannot see it, change the Files of type option to **CSV FILES (*.CSV)**.

4. Check the **SOURCE FILE HAS COLUMN HEADERS** option shown in Figure 10-62.

   The **REPLACE PRODUCTS WITH THE SAME NAME** option will overwrite products that are already in the Product list with the changes in the file that you import. This is how you can update existing product information.

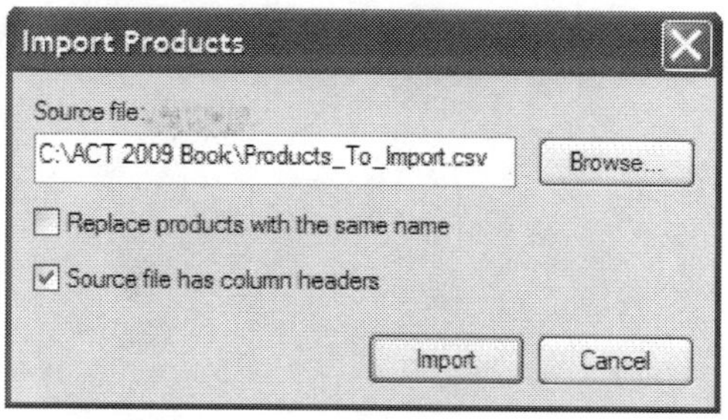

Figure 10-62 Import Products dialog box

The Source file has column headers option will not import the first row of data in the file. Check this option if the file that you are importing has column headings. If you are not sure, open the file before importing it. You can also view the products on the Manage Product List dialog box and delete the product that is really a column heading.

5. Click the Import button on the Import Products dialog box. Click OK when prompted that the products have been successfully imported.

   You should see the three products illustrated at the bottom of Figure 10-63.

   Leave the dialog box open to complete the next exercise.

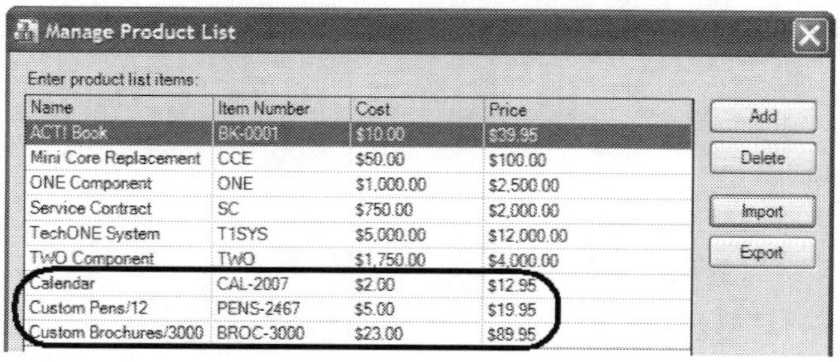

Figure 10-63 Manage Product List dialog box

Exercise 10.17: Exporting Products

Exporting products can be useful if you need to change data in several records. You can export the products, make the changes in Excel for example and then import the list back into ACT!. In this exercise you will export products.

1. Open the Manage Product List dialog box if it is not already open, then click the **EXPORT** button.

2. Type `My Exported Products` as the file name, then press Enter.

3. You can open the exported file in Excel to view it, if you want. Close the Manage Product List dialog box.

CREATING QUERIES

In this lesson you will learn the following query techniques:

- ☑ Create queries using the Lookup By Example tool
- ☑ Query operators
- ☑ Running and saving queries
- ☑ Advanced queries
- ☑ Creating dynamic groups
- ☑ Sorting records retrieved from a query

LESSON 11

Queries Overview

Queries and lookups for that matter, allow you to get answers to questions like "Which contacts are in a particular state and were referred by Agency 1 or Agency 2?". Another question a query could answer would be "Which customers have not been contacted in the last 60 days?". You have learned how to use the Lookup command to find contacts. Depending on the types of contacts that you are trying to find, you will have to perform several lookups. If you needed to find contacts in two cities, you would have to perform two lookups and add the results of the second lookup to the results of the first lookup.

The Lookup By Example window resembles the Contact Detail view. It contains all of the fields that are on the layout. If you add a field to the top of a layout or to a tab, it will also appear on the Lookup By Example window.

Queries have several advantages over lookups. Queries allow you to find contacts based on multiple values in the same field. Queries allow you to find contacts that match criteria in more than one field at the same time. Another advantage of using queries is that you can save them and use them again. You can create contact, company and group lookups on the Lookup By Example window. If you need to lookup data in a range of values, you have to use the Advanced Query tool.

Like other features in ACT!, there is more than one way to create a query. You can use the Lookup By Example window or the Advanced Query tool. In this lesson you will learn how to create queries using both options.

> **Saved Query File Extensions**
>
> Saved queries have three file extensions, as listed below.
> **.QRY** are contact queries.
> **.CRY** are company queries.
> **.GRY** are group queries.

Exercise 11.1: Creating Queries Using The Lookup By Example Tool

The primary reason to use the Lookup By Example tool is to save a query without having to create all of the syntax that is required when using the Advanced Query tool. The other reason to use the Lookup By Example tool instead of the Lookup technique is if you need to perform the lookup on more than one field. In this exercise you will create a query to find all customers in Arizona.

1. Make sure that all of the contacts are displayed. Lookup ⇒ By Example. You should see the Lookup By Example window.

2. Select AZ in the State field.

3. Check the Customer option in the **ID/STATUS** field drop-down list. You should have the options selected that are shown in Figure 11-1.

   Some of the tabs (Personal Info, Contact Access, and User Fields) display fields and some do not, like the History and Notes tabs.

   The tabs that have fields displayed can be used in the lookup.

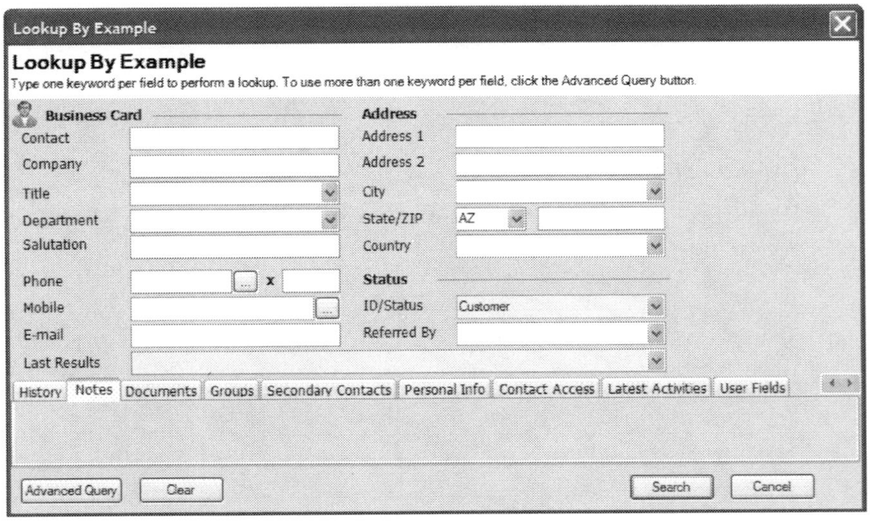

Figure 11-1 Lookup By Example search criteria

Saving Lookup By Example Queries

If you create a query that you will want to run again, you should save it. If you save the query you can also edit and use it as the basis for another query. Actually, you should save the query before you run it. If you do not save the query before it is run and discover that you did not select the correct options, you will have to start over. You cannot save the query on the Lookup By Example window. You have to save it using the Advanced Query tool.

1. Click the Advanced Query button, then click the **SAVE** button on the Advanced Query window. The default folder for saving queries that ACT! uses is automatically displayed.

2. Navigate to your folder and type `Customers in AZ` as the query name, then press Enter.

3. You should see the query name in the Title bar at the top of the Advanced Query window. Click the Preview button.

4. The contact records that meet the criteria of the query will appear at the bottom of the window.

   There should be eight customers in AZ. If you scroll through the records in the Contact Detail view, you will see that each record has **CUSTOMER** in the ID/Status field and **AZ** in the State field, as shown in Figure 11-2.

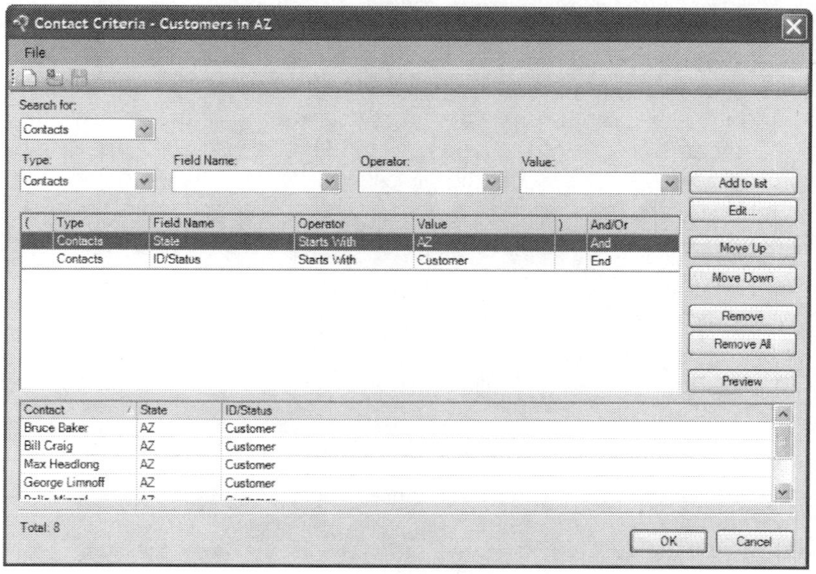

Figure 11-2 Query results

The **ADD TO LIST** button will add the criteria from the Type, Field Name, Operator and Value fields to the grid in the middle of the dialog box.

The **EDIT** button opens the Edit dialog box so that you can modify the selected row of criteria in the grid.

The **MOVE UP** and **MOVE DOWN** buttons are used to change the order of the criteria in the grid.

The **REMOVE** button will delete the criteria on the row that is selected.

The **REMOVE ALL** button deletes all of the criteria.

The **PREVIEW** button runs the query and displays the results at the bottom of the dialog box.

5. Click OK. You will see the dialog box shown in Figure 11-3.

   Click OK.

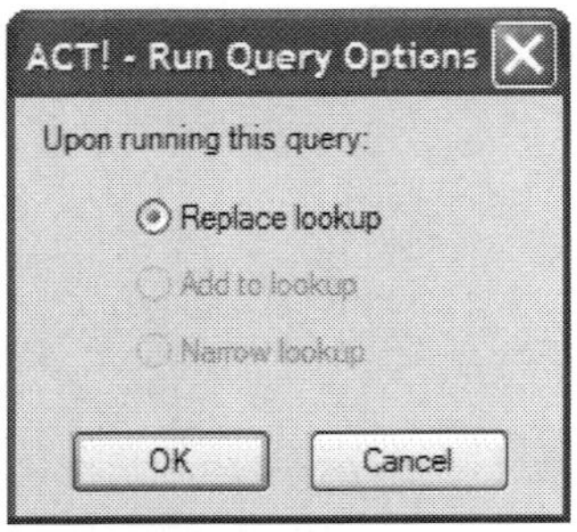

Figure 11-3 ACT! Run Query Options dialog box

Wildcards

The Lookup By Example tool has two wildcard characters that you can use to search for characters in a field. They are discussed below. The default search method will only search for the characters that you enter.

① The **%** (percent sign). This wildcard character is used to find characters any place in the field. If you wanted to find all companies that had a specific word or character, you would type the percent sign followed by the characters that you want to search for like this, %Toys. If you entered this in the Company field, all of the records with "Toys" any place in the Company field would be retrieved.

② The _ (underscore). Use this wildcard character to replace one character in the string of characters that you are searching for. If you entered t_n as the search criteria, the search would return records that have ten, tan and ton in the field, but not toon.

If you used a version prior to ACT! 2007 and used the asterisk (*) in a lookup or query and tried it in ACT! 2009, you saw that it did not work. I do not know why, but the functionality of the asterisk has been changed to the percent sign (%).

Exercise 11.2: How To Run A Saved Query

There are two ways that you can run a saved query as discussed below.

① From the Advanced Query window (Lookup ⇒ Advanced ⇒ Advanced Query).

② Add it to the Lookup menu and run it from there. You will learn how to modify menus in Lesson 17.

How To Run A Query From The Advanced Query Window

1. Lookup ⇒ Advanced ⇒ Advanced Query.

2. Click the Open button, then double-click on the query, Customers in AZ, in your folder.

3. Click OK, then select **REPLACE LOOKUP** and click OK. You will see the same eight contacts. If more records were added to the database that met the criteria, they would appear at the bottom of the window. Lookup ⇒ All Contacts.

Advanced Queries

You will need to create an advanced query when the Lookup command and Lookup By Example query options will not retrieve the records that you need. This is usually the case when you need to search for two or more values in the same field. An example of when you would need to create an advanced query is if you need to find all customers and prospects in AZ.

Advanced queries are a little harder to construct then Lookup By Example queries because syntax is required. It is not as difficult as you may think. Some conditions must be enclosed in parentheses as shown below.

(ID/STATUS = CUSTOMER OR ID/STATUS = PROSPECT) AND STATE = AZ

The equation above will find all contacts that have "Customer" or "Prospect" in the ID/Status field and AZ in the State field. There is a syntax checker to help you fix syntax errors. You can convert a Lookup By Example query to an advanced query. This may save you some time when creating an advanced query.

Earlier you created a query to find all customers that are in AZ. You can recreate this query on the Lookup By Example window and then open the **ADVANCED QUERY** window to add the prospect criteria to the query.

Even though you can create the entire query in the Advanced Query window, some people feel more comfortable creating as much of an advanced query in the Lookup By Example window as possible and then open the Advanced Query window to finish it.

Advanced Query Options

There are four options (drop-down lists) on the Advanced Query window that are used to create the criteria for a query, as discussed below.

① **Type** Is used to select the record type (Contact, Company, Opportunity, etc) for the field that you need to create criteria for. The option selected in this field controls the fields that are displayed in the Field Name drop-down list. For example, if you select Company in the Type field, the fields in the Field Name drop-down list will be Company fields.

② **Field Name** Is used to select the field that you will create the criteria for.

③ **Operator** Operators are used to describe the relationship between the criteria in the query. This relationship is a comparison of the data in the database to the value selected in the query. "Starts With" is the default operator. Table 11-1 explains the query operators. You will only see operators that the selected field can use.

④ **Value** This field contains the data that you want to use in the comparison. If the field selected has a drop-down list, the options in the Value drop-down list come from the data in the field in the database. If the field does not have a drop-down list, you will have to type in the value.

This Operator	Will Find Records That . . .
Contains	Have the criteria that you enter any place in the field.
Contains Data	Have data in the field, meaning the field is not empty. (1) (2)
Does Not contain data	Do not have any data in the field, meaning that the field is empty. (1) (2)
Ends With	Have data in the field that ends with the criteria that you enter. (1)
Equal To (=)	Are equal to the criteria that you enter. (1)
Greater than	Have an amount higher than the amount that you specify in the Value field. If you want to see all orders with an order amount over $500, enter $500 in the Value field and the query will display records with an order amount of $500.01 or more. (3)
Greater than or equal to	(Works similar to "Greater than"). The difference is that this operator will also select records that have the amount that you specify. In the greater than example above, the query would not retrieve records with an order amount of exactly $500. The greater than or equal to operator will. (3)
Less than	Have an amount less than the amount that you specify in the Value field. If you want to see products that have a reorder level of less than 10 items in stock, enter 10 in the Value field and the query will display products with a reorder level of nine or less. (3)
Less than or equal to	(Works similar to "Less than"). The difference is that this operator will also select records that have the amount that you specify. In the less than example above, the query would not retrieve records with a reorder level of 10 items. The less than or equal to operator will. (3)
Not Equal To (!=)	Do not have data that matches the criteria that you enter. (1)
Starts With	Have data in the field that starts with the criteria that you enter. (1)
On or After	Have a date that is greater than or equal to the date that you enter. (4)
On or Before	Have a date that is equal to or less than the date that you enter. (4)

Table 11-1 Query operators explained

This Operator	Will Find Records That . . .
Within Last [days]	Have a date that is within the previous number of days that you specify. (4)
Within Next [days]	Have a date that is within the next number of days that you specify. (4)

Table 11-1 Query operators explained (Continued)

(1) This operator is for text fields.
(2) The Value field is not enabled when this operator is selected.
(3) This operator is only for numeric fields.
(4) This operator is only for date fields.

Exercise 11.3: How To Create An Advanced Query

1. Lookup ⇒ Advanced ⇒ Advanced Query, then open the Customers in AZ query.

2. Select the criteria in the Field Name, Operator and Value fields shown at the top of Figure 11-4. The criteria shown at the bottom of the figure is from the Customers in AZ query.

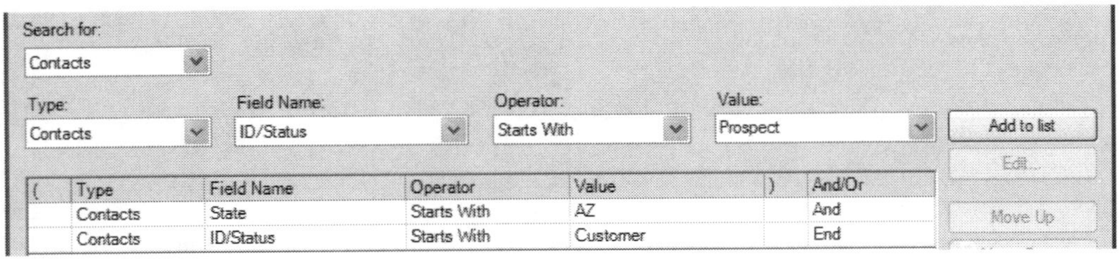

Figure 11-4 Criteria options to select

If you look in the **AND/OR** column in the grid, you will see that contacts must meet the criteria of the State starting with AZ and the ID/Status field start with Customer. Changing the value of the And/Or field in the first ID/Status criteria row to **OR** will retrieve contacts if the value in the ID/Status field is Customer or Prospect, which is what you want in this exercise.

If you previewed the contacts now, based on the criteria shown in Figure 11-5, the query would not retrieve any records. That is because the query criteria needs to enclose the two ID/Status rows of criteria in parentheses so that if a contact has the status of Customer or Prospect, the state still has to be equal to AZ.

(	Type	Field Name	Operator	Value	)	And/Or
	Contacts	State	Starts With	AZ		And
	Contacts	ID/Status	Starts With	Customer		And
	Contacts	ID/Status	Starts With	Prospect		End

Figure 11-5 And operator illustrated

Using **AND** means that you want both conditions to be met: The condition on the first line with the And condition (in the And/Or column) and the condition on the line below it.

For example, if you want to find all customer and prospect records in AZ that were edited between 1/1/2006 and 5/21/2007, you would create the criteria shown in Figure 11-6.

(	Type	Field Name	Operator	Value	)	And/Or
(	Contact	ID/Status	Starts With	Customer		Or
	Contact	ID/Status	Starts With	Prospect	)	And
	Contact	State	Starts With	AZ		And
(	Contact	Edit Date	On or After	1/1/2006		And
	Contact	Edit Date	On or Before	5/21/2007	)	End

Figure 11-6 Date range criteria

I am not sure why "Starts With" is used as the default operator on the Lookup By Example window and Lookup Opportunities dialog box when most people really want to use **EQUAL TO**. The "Starts With" operator does just that. The operator will look for all records that have the value that you enter at the beginning of the field. Using the Starts With operator can return unexpected results. The problem that I have with using the Starts With operator is that if there are other values that "Start with" the same characters as those in the Value field, those records will also be retrieved when the query is run.

I personally do not use the Starts With operator for this reason. From a programmers perspective, the query criteria shown earlier in Figure 11-5 is not what most users want. The criteria shown in Figure 11-7 is what should be used. You will find out how to correct this query later in the lesson when you learn how to edit a query.

(	Type	Field Name	Operator	Value	)	And/Or
	Contacts	State	Equal To (=)	AZ		And
((	Contacts	ID/Status	Equal To (=)	Customer		Or
	Contacts	ID/Status	Equal To (=)	Prospect	))	End

Figure 11-7 Equal to criteria

3. Click the **ADD TO LIST** button.

4. Click in the **(** column of the first ID/Status criteria row, as shown in Figure 11-8, and select ((.

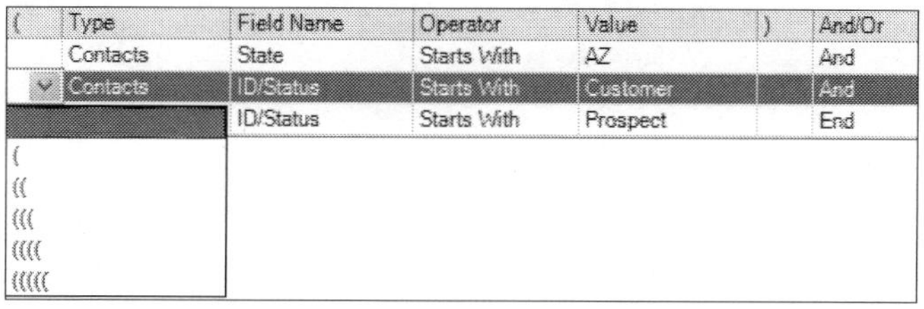

Figure 11-8 Left parenthesis criteria options

5. Open the And/Or drop-down list for the first ID/Status criteria row and select **OR**, as shown in Figure 11-9.

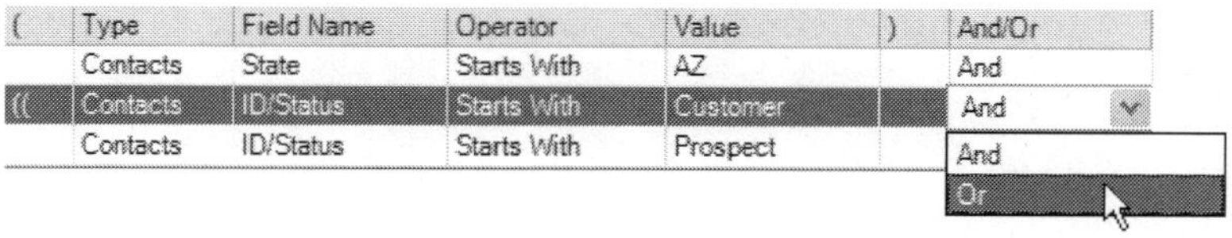

Figure 11-9 And/Or criteria options

Check The Query Syntax

If you preview a query and see a message similar to the one shown in Figure 11-10, it means that there is something wrong with the syntax (code) of the query.

In this example, the message is telling you that there is something wrong with the parentheses.

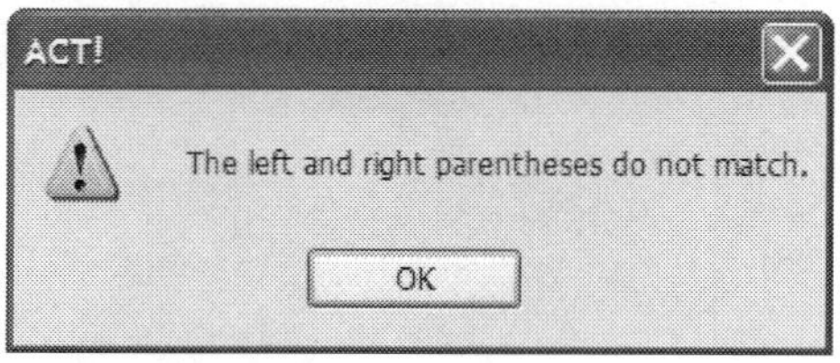

Figure 11-10 Query syntax error message

Look at the parentheses in the query. There should be an equal number of each type of parentheses that you select and the parentheses should be on different lines. (See the options in the drop-down list shown earlier in Figure 11-8).

1. If you see the message shown above in Figure 11-10, click OK and fix the query criteria based on the message.

2. Click in the) column on the last criteria row and select)), as shown in Figure 11-11.

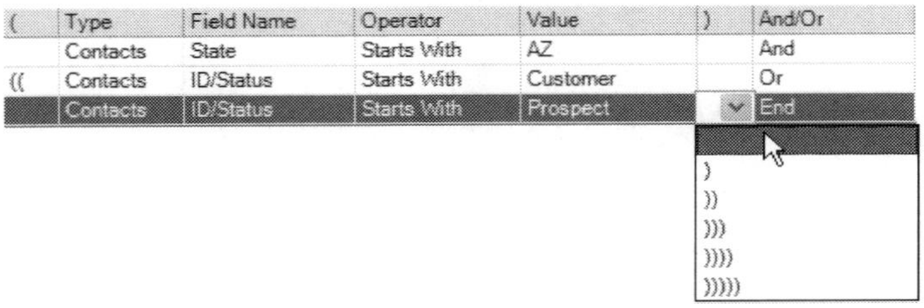

Figure 11-11 Right parenthesis criteria options

Save And Run The Query

1. File ⇒ Save As.

2. Type `Customers & Prospects in AZ` in the File name field, then click the Save button.

3. Click OK. Select Replace Lookup and click OK. There should be 11 contacts displayed in the Contact List view.

Exercise 11.4: Find Records Created In The Last 30 Days Query

You may have the need to know which contacts you added to the database or modified in the past. An example would be if you wanted to review all of the contacts that you added to the database in the last 30 days. The field that stores when a contact record is added to the database is the **CREATE DATE** field.

1. Lookup ⇒ Advanced ⇒ Advanced Query.

2. Select the Create Date field.

3. Select the **WITHIN LAST [DAYS]** operator, then type `30` in the Value field.

4. Click the Add to list button.

   You should have the criteria shown in Figure 11-12.

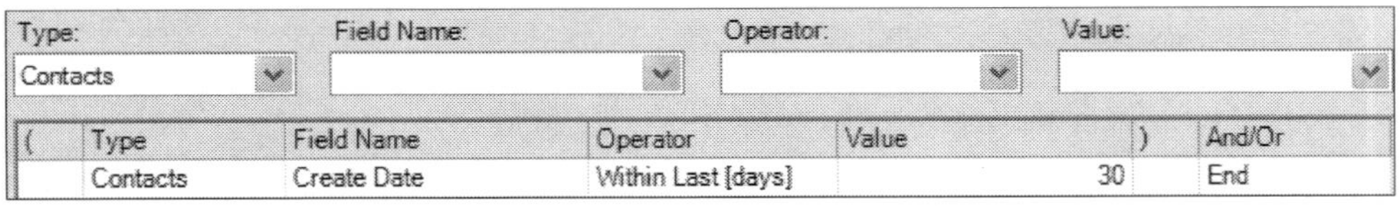

Figure 11-12 Last 30 days criteria

5. Save the query in your folder as `New contacts in last 30 days.`

6. Preview the results. You will see the contact records that you have added in the last 30 days. Close the Advanced Query window.

> If you edit the criteria shown above in Figure 11-12 and change the Field Name to **EDIT DATE**, you will see all of the contacts that you have edited in the last 30 days.

Exercise 11.5: Find Contacts In CA With Open Opportunities

In this exercise you will create a query that finds contacts in California that have opportunities with an open status.

1. Lookup ⇒ Advanced ⇒ Advanced Query.

2. Select the State field.

3. Select the Equal To operator, then select CA from the Value drop-down list.

4. Click the Add to List button.

5. Open the Type drop-down list and select Opportunities.

6. Select the Status field.

7. Select the Equal To operator, then type `Open` in the Value field. I don't know about you, but I was expecting to be able to select the status from the drop-down list.

8. Click the Add to List button, then click the Preview button.

   You should have the options shown in Figure 11-13.

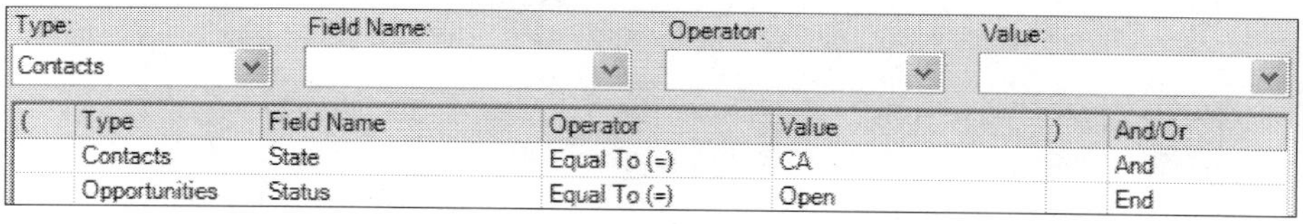

Figure 11-13 Contacts in CA with open opportunities criteria

9. Save the query as `Open Opportunities in CA`.

10. Run the query. You will see the contacts in CA that have open opportunities. If you double-click on a contact, on the Opportunities tab, you will see at least one open opportunity for the contact.

How To Edit A Query

If you need to edit a query you can follow the steps below. For now you can just read this section. If you want to practice editing a query you can change the operator on each criteria row to Equal To (=) in the Customers & Prospects in AZ query.

1. Open the query that you want to edit in the Advanced Query window.

2. Click on the criteria row that needs to be changed, then click the Edit button.

   You will see the dialog box shown in Figure 11-14.

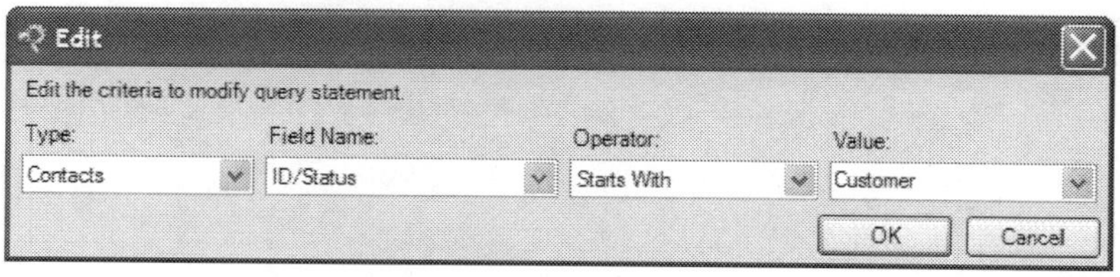

Figure 11-14 Edit dialog box

3. Make the criteria changes that you need, then click OK. Save the changes.

Exercise 11.6: Sorting Records Retrieved From A Query

You can sort the records that the query finds. This will be useful if you will be doing a bulk mailing and need the records sorted in order by zip code when you print the mailing labels. You can sort the records from the query in the detail or list view by following the steps below.

1. Lookup all contacts. Edit ⇒ Sort.

2. Open the **SORT BY** drop-down list and select Zip Code.

3. Change the **AND THEN BY** option to <None>.

   You should have the options selected that are shown in Figure 11-15.

   Click OK. The records in the Contact List will now be sorted by zip code.

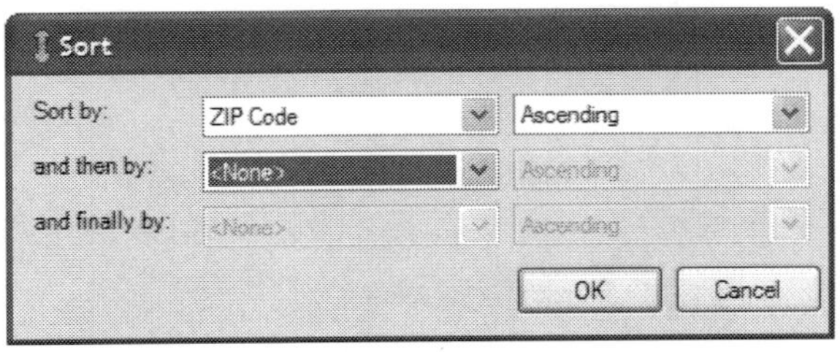

Figure 11-15 Sort dialog box options

Dynamically Linking Contacts To Companies

In Lesson 4 you learned how to manually link contacts to companies. If you want to be able to have contacts automatically linked to a company, you have to create a query.

An example of when this would be useful is when you want to have certain fields filled in for the contact. This is one way to make sure that the data is being maintained. If you needed to make sure that every contact record has a company name, you could create a query that looks for records that do not have data in the Company field.

This works for the Company field, but not for other types of linked fields. For example, if you wanted to put all contact records that do not have a zip code into a company. If the Zip Code field is a linked field, this would not work. You would have to put the records in a group instead of a company.

Exercise 11.7: Find Prospects Query

In this exercise you will create a query to find prospect contacts in the US that do not have an email address. You can use the Lookup By Example and Advanced Query windows to get the contacts that meet the criteria. Using the Lookup By Example window to create as much of the query as possible and then use the Advanced Query window to complete the query is a good idea. This will keep you from having to create the entire query manually.

1. Create a query to display all customers with a prospect status in the United States that do not have an email address.

2. Save the query in your folder as `US Prospects with no email address`. Your query should retrieve 12 records. Figure 11-16 shows the query syntax.

(	Type	Field Name	Operator	Value	)	And/Or
	Contacts	E-mail	Does Not Contain Data	Nothing		And
	Contacts	ID/Status	Equal To (=)	Prospect		And
	Contacts	Country	Equal To (=)	United States		End

Figure 11-16 Prospects without an email address query

Exercise 11.8: How To Create A Dynamic Group

In Exercise 5.6 you created a Sales Reps group and added contacts to it. As time goes on, more contacts will be added to the database and some of them will be sales reps. You could create a lookup to find the new contacts that are sales reps, but you would have to do that on a regular basis so that all of the contacts with this title will be in the group. ACT! has a dynamic option that can be used to create criteria to automatically add records to a group. This is done by creating a query. You can also use the dynamic option to automatically remove records from a group. In this exercise you will modify the Sales Reps group so that it is dynamic. You can add as much criteria as needed to create a dynamic group.

1. On the Group Detail view, click on the Sales Reps group in the tree, then click the Add/Remove Contacts button below the tabs on the right.

2. Click the Edit Criteria button on the Add/Remove Contacts dialog box.

3. Open the Field Name drop-down list and select **TITLE**.
   Open the Operator drop-down list and select **EQUAL TO (=)**.
   Open the Value drop-down list and select **SALES REPRESENTATIVE**.

4. Click the **ADD TO LIST** button. You should have the criteria shown in Figure 11-17.

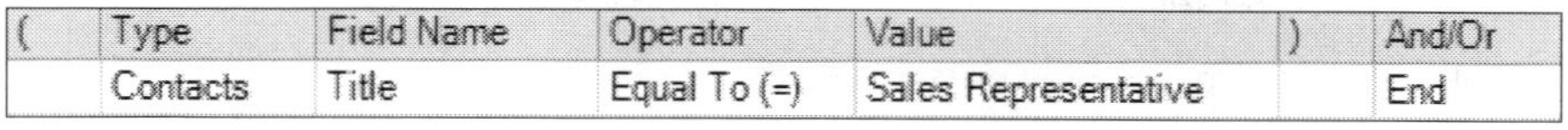

Figure 11-17 Sales rep group criteria

> If you made a mistake, click on the criteria under the drop-down lists that needs to be changed, then click the **EDIT** button to correct the mistake.

5. Click the **PREVIEW** button. You should see five contacts at the bottom of the dialog box.

6. Click OK to close the Group Criteria dialog box.

7. You should see the criteria in the **DYNAMIC MEMBERS** section of the Add/Remove Contacts dialog box, as shown in Figure 11-18.

   Click OK.

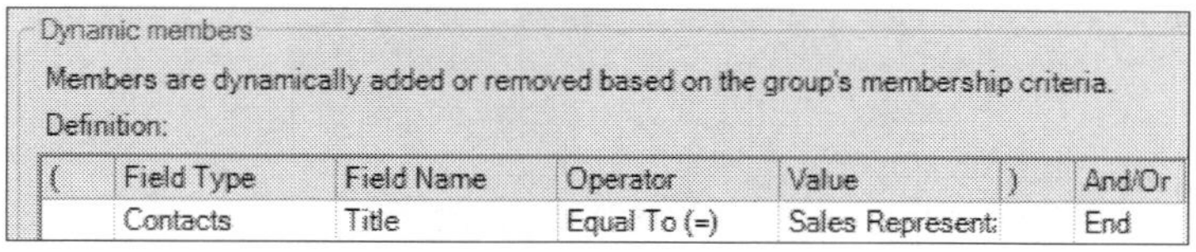

Figure 11-18 Dynamic criteria

> Contacts that are added to the group via a query will stay in the group as long as they meet the criteria. In the exercise that you just completed, if any of the contacts that were added dynamically has a change in title, they will automatically be removed from the Sales Reps group. If you add a contact to this group manually, they will stay in the group whether or not they meet the criteria.

It is probably best to link contacts to a company on more than the Company name field. It is possible that there is more than one company with the same name in the database, meaning one company could end with "Inc" and the other one doesn't. If you also linked on the street address, the chances of linking to the wrong company is greatly reduced.

Test The Dynamic Group Criteria

1. Create new records for the contacts in Table 11-2.

   The last two records in the table should be added to the Sales Reps group automatically.

Contact	Title
Tim Dynamic	Sales Manager
Tina Dynamic	Sales Representative
Tom Dynamic	Sales Representative

Table 11-2 Test records for the dynamic group criteria

2. Click the Groups button, then click on the Sales Reps group.

   You should see the records for Tina and Tom Dynamic, as illustrated in Figure 11-19.

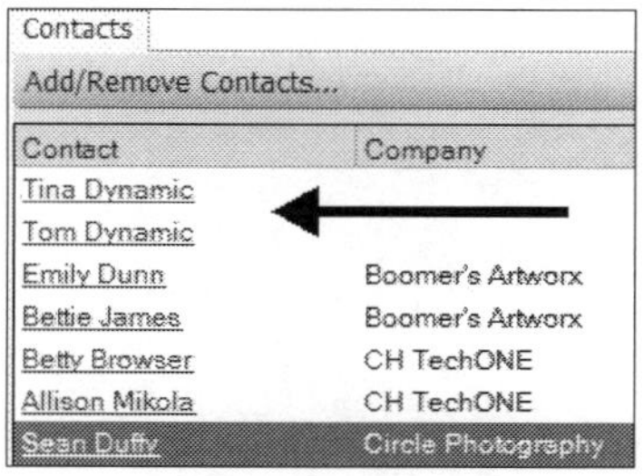

Figure 11-19 Result of the dynamic group criteria

The Groups/Companies tab on the Contact Detail view does not automatically show dynamic groups that the contact is a member of. You have to click the **DISPLAY DYNAMIC GROUP MEMBERSHIP** button, illustrated in Figure 11-20, to see if the contact is a member of a dynamic group. When you click this button you will see the dialog box shown in Figure 11-21. This dialog box lets you know which dynamic groups the contact is a member of.

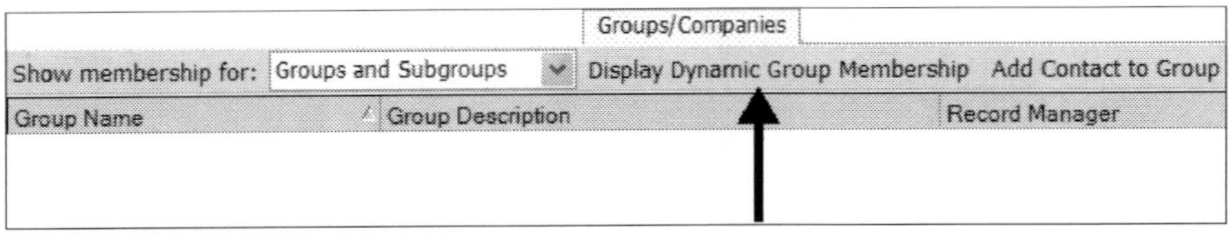

Figure 11-20 Groups/Companies tab options

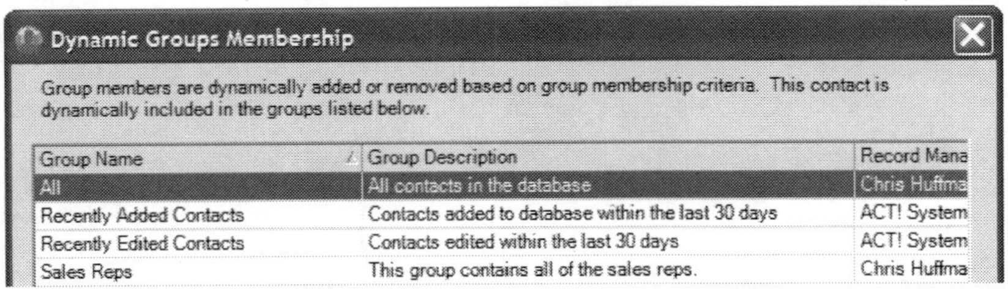

Figure 11-21 Dynamic Groups Membership dialog box

The query for the dynamic group that you just created will automatically run each time either of the following actions occur:

① The Group Detail view is opened.
② The Groups/Companies tab is displayed.

How To Create A Dynamic Company

You can create a dynamic company if the need arises by following the steps below.

1. On the Company Detail view, click on the company in the tree that you want to create a dynamic company for.

2. On the Contacts tab, click the Add/Remove Contacts button below the tabs on the right.

3. Click the Edit Criteria button on the Add/Remove Contacts dialog box.

4. Create the criteria for the company, then click the Add To List button.

5. Once you have the criteria correct, click OK to close the Company Criteria and Add/Remove dialog boxes.

WRAP UP OF THE BASICS

In this lesson you will learn the about following features in ACT!:

- ☑ Tagging records
- ☑ Copying data
- ☑ Swapping data
- ☑ Supplemental files
- ☑ Promoting secondary contacts
- ☑ Using the Timer
- ☑ Editing notes
- ☑ Filtering notes
- ☑ Record creation options
- ☑ Internet services
- ☑ Attaching web pages to a contact
- ☑ Managing links
- ☑ Export contact data to Excel
- ☑ Mapping ACT! fields to an Excel spreadsheet
- ☑ Uninstalling ACT!
- ☑ Adding graphics to ACT! notes
- ☑ Editing attached documents

LESSON 12

Wrap Up Of The Basics Of ACT!

This lesson concludes the basics of ACT!. The majority of tasks that you will use the most in ACT! are covered in the first 11 lessons of this book. The remaining lessons contain tasks that you may use a lot when first creating a database, but will use much less frequently over time. The exceptions to this are the dashboard and backing up a database, which, depending on how frequently data is modified, you may need to do daily.

The topics covered in this lesson are important to know, but in my mind were better left out of the previous lessons because they were not essential to learning and mastering the core concepts of ACT!.

Understanding The ID/Status And Referred By Fields

The majority of fields on the Contact Detail view are pretty straight forward. The fields discussed below may not be as straight forward.

The **ID/STATUS** field is most often used to categorize contacts. This means that you can enter customers, prospects, vendors and lawyers in the same database. Many people would keep each of these types of contacts in different databases or spreadsheets. Using this field allows you to maintain an unlimited number of types of contacts. This field provides an informal way to group or categorize contacts. You can add to and edit the entries that are in the drop-down lists.

When you first enter names in the database, you would select the "Prospects" ID/Status if the goal was to get the contact to purchase a product from you. If they purchase a product, you would change the value in this field to Customer.

When the value in this field is changed, an entry is automatically created on the History tab unless you change the option to not record a history record. Having this field generate a history record can be helpful if you need to know when the status of contacts change. A month after your marketing campaign, you could look up all of the contacts that are "Prospects" and contact them by phone or email to see whether or not they received your mailing.

What may not be obvious is that the ID/Status field is what ACT! refers to as a **MULTI-SELECT** field.

This means that the field can store more than one value. Multi-select fields look like the one shown in Figure 12-1. Open the drop-down list and check the option(s) that you want to categorize the contact by.

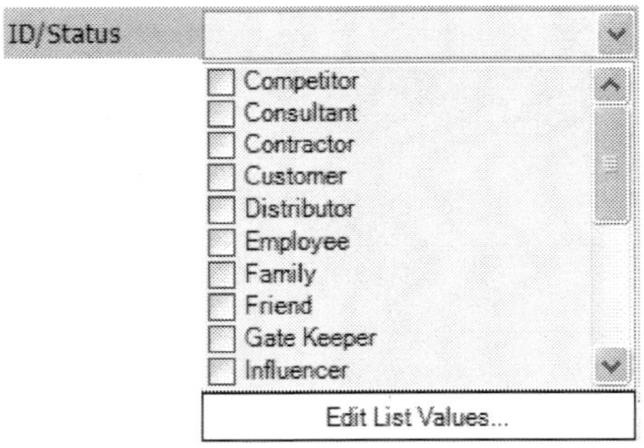

Figure 12-1 Multi-select drop-down list field

The **REFERRED BY** field shown in Figure 12-2 is used as a way to know how the contact was acquired. You could have purchased a mailing list of leads from two companies and need to track which company the lead (contact) came from.

You could also have contacts from a newsletter subscription service. How will you know how each contact was acquired if this field was left blank?

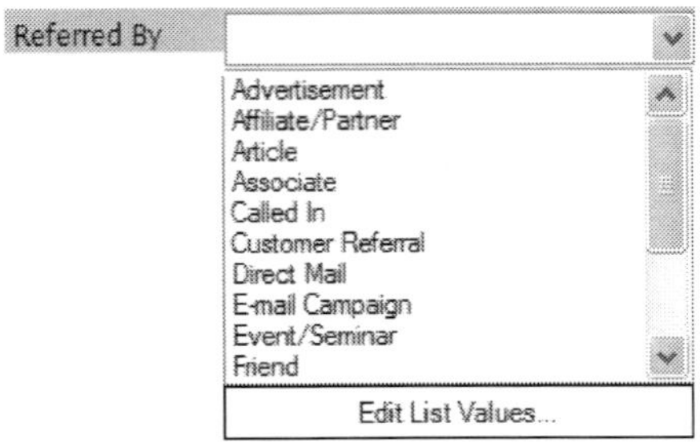

Figure 12-2 Referred By field options

Why Are Drop-Down Lists Important?

Drop-down lists provide the most used values that would be entered in a field. Drop-down lists are important because they help ensure that the data in a field is entered the same way for every record. Consistent data is especially helpful if the field will be used in queries, reports or sorting.

For example, one user types "USA" in the Country field and another user types "United States" in the Country field. When you run a query that looks for all records with "USA" in the Country field, the query will skip records that have "United States" in the field. This means that the result of the query will not contain all of the records that it should. In Lesson 2, I had you type USA in the Country field instead of selecting United States from the Country drop-down list. [See Lesson 2, Figure 2-9] If the entries in the drop-down lists do not have the types of information that you need, you can create new entries. In the next lesson you will learn how to add and delete entries in drop-down lists. [See Lesson 13, Creating and Editing Drop-Down List Fields]

ACT! has two types of drop-down lists as shown above in Figures 12-1 and 12-2. The drop-down list shown in Figure 12-1 allows more than one option to be selected. The drop-down list in Figure 12-2 only allows one option to be selected. This is the more popular type of drop-down list and the one that you are probably the most familiar with. Both types of drop-down lists can be used to select or type in the value that you want. If the value that you enter is already in the list, after typing in enough characters to make the value unique, it will automatically be filled in the field.

Drop-down lists allow you to enter information into a field without typing. You can also type the first letter of the value that you are looking for. Doing this will bring you to the first entry that matches the letter that you typed in. You do not have to open the drop-down list to select an entry if you already know what you are looking for. You can type in the first few letters.

If you enter text in a field that has a drop-down list like the City, Country, Department or Title fields, the text that you type in, may or may not be accepted. It depends on whether the **LIMIT TO LIST** option on the Define Fields dialog box is enabled for the field. This option will force the user to select an option from the list or leave the field blank. This is done to ensure accuracy in the field.

Tagging Contacts

There may be times when you need to select contacts that do not have anything in common based on the value in any field. Tagging records is used to create a manual lookup. If you have tried to create a lookup for contacts but can't find a common denominator, you can tag the records. To tag a record, enable the tag mode, then manually click on the records. After you tag the records that you need, you can create a lookup of the tagged records. With a small database like the demo database that you are using to complete the exercises in this book, manually viewing all of the records to find the ones to tag is bearable. If the database has 5,000 records, it could take a while to find the records that you need.

Exercise 12.1: Tagging Contacts

In this exercise you will tag random contact records, add a note to the records and save them as a group. It is not a requirement to group tagged records.

1. Create a group called My Tagged Record Group.

2. Open the Contact List view. Sort the contacts by state, then check the **TAG MODE** option shown in Figure 12-3.

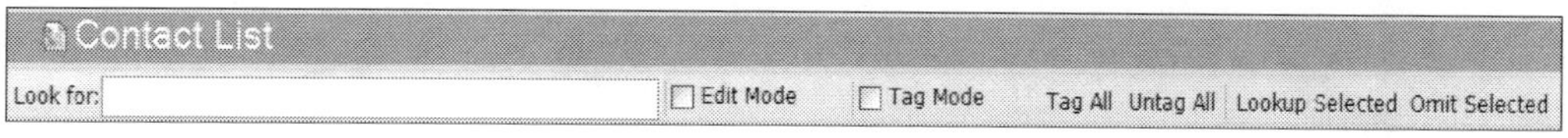

Figure 12-3 Tag options

The **LOOK FOR** field is used to search for a contact based on the field that the list is sorted on. If the Contact List is sorted on the Company field, you would enter the company name that you were looking for in this field.

The **EDIT MODE** option is used to modify records in the list view.
The **TAG MODE** option turns the tag functionality on and off.
The **TAG ALL** button will mark all of the contacts displayed in the list as tagged.
The **UNTAG ALL** button will remove the tag from all of the selected contacts.
The **LOOKUP SELECTED** button creates a lookup of the records that have been tagged.
The **OMIT SELECTED** button is used to remove the tagged contacts from the view. This option does not delete the records from the database.

> If you click on a record that you do not need to tag, click on the record again to remove the tag. When in tag mode, records that are tagged are highlighted, as shown in Figure 12-4.

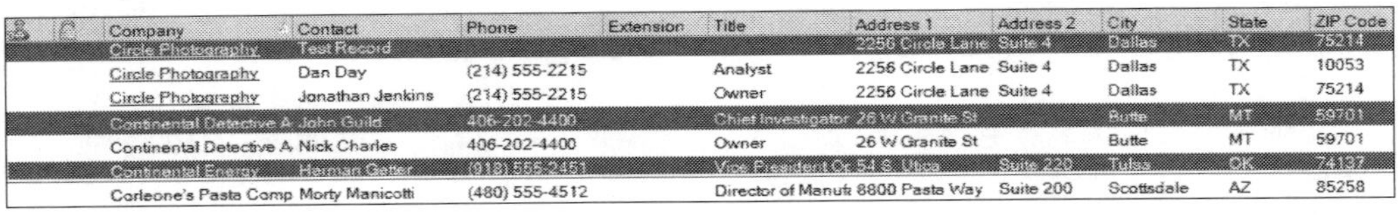

Figure 12-4 Tagged records

3. Tag the first record in the following states: AZ, CA and LA.

4. Click the **LOOKUP SELECTED** button.

At this point you could add the same note to the contact records that are tagged, create an activity that included these records, save them as a group, subgroup, company or division.

5. Click the Insert Note button on the Contact List toolbar, then type `This contact is a tagged record that is in the Tagged Record Group.`

6. Click the **GROUP/COMPANY** button on the Insert Note dialog box, then click OK on the Public Note message box.

7. Select the My Tagged Record Group and add it to the list on the right, then click OK.

8. The dialog box should have the options that are shown in Figure 12-5.

   Click OK to close the Insert Note dialog box.

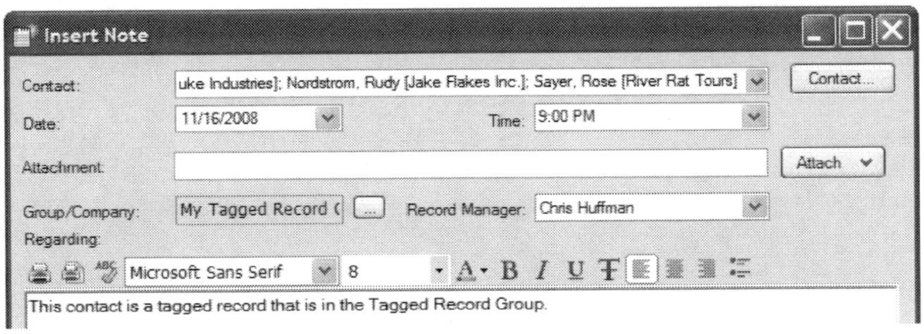

Figure 12-5 Insert Note dialog box

9. Right-click on the tagged records and select Add Contacts to group. Select the My Tagged Record Group option.

10. Click OK, then clear the Tag Mode option. Now when you need to access these records you can select the group that they are in. If you view the tagged group, you will see the three contacts.

Using The Omit Selected Option

If there are records that you do not want to view, you can remove them from the list view. Removing records from a view does not delete them from the database. Using the Omit Selected option has the same effect as creating a lookup. The difference is that the Omit Selected option does it record by record, manually. To restore the records, lookup all of the contacts.

1. Click on the first record in the Contact List view. The record should now be highlighted.

2. Click the **OMIT SELECTED** button on the toolbar. The record should not be visible in the window. You will see that the record count decreases by one.

Copying Data From One Field To Another

You may have a need to copy data from one field to another. Instead of doing this manually, record by record, you can create a lookup for the records that you want to copy the data to, then use the **COPY FIELD** command. Not creating a lookup first means that data will be copied to every record in the database. It is not a requirement to create a lookup first.

Exercise 12.2: How To Copy Data

In this exercise you will look up the Liberty Savings company and copy the data in the Title field to the User 6 field.

1. Create a lookup for the Liberty Company.

2. On the Contact Detail view, Edit ⇒ Copy Field.

3. Open the **COPY CONTENTS OF** drop-down list and select the Title field, then open the **TO** drop-down list and select the User 6 field.

4. You should have the options shown in Figure 12-6.

   Click OK.

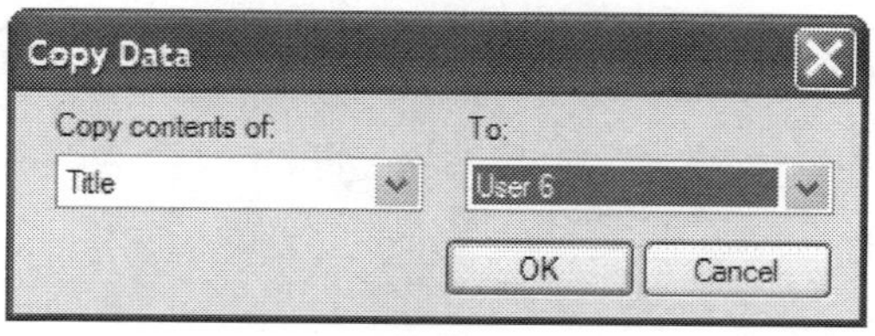

Figure 12-6 Copy Data dialog box

5. Click Yes when you see the Replace/Swap/Copy message that lets you know that all of the records in the current lookup will be modified.

   You will see the message shown in Figure 12-7. This message lets you know that the **TARGET** field (User 6) size is smaller than the **SOURCE** field (Title). If the target field is smaller, all of the data will not be copied to the target field. The data will be truncated.

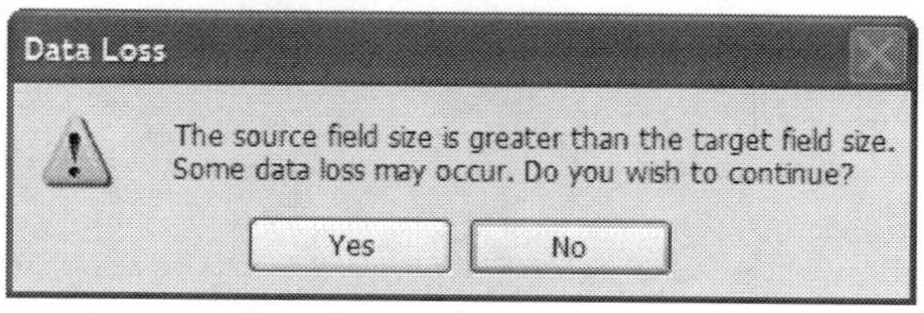

Figure 12-7 Data Loss message

6. Click Yes on the Data Loss message window. Normally you would not want to have data loss and would click No when you see the message shown above in Figure 12-7.

View The Copied Data

1. Click the Contacts button.

2. On the User Fields tab, you will see the title in the User 6 field, as shown in Figure 12-8.

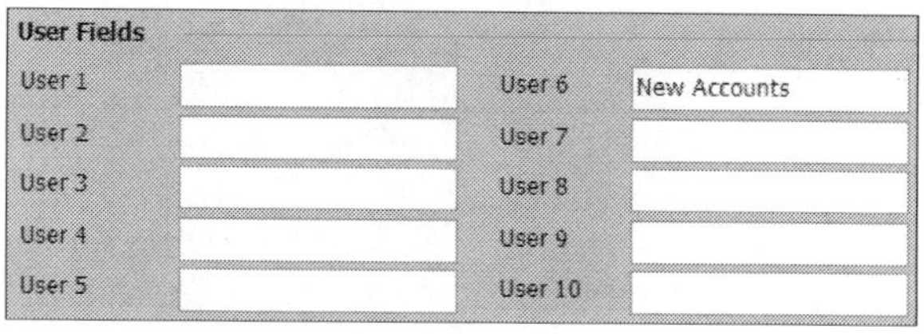

Figure 12-8 User Fields tab

Swapping Data

This command is used to swap the data in one field with data from another field. Like the Copy Field command, if the target field is smaller, all of the data will not be copied to the target field.

Exercise 12.3: How To Swap Data

In this exercise you will swap the data in the Alternate Phone field with the data in the Home Phone field.

1. Create a lookup for the city of Scottsdale. You should see six records in the Contact List view.

2. Edit ⇒ Swap Field.

3. Open the **SWAP CONTENTS OF** drop-down list and select the Alternate Phone field, then open the **WITH CONTENTS OF** drop-down list and select the Home Phone field, as shown in Figure 12-9.

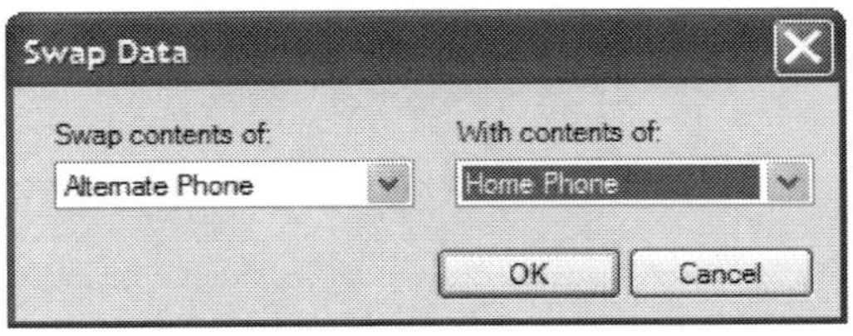

Figure 12-9 Swap Data dialog box

4. Click OK. Click Yes to modify records in the current lookup.

View The Swapped Data

1. Click the Contacts button, then click on the Personal Info tab.

2. Scroll through the records.

You will not see a phone number in the Home Phone field because none of the records had data in the Alternate Phone field. If any of the records had data in the Alternate Phone field, it would have been swapped (moved) to the Home Phone field.

It is recommended that you back up the database before using the **COPY FIELD** or **SWAP FIELD** command.

What Are Supplemental Files?

Supplemental files are files that ACT! uses that are not saved in the database (.adf) file. The database file only stores the data that you see in the views. Examples of supplemental files include attachments, templates, reports and layouts. Many of these supplemental files are installed when you installed the software. ACT! has two supplemental file types, as discussed below.

① **Database** This file type includes the templates, reports and layout files that you see when you first open ACT!. These files are only available when ACT! is open. They are stored in folders. The default main folder name is **Name of database-database files**. Under this folder are folders for each type of file, as shown in Figure 12-10. If you copy a database, these files are also copied. If the ACT! database is stored on a server, more than likely, the database supplemental files are stored on the same server.

② **Personal** This file type includes files that are not associated to records in the database. Personal files are not backed up when a database is backed up. If you create a file that you do not want to share with other users of the database, save it in your personal supplemental folder. The other option is to create a folder outside of the default ACT! folders and save files that you do not want to share in that folder. An example of this would be the folder that you created for this book. The default folders that ACT! creates for supplemental personal files are stored in the following locations on your hard drive:

C:\Documents and Settings\YourUserName\My Documents\ACT\ACT for Windows 11
C:\Documents and Settings\YourUserName\Application Data\ACT\ACT for Windows 11

After looking at the long paths above, I hope that you understand why I had you create the ACT 2009 Book folder at the root of the C drive, because it is easier to navigate to.

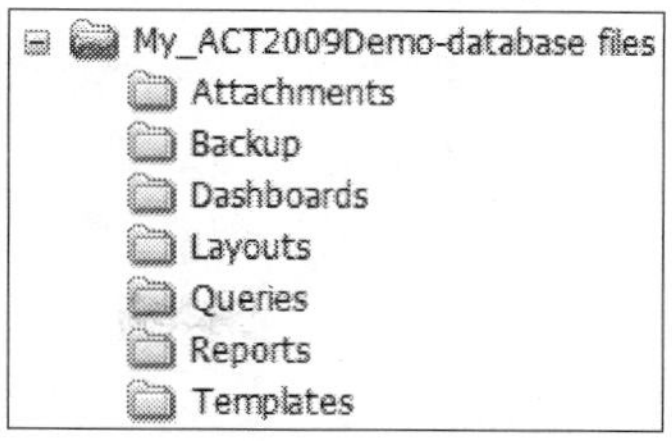

Figure 12-10 Database folders

What Are Secondary Contacts And Why Should I Use Them?

Secondary contacts are contacts that are associated to a primary contact in the database. Examples of secondary contacts include an alternate contact if the primary contact is unavailable or a primary contacts assistant. You can also create secondary contacts to list the primary contacts spouse and children.

It would be helpful if the Secondary Contacts tab would automatically change colors as soon as one secondary contact was added to a primary contact record. That would make it easier to know if there were any secondary contacts associated to the primary contact.

Exercise 12.4: Entering Information On The Secondary Contacts Tab

You can create a separate secondary contact record for the contacts children, assistant and spouse. Keep the following two things in mind when creating secondary contact records.

① Secondary contact records cannot be used in a mail merge or email campaign.
② Activity, note, opportunity and history records cannot be created or associated with secondary contact records.

1. Lookup the contact Sarah Baker.

2. On the **SECONDARY CONTACTS** tab shown in Figure 12-11, click the **NEW SECONDARY CONTACT** button.

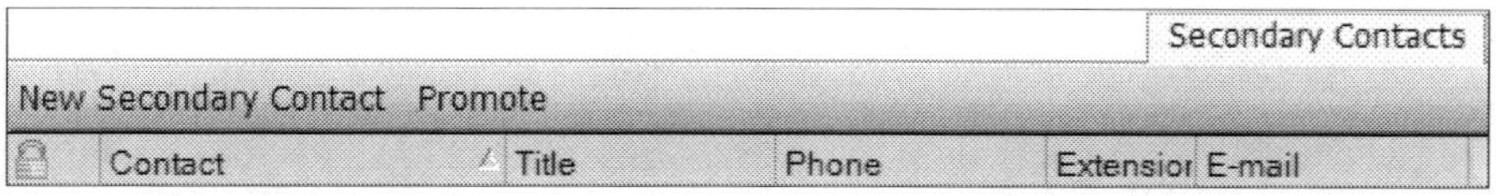

Figure 12-11 Secondary Contacts tab

3. Enter the information in Table 12-1 in the appropriate fields on the Secondary Contacts dialog box.

   If you have access to the Internet, you could click on the link in the Web site field and the web site would open in your browser.

Field	Type This
Contact	Terry London
Title	Purchasing Agent
E-mail	tlondon@xcapri.com
Web site	www.xcapri.com

Table 12-1 Secondary contact information

4. The dialog box should look like the one shown in Figure 12-12.

   Click OK.

   You should see the contact on the Secondary Contacts tab of the contact record.

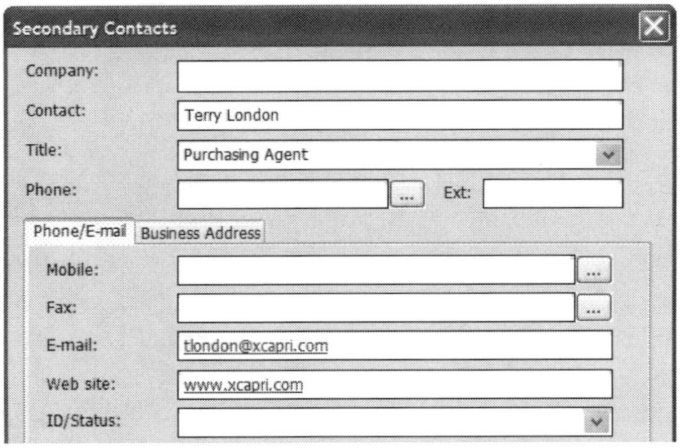

Figure 12-12 Secondary contact information

Exercise 12.5: Promoting A Secondary Contact

There may be a time when a secondary contact needs to become a primary contact. Instead of creating a new primary contact record for the secondary contact (which would also leave the secondary contact record in place if you did not delete it) you can promote the secondary contact to a primary contact by following the steps below. When a secondary contact is promoted, it is automatically deleted from the primary contact record.

1. Add a secondary contact record to the contact John Doe by clicking the **NEW SECONDARY CONTACT** button on the Secondary Contacts tab.

   Add the secondary contact information shown in Figure 12-13.

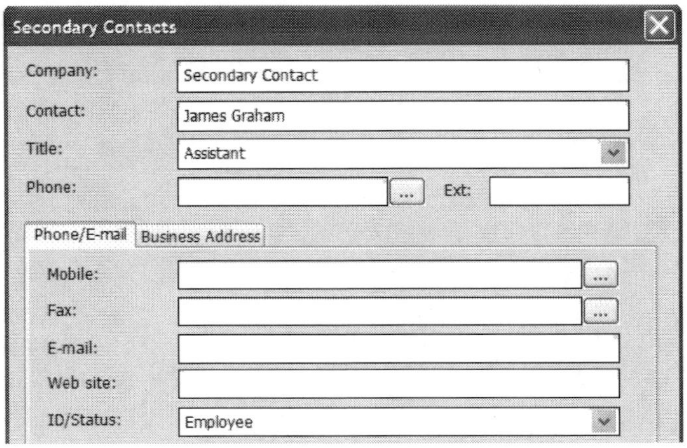

Figure 12-13 Secondary contact to be promoted

2. Click on the secondary contact that you want to promote. In this exercise select the secondary contact record that you just created, then click the **PROMOTE** button shown earlier in Figure 12-11. You will see the dialog box shown in Figure 12-14.

   The **DUPLICATE DATA** option will copy data from the primary contacts record (like the company name and address fields) to the record that you are promoting.

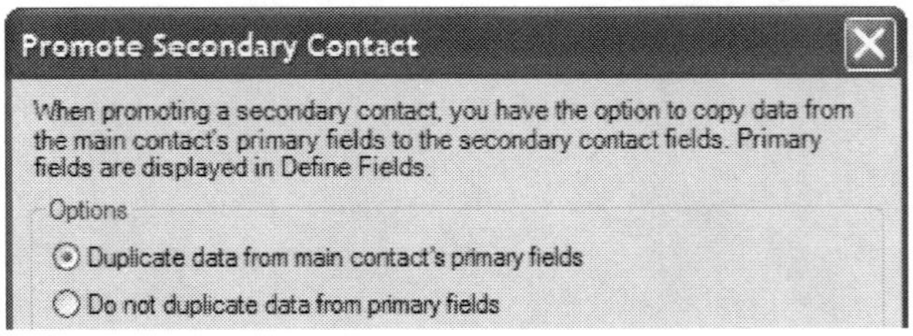

Figure 12-14 Promote Secondary Contact dialog box

3. For this exercise select the Duplicate data option, then click OK. You will see that the record is no longer on the Secondary Contacts tab.

Deleting A Secondary Contact

If a secondary contact should no longer be associated to the primary contact and you currently do not have a replacement contact, you should delete the secondary contact by following the steps below. For now you can just read the steps to become familiar with the process.

1. Right-click on the secondary contact that you want to delete, then select **DELETE SECONDARY CONTACT**.

2. Click Yes to permanently delete the secondary contact.

Notes And History Tabs

You have learned a little about these tabs and what types of data they have. In this lesson you will learn more about these tabs. You will see that they have a lot in common.

Notes Tab

The Notes tab contains details including business and personal information about contacts, companies and groups. The goal of entering notes is to build a profile of your relationship with the contact, company or group. Notes can be edited unless the **ALLOW NOTES EDITING** option is not enabled. [See Lesson 1, General Tab Preferences]

The Notes tab may be under utilized because many people are use to writing messages on a note pad or on a loose piece of paper or worse, think that they will remember details of a phone call or meeting. Days later when they need this information they cannot find the piece of paper that it was written on or they mentally draw a blank. I fall into the category of not being able to find the envelope that I wrote the information on. If you start off using the Notes tab when you first start using ACT!, the easier it will be to continue the good habit.

Whether you think that you are going to use ACT! daily or not, it may help if you open ACT! when you first turn your computer on. What I do is open the Contact List view and sort it by last name, then when I need to add a note, I do not have to wait to open ACT! and find the contact record. By the time I waited for ACT! to open, I would forget what I wanted to put in the note <smile>.

Attaching A Document To An Existing Note

In Lesson 2 you learned how to add an attachment to contact records and how to attach a document on the Documents tab. In Lesson 5 you learned how to attach a document to a group record. Now you will learn how to attach a document to an existing note. The process is the same when you are first creating a note. You can read the steps below to become familiar with the process.

1. Double-click on the note on the Notes tab that you want to attach a document to.

2. Click the **ATTACH** button, then select File on the Edit Note dialog box.

3. Double-click on the file that you want to attach, then click OK to close the Edit Note dialog box.

How To Copy A Note From One Contact Record To Another

If you attach a note to a contact record and want to attach it to a different contact record, you can, by following the steps below.

1. On the Notes tab, click on the note that you want to copy, then press **CTRL** + **C**.

2. Click on the Notes tab of the contact record that you want to copy the note to, then press **CTRL** + **V**.

Editing A Shared Note

If you edit a note that is shared, you will see the dialog box shown in Figure 12-15, when you click OK after editing the note.

The options on this dialog box are to save the changes for all contacts that are associated with the note or to create a new note for the contact record that you opened the note from, to edit. You can try this by editing the note with green text, that you created in Lesson 2 for George, Mary and Peter Bailey.

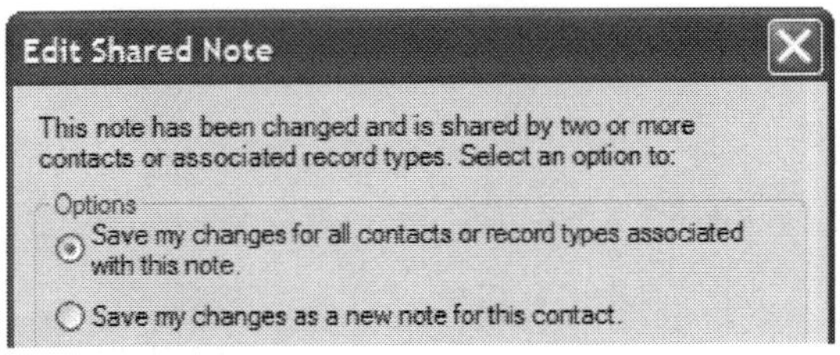

Figure 12-15 Edit Shared Note dialog box

Filtering Notes

Over time, contact, company or group records can accumulate a lot of notes. While they can be sorted, it may be more effective to filter the notes. If you right-click in the detail section of the Notes tab on the Contact or Company Detail view and select **FILTER NOTES**, you will see the dialog box shown in Figure 12-16 on the Contact Detail view and Figure 12-17 on the Company Detail view.

While filters narrow and reduce the number of records displayed (in this case notes), filters can be tricky and give the appearance that records are lost. If you cannot find records, check the filter options on the tabs and change them to display all of the records.

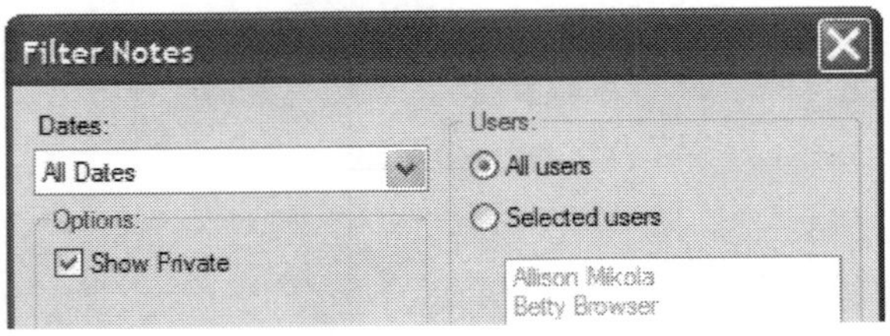

Figure 12-16 Contact Filter Notes dialog box

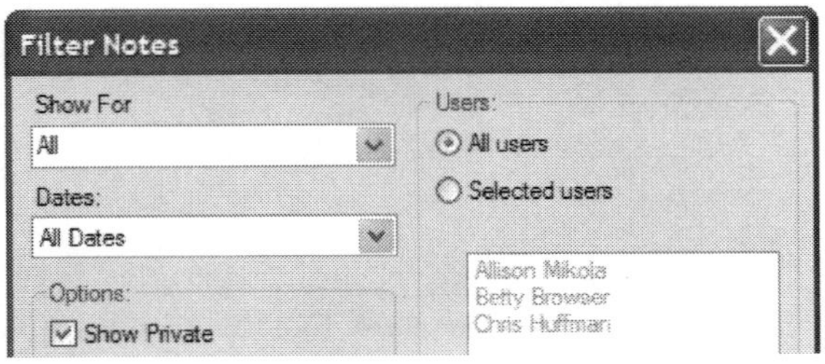

Figure 12-17 Company Filter Notes dialog box

History Tab

You have already viewed the records on the History tab for the My Record. History records display changes that you have made. [See Lesson 3, View The My Record] The History tab picks up where the Notes tab leaves off. The entries on the History tab are a chronological recap of the communication and events for contacts, companies and groups. The majority of entries on this tab come from other tabs, but you can manually create a History record.

Some entries on the History tab are created automatically when you delete a contact, when the Last Results field is updated, create a mail merge, change the value in the ID/Status field or complete an activity. The date and time are automatically added to each entry that is added to the History tab.

You can add an entry to the History tab from any detail view by right-clicking in the detail section of the History tab and selecting **RECORD HISTORY** on the shortcut menu shown in Figure 12-18. You will see the dialog box shown in Figure 12-19. It looks similar to the Schedule Activity dialog box. You can also create a history record from the list views. The **FOLLOW-UP** button opens the Schedule Activity dialog box.

Figure 12-18 History tab shortcut menu

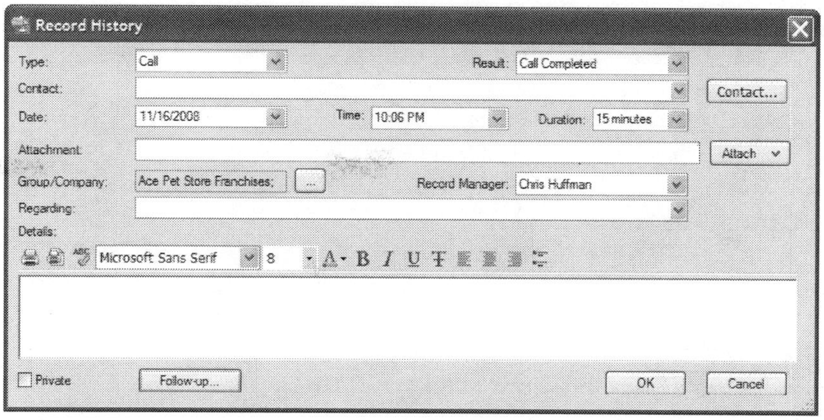

Figure 12-19 Record History dialog box

Automatic Additions To The History Tab

As you just learned, you can manually add records to the History tab. By default, ACT! has designated the ID/Status and Last Results fields as history fields when you create a new database. When the data in a history field is changed, a record is automatically created and added to the History tab. In the next lesson you will learn how to designate a fields as a history field. [See Lesson 13, Field Behavior Options]

Finding Records On The History Tab

At the top of the History tab shown in Figure 12-20, there are options that you can use to find specific records as discussed below.

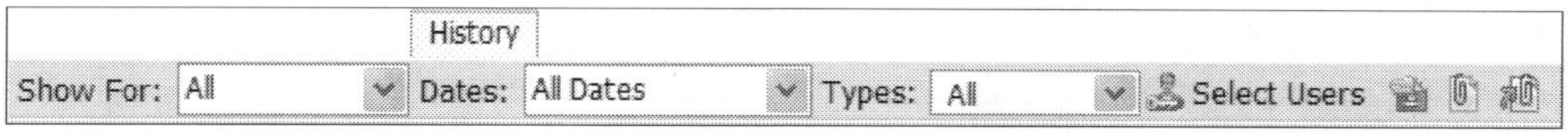

Figure 12-20 History tab

The Dates Field

The options in this drop-down list are used to select the date range for the records that you want to view on the History tab.

As time goes on, you will have more and more entries on the History tab, but you may not want to see all of them all the time. You can reduce the number of records displayed by selecting a date range. You can also create a **CUSTOM** date range to select history records, as shown in Figure 12-21.

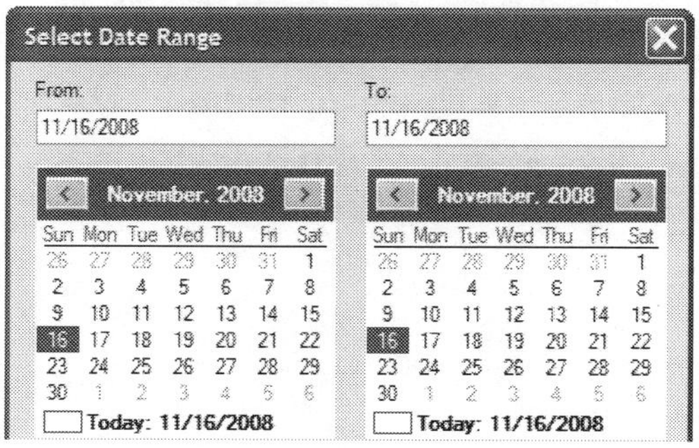

Figure 12-21 Select Date Range dialog box

History Record Types

There are three types of history records that you can view, as discussed below.

Figure 12-22 shows the history type options.

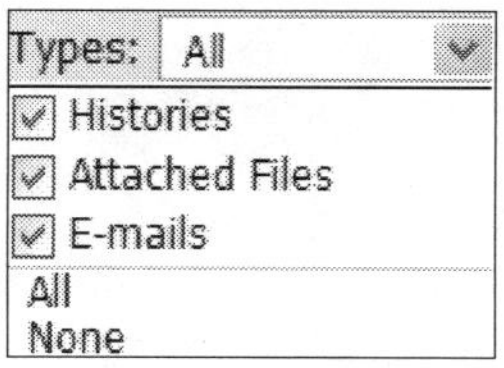

Figure 12-22 History record options

① **Histories** This type of record is created when you change the value in a field that has been designated to automatically have a history record created.
② **Attached Files** This type of history record is created when a document is attached to a contact, company or group record.
③ **E-mails** This type of history record can be created when you send an email message.

Select Users Button

This option is useful if more than one person is using the database.

The dialog box shown in Figure 12-23 is used to you select which users entries you want to view on the History tab.

To select multiple users calendars to view, select the first user then press and hold down the Shift key and click on the other users names. The maximum number of users that you can select is 10.

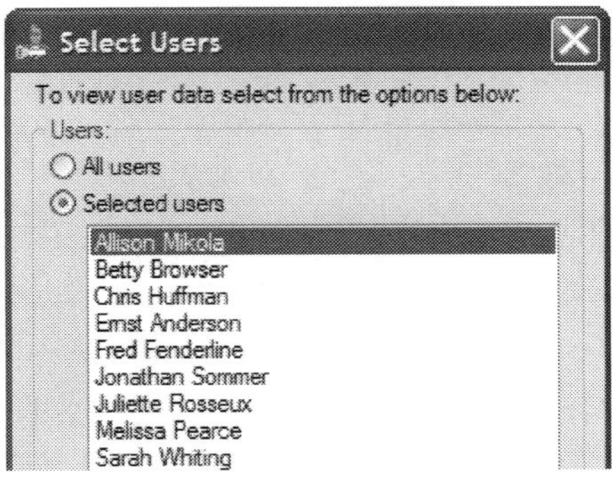

Figure 12-23 Select Users dialog box

Using The Record History Tool

This tool is used to create a history record for tasks that you complete that do not have a scheduled activity. This is helpful when you need to remember something like an email or phone conversation that you had with a contact that was not scheduled. History records can also be created from the company and group views.

How To Open The Record History Tool

Earlier in Figure 12-19 you saw the Record History dialog box. You can open this dialog box by doing any of the following:

① Pressing the Ctrl + H keys.
② On the History tab of the Contact Detail view, right-click and select Record History.
③ From either contact view, Contacts ⇒ Record History.

How To Create A History Record For Multiple Contacts

Just like you can schedule one activity with multiple contacts, you can create a history record for multiple contacts. There are two ways to accomplish this, as discussed below.

① Open the Record History dialog box, click the Contact button, then select the contacts that you want to create the history record for.
② Tag the records that you want to create the history record for, then open the Record History dialog box. Earlier in this lesson you learned how to tag records.

How To Edit History Records

After viewing the history records that ACT! creates, you may decide that they need more information or that the information needs to be changed.

If this is the case, double-click on the history record that you want to change. You will see the dialog box shown in Figure 12-24. Make the changes that are needed, then click OK.

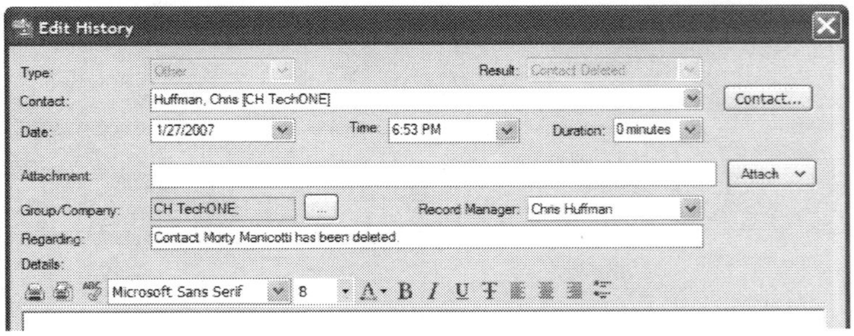

Figure 12-24 Edit History dialog box

How To Edit A History Record Associated With Multiple Contacts

After you create a history record that is associated with multiple contacts you may have the need to change it.

After you make the change, you will see the dialog box shown in Figure 12-25. These options are used to select whether to save the change for the current contact or for all contacts associated with the history record.

Select the option that fits your need, then click OK. These options are similar to the options on the Edit Shared Note dialog box shown earlier in Figure 12-15.

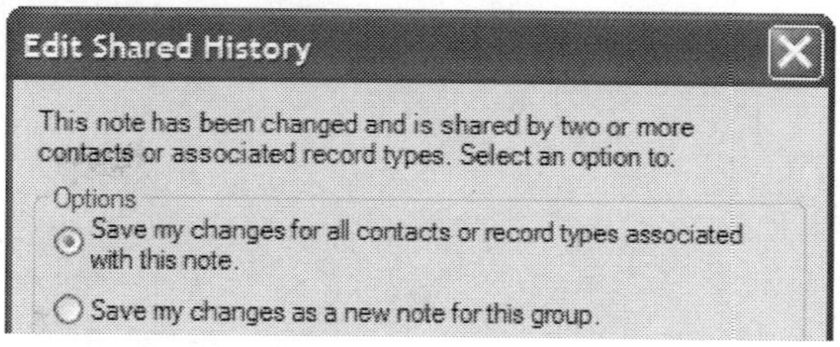

Figure 12-25 Edit Shared History dialog box

Preventing History Records From Being Deleted

You can delete history records. If you are the only person that is using the database, it may not be necessary to prevent history records from being deleted. If other people will be using the database, you may want to consider preventing history records from being deleted by clearing the **ALLOW HISTORY EDITING** option on the General tab of the Preferences dialog box.

The Documents Tab

If you will attach a lot of documents to contact, company and group records, this section will give you a better understanding of the features that the Documents tab offers. The Documents tab is the repository for attachments in the database. Unless an attachment is marked as private, all users of the database will have access it. The attachments are usually stored in the Attachments folder for the database.

Figure 12-26 shows the Documents tab with several types of attached documents. The first column displays the icon for the file type. Sometimes the icons are not correct. An example is the last document listed in Figure 12-26. It has a generic icon. The file was created in a software package called Crystal Reports, which it seems ACT! recognizes. The **FILE TYPE** column will automatically be filled in as long as the file type is one that ACT! recognizes. Table 12-2 explains the buttons on the Documents tab.

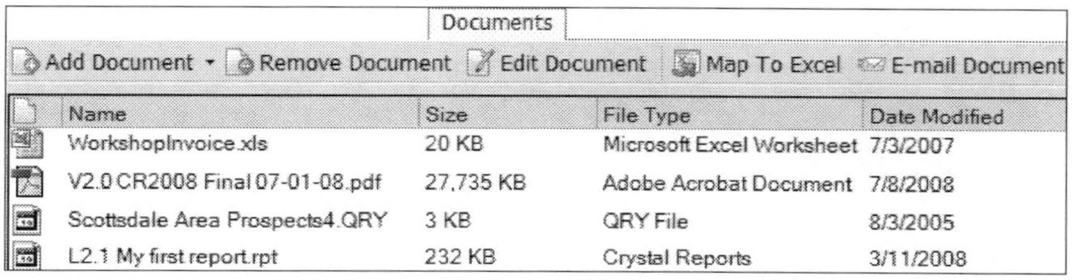

Figure 12-26 Documents tab

Button	Description
Add Document	Attach a document. If the **FILE** option is selected, remote database users can access the document.
Remove Document	Delete the selected attachment. This action deletes the document from the Documents folder. (1)
Edit Document	Opens the attached document so that you can view or edit it. To view or edit the document, you have to have the software that the document was created in installed on your computer. For example, in Figure 12-26 above the fourth document was created in Crystal Reports. If you do not have this software installed, you will not be able to open this document.
Map To Excel	Map fields in the database to fields in an Excel spreadsheet. You will learn how to do this later in this lesson.
E-mail Document	Used to send the selected file via email.

Table 12-2 Documents tab buttons explained

(1) If you do not have another copy of the document on your hard drive, the file cannot be retrieved after it is deleted. Unlike many Windows applications, deleting files from ACT! does not send the deleted files to the Recycle Bin.

You can also right-click on the document (on the Documents tab) that you want to delete and select **REMOVE DOCUMENT**, as shown in Figure 12-27. When you select this option you will see the message shown in Figure 12-28. Click Yes to delete the document. You can also delete an attachment from the History tab by right-clicking on the file and selecting **DELETE SELECTED**, as shown earlier in Figure 12-18.

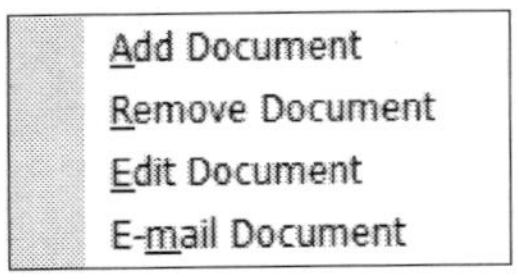

Figure 12-27 Documents tab shortcut menu options

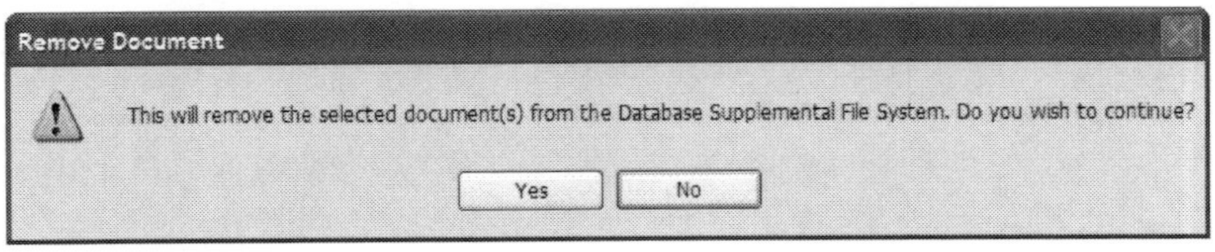

Figure 12-28 Remove Document message

Record Creation Options

The options shown in Figure 12-29 are used to make contact, company, groups and opportunity records public or private by default.

If you know that one of these types of records needs to be private, most or all of the time, select the **PRIVATE** option on this dialog box.

Figure 12-29 Record Creation Options dialog box

Internet Services

As the name suggests, these tools are used to access the Internet. The Internet has become an important part of many businesses. ACT! has several Internet related tools that you may find useful, as shown in Figure 12-30.

View ⇒ Internet Services, displays the menu options shown at the bottom of Figure 12-30. To use these tools you need to have Internet Explorer version 6.0 or higher installed.

The first eight options on the Internet Services submenu will take you to various pages on the ACT! web site.

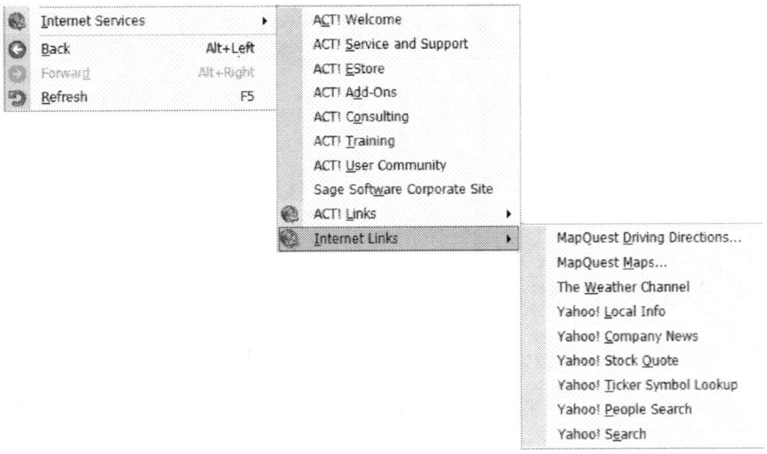

Figure 12-30 Internet Services options

The **ACT! LINKS** submenu options are used to manage the web site links that you save in ACT!. The main reason to save links here is if you have a need to use them in ACT!.

The **INTERNET LINKS** submenu options are web sites that you can use for research.

The **MAPQUEST DRIVING DIRECTIONS** option will open the dialog box shown in Figure 12-31. This tool does not display the destination of a company record.

By default, the **ORIGIN** contact fields are your information.

The **DESTINATION** contact fields are for the contact record that was displayed or selected before this dialog box was opened.

You can open the Contact drop-down list and select a different contact.

The **DRIVE IT!** button will open the MapQuest web site and fill in some of the address information so that you can get directions.

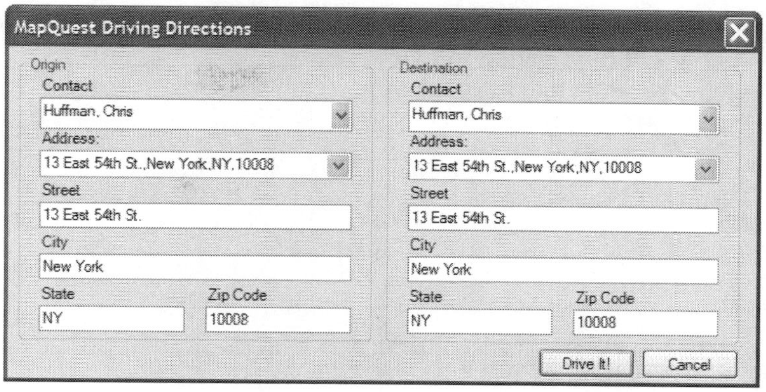

Figure 12-31 MapQuest Driving Directions dialog box

Exercise 12.6: Using The Attach Web Pages To ACT! Contact Option

This option is added to the Tools menu in Internet Explorer when ACT! is installed. Attaching a web page to a contact in ACT! is different then book marking or saving a link in your web browsers Favorites folder. When you save a link to a web page in your Favorites folder and go back to it later, you will see the current version of the web page, which could be different if it was changed (or worst, deleted) since the last time that you viewed it.

Attaching a web page in ACT! saves the actual web page as it is right now, which means that three years from now you are still able to see the exact page that you saved today. You do not have to be connected to the Internet to view web pages that are attached to a contact in ACT!. The steps below will show you how to use this feature to attach a web page to all contacts in a group.

If you have pop-up blocker software turned on, you may have to disable it to complete this exercise.

1. Open the web page in Internet Explorer that you want to attach to a contact record. For this exercise, you can use www.tolana.com.

2. Tools ⇒ Attach Web page to ACT! contact, as illustrated in Figure 12-32.

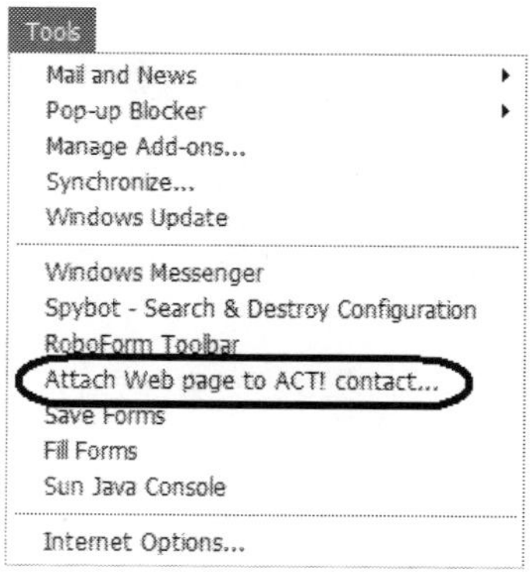

Figure 12-32 Internet Explorer menu options

3. Open the **SELECT FROM** drop-down list and select Groups.

4. Open the drop-down list to the right and select the Sales Reps group.

   Add all of the contacts in the left column to the **SELECTED CONTACTS** list, as shown in Figure 12-33.

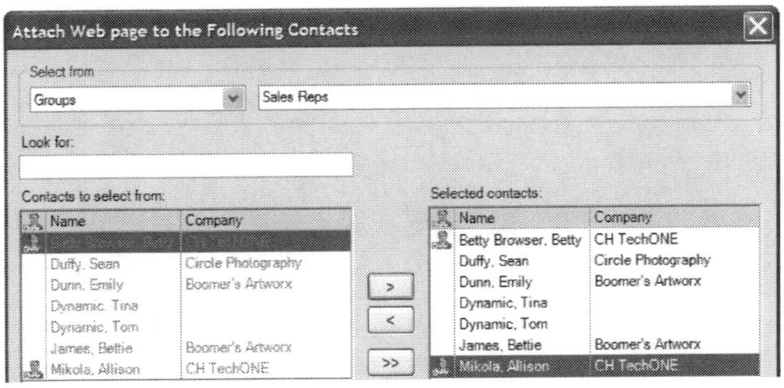

Figure 12-33 Attach Web page to the Following Contacts dialog box

5. Click OK, then close the browser.

6. Select one of the contacts in the Sales Reps group shown above in Figure 12-33, then click on the History tab.

Near the top of the History tab you should see an entry with "Web Attachment" in the **REGARDING & DETAILS** column, as shown in Figure 12-34. The entry will have today's date.

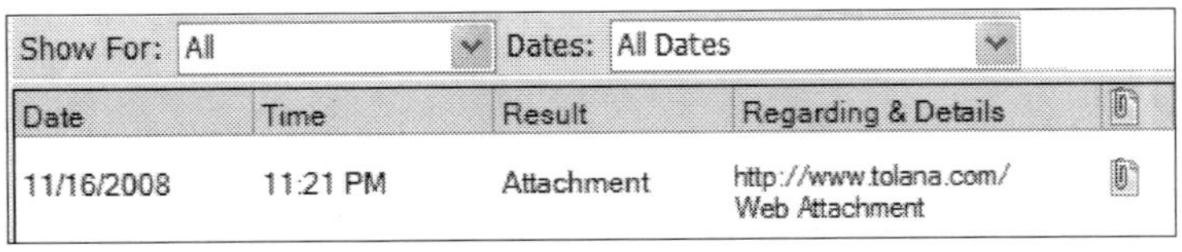

Figure 12-34 Web page attachment illustrated

7. If you click on the paper clip icon in the **ATTACHMENTS** column (to the far right of Figure 12-34 above), your browser will open the web page. Close the browser.

Exercise 12.7: Managing Links

In the previous exercise you attached a web page to contact records. If you think that you will have a need to reference the same web page more than once, you should keep the link in the Manage Internet Links dialog box.

1. View ⇒ Internet Services ⇒ ACT! Links ⇒ Manage Links.

2. Click the Add button, then type the link name and web site address shown in Figure 12-35.

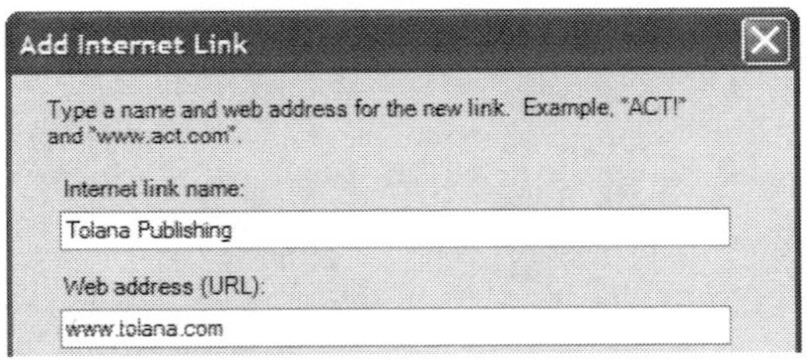

Figure 12-35 Add Internet Link dialog box

3. Click OK. You will see the link that you just created in the dialog box shown in Figure 12-36.

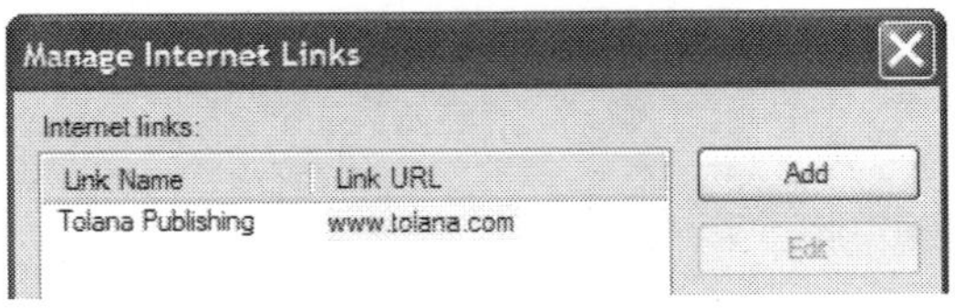

Figure 12-36 Manage Internet Links dialog box

4. Click the Close button when you are finished.

Exporting Data To Excel

If you need to work with contact, company or group data in a spreadsheet, you can export the data to Excel. Exporting contact data is similar to exporting opportunity data that you learned about in Lesson 10.

> The **EXPORT TO EXCEL** option is only available on the Contact, Company, Group or Opportunity list views. To view the exported records, you need to have Excel installed. The only columns that are exported are the ones that are visible. If you want to export data that is not currently visible, add the column(s) of data that you want to export to the view before exporting data, then remove the column(s) that you added if you no longer need them in the view, once the export is completed.

Exercise 12.8: Export Contact Data To Excel

In this exercise you will export all of the contacts for a specific company to Excel.

1. Create a lookup for the `CH TechONE` company. Nine records should be displayed.

2. Click the **EXPORT TO EXCEL** button on the toolbar. The records from the lookup will be exported to Excel, which will automatically open and display the records, as shown in Figure 12-37. When you are finished viewing the spreadsheet close Excel.

	A	B	C	D	E	F	G	H	I	J	K	L
1	**Contact Type**	**Private**	**Company**	**Contact**	**Phone**	**Extension**	**Title**	**Address 1**	**Address 2**	**City**	**State**	**ZIP Code**
2	User	Public	CH TechONE	Ernst Anderson	(212) 555-2485		Vice President of US Operations	13 East 54th St.	Suite 300	New York	NY	10008
3	User	Public	CH TechONE	Betty Browser	(212) 555-2485		Sales Representative	13 East 54th St.	Suite 300	New York	NY	10008
4	Contact	Public	CH TechONE	Jane Chan	(212) 555-4447		Controller	13 East 54th St.	Suite 300	New York	NY	10008
5	User	Public	CH TechONE	Chris Huffman	(212) 555-2485		CEO	13 East 54th St.	Suite 300	New York	NY	10008
6	User	Public	CH TechONE	Alison Mikola	(212) 555-2485		Sales Representative	13 East 54th St.	Suite 300	New York	NY	10008
7	User	Public	CH TechONE	Melissa Pearce	(212) 555-2485		Assistant	13 East 54th St.	Suite 300	New York	NY	10008
8	User	Public	CH TechONE	Juliette Rosseux	(212) 555-2485		CFO	13 East 54th St.	Suite 300	New York	NY	10008
9	User	Public	CH TechONE	Jonathan Sommer	(212) 555-2485		Vice President AsiaPac Operations	13 East 54th St.	Suite 300	New York	NY	10008
10	User	Public	CH TechONE	Sarah Whiting	(212) 555-2485		Vice President European Operations	13 East 54th St.	Suite 300	New York	NY	10008

Figure 12-37 Exported contact records in Excel

Exercise 12.9: Mapping ACT! Fields To An Excel Spreadsheet

This tool is used to update fields in an Excel spreadsheet if they are mapped to fields in an ACT! database. Contact, company and group fields can be mapped to fields in a spreadsheet. In order for mapping to occur and for fields to be updated, the spreadsheet has to be attached on the Documents tab.

The ACT! menu in Excel is used to map fields from the database to an Excel worksheet. [See Lesson 7, The ACT! Menu In Word And Excel]

Attach The Spreadsheet To The Documents Tab

The ACT! database and Excel have to be open to complete this exercise.

1. Lookup the contact Tim Dynamic.

2. Display the Documents tab for the contact.

3. Click the **ADD DOCUMENT** button and select File, then double-click on the Map ACT! Fields To Spreadsheet file.

Map The Fields In ACT! To The Spreadsheet

The fields that are selected to be mapped in the spreadsheet are the ones that need to be updated when data is changed in the ACT! database.

1. Right-click on the spreadsheet on the Documents tab and select **EDIT DOCUMENT**.

   You should see the spreadsheet shown in Figure 12-38.

	A	B	C	D
1	Company	Contact	Title	E-mail
2		Tim Dynamic	Sales Manager	
3		Tina Dynamic	Sales Representative	
4		Tom Dynamic	Sales Representative	

Figure 12-38 Spreadsheet to map the fields to

2. Click on the Sales Manager title in the spreadsheet. Open the ACT! Menu in Excel, then select **MAP TO CONTACT**.

3. Scroll down the list of fields and click on the Title field, as highlighted in Figure 12-39, then click the **ADD** button.

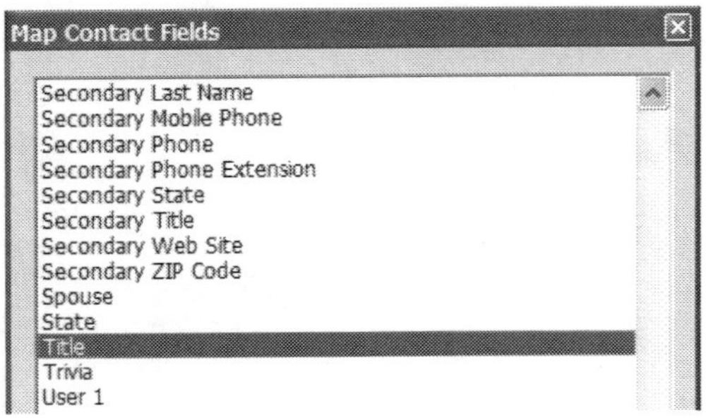

Figure 12-39 Map Contact Fields dialog box

4. Repeat the steps above for each field that you want to map.

   For now, just map the E-mail field. The spreadsheet should look like the one shown in Figure 12-40.

	A	B	C	D
1	Company	Contact	Title	E-mail
2		Tim Dynamic	<Title>	<E-mail>
3		Tina Dynamic	Sales Representative	
4		Tom Dynamic	Sales Representative	

Figure 12-40 Spreadsheet with fields mapped

5. Click the Close button. Save the changes to the spreadsheet and close it.

Test The Field Mapping

The way to test if the fields in the spreadsheet are mapped correctly is to add or change data in ACT! and see if the changes appear in the spreadsheet.

1. Type `testmap@email.com` in the E-mail field for Tim and Tina Dynamic.

2. On the Documents tab select the spreadsheet, then click the **MAP TO EXCEL** button.

When the spreadsheet opens you will see that the E-mail field has been updated for Tim Dynamic, but not Tina. That is because Tina's record in the spreadsheet was not mapped to a field in the ACT! database.

Sharing A Database Tip

If you create a database and need to let other people use it, you have to share the database. In order to share a database it should be on a network or on a shared drive.

> When designing a database, one thing that you need to consider is whether or not the database will be used by more than one person. If so, when the database is created, you should put it on a server or shared drive. Creating a database on your computers hard drive and then trying to move it, is more work then it is worth. You would have to back up and restore the database and all associated files to put them on the server.

Using The Timer

ACT! comes with a timer that you can use to record a history item, time an unscheduled activity or to time and clear a scheduled activity. You can also use it to record how long a phone call is. I am not sure that this feature is important to know, but since it exists, I decided to cover it. The steps below will show you how to use the timer to clear a scheduled activity (task).

1. Click on the Task List view. Click on the 6/12/2009 scheduled task for David Yale.

2. Tools ⇒ Timer.

3. Click the Start button illustrated in Figure 12-41, then move the timer away from the middle of the screen.

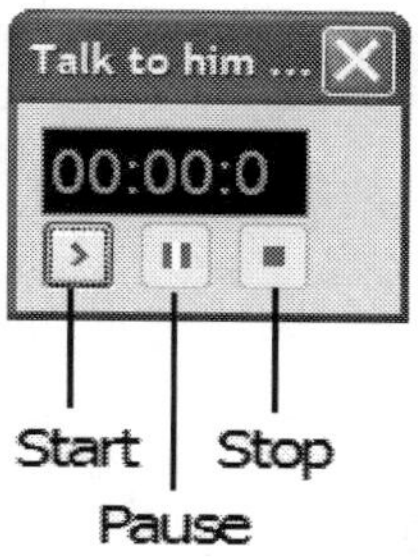

Figure 12-41 ACT! Timer

4. Click in the check box in the first column (It is called Cleared.) for the task for David Yale.

   You will see the dialog box shown in Figure 12-42.

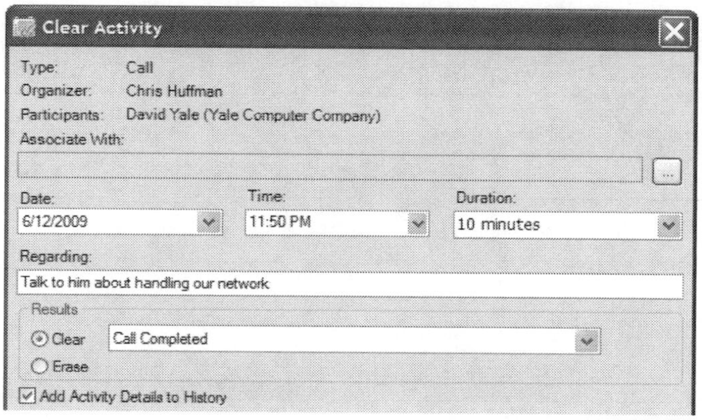

Figure 12-42 Clear Activity dialog box

5. Type `Testing the timer` in the Note field, then click OK. The task will be moved to the History tab.

6. Click the Stop button on the timer. You will see the message shown in Figure 12-43.

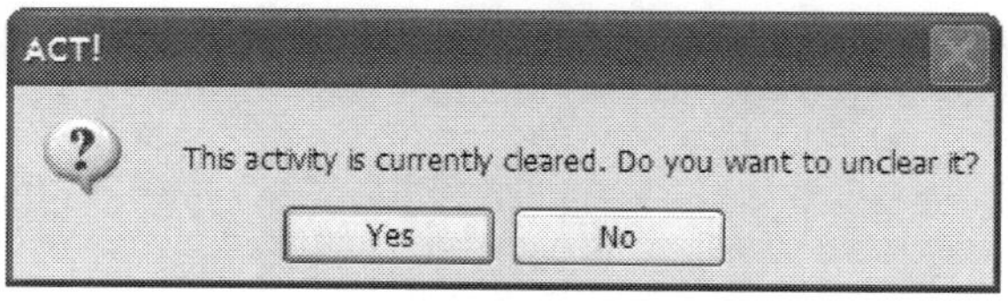

Figure 12-43 Clear activity message

7. For now, click Yes to restore the activity. The activity will reappear on the Task List.

How To Uninstall ACT!

If you decide that you do not want to use ACT! and want to uninstall (delete) it, follow the steps below.

Use The Add Or Remove Programs Utility

1. Open the Control Panel in Windows.

2. Double-click on the Add or Remove Programs icon. Scroll down the list of installed programs and click on the ACT! option.

3. Click the **CHANGE/REMOVE** button, illustrated in Figure 12-44, then follow the instructions to remove the software.

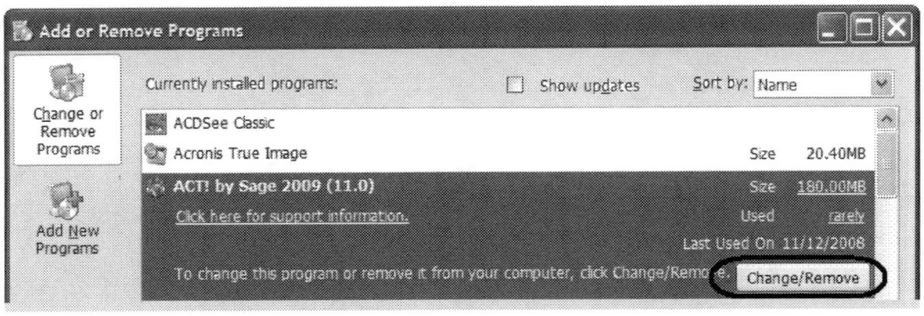

Figure 12-44 Add or Remove Programs dialog box

> Prior versions of ACT! had a built-in uninstall tool as shown in Figure 12-45. I do not know why it was removed. Start button ⇒ Programs (or All Programs) ⇒ ACT! by Sage ⇒ Uninstall.

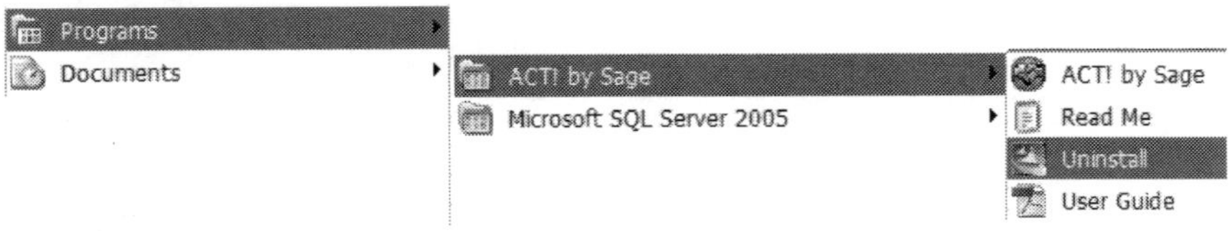

Figure 12-45 Uninstall menu options

Removing All Traces Of ACT!

In the previous section you learned how to uninstall ACT!. I think that it is important to note that using the Add or Remove Programs Utility does not remove all traces of the software from your hard drive. This means that ACT! files and folders are still on your hard drive. The same is true for the uninstall utility, like the one you saw above in Figure 12-45, that comes with some software.

For reasons that I do not understand, most software uninstall tools do not remove everything. The three places on your hard drive that you will probably still find ACT! folders or files or any software that you uninstall for that matter, are in the following locations. The path to the folders are at the top of the figure. You can delete the files, folders and registry keys shown in the figures below.

① Documents and Settings folder. Figure 12-46 shows the folders and files.
② Program Files folder. Figure 12-47 shows the folders and files.
③ The registry. Figures 12-40 to 12-50 show the **ACT! REGISTRY KEYS**.

> You should have a good understanding of the registry before making changes to it. If you make a mistake, you could cause Windows to not work properly. If you decide to modify the registry, you should make a back up copy of it first.

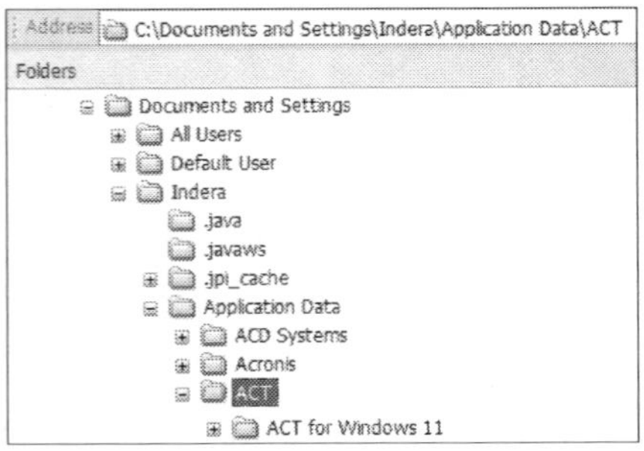

Figure 12-46 Documents and Settings folder

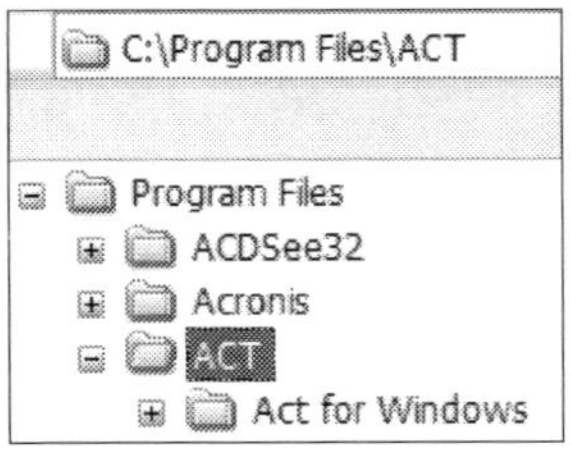

Figure 12-47 Program Files folder

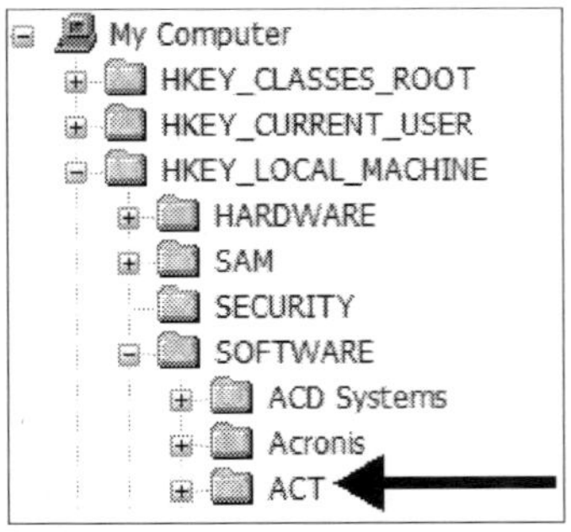

Figure 12-48 HKEY_LOCAL_MACHINE registry key

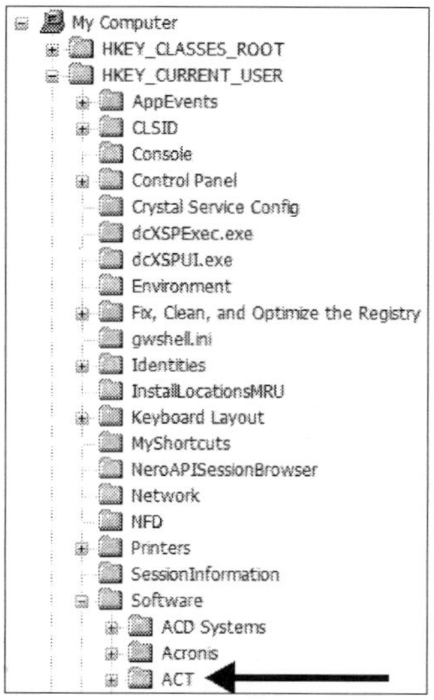

Figure 12-49 HKEY_CURRENT_USER registry key

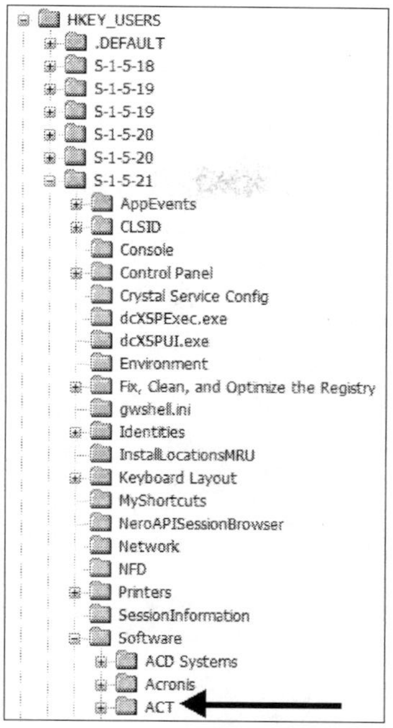

Figure 12-50 HKEY_USERS registry key

Each of the folders in the registry branch shown above in Figure 12-50 has a software folder. This means that you will have to open all of them to find the one with ACT!.

Adding Graphics To ACT! Notes

You can add graphics or images to notes by following the steps below.

1. Open an existing note or create a new one. Leave the note open.
2. Open the graphic file that you want to add to the note in a graphics viewer or other software package that will let you see the graphic.
3. Right-click on the graphic and select Copy (or Edit ⇒ Copy), then right-click in the note in ACT! and select Paste.

   Your note field should look similar to the one shown in Figure 12-51.

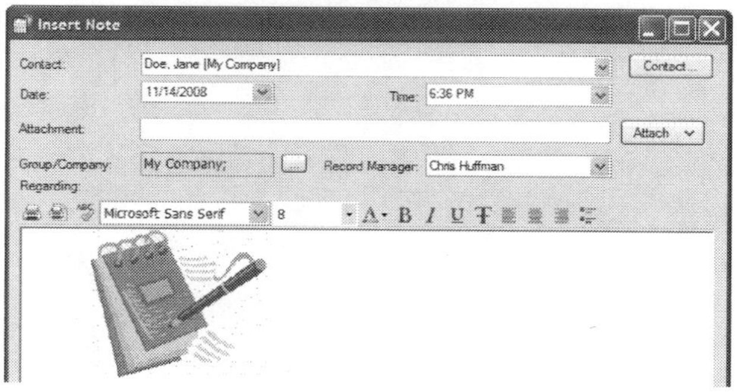

Figure 12-51 Graphic file added to a note

How To Edit Attachments

In Lesson 2 you learned how to attach documents to notes. The steps are the same to edit word processing documents and other types of attachments. Attachments can be on the Notes, History, Activities or Documents tab. The only difference is that you need the software that other file types were created in. There are two ways to open attachments as discussed below.

① Clicking on the attachment icon for the document that you want to edit.

② Double-clicking on the row that has the attachment that you want to edit will open the Edit dialog box. Click on the attachment.

CUSTOMIZING ACT!

In this lesson you will learn several ways to customize ACT!, including how to:

- ☑ Modify preferences
- ☑ Create and edit drop-down list fields
- ☑ Modify fields
- ☑ Customize columns
- ☑ Create an annual event

LESSON 13

Why Waiting To Customize ACT! Is A Good Idea

I suspect that this may be the lesson that many readers are very interested in. There was a time when I wanted to customize (aka tweak) software as soon as I installed it, even if I did not know how to use the software. When you think about it, how could one customize software that they really do not know? I call it "Click Fever". We really like clicking on options to see what will happen. Depending on how well you already know the software, that may not be a problem.

If you are not very familiar with the software, waiting until you have used it for a while before customizing it is probably a good idea. If you have a question or something does not work as expected, you will not know if it is a problem with the software or if the cause is from a change that you made and were not aware of all of the ways that a certain customization effects the software.

Modifying Preferences

There are several options in ACT! that you can modify. In Lesson 1 you learned how to modify the General preferences. In this lesson you will learn how to modify other options on the Preferences dialog box.

Name And Salutation Preferences

In Lesson 2 you learned how ACT! displays the contact names that you enter. [See Lesson 2, Exercise 2.1] If the default prefix and suffix options do not meet your needs, the options shown in Figures 13-1 to 13-4 should help. The options that are selected in the figures are the defaults.

Tools ⇒ Preferences ⇒ General tab. Click the Name Preferences or Salutation Preferences button.

The options shown in the list on the right of Figure 13-2 are the prefixes that ACT! will ignore as being the contacts first name. You can add or delete items in these lists.

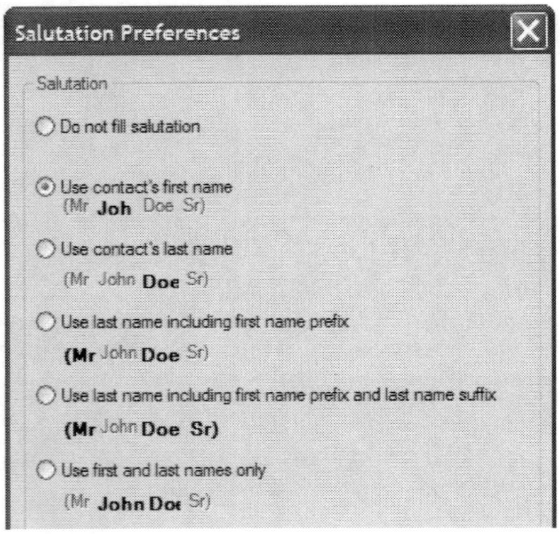

Figure 13-1 Salutation Preferences

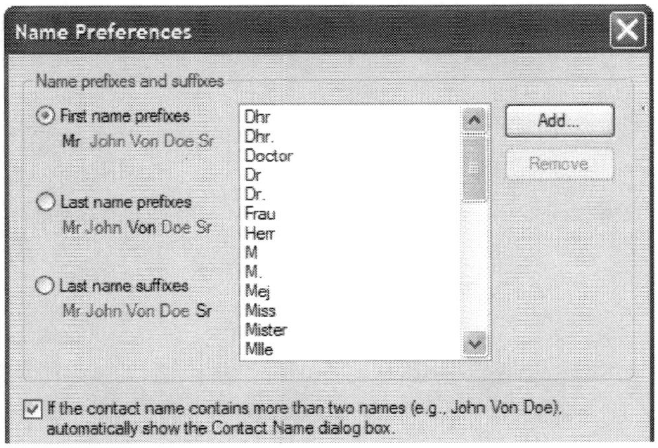

Figure 13-2 Name Preferences

The **LAST NAME PREFIX** options shown in Figure 13-3 are the first part of a two word last name. An example would be Dr. Van Ost. "Van" is the type of prefix that you would add to this list if it was not already there.

The **LAST NAME SUFFIX** options shown in Figure 13-4 are a list of abbreviations that people use after their last name. If they are the last word entered in the Contact field, they are ignored with the default options that ACT! uses.

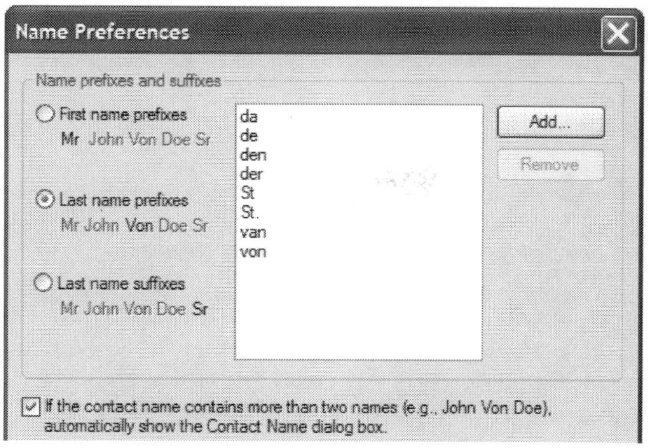

Figure 13-3 Last name prefix options

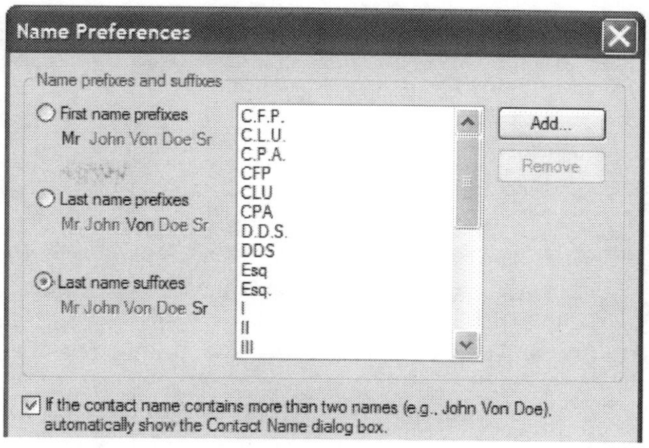

Figure 13-4 Last name suffix options

Exercise 13.1: Calendar Preferences

ACT! allows you to change some of the default calendar settings. The ones that you can change are the day the calendar week starts on, the time slot increments on the daily and weekly calendars and whether or not you want to only show the current month in the mini-calendar.

1. Tools ⇒ Preferences. On the Calendar & Scheduling tab, click the **CALENDAR PREFERENCES** button.

2. Change the options shown in Table 13-1. The Calendar Preferences dialog box should have the options shown in Figure 13-5.

Option	Change To
Start Time	9 AM
Daily Calendar	60 minutes

Table 13-1 Calendar options to change

Changing these options will cause the daily calendar to display the time slots in one hour increments.

The default starting time of the calendar will now be 9 AM.

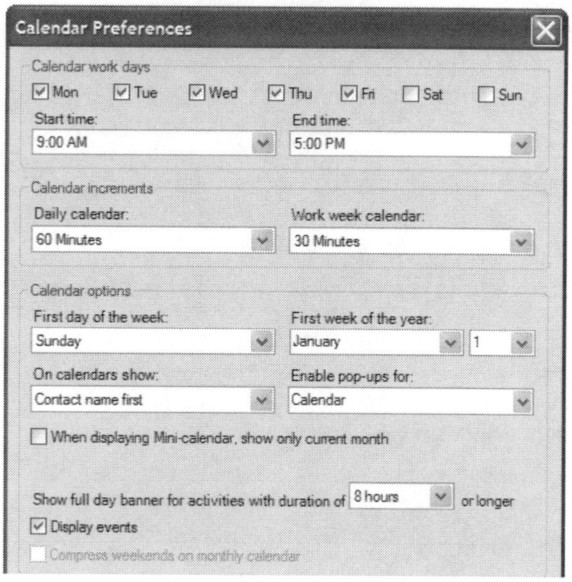

Figure 13-5 Calendar Preferences options

Pop-Up Options

This option is on the Calendar Preferences dialog box shown above in Figure 13-5. ACT! has pop-ups that you may find useful. They will not slow down your computer like the pop-ups that you may see when surfing the Internet. Figure 13-6 shows the parts of ACT! that you can enable pop-ups for. By default, the calendar pop-ups are enabled. Check the options that you want and clear the check mark for the option(s) that you do not want pop-ups for.

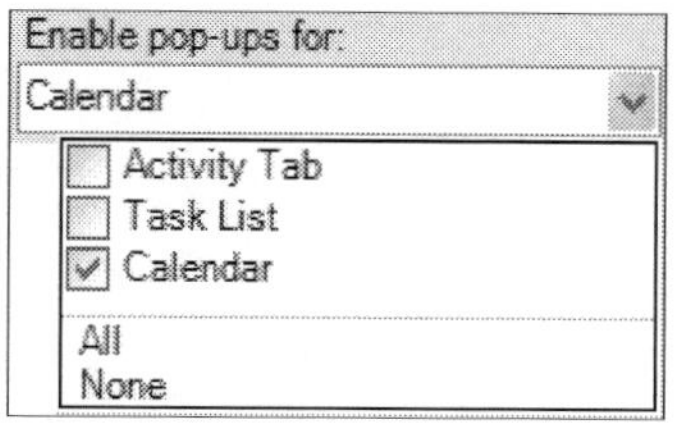

Figure 13-6 Pop-up options

Exercise 13.2: Scheduling Preferences

You can modify the following scheduling preferences:

① Activity type (Call, Meeting, To-Do).
② Priority levels.
③ Alarm options.
④ Have certain types of activities automatically roll over to the next day if they are not completed.
⑤ Designate how cleared activities should appear.

1. Click the Scheduling Preferences button on the Calendar & Scheduling tab.

To change the settings, click on the activity type that you want to change (call, meeting etc.), then select the options that you want to change. If modified, the options in the **DEFAULT ACTIVITY SETTINGS TO** section will change the default values that you see when you create an activity.

2. Change the options in Table 13-2 for the To-Do activity type. Your dialog box should have the options selected that are shown in Figure 13-7.

Option	Change To
Ring alarm	15 minutes
Duration	1 Hour

Table 13-2 To-do activity options to change

If set, the alarm will start warning you 15 minutes prior to the start time of the activity.

If checked, the **AUTOMATICALLY ROLL OVER TO TODAY** option will cause all uncompleted activities of the activity type selected to be moved to the next day.

Depending on how many activities you schedule, you may want to check the option. I find this option most useful for phone calls that I did not complete.

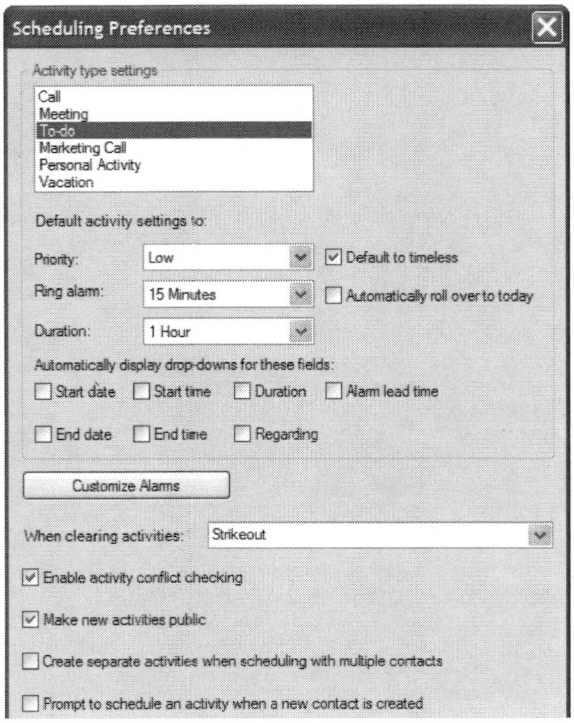

Figure 13-7 To-Do activity preference options

Take caution when using the roll over option because it is cumulative, meaning that all past activities that were not completed will be rolled over.

If there were 500 activities that were not completed, all of them will be rolled over. The roll over is not automatic though.

When you open the database, you will be asked if you want to roll over the activities. You will see how many activities would be rolled over, as shown in Figure 13-8.

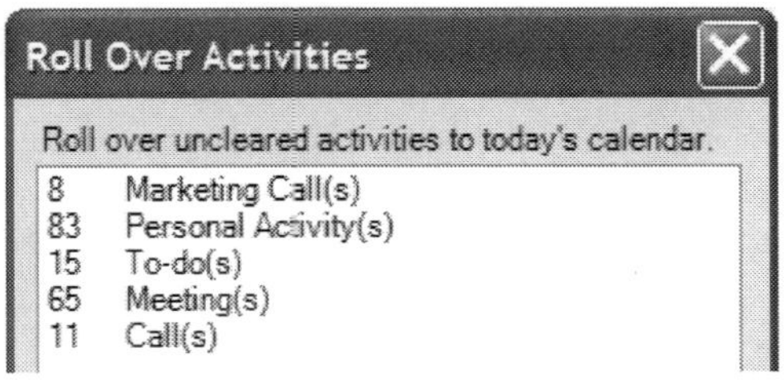

Figure 13-8 Roll Over Activities dialog box

3. Click OK twice to close both dialog boxes.

Quick Print Preferences

The options shown in Figure 13-9 are used to select the header and footer printing options for data on different tabs.

You can access this dialog box by clicking the Quick Print Preferences button on the Communication tab on the Preferences dialog box.

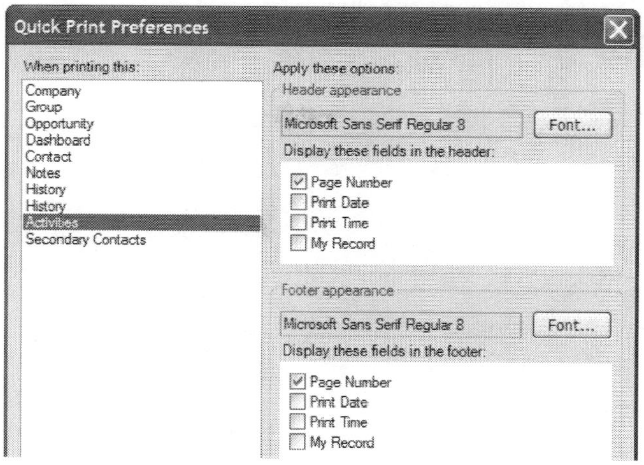

Figure 13-9 Quick Print Preferences dialog box

Exercise 13.3: How To Customize The Contact List View

The Contact List view, as well as the Task List view, which you will learn about later, can be customized to sort according to your needs. You can rearrange the order of the columns. You can make a column smaller or wider. You can also add or remove columns.

Rearrange The Order Of Columns

1. In the Contact List view, click on the Title column heading and drag it to the left, so that it is before the Contact column. The Contact List view should look like the one shown in Figure 13-10.

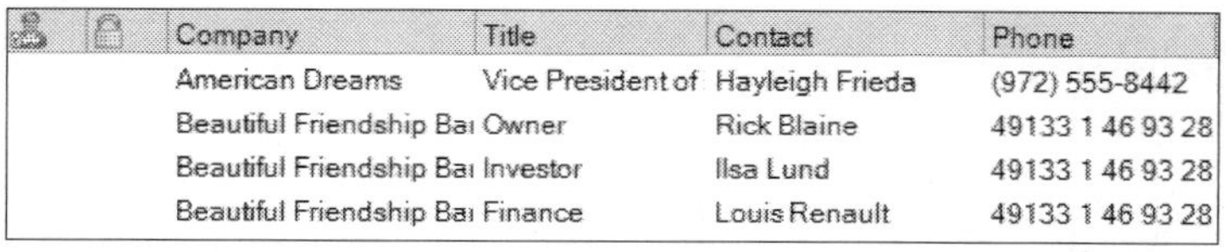

Company	Title	Contact	Phone
American Dreams	Vice President of	Hayleigh Frieda	(972) 555-8442
Beautiful Friendship Ba	Owner	Rick Blaine	49133 1 46 93 28
Beautiful Friendship Ba	Investor	Ilsa Lund	49133 1 46 93 28
Beautiful Friendship Ba	Finance	Louis Renault	49133 1 46 93 28

Figure 13-10 Title column moved

Resize A Column

1. Place the mouse pointer on the line between the Company and Title column headings. The mouse pointer is in the right place when you see a double-headed arrow, as shown in Figure 13-11.

Figure 13-11 Mouse pointer in position to resize a column

2. Hold down the left mouse button and drag the line to the right, as shown in Figure 13-12.

   Release the mouse button. The Company column should be wider.

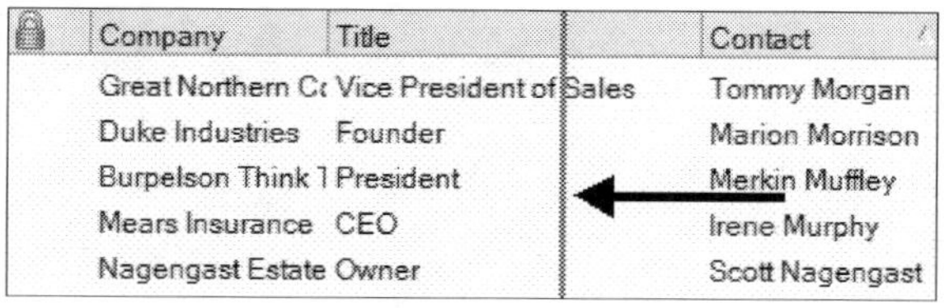

Figure 13-12 Company column made wider

Add A Column

1. Right-click in the list and select **CUSTOMIZE COLUMNS**.

   You should see the dialog box shown in Figure 13-13.

   The **AVAILABLE FIELDS** list contains all of the fields that have not already been added to the view.

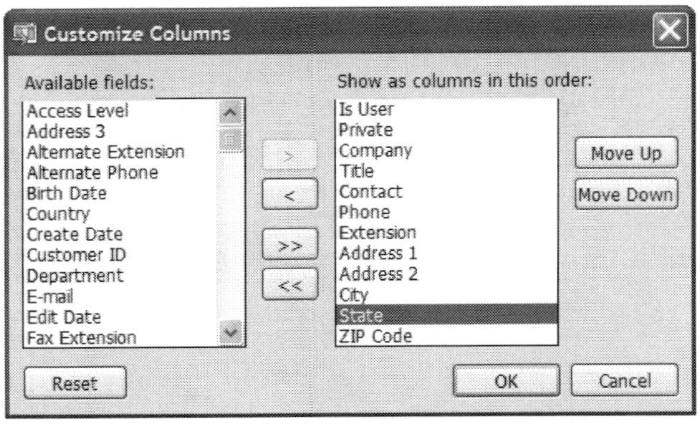

Figure 13-13 Customize Columns dialog box

The fields in the **SHOW AS COLUMNS IN THIS ORDER** list are the order that the columns will be displayed in, on the tab, from left to right.

The **MOVE UP** and **MOVE DOWN** buttons allow you to rearrange the order of the columns in the view. Click on the field that you want to move, then click on the appropriate button.

The **RESET** button will restore the columns back to the order they were when ACT! was first installed.

Tools ⇒ Customize ⇒ Columns, will also open the Customize Columns dialog box.

2. Click on the Department field in the **AVAILABLE FIELDS** list. Press and hold down the CTRL key. Scroll down the list and select the Last Meeting and Last Results fields.

3. Click the Add button (the top arrow button), then click OK. Scroll to the right so that you can see the three fields that you just added to the view.

Another Way To Add Or Remove Columns

If you double-click on a field in the Available Fields section on the Customize Columns dialog box you will add the field to the view. If you double-click on a field in the Show as columns in this order section, you will remove the field from the view. When you remove a column from a view, the data is still in the database. If you need to view the data from a field that you removed, you can add it back.

Delete A Column

1. Open the Customize Columns dialog box.

2. Click on the Last Meeting field in the list on the right, then click the Remove button (the second arrow button from the top) and click OK. The column will be removed from the Contact List view. Click OK.

Customizing The Columns On The Notes Tab

There are two ways to customize the columns on the Notes tab, as discussed below.

① **Resize the columns** by placing the mouse pointer on the line to the right of the column as shown earlier in Figure 13-12 that you want to resize. Drag the mouse pointer to the right to make the column wider or to the left to make the column smaller.

② **Add or remove columns** You can change which columns are displayed on the tab by using the Customize Columns dialog box shown above in Figure 13-13.

Exercise 13.4: How To Customize Columns On A Tab

Customizing columns on a tab is very similar to adding a column to a view.

1. Click the arrow on the Options button and select **CUSTOMIZE COLUMNS**, as shown in Figure 13-14.

   You will see the Customize Columns dialog box that you saw earlier in Figure 13-13.

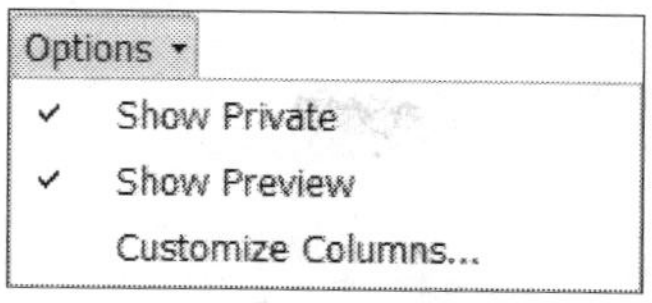

Figure 13-14 Options drop-down list

> All tabs do not have the Options button. Some tabs only have the Customize Columns option on the drop-down list and other tabs have additional options.

2. Add the fields that you want to see on the tab, then remove the fields from the list on the right that you do not want to see on the tab.

3. Rearrange the order of the fields if necessary, then click OK.

Creating New Fields

If you have the need to customize a layout, fields are probably the item that you will customize the most. Depending on your needs, the fields that come with ACT! may not be sufficient. You may have to create additional fields to store data. You have to have administrator or manager rights to create fields. Users cannot be logged into the database while you are creating or editing fields. If anyone else is logged in, you will see a message that contains a list of who is logged in.

While the process of creating fields is easy, you should have a plan for the fields that you need to create. If the database has been in use for a while or has a lot of contacts, you can still add fields. You may have to go through all of the records that were in the database before the field was added and fill in the data for the new field. This could be very time consuming. At a minimum, you should have the following items in your plan for each field that you want to add:

① What type of field (drop-down, date, free form, etc.) is best suited for the data that the field needs to store.
② Which view(s) should the field be placed on.
③ Will the field be used as a lookup field or in a report? If so, determine if the field would be more useful if it was a drop-down list.

Field Data Type Options

If you are creating a new field you can use the data types that are explained in Table 13-3. When editing a field, not all of the data types in the table are available. Each field that is created can only have one data type.

Data Type	Description
Address	When you select this field type, seven fields are automatically created: Address 1, 2 and 3, City, State, Zip Code and Country. (1)
Annual Event	A date field for events that only happen once a year. (2) (3)
Character	A free form data type, which means that any combination of data (text and numbers) can be entered in the field. While it is tempting to use this data type for all fields, it should really only be used when none of the other data types discussed in this table are a better option.
Currency	Only accepts monetary values. By default, a dollar sign, commas and decimal point (for cents) are automatically filled in. If the user entered 123456 in a currency field, the number would be displayed as $1,234.56. (2)
Date	Allows a date to be entered in the field. (2) (3)
Date/Time	Allows a date and time to be entered in the same field. (2) (3)
Decimal	Only allows numbers and decimal points to be entered. (2)
Email	Used to enter an email address. (1)
Initial-Caps	This data type forces the first character of each word entered in the field to be a capital letter and the remaining letters in each word to be lower case.
Lower Case	Converts all upper case characters to lower case.
Memo	Similar to the Character data type because it is free form. The difference is that a memo field allows a lot more data to be entered in the field.
Number	Only accepts numeric values.
Phone	Used to enter telephone numbers. By default, a dash is automatically filled in after the area code and after the first three digits of the phone number. (1)
Picture	Used to store graphic files, images or photos. (1)
Time	Allows a time to be entered in the field. The drop-down list shown in Figure 13-16 is added to this field type. A time can be selected from the drop-down list or the time can be typed in. (2)
Upper Case	Converts all lower case characters to capital letters.
URL Address	Enter a web site address.
Yes/No	Creates a check box field. ACT! queries do not use Yes and No values, instead they use True and False. If this field is used in a query, keep in mind that Yes equals True and No equals False. (1)

Table 13-3 Field data types explained

(1) This field type is only available if you are creating a new field.
(2) The format for this field comes from the Regional and Language Options dialog box shown in Figure 13-15. The currency field formats on the Opportunities dialog box also come from this dialog box.
(3) A calendar object is automatically added to this field type so that all dates will be entered in the same format.

To view the dialog box shown in Figure 13-15, open the Control Panel in Windows, then double-click on the **REGIONAL AND LANGUAGE OPTIONS** icon.

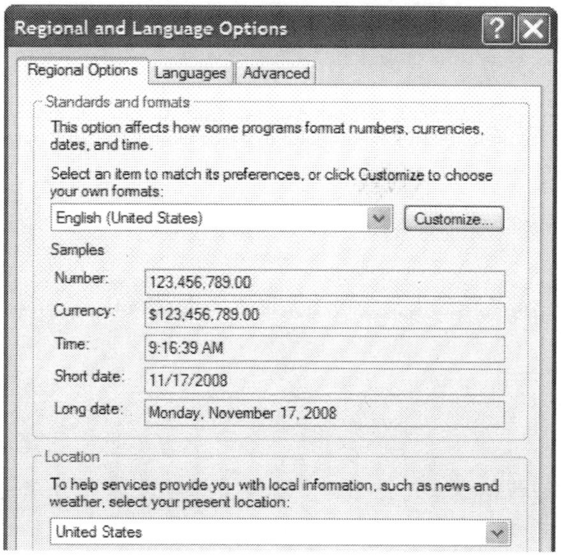

Figure 13-15 Regional and Language Options dialog box

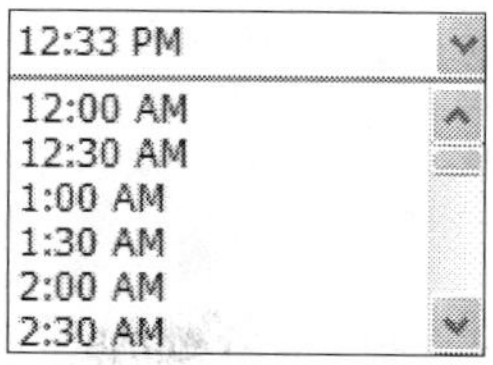

Figure 13-16 Time data type drop-down list

Field Behavior Options

The field behavior options discussed below are used to customize the fields that you create or modify. All of the attributes are not available for each data type.

① **ALLOW BLANK** If checked, this option will not require data to be entered into in the field.
② **GENERATE HISTORY** Automatically creates a history record each time the value in the field is changed. By default, several fields have this option enabled.
③ **PRIMARY FIELD** Designates the field as a primary field. Fields that have this option checked will be duplicated. This is useful when you duplicate a contact record.
④ **USE DROP-DOWN LIST** Is used to select an existing drop-down list or create a new drop-down list.

Customize Field Behavior

The options discussed below are some of the options on the Customize Field Behavior screen.

They allow for more functionality to be added to fields.

The options on the Customize Field Behavior screen shown in Figure 13-17 change depending on the data type that is selected.

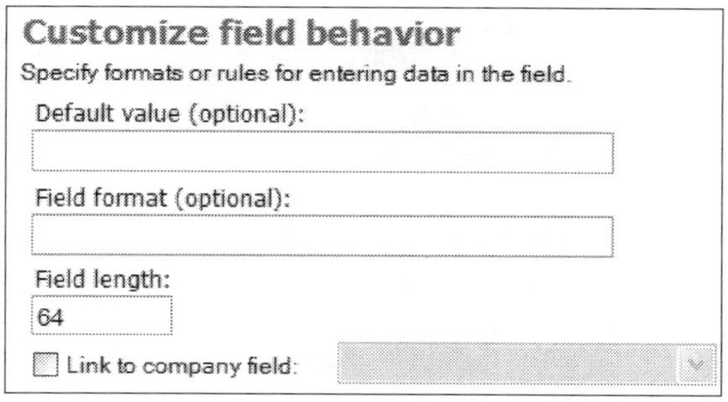

Figure 13-17 Customize field behavior options

① **DEFAULT VALUE** The value that you enter in this field will automatically be filled in the field for each new record added to the database. This is useful if the majority of records need to have the same value in the field.
② **FIELD FORMAT** Is used to enter symbols that will automatically appear in the field. This formatting is used to help the user enter the correct type of numeric data.
③ **FIELD LENGTH** The number entered in this field is the maximum number of characters that can be entered in the field. Try not to make the field length too long because that will waste space in the database and make the database larger than it needs to be. This will cause the database to run slower then it should.
④ **LINK TO COMPANY FIELD** This option is used to link a contact field to a field in the company record. When the company field is updated, the linked field in the contact record is automatically updated. [See Lesson 4, Linking and Unlinking Contact And Company Fields]

Triggers

Triggers allow an action to take place on a field in one of three ways, as shown in Figure 13-18.

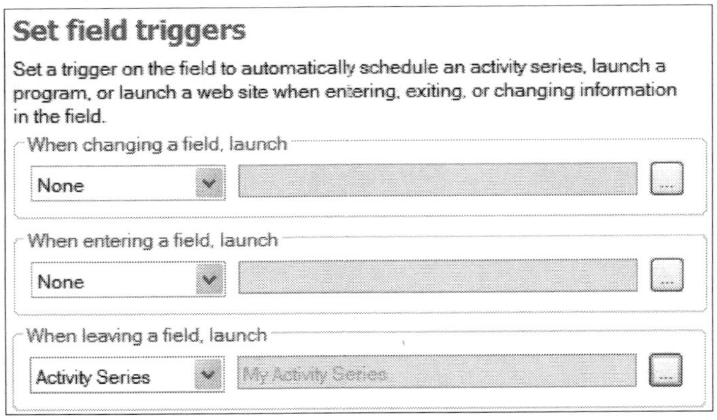

Figure 13-18 Set field triggers screen

Types Of Triggers

There are three types of triggers that can be set, as discussed below.

① **NONE** This is the default trigger type. It means that the trigger will not have an event occur.
② **PROGRAMS** Is used to select a program (software package), file or web site to open.
③ **ACTIVITY SERIES** Is used to select a list of activities that you want to schedule. [See Lesson 8, Activity Series]

Trigger Options

There are three triggers that can be set for a field, as discussed below.

① **WHEN CHANGING A FIELD**, an event will happen when the value in the field changes.
② **WHEN ENTERING A FIELD**, an event will happen when the cursor first enters the field.
③ **WHEN LEAVING A FIELD**, an event will happen when the cursor leaves the field.

An example of when to use the **WHEN CHANGING A FIELD** trigger would be when the data in a field changes, you want a document to automatically open. You would select the programs option from the drop-down list and add the file name in the field to the right. You could also use this trigger to open a file that provides helpful information about what type of data should be entered in the field.

An example of when to use the **WHEN ENTERING A FIELD** trigger would be when the cursor leaves a field, a web site will open to display information about the value being entered in the field.

An example of when to use the **WHEN LEAVING A FIELD** trigger would be to set up an activity series automatically when the cursor leaves the field, like the activity series that you created in Lesson 8.

Exercise 13.5: Create A Trigger

In this exercise you will create the **WHEN LEAVING THE FIELD** trigger shown above in Figure 13-18. You will add the trigger to the User 7 field.

1. Tools ⇒ Define Fields. Scroll down and click on the User 7 field.

2. Click the **EDIT FIELD** link, then click the Next button twice. You will see the Set field triggers window.

3. Open the **WHEN LEAVING A FIELD** drop-down list and select Activity Series.

4. Click the button at the end of the section and select the Activity Series that you created, as illustrated in Figure 13-19.

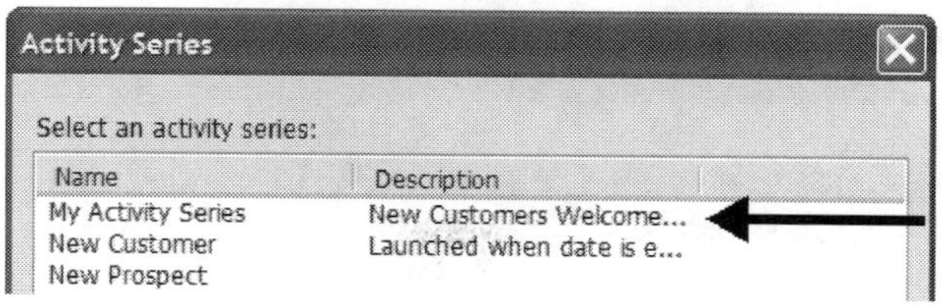

Figure 13-19 Activity Series dialog box

5. Click OK. You will see the Activity Series name shown earlier in Figure 13-18. Click Finish, then close the Define Fields dialog box.

Test The Trigger And Submit An Activity Series

1. Display the record for Tom Dynamic.

2. On the User Fields tab, type `Test trigger` in the User 7 field, then press the Tab key.

   You should see the Schedule Activity Series dialog box shown in Figure 13-20.

   If you need to add more contacts for the activities you can.

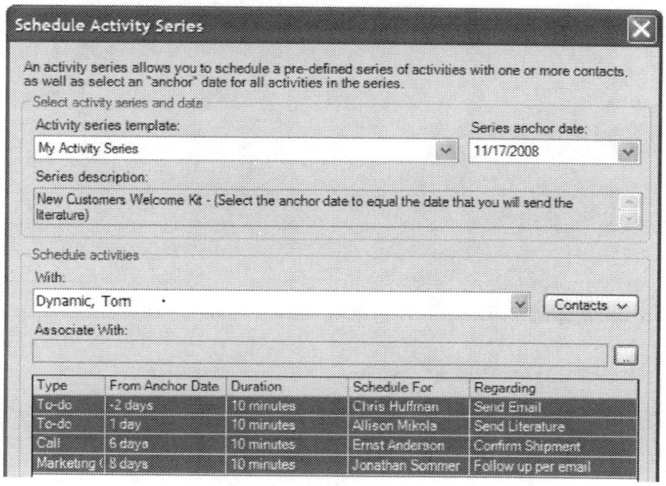

Figure 13-20 Schedule Activity Series dialog box

3. Click the Cancel button to close the Schedule Activity Series dialog box.

Creating And Editing Drop-Down List Fields

You have already seen and used many of the default drop-down lists that come with ACT!. You can create drop-down lists for a field that you need. You may have a database that has all types of doctors and may want to list their specialty. You could modify a user defined field and add a drop-down list to it that contains specialties. A list can be used by more than one field.

Exercise 13.6: How To Create A Drop-Down List Field

In this exercise you will create a drop-down list field for doctor specialties.

1. Tools ⇒ Define Fields. If the **DEFINE FIELD** option is not enabled, you are not logged in as an administrator or manager and cannot complete this exercise until you are.

2. Click the **MANAGE DROP-DOWN LISTS** option, then click the **CREATE DROP-DOWN LIST** option.

3. Type `Specializes In` in the **DROP-DOWN LIST NAME** field.
   Type `What the doctor specializes in` in the Description field.
   The options in the **TYPE** drop-down list were explained earlier in Table 13-3.

> You should avoid using special characters in field names because they can create problems in reports and queries.

4. Clear the **AUTOMATICALLY ADD NEW ITEMS USERS ENTER TO THE LIST** option. You should have the options shown in Figure 13-21. Click Next.

   The **ALLOW USERS TO EDIT ITEMS IN THIS LIST** option has to be checked for each field that you want to let users add, delete or edit the values in the drop-down list.

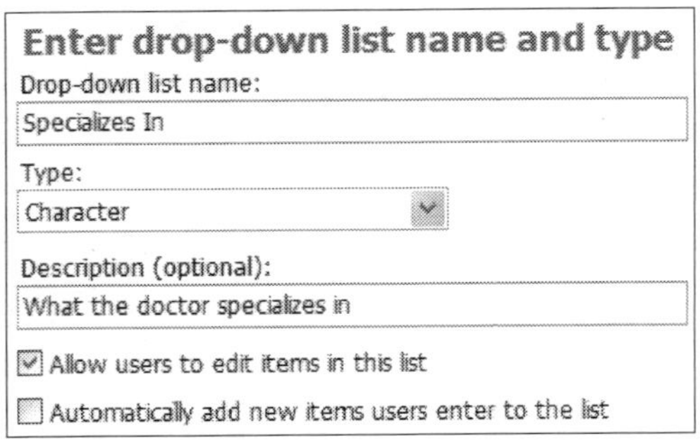

Figure 13-21 Drop-down list name and type options

If checked, the Automatically add new items users enter to the list option is used to allow users type in a value that is not already in the list. When this happens, the value will automatically be added to the list. This could be a problem because typos will not be caught and the lists can get out of hand to manage.

> The following options cannot be accessed when the **ALLOW USERS TO EDIT ITEMS IN THIS LIST** option is selected: **ALLOW MULTI-SELECT, SHOW DESCRIPTIONS** and **TYPE-AHEAD**. These options can only be enabled from the Define Fields dialog box.

5. Click the Add button, then type `Brain Surgery` in the Value column.
   Click the Add button, then type `OB-GYN` in the Value column.

   You should have the options shown in Figure 13-22.

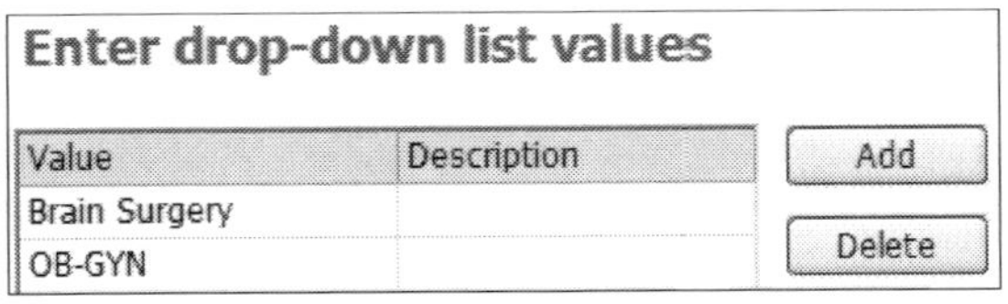

Figure 13-22 Drop-down list values

6. Click Finish. You should see the drop-down list that you just created on the window shown in Figure 13-23.

   If you look in the **DETAILS** section on the left, you will see information about the drop-down list that is selected.

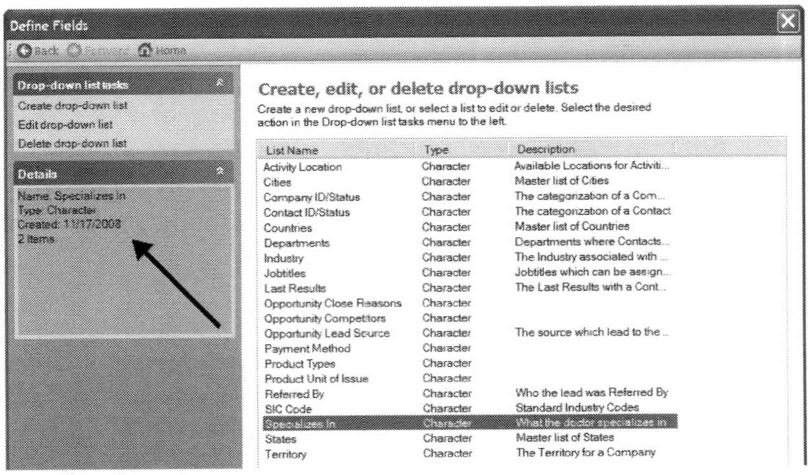

Figure 13-23 Details for the drop-down list

7. Click the Back button. Leave the Define Fields dialog box open to complete the next exercise.

Managing Drop-Down List Options

If the field has a drop-down list you can decide whether users can add or delete entries in the list. If you need to change the contents of a field like the address field, click in the field and back space out what you do not want and type in the new information. ACT! is in **INSERT** mode by default. In the next exercise you will learn several drop-down list editing techniques.

You can modify drop-down lists on the Define Fields dialog box or as you learned earlier, you can select the Edit List Values option at the bottom of a drop-down list. System fields can be modified on the Define Fields dialog box. Other fields are modified in a view. To use the Define Fields dialog box, other users cannot have the database open.

Exercise 13.7: How To Add Items To A Drop-Down List

In this exercise you will add a value to the Contact ID/Status field.

1. Open the Define Fields dialog box if it is not already open, then click the Manage drop-down lists option in the List Tasks section.

2. Select the Contact ID/Status list name, then click the **EDIT DROP-DOWN LIST** option.

3. Click Next on the Enter drop-down list name and type screen.

4. Click the Add button, then type `Purchased Book` in the Value field.

   Press the Tab key, then type `Purchased the ACT! Book` in the Description field.

   The entry should look like the one shown at the bottom of Figure 13-24.

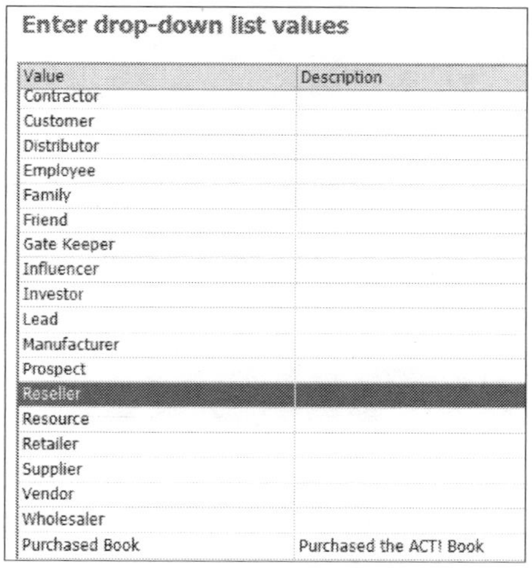

Figure 13-24 Drop-down list values

5. Click Finish. The item will be added to the drop-down list. Close the Define Fields dialog box.

View The New Entry

1. Switch to the Contact Detail view, then open the ID/Status drop-down list on any contact record.

2. Scroll down the list. You will see the item that you created, as illustrated in Figure 13-25.

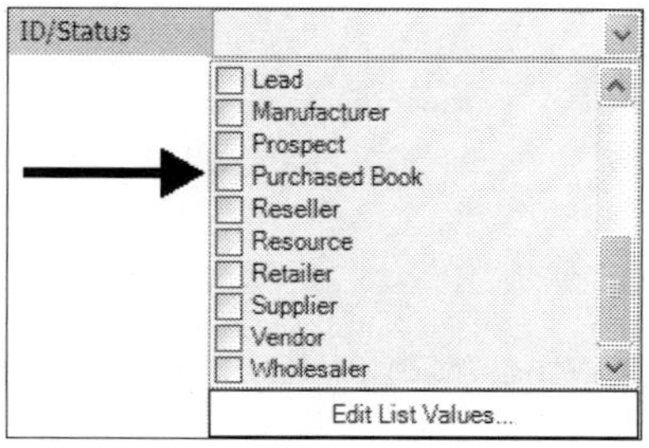

Figure 13-25 ID/Status drop-down list options

Exercise 13.8: How To Edit The Values In A Drop-Down List (From A View)

Many of the fields in the contact and company detail views have drop-down lists. You can add, modify or delete the entries in these lists.

How To Add An Item To A Drop-Down List

In this part of the exercise you will learn how to add an item to a drop-down list.

1. Click on the arrow at the end of the Department field on the Contact Detail view, then click the **EDIT LIST VALUES** option. You should see the Edit List dialog box. This is a list of all of the items that can currently be selected for the Department field. The list looks similar to the one that you saw earlier in Figure 13-24.
2. Click the Add button. Type `Computer` in the Value field. If you wanted, you could type in a description to help clarify the item that you are adding.
3. Click OK to close the Edit List dialog box. The item that you just added will be available in the Department drop-down list.

How To Modify Or Delete An Item In A Drop-Down List

The steps below explain how to modify or delete an item in a drop-down list. Read through the steps now, but do not modify or delete anything.

How To Modify An Item In The List

1. Open the Edit List dialog box for the drop-down list that you want to modify.
2. Select the value that you want to modify, then change the item to what you want it to be, as illustrated in Figure 13-26.

   Click OK.

   Notice in Figure 13-24 shown earlier, that the value below the Manufacturer option was Prospect.

   In Figure 13-26, the value was changed to Brand Marketing.

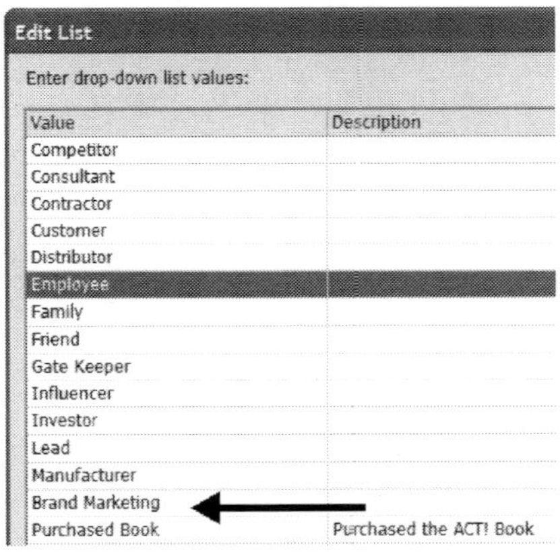

Figure 13-26 Prospect value changed to Brand Marketing

How To Delete An Item In The List

I do not advise deleting items from a drop-down list unless you know that the value is not being used for any contact. If you delete a value and it is being used, the records that are using it will retain the value, but the value will not be available for any other records. If the value that you want to delete is "Computer", I would change it to "Not in use - Computer" or something similar. That way, it is still available and if at some point in the future you need to reclassify contacts that have the value, you will be able to easily find the records.

1. To delete an item in a drop-down list, open the Edit List dialog box shown above in Figure 13-26.
2. Select the value that you want to delete, then click the **DELETE** button. Click Yes, when prompted to delete the list value, then click OK.

> You can also delete an item using the Define Fields dialog box.

Exercise 13.9: How To Modify A User Field

There are 10 contact user fields that you can customize to store data that does not exist in the fields that come with ACT!. If you customize these fields, the name changes on the Define Fields dialog box, but not on the User Fields tab. This is because the "User 1" label on the layout has to be modified. You will not see the label change on the User Fields tab until you edit the layout, which you will learn how to do in Lesson 18. In this exercise you will modify the User 1 field.

1. Tools ⇒ Define Fields.

2. Select the **CONTACTS** field from the drop-down list, if it is not already selected.

3. Scroll down the list and click on the User 1 field, then click the **EDIT FIELD** link.

4. In the Field Name field, type `Specializes In`.

5. Open the Select a field drop-down list and select **INITIAL-CAPS**. This will cause the first letter of each word that you type in this field to automatically be capitalized. Click Yes when prompted that data may be lost.

6. Check all of the options in the **CUSTOMIZE FIELD BEHAVIOR** section, as illustrated in Figure 13-27, then click Next.

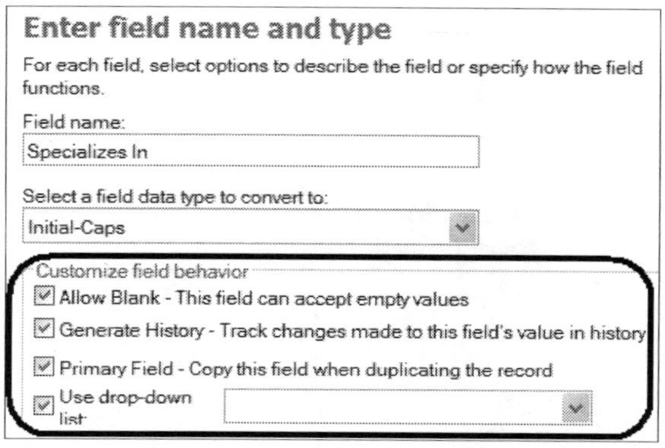

Figure 13-27 Customize field behavior options illustrated

7. In the **DEFAULT VALUE** field type `General Practitioner`, as shown in Figure 13-28.

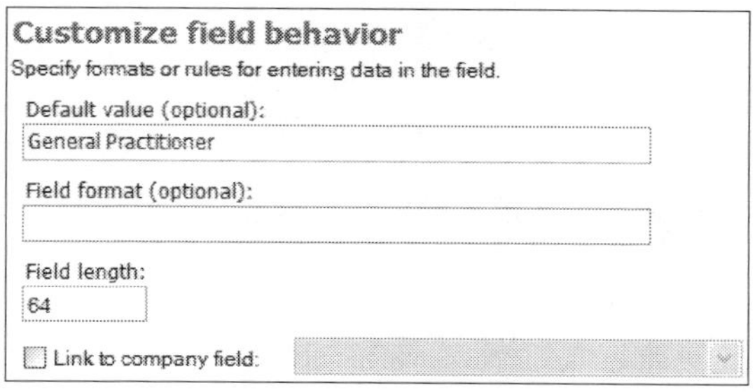

Figure 13-28 Default value for the user field

8. None of the triggers need to be set. Click Finish. The field will be created.

Exercise 13.10: How To Create A Field

So far in this lesson you have learned how to create and manage drop-down list fields and modify user fields. These are probably the types of fields that you will need to create and modify the most. It is possible though that you may need to create a field that is not a drop-down list. You can create fields and link them to an existing drop-down list. The steps below will show you how to create a field that will be linked to an existing drop-down list.

1. Open the Define Fields dialog box, then click the **CREATE NEW FIELD** link.

2. Type `Specialty` in the Field name field.

3. Check the **USE DROP-DOWN LIST** option shown in Figure 13-29, then select Specializes In from the drop-down list.

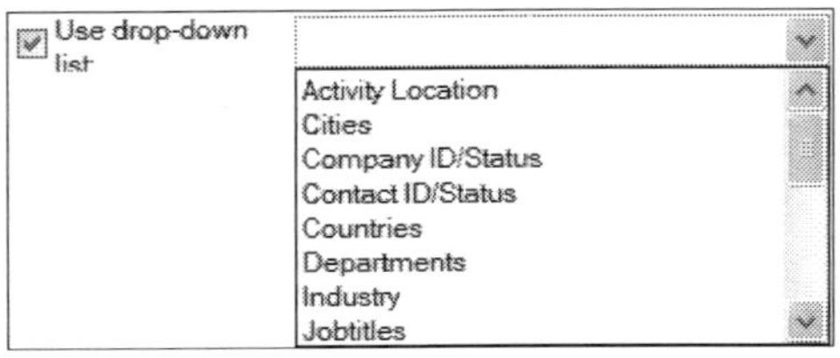

Figure 13-29 Fields with drop-down lists

The options shown above in Figure 13-29 are the default fields in ACT! that have data for a drop-down list. If one of them is appropriate for the field that you are creating, you can use it.

4. Click Next, then select the **LIMIT TO LIST** option shown in Figure 13-30.

   This will prevent a value from being entered that is not already in the list.

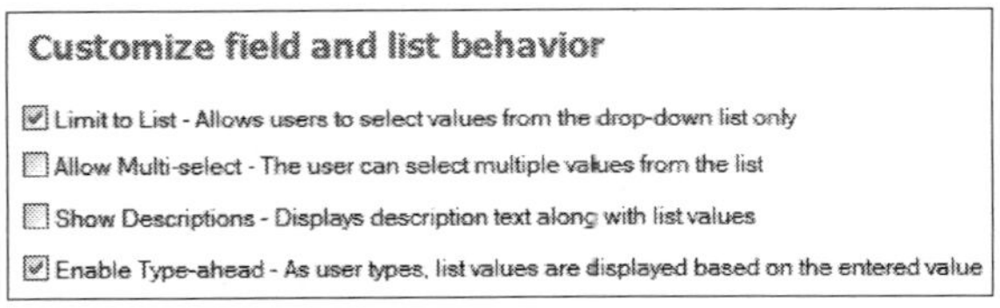

Figure 13-30 Customize field and list behavior options

5. Click Finish. The field will be created. In Lesson 18 you will add this field to the Basic Contact layout. Close the Define Fields dialog box.

As shown above in Figure 13-30, the **SHOW DESCRIPTIONS** option is not enabled by default. This description refers to the one that you created in Exercise 13.7.

If the Show Descriptions option is checked, the drop-down list will also display the description, as shown in Figure 13-31. Notice that some options do not have a description.

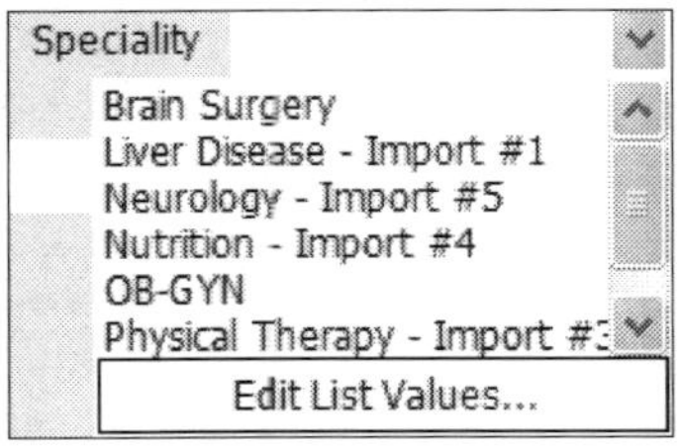

Figure 13-31 Show Descriptions option illustrated

Deleting Fields

As a programmer, I do not delete fields that have data from a database when I first come to the conclusion that the data is no longer needed. Instead, I will modify the layouts that display the field, so that the field is not visible on the layout. I will also remove the field from the queries and reports, but not from the database. If you want to delete a field right away, make a backup copy of the database, then delete the field. While deleting the field from the database is easy to do, you should also remove it from the layouts, queries and reports that it is used in. The steps below show you how to delete a field.

1. Tools ⇒ Define Fields.

2. Open the **VIEW FIELDS FOR** drop-down list and select the record type of the field that you want to delete.

3. Click on the field that you want to delete in the list, then click the Delete Field link on the left.

4. Click Yes, when prompted if you are sure that you want to delete the field. Once the field is deleted, close the Define Fields dialog box.

Managing Priority Types

Schedule ⇒ Manage ⇒ Priorities, will open the dialog box shown in Figure 13-32.

In Lesson 8 you learned how to schedule activities and set the priority for the activity. Renaming or disabling a priority does not effect activities that already have a priority.

They will still display with the priority they had when the activity was created. The changes that you make on this dialog box only effect new activities.

There are five priority options that come with ACT!.

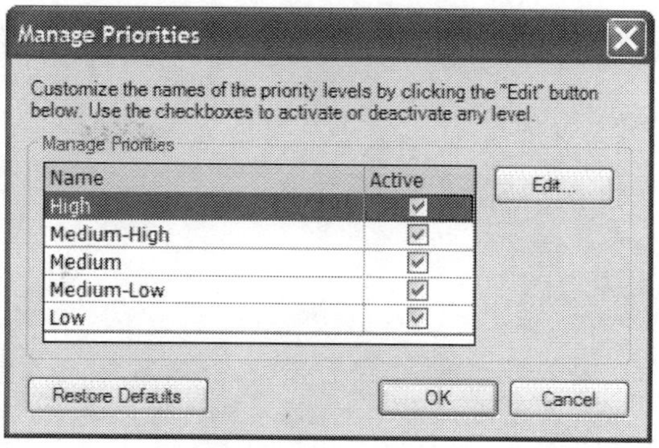

Figure 13-32 Manage Priorities dialog box

You cannot create new entries, but you can modify the names of the existing ones to better meet your needs or to be more descriptive.

If you need to rename a priority, click on it, then click the **EDIT** button and type in the new name.

If you do not need a priority, clear the check mark for it in the **ACTIVE** column. This prevents users from selecting the priority on the Schedule Activities dialog box.

The **RESTORE DEFAULTS** button will reset the priorities back to what they were when ACT! was first installed.

Exercise 13.11: Creating Activity Types

In Lesson 8 you learned about the six activity types that come with ACT!. Only users with administrator or manager level security rights can create new activity types. In this exercise you will learn how to create activity types.

1. Schedule ⇒ Manage ⇒ Activity Types, then click the Add button.
2. Type `Post Card Mailing` in the **NAME** field.
3. If you want the activity type to have an icon, click the **BROWSE** button. Navigate to and double-click on the icon file that you want to use.
4. Click the Add button on the Add Activity Type dialog box. Type `Post Card Mailing Completed` in the **RESULT NAME** field, then click OK.
5. Check the option that you just created on the Add Activity Type dialog box to make it the default. You should have the options shown in Figure 13-33.

   The options on the bottom half of this dialog box are the values in the Results drop-down list field on the Schedule Activities dialog box. These options are also used to clear an activity on the Clear Activity dialog box. You can enter as many options as you need.

   When a new activity type is created, the **COMPLETED** and **NOT COMPLETED** result types shown at the bottom of Figure 13-33 are automatically added.

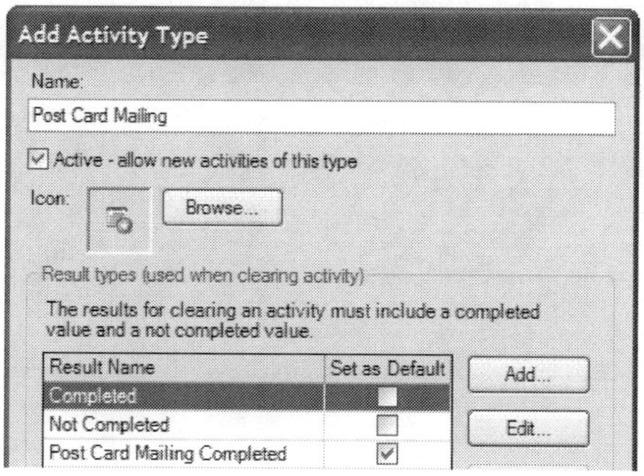

Figure 13-33 Add Activity Type dialog box

6. Click OK. The dialog box should have the Post Card Mailing activity shown in Figure 13-34.

   The activity types that come with ACT! cannot be deleted.

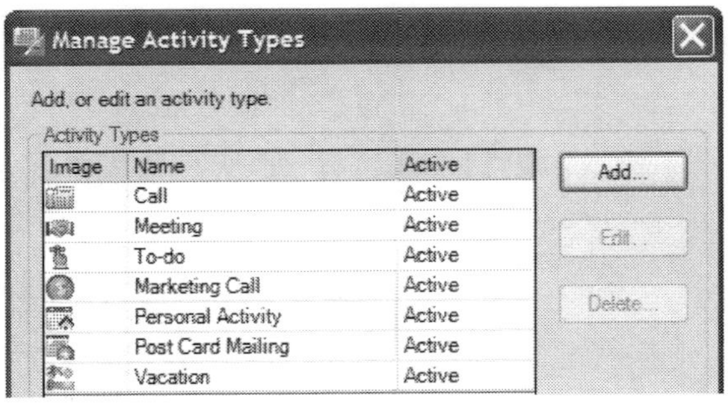

Figure 13-34 Manage Activity Types dialog box

7. Click the Close button.

Annual Events

Annual Events are activities that can be displayed on your calendar, but not on the Task List. Events can be recurring like birthdays or one-time events like a business trip. A good use of the events option is to set up holidays on your calendar. Events do not cause scheduling conflicts and do not appear on reports. Administrator or manager level accounts are needed to create events.

Exercise 13.12: Create An Annual Event Activity

In this exercise you will create an event for July 4th.

1. Schedule ⇒ Manage ⇒ Events.
2. Click the **ADD** button, then type `4th of July` in the **EVENT NAME** field.
3. Select July 4th for next year in the Date field.
4. Change the **DURATION** to 1 day.
5. Change the **OCCURS** option to yearly.

   You should have the options shown in Figure 13-35.

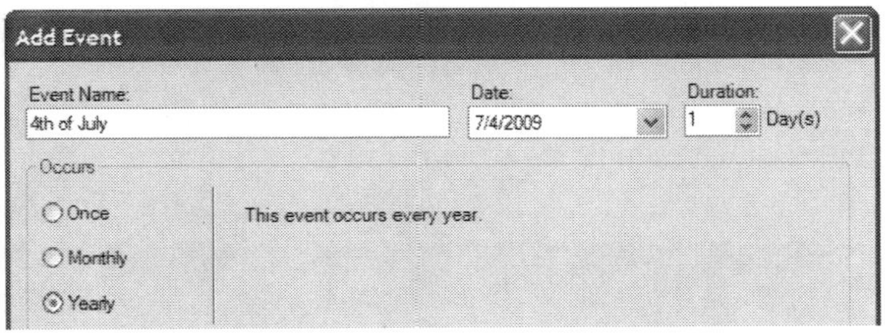

Figure 13-35 Add Event dialog box

6. Click OK. You will see the event on the dialog box shown in Figure 13-36.

   Click the Close button.

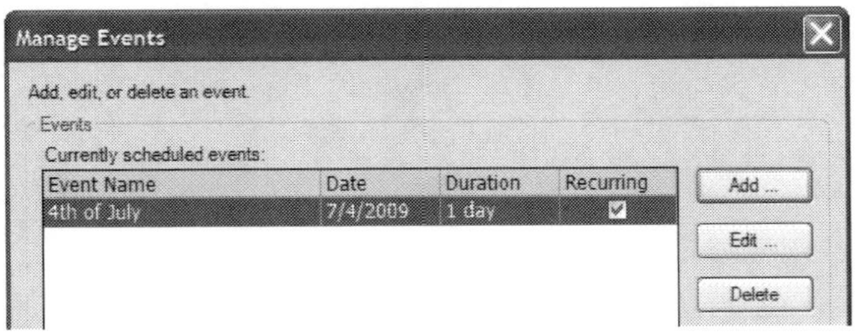

Figure 13-36 Manage Events dialog box

Add The Event To Your Calendar

In this part of the exercise you will add the event that you just created to your calendar.

1. Tools ⇒ Preferences.

2. On the Calendar and Scheduling tab, click the Calendar Preferences button.

3. Check the **DISPLAY EVENTS** option, illustrated in Figure 13-37, if it is not already checked, then click OK twice to close both dialog boxes.

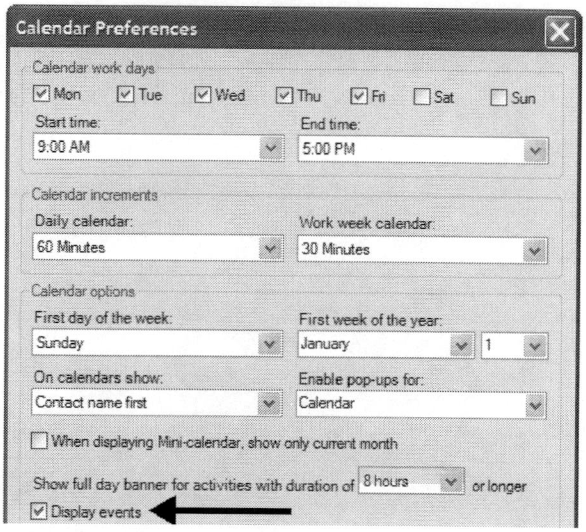

Figure 13-37 Calendar Preferences dialog box

4. Open a calendar view and display July 4th for next year. You will see the entry shown in Figure 13-38. If you do not see the entry, make sure that all of the filter options are set to show all.

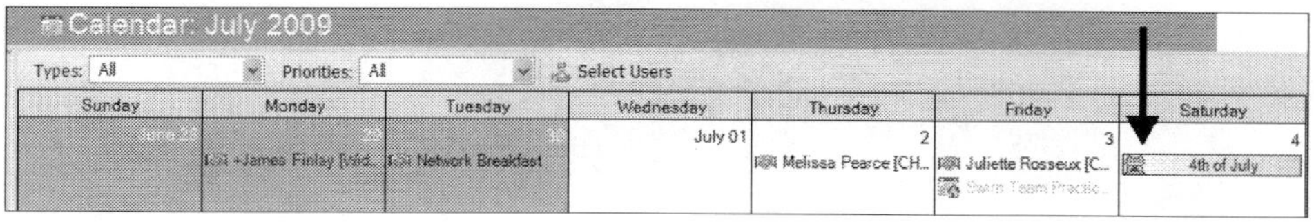

Figure 13-38 Event added to the calendar

DASHBOARDS

In this lesson you will learn how to use Dashboards and how to modify them by exploring the following topics:

- ☑ What is a dashboard?
- ☑ Dashboard toolbar
- ☑ Dashboard views
- ☑ Components
- ☑ Adding data from the dashboard
- ☑ Filtering data in a dashboard
- ☑ Modifying dashboard layouts
- ☑ Modifying dashboard components

LESSON 14

What Is A Dashboard?

A dashboard displays a snapshot of data in a graphical format. So far in this book you have created, viewed and edited different types of data, including contacts, activities and opportunities. While it is easy to switch between views to see all of these types of data, you cannot view more than one of these types of data at the same time. You also cannot get a feel for the big picture of your data, as they say.

This is where dashboards come into play. Like other features in ACT!, the data that is displayed in a dashboard can be filtered. You can create, view and edit data from a dashboard. You can edit the default dashboard layouts by adding, modifying and removing components in a dashboard. To create a dashboard from scratch involves selecting the components that are needed, adding them to the layout, then select the options on the Component Configuration Wizard.

Dashboard Toolbar

Figure 14-1 shows the Dashboard toolbar. Table 14-1 explains the toolbar buttons.

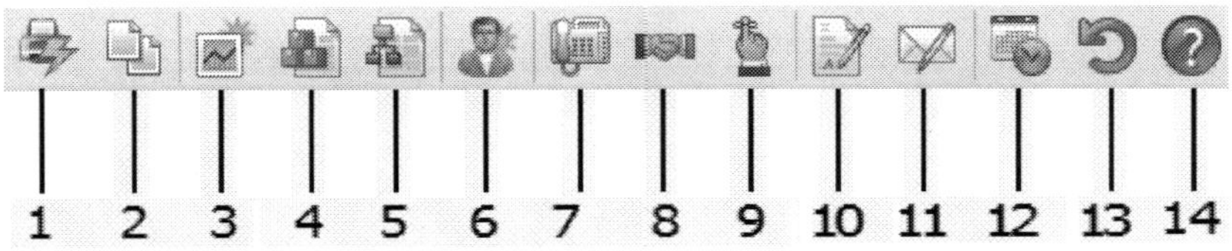

Figure 14-1 Dashboard toolbar

Button	Description
1	Prints the dashboard.
2	Copies the dashboard that is displayed.
3	Opens a new opportunity record.
4	Opens the Manage Product List dialog box.
5	Opens the Manage Process List dialog box.
6	Opens a new contact record.
7	Schedules a telephone call activity. (1)
8	Schedules a meeting activity. (1)
9	Schedules a To-Do item activity. (1)
10	Create a letter.
11	Send an email.
12	Copies calendar information between the ACT! and Outlook calendars.
13	Refreshes the data in the dashboard.
14	Opens the Help system.

Table 14-1 Dashboard toolbar buttons explained

(1) This option does not open with a specific contact name already filled in.

Dashboard Layouts

ACT! comes with three default layouts as shown in Figures 14-2 to 14-4. Each layout can be customized. The layouts contain components which have preset filters. Later you will learn how to customize the layouts and how to change the preset defaults and filters.

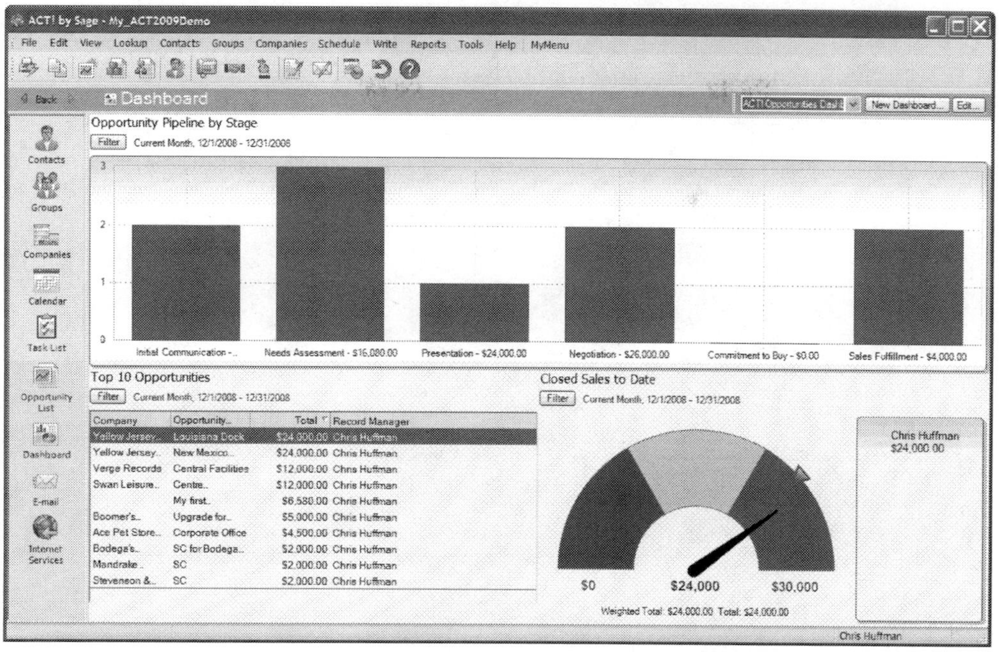

Figure 14-2 ACT! Opportunities Dashboard

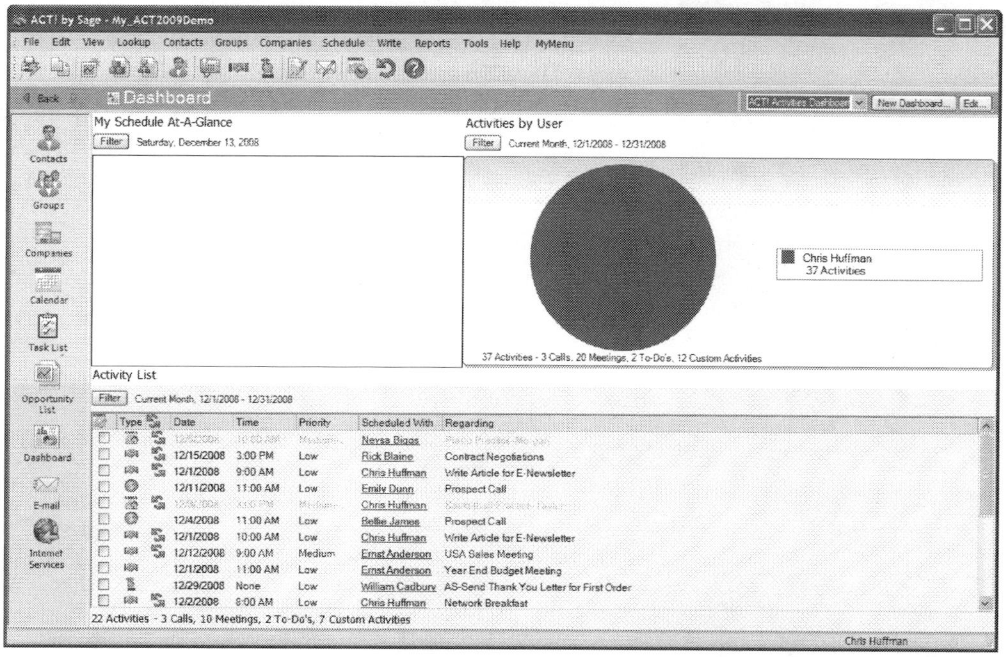

Figure 14-3 ACT! Activities Dashboard

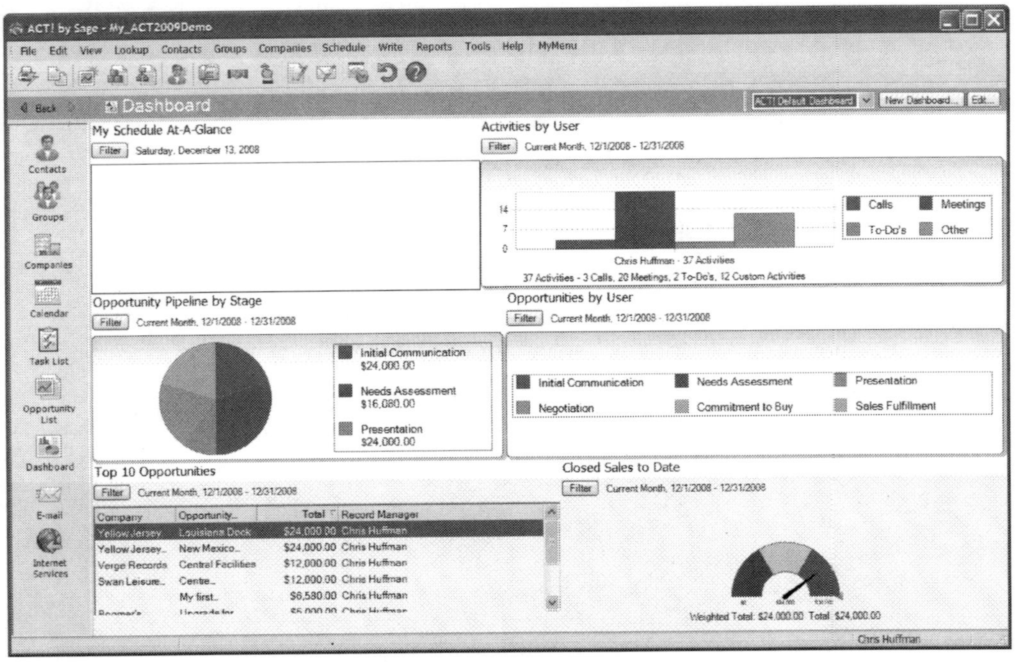

Figure 14-4 ACT! Default Dashboard

The **NEW DASHBOARD** button opens the Dashboard Designer so that you can create a dashboard from scratch.

The **EDIT** button opens the current dashboard in the Dashboard Designer so that you can modify it.

Exercise 14.1: Selecting A Dashboard Layout

As stated earlier, ACT! comes with three Dashboard layouts that you can select from. The steps below show you how to select one.

1. Click the **DASHBOARD** icon on the Navigation bar.
2. To select a different dashboard, open the Dashboard drop-down list and select one of the options shown in Figure 14-5.

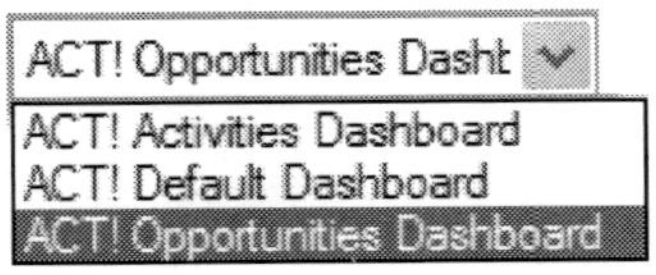

Figure 14-5 Default dashboard layouts

Dashboard Components

Components display different types of data from the database. The majority of components display opportunity data. As shown above in Figures 14-2, 14-3 and 14-4, each dashboard can have different components in different locations on the dashboard.

There are six components in two categories that can be added to a layout as discussed below. The options shown are the defaults for the component, which can be modified. For example, the Closed sales to date component displays opportunities in the ACT! Sales Process. If you created a process, you can modify this component to display your process by default, instead of the ACT! Sales Process.

Activity Components

There are two activity components that come with ACT!, as discussed below.

① **MY ACTIVITIES** Displays a chart with your activities for the current month. (This component displays as Activities by User.)
② **MY SCHEDULE AT-A-GLANCE** Displays your scheduled activities for today.

Opportunity Components

There are four opportunity components that come with ACT!, as discussed below. The opportunity data that each component displays is from the ACT! Sales Process.

① **CLOSED SALES TO DATE** Displays opportunities that have the Closed - Won status for the current month.
② **MY OPPORTUNITIES** Displays a bar chart that has open opportunities for the current month. (This component displays as Opportunities by User.)
③ **OPPORTUNITY PIPELINE BY STAGE** Displays a pie chart with open opportunities for the current month.
④ **TOP OPPORTUNITIES** Displays a list of your top 10 opportunities for the current month that have the Closed - Won status.

Getting Things Done From A Dashboard

Yes, the dashboard provides a great way to view a lot of data in a graphical format, but you still need to be able to get work done. Many of the components have a shortcut menu that will allow you to get tasks done. This is in addition to the menu and toolbar options on the dashboard.

Exercise 14.2: Activity Component Shortcut Menu Options

The activity shortcut menu options discussed in this section are available, regardless of the dashboard that they are on.

1. Open the ACT! Activities Dashboard.
2. Right-click in the My Schedule At-A-Glance section.

   You should see the shortcut menu shown in Figure 14-6.

   These are the activity options that you can use.

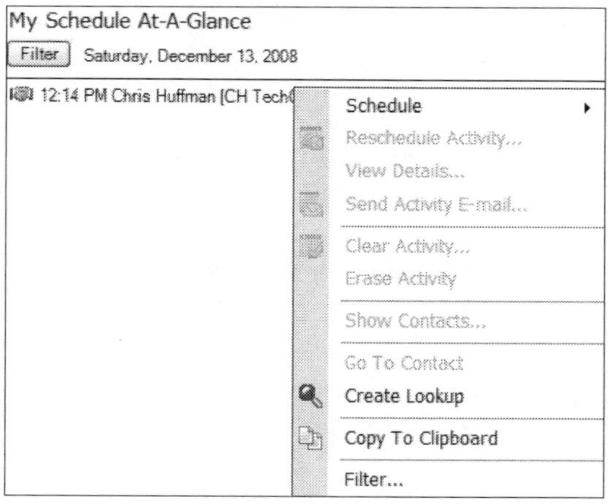

Figure 14-6 Activity shortcut menu

3. If you right-click in the Activities by User section, you will see that the **COPY TO CLIPBOARD** option, shown in Figure 14-7, is the only one available.

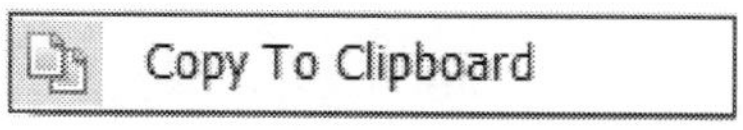

Figure 14-7 Copy shortcut option

4. If you right-click in the Activity List section, you will see the shortcut menu shown earlier in Figure 14-6. The Activity List shortcut menu also has the **CUSTOMIZE COLUMNS** option available on the menu.

Exercise 14.3: Opportunity Component Shortcut Menu Options

The opportunity shortcut menu options discussed in this section are available, regardless of the dashboard that they are on.

1. Open the ACT! Default Dashboard.

2. Right-click in the grid in the Top 10 Opportunities section. You should see the shortcut menu shown in Figure 14-8.

   These are the opportunity options that you can use.

   The other opportunity sections only have the Copy To Clipboard option shown above in Figure 14-7.

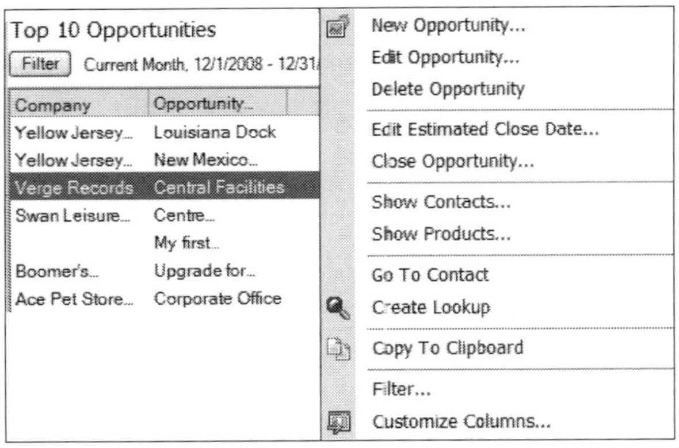

Figure 14-8 Opportunity shortcut menu

Filtering Data In A Dashboard

As you have seen, each activity component has a filter button. The filter button is used to change the data that is displayed in the component. The options that you will see on the Filter dialog boxes are the default options that were set for the component.

If you select different options on a filter dialog box, the next time that you open a dashboard, those options will still be selected. The exception to this is if you or another administrator or manager of the database modifies the default filter options for the component.

Exercise 14.4: Filtering Activity Component Data

In this exercise you will learn how to filter the activity component data.

My Schedule At-A-Glance Filter Component Options

1. Open the ACT! Activities Dashboard.

2. Click the **FILTER** button for the My Schedule At-A-Glance component.

   You will see the dialog box shown in Figure 14-9.

   The filter options on this dialog box are a subset of the filter options that are on the Activities tab.

Figure 14-9 My Schedule At-A-Glance component filter options

If the My Schedule At-A-Glance component displays has a lot of activities, you can clear some of the options to reduce the number of activities that appear in this component.

Activities By User Filter Component Options

1. Click the **FILTER** button in the Activities By User component.

   You will see the dialog box shown in Figure 14-10.

   The filter options on this dialog box are the same filter options that are on the Activities tab.

   The **SHOW OUTLOOK TASKS** option is helpful if you are using Microsoft Outlook as your email reader in ACT!. Selecting this option means that you want to display tasks that were created, based on an email in Outlook.

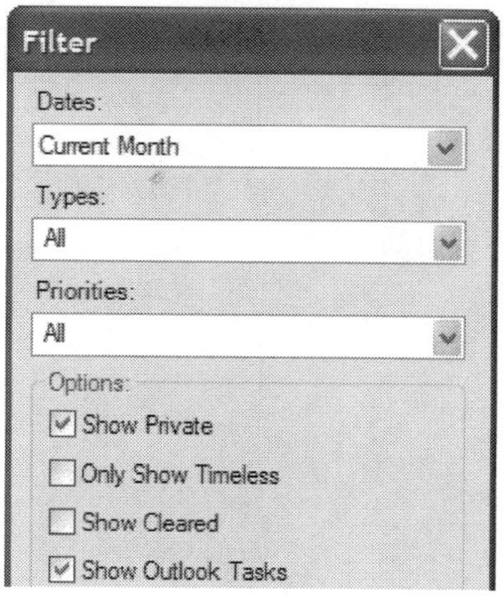

Figure 14-10 Activities By User component filter options

2. Open the Dates drop-down list and select Custom, then select the date range for all of 2007.

3. Clear the **SHOW PRIVATE** option, then click OK. The Activities by User component should look like the one shown in Figure 14-11.

   This display of activities may be more helpful if they were displayed in a bar chart because that would allow you to better see how many of each type of activity was listed. Later in this lesson you will learn how to modify this component.

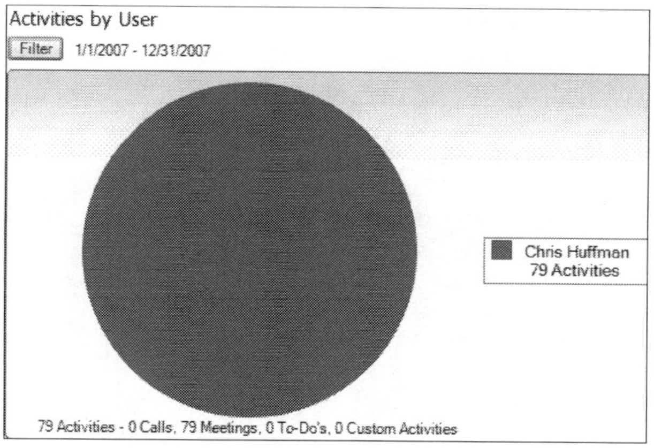

Figure 14-11 Activities by User component with different filter options

Activity List Filter Options

The Activity List filter is the List view display type of the My Activities component.

1. Click the **FILTER** button in the Activities List section. As you see, the Filter dialog box has the same options as the one shown earlier in Figure 14-10.

2. Clear the Call and To-Do **TYPES**, then click OK. You will see less activities in this section of the dashboard.

Exercise 14.5: Filtering Opportunity Component Data

In this exercise you will learn how to filter the opportunity component data.

1. Open the ACT! Default Dashboard.

2. Click any **FILTER** button in an Opportunity component.

   You will see the dialog box shown in Figure 14-12.

   The options on this dialog box are the same filter options that are on all of the Opportunity components.

   They are the same options that are on the Opportunity List view. [See Lesson 10, Using The Opportunity List Filters section]

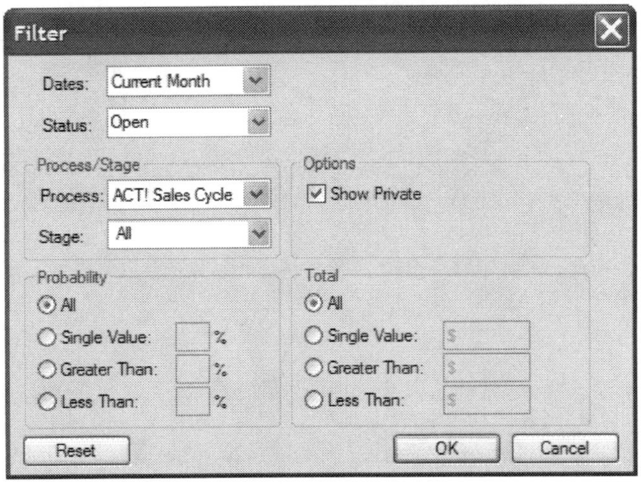

Figure 14-12 Opportunity component filter options

3. Select the options that you want to filter the opportunity records by, then click OK.

The Dashboard Designer

The Dashboard Designer is used to create new dashboards and modify the dashboards that come with ACT!. The Dashboard Designer has two functions as discussed below.

① **CREATE OR MODIFY THE LAYOUT.** Select this option when you want to create a new dashboard layout or modify an existing layout.

② **MODIFY A DASHBOARD COMPONENT.** As you learned earlier, six components come with ACT!. You may have a need to modify some of the component options, like changing the default filter options.

Dashboard Designer Toolbar

Not to be out done, the Dashboard Designer has its own toolbar, as shown in Figure 14-13. Table 14-2 explains the options on the toolbar.

Figure 14-13 Dashboard Designer toolbar

Button	Description
1	Create a new dashboard.
2	Opens an existing dashboard.
3	Saves the changes.
4	Deletes the selected component.
5	Copies the selected component.
6	Pastes the selected component.
7	Undoes the last action.
8	Redoes the previous action.

Table 14-2 Dashboard Designer toolbar buttons explained

Dashboard Designer Window

When you open the Dashboard Designer in Edit mode, you will see the window shown in Figure 14-14.

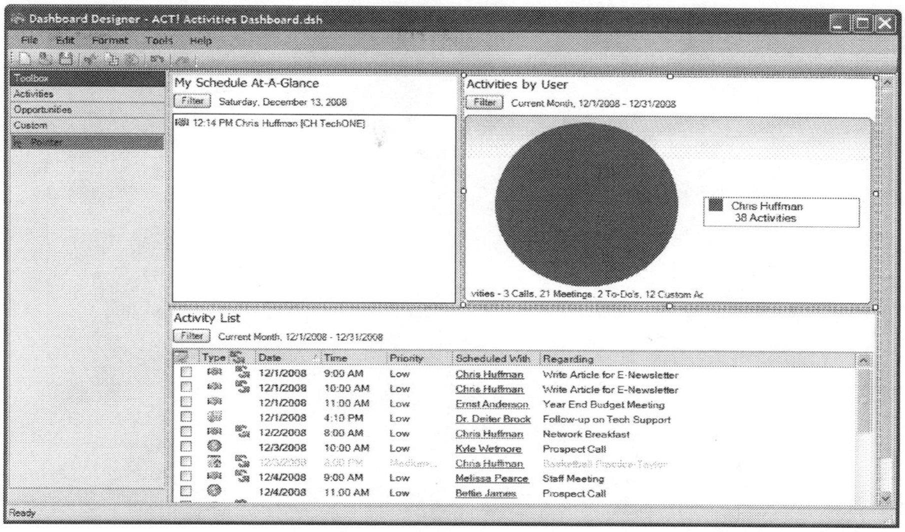

Figure 14-14 Dashboard Designer window

Dashboard Designer Menu Options

The Dashboard Designer has some menu options that are unique. They are explained in Table 14-3.

Menu	Option	Description
File	Layout Settings	Opens the dialog box shown in Figure 14-15. These options are used to change the size of the dashboard.
Format	Insert/Delete	Both options have the submenu shown in Figure 14-16. The options are explained below.
Tools	Add Component	Opens the submenu shown in Figure 14-17. This is one way to add a component to the dashboard. The components are divided into the activity, opportunity and custom categories that you learned about earlier in this lesson.
Tools	Component Configuration	Opens the **COMPONENT CONFIGURATION WIZARD**, which is covered later in this lesson.

Table 14-3 Dashboard Designer menu options explained

The dimensions shown in the **TARGET SIZE** drop-down list are the same size as computer screen resolutions.

This means that if you are creating or modifying a dashboard and all of the people that will use it have the same screen size resolution, you can select that size instead of using the smaller default size.

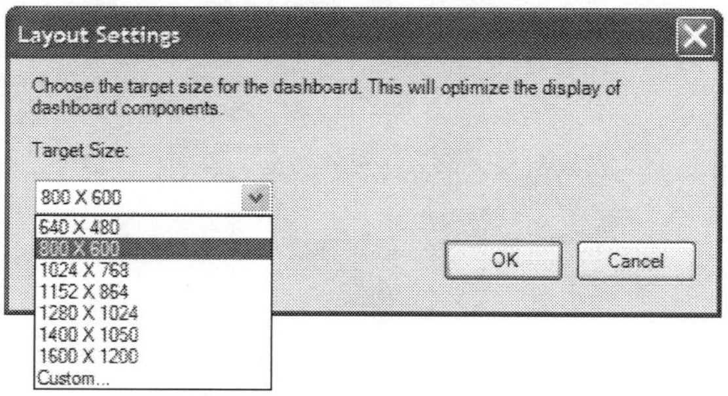

Figure 14-15 Layout Settings dialog box

The **COLUMN ON THE FAR RIGHT** option will add/delete a column on the right side of the dashboard.

The **ROW AT THE BOTTOM** option will add/delete a row at the bottom of the dashboard.

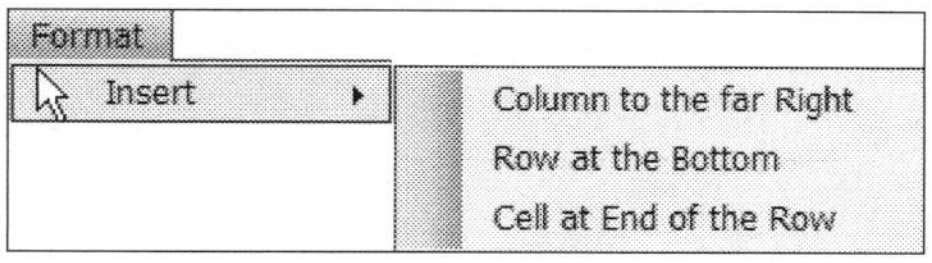

Figure 14-16 Insert and Delete layout options

The **CELL AT END OF THE ROW** option will add/delete a cell at the end of the row that is selected.

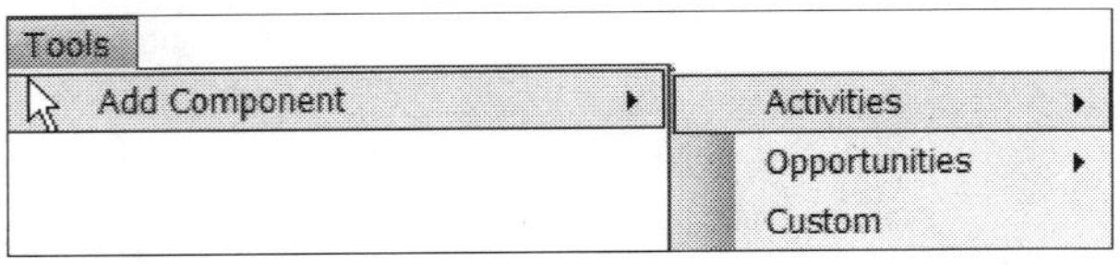

Figure 14-17 Add Component options

Dashboard Designer Toolbox

The Dashboard Designer toolbox options are shown in Figures 14-18 and 14-19. Each component was explained earlier in the Dashboard Components section. These are the components that you can add to the dashboard.

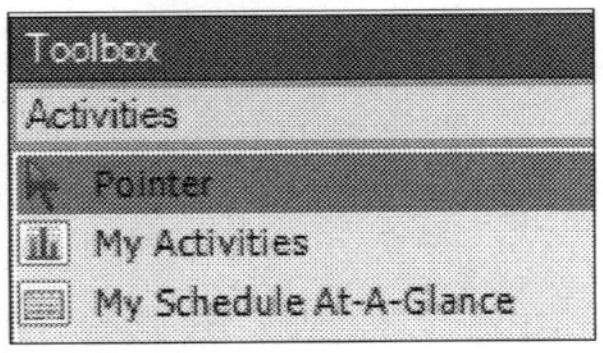

Figure 14-18 Activity toolbox Components

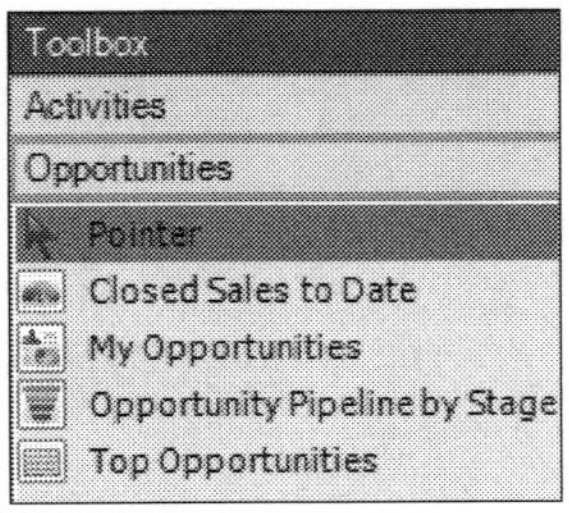

Figure 14-19 Opportunity toolbox components

Dashboard Layout Overview

By default, a new layout has six sections that you can add a component to. It is not a requirement that all six sections be used in a layout. Each section can be resized. I think the Dashboard Designer is a good first step in being able to modify dashboards. It has some quirks that I hope will be worked out in the next release. It is not as user friendly as the other designers in ACT!. For example, in the exercise below, the goal is to move the component that is at the bottom of the dashboard to the top of the dashboard. Sounds easy right? Well, as you will see, it requires more steps then you think it should.

Exercise 14.6: Modify The ACT! Activities Dashboard Layout

In this exercise you will modify the Activities dashboard layout to put the Activity List component at the top of the layout.

1. Open the ACT! Activities Dashboard, then click the **EDIT** button. You will see the Dashboard Designer window, shown earlier in Figure 14-14.

2. File ⇒ Save As.

   You will see the dialog box shown in Figure 14-20.

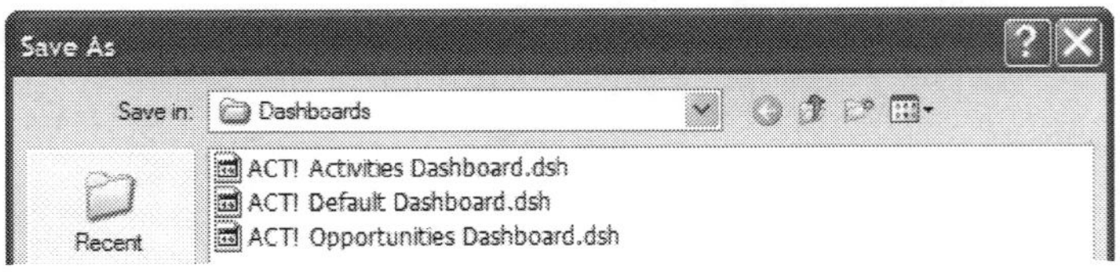

Figure 14-20 Dashboards folder

   This is where the dashboard layouts are stored that appear in the drop-down list at the top of the dashboard. If you want the dashboard layouts that you create to appear in the drop-down list, you have to save them in this folder.

3. Type `My Activities Dashboard`, then press Enter.

4. The My Schedule component should be selected.

   Format ⇒ Insert ⇒ Row at the bottom.

   You should see a new row at the bottom of the window, as shown in Figure 14-21.

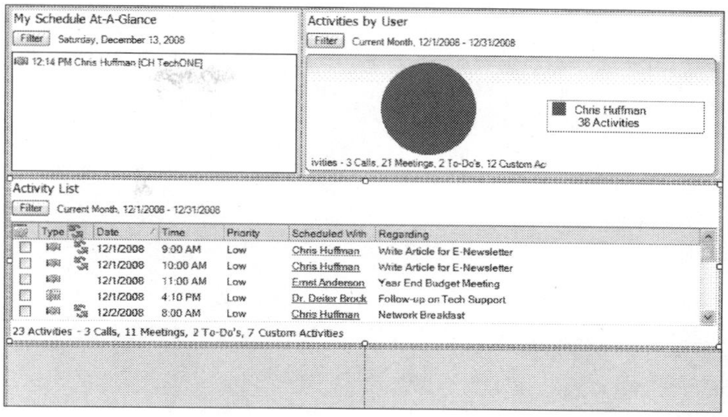

Figure 14-21 New row added to the dashboard layout

5. Drag the Activity List component in the layout to the bottom row.
6. Right-click in the middle row and select Insert ⇒ Cell at end of the row.
7. Place the mouse pointer on the line between the two cells in the middle row, as shown in Figure 14-22, then drag the line to the left so that it lines up with the one at the end of the My Schedule component.

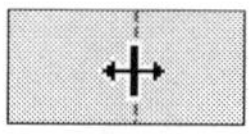

Figure 14-22 Mouse pointer in position to resize a cell

8. Drag the two components at the top of the layout down to the cells in the middle section.
9. Right-click in the top row and select Delete ⇒ Cell at end of the row.
10. Drag the Activity List component in the layout to the top row.
11. Format ⇒ Delete ⇒ Row at the bottom.
12. File ⇒ Exit. Click Yes, when prompted to save the changes to the dashboard. Wasn't that a lot of steps to rearrange the components on the layout? <smile>

View The Changes

1. On the Dashboard view, open the Dashboard drop-down list.

   You should see your dashboard, as shown in Figure 14-23.

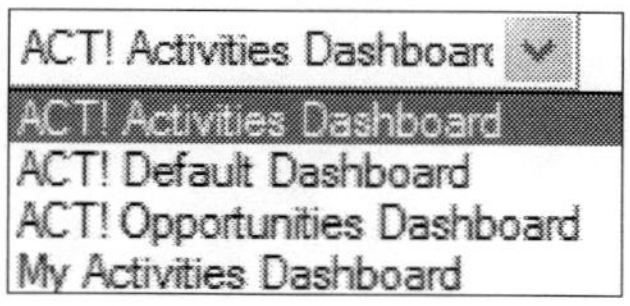

Figure 14-23 Dashboard added to the list

2. Select your dashboard.

   It should look like the one shown in Figure 14-24.

   Compare it to the one shown earlier in Figure 14-3.

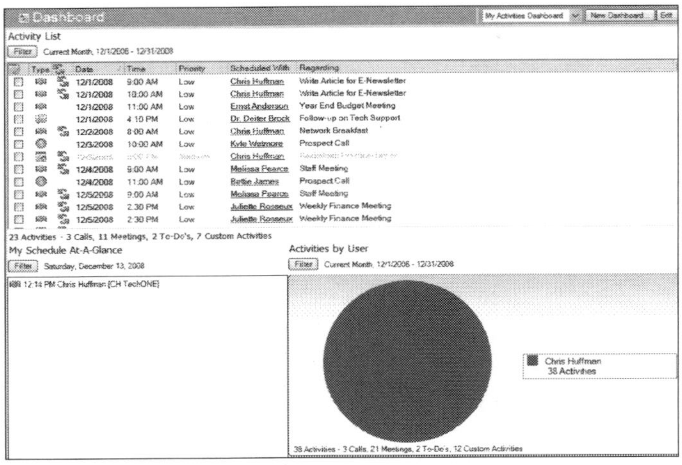

Figure 14-24 Modified Activities dashboard

Exercise 14.7: Modify The ACT! Default Dashboard Layout

In this exercise you will modify the Default Dashboard by removing some of the components and rearranging the remaining components.

1. Open the ACT! Default Dashboard, then click the **EDIT** button.
2. File ⇒ Save As. Type `My Default Dashboard` as the file name, then press Enter.
3. Delete the following components by clicking on them and then pressing the Delete key: My Schedule At-A-Glance, Opportunities by User and Top 10 Opportunities.
4. Drag the Activities by User component to the cell on the left of the same row.
5. Drag the Closed Sales to Date component up to the first row.
6. Click in the middle row, then delete the cell on the right in the middle row.
7. Delete the bottom row.
8. Make the first row longer so that it takes up more than 50% of the space in the dashboard.
9. File ⇒ Exit. Save the changes.
10. Select the My Default Dashboard from the drop-down list.

    It should look like the one shown in Figure 25.

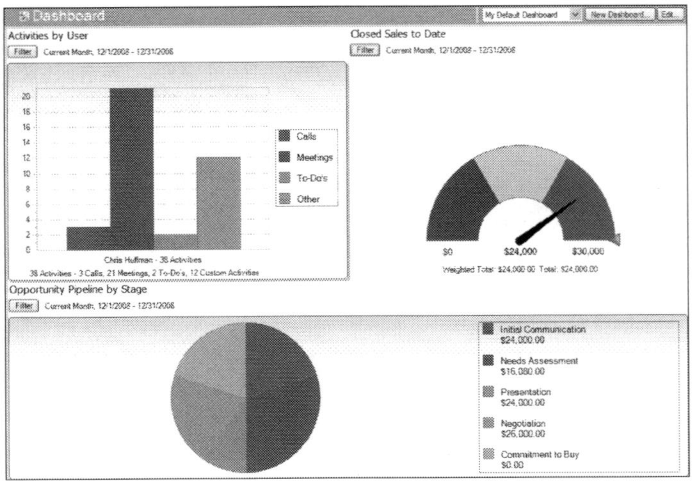

Figure 14-25 My Default Dashboard

Component Configuration Wizard

This wizard is used to add components to a dashboard. Once you select an option on a component wizard screen, you can preview the change by clicking the **PREVIEW** button. The following seven steps are available on the Component Configuration Wizard for components that have been added to a dashboard. All steps are not available for each component. The options available for some steps vary depending on the component that is being added to the dashboard.

Step 1: Select Display Type

This step is used to select the chart type, as shown in Figure 14-26.

All chart types are not available for all components.

You can also select where to place the filter bar, as illustrated at the bottom of Figure 14-26.

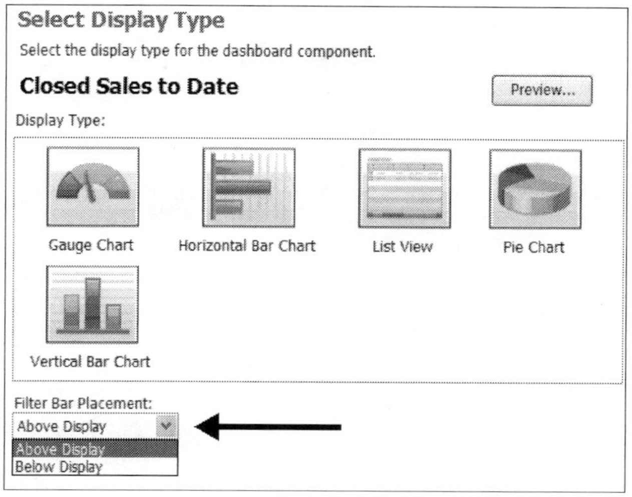

Figure 14-26 Display type options for the Closed Sales to Date component

Step 2: Edit Default Filters

This step displays the current default filter options for the component and is used to select new default filter options.

The filter options change, depending on the display type (chart) that is selected.
Figure 14-27 shows the filter options for the My Activities component.
Figure 14-28 shows the filter options for the Opportunity Pipeline by Stage component.

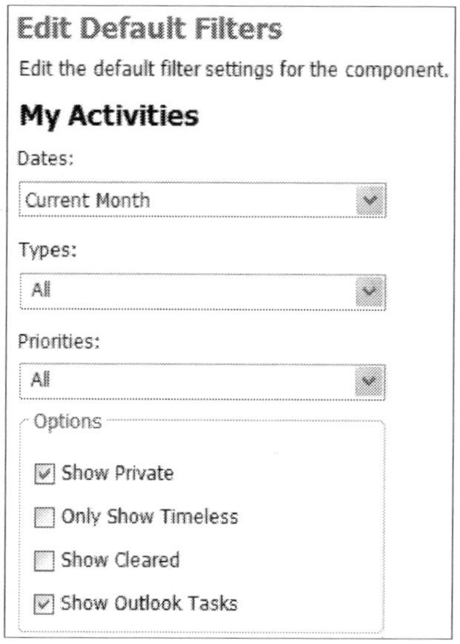

Figure 14-27 Filter options for the My Activities component

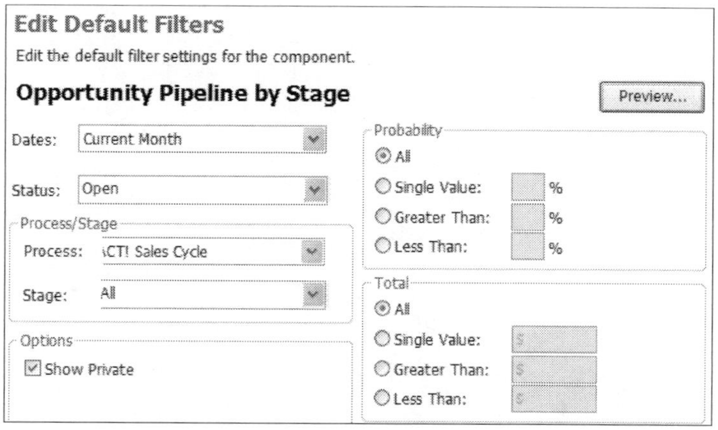

Figure 14-28 Filter options for the Opportunity Pipeline by Stage component

Step 3: Edit Header/Footer

This step is used to add or edit the header and footer information for the component, as shown in Figure 14-29.

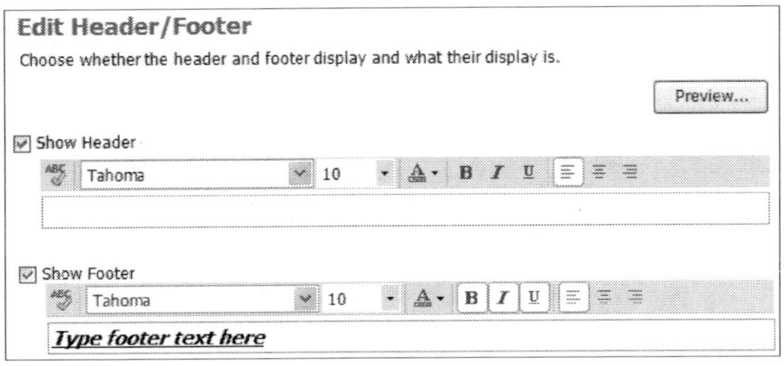

Figure 14-29 Header and footer options

Step 4: Change Legend

This step is used to select whether or not the component displays a legend and where the legend should be placed, as shown in Figure 14-30.

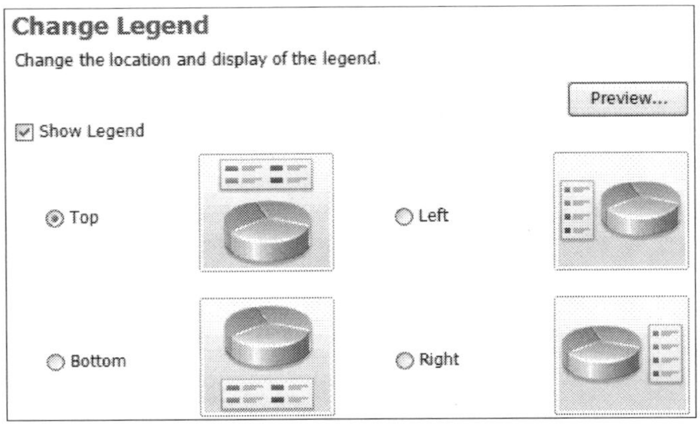

Figure 14-30 Legend options

Step 5: Change Totals

This step is used to select whether or not the component displays totals. The totals for each component type are pre-determined, which means that you can only select whether or not to display totals. Figure 14-31 shows the totals for the Closed Sales to Date component. Figure 14-32 shows the totals for the My Activities component.

Figure 14-31 Change totals options for the Closed Sales to Date component

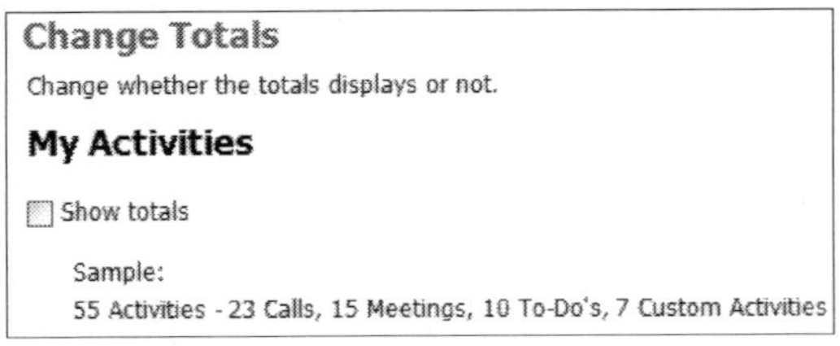

Figure 14-32 Change totals options for the My Activities component

Step 6: Specify Targets

This step is used to select whether or not the component displays the minimum acceptable amount or value that will reach the expected goal. Figure 14-33 shows the target options. Figure 14-34 shows the target option applied to a chart. The line illustrated in Figure 14-34 across the chart, represents the target. This allows the user to see which items meet the goal and which ones do not.

As illustrated in Figure 14-35, the target is $30,000. The target is indicated by a triangle pointer on the chart. In this example, the target has not been met. In Figure 14-36, the target is $17,500, which means that the target has been exceeded.

Figure 14-33 Target options

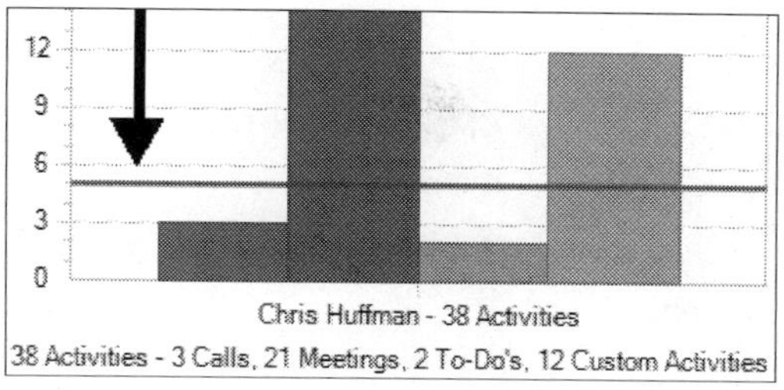

Figure 14-34 Target option on the chart

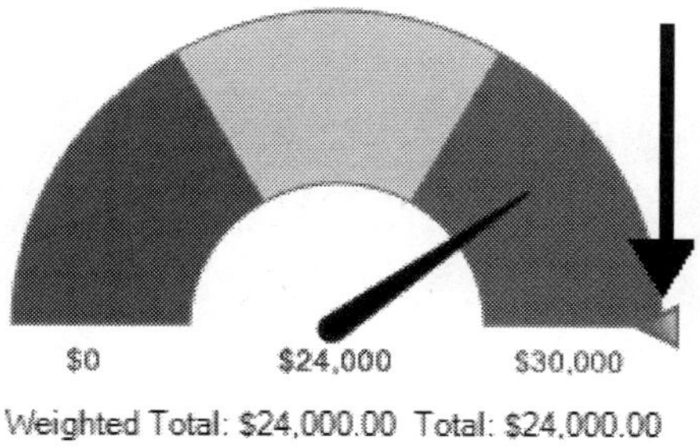

Figure 14-35 Target has not been met

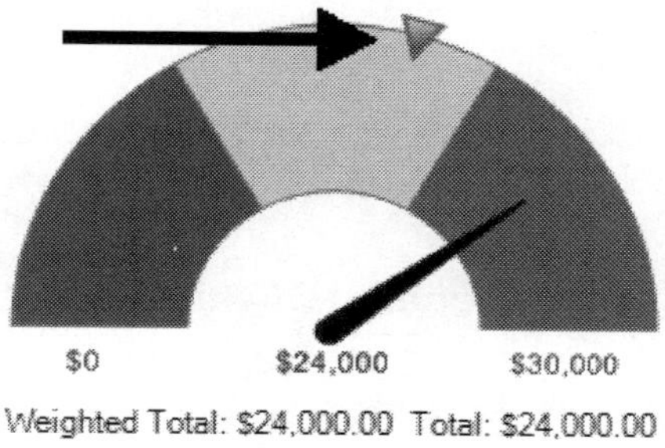

Figure 14-36 Target has been met

Step 7: Scale/Limits

This step is used to select the range that numeric data should be displayed in, on the chart. The scale and limits change depending on the display type that is selected.

Figures 14-37 to 14-39 show different types of scale/limits.

The **BREAKPOINT** options are used to measure progress.

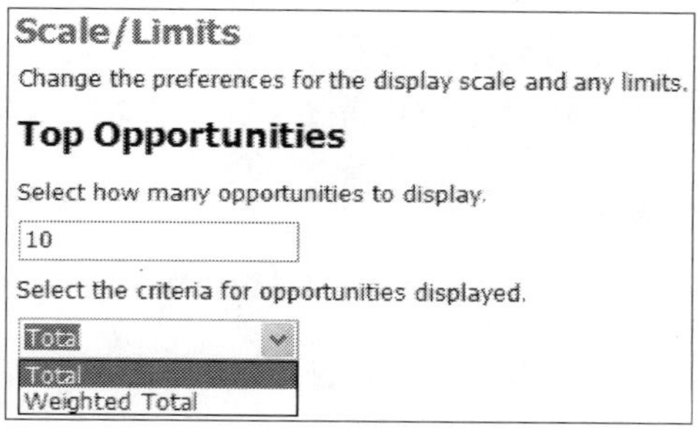

Figure 14-37 Top Opportunities component Scale/Limits options

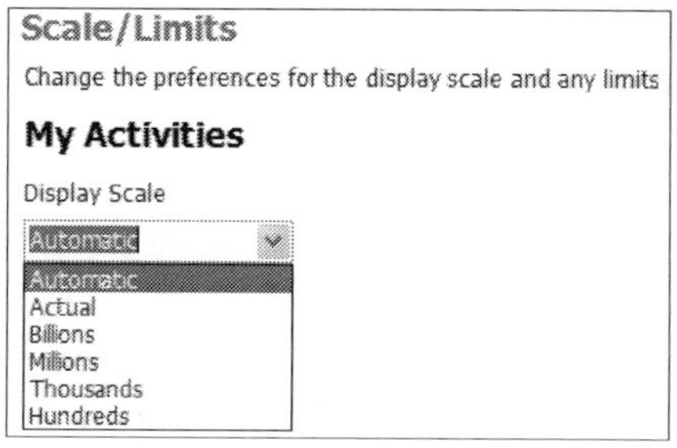

Figure 14-38 My Activities Scale/Limits component options

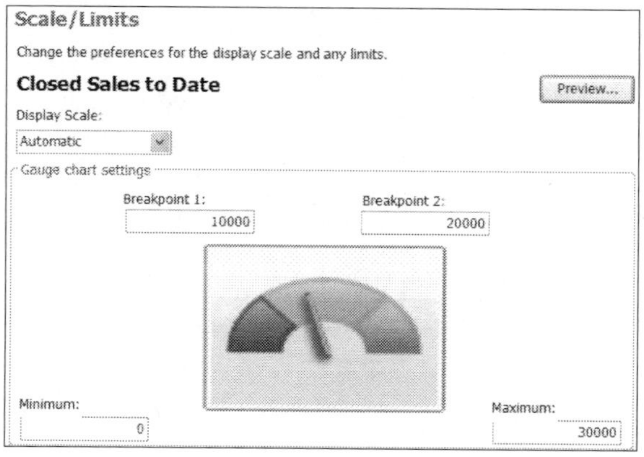

Figure 14-39 Closed Sales to Date Scale/Limits component options

Top Opportunities Component

This component has an additional step, as shown in Figure 14-40. The options shown are used to change the columns that are displayed in the grid and how the opportunity records are sorted.

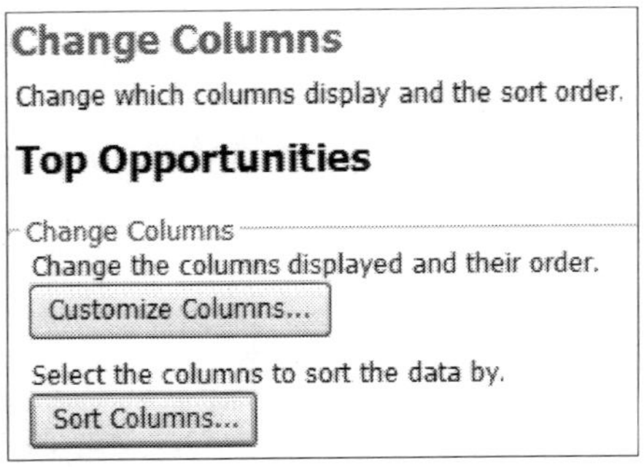

Figure 14-40 Change Columns options for the Top Opportunities component

Exercise 14.8: Modify The Components Of The My Default Dashboard

In this exercise you will modify the default filter options for the My Default Dashboard. Currently, all of the filters are using the current month as the date range.

1. Open the My Default Dashboard, if it is not already open, then click the **EDIT** button.
2. File ⇒ Save As. Type `My New Filter Dashboard` as the file name, then press Enter.

Modify The Activities By User Component Filter Options

1. Right-click on the Activities by User component and select **COMPONENT CONFIGURATION**.
2. Click on the Select Display Type link, then select the **HORIZONTAL BAR CHART** display type.
3. Open the **FILTER BAR PLACEMENT** drop-down list and select Below Display.
4. On the Edit Default Filters screen, open the Dates drop-down list and select Today and Future.
5. On the Change Legend screen, select Top, then click Finish.
6. Click Yes, when prompted that the changes will affect all users.

   As shown in Figure 14-41, the Details section of the Configuration Wizard screen shows the options that have been selected for the component.

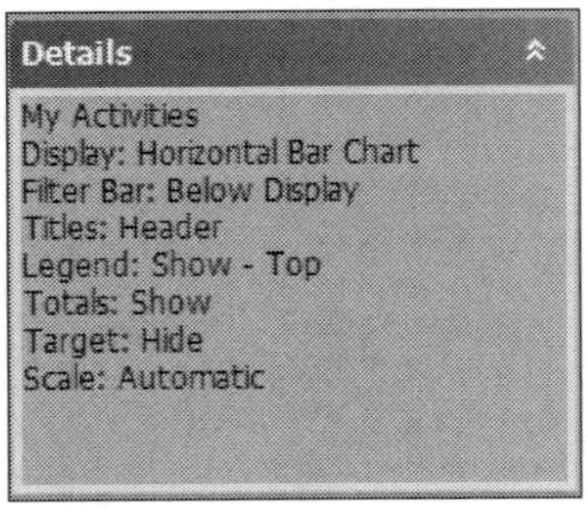

Figure 14-41 Details section

7. Click Close to close the Component Configuration dialog box.

Modify The Closed Sales To Date Component Filter Options

1. Right-click on the Closed Sales to Date component and select Component Configuration.
2. On the Edit Default Filters screen, open the Dates drop-down list and select Today and Future.
3. On the Edit Header/Filter screen, type `Pending Sales` in the Header field, then change the font size to 14. Change the color to red.

4. On the Specify Targets screen, change the Target value to `$100,000.00`.

5. On the Scale/Limits screen, make the following changes. You should have the options shown in Figure 14-42.

   Breakpoint 1 25000
   Breakpoint 2 75000
   Maximum 250000

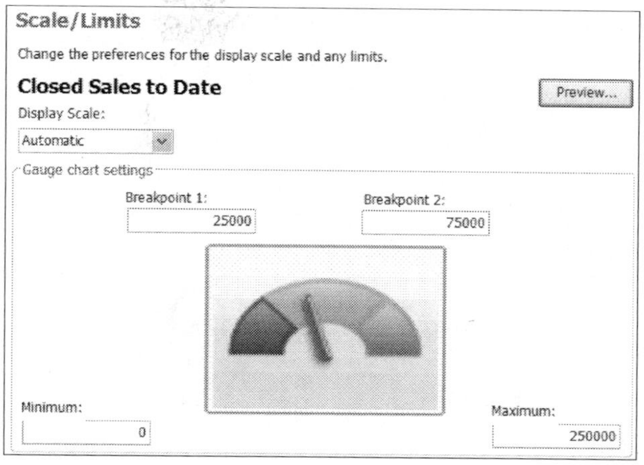

Figure 14-42 Scale/Limit options

6. Click Finish. Click Yes to continue with changes, then click Close.

7. File ⇒ Exit, then click Yes. The dashboard should look similar to the one shown in Figure 14-43. Compare this to the dashboard shown earlier in Figure 14-25.

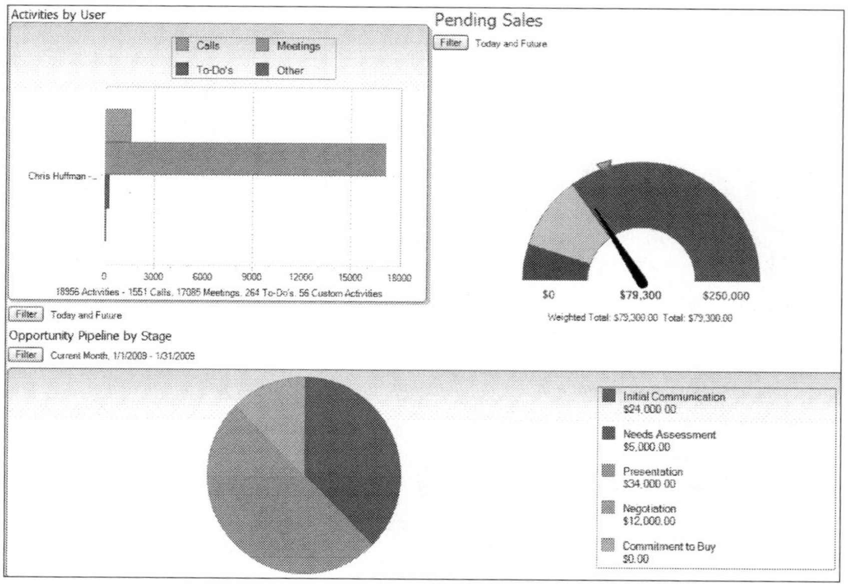

Figure 14-43 Modified dashboard components

Create A New Dashboard

If you need to create a dashboard from scratch, you can follow the steps below.

1. Click the **NEW DASHBOARD** button on the Dashboard view. You will see an empty layout in the Dashboard Designer.
2. Drag the component from the Toolbox to the layout, where you want it to be.
3. The Component Configuration wizard will automatically open. Select the default options that you need, for the component.
4. Repeat steps 2 and 3 for each component that you want to add to the layout.

5. Remove any sections from the layout that are not needed.

6. Save the dashboard and give it a descriptive name.

USING THE TASK LIST & CALENDARS

In this lesson you will learn the following Task List and calendar features:

- ☑ How to use the Task List view to work with activities
- ☑ How to use the calendar views
- ☑ How to filter activities in a calendar view
- ☑ Granting calendar access

LESSON 15

The Task List View

You have learned how to create activities and view them. You have also learned how to view several contacts at the same time using the Contact List view. If you need to view activities for several contacts at the same time, you can use the Task List view. The entries displayed in the Task List are linked to the current My Record. This means that by default, each person that uses the database has their own Task List and calendar that only displays activities that they scheduled or activities that are assigned to them.

The Task List view allows you to add and delete columns, sort by column headings and change the order of the column headings, just like you can with the Contact List view. In addition to being able to view activities for several contacts in the Task List view, you can also modify, sort, filter, clear, schedule and delete activities on the Task List view, the same way that you can on the Activities tab.

Figure 15-1 shows the Task List toolbar.
Table 15-1 explains the buttons on the toolbar.

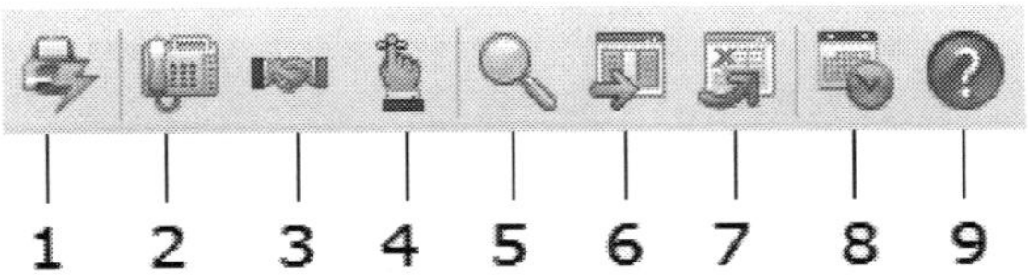

Figure 15-1 Task List toolbar

Button	Description
1	Prints the current view.
2	Schedules a telephone call activity.
3	Schedules a meeting activity.
4	Schedules a To-Do item activity.
5	Opens to the Contact List view.
6	Opens the Customize Columns dialog box, which is used the change the order of the columns on the Task List.
7	Exports the Task List to Excel.
8	Copies calendar information between the ACT! and Outlook calendars.
9	Opens the Help system.

Table 15-1 Task List toolbar buttons explained

Status Bar

At the bottom of the Task List window is the status bar shown in Figure 15-2. It displays the date range and totals for each type of activity that is displayed on the Task List view.

Figure 15-2 Task List status bar

1. Click the Task List button. You will see the view shown in Figure 15-3. If you do not see the filter options (Dates, Types, etc.) at the top of the Task List, click the **SHOW FILTERS** button.

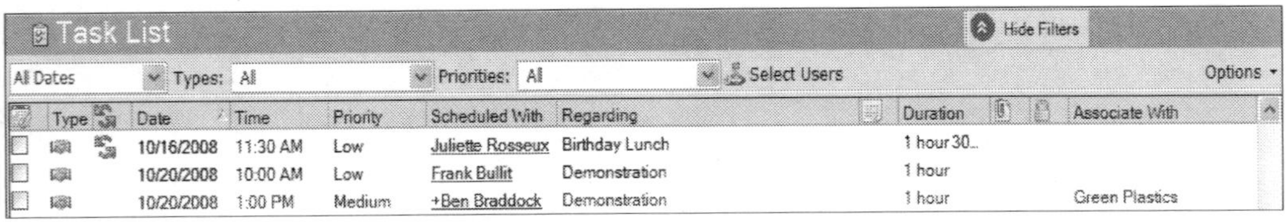

Figure 15-3 Task List view

> If you double-click on an activity in the Task List, you can edit it or see more information about the activity.

Filter Options

The filter options for the Task List are explained in Table 15-2.

Filter	Description
Dates	Select the date or date range that you want to see activities for, as shown in Figure 15-4. If none of the options shown fit your needs, select the **CUSTOM** option at the bottom of the drop-down list.
Types	Check the activity options that you want to see and clear the check mark of the option(s) that you do not want to see, as shown in Figure 15-5.
Priorities	Check the priority of the activity types that you want to see. Clear the check mark of the option(s) that you do not want to see, as shown in Figure 15-6.
Select Users	View the public activities of others users in the database. If you select other users, keep in mind that their activities will continue to be displayed in your Task List until you remove the user from your view.

Table 15-2 Task List filter options explained

Figure 15-4 Date filter options

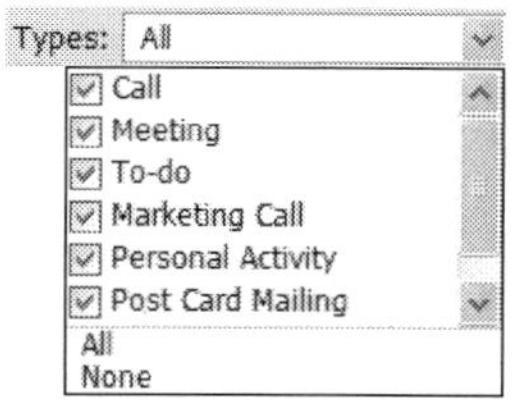

Figure 15-5 Activity Type options

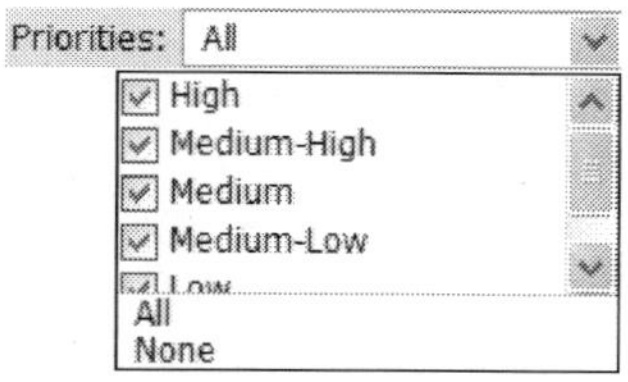

Figure 15-6 Priority options

Options Button

The options shown in Figure 15-7 are other options that can be selected to filter activities on the Task List view. They are explained below.

① **Show Private** Displays or hides private activities.

② **Only Show Timeless** Hides tasks that have a time.

③ **Show Cleared** displays tasks that have been cleared, but not deleted. Cleared tasks have a line through them, as illustrated in Figure 15-8.

④ **Show Outlook Tasks** Displays tasks that were imported from Microsoft Outlook.

⑤ **Customize Columns** Opens the Customize Columns dialog box that you learned about in Lesson 13.

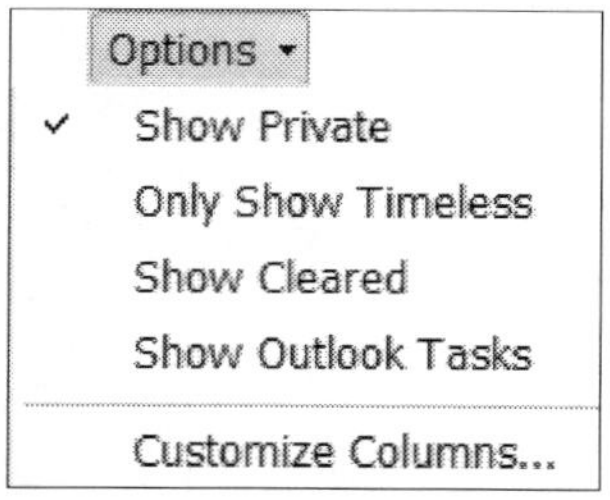

Figure 15-7 Task List Options button

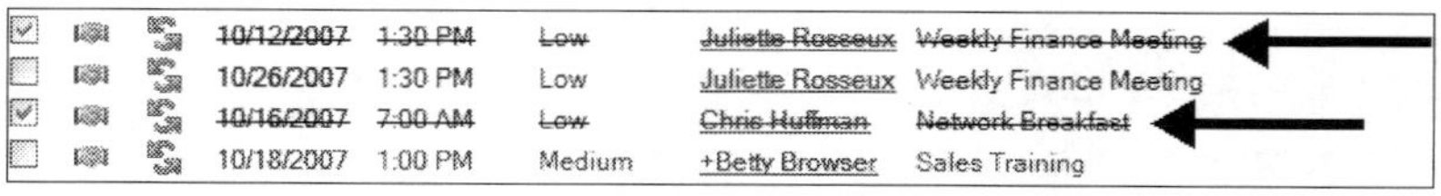

Figure 15-8 Cleared tasks illustrated

Exercise 15.1: Create A Task List Lookup Using Filters

By default, the activities are in ascending order by date. If you have hundreds of activities, you will probably not want to see all of them. You can create a lookup to only display certain activities.

1. Open the Dates drop-down list, then select the **CUSTOM** option at the bottom of the list. You will see the Select Date Range dialog box.

2. Select the range 9/1/2008 to 9/8/2008, as shown in Figure 15-9.

   Click OK.

   You should only see activities that have a date in the range that you selected.

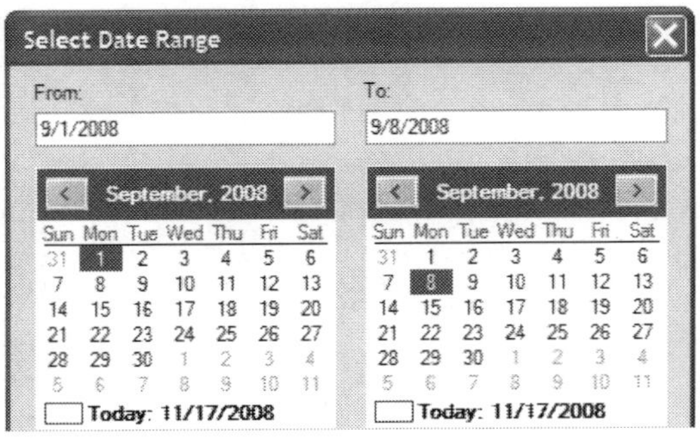

Figure 15-9 Select Date Range dialog box

3. Display all of the activities, then clear the Activity Type options that you do not want to see. In this exercise clear all of the options except Call and To-Do.

4. Select the priority of the activities that you want to see. For this exercise clear all of the options except Medium-High.

5. If you want to see activities for other users, click the **SELECT USERS** button. Select the first two users, then click OK.

6. View all of the activities.

> If you prefer to see all of the Task List filter options in one place, use the dialog box shown in Figure 15-10. Right-click in the Task List view and select **FILTER TASK LIST**. It is similar to the Filter Activities dialog box that you learned about. [See Lesson 8, Figure 8-39]

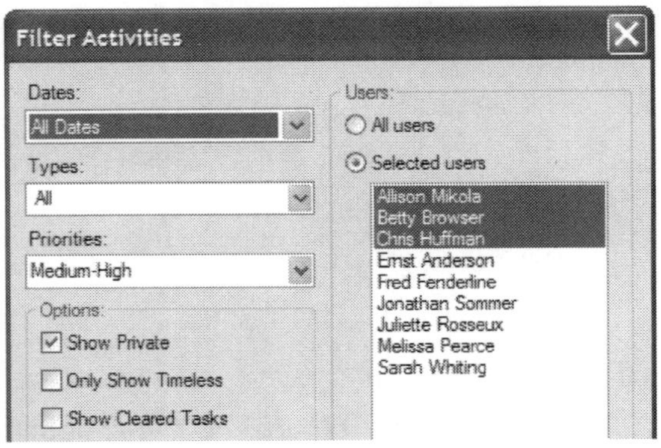

Figure 15-10 Filter Activities (Task List) dialog box

Exercise 15.2: Clearing Tasks From The Task List View

Once you have completed a task or no longer need it, you can clear the activity. You can also create a follow up task. Use the activity dated 9/19/2008 to complete this exercise.

1. Click in the **CLEARED** column (the column with the ✓) next to the activity that you want to clear. You will see the Clear Activity dialog box.

2. In the Details field type `Clearing this task`, as illustrated in Figure 15-11.

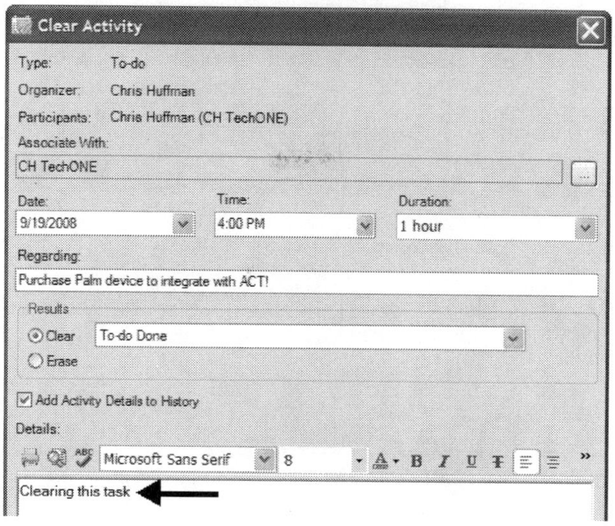

Figure 15-11 Clear Activity dialog box

3. Click OK. You will not see the task in the list unless the **SHOW CLEARED** option is selected on the Options button.

How To Print The Task List

The Task List can be printed by following the steps below.

1. From the Task List view, File ⇒ Quick Print Current Window.

2. Select any options that are needed on the Print dialog box, then click OK.

Looking Up Records On The Task List

If you like working from the Task List, you can accomplish the same tasks that you can from other views by using the options on the shortcut menu shown in Figure 15-12.

Like other views, you can look up contacts from the Task List. If you do, the contacts will open in the Contact List view.

There are two ways to create a lookup from the Task List view as discussed below.

① Click the **CREATE LOOKUP** button on the toolbar.

② Right-click in the Task List view and select Create Lookup, as shown in Figure 15-12.

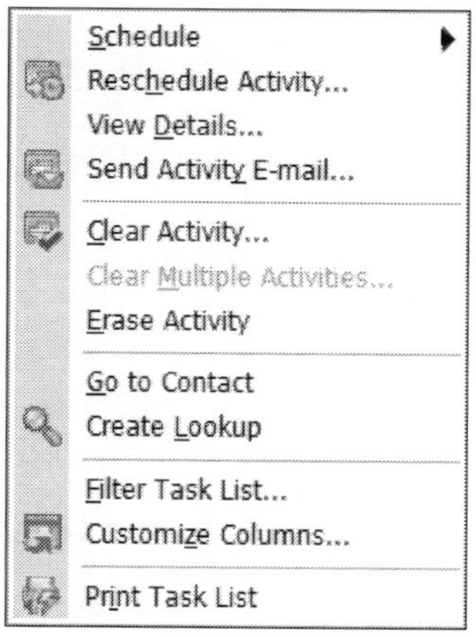

Figure 15-12 Task List view shortcut menu

Exercise 15.3: Customizing The Task List View

The columns on the Task List view can be customized by following the steps below.

1. Open the Task List view.

2. Right-click in the view and select **CUSTOMIZE COLUMNS**. You will see the Customize Columns dialog box.

Adding the **SCHEDULED BY** field to the Task List will show who created the activity.
Adding the **SCHEDULED FOR** field will show who the activity has been assigned to.

These two fields are useful to see on the Task List view if you view other users activities on a regular basis. Figure 15-13 shows these two fields.

Regarding	Scheduled By	Scheduled For
Lunch Meeting to review proposal	Chris Huffman	Allison Mikola
Customer Thank You	Chris Huffman	Chris Huffman
AS-Check Creditand Set Up New...	Chris Huffman	Juliette Rosseux

Figure 15-13 Modified Task List view

Calendar Preferences

In Lesson 1 you learned that there are preferences that you can set for the calendar views. ACT! has calendar options that you can customize as needed.

Using The Calendar Views

The default date when you open any calendar is today's date. Each calendar view has a daily check list and date selector. **TIMELESS** activities are not displayed on calendars. They are displayed under the calendar on the right side of the window with the rest of the activities. There is also a mini calendar that you can use. The calendar views can also be used to schedule and modify activities. The calendar views (Daily, Work Week, Weekly and Monthly), allow you to see and schedule activities.

Calendar Toolbar

Figure 15-14 shows the calendar toolbar. Table 15-3 explains the buttons on the toolbar.

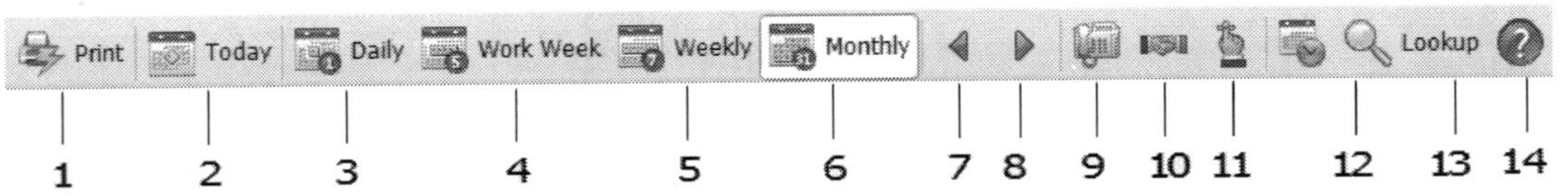

Figure 15-14 Calendar toolbar

Button	Description
1	Prints the calendar.
2	Highlights today in any calendar view except the daily calendar.
3	Opens the daily calendar.
4	Opens the work week calendar.
5	Opens the weekly calendar.
6	Opens the monthly calendar.
7	Moves back one day, week or month, depending on which calendar view is open.
8	Moves forward one day, week or month, depending on which calendar view is open.
9	Schedules a telephone call activity.
10	Schedules a meeting activity.
11	Schedules a To-Do activity.
12	Copies calendar information between the ACT! and Outlook calendars.
13	Look up contacts.
14	Opens the Help application.

Table 15-3 Calendar toolbar buttons explained

Mini-Calendar

This calendar is used to view calendars for the previous month, current month and next month. This is a quick way to display activities from previous or future months. The single arrows will move to the previous and next month. The double arrows will move to the previous and next year. You can use this calendar to navigate to a day, week or month, by clicking on it.

1. Click the Calendar button on the Navigator bar.

2. View ⇒ Mini-Calendar, or press F4 if the calendar shown in Figure 15-15 is not visible.

   If you click on a date and the weekly calendar view is open, you will see the weekly calendar for the date that you click on.

   If necessary, close the mini calendar by clicking on the red X in the upper right corner of the calendar.

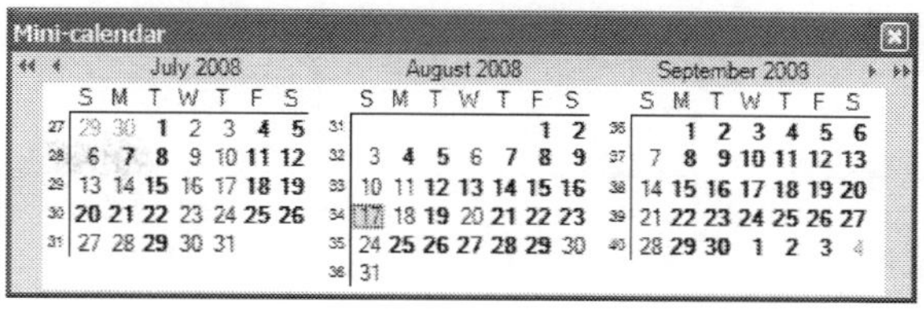

Figure 15-15 Mini-calendar

Calendar Tips

Mini-Calendar and **Recap List Calendar** If you right-click on the month name in the mini calendar shown above in Figure 15-15, you will see the Recap List calendar shown in Figure 15-16. You can jump to one of the months in the list. The dates in bold on the mini-calendar have activities. If you right-click on a date that is bold, you will see all of the activities for that day.

Shortcut Menu If you right-click on an activity in the calendar, you will see the shortcut menu shown in Figure 15-17. Many of the options that you will use the most are on this shortcut menu.

The **Filter Calendar** view option opens the dialog box shown in Figure 15-18. This dialog box contains all of the filter options that are at the top of a calendar view.

Drop And Drag An Activity You can move an activity from one day or time to another day or time by dragging the activity to a new location. If you select an activity to move that is part of a recurring activity, you will be prompted to change all occurrences of the activity or only the current occurrence. If you click OK to move the activity, it will no longer be part of the recurring activities, as shown by the message in Figure 15-19.

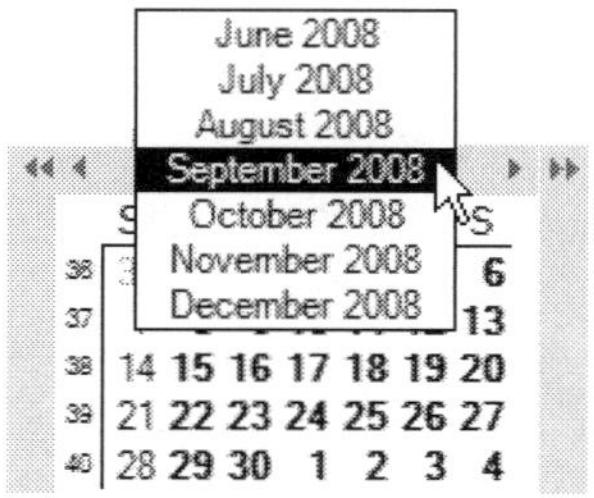

Figure 15-16 Recap List calendar

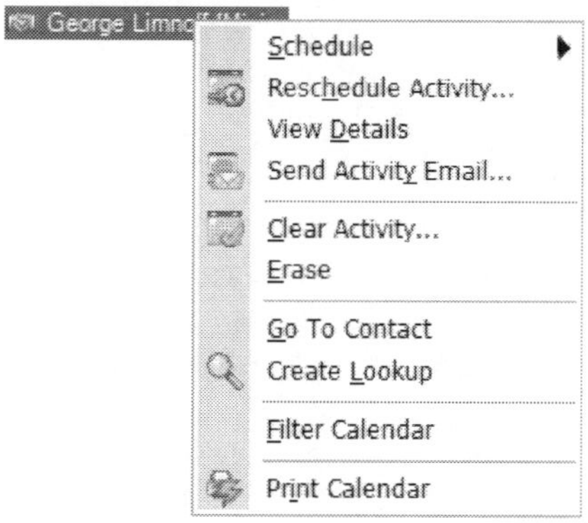

Figure 15-17 Calendar shortcut menu

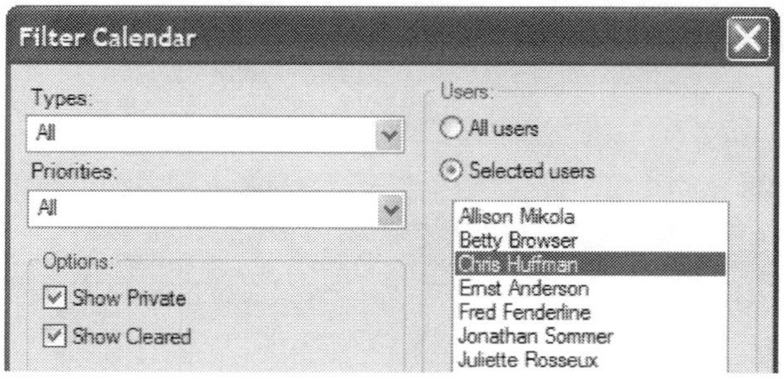

Figure 15-18 Filter Calendar dialog box

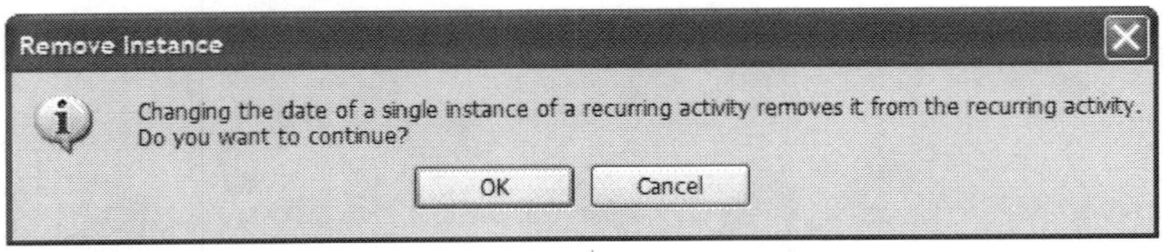

Figure 15-19 Remove Instance message

Daily Calendar

The daily calendar displays activities and tasks for one day. By default, the day is divided into 30 minute intervals. You can change the time interval on the Preferences dialog box.

1. Display the My Record, then click on the Calendar button on the Navigation bar.

2. View the daily calendar for January 13, 2009, by clicking the **DAILY** button and then selecting the day in the mini calendar.

   The calendar should look similar to the one shown in Figure 15-20.

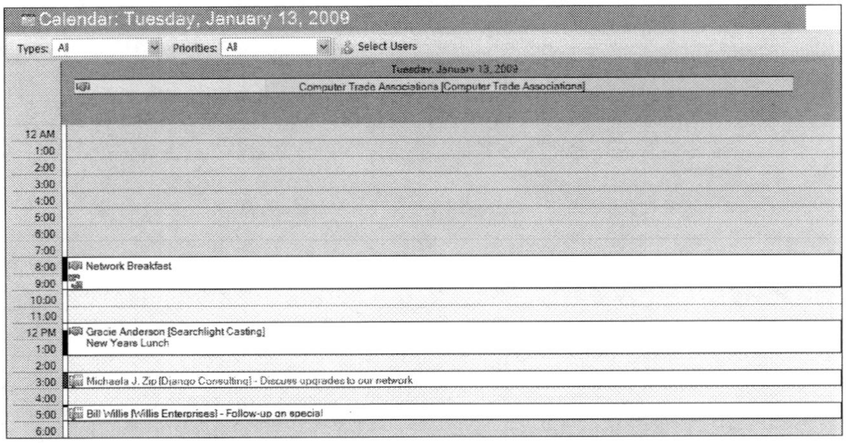

Figure 15-20 Daily calendar view

Notice that all of the activities in the **RECAP LIST** (which is under the calendar on the right) are for one day, as shown in Figure 15-21.

The items in this section are from the Task List. This list is helpful when there are activities that you can't see without scrolling.

When you click on a different day on the Recap calendar, the activities below it will change.

When you need to view a different date in the daily calendar, click on the date in the Recap calendar.

Figure 15-21 Recap list

Banner Option

The banner option will display a single line entry at the top of the daily calendar. This lets you see more information about the activity. The banner option can be disabled on the Schedule Activity dialog box. Double-clicking on a banner, like the one shown earlier at the top of Figure 15-20, will open the Schedule Activity dialog box for the activity. (I added the banner to the screen shot for illustration purposes.)

Calendar Pop-Ups

If you hold the mouse pointer over an activity on a calendar you will see a pop-up like the one shown in Figure 15-22.

This allows you to see some of the information about the activity.

Figure 15-22 Calendar pop-up illustrated

Today (Calendar) Button

When clicked, this button will jump to today's date in the calendar view that you are in, except for the daily calendar view. For example, if today is September 19, 2008 and you are viewing the monthly calendar for June 2009, if you click the **TODAY** button, the calendar will go back to the September 2008 monthly calendar and highlight September 19th.

Work Week Calendar

The work week calendar view shown in Figure 15-23 displays all activities and tasks that have a start time between Monday and Friday or the work days that are selected in the Calendar preferences.

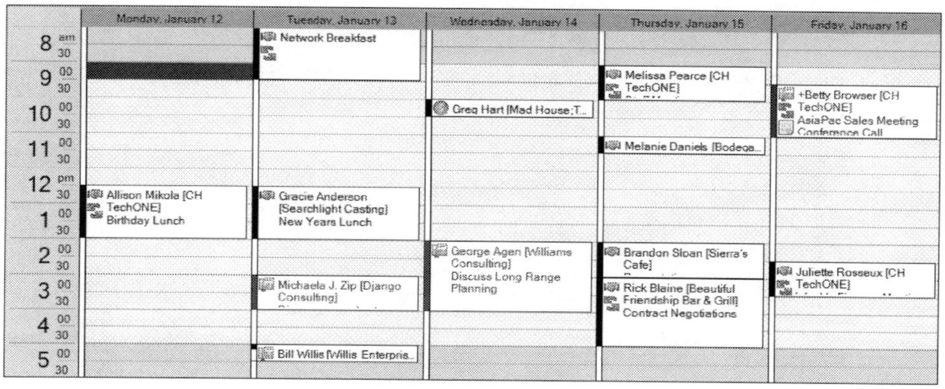

Figure 15-23 Work Week calendar view

If you double-click on the day of the week at the top of the calendar, that day will open in the Daily calendar. Double-clicking on an activity will open the Schedule Activity dialog box.

Weekly Calendar

The weekly calendar view shown in Figure 15-24 displays all activities for the week. The activities under the Recap calendar on the right are for the day that is selected in the calendar.

In this calendar view, the activities under the calendar are for Tuesday, January 20, 2009.

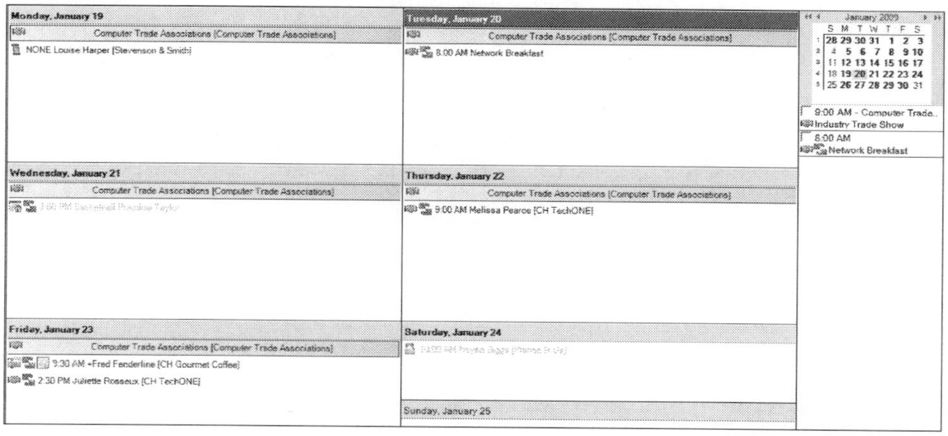

Figure 15-24 Weekly calendar view

> If you double-click on a date header on the weekly calendar you will open the daily calendar for the day that you double-click on.

Monthly Calendar

The monthly calendar displays all activities and tasks that have a start time in the month selected, as shown in Figure 15-25.

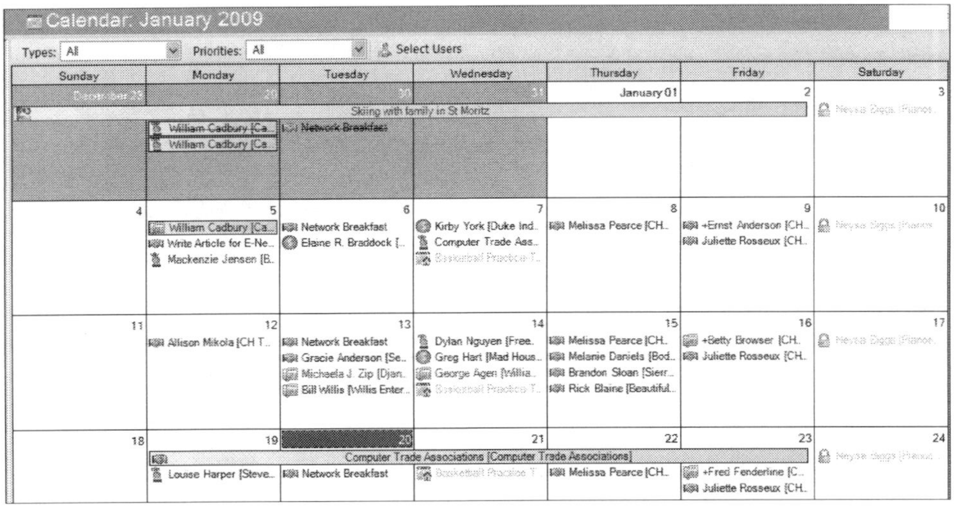

Figure 15-25 Monthly calendar view

> **Cool Calendar Tip**
>
> I stumbled across this by accident, with the slip of the mouse. By default, the Recap calendar on the right side of the calendar view only displays one month. The border to the left of this calendar moves. Who knew? Place the mouse pointer in the position illustrated in Figure 15-26, then drag the mouse to the left until you see as many months as you need, as shown in Figure 15-27. You can also display more calendars below, by dragging the bottom of the calendar down.

Figure 15-26 Mouse pointer in position to display more calendars

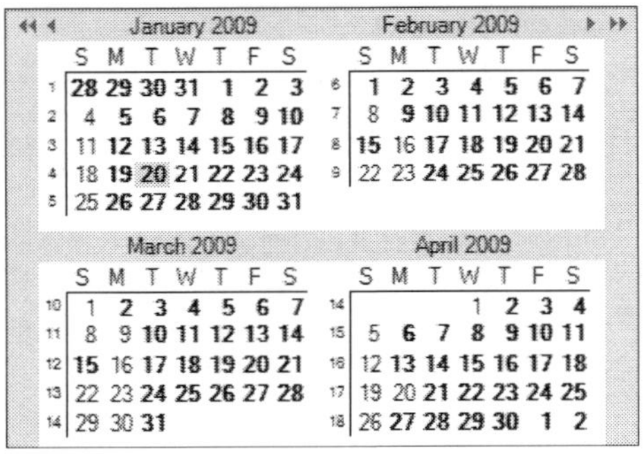

Figure 15-27 Multiple calendars displayed

Calendar Status Bar

At the bottom of each calendar view is a status bar, as shown in Figure 15-28. It displays a count of the activities that are scheduled, based on the view that is displayed.

Figure 15-28 Status bar for the weekly calendar

Filtering Activities In A Calendar View

Some calendar views are better able to handle a lot of activities then others. You may only want to view a certain type of activity on a calendar. If either of these options is what you want to do, you can filter the activities that appear on calendars. You can filter activities in a calendar the same way that you filter activities on the Activities tab. The filter that you set will be applied to each calendar view until you remove or change the filter. You can select which activity types and priorities to display.

Calendar Filter Options

Figure 15-29 shows the calendar filter options. They are explained below. They are similar to the Task List view filters that you learned about earlier in this lesson.

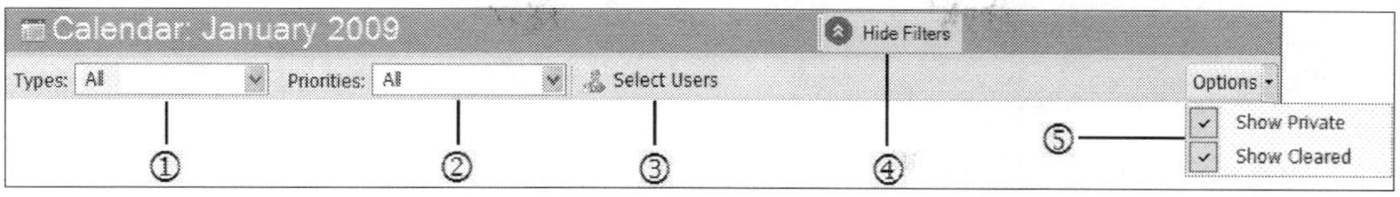

Figure 15-29 Calendar filter options

① **TYPES** The options in this drop-down list are used to select the activity type(s) that you want to display. The default is to display all activity types. Clear the check box of the activities that you do not want to display.
② **PRIORITIES** This option is used to select the priority of the activity types that you want to display, as shown earlier in Figure 15-6.
③ **SELECT USERS** This button opens the Select Users dialog box that you learned about in Lesson 12. [See Lesson 12, Select Users Button]
④ **SHOW/HIDE FILTERS** This button displays and hides the other filter options.
⑤ The **OPTIONS** drop-down list options are used to display private and cleared activities.

How To Filter Activities On The Calendar

1. Select a month that has a lot of activities, like January 2009.

2. Only display the scheduled meetings that do not have a low priority. You will see fewer activities.

Using The Calendar To Schedule Activities

In addition to being able to schedule activities from a contact view, activities can also be scheduled from any calendar view. A benefit of scheduling activities from a calendar view is that you are able to see if the start date and time are already booked. I find the daily calendar the easiest to use to schedule activities because you can select the start and end times before opening the Schedule Activity dialog box.

1. Display the start date of the activity that you want to create on a calendar.

2. If you are using the daily or work week calendar, double-click on the time that you want the activity to start. If you are using the weekly or monthly calendar, right-click on the day that you want to schedule the activity on, then select the schedule option and the type of activity that you want to create.

> If you highlight the start and end time for the activity that you want to create in the daily calendar, as illustrated in Figure 15-30, before you double-click on a time, you will not have to type this information in on the Schedule Activity dialog box.

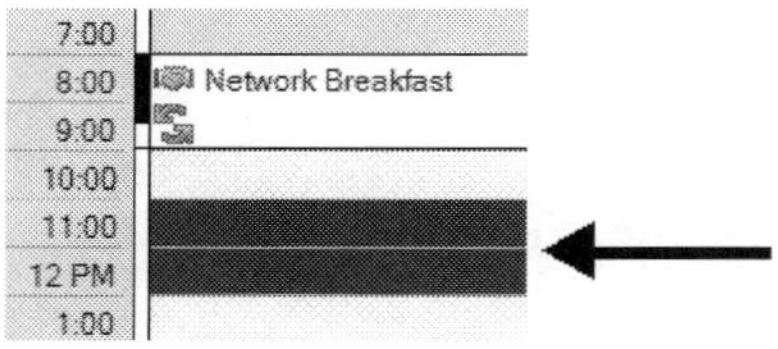

Figure 15-30 Activity time range selected

3. Enter the remaining information for the activity, then click OK.

Exercise 15.4: Granting Calendar Access

This tool is used to give another user access to your calendar. Granting access is helpful when you need to allow someone to schedule or manage your appointments or activities.

> All users of the database can view everyone's calendar. By default, only administrators and managers have the security level to schedule activities for other users.

1. Schedule ⇒ Grant Calendar Access.

   The names that you see in Figure 15-31 are the people that currently have rights to use the database.

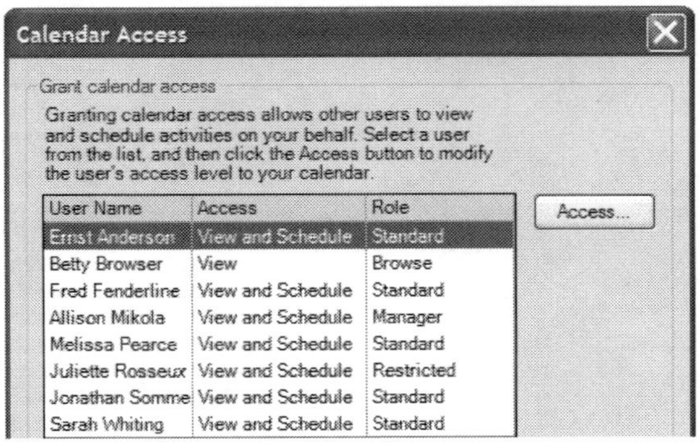

Figure 15-31 Calendar Access dialog box

2. Select the people that you want to have access to your calendar. For this exercise select the five Standard users.

3. Click the **ACCESS** button, then click OK to grant access to **VIEW AND SCHEDULE** activities for other users, as shown in Figure 15-32.

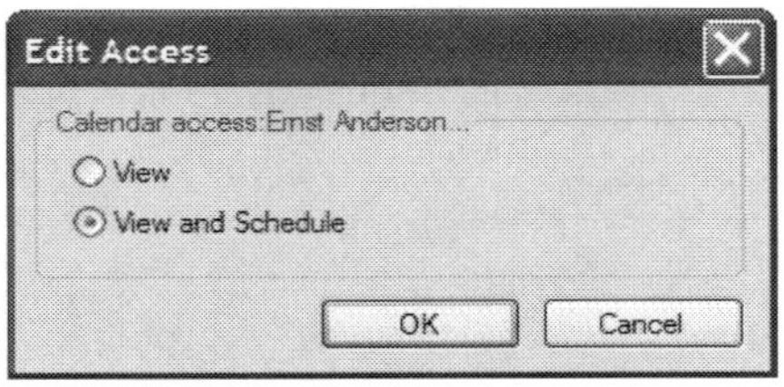

Figure 15-32 Edit Access dialog box

4. Click OK again to close the Calendar Access dialog box.

Viewing Other Users Calendars

When you have the access to view other users calendars, one day in a calendar will look like the one shown in Figure 15-33. (The date shown is January 23, 2009.) Activities for other users will have their name in brackets after the time.

If you look under the calendar on the right side of the window you will see a button for each users activities that you have access to, as shown in Figure 15-34. If you click on one of these buttons, you will see the activities for the user below the button.

Figure 15-33 Calendar with multiple users

Figure 15-34 Buttons to select a user

Exercise 15.5: Printing Calendars

ACT! provides several options to print calendars. If you already use Day Runner or Day-Timer products, you can print calendars in these formats in addition to printing calendars on plain paper. ACT! has three types of calendars that you can print: Daily, Weekly and Monthly.

1. Open the daily calendar.

2. File ⇒ Print. The Day Calendar option should be selected in the **PRINTOUT TYPE** section of the Print dialog box.

3. Select the **PLAIN LETTER FULL PAGE (P) (2 COL)** option in the Paper Type section, as shown at the bottom of Figure 15-35.

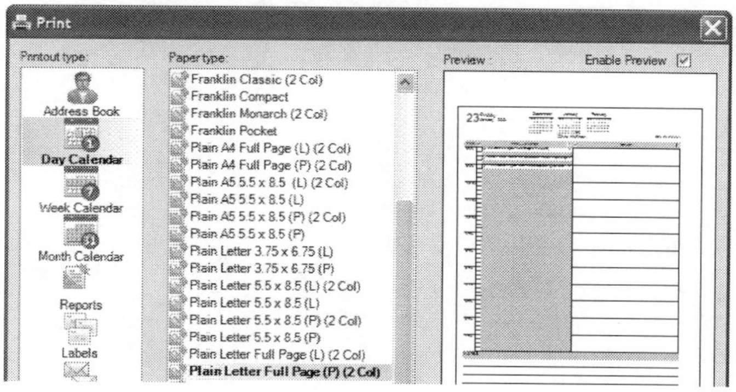

Figure 15-35 Calendar print options

4. Click the Options button.

   The options shown in Figure 15-36 are used to customize how the calendar will print.

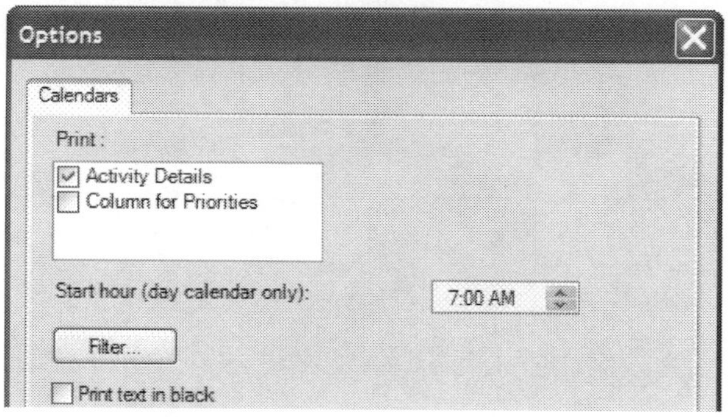

Figure 15-36 Calendar options

If you want to print the Activity Details or Column for Priorities for each calendar entry, check the option.

The **START HOUR** field is the hour of the day that you want the calendar to start printing from.

The **FILTER** button opens the Filter Calendar Printout dialog box shown below in Figure 15-37. These options are used to filter the activities that will print on the calendar. You can select which users activities, the date range and activity options, including the type and priority that you want to print on the calendar.

5. Check the Activity Details **PRINT** option, then clear the Column for Priorities option, if it is checked.

6. Select 7 AM in the **START HOUR** field. You should have the options selected that are shown above in Figure 15-36.

7. Click the **FILTER** button and change the Date Range to 1/19/2009 to 1/23/2009.

8. Clear the **SHOW CLEARED** option.

   You should have the options selected that are shown in Figure 15-37.

   Click OK.

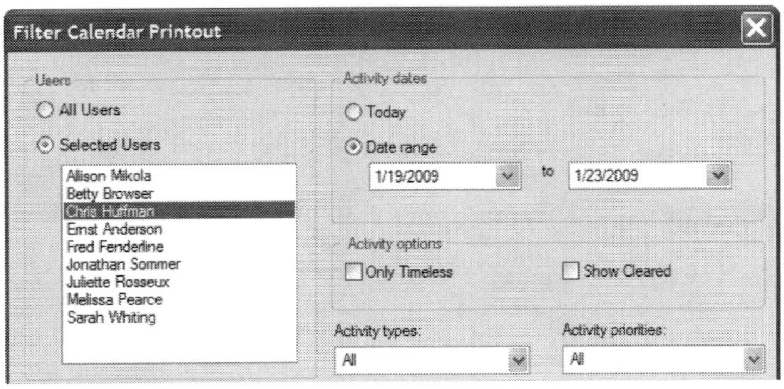

Figure 15-37 Filter Calendar Printout dialog box

9. Click OK to close the Options dialog box.

   If you want to print the calendar, click the Print button on the Print dialog box.

   The calendar will look like the one shown in Figure 15-38.

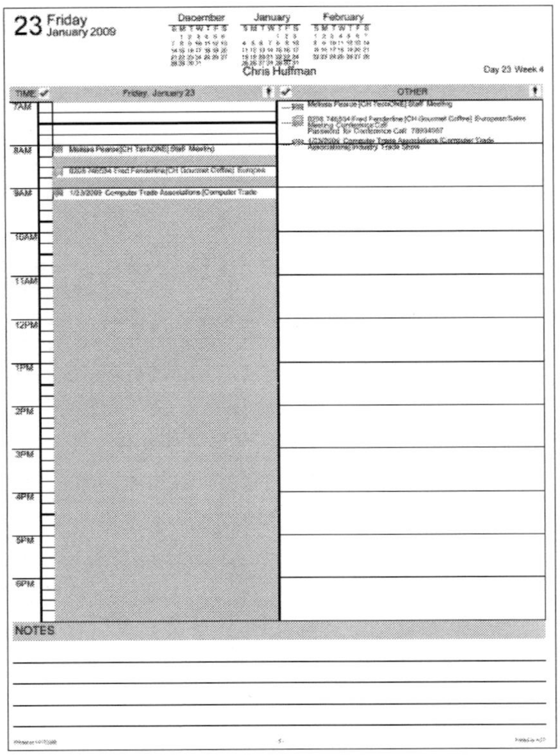

Figure 15-38 ACT! daily calendar

CUSTOMIZING REPORT TEMPLATES

In this lesson you will learn the following report template customization techniques:

- ☑ Sizing fields
- ☑ Adding fields to a report
- ☑ Saving templates
- ☑ Hiding report sections
- ☑ Creating subreports

LESSON 16

Report Design Overview

As you have seen, ACT! comes with over 30 reports. Many of the reports may be exactly what you need and others you may wish were slightly different. For example, you may need an existing report to have totals. ACT! has a tool called the **REPORT DESIGNER**. It is used for the following:

① To modify existing reports.
② Creating a new report based off of an existing report.
③ If you need a report that is not similar to any of the reports that come with ACT!, you can create a report from scratch.

Many of the report design techniques that you will learn about are similar to the techniques that the Layout Designer has to modify the layouts (data entry screens and tabs). You will learn how to use the Layout Designer in Lesson 18.

Having modified and designed reports for close to two decades, I can tell you that it is much easier to modify and create reports when you are familiar with the data that the report needs and the structure of the database. By structure, I mean knowing which table each field is in that you need for the report. The other thing that will be helpful is to have a draft of what the new or modified report should look like.

Report Creation Options

There are two ways that you can create a report: From an existing report and from scratch. Each option has pros and cons. Once you understand all of the options, you can select the report creation option that best meets the need for each report that you need to create.

Create A Report Based Off Of An Existing Report

If a report exists that is similar to the report that you need to create, select this report creation option. Save the existing report with a new file name and make the necessary changes to the new report. An example of when to create a report based off of an existing report would be when two groups of people need to see the majority of the same fields, but one of the groups needs additional information that the other group does not need. Another example is when one group needs the same fields but in a different layout then the other group. You can use one of the templates that come with ACT! and format the report as needed.

Reports ⇒ Edit Template ⇒ Select report, are the menu options to select when you want to modify an existing report.

Create A Report From Scratch

This option gives you the most flexibility to create a report. You start with a blank canvas so to speak and add the fields and other objects to the layout. For many, this can be intimidating, especially in the beginning. But being the fearless person that you are, I am sure that when you get to the exercise that has you create a report from scratch, that you will do just fine.

Reports ⇒ New Template, will open the dialog box shown in Figure 16-1.

The **REPORT TYPES** list shown in Figure 16-1 is how you select the type of report that you want to create.

The report types are based on the type of data. Select the type for the new report, then select the **EMPTY REPORT** option in the Templates list on the right.

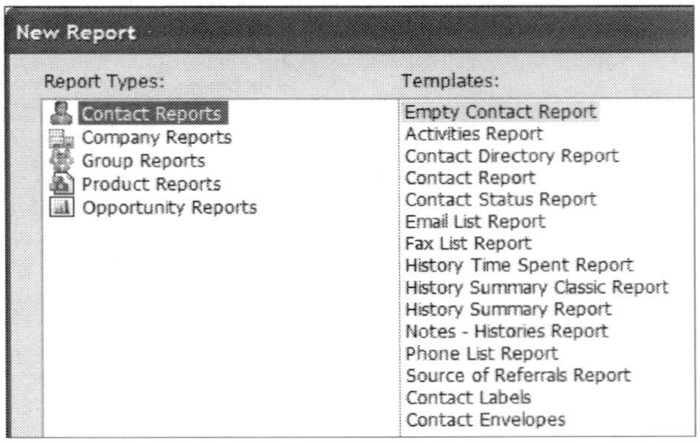

Figure 16-1 Options to create a report from scratch

Report Designer

The Report Designer window shown in Figure 16-2 is used to create new reports and modify existing reports.

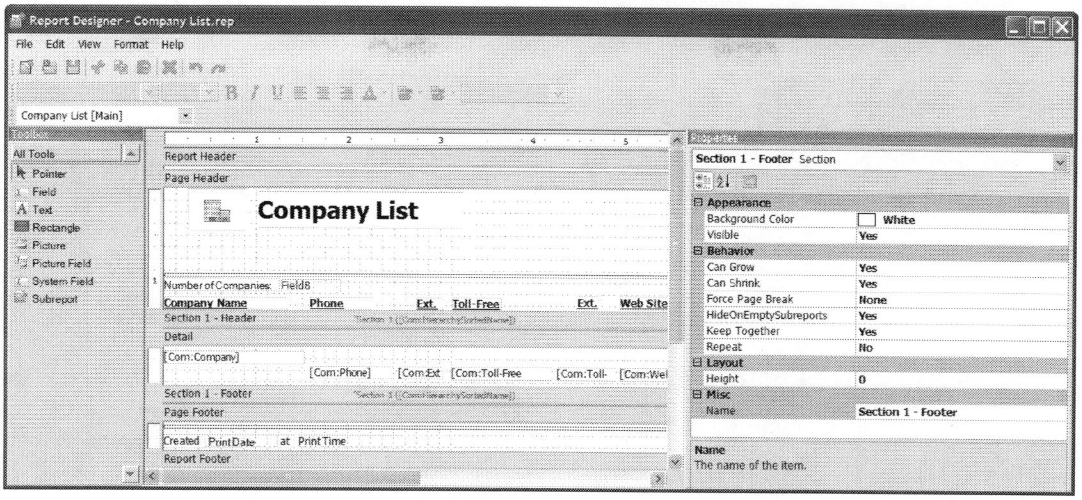

Figure 16-2 Report Designer window

Report Designer Toolbars

The Report Designer has two toolbars that you can use to create and modify reports. Many of the options are the same as options in most word processors. Figure 16-3 shows the Editing toolbar. Table 16-1 explains the buttons on the Editing toolbar. The first eight buttons on the Formatting toolbar shown in Figure 16-4 are the same buttons that are on the Formatting toolbar in most word processors. The remaining buttons on the Formatting toolbar are explained in Table 16-2. The buttons on this toolbar are used to change the look of objects, like fields or labels on the report.

Figure 16-3 Report Designer Editing toolbar

Button	Description
1	Creates a new report.
2	Opens an existing report.
3	Saves the changes.
4	Cuts the selected object(s). (1)
5	Copies the selected object(s).
6	Pastes the selected object(s).
7	Deletes the selected object(s). (1)
8	Undoes the last change.
9	Redoes the last change.

Table 16-1 Report Designer Editing toolbar buttons explained

(1) The difference between these options is that the Delete option does not allow the selected object(s) to be pasted back into the report.

Figure 16-4 Report Designer Formatting toolbar

Button	Description
1	Changes the color of the font.
2	Changes the background color of the object.
3	Changes the border color.
4	Changes the border style.

Table 16-2 Report Designer Formatting toolbar buttons explained

Sections Of A Report

There are five sections of a report that you can modify and place fields and other objects in, as shown in Figure 16-5.

The sections are the Report Header, Page Header, Detail, Page Footer and Report Footer.

You cannot change the order of or delete these sections. If you place the same calculated field in different sections of the report, it could produce different results.

It is important that you understand how each section of the report functions, because they function independently of each other. Keep the following in mind when deciding where to place fields and objects on the report.

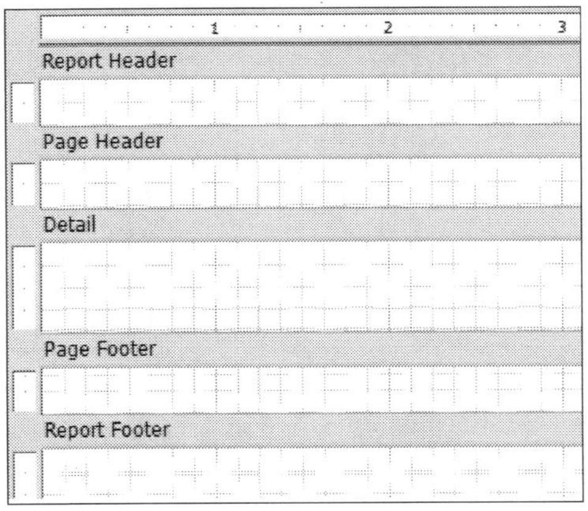

Figure 16-5 Report layout

① Not all sections are needed for every report.

② If a report does not need a section, the section can be suppressed so that it does not display blank space on the report.

③ Sections can be resized as needed.

Section 1: Report Header

By default, data fields and other objects placed in this section will only print at the top of the first page of the report. It is quite possible that many of the reports that you create will not have anything in this section. Something that you may want to include in this section of the report is the criteria and parameters of the report. If the report needs a cover page, the report header section can be used for the cover page. If this is what you need to do, add a page break after this section so that the actual report data from the other sections of the report starts on a new page.

Section 2: Page Header

Data fields and other objects placed in this section will appear at the top of every page in the report. This is where the report title and headings for the fields in the detail section of the report are usually placed. Other objects that are commonly placed in this section include the date and page number.

Section 3: Detail

Data fields and other objects placed in this section will print for each record in the database that meets the criteria. This section is automatically repeated once for each record that will be printed on the report. The data fields in this section usually have field headings in the page header section.

Section 4: Page Footer

Data fields and other objects placed in this section will print at the bottom of each page of the report. The page footer section is similar to the page header section. Items like page numbers and footnotes can be placed in this section.

Section 5: Report Footer

Data fields and other objects placed in this section will print once at the end of the report. This is usually where grand totals and other types of report summary information is placed.

Customizing Report Templates

In Lesson 9 learned how to run several reports. Now you will learn how to customize report templates. By customizing report templates, you can add fields to a template and delete fields that you do not need. ACT! also allows you to create your own envelope and label templates from scratch.

Exercise 16.1: Customizing The Report Templates

In this exercise you will learn how to add fields to a report. You will also learn about the tools in the Report Designer window.

Saving Templates

If you modify a template that comes with ACT!, it is a good idea to save it with a different name before making any changes. That way, the existing template is not changed. The **UNDO** option does not work in the Report Designer as you may expect.

Unless instructed otherwise, save the reports that you create or modify in your folder.

1. Lookup all contacts.
2. Reports ⇒ Edit Template.

   You will see the dialog box shown in Figure 16-6.

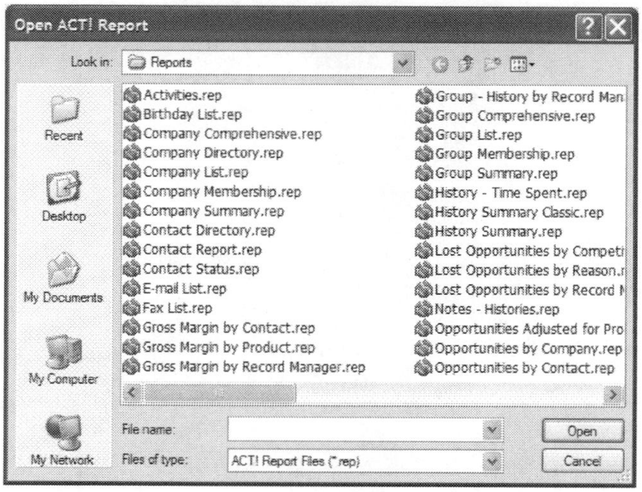

Figure 16-6 Report templates that come with ACT!

This is the dialog box that opens when you select the "Other Reports" option on the Reports menu.

3. Double-click on the file **CONTACT STATUS.REP**.
4. File ⇒ Save As. Type `Missing Email Address` as the file name, then press Enter or click the Save button.

Field vs Label

Figure 16-7 shows the fields and labels. The **LABEL** for a field is on the left by default. It is not a requirement to keep the label on the report, nor does the label have to have the same name as the field name. If you do not need the label you can delete it by right-clicking on it and selecting **CUT**, as shown in Figure 16-8.

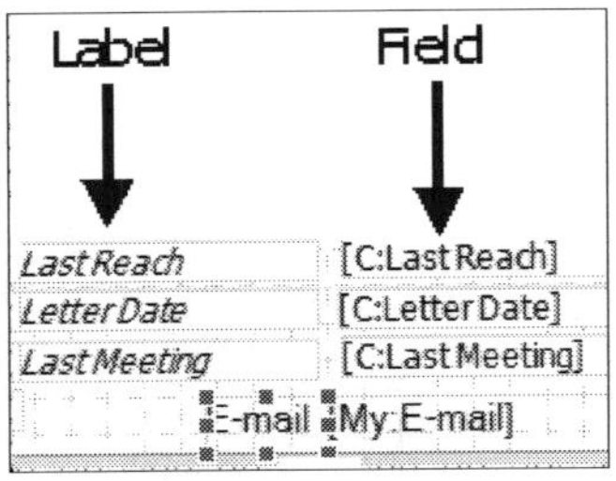

Figure 16-7 Label and field illustrated

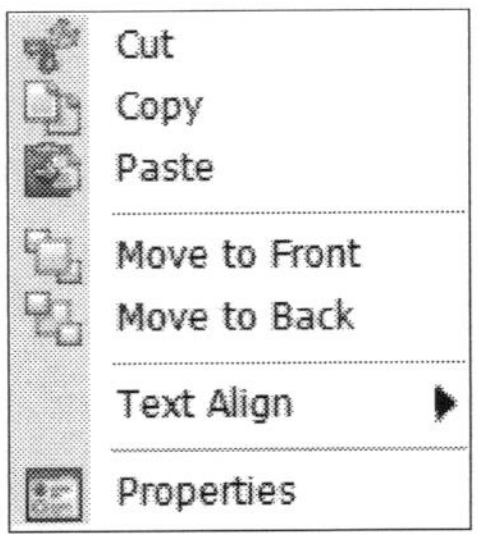

Figure 16-8 Label and field shortcut menu

The **FIELD**, which is in brackets, will display data (from the database) on the report. You can modify the field by right-clicking on it and selecting an option on the shortcut menu shown above in Figure 16-8. Table 16-3 contains the field codes. The field codes are the letter(s) before the colon in the field name. The Table column indicates the table that the field is stored in. The abbreviations in the middle of Table 16-3 are the codes. For example, the code GA is a group activity. This is how you know if the field is a contact, company, group or opportunity field. System fields do not have an abbreviation in front of them.

Table	Contact	Notes	History	Activity	Secondary Contact	Opportunity
Contact	C	CN	CH	CA	SC	CO
Company		COMN	COMH	COMA		COMO
Group		GN	GH	GA		GO
Opportunity						O

Table 16-3 Field codes

How To Manually Resize A Field

Often when you add a field to a report, you will probably have to resize it. Just be careful not to make the field so small that all of the data in the field does not print.

1. Click on the field, **C:LAST RESULTS** in the Status section of the report. You should now see squares around the field.

2. Place the mouse pointer on the middle square on the right side of the field. You may have to scroll to the right to see the end of the field.

3. When the pointer changes to a double headed arrow, press and hold down the left mouse button, then drag the mouse to the left until the pointer is near the end of the field, as illustrated in Figure 16-9.

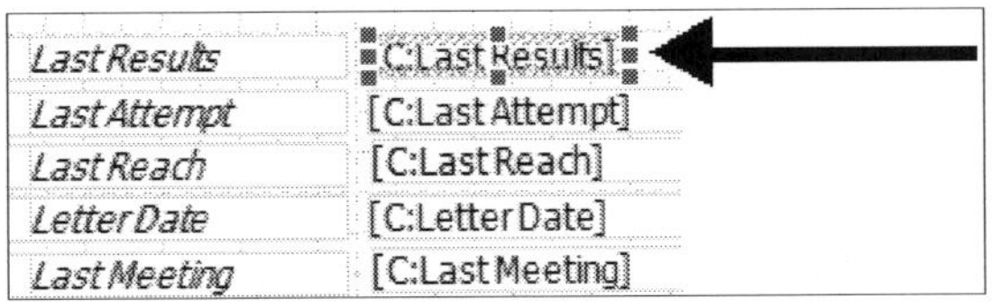

Figure 16-9 Last Results field made smaller

To **MOVE A FIELD OR LABEL**, click on it. Press and hold down the left mouse button. The mouse pointer will change to a hand when you start to move the field, as shown in Figure 16-10.

Figure 16-10 Mouse pointer in position to move the field or label

Report Designer Toolbox

A report can have different types of objects. Earlier you learned about fields.

The options in the toolbox shown in Figure 16-11 are used to add fields and other types of objects to the report.

Table 16-4 explains the options in the toolbox.

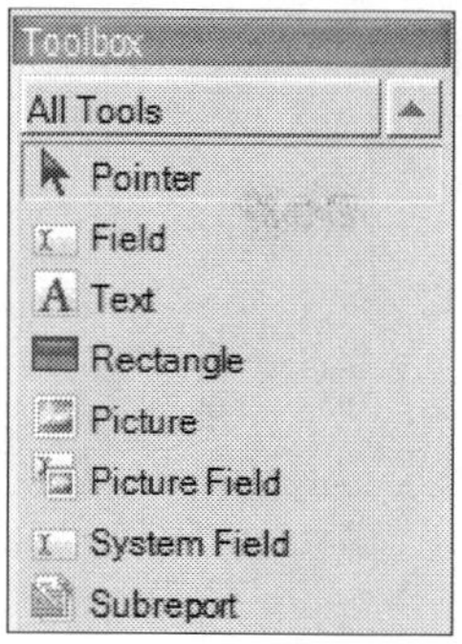

Figure 16-11 Report Designer Toolbox

Option	Description
Pointer	You have to click this button before clicking on an object on the report to select it.
Field	Adds a field from the database to the report.
Text	Free form field for adding text to the report.
Rectangle	Adds a rectangle or box to the report. This object is often used to visually group fields together.
Picture	Adds a graphic or image to the report. In the upper left corner of the Contact Status report you will see the logo, which is a graphic.
Picture Field	Adds an image to the report. A different image will be displayed for each record on the report. This field is often used for photos.
System Field	Adds a field shown in Figure 16-12 to the report.
Subreport	Adds a report to an existing report. This feature is often used when you want to add multiple rows of the same type of data to a report. Subreports allow a field or fields to be repeated an unlimited number of times. A popular use for a subreport is to add data stored on any of the System tabs. [See Lesson 18, Tabs Overview]

Table 16-4 Report Designer Toolbox options explained

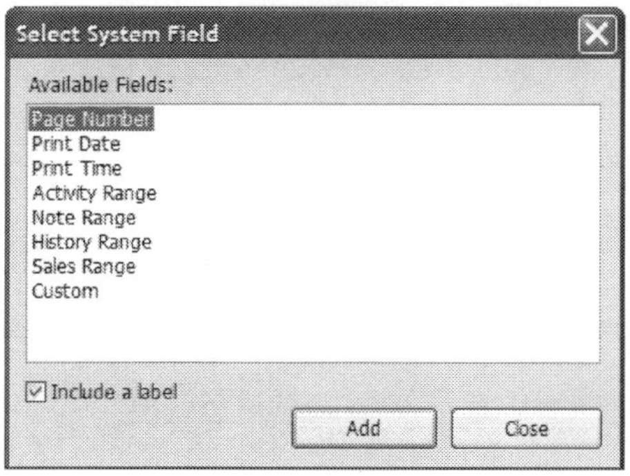

Figure 16-12 System fields

How To Add A Field

In this part of the exercise you will learn how to add different types of fields to a report template. You will also learn basic report editing techniques.

1. Click the **FIELD** button in the Toolbox. The mouse pointer will change to a cross hair (+) when it is on the report.

2. Place the mouse pointer under the C:Last Meeting field. Press the left mouse button and draw a rectangle the same size as the C:Last Meeting field. You will see the dialog box shown in Figure 16-13.

   The options in the **SELECT A RECORD TYPE** drop-down list are tables in the database. Each table contains different fields.

   Some of the tables correspond to a tab on a detail view.

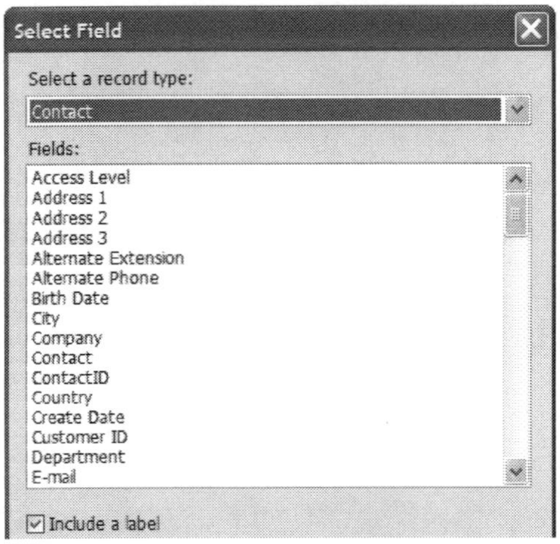

Figure 16-13 Select Field dialog box

3. Open the drop-down list and select MyRecord, then click on the E-mail field.
4. Check the **INCLUDE A LABEL** option at the bottom of the Select Field dialog box, if it is not already checked, then click the Add button.
5. Click the Close button.

How To Align Fields

As you can see, the field that you just added to the template is not lined up with the field above it. The steps below show you how to align and resize fields using menu options.

> When aligning fields, select the fields that need to be aligned first, then select the field that you want those fields to line up with. Figure 16-14 shows several fields selected. The one that has the dark handles (the Com:Address 3 field) is the one that the other selected objects will be aligned to.

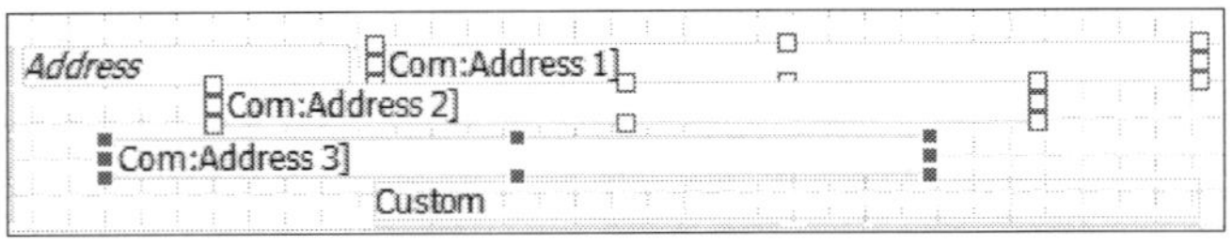

Figure 16-14 Fields selected to be aligned

1. Click on the E-mail label, then press and hold down the Shift key.
2. Click on the Last Meeting label. Format ⇒ Align ⇒ Left. The E-mail label should now be lined up with the Last Meeting label.
3. Click on a blank space in the report, then click on the E-mail label. Change the font and size to match the Last Meeting label. (For me that is the Tahoma font, size 8, italic.)
4. Click on a blank space in the report, then click on the E-mail field. Change the font and size to match the Last Meeting field. (For me that is the Tahoma font, size 8, no italic.)
5. Click on the My:Email field. Press and hold down the Shift key, then click on the C:Last Meeting field. Format ⇒ Make Same Size ⇒ Height.
6. With the two fields still selected, Format ⇒ Align ⇒ Left. Click on a blank space on the report, then save the changes.

How To Add Text To A Template

You may have the need to add text to a report to help explain something about the report. For example, the report may need a sub title.

1. Click the **TEXT** button in the Toolbox. Place the mouse pointer below the Contact Status report title and draw a box.

2. If you do not see the Properties window, View ⇒ Properties Window.

3. Type `Missing E-mail Addresses` in the **TEXT** field on the Properties window, as illustrated in Figure 16-15. Make the field smaller on the report so that the frame is closer to the text on the right.

The Properties Window

Earlier you learned that the options on the toolbox are used to add a variety of fields and objects to a report. You also learned that each field or object on the report can be modified.

The Properties window shown in Figure 16-15 is used to customize the fields and objects, which are sometimes called **ELEMENTS**.

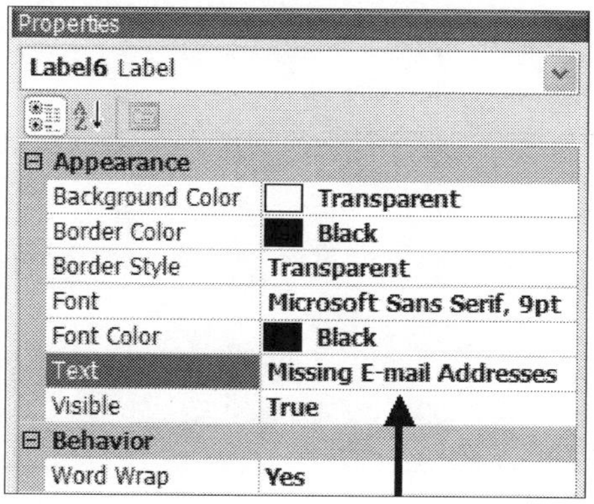

Figure 16-15 Properties window

The **F4** key opens and closes the Properties window. The options on this window will change depending on the type of object that is selected. If you want to apply the same change to several objects on the report at the same time, select the objects first, then make the changes in the Properties window.

How To Resize A Section Of The Report

If you are creating a new report or making a lot of changes to an existing report, you may find it easier to work if a section of the report was larger. To make a section larger, place the mouse pointer on the top edge of the section bar of the section below the one that you want to resize. Drag the section down. When you are finished making the changes, drag the section bar back up so that a lot of blank space does not appear at the bottom of the section when you preview or print the report.

If you need to have more than one text field have the same formatting, create the first field and format it as needed. To duplicate the field, right-click on it and select **COPY**, then right-click on the report and select **PASTE**.

How To Add A Summary Field

Summary fields are used for calculations. You can use summary fields to get totals and averages, as well as, minimums, maximums and counts. Summary fields are usually placed in the report and page header or footer sections.

The purpose of the report in this exercise is to provide a list of contacts to call, to either verify the email address that you have or get an email address from contacts that do not have one. The report already prints the total number of contacts. You will add a summary field to count the number of contacts that have an e-mail address.

1. Click the **FIELD** button in the Toolbox, then draw a rectangle to the right of the **NUMBER OF CONTACTS** field in the Page Header section.

2. Select the E-mail field on the Select Field dialog box. Click Add, then click Close.

3. Right-click on the C:Email field and select Properties.

4. On the Data tab, select the **SUMMARY** Field Type option. The **COUNT** option should be selected, as shown in Figure 16-16.

   Options that are not enabled cannot be used on the field that is currently selected.

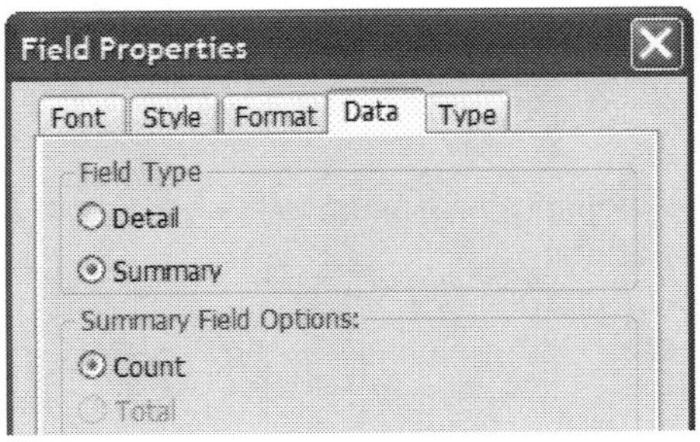

Figure 16-16 Data tab options

5. Click Apply, then click OK.

6. Change the label of the field to `Contacts with E-mail Addresses:`.

7. Move and resize the field and label as needed. Left align the field, then save the changes.

Test The Report

You should test the report template that you create before you close the Report Designer window.

1. File ⇒ Print Preview.

   The top of the report should look like the one shown in Figure 16-17.

   The arrows indicate the items that you added. You may have different totals then the ones shown in the figure.

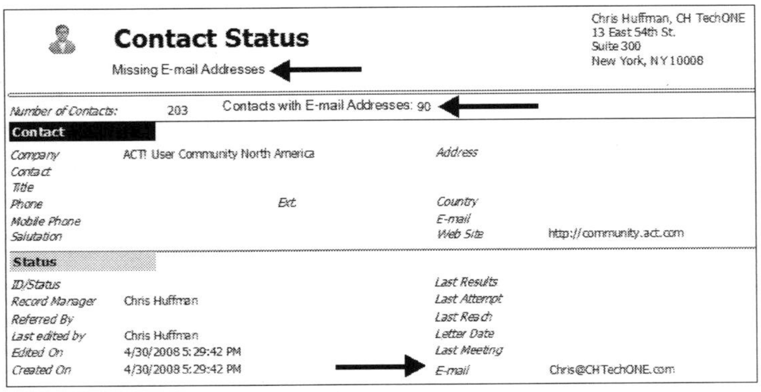

Figure 16-17 Revised Contact Status report

2. Close the Print Preview window. Make any changes that are needed, then save the changes.

> **How To Align Text In A Label And Field**
>
> If you are having trouble aligning the text in the label and field, follow the steps below.
>
> 1. Select the label and field.
> 2. On the Properties window, open the **ALIGNMENT** drop-down list shown in Figure 16-18 and select the option that will best line up the text in both fields.

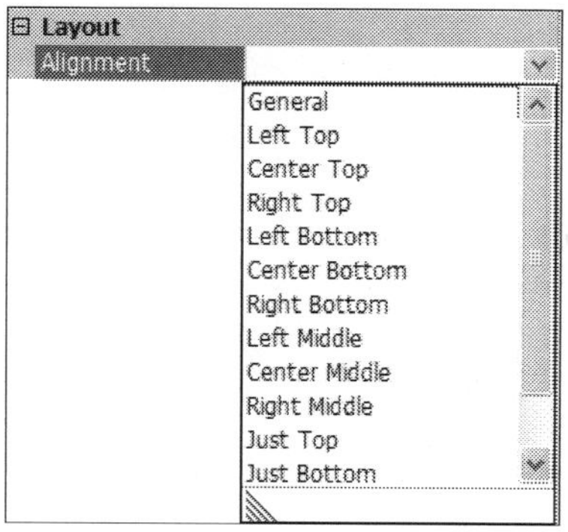

Figure 16-18 Alignment options

Custom Fields

Custom fields are not stored in the database. Many of the reports that come with ACT! have custom fields. The custom field in the upper right corner of the Contact Status report is an example. This field contains the City, State and Zip Code fields.

One of the more popular custom fields that is created is to combine two or more fields into one. Combining the city, state and zip code fields is probably the most popular custom field. If you added these three fields to a report individually, they would be printed as shown in Figure 16-19.

Figure 16-19 City, state and zip code fields added to the report

This is probably not the way that you want the fields to print. You probably want these fields to look the way that they do at the top of the Contact Status report shown earlier in Figure 16-17. You can create custom fields in one of two ways, as discussed below:

① Use fields that are already on the report.
② Add fields to the report and then hide them.

The benefit of using option 1 is that it is less work. To get the name of the field(s) that you want to use, click on the field in the report.

Figure 16-20 shows that the Email count field is selected. If you look at the top of the Properties window on the right of the figure, you will see the field name E-mail2. If you wanted to use this field in a custom field, you would reference it as E-mail2.

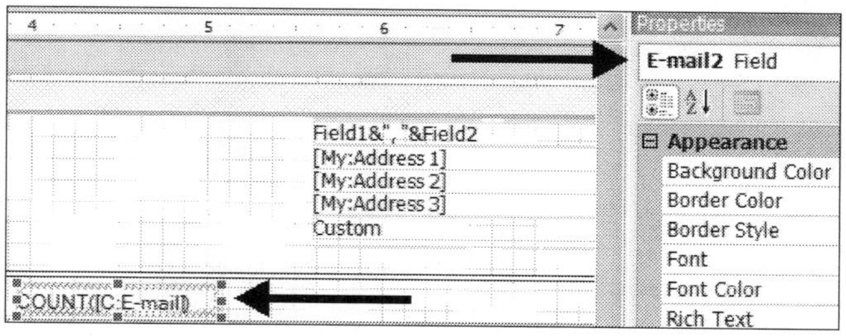

Figure 16-20 Properties for the E-mail count field

Select the second option listed above when the fields that you need are not already on the report. If you look closely below the custom field in the Contact Status report, in the design view, you will see light gray lines.

If you click on the first gray line and then look at the top of the Properties window you should see Field6, as illustrated in Figure 16-21.

If you see Field7 or 8, you are in the right place. Field6 is the City field. Field7 is the State field and Field8 is the Zip Code field.

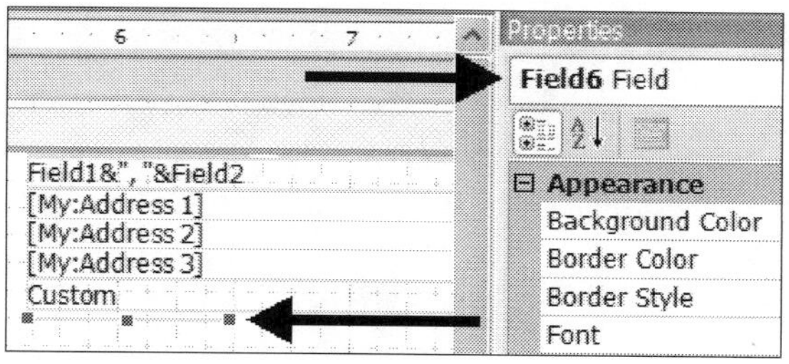

Figure 16-21 Hidden field selected

Exercise 16.2: How To Create A Custom Field

In this exercise you will create a custom field for fields that are not on the report. You will create a custom field that combines the city, state and zip code fields into one field.

1. Save the Birthday List report as `My custom field report.`

2. Delete the three fields below the custom field shown above in Figure 16-21. If you cannot see them, click in the area below the custom field.

3. Delete the Custom field shown above in Figure 16-21.

Hiding Fields

When you have to use fields that are not already on the report to create a custom field, you have to add them to the report and then hide them. The reason that you hide the fields is because they should not be printed in their current format. When you draw the box for a field that you have to hide, you should make it as small as possible and place it in a location that is not in the way of the other fields on the report. In step 2 above, you deleted three fields. You do not have to make the fields as small as the ones that you deleted, if you do not want to.

> Once you double-click on the first field that you need to add to the report, you do not have to close the Select Field dialog box. Double-click on the next field in the dialog box that you need to add.

4. Add the My Record type City, State and Zip Code fields, but not the labels, to the Page Header section.

5. Select the three fields that you just added, then change the **VISIBLE** option on the Properties window to False.

Figure 16-22 shows the hidden fields, which should have slanted lines through them. This lets you know that the fields will not print on the report. I don't know about you, but I find these fields easier to work with and know what they are, then the three fields that you deleted under the custom field earlier in this exercise.

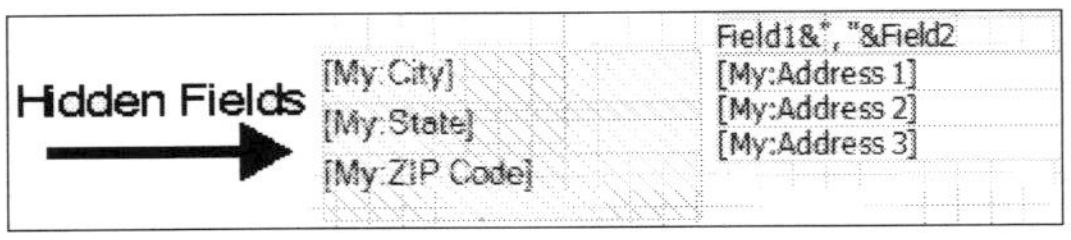

Figure 16-22 Hidden fields

6. Click the System Field button in the Toolbox, then draw a box under the Address 3 field in the Page Header section.

7. Select the Custom field option, then clear the **INCLUDE A LABEL** option. Click Add, then click Close.

8. Select the custom field. Type the following in the **EXPRESSION** field on the Properties window, as shown in Figure 16-23. `City1 & ", " & State1 & " " & ZipCode1.`
   The only place that there should be a space is between each set of quotes and after the comma.

Figure 16-23 Expression for the custom city, state and zip code field

> If you look at the fields above the Custom field that you created, you will see that there is no space between them. This is done to make the report look better. It is not mandatory though.

9. Align the custom field on the left with the Address 3 field.

10. Make the font and size of the custom field the same as the My:Address 3 field if it is not already.

11. Save the changes and preview the report.

    The name and address section should look like the one shown in Figure 16-24.

Figure 16-24 Custom city, state and zip code field

Modifying Report Sections

There will be times when an existing report has the layout and many of the fields that you need for a new report. Instead of creating a report from scratch, you can save an existing report with a different name and modify it. You can hide or delete the fields in sections of a report that are not needed. You can also force a section to start on a new page.

Exercise 16.3: Hiding A Report Section

As you learned earlier, sections of the report cannot be removed. If a report does not need a section, you can hide it by following the steps below.

1. Lookup all contacts.

2. Save the Contact Status report as `My Contact Report - Hidden Section`.

3. Click on the Page Footer section bar, then press the F4 key if the Properties window is not open.

> If the Properties window is already open, you can open the drop-down list at the top and select the section of the report that you want to change the properties of.

4. Click in the **VISIBLE** property to open the drop-down list, then select No.

5. Save the changes. If you preview the report you will not see the fields in the Page Footer section.

Exercise 16.4: Adding A Section To A Report

Sections are added to a report to group and sort the detail records. In this exercise you will add a section to a report. Once you add a section to the report, you can add fields and other objects to it. You will group the report by company name, sorted in ascending order.

1. Save the My Contact Report - Hidden Section report as `My Contact Report - Added Section`.

2. Edit ⇒ Define Sections. Click the Add button.

3. Select Company in the Fields list on the dialog box shown in Figure 16-25, then click OK.

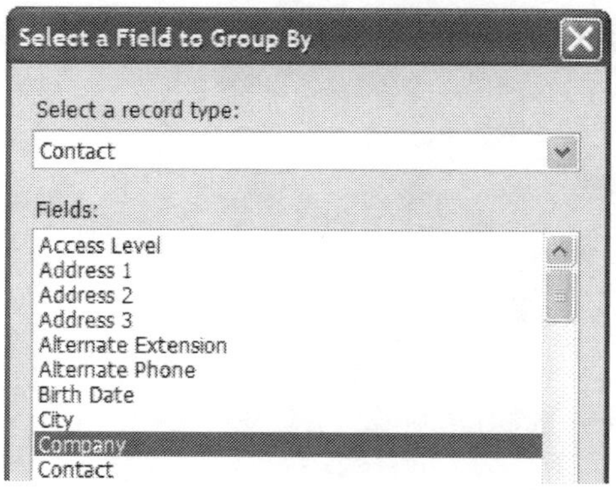

Figure 16-25 Select a Field to Group By dialog box

4. Click on the **SECTION 2** option on the left. At the bottom of Figure 16-26 you will see that the section will be sorted in ascending order, which is what you want. Leave the dialog box open to complete the next part of the exercise.

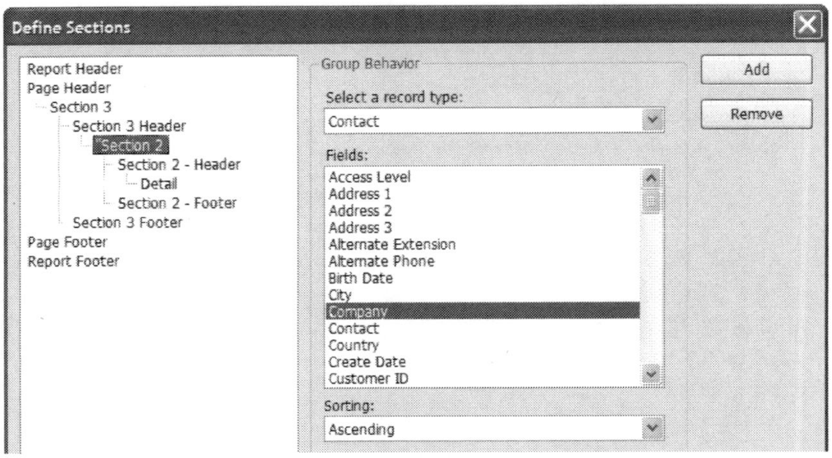

Figure 16-26 Define Sections dialog box

Double-clicking on any section header in the Report Designer window will open the Define Sections dialog box.

Define Sections Dialog Box Options

The options shown in Figure 16-27 are used to customize the sections of the report.

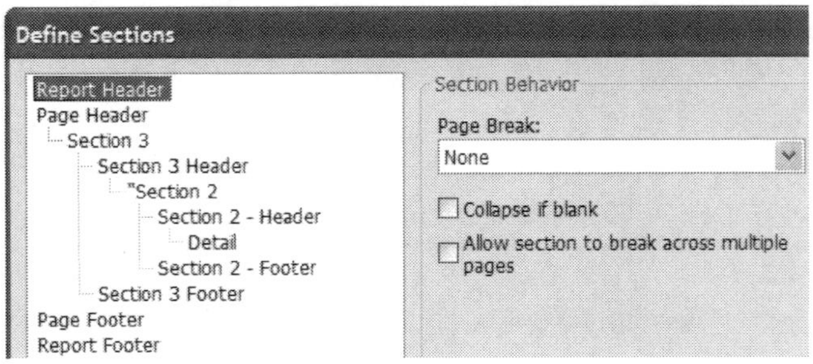

Figure 16-27 Section Behavior options

① The **PAGE BREAK** options shown in Figure 16-28 are used to determine whether or not a section will start on a new page. I often use the **AFTER** option on the Report Header section as the way to make that section print on a page by itself, so that it can be used as a cover page for the report.
② If checked, the **COLLAPSE IF BLANK** option shown on the right of Figure 16-27 above, will hide the section when the report is printed if it does not have any fields or objects in it.
③ If checked, the **ALLOW SECTION TO BREAK ACROSS MULTIPLE PAGES** option allows a report section print on more than one page.

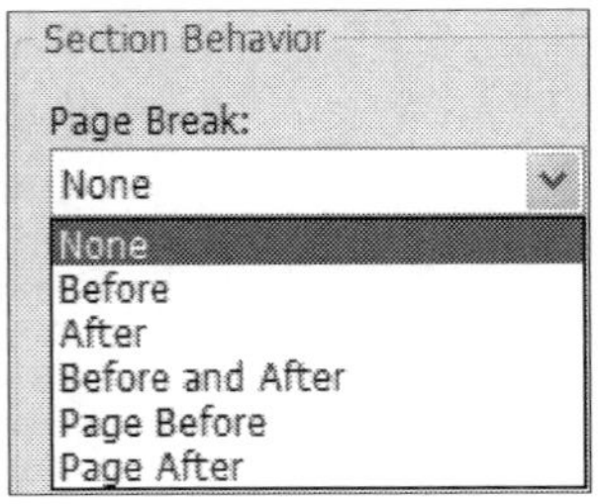

Figure 16-28 Page Break options

How To Remove A Section Of The Report

If you slide the dialog box out of the way, you will see that the report is also grouped on the Contact field. (See Section 3 Header.) This group is not needed. The steps below show you how to remove a section.

1. Click on the section that you want to remove on the Define Sections dialog box. In this exercise click on the Section 3 option, then click the **REMOVE** button.

2. Click Yes when prompted to delete the report section, then click OK to close the Define Sections dialog box.

Resize A Section Of The Report

As you can see, the Section 2 Header and Footer sections are long and do not contain any fields. You can manually resize them to make them smaller or you can hide them by dragging the section bar above or below the section that you want to resize. In Exercise 16.3 you used the **VISIBLE** option on the Properties window to hide a section of the report.

1. Select any of the resize options discussed or follow the steps in Exercise 16.3 to hide the Section 2 Header and Footer sections, then save the changes.

2. Preview the report.

You should see that the contacts on the first few pages do not have a company name, which is why the records are at the beginning of the report. When you get past the contacts without a company name, you should see that the report is now in order by company name.

Report Margins

File ⇒ Page Setup, will let you change the margins for the report. The options on this dialog box work the same way that they do in word processing software.

Exercise 16.5: How To Create A Section Break

In this exercise you will create a section break. You will use the Report Header section to create a cover page for the report. You will also add a system field to the Report Header section.

Create The Cover Page

The Contact Status report already has the Print Date, Print Time and Page Number system fields in the Page Footer section. In this part of the exercise you will add the Print Date system field to the Report Header section of the report. Yes, I know that the report already has this field, but I did not want to select a field that would not make sense on a cover page.

1. Save the Contact Status report as `My Cover Page Report`.

2. Make the Report Header section longer, then add a Text field to the section and type `Report Cover Page` in the Text field in the Properties window.

3. Change the Border Style to **DASH DOT DOT**.

4. Change the font to Comic Sans MS, bold, size 18, then center the text.

Add A System Field

1. Click the System Field button in the Toolbox and draw a box below the text that you just added. Select the Print Date field. Click Add, then click Close.

2. Change the label of the field to `This report was printed on`. Resize the label so that you can see all of the text.

Add A Page Break

In this part of the exercise you will add a page break after the Report Header section so that it is the only content that prints on the first page of the report.

1. Double-click on the Report Header bar.

2. Open the Page Break drop-down list and select **AFTER**, then click OK.

> Selecting the Page Header section and the **BEFORE** Page option will produce the same result as the two steps above.

3. Save the changes and preview the report. The first page should look like the one shown in Figure 16-29.

   At the bottom of the page you should see the Page Footer information.

   I could not find a way to keep this from printing on the first page. The second page of the report contains the data.

Figure 16-29 Report cover page

Exercise 16.6: Using The Picture Field

The Picture field will display a different image or photo for each detail record on the report. In this exercise you will modify the Birthday List report to print the contacts photo on the report.

1. Save the Birthday List report as `My Photo Birthday List Report.`

2. Make the Detail section a little longer. Click the Picture Field button on the Toolbox, then draw a box to the right of the Birth Date field.

3. Select the Photo Field, then clear the Include a label option. Click Add, then click Close.

4. Save the changes and preview the report. It should look like the one shown in Figure 16-30.

   If you scroll through the report, you will see some photos that are a lot larger than the one shown in Figure 16-30.

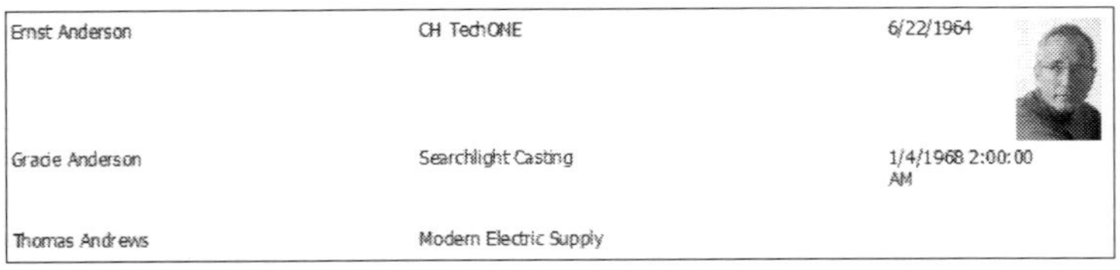

Figure 16-30 Report with photo added

The best way to handle this is to make all of the photos the same size before adding them to the database.

Exercise 16.7: Create A New Report

So far you have modified existing reports. At some point you may need a report that is completely different then the ones that come with ACT!. If so, you will have to create a report from scratch. What many people do is create their own template to use as the basis for new reports. The template that you will create in this exercise will include fields and objects that you want to include on every new report. That way, you do not have to spend time adding page numbers, print dates and logos to every report that you create.

Create A Custom Report Template

In this part of the exercise you will use an existing report as the basis for the template for new reports that you will create.

1. Save the Contact Status report as `My Report Template.`
2. Change the Contact Status title to `Report Title goes here.`
3. Leave the logo and blue line on the report. Delete all of the other fields in the Page Header section including the three hidden fields below the Custom field.
4. Delete everything in the Detail section.
5. Save the changes. Minimize the Report Designer window.

Look Up The Records

In this part of the exercise, you will use an existing query as the basis for the records that will appear on the report. In Lesson 3, you created a lookup to find all records that were created in the last 30 days. If you recall, you typed in a specific date. If that lookup was saved as a query, 60 days from now you would still see the same records, which is not what you want. The query tool has an operator that is used to select how many days you want to go back, instead of typing in a specific date. To complete this report, I created a query that you will use to find the records.

1. Lookup ⇒ Advanced ⇒ Advanced Query.
2. File ⇒ Open. Double-click on the Last 30 Days query file in your folder.
3. Click the Preview button.

   You should see the query and results shown in Figure 16-31.

   The records at the bottom of the dialog box are the ones that you created in the last 30 days.

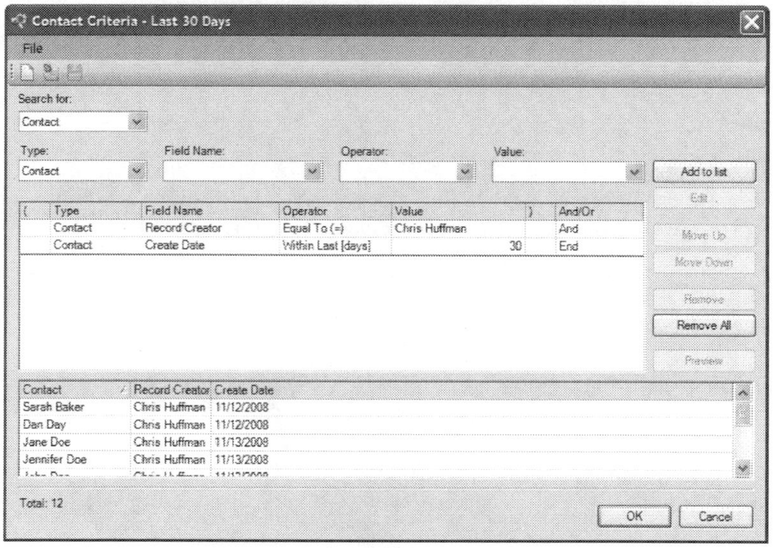

Figure 16-31 Last 30 Days query

4. Click OK. Click OK again to replace the current lookup.
5. Restore the Report Designer window.

Create A Report From Scratch

Before creating a new report, it is a good idea to look up all of the contacts so that you will have some data to test the report with. In this part of the exercise you will create a new report. You will use the template that you created earlier in this exercise.

1. Save the My Report Template that you created as `My Custom Contact Report.`
2. Change the report title to the file name.
3. Click the Field button in the Toolbox and draw a box in the Detail section. Add the following fields with labels: Contact, Company, Create Date and Record Creator.

> To select the field and label, hold down the left mouse button and draw a box around the label and field. This allows you to move both objects at the same time. This is sometimes referred to as the **LASSO** technique.

4. Rearrange the fields and labels so that your report looks like the one shown in Figure 16-32.

   Drag the labels to the bottom of the Page Header section.

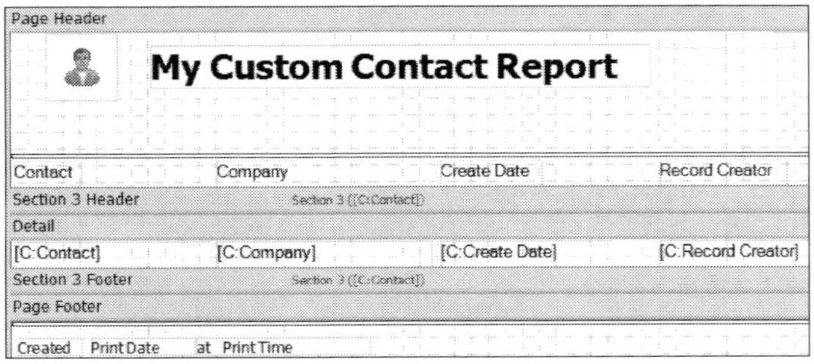

Figure 16-32 Layout for a new report

5. Save the changes and preview the report. You should see the same records that were in the Contact List view.

Subreports

A subreport is a report inside of another report. Subreports have many uses. Often a subreport contains data from a tab on a detail view, but you are not limited to only using data from a tab on a subreport. For example, if you are a realtor, you could add three image fields to the top of the Contact Detail view to display three photos for each house. Subreports can be used to display an unlimited amount of the same type of information, like all of the opportunities for a contact.

For example, you may have the need to display all of the notes for each contact.

The Notes field would be added to the subreport.

If you look at the bottom of the Detail section of the layout shown in Figure 16-33, you will see five subreports.

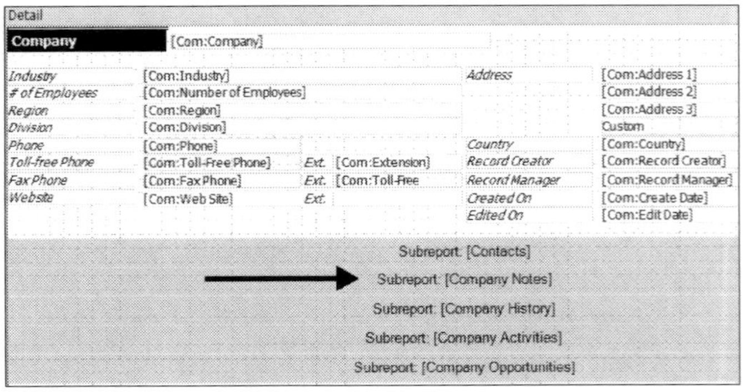

Figure 16-33 Subreports illustrated

Exercise 16.8: Create A Subreport

In this exercise you will create a subreport and add it to the report that you created in the previous exercise. The subreport will contain data from each contacts History tab.

1. Open the My Custom Contact report, if it is not already open and make the Detail section a little longer.
2. Click the Subreport button in the Toolbox and draw a box below the fields in the Detail section. The box should start at the one inch mark go to the 7.5 inch mark on the ruler.
3. Type `My History Subreport` in the Subreport name field, as shown in Figure 16-34.

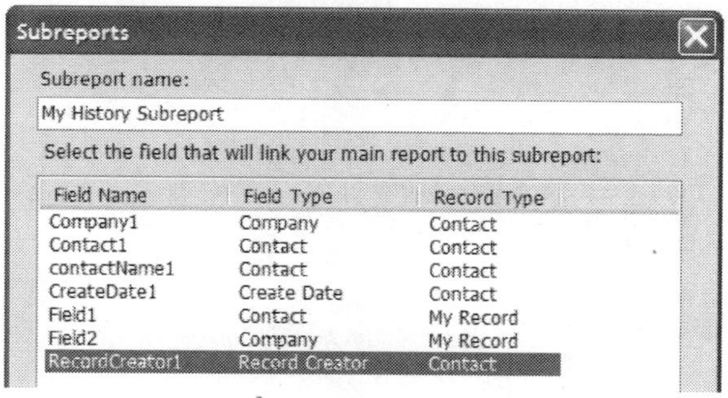

Figure 16-34 Subreports dialog box

4. Double-click on the Contact1 field.
5. Save the changes, then double-click on the Subreport field in the Detail section.
6. Make the Header and Detail sections longer, then change the Visible option to Yes for both sections.
7. Add a text field to the Header section. Type `History Records`. Make the field bold.
8. Add a field to the Detail section. Open the Record Type drop-down list and select Contact History.
9. Add the following fields with labels to the Detail section of the subreport: Date, Result, Regarding & Details, Record Manager.

Add The Subreport To The Main Report

In this part of the exercise you will add the subreport that you just created to the Detail section of the My Custom Contact report. Adding the Subreport is not sufficient. The subreport must also be linked to the Custom Contact report by a field that is unique and in both tables. This is usually an **ID** field. ID fields hold unique values like a social security number. The ID field that both tables have that is unique is the Contact ID field. This is how the correct records are retrieved for the subreport.

1. Add the Contact ID field without a label to the right of the Record Manager field. Change the Visible option to False.
2. When you move the labels to the Header section below the History Records text field, make them bold and underlined.
3. Add a rectangle above the labels in the Header section. Make it narrow so that it looks like two lines.
4. Rearrange and align the fields and labels to match the layout shown in Figure 16-35. You can make the Date field smaller and the Regarding & Details field wider.

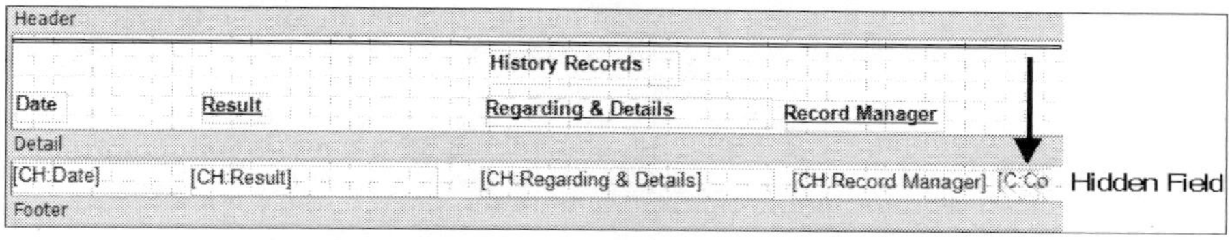

Figure 16-35 Subreport layout

5. Change the **RICH TEXT** property of the Regarding & Details field to Yes.

6. Save the changes. Open the drop-down list above the Toolbox shown in Figure 16-36, then select My Custom Contact Report [Main].

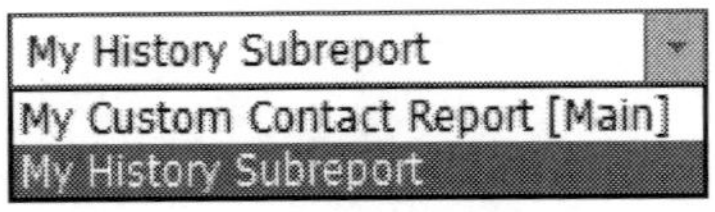

Figure 16-36 Subreports drop-down list

7. File ⇒ Run. Clear the Exclude My Record option because this report retrieves the records that you created in the last month.

The History tab was automatically added to the Define Filters dialog box when you created the subreport for history records.

8. On the History tab, check all three history type options, then change the Date Range to All.

   Click OK.

   The report should look like the one shown in Figure 16-37.

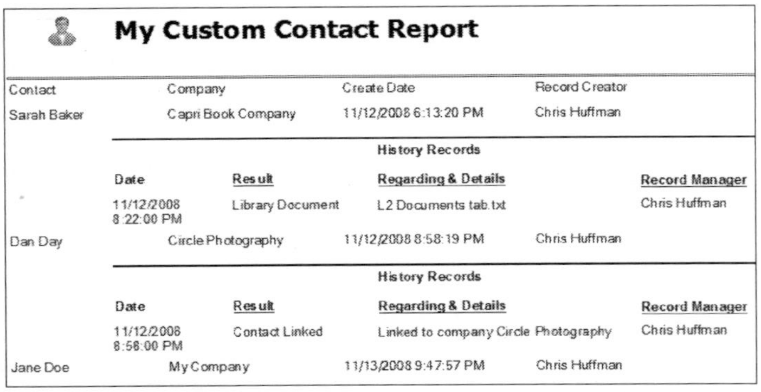

Figure 16-37 My Custom Contact report

9. Close the Report Designer.

Modifying Labels And Envelopes

In previous exercises in this lesson you learned how to modify reports. Modifying labels and envelopes is very similar. The main difference is that there are less options. The steps to modify labels are the same as envelopes. In the next exercise you will learn how to modify an envelope. If you want to modify a label, in step 2 below, select "Labels" instead of "Envelopes" on the Print dialog box. Like reports, the first thing that you should do when you open a label or envelope template is to save it with a new name if you are going to modify it.

Exercise 16.9: Modify An Envelope (Or Label) Template

In this exercise you will add text to an envelope. If you were sending out letters to invite people to an event, you could add a line of text to the envelope that lets the recipient know that they have been invited.

1. Look up the records in the Potential Book Customer group.

2. File ⇒ Print. Select **ENVELOPES**, then select the size. In this exercise select Paper Type 10.

3. Click the **EDIT TEMPLATE** button.

4. File ⇒ Save As. Save the file as `My Custom Envelope`.

5. Add a Text field above the first custom field in the center of the envelope.
   Type `You are invited to our Spring Gala` in the Text field.

6. Change the Font size to 10 and make the text italic. Save the changes.

7. File ⇒ Run.

   Select the Current Lookup option, then click OK.

   When you preview the envelope, it should look like the one shown in Figure 16-38.

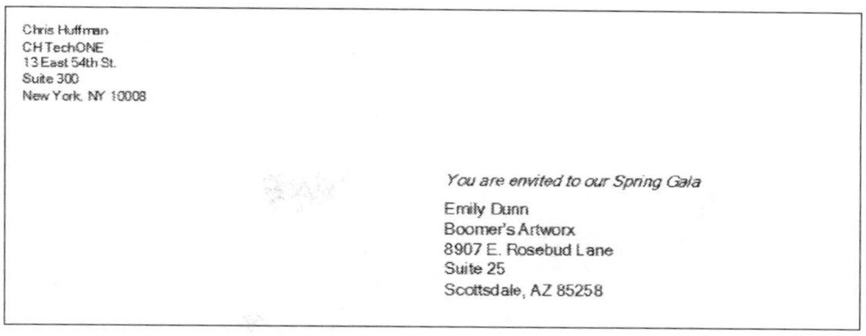

Figure 16-38 Custom Envelope

Creating Label And Envelope Templates

If the label or envelope size that you need is not in ACT! you can create your own. The majority of the steps are the same as creating a report. The steps below are for envelopes. If you need to create labels, in step 2 select a label template.

1. File ⇒ New, from the Report Designer window or Reports ⇒ New Template from an ACT! view. You will see the New Report dialog box.

2. Select the Contact Reports type, then double-click on the Contact Envelopes option.

3. Open the Select an envelope size drop-down list and select Custom. Accept the default height and width options, then click OK. The rest of the process is the same as creating a report.

CUSTOMIZING THE MENU & TOOLBARS

In this lesson you will learn several ways to customize the menu and toolbars, including how to:

- ☑ Modify menus
- ☑ Create custom menus
- ☑ Create custom commands
- ☑ Modify toolbars
- ☑ Create keyboard shortcuts
- ☑ Modify the Navigation bar

LESSON 17

Modifying Menus

You can modify menus by adding more commands to them. You can also create custom submenus. If you created several of your own reports, you could create a submenu off of the Reports menu and add your reports there. The commands that are on the menus that come with ACT! can also be modified. If you run the same queries all the time you can add them to a menu or a toolbar.

Modifications to menus and toolbars are not saved in the database. If you make changes to the menus and toolbars and want other users to have the same changes, the changes have to be added to each computer.

Exercise 17.1: Using The Customize Dialog Box To Modify Menus

In this exercise you will learn how to perform the following tasks to modify menus.

① Add a command to a menu.
② Create a custom menu.
③ Create a custom submenu.
④ Rearrange commands on menus.
⑤ Delete commands on a menu.

How To Add A Command To A Menu

In ACT!, a command is a series of instructions that perform a task like open a dialog box. Usually, commands are created for repetitive tasks. In this part of the exercise you will add a command to the Contacts menu.

1. Open the Contact Detail view.

   Tools ⇒ Customize ⇒ Menus and Toolbars.

   You will see the dialog box shown in Figure 17-1. These are the toolbars that come with ACT!.

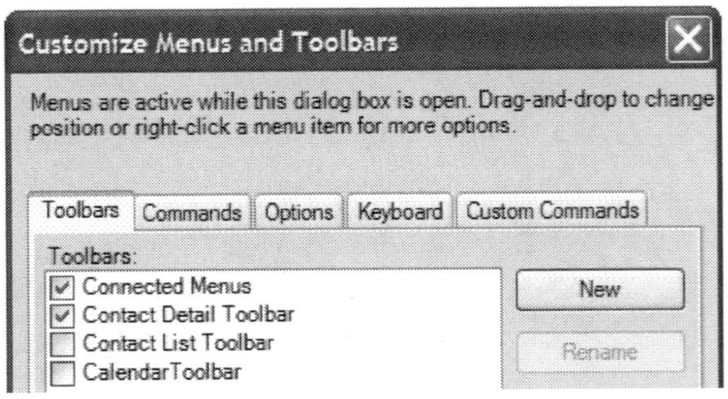

Figure 17-1 Customize Menus and Toolbars dialog box

2. On the Commands tab, click on the Contacts option in the **CATEGORIES** list.

3. Scroll down the list of commands and click on the **CREATE QUOTE** command shown in Figure 17-2.

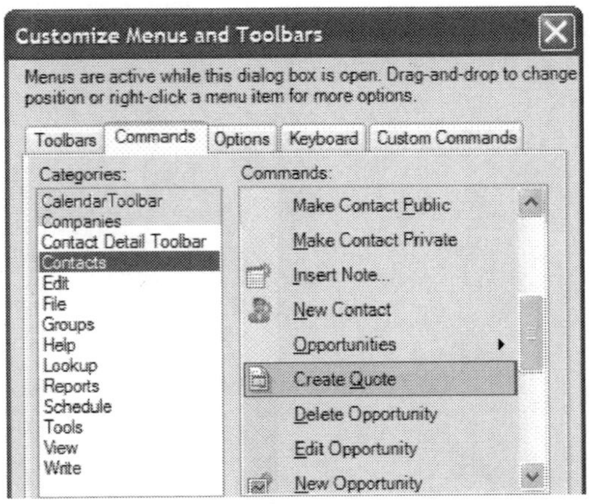

Figure 17-2 Commands tab options

4. Drag the Create Quote command to the Contacts menu illustrated below in Figure 17-3. The Contacts menu will open.

5. Drag the mouse down past the **NEW SECONDARY CONTACT** option, as illustrated below in Figure 17-4, then release the mouse button.

6. Close the Customize Menus and Toolbars dialog box. The Contacts menu should look like the one shown in Figure 17-5.

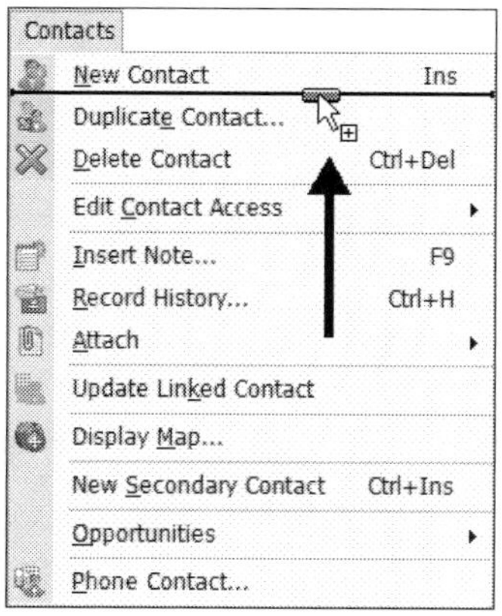

Figure 17-3 Command dragged to the Contacts menu

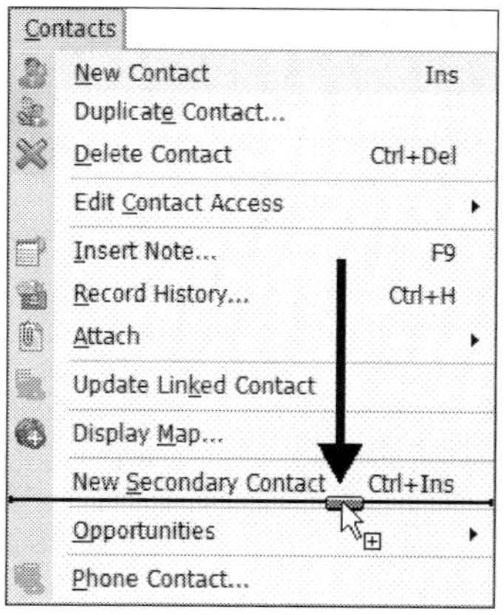

Figure 17-4 Command moved on the menu

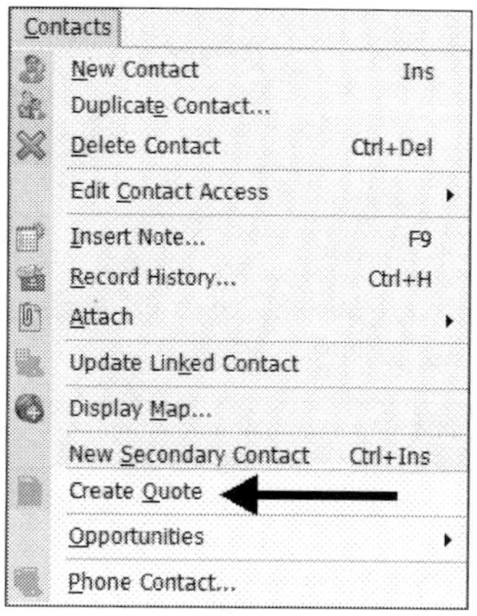

Figure 17-5 Modified Contacts menu

How To Create A Custom Menu

If you have the need to add several commands to menus, it may be easier to find the commands by creating your own menu and placing all of your commands there. The steps below show you how to create a custom menu. You can add commands to menus that you create, just like you did in the previous part of this exercise.

1. Tools ⇒ Customize ⇒ Menus and Toolbars.

2. Click the **NEW** button on the Custom Commands tab.

3. Type `MyMenu` in the Command name field, then click the **ADD COMMAND** button.

   Your dialog box should look like the one shown in Figure 17-6.

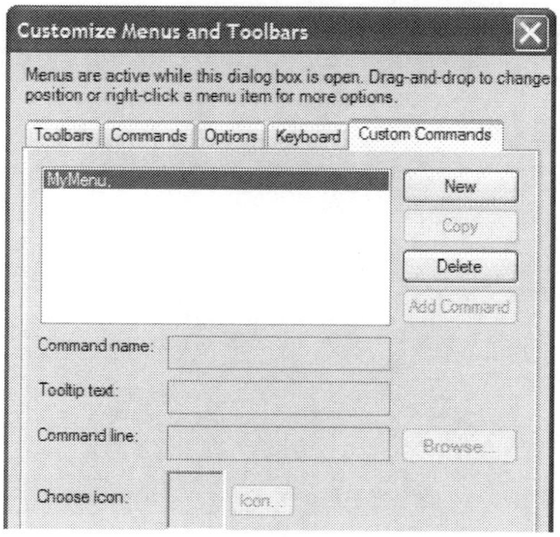

Figure 17-6 Command name added

4. On the Commands tab, click on the Custom Commands category.

   You should see the menu that you created on the Custom Commands tab, as shown in Figure 17-7.

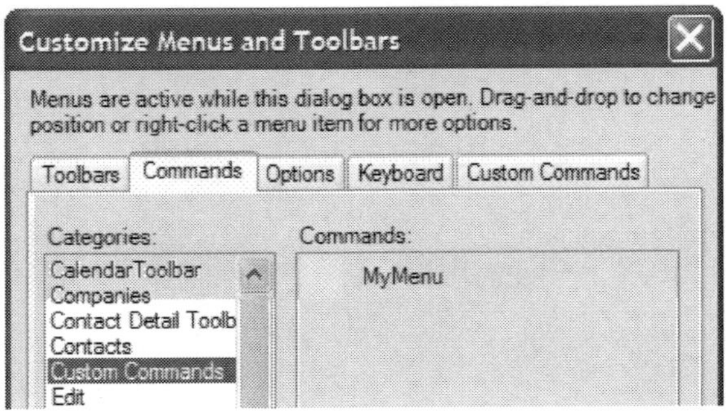

Figure 17-7 Customized menu created

5. Drag the MyMenu command shown above in Figure 17-7 to the menu bar in ACT!. Place it to the right of the Help menu, as shown in Figure 17-8. Leave the dialog box open.

Figure 17-8 Custom menu added to the menu bar

> You can add menus that you create between existing menu options, meaning you could add your menu after the Reports menu for example.

How To Create A Custom Submenu

Submenus are menus that open from an option on a menu. You can add as many commands to a submenu as you need. Commands that have a triangle, as shown earlier in Figure 17-5, have submenus.

In this part of the exercise you will add a submenu to the custom menu that you just created. Adding submenus is the same process as adding other commands.

1. On the Commands tab, select the Reports category.

2. Drag the Company Reports command to the menu that you created. You will see a white box below the menu that you created, as shown in Figure 17-9.

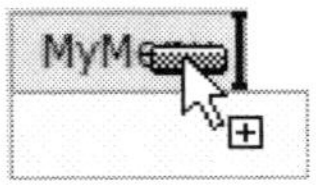

Figure 17-9 Menu command in position

3. Drag the submenu to this box and release the mouse button.

4. Close the Customize Menus and Toolbars dialog box. Your menu should look like the one shown in Figure 17-10.

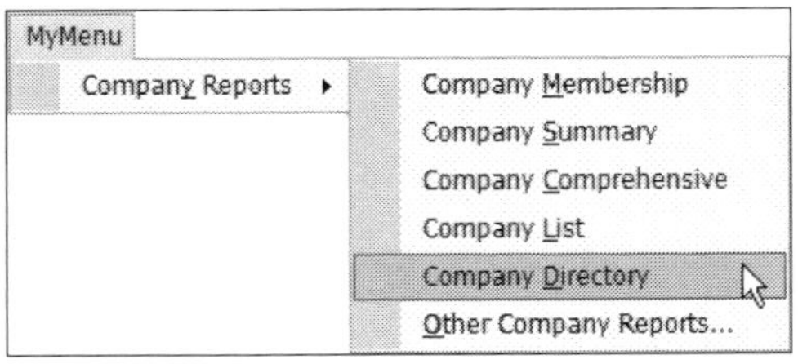

Figure 17-10 Submenu added to the menu

Rearrange Commands On A Menu

If you decide that you do not like the order of the commands on a menu, you can change the order by following the steps below. In this part of the exercise you will move the Create Quote option on the Contacts menu.

1. Open the Customize Menus and Toolbars dialog box.

2. Open the Contacts menu and drag the Create Quote command up and place it below the **EDIT CONTACT ACCESS** command, as illustrated in Figure 17-11.

   In addition to being able to add commands to a menu from the dialog box, you can drag items from one menu to another.

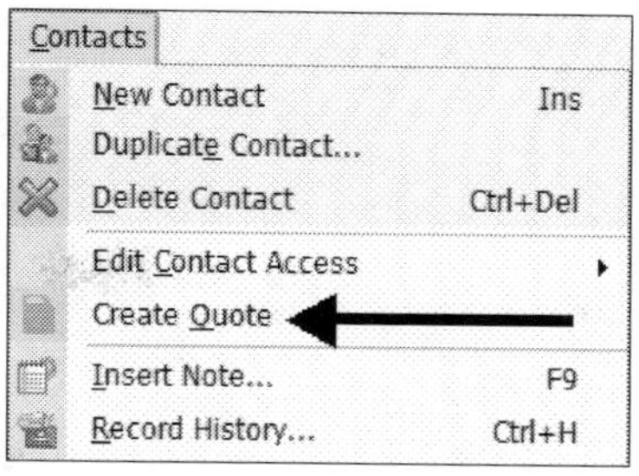

Figure 17-11 Command moved on the menu

How To Delete Commands From A Menu

You can delete a command from a menu by following the steps below. In this part of the exercise you will delete the Create Quote command from the Contacts menu.

1. Open the Customize Menus and Toolbars dialog box.

2. Open the Contacts menu, then right-click on the **CREATE QUOTE** command and select Delete, as shown in Figure 17-12.

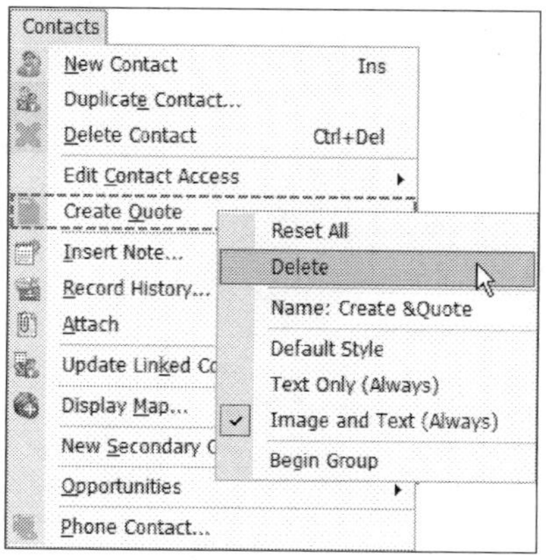

Figure 17-12 Option to delete a menu command

Exercise 17.2: Creating Custom Commands

If you use documents like a template or another software application on a regular basis in conjunction with ACT! and do not want to keep opening the file from outside of ACT!, you can create a custom command to open the template or software package from inside of ACT!.

In this exercise you will create two custom commands. One to open a document and one to open an application. You will then add the commands to the custom menu that you created earlier in this lesson.

Create A Custom Command For A Document

1. Tools ⇒ Customize ⇒ Menus and Toolbars.

2. On the Custom Commands tab, click **NEW**.

3. In the Command name field type `My Document Command.`

4. In the **TOOLTIP TEXT** field type `Opens the Specialties document.`

5. Click the Browse button at the end of the **COMMAND LINE** field, then double-click on the Specialties.txt file in your folder.

   You should have the options shown in Figure 17-13.

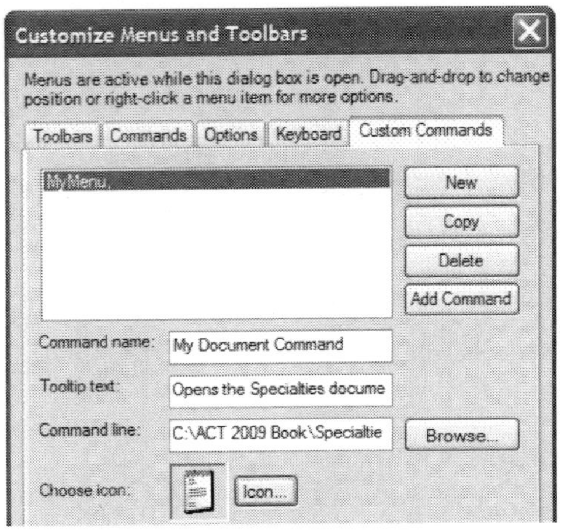

Figure 17-13 Options to open a document

> If you know the full path to the file or application that you are creating the command for, you can type it in the **COMMAND LINE** field instead of clicking the Browse button. If you wanted to use a different icon then the one in the **CHOOSE ICON** section, click the **ICON** button to select the icon file that you want to use.

6. Click the Add Command button. Leave the dialog box open to complete the next part of the exercise.

Create A Custom Command For An Application

1. On the Custom Commands tab, click New.
2. In the Command name field, type `My Application Command`.
3. In the Tooltip text field, type `Opens Notepad`.
4. Click the Browse button at the end of the Command line field, then double-click on the **NOTEPAD.EXE** file in the C:\WINNT folder if your file system is NTFS or C:\Windows if your file system is FAT32.

   You should have the options shown in Figure 17-14.

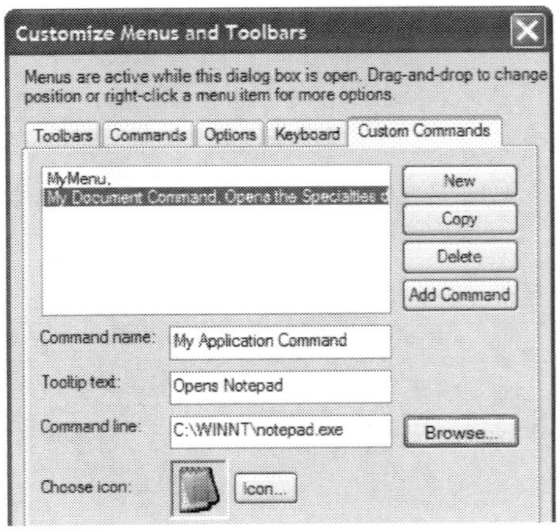

Figure 17-14 Options to open an application

5. Click the Add Command button.

Add The Commands To The Menu

Earlier you added a command to the custom menu that you created. Follow the same steps to add the two commands that you just created to your custom menu.

Place the commands below the Company Reports option. Your custom menu should look like the one shown in Figure 17-16.

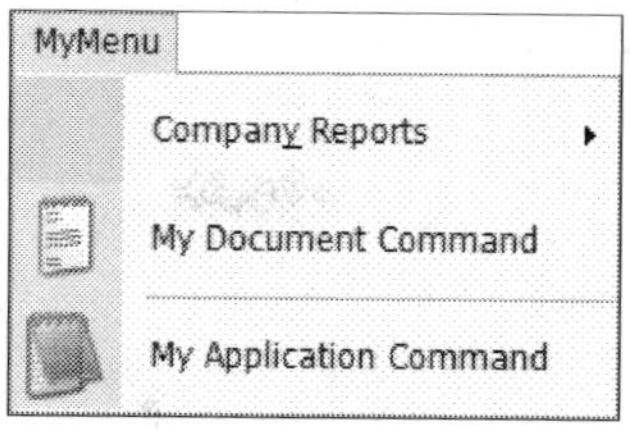

Figure 17-15 Custom menu with commands added

Close the Customize Menus and Toolbars dialog box. Notice that the icons that are at the bottom of the dialog boxes shown earlier in Figure 17-13 and 17-14 are displayed on the menu.

Test The Commands

1. My Menu ⇒ My Document Command. The Specialties document will open.

2. My Menu ⇒ My Application Command. The Notepad application will open.

Deleting Custom Menus

If you have created a custom menu that you no longer need, you can delete it by following the steps below.

1. Open the Customize Menus and Toolbars dialog box, then click on the Custom Commands tab. You should see the menu that you created, as shown earlier in Figure 17-14.

2. Select the command that you want to delete, then click the Delete button. Click OK when you see the Delete Custom Command message.

3. Close the dialog box. The custom menu that you created should no longer be on the menu bar.

Modifying Toolbars

As you learned, each of the views has a toolbar. You can modify the toolbars by adding or removing commands. You can also rearrange the order of the buttons on the toolbar. Each of the views each have their own toolbar. That means that if you add a button to the Groups toolbar you will not see it on the Contacts toolbar. You can also add custom commands to a toolbar like you can to a menu. The difference between customizing a menu and a toolbar is that the changes to menus are visible throughout ACT! regardless of the view that is open. Changes to toolbars are only visible on the views that have the toolbar that you change.

One reason people customize toolbars is to place the commands, files and applications that they use the most out in the open where they can be seen. This allows you to be more efficient because you do not have to remember which menu has the option that you are looking for.

Exercise 17.3: Customizing Toolbars

In this exercise you will learn how to perform the following tasks to customize toolbars.

① Add a command to a toolbar.
② Add a custom command to a toolbar.
③ Rearrange commands on a toolbar.
④ Customize toolbar buttons.
⑤ Distribute and install custom menus and toolbars.
⑥ Delete commands from a toolbar.

How To Add A Command To A Toolbar

In this part of the exercise you will add a command to the Contacts toolbar.

1. Open the Contact List view.
2. Right-click on the toolbar (not a button) and select Customize, as shown in Figure 17-16.

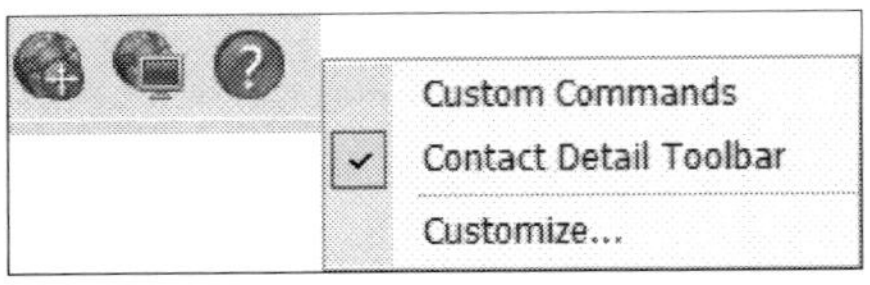

Figure 17-16 Toolbar shortcut menu

3. Move the dialog box off of the toolbar if necessary.
4. On the Commands tab, click on the **REPORTS** category.
5. Drag the Contact Report command to the toolbar and place it after the **EXPORT TO EXCEL** button.
6. Close the dialog box. The Contact List toolbar should look like the one shown in Figure 17-17.

Figure 17-17 Command added to the Contacts toolbar

How To Add A Custom Command To A Toolbar

Just like you added a custom command to a menu, you can add a custom command to a toolbar. In this part of the exercise you will add the custom command that opens an application that you created earlier in this lesson to the Groups toolbar.

1. Open the Group Detail view.
2. Right-click on the toolbar and select Customize.
3. On the Commands tab, click on the Custom Commands category.
4. Drag the **MY APPLICATION COMMAND** to the toolbar and place it after the Save button.
5. Close the dialog box. The Group Detail toolbar should look like the one shown in Figure 17-18.

   If you click on the button that you just added, the Notepad application will open.

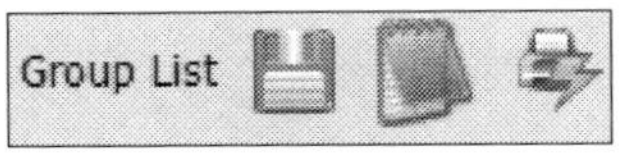

Figure 17-18 Custom command added to the Group Detail toolbar

How To Rearrange Commands On A Toolbar

If you do not like the order that the commands (buttons) are in on the toolbar, you can change the order, just like you rearranged the order of the commands on a menu in Exercise 17.1. In this exercise you will move the report command to the left of the Export to Excel command on the Contact List view toolbar.

1. Open the Contact List view, then open the Customize Menus and Toolbars dialog box.
2. Drag the Contact Report command to the left of the Export to Excel command and release the mouse button.

How To Customize Toolbar Buttons

You can customize each button on a toolbar. Figure 17-19 shows the toolbar button customization options. Table 17-1 explains the customization options that are available when the Customize Menus and Toolbars dialog box is open.

To open this shortcut menu right-click on a button on the toolbar.

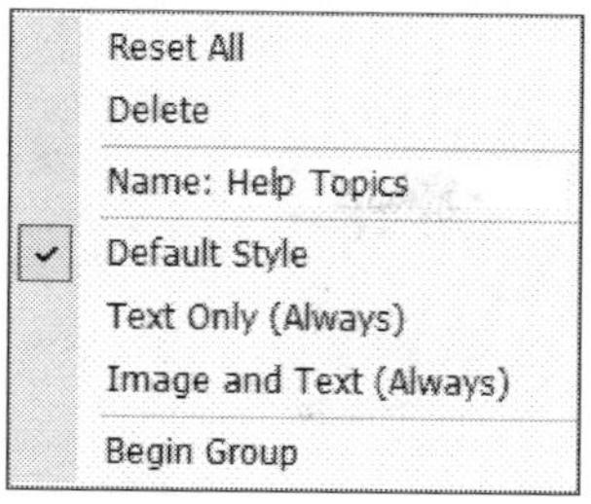

Figure 17-19 Toolbar button shortcut menu

Option	Description
Reset All	Resets all toolbars and menus to the way they were when ACT! was first installed. I don't know why the menus are reset with this option when all of the other options on this shortcut menu are only for toolbar buttons. The only thing that I can think of is because the Reset All command shares code with the Reset Menus and Toolbars command.
Delete	Deletes the command that you right-click on.
Name	Change the name of the button.
Default Style	Only displays the icon for the command without any text. This is how many of the toolbar buttons are, by default.
Text Only (Always)	Only displays text with no icon as shown earlier in Figure 17-17.
Image and Text (Always)	Displays the icon and name of the button, as illustrated in Figure 17-20.
Begin Group	Creates a group of buttons by inserting a vertical line on the toolbar, as illustrated in Figure 17-21. The buttons in the group do not have to have anything in common. One use for this may be if you need to add a few buttons to the toolbar that open the applications that you use often. You could add vertical lines to group them together.

Table 17-1 Toolbar button shortcut menu options explained

Figure 17-20 Image and Name button illustrated

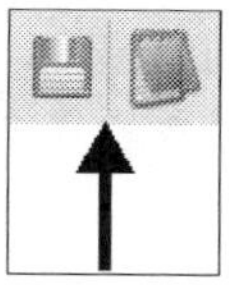

Figure 17-21 Vertical line added to the toolbar

If you right-click on a blank space at the end of the toolbar and select **CUSTOM COMMANDS** on the shortcut menu shown earlier in Figure 17-16, you will see all of the commands that you have created on the second row of the toolbar, as illustrated in Figure 17-22.

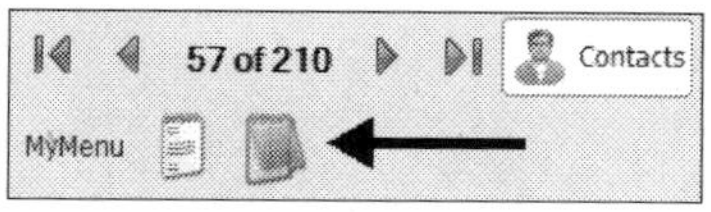

Figure 17-22 Custom commands on the toolbar

How To Distribute Custom Menus And Toolbars

Earlier in this lesson you learned how to customize menus and toolbars. If you want other people that use the database to have the same customized menus and toolbars that you created, follow the steps below. For now you can just read the steps.

1. File ⇒ Back Up ⇒ Personal Files.

2. Click the **BROWSE** button. Select a folder on a server or external device like an external hard drive that you want to store the files on that will be copied to other computers.

3. You can rename the zip file to something else or accept the default name shown in Figure 17-23.

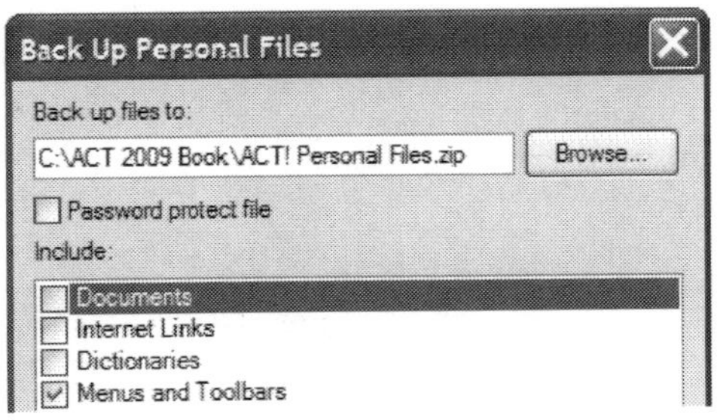

Figure 17-23 Back Up Personal Files dialog box

4. Clear all of the options except the Menus and Toolbars option, then click OK.

How To Install The Custom Menu And Toolbar On Another Computer

Before installing the customizations on another computer, you should confirm that the computer does not already have a custom menu or toolbar.

1. Go to the computer that you want to install the custom menu and toolbar on, then open ACT!.

2. File ⇒ Restore ⇒ Personal Files.

3. Click the Browse button, then navigate to the folder that has the zip file with the customizations that you created and double-click on the zip file.

4. Click OK on the Restore Personal Files dialog box. The custom menus and toolbars will be installed on the computer. Repeat this process on each computer that you want to have the custom menus and toolbars.

How To Delete A Command From A Toolbar

Deleting a command from a toolbar is the same as deleting a command from a menu. In this part of the exercise you will delete the Open NotePad command shown earlier in Figure 17-18 from the toolbar.

1. Open the view that has the toolbar that you want to delete a command from. In this exercise open the Group Detail view.

2. Open the Customize Menus and Toolbars dialog box.

3. Right-click on the command on the toolbar that you want to delete and select Delete.

4. Close the Customize Menus and Toolbars dialog box.

Exercise 17.4: How To Reset Menus And Toolbars

If you have made changes to a menu or toolbar and no longer want or need the changes, you can manually remove the changes one by one or you can reset the menus and toolbars back to the way that they were when ACT! was first installed. Any keyboard shortcuts that you created will also be reset. If you need to reset these tools, follow the steps below. The commands that you create are not deleted, just removed from the menus and toolbars.

1. Tools ⇒ Customize ⇒ Reset Menus and Toolbars.

   You will see the dialog box shown in Figure 17-24.

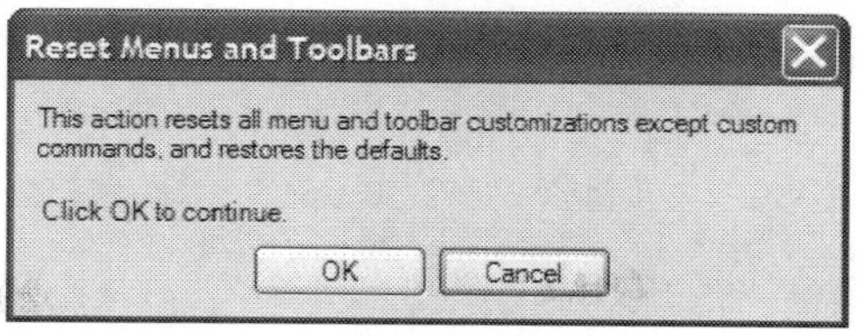

Figure 17-24 Reset Menus and Toolbars dialog box

2. Click OK and the menus and toolbars will be reset.

Creating Keyboard Shortcuts

In addition to being able to customize menus and toolbars, you can create keyboard shortcuts. Keyboard shortcuts are the keystrokes shown at the end of some options on a menu, as shown earlier in Figure 17-11. The steps below show you how to create a keyboard shortcut.

1. Tools ⇒ Customize ⇒ Menus and Toolbars.
2. On the Keyboard tab, click on the Custom command category at the bottom of the list.
3. Click on the My Document command, as shown in Figure 17-25.

Figure 17-25 Command selected

4. Click the **ASSIGN SHORTCUT** button.
5. Press and hold down the Alt key, then press the letter D.

   You should see OK in the bottom field on the dialog box shown in Figure 17-26.

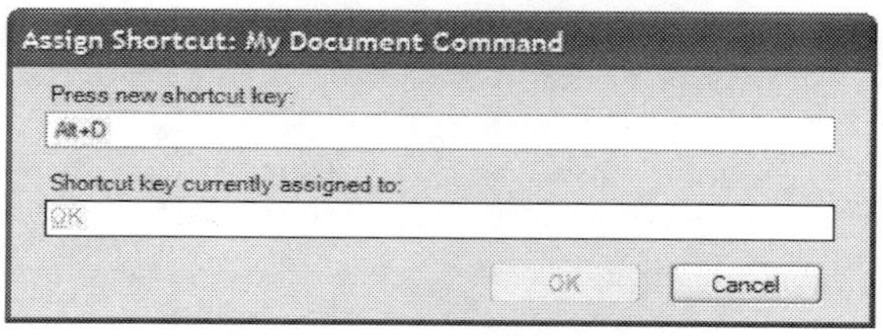

Figure 17-26 Assign Shortcut dialog box

6. Click OK, then click Close. If you open the menu that you created, you will see the keyboard shortcut next to the My Document command, as shown in Figure 17-27.

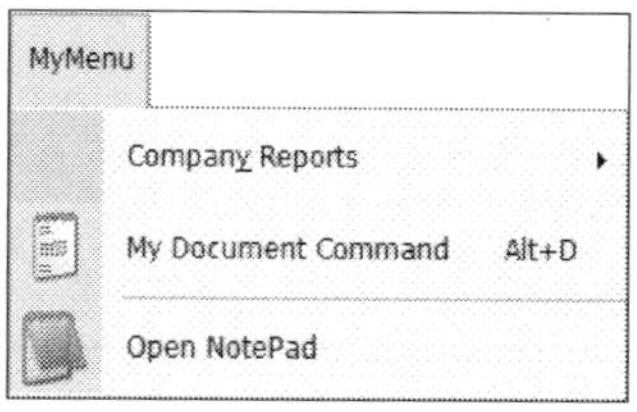

Figure 17-27 Keyboard shortcut added to a command

Keyboard Shortcuts

ACT!, like other software has keyboard shortcuts. Many of them use the Control (CTRL) key. Table 17-2 contains some of the keyboard shortcuts. If you want to know whether or not a specific command has a shortcut, open the menu that the command is on to find out. If you want to print a copy of these keyboard shortcuts, the file ACT_Keyboard_Shortcuts.pdf is in the zip file that you downloaded that has the practice files.

Shortcut	What It Does
CTRL + C	Copies the selected text.
CTRL + D	Clears an activity.
CTRL + H	Creates a history record.
CTRL + I	Attaches a file.
CTRL + L	Schedules a telephone call activity.
CTRL + M	Schedules a meeting activity.
CTRL + P	Prints an address book, calendar, envelope, label and reports.
CTRL + T	Schedules a To-Do activity.
CTRL + V	Pastes the contents of the clipboard into a field in ACT!.
CTRL + X	Cuts (deletes) the selected text.
CTRL + Z	Undoes the last action.
CTRL + F5	Refreshes the window.
CTRL + F11	Opens a new sales opportunity.
F1	Opens the Help system.
F3	Opens the weekly calendar.
F5	Opens the monthly calendar.
F7	Opens the Task List view.
F8	Opens the Contact List view.
F9	Inserts a note.
F10	Opens the Group List view.
F11	Opens the Contact Detail view.

Table 17-2 ACT! keyboard shortcuts explained

Exercise 17.5: Modifying The Navigation Bar

The default buttons on the Navigation bar provide the options that you may use most often. If you have created a custom command or want to add additional buttons to the Navigation bar, you can. In this exercise you will learn how to perform the following tasks.

① Add buttons to the Navigation bar.
② Remove buttons from the Navigation bar.
③ Learn about the Navigation bar menu layouts.
④ Reset Navigation bar customizations.

Add Buttons To The Navigation Bar

In this part of the exercise you will add the **WEEKLY CALENDAR** command to the Navigation bar by following the steps below.

1. Tools ⇒ Customize ⇒ Navbar.

   The options on the dialog box shown in Figure 17-28 are the commands that can be added to the Navigation bar.

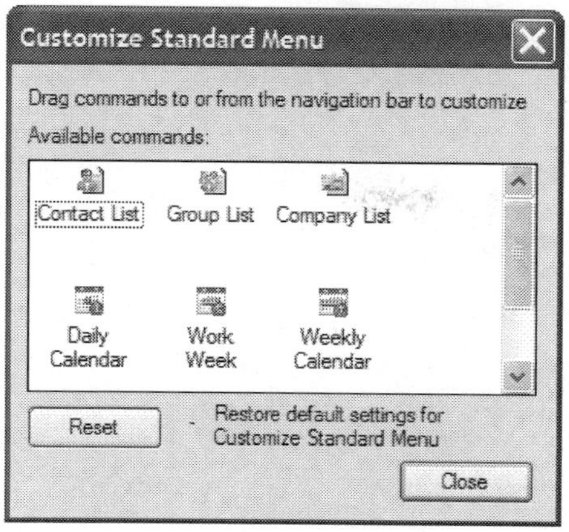

Figure 17-28 Customize Standard Menu dialog box

You can also open the Customize Standard Menu dialog box shown above in Figure 17-28 by right-clicking on the Navigation bar and selecting Customize, as shown in Figure 17-29.

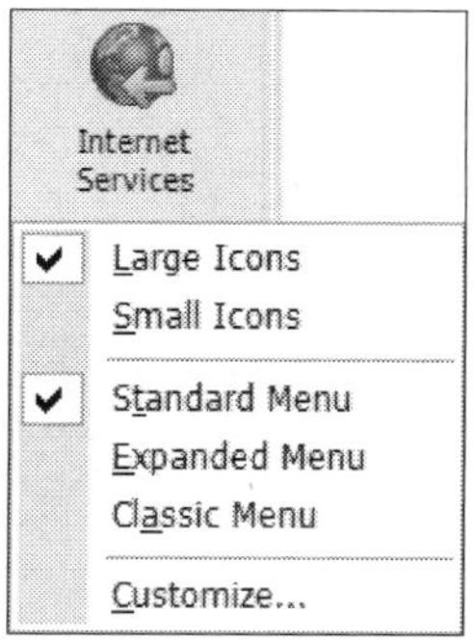

Figure 17-29 Navigation bar shortcut menu

If you cannot see the Internet Services icon on the Navigation bar, open the Navigation bar shortcut menu and select **SMALL ICONS**, as shown above in Figure 17-29.

2. Drag the Weekly Calendar command from the Customize Standard Menu dialog box to the Navigation bar and place it below the calendar option, as illustrated in Figure 17-30.

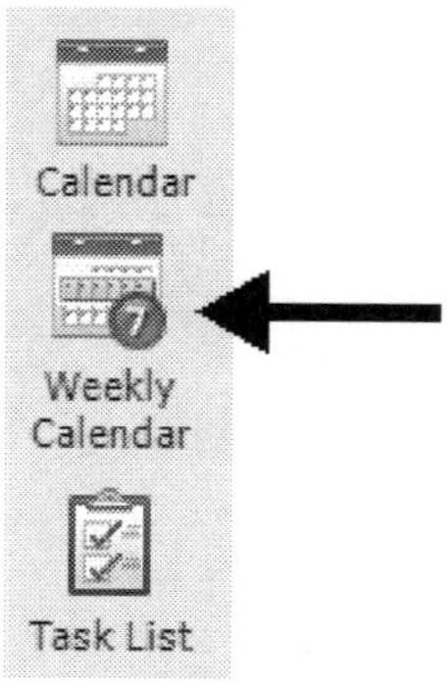

Figure 17-30 Weekly calendar command added to the Navigation bar

3. Close the Customize Standard Menu dialog box.

Remove Buttons From The Navigation Bar

If you do not use options on the Navigation bar and want to remove them, follow the steps below.

1. Open the Customize Standard Menu dialog box shown earlier in Figure 17-28.

2. On the Navigation bar, click on the button that you want to remove, then drag it to the Customize Standard Menu dialog box.

Navigation Bar Menu Layouts

The default Navigation bar menu is the **STANDARD MENU**, which is shown above in Figure 17-30.

Figure 17-31 shows the **EXPANDED MENU** layout.

Figure 17-32 shows the **CLASSIC MENU** layout.

Figure 17-31 Expanded menu layout

Figure 17-32 Classic menu layout

> If you customize the Standard menu and then switch to the Expanded or Classic menu navigation layout, your customizations will disappear.

Reset The Navigation Bar

If you made changes to the Navigation bar that you no longer like, need or want, you can put the Navigation bar back to the way it was when ACT! was installed, by following the steps below.

1. Open the Customize Standard Menu dialog box shown earlier in Figure 17-28.

2. Click the **RESET** button, then click the Close button. The customizations that were added to the Navigation bar will be removed.

USING THE LAYOUT DESIGNER

In this lesson you will learn how to use the Layout Designer to modify the views. To modify the views, you will learn about the following:

- ☑ Layout Designer options
- ☑ Formatting toolbar
- ☑ Layout Designer toolbox
- ☑ Customizing tabs on a view
- ☑ Adding fields to a tab
- ☑ Adding graphics to a layout
- ☑ Changing the background color of a tab
- ☑ Using the Properties window
- ☑ Changing the label for a field on a layout
- ☑ Aligning fields on a layout
- ☑ Changing the tab stop order

LESSON 18

What Is A Layout?

A layout is how the fields and tabs are arranged on the view.

ACT! Layouts

ACT! comes with the layouts shown in Figure 18-1. Each layout can have different fields. An example of this is the Photo field shown in Figure 18-2. This is on the ACTDemo layout. The Basic Contact Layout - 800x600 layout does not have this field on the Personal Info tab.

ACTDemo.aly
ACTDemo.cly
ACTDemo.gly
Basic Company Layout - 800x600.aly
Basic Company Layout - 1024x768.aly
Basic Contact Layout - 800x600.cly
Basic Contact Layout - 1024x768.cly
Basic Group Layout - 800x600.gly
Basic Group Layout - 1024x768.gly

Figure 18-1 ACT! Layouts

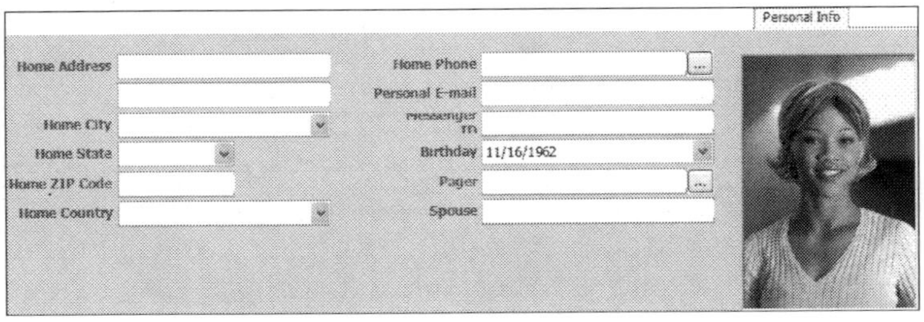

Figure 18-2 Photo field on the Personal Info tab of the ACTDemo layout

Layout File Type Extensions

As shown above in Figure 18-1, layout files can have one of three file type extensions, as explained below.

The **.CLY** extension is for contact layouts.
The **.GLY** extension is for group layouts.
The **.ALY** extension is for company layouts.

The numbers after the Basic Layouts shown above in Figure 18-1, refer to the screen resolution. If your monitor or LCD has a resolution of 1024x768, that is the layout that would look best on your computer screen. What I noticed between these two layout resolutions is that some fields are in different places. This was probably done to accommodate the different screen resolutions. Figure 18-3 shows the 800x600 basic contact layout. Figure 18-4 shows the 1024x768 basic contact layout.

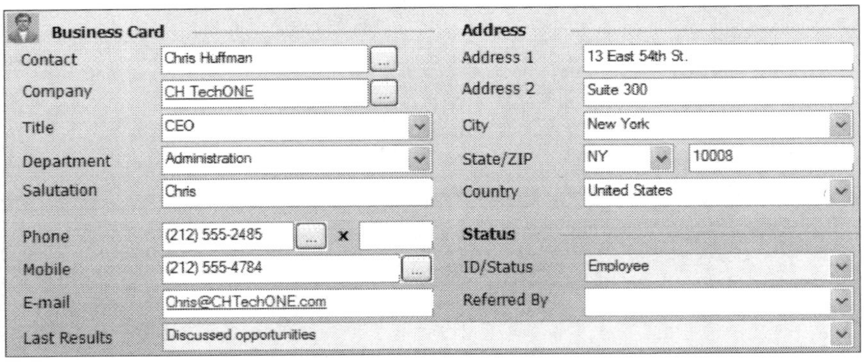

Figure 18-3 800x600 resolution basic contact layout

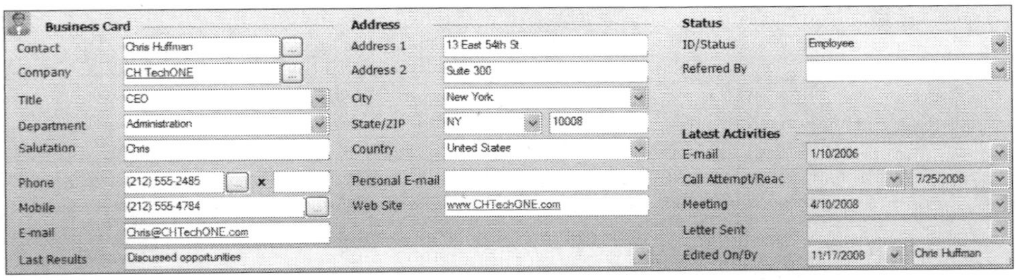

Figure 18-4 1024x768 resolution basic contact layout

Layout Designer

The Layout Designer shown in Figure 18-5 is used to change what the views, including the tabs, look like. You can change the background color, add fields, remove fields, rearrange the order of fields and much more.

In Lesson 13 you learned how to create new fields. Fields can only be used when they are on a layout. If an existing layout meets most of your needs, you can add the new fields to it or you can save an existing layout with a new file name and add the fields to the layout with the new file name. You can also create a new layout from scratch. Creating and modifying layouts require administrator or manager rights. While the layout modification exercises in this lesson are for the contact view and tabs, you can modify the company and group layouts also.

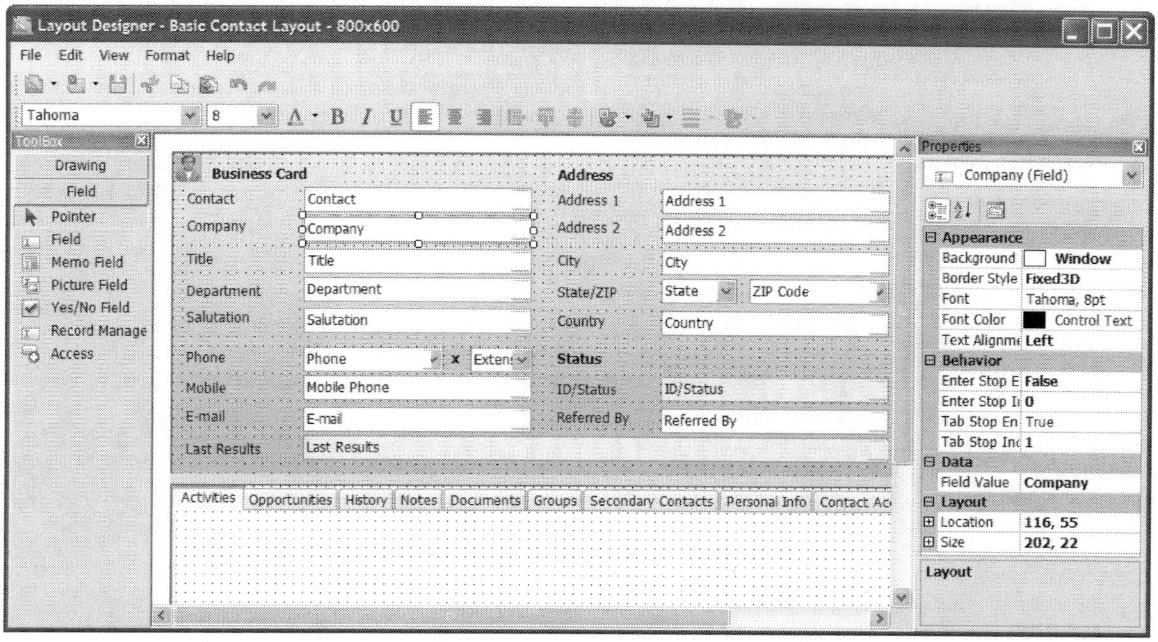

Figure 18-5 Layout Designer window

Layout Design Tips

There are some things to take into consideration when creating or modifying a layout as discussed below.

① Many new layout designers are often more concerned with how a layout looks, rather then how functional it is. A primary goal of a layout is to make the data entry as easy as possible.

② If you find that you are constantly going from tab to tab to enter basic information, the layout may need to be modified. If there are fields on a layout that are not being used, consider deleting them from the layout.

③ Layouts that you modify or create can be used by other databases. If you plan to use a layout created or modified in one database in a different database, make sure that the second database has the same fields.

Layout Designer Options

There are a lot of options that you can use to design or modify the layout for a view. Many of them are similar to the options used to modify a report.

Edit Menu The options on this menu are the same as the editing options in word processing software. The exception to this is the **TABS** option. The tabs option opens the Edit Tabs dialog box. You can create new tabs, delete tabs and rearrange the order of tabs on a view.

View Menu The first option on this menu opens the Properties window shown in Figure 18-6.

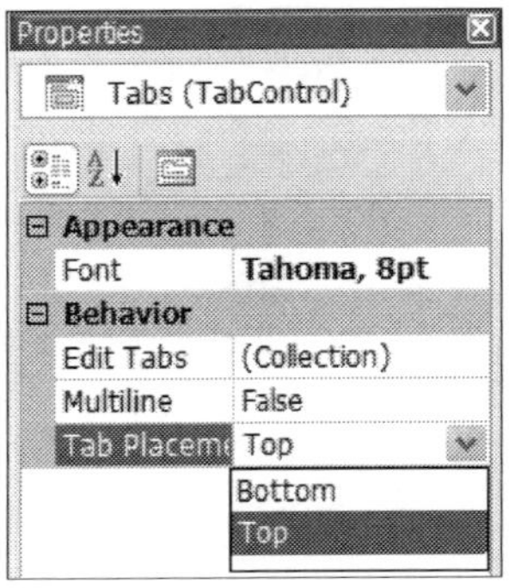

Figure 18-6 Properties window

Different options are available on the Properties window depending on the object that is selected in the layout before the Properties window is opened.

If the Properties window is too small, you can resize it by putting the mouse pointer on the edge of the window and dragging the edge to the size that you want.

As shown at the bottom of Figure 18-6, the tabs can be placed at the top or bottom of the tab section. The default is to display the tabs at the top. Figure 18-7 shows the tabs displayed at the bottom of the layout.

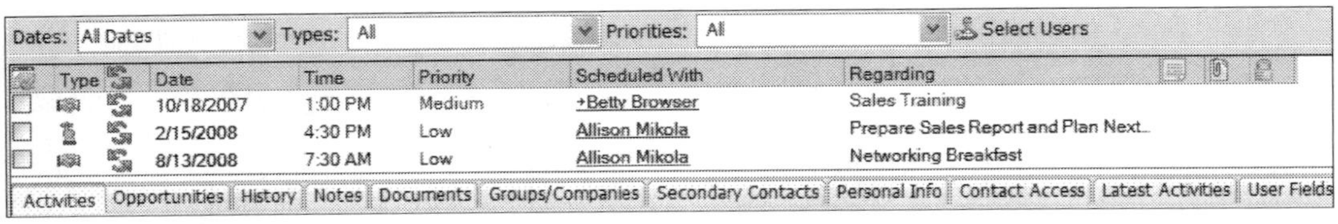

Figure 18-7 Tabs displayed at the bottom of the layout

The **Toolbox** option opens and closes the Toolbox that is on the left side of the Designer window.

The **View ⇒ Tab Stops ⇒ Show Tab Stops** option will display the order (in red numbers) that the Tab key will move, through the fields on the layout, as shown in Figure 18-8.

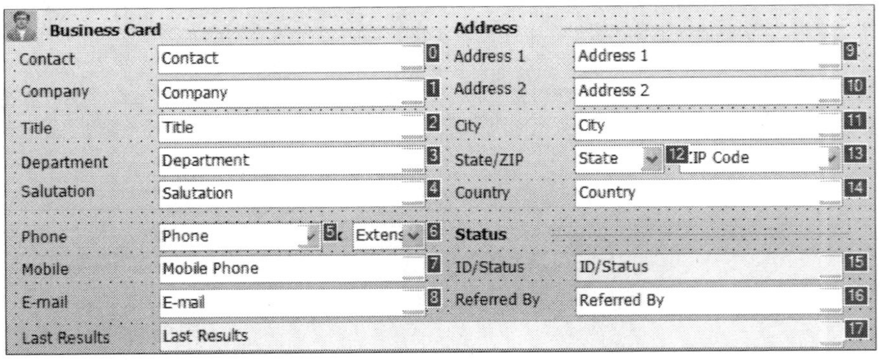

Figure 18-8 Tab key order for a layout

The **View ⇒ Enter Stops ⇒ Show Enter Stops** option will display the order (in green numbers) that the Enter key will move, through the fields on the layout. It looks like the one for Tab stops.

Format Menu The options on this menu are used to align, size and space the fields on the layout.

Layout Designer Formatting Toolbar

The first nine buttons on the toolbar shown in Figure 18-9 are the same buttons that are on the formatting toolbar in most word processors. The remaining buttons are explained in Table 18-1. The buttons on this toolbar are used to change the look of objects like fields or labels on the layout.

Figure 18-9 Layout Designer Formatting toolbar

Button	Description
1	Aligns the selected object(s) on the left side of the object. (1)
2	Aligns the selected object(s) on the top of the object. (1)
3	Aligns the selected object(s) on the center of the object. (1)
4	Select the background color of the object. (2)
5	The options shown in Figure 18-10 are used to add a border around the object.
6	Change the size (height) of a line. (3)
7	Change the color of a line. (3)

Table 18-1 Layout Designer Formatting toolbar buttons explained

(1) This option is only available if two or more objects are selected. The align options are also available on the shortcut menu shown in Figure 18-11 when you have more than one object selected and right-click on one of the selected objects.

(2) If you want to match the color of an existing background on the layout, view the **BACKGROUND COLOR** option on the Properties window in the top portion of the view or the tab that has the color that you want to match.

(3) The border is created by using a Drawing Object. This option is not used for fields.

Figure 18-10 Border Style options

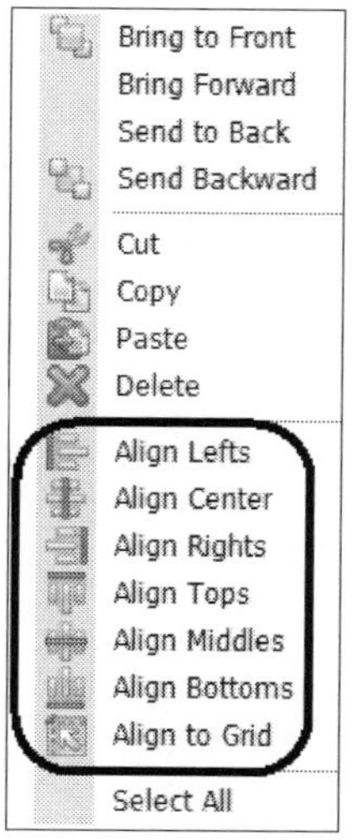

Figure 18-11 Object shortcut menu

Layout Designer Toolbox

Figures 18-12 and 18-13 show the tabs on the Toolbox.

The **FIELD** tab has all of the field types that can be added to a layout.

The **DRAWING** tab contains other objects that can be added to a layout.

The **MEMO FIELD** is a free form field that is used as a comments field. It is similar to the fields on the User Fields tab. The difference is that you can allow more text to be entered into a memo field.

The **YES/NO FIELD** is a check box field. The Yes/No fields that you have seen on the layout are some of the fields used to filter records.

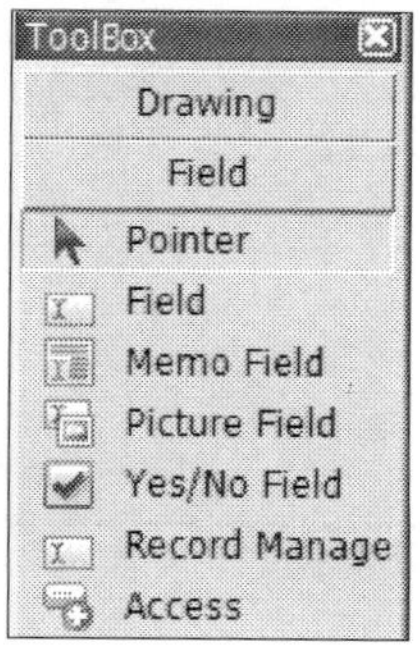

Figure 18-12 Field tab options

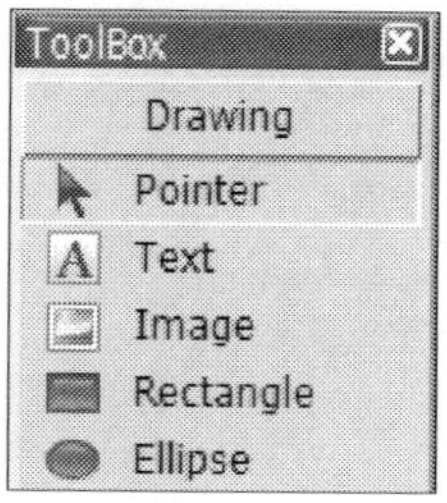

Figure 18-13 Drawing tab options

Tabs Overview

In previous lessons you have entered data in fields on the tabs. The tabs in ACT! have features that you need to be aware of before you modify them. The following tabs are **SYSTEM TABS**: Notes, History, Activities, Opportunities, Groups/Companies, Secondary Contacts and Documents. If you do not need these tabs you can hide them. Each of these tabs has its own table in the database and because of this, you cannot customize these tabs like you can the other tabs that come with ACT! or tabs that you create. This is the reason that you can enter an unlimited number of records on each of these tabs for the same contact. This is known as **RELATIONAL** data.

The detail views in ACT! come with tabs. If you need to add more fields to an existing tab or if you want to put certain fields on a tab by themselves, you can. The only limitation is that you cannot add a field to a tab that is already on a tab.

Customizing Tabs

Tabs are used to organize fields. If there are fields that are only used for a season or promotion, it may be a good idea to put them on their own tab or create a layout for them. If the order of the tabs on a layout does not meet your needs or your users needs, you can change the order that the tabs are in. An example would be if you rarely use the History tab. Moving it to the last position in the row of tabs may be a good idea.

Exercise 18.1: Create A Tab For A Layout

In this exercise you will create a new tab on the Basic Contact Layout and add the Specialized In field that you created in Exercise 13.6 to the layout.

1. Tools ⇒ Define Layouts ⇒ Contact. You should see the words **BASIC CONTACT LAYOUT - 800x600** in the Title bar of the Layout Designer window.

2. Edit ⇒ Tabs, then click the **ADD TAB** button on the Edit Tabs dialog box.

3. Type `My Tab` in the Tab name field, as shown in Figure 18-14, then click OK.

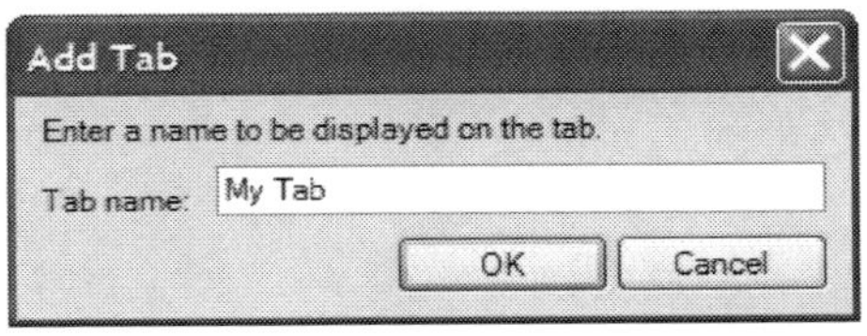

Figure 18-14 Add Tab dialog box

4. In the Edit Tabs dialog box, click on the tab that you just created, then click the Move Up button once.

Hiding A Tab

To keep a tab from being displayed on the layout, click on the Tab name in the **SHOW TABS IN THIS ORDER** list, shown in Figure 18-15, then click the **<** button.

The tab will now be in the **HIDDEN TABS** list.

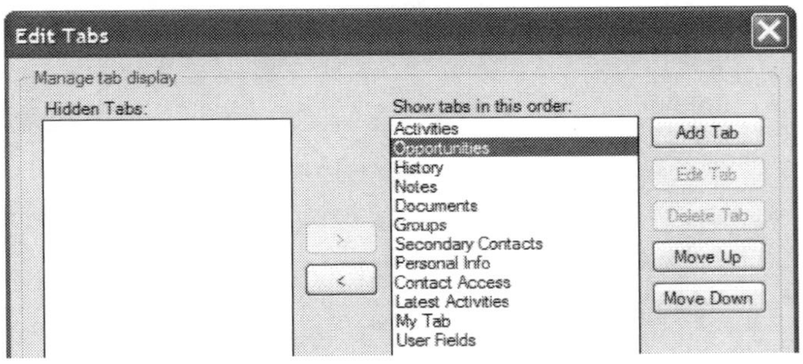

Figure 18-15 Edit Tabs dialog box options

5. Your tab should be the second one from the bottom in the list, as shown above in Figure 18-15. Click the Close button.

Changing The Order Of The Tabs

The **MOVE UP** and **MOVE DOWN** buttons shown above in Figure 18-15 are used to change the order that the tabs are displayed in, from left to right on the layout.

Edit Tab Options

In addition to being able to add and hide tabs on the Edit Tabs dialog box you can also rename and delete tabs as discussed below.

① The **EDIT TAB** button is used to rename any tab except the System tabs.

② The **DELETE TAB** button is used to delete any tab except the System tabs. When deleting a tab, the fields on the tab are not deleted from the database. If you are not comfortable deleting a tab or are not 100% sure that the tab should be deleted, you should hide it instead.

Fields On A Layout

Like fields on a report, fields on a layout have two parts and work the same way that they do on a report. [See Lesson 16, Field vs Label]

Exercise 18.2: Adding Fields To A Tab

1. Click on the tab that you created at the bottom of the layout. You may have to click on the right arrow button at the end of the row of tabs to see your tab.

2. Click the **FIELD** button in the Toolbox.

3. Place the mouse pointer in the position where you want the upper left corner of the field to be placed on the layout. Draw a rectangle in the grid below the tab name. When you release the mouse button you should see the dialog box shown in Figure 18-16.

   The fields on this dialog box are fields that have not already been added to the layout.

   You may be wondering why you do not see the Specializes In field that you created. The reason that you do not see the field in the list is because it was created as a drop-down list, not a field.

   The **NEW FIELD** button is used to create a new field.

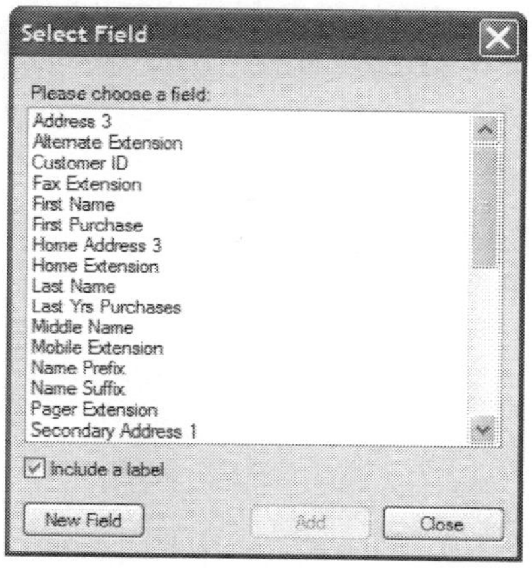

Figure 18-16 Select Field dialog box

4. Click on the Specialty field at the bottom of the list, then click the Add button.

5. Click on a blank space on the layout so that the field is not selected. If necessary, click on the label and drag it to the left so that it is not touching the field. It should look like the one shown in Figure 18-17.

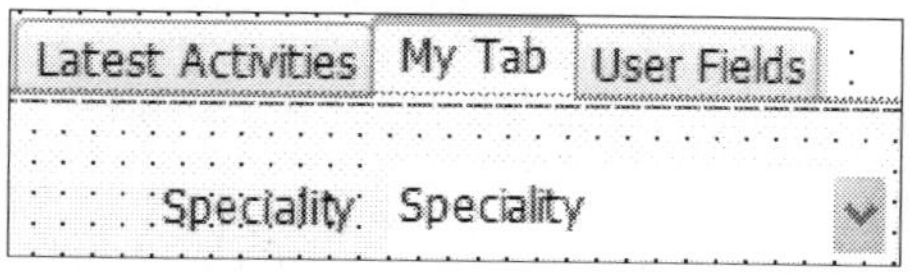

Figure 18-17 Field added to a tab

You can add more than one field to the layout at the same time. Click on the first field that you want to add in the Select Field dialog box. Press and hold down the **CTRL** key, then click on the other field(s) that you want to add, as shown in Figure 18-18. Once you have selected all of the fields, click the Add button.

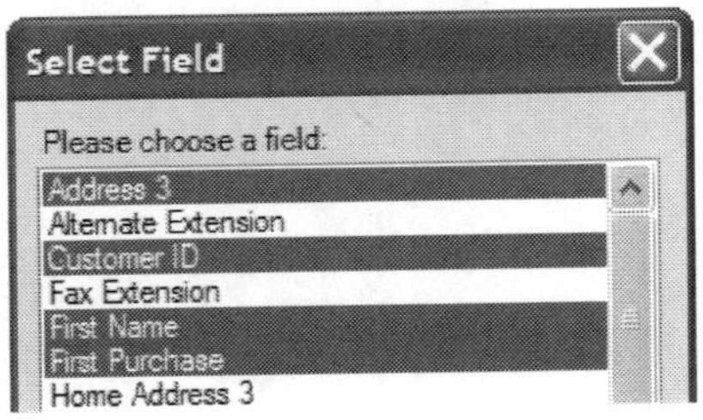

Figure 18-18 Multiple fields selected to be added to the layout

Text Boxes

Text boxes serve the same purpose that text fields serve in reports. They are used to add free form text to the layout. The one thing that text boxes are useful for in a layout is to provide helpful information or a reminder for the type of information that should be entered in a field. The other reason that I have added a text box to a layout is to add a name to a group or section of fields.

For example, there is no requirement that the fields have to be in a two column layout like you see on the Contact Detail view. I have had the need to create a custom layout. The majority of contacts did not have street addresses (don't ask), so I put the address fields all the way on the right side of the layout to make room for new fields that were needed.

To save space, I used a text box to indicate that the fields on the right side of the layout were address fields. Another use for a text box is to indicate that a field is required. If you need to add a text box to a layout, follow the steps below. For now you can just read the steps to become familiar with the process.

1. Click on the **DRAWING** button on the Toolbox, then click the Text button.
2. Draw a box on the layout where you need it. To add the text, double-click on the text box, then type in the text.
3. If you need to change an attribute of the text box like the font, you can change it on the Properties window.

Resizing Fields On A Layout

When you select a field or object, you will see **HANDLES** around the object, as shown in Figure 18-19.

If you need to resize several objects, select all of them first and then resize the objects. When you place the mouse pointer on a handle, you can drag the border of the object(s) to change the size.

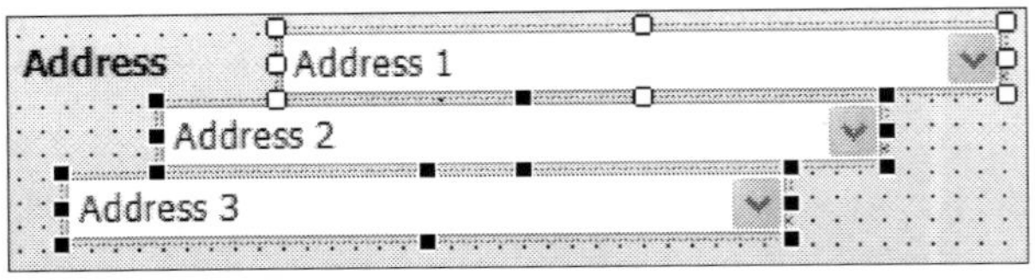

Figure 18-19 Handles illustrated

When you add fields to a layout, it is very possible that the fields are not the exact size that you need them to be. There are two ways to resize fields as discussed below.

① **Use the anchor** This option is used to resize fields to match the size of an existing field in the layout. To use this method, select the field(s) that need to be resized. Press and hold down the **CTRL** key, then click on the field that has the dimensions that you want the other field(s) to be the size of. The handles on the field that you want to use to resize the other fields to should be white, as shown above in Figure 18-19. Format ⇒ Make Same Size ⇒ Select the option that you need (width, height or both).

② **Resize a field manually** Use this option when none of the fields on the layout is the size that you want. Select the field(s) that you want to resize. Place the mouse pointer on the side of the field that you want to resize and drag the handle to the size that you want all of the selected fields to be.

If you want to move a field and label, you have to select both of them because they are separate objects.

Exercise 18.3: Adding Graphics To A Layout

If your company has a logo, you may want to add it to a layout. The steps below show you how to add a graphic file to a layout. You will add the ACT! icon to the tab that you created.

1. If there are fields where you want to put the graphic in the layout, move the fields out of the way.
2. Click the Drawing button in the Toolbox, then click the Image button. Draw a small box to the left of the drop-down field that you added to the tab.
3. Right-click on the image field and select Edit Properties. Navigate to the location of the graphic file that you want to add. To complete this exercise, use the ACT! icon, which is in this location: C:\Program Files\ACT\Act for Windows\act.ico.
4. Make the frame of the image smaller, then click on a blank space on the tab.

Exercise 18.4: Changing The Background Color Of A Tab

While this exercise will change the background color of a tab, the steps are the same to change the background color of the top portion of a layout.

1. Click on the tab that you created, then click on the arrow on the **BACKGROUND COLOR** button on the toolbar, as shown at the top of Figure 18-20.

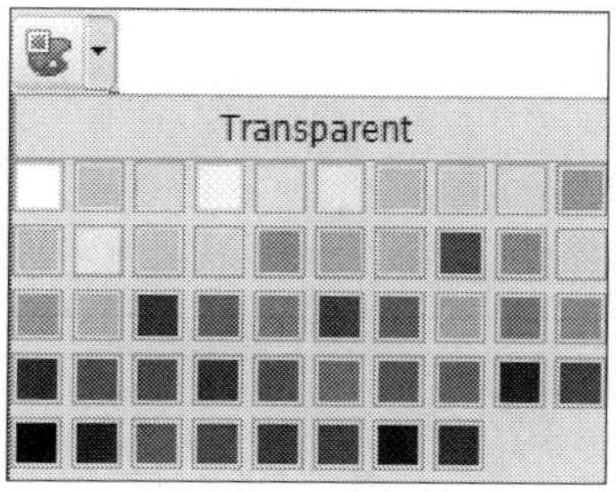

Figure 18-20 Background color options

2. Click on the first yellow square in the second row. The background color of the tab that you created should now be yellow.

How To Use An Image For The Background

If you wanted to use an image for the background instead of a color, follow the steps below.

1. Click the button at the end of the Background Image option, in the **APPEARANCE** section of the Properties window illustrated in Figure 18-21.
2. Select the image file for the background.

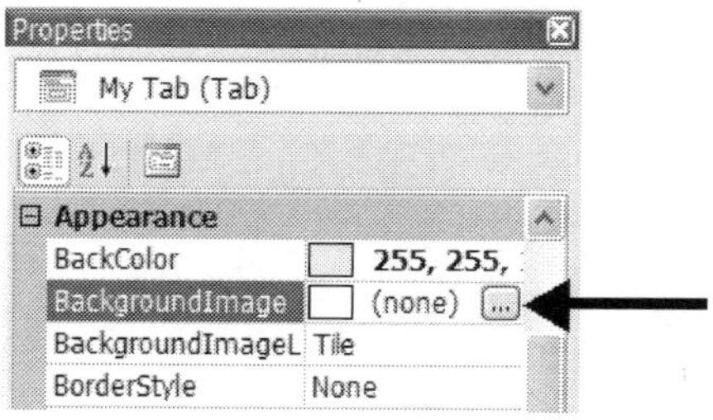

Figure 18-21 Background options

Saving The Layout Changes

You have two options for saving changes to a layout. You can save the changes to the existing layout or save the changes as a new layout. In this exercise you will save the changes to a new layout.

1. File ⇒ Save As. You should see the Layouts folder. Type `My Basic Contact Layout` as the file name, then press Enter or click the Save button.

2. Close the Layout Designer window. (File ⇒ Exit.)

View The Layout

1. Click on the Layout button in the lower left corner of the Contact Detail view, then select the layout that you just created, from the list shown in Figure 18-22.

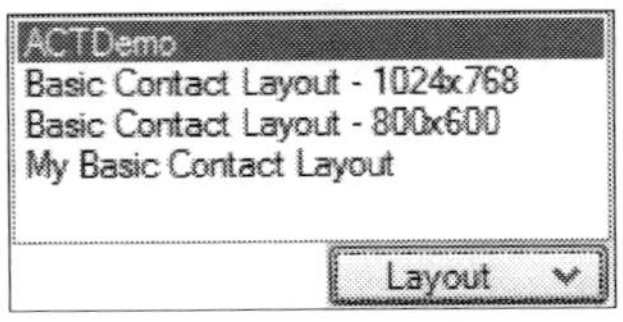

Figure 18-22 Layout options

2. Click on the tab that you created, then open the Specialty drop-down list, as shown in Figure 18-23.

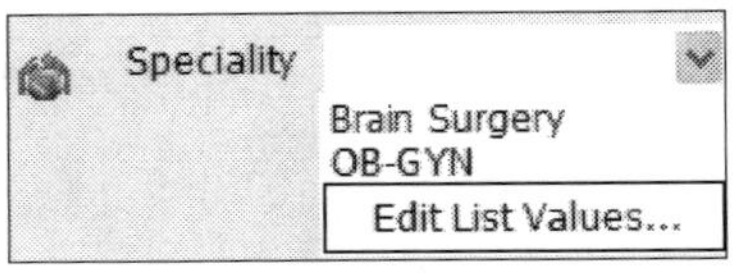

Figure 18-23 Drop-down list field added to a tab

3. Switch back to the Basic Contact 800x600 layout.

Using The Properties Window To Change The Appearance Of A Field Or Label

Earlier in this lesson you used the Properties window to change the behavior of a tab. You can also use the options on this window to modify the appearance of a field. When you click on the field(s) that you want to modify, you can change the border style and font.

If you click on the label(s) that you want to modify, you can change the label text. The differences between the Properties window and the Edit Properties dialog box is that the Properties window has more options and you can modify more than one field or label at the same time.

Using The Edit Properties Dialog Box

The options shown in Figure 18-24 are used to modify the font properties. The tab shown in Figure 18-25 has options to modify the borders. To change any of these properties, right-click on the field or label that you want to modify and select **EDIT PROPERTIES**.

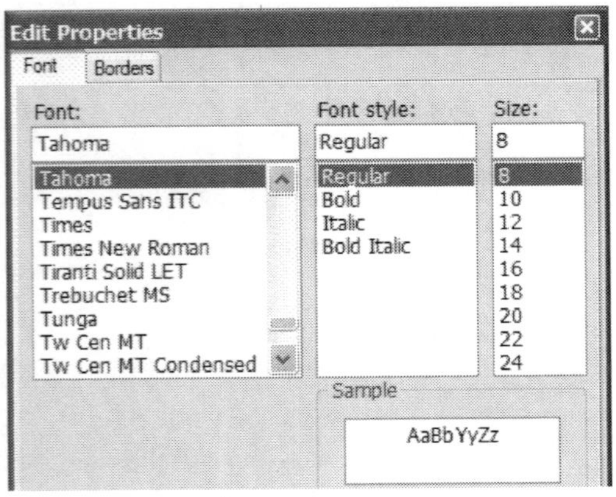

Figure 18-24 Font tab options

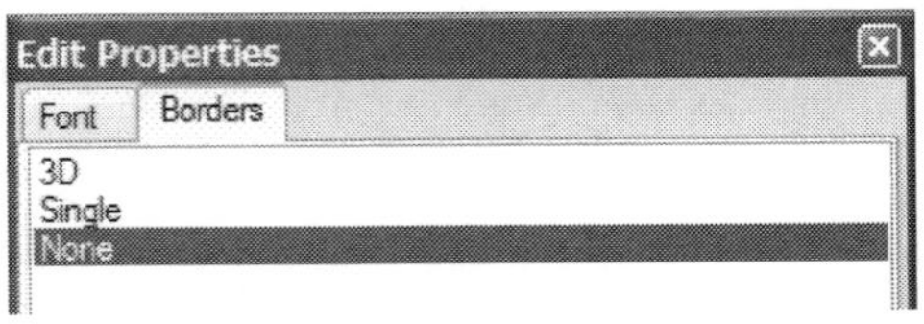

Figure 18-25 Borders tab options

Exercise 18.5: How To Change The Label For A Field On A Layout

In Lesson 13 you modified the User 1 field. When you viewed the field on the User Fields tab, the label was still User 1. In this exercise you will change the text that is displayed on the label for the User 1 field.

1. Open the Basic Contact Layout 800x600 in the Layout Designer.
2. On the User Fields tab, double-click on the User 1 label. The background color should have changed to white.
3. Highlight the text and type `MD Type`. Press Enter, then click on a blank space on the layout. The label for the field should look like the one shown in Figure 18-26.

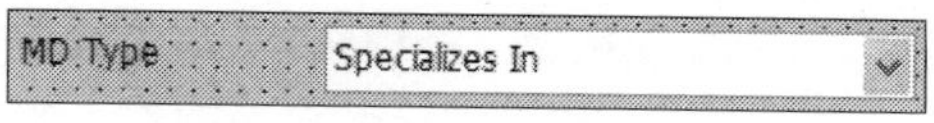

Figure 18-26 Label changed

4. Save the changes to the layout and close the Layout Designer.
5. Click on the User Fields tab. The label for the first user field should have "MD Type", as shown above in Figure 18-26.

Annual Event Fields

This type of field is used to track dates of events that happen once a year. To create an annual event field you need administrator or manager level rights. You can create a reminder of the annual event by creating a recurring To-do activity.

Exercise 18.6: Create An Annual Event Field

In this exercise you will create a renewal date annual field.

1. Tools ⇒ Define Fields. Click the Create new field link.
2. Type `Renewal Date` in the Field name field.
3. Open the Field data type drop-down list and select Annual Event.
4. Check the **GENERATE HISTORY** option, then click Finish.
5. Close the Define Fields window, then open the Basic Contact Layout that you created earlier in this lesson.
6. Add the Renewal Date (Annual Event) field below the Specialty field on the tab that you created.
7. Add a 3D border to the Renewal Date field and save the changes.

   When you view the layout, it should look like the one shown in Figure 18-27.

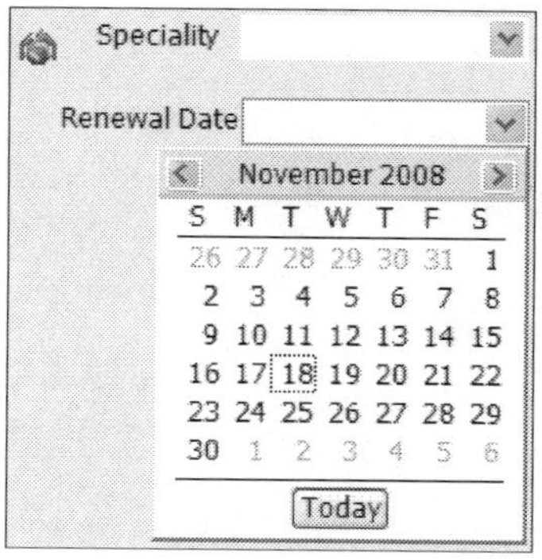

Figure 18-27 Annual Event field added to the layout

Annual Event Field Tips

These tips are for the options on the Define Fields dialog box.

① A text (character) field cannot be converted to an Annual Date field.
② A date field can be converted to an Annual Event field by changing the **SELECT A FIELD DATA TYPE TO CONVERT TO** option to Annual Event, as shown in Figure 18-28.

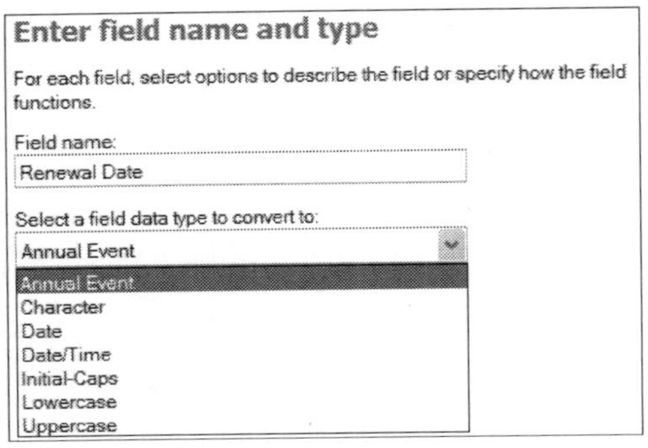

Figure 18-28 Data Type options

Exercise 18.7: Aligning Fields

In Lesson 9 you learned how to align fields on a report. Aligning fields on a layout is similar. I don't know for sure, but I get the feeling that aligning fields is not something that most people like to do, even though it makes the layout or report look more professional. Table 18-2 explains the align options. If you have to align fields, follow the steps below.

Align Option	How It Aligns
Lefts	On the left side of the object.
Center	On the center of the object.
Rights	On the right side of the object.
Tops	On the top of the object.
Middles	On the middle of the object.
Bottoms	On the bottom of the object.
To Grid	To the closest grid point (the dots on the layout) of the object that you right-click on. You need to have the **GRID** option turned on to see how this works.

Table 18-2 Alignment options explained

1. Open the layout that you created. Currently, there are no fields that need to be aligned on the layout.
2. On the User Fields tab, drag the User 2 field to the right, as shown in Figure 18-29.

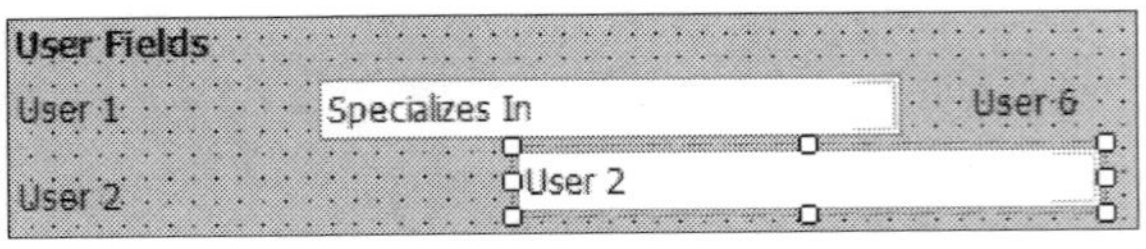

Figure 18-29 User 2 field moved

3. Click on the field that needs to be aligned. In this exercise click on the User 2 field, then press and hold down the Shift key.
4. Click on the field that you want to align the field with. In this exercise click on the Specializes In field.

The boxes around the field that you just selected should be white. The second field is known as the **ANCHOR** field because it is the field that the other fields will be aligned to.

5. Right-click on the Specializes In field, then select the align option that corresponds to how you need to align the field. In this exercise select **ALIGN LEFTS**. The User 2 field should now be aligned with the Specializes In field.

6. Close the layout, but do not save the changes.

7. Switch back to the Basic Contact 800x600 layout.

Exercise 18.8: How To Change The Tab Stop Order

In Lesson 2 you learned the purpose of the Tab key. Earlier in this lesson you learned that the tab order can be changed. In this exercise you will learn how to change the tab stop order on the Basic Contact layout.

1. In the Design Layout window save the Basic Contact Layout - 800x600 as `Revised tab order layout` in the Layouts folder.

2. View ⇒ Tab Stops ⇒ Show Tab Stops.

3. View ⇒ Tab Stops ⇒ Clear.

I find it easier to remove all of the existing tab stops and start from scratch, but you can change the order without clearing all of the tab stops. The way to include a field in the tab stop order is to click in the fields in the order that you want the Tab key to follow. When you click in a field without a number, the next available number is assigned.

4. Click in the following fields in this order: Company, Contact, Address 1, Address 2, Title and Department. The fields should have the order shown in Figure 18-30.

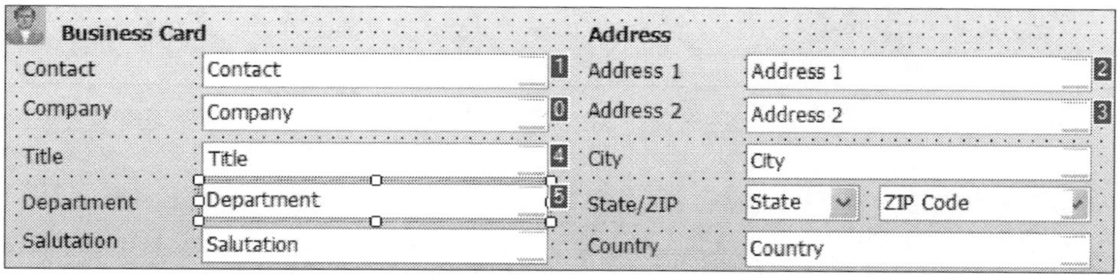

Figure 18-30 Tab stop order

5. Right-click in the City field and type a 3 in the **ENTER THE NEW INDEX** field shown in Figure 18-31, then click OK.

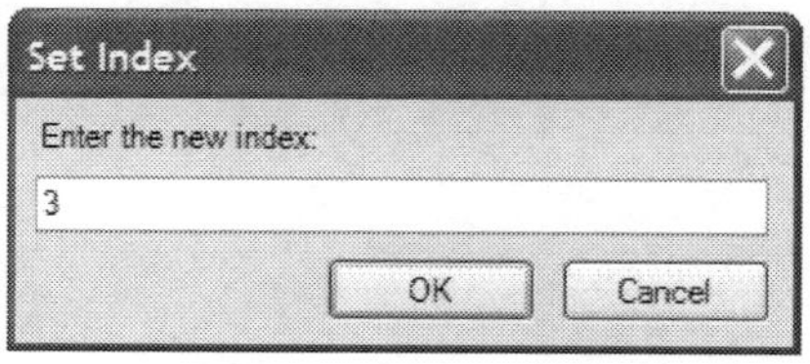

Figure 18-31 Set Index dialog box

You should see the tab order shown in Figure 18-32.

If you do not see a number by the City field, click in the field.

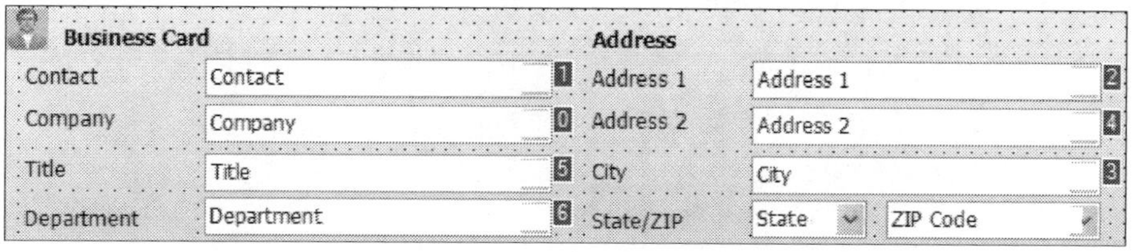

Figure 18-32 Modified tab stop order

Notice that the City field is the third field that the Tab key will go to instead of the Address 2 field shown earlier in Figure 18-30.

The **SET INDEX** dialog box allows you to insert a field into the existing tab order, but there is no way to remove a field from the tab order without clearing all of the tab stops in the index and starting over.

6. View ⇒ Tab Stops ⇒ Show Tab Stops.

7. Save the changes and close the layout. You can test the new tab order. When you finish, switch back to the Basic Contact 800x600 layout.

IMPORTING, EXPORTING AND SYNCHRONIZING DATA

In this lesson you will learn the following importing, exporting and synchronizing data techniques:

- ☑ Upgrading older ACT! databases
- ☑ Importing data from another ACT! database
- ☑ Mapping fields to import
- ☑ Importing data from a text delimited file
- ☑ Exporting data from one ACT! database to another ACT! database
- ☑ Exporting data to a text delimited file
- ☑ Synchronizing data
- ☑ Creating Sync Sets
- ☑ Create remote databases
- ☑ Unpack and restore remote databases
- ☑ Creating and using subscription lists

LESSON 19

Importing Data

Importing data is used to copy records from one data source (often a database) to another data source. This process can consolidate records from several data sources into one. You can also import data and add it to a drop-down list. You have already learned to manually add items to a drop-down list using the Define Fields dialog box. In Exercise 19.1 you will learn another way to add data to a drop-down list.

The **DESTINATION** data source is the file that records will be copied to. This data source must be open before the import process begins. The **SOURCE** data source is the file that has the records that you want to copy.

You can import all of the records in the data source or you can select specific records to import. Suppose you are planning to do a mailing to all contacts in NY and a co-worker has a database of contacts in NJ, NY and PA. You can select to only import the contacts in NY from the co-workers database.

If you think that you will have the need to use the Help system while using the Import or Export Wizard, you should open the Help system and minimize it before starting the wizard because you cannot open the Help system after either of these wizards open.

While not required, it is best to close ACT! and reopen it after importing or exporting data.

Upgrading Older ACT! Databases

If you want to import data from a database from a previous version of ACT!, you have to upgrade the database by opening it in ACT! 2009 first. If you try to import records from a database from a previous version of ACT! without opening the database in the current version of ACT! first, you will see the message shown in Figure 19-1. This does not apply to ACT! Premium databases. Premium databases have to be downgraded to a non premium database to be imported.

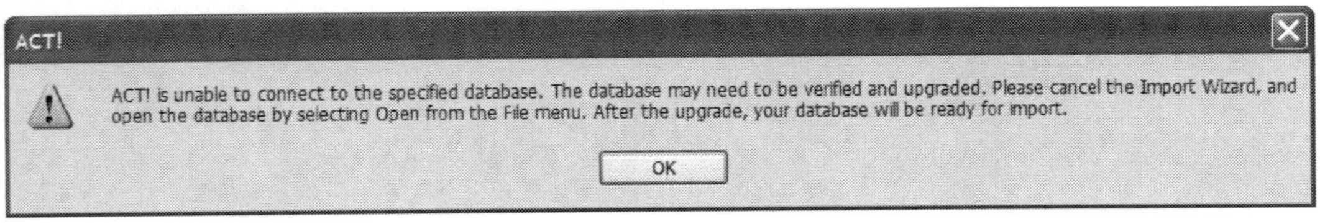

Figure 19-1 Unable to connect message

Exercise 19.1: How To Upgrade A Database To The Current Version

In this exercise you will upgrade a database that was created in ACT! 2007. This will let you use the database in the current version of ACT! or import records from it, into the database that you use with ACT! 2009.

1. File ⇒ Open Database.
2. Navigate to your folder if necessary, then double-click on the RecordsToImport.pad file.
3. Click OK when you see the message shown in Figure 19-2.

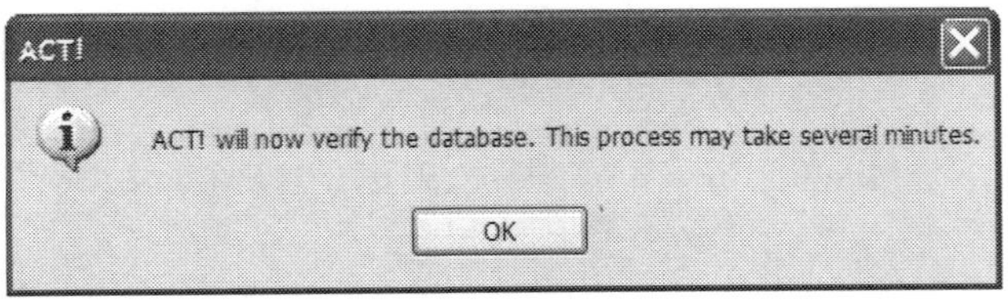

Figure 19-2 Verify database message

4. When you see the dialog box shown in Figure 19-3, accept the user name. Do not enter a password, then click OK.

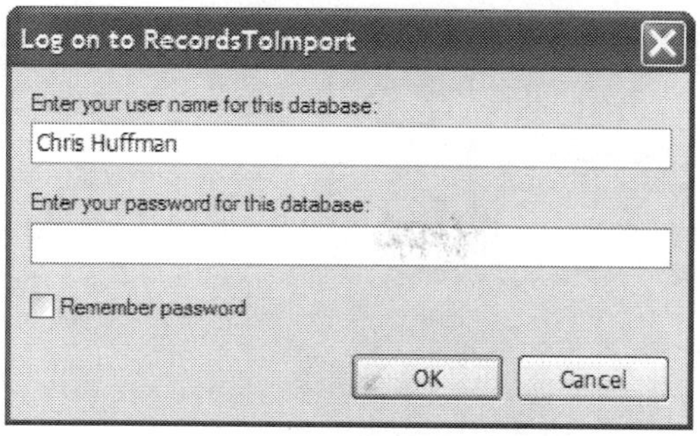

Figure 19-3 Log On dialog box

5. Click No when you see the message shown in Figure 19-4.

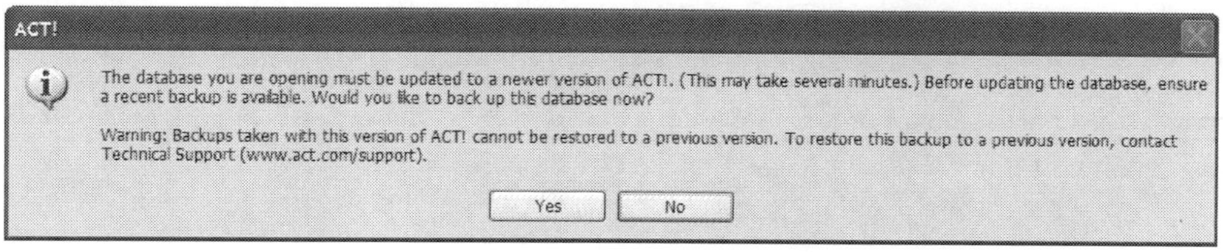

Figure 19-4 Backup database message

This message is asking if you want to back up this database. You can select No because this is not live data. Make sure that you have another copy. Making a copy of the database outside of ACT! is quicker then letting ACT! make a backup copy.

This message is also letting you know that the database that you are trying to open must be updated to the version of ACT! that you are currently running.

6. Click Yes when prompted to update to the database, as shown in Figure 19-5.

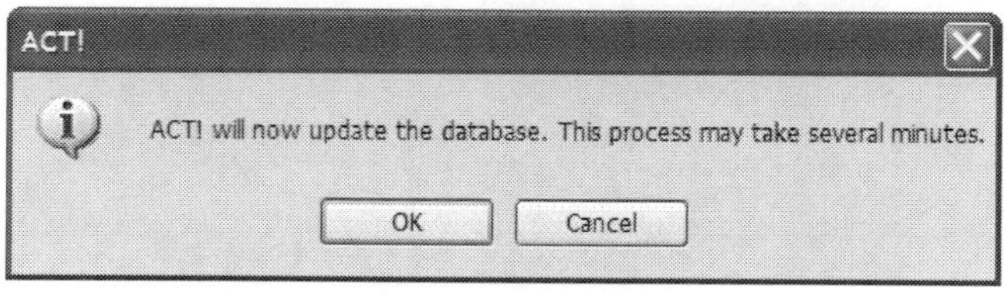

Figure 19-5 Update database message

If you get an error message during the update process, start the process again. Under Windows XP, I got an error message. Under Windows Vista, I did not.

7. When you see the message shown in Figure 19-6, click OK. In a few seconds, the RecordsToImport database will open.

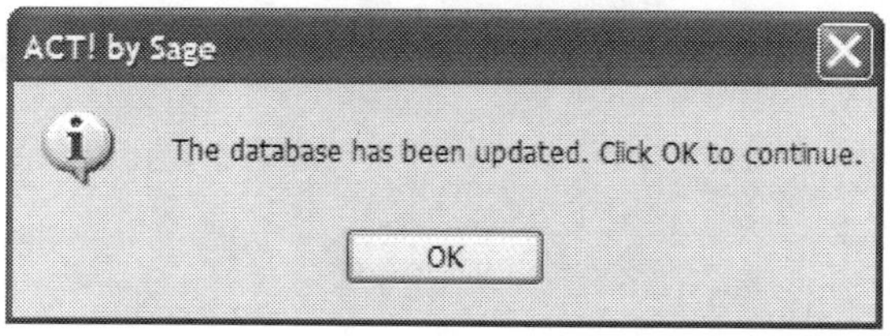

Figure 19-6 Updated database message

Exercise 19.2: How To Import Data From Another ACT! Database

Importing data is not as complicated as it may sound. The primary reason that many people import data is so that they can work with fewer databases.

In this exercise you will import data from the database that you updated in Exercise 19.1. In this exercise, the **MY_ACT2009DEMO** database is the destination data source and the **RECORDSTOIMPORT** database is the source database. The **IMPORT WIZARD** will walk you through the import process.

Step 1: Select The Import File Type And File

1. Open the My_ACT2009Demo database. This is the database that the records will be imported into.

2. File ⇒ Import. You should see the Import Wizard dialog box. Click Next.

3. Select the ACT! Database (11x) file type if it is not already selected. The options in the File Type drop-down list shown in Figure 19-7 are the types of files (data sources) that you can import into ACT!.

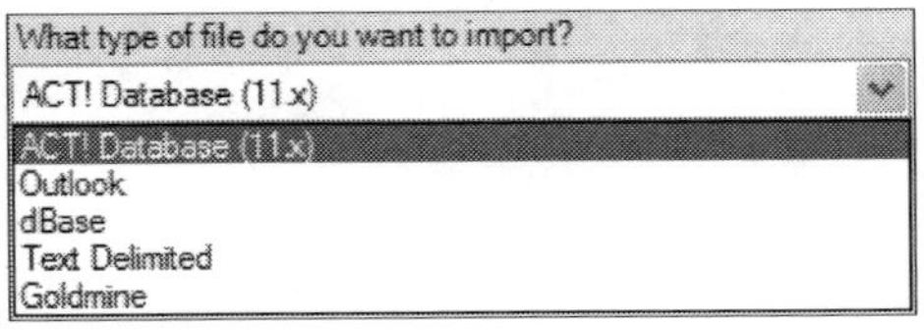

Figure 19-7 Import file types

Step 2: Specify Source

1. Click the **BROWSE** button, then double-click on the file RecordsToImport.pad in your folder. This file name should now be in the **FILE NAME AND LOCATION** field, as shown in Figure 19-8.

   If the ACT! database that you are importing is password protected, you will have to enter a user name and password before you can import it.

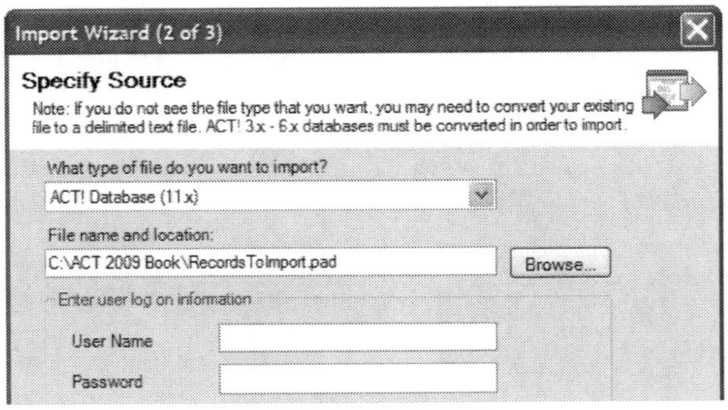

Figure 19-8 Specify Source screen

2. Click Next.

Step 3: Specify Record Type(s)

As shown in Figure 19-9, you can import Contact, Group and Company records.

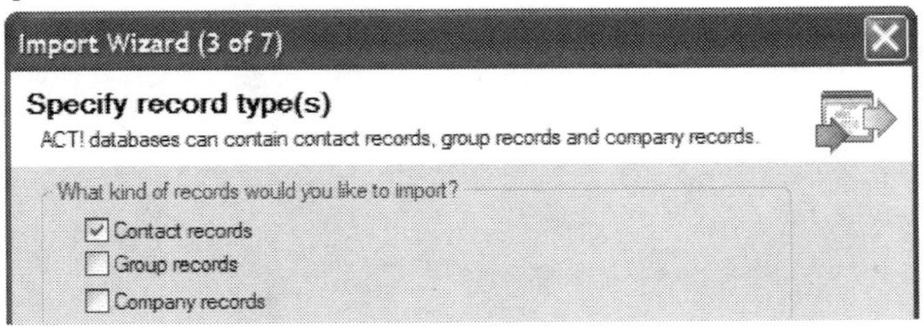

Figure 19-9 Specify record type(s) screen

1. Check the **CONTACT RECORDS** option, then click Next.

Step 4: Mapping Fields

Mapping fields as shown in Figure 19-10 matches fields in the source database (the column on the left) to fields in the target database (the column on the right).

Mapping ensures that the data that you are importing is placed in the correct fields in the destination database.

When importing data, you should pay close attention to the field mappings.

If you need to make changes or plan to import data from the same data source on a frequent basis, you should create a map. A map will save how the fields are matched between the two data sources.

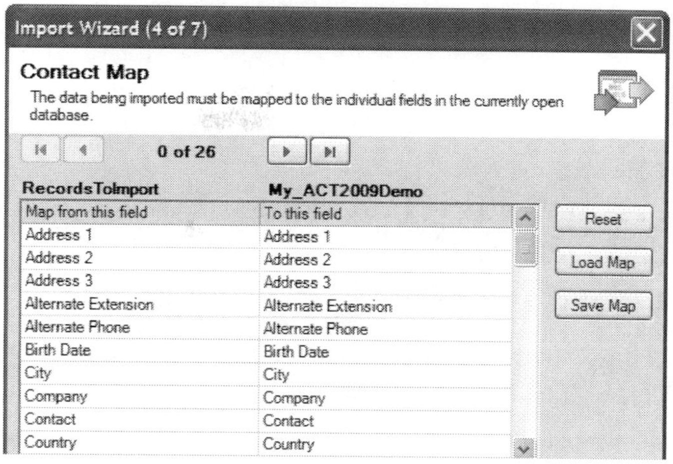

Figure 19-10 Contact Map screen

The mapping tool is useful because the next time that you import the same fields from the same source database, you can load the map and not have to worry about mapping the fields. Even though you may load a map of the settings, it is a good idea to scan the list in case a field in the destination or source database has been modified. There are five import maps that you can use: Company, Contact, Group, Opportunity and Secondary.

Field names that are the same in both databases will automatically be mapped to each other, as shown above in Figure 19-10. If you have to create the data source that will be imported, it will make setting up the import easier if you use field names that are in the destination database. You can also rename the fields in the source database to match the names in the destination database before starting the import process.

How To Map A Field

The steps below show you how to map a field. The process is the same for all of the data that can be mapped. The goal of mapping fields is to make sure that each of the fields that you need to import has a field in the database that it will be added to, otherwise, all of the data that should be imported will not be.

To map a field, open the drop-down list in the second column and select the field that best matches the field in the first column, as shown in Figure 19-11.

If you do not see a field that is appropriate, you can select an available **USER** field, then modify the layout once the data has been imported. You can also create a new field.

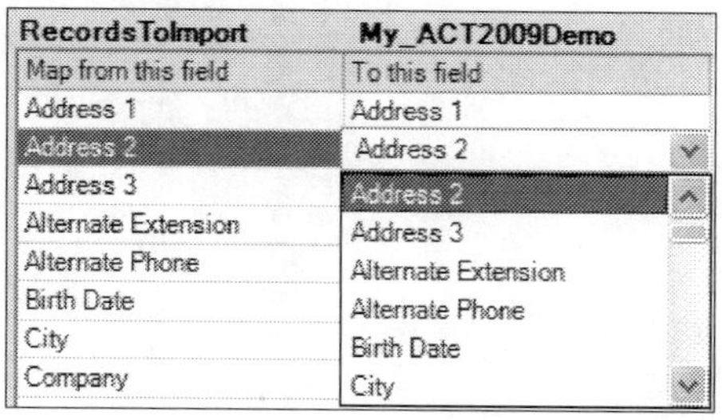

Figure 19-11 Field mapping illustrated

1. Scroll to the end of the list of fields. Open the drop-down list for the Web Site field and select **USER 4**. This will place the data that is in the Web Site field in the User 4 field.

2. Click Next.

Loading Maps

The steps below demonstrate how to load an existing map and how to save a map. You will learn how to create a map later in this lesson. For now you can just read this section, then go to Step 5: Opportunity Map, because you do not have a map to load.

1. Click the **LOAD MAP** button.

2. Navigate to the folder that has the map that you want to use, then double-click on the map file.

3. If any fields need to be remapped change them now, then click Next.

Saving Maps

If you create a map, you can save it so that you can use it later. In this part of the exercise you will save the map that you are currently using.

1. Click the **SAVE MAP** button.

2. Save the map in your folder. Type `ImportMap` in the File name field, then press Enter. If you click the Load Map button you should see the map that you just created. Click Next.

Step 5: Opportunity Map

The options on the screen shown in Figure 19-12 are used to map the opportunity fields, as well as, load and save maps for opportunities.

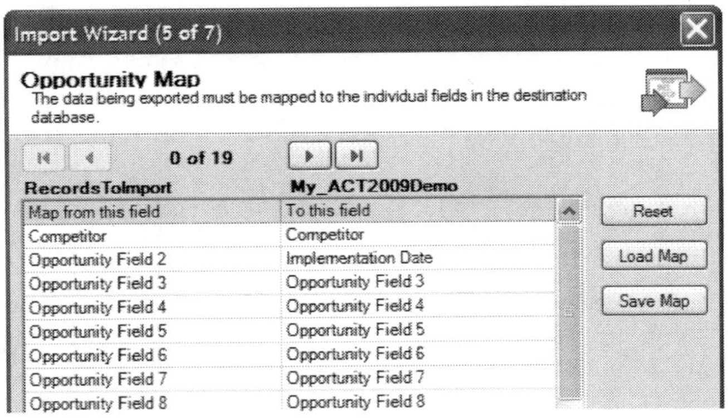

Figure 19-12 Opportunity Map screen

1. Click Next because there are no opportunity fields that need to be mapped.

Step 6: Specify Merge Options

The options shown in Figure 19-13 are used to select the merge options for contacts, groups and companies.

The options available at the top of this screen depend on the types of records that were selected to be imported, as shown earlier on the third wizard screen shown in Figure 19-9.

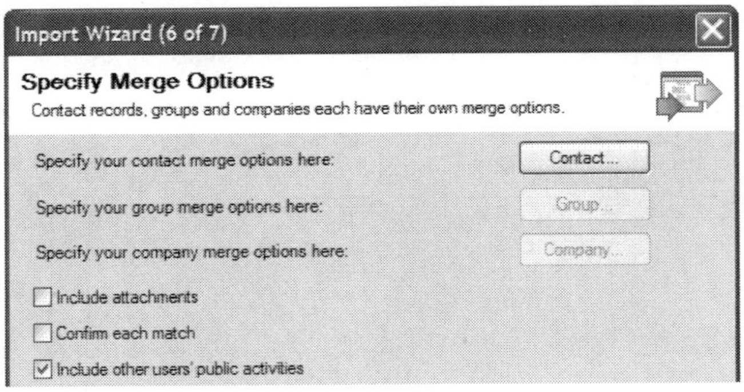

Figure 19-13 Specify Merge Options screen

The **INCLUDE ATTACHMENTS** option allows attachments to be imported.

The **CONFIRM EACH MATCH** option is used to view each duplicate record to make sure that it is a duplicate.

The **INCLUDE OTHER USERS PUBLIC ACTIVITIES** option is used to import the activities that other people have created for the contacts that will be imported.

The options shown in Figures 19-14, 19-15 and 19-16 are used to decide what you want to happen if the source records match or do not match the destination records. By default, ACT! considers contact records a "match" if two records have the same Contact name, Company and Phone number.

You can specify that the most recent record, whether it is the destination or source record, be imported. You can also specify how you want to handle data on the Notes, History, Activities, Opportunities and Secondary Contacts tabs. These options are useful when you only want to import certain information from the source records.

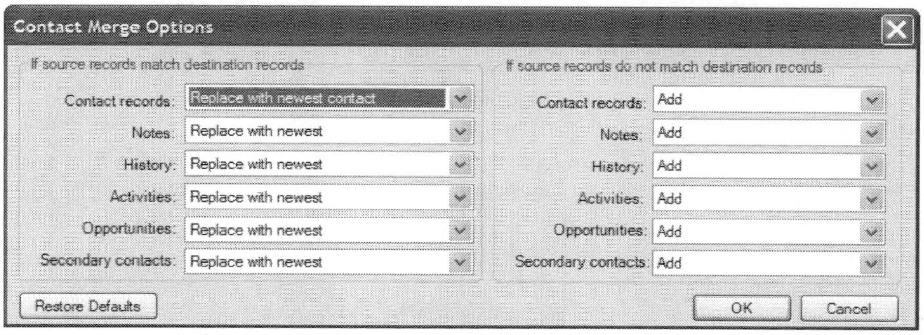

Figure 19-14 Contact record merge options

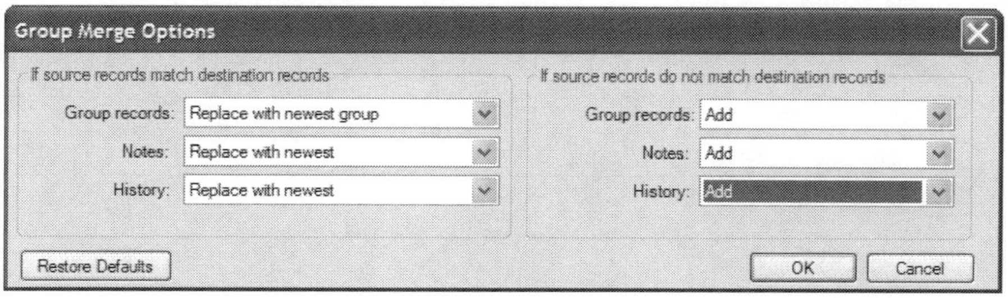

Figure 19-15 Group record merge options

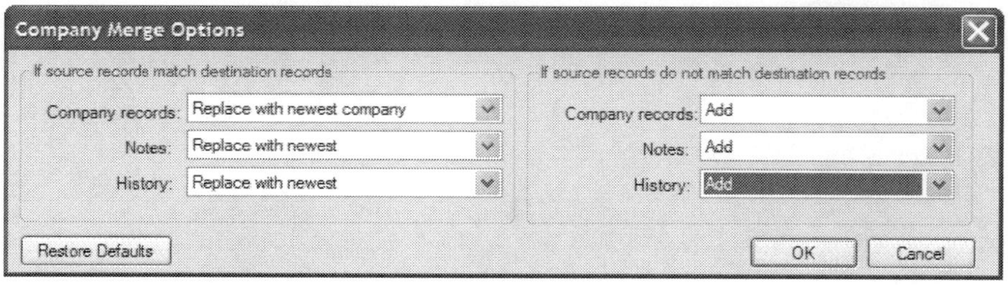

Figure 19-16 Company record merge options

If you change any of the default options on Figures 19-14, 19-15 or 19-16 for an import or export and then run another import or export, the options that you selected the first time will still be selected. Therefore, it is a good idea to check every screen in the Import or Export Wizard if you previously imported or exported data without closing and reopening ACT!.

Contact Merge Options

1. Click the Contact button.

2. In the second column on the Contact Merge Options dialog box shown earlier in Figure 19-14, change the Opportunities and Secondary contacts options to **DO NOT ADD**.

3. Click OK, then click Next.

Step 7: Completing The Import Wizard

You should see the last wizard screen shown in Figure 19-17. In this exercise the last step is step 7. If group or company records will be merged, there would be more steps.

Above the Details button is a message indicating that the import can be completed. If there was a problem, clicking the Details button will let you see more information about the problem.

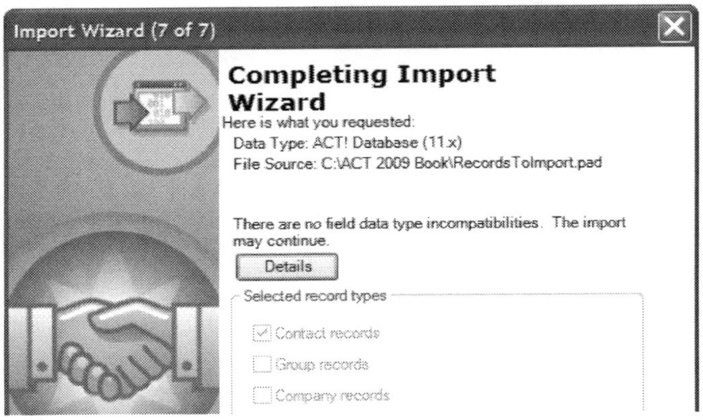

Figure 19-17 Import options that you selected

Figure 19-18 shows a potential problem with the import that you are creating now. In this example the reason that you cannot import data for the Last Yrs Purchases field is because the field is set to read-only. If you needed to import data into the field, you would have to change the field access to **FULL ACCESS**.

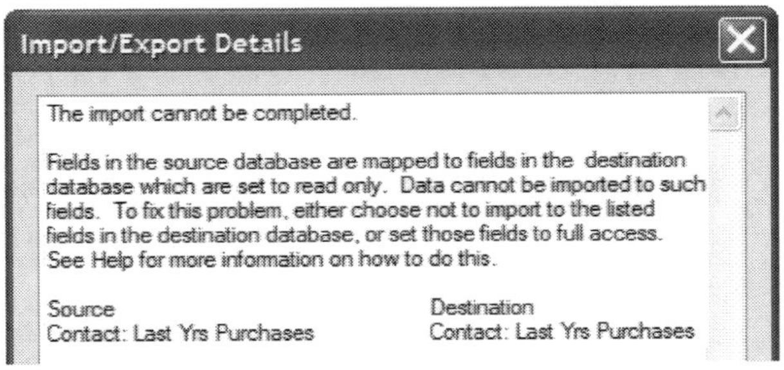

Figure 19-18 Import/Export Details information

Run The Import

If you are satisfied with all of the options that you have selected, you can click the Finish button. If you want to review the options that you have selected or want to change something, click the Back button until you see the screen that has the option(s) that you want to review or change.

1. If you made changes, click Next until you get to the screen shown earlier in Figure 19-17. You should see the message that states that there are no incompatibilities.

2. Click Finish on the last wizard screen. The records will be imported. You will see the dialog box shown in Figure 19-19. It lets you know that the records are being imported.

Figure 19-19 Importing Data dialog box

Exercise 19.3: How to Import Data From A Text Delimited File

The is probably the most used import file type other than an ACT! database. This is because most word processing and spreadsheet software packages allow you to save files in the text delimited format. A text delimited file means that the text (fields) are delimited (separated) by a specific character like a tab or comma.

> You should open the text delimited file before you start the import and look at the data so that you will be able to select the correct options for the import.

1. File ⇒ Import, then click Next on the first wizard window.

2. Select **TEXT DELIMITED** as the file type to import.

3. Click the Browse button. Change the Files of type to Text files (*.txt) if necessary, then double-click on the Contacts table.txt file.

4. Click Next. Select the Contact Records option, then click Next.

5. Select the **TAB** option shown in Figure 19-20, then click Next.

   These are the options for text-delimited files.

   The **SELECT FIELD SEPARATOR** options are used to select how the fields in the text-delimited file are separated.

   Before you can import a delimited file, you need to know how the fields are separated.

   If the first record in the text file has field names or column headings, clear the **YES, IMPORT THE FIRST RECORD** option.

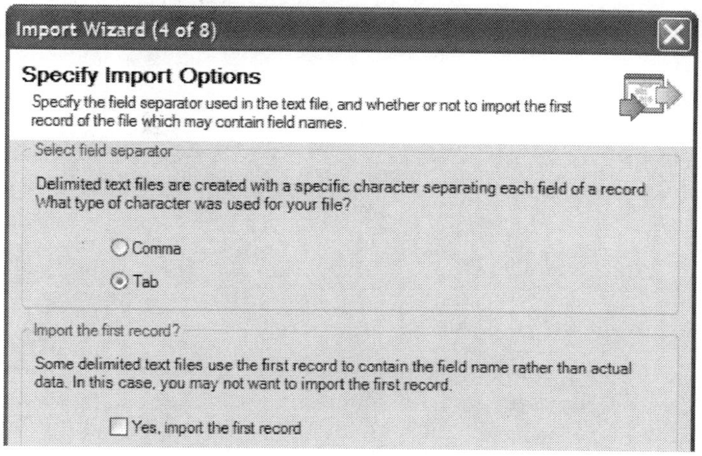

Figure 19-20 Specify Import Options screen

Selecting A Predefined Map

The dialog box shown in Figure 19-21 is used to select an existing map.

This option is helpful if you will be importing data frequently.

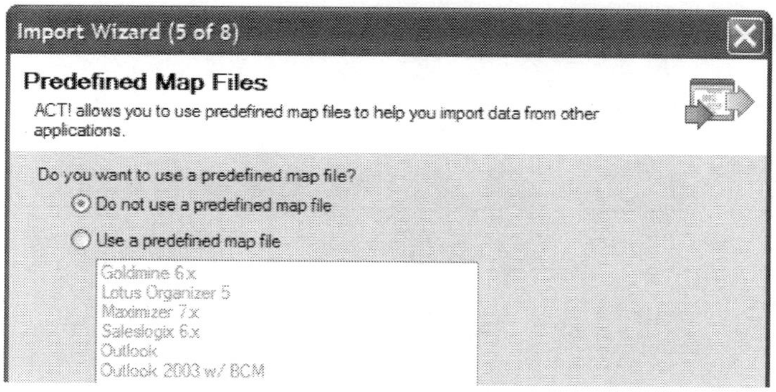

Figure 19-21 Predefined Map Files screen

6. Select the option, **DO NOT USE A PREDEFINED MAP FILE**, then click Next.

How To Map Fields

The dialog box shown in Figure 19-22 shows the fields that are in the text delimited file.

The fields shown in the **TO THIS FIELD** column are the fields that ACT! could map on its own. The blank fields in this column may or may not have a corresponding field in the file that you are importing data from.

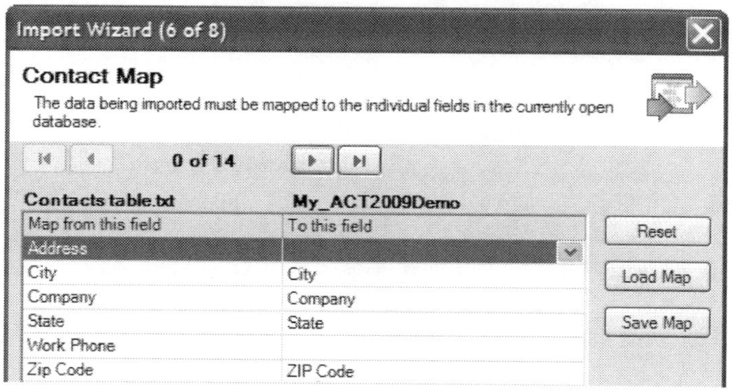

Figure 19-22 Contact Map screen

7. Open the drop-down list for the Address field, then select the Address 1 field.

8. Map the Work Phone field to the Phone field.

   You should have the options selected that are shown in Figure 19-23.

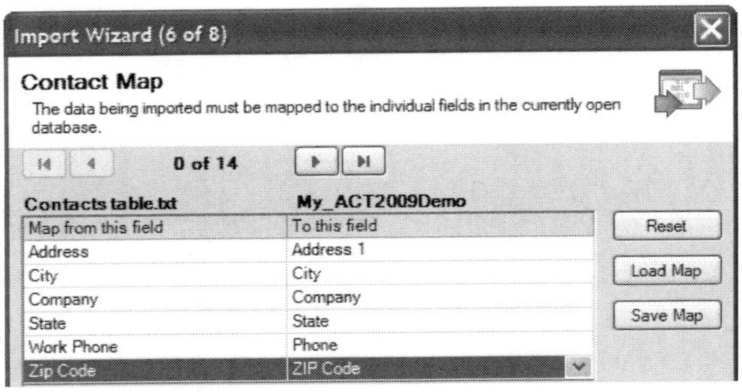

Figure 19-23 Address and Work Phone fields mapped

View The Records To Be Imported

You can view the records that will be imported before you actually import them. Fields that are empty in the Preview Data column means that there is no data in that field to be imported. After looking at a few records, you will be able to tell whether or not you have mapped the fields correctly.

9. Click the ▶ button, illustrated in Figure 19-24.

   You should see the preview data as shown in Figure 19-24.

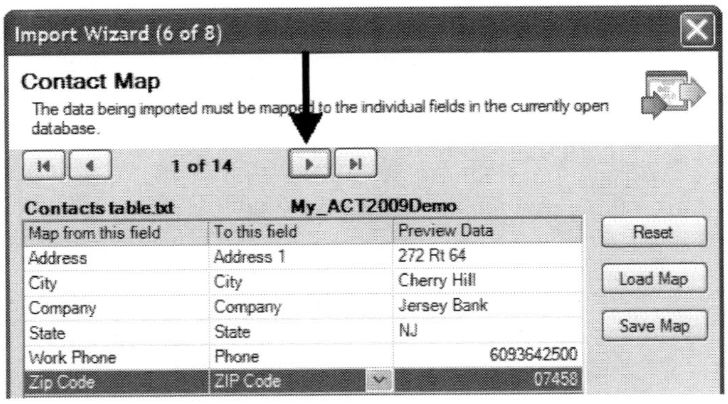

Figure 19-24 Preview data

10. Look at a few more records to make sure that the fields are mapped correctly.

Finish The Import

11. Click Next on the Contact Map screen. Click Next on the Specify Merge Options screen because you want to add all of the records in the text file to the database.

12. Click Finish. The records will be imported.

Exercise 19.4: How To Import A List

If you are creating a new database you will have a lot to do. One task that is time consuming is typing in the entries for drop-down lists. Importing the entries from a list is faster. The Import option can be used to add or append items that you have in a text file to a drop-down list.

1. Open the Define Fields dialog box, then select the Manage drop-down lists link.

2. Select the Specializes In list, then click the Edit drop-down list link.

3. Click Next on the drop-down list name and type screen.

4. Click the Import drop-down list items link, then click the **BROWSE** button on the Import List Items dialog box.

5. Double-click on the Specialties.txt file in your folder.

   Check the **INCLUDE DESCRIPTIONS** option shown in Figure 19-25.

   The Include descriptions option will import any descriptions that are in the file that you are importing data from.

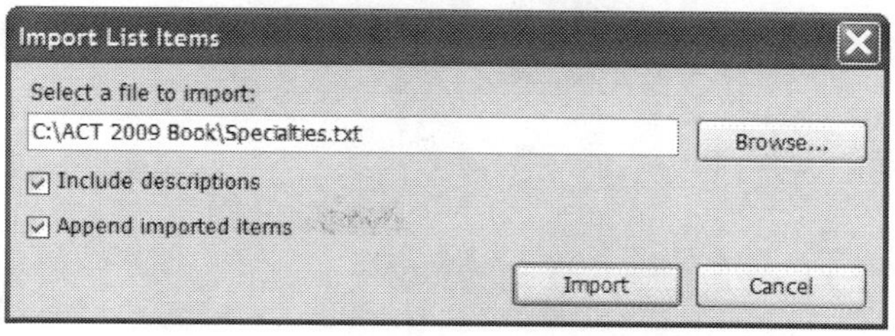

Figure 19-25 Import List Items dialog box

   The **APPEND IMPORTED ITEMS** option should be checked if the list that you are importing to already has records and you want to add more records or if you want to overwrite some of the items that currently exist in the drop-down list. If this option is not checked, all of the current records in the list will be over written.

6. Click the Import button.

   Your list should look like the one shown in Figure 19-26.

Value	Description
Brain Surgery	
OB-GYN	
Liver Disease	Import #1
Root Canal	Import #2
Physical Therapy	Import #3
Nutrition	Import #4
Neurology	Import #5

Figure 19-26 Imported drop-down list values

7. Click Finish, then close the Define Fields dialog box.

How To Create A Text Delimited File

In the previous exercises, you learned how to import text files to fill drop-down lists. The steps below show you how to create a text delimited file that can be imported. Each line of data in the text file equals one option in the drop-down list.

1. Open NotePad.

2. Type the data shown in Figure 19-27 in the text file. You have to type the quotes.

   At the end of each line, you must press Enter.

```
"Product 1", "New Shoes"
"Product 2", "Boots"
```

Figure 19-27 Data for the text delimited file

3. Save the file in your folder as `New Products.txt`.

Exporting Data

The Exporting Data option is used to copy records from one ACT! database to another ACT! database or to a file. This is useful if you want to give someone some of the records in the database or if someone else needs to use or view the contacts in another software package.

You can also use the Export option if you want to remove records that you do not use anymore. You can keep the records that you do not use in a separate database so that you will still have access to them. Once you export them, you can delete them from the current database.

You cannot export records to a database that has not already been created.

Exercise 19.5: How To Export Data To Another ACT! Database

In this exercise you will select records that will be exported to another ACT! database. This is one way that you can archive records that are not needed.

Step 1: Look Up The Records To Export

Unless you are going to export the entire database, you need to look up the records that you want to export before you start the export process.

1. Create a lookup to find all contacts in NY.

Step 2: Select The Export File Type And File Name

1. File ⇒ Export. You should see the Welcome Export screen. Click Next.
2. Select ACT! Database 11.x as the File type to export.
3. Click the **BROWSE** button, then double-click on the RecordsToImport.pad file.

   You should have the options selected that are shown in Figure 19-28. Click Next.

   This is the database where the records will be exported to.

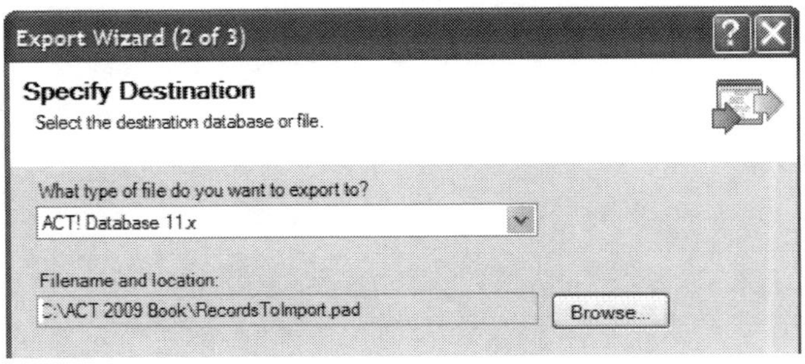

Figure 19-28 Specify Destination screen

Step 3: Select The Type Of Records To Export

You can export contact, group and company records the same way that you can import record types.

1. Select the **CONTACT RECORDS** option, then select the **CURRENT LOOKUP** option, as shown in Figure 19-29.

   In this exercise you only selected one record type to export. You can select as many record types as you need.

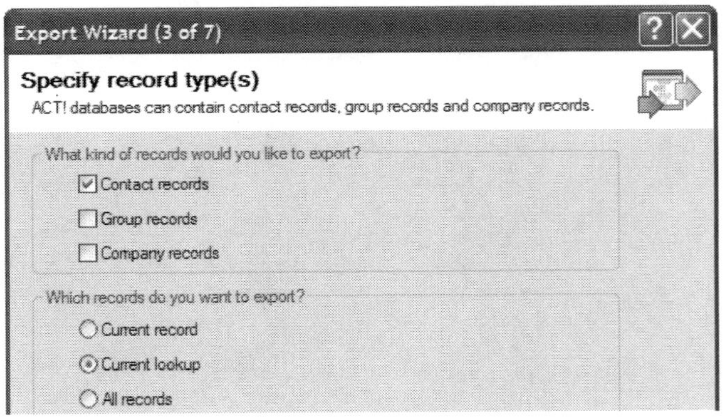

Figure 19-29 Specify Record Type(s) screen

2. Click Next. In a few seconds you will see the dialog box shown in Figure 19-30.

Step 4: Contact Map Options

Use the screen shown in Figure 19-30 to verify that the correct number of records will be exported. You should also check to make sure that the contact fields are mapped properly.

As you can see, 20 contact records will be exported. That is the same number of records that is in the lookup.

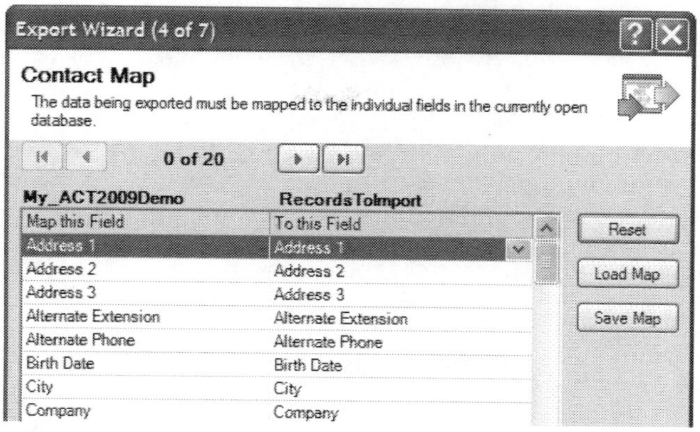

Figure 19-30 Contact Map screen

1. Change the Last Years Purchases field to blank so that the data in the field will not be exported.
2. Click Next once you have verified that all of the information is correct.

Step 5: Opportunity Map Options

You should verify that the opportunity fields are mapped correctly, as shown in Figure 19-31. If there are fields that you do not want to export, you should change the value in the **TO THIS FIELD** column to blank.

The reason that there are only five opportunity records is because not all of the contacts in the lookup have an opportunity.

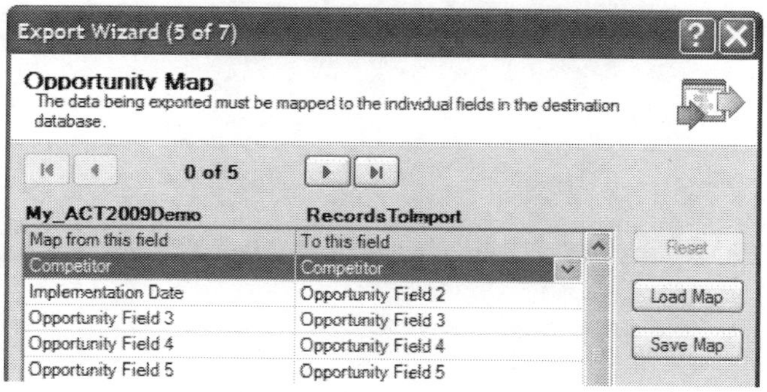

Figure 19-31 Opportunity Map screen

1. Click Next because you want to export all of the fields.

Specify Merge Options

The options on this screen work the same way that they do on the Import wizard.

1. Clear the Include other users' public activities option.
2. Click the Contact button.

   Change the options in Table 19-1.

Source Records Match	Change To
Notes	Do not change
Opportunities	Merge
Source Records Do Not Match	**Change To**
Opportunities	Add
Secondary Contacts	Add

Table 19-1 Contact options to change

3. The dialog box should have the options shown in Figure 19-32.

   Click OK.

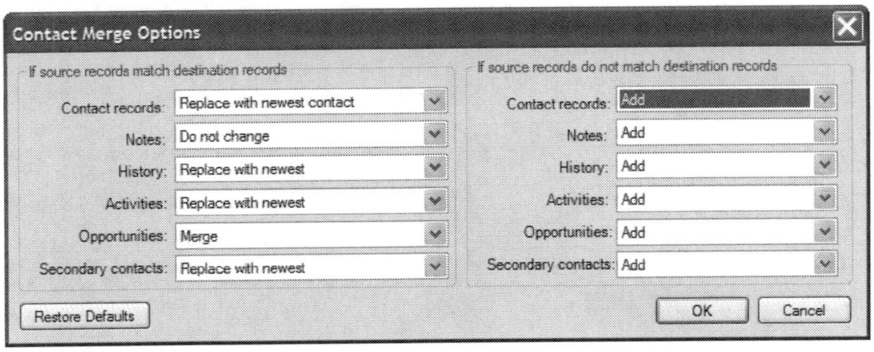

Figure 19-32 Contact Merge Options dialog box

4. Click Next.

   On the screen shown in Figure 19-33, you should see that there are no data type incompatibilities.

Figure 19-33 Export options that you selected

5. Click Finish. The contact records will be exported to the RecordsToImport database.

Viewing The Records That Were Exported

1. Open the RecordsToImport.pad file and view some of the records that were added to the database. Leave the RecordsToImport database open to complete the next exercise.

Exercise 19.6: How To Export Data To A Text Delimited File

Just like you can import data from a text delimited file, you can export data to a text delimited file. You can export contact, group and company records, but not at the same time. They have to be exported separately. In this exercise you will export all of the contact records in the RecordsToImport database to a text delimited file.

1. File ⇒ Export. Click Next.

2. Select the File type, Text Delimited, then click the Browse button. Make sure that the File type is **TEXT FILES**.

3. Type `MyTextExport` in the File name field on the Open dialog box, then press Enter.

4. Click Next. Select the Contact Records and All records options, then click Next.

Select The Export Options

5. Select the Tab field separator option. Select the option, **YES, EXPORT FIELD NAMES**, then click Next.

How To Remove A Field From The Export

The options on the fifth screen will vary depending on the type of records that are selected to be exported.

On the dialog box shown in Figure 19-34, you can select which fields will be exported. You can also rearrange the order that the fields will be exported in and delete fields that you do not want to export.

If there are fields that you do not want to export, you can follow the steps below.

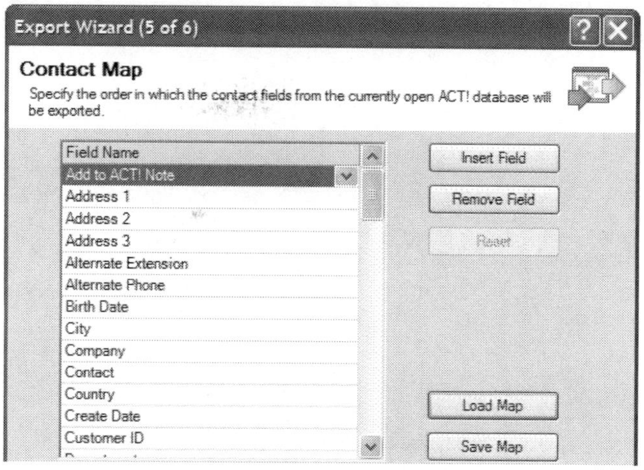

Figure 19-34 Contact Map screen

6. Click on the field that you do not want to export. In this exercise click on the Create Date field.

7. Click the **REMOVE FIELD** button, then remove the following fields: Add to ACT! Note and E-mail.

If you remove fields from the **CONTACT MAP** screen and then come back to the Map screen, the fields that you removed will reappear on the screen shown above in Figure 19-34.

Exercise 19.7: How To Reorder Fields And Create A Map

Reordering fields is not the easiest task to complete on the Contact Map screen because it does not have Move up and Move down buttons. The fields that will be exported in this exercise would be more helpful if the address fields were together. Like the Contact Map screen that you saw earlier in Figure 19-30, you can select a different field from the drop-down list.

1. Change the Alternate Extension field to the City field, as shown in Figure 19-35.

   Change the Alternate Phone field to the State field.

   Change the Birth Date field to the Zip Code field.

   Change the second City field to the Country field.

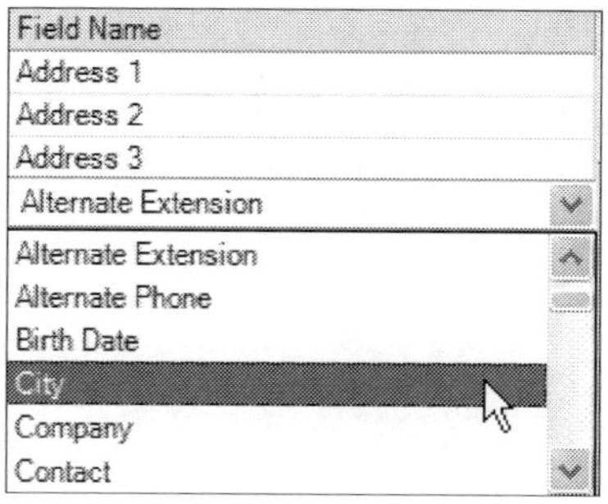

Figure 19-35 How to select a different field

2. Delete the second Country field and all of the fields below it. You should have the fields that are shown in Figure 19-36.

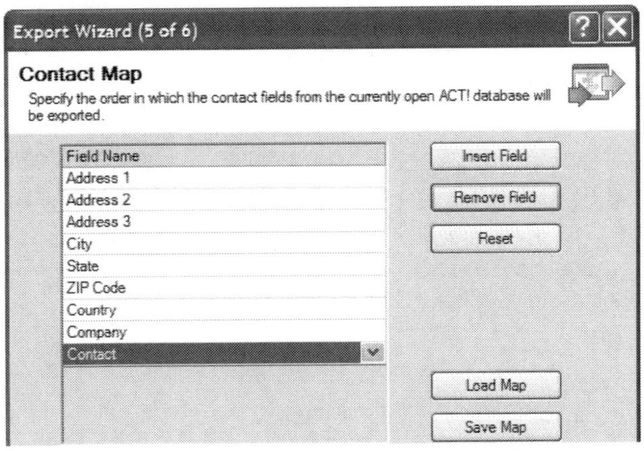

Figure 19-36 Fields that will be exported

3. Click the Save Map button. Type `MyTextExportMap` as the file name.

4. Click Next, then click Finish.

5. Open the My_ACT2009Demo database.

View The Exported Data

1. In Windows Explorer double-click on the file, MyTextExport.txt in your folder. The file should look like the one shown in Figure 19-37.

Figure 19-37 Exported data

In prior versions of ACT!, the City and Country fields were the first two fields in the export file, even though that was not the order that was selected. Fortunately, this has been fixed.

Synchronizing Data

In order to synchronize data, the main database has to be on a server. If your database is on your computers hard drive, you can skip the rest of this lesson.

This process allows data to be exchanged between databases so that both copies of the database have the same information. Synchronization sends and receives data changes between the databases which keeps both sets of data the same.

An example of when to use synchronization is if you are sharing a database at work with other people and you put a copy of the database on your laptop to go on a business trip. While you are on the trip, you add new contacts and modify existing ones in the copy of the database on your laptop. The people in the office make changes to the database on the server. When you return to the office, the two copies of the database do not have the same information. They need to be synchronized so that both copies of the database have the changes that were made to both databases.

Prior to synchronizing databases, you have to set up how you want to synchronize the databases. The database must be open and locked before you can synchronize it.

There are two databases involved in the synchronization process: The **MAIN** database (also known as the master) is the one that will send and update the remote database. The **REMOTE** database receives changes from the main database. The synchronization usually takes place on a network.

Files stored in Personal folders will not be synchronized.

If the same field was changed for the same contact in the main and remote databases, the change with the most recent date is the change that is kept.

Sync Set

You can synchronize all of the contacts in the main database or you can synchronize a subset of contacts. A Sync Set is the tool used to specify the data and users that can access the remote database. You can use a query to create the Sync Set. Sync Sets can be created in the main or remote database. Only an administrator or manager of the main database can create a remote database using a Sync Set.

Setting Up The Synchronization

The options needed to set up the synchronization are part of the Synchronization tool that is available in the main and remote databases. Only the tasks that can be used in each database are available.

Exercise 19.8: How To Synchronize Databases

In this exercise you will complete all of the tasks for the main database portion of the synchronization process. The three steps to setting up synchronization on the main database are discussed below.

① **Enable synchronization** Turns on synchronization so that data can be transmitted.
② **Create the Sync Set** This file stores the instructions for what data should be synchronized.
③ **Create the remote database** The remote database has to be created so that records can be synchronized.

Enable Synchronization

1. Tools ⇒ Synchronization Panel.

2. Click on either of the **ENABLE SYNCHRONIZATION** options illustrated in Figure 19-38, then click Yes to enable synchronization.

   Once synchronization has been turned on, more options on this screen will be available. The order that the administrative tasks are numbered in, is the order that the tasks have to be completed.

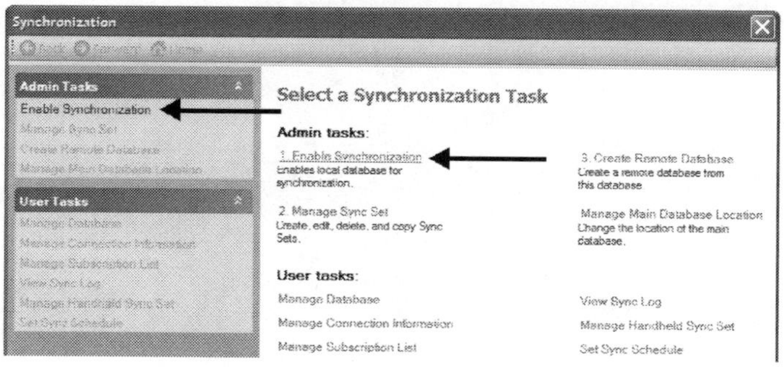

Figure 19-38 Synchronization screen

Create A Sync Set

In this part of the exercise you will create a sync set that uses an existing query to determine which records will be sent to the remote database.

1. Click the **MANAGE SYNC SET** link, then click the **CREATE NEW SYNC SET** link.

2. Type `MyCustomers` in the Sync Set name field.

   Type `Customers & Prospects in AZ` in the Description field, as shown in Figure 19-39, then click Next.

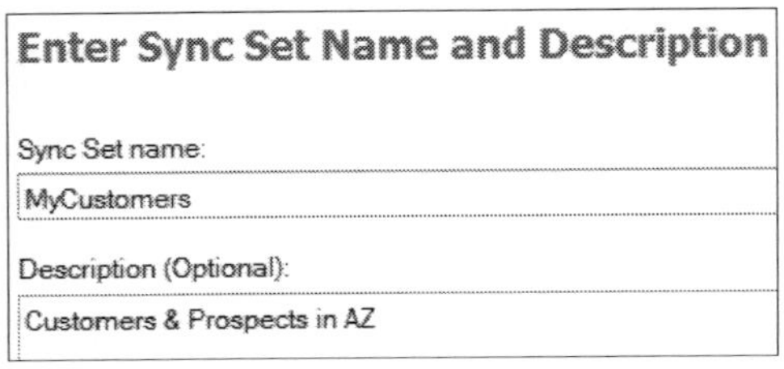

Figure 19-39 Sync Set Name and Description screen

Select The Users

On this screen, select the people that you want to have access to the remote database.

3. Select Chris Hoffman and Betty Browser. You should see the two names in the list on the right. Click Next.

Select The Contacts

The options shown in Figure 19-40 are used to select the contacts that will be copied to the remote database. The number of contacts in the main database is displayed on this screen.

The **DEFINE SYNC SET CRITERIA** option is used to select specific contacts to send to the remote database.

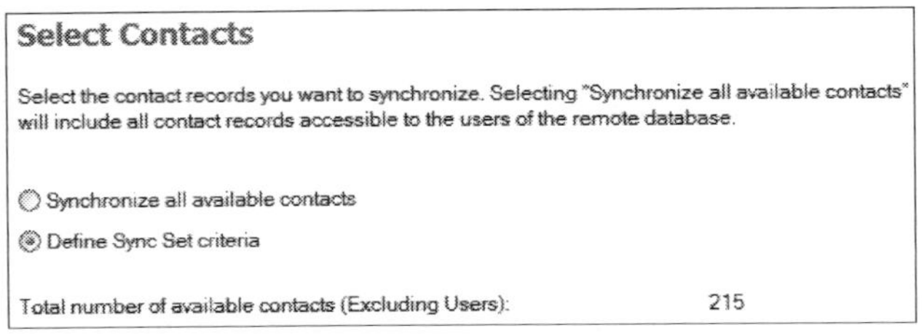

Figure 19-40 Select contacts screen

4. Select the Define Sync Set criteria option and click Next.

Create Or Edit The Sync Set Criteria

In this part of the exercise you will create the criteria that will be used to select the records that will be sent to the remote database.

1. Click the **CREATE CRITERIA** link. You will see the Sync Set Criteria dialog box shown in Figure 19-41. It looks like the Advanced Query dialog box that you used in Lesson 11.

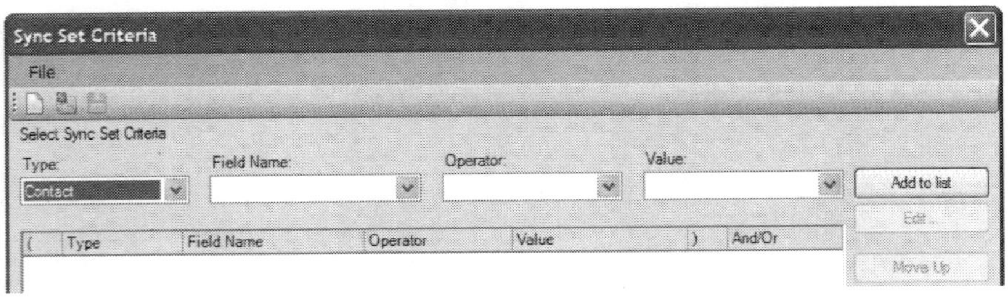

Figure 19-41 Sync Set Criteria dialog box

You can create the criteria from scratch on this dialog box or you can use a query that has already been created.

2. Click the Open button, then double-click on the Customers & Prospects in AZ query in your folder. You will see the query criteria. You can use the query as is or you can edit it, then save it with a new name and use the new query as the sync set criteria.

3. Click OK to close the Sync Set Criteria dialog box.

4. You will see the query criteria on the screen shown in Figure 19-42.

   Click Next.

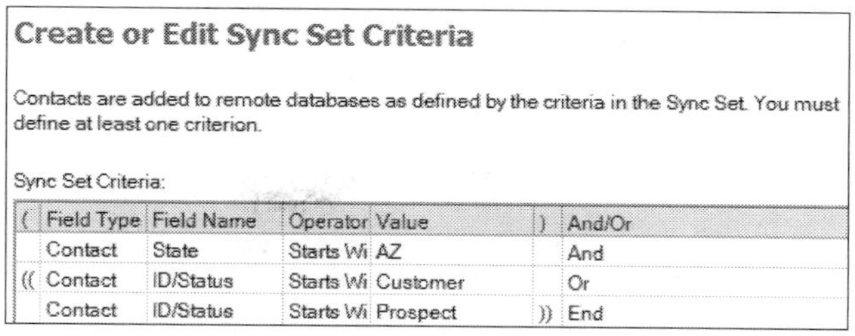

Figure 19-42 Create or Edit Sync Set Criteria screen

5. Click Finish.

   You will see the screen shown in Figure 19-43.

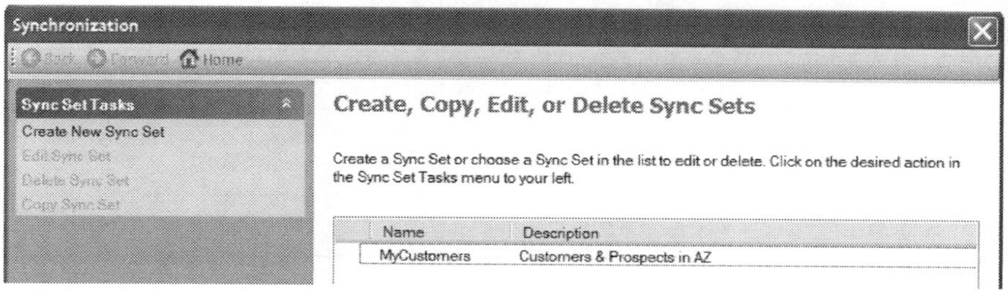

Figure 19-43 Sync Sets screen

The options on the Sync Sets screen are the sync sets that have been created for the synchronization process that is currently open. There can be more than one sync set associated with a database.

6. Click the **HOME** button.

Create The Remote Database

1. Click either of the **CREATE REMOTE DATABASE** links on the Synchronization Task screen.
2. Type `MyRemoteDB` in the Remote Database Name field.
3. If your folder is not in the Location field, as shown in Figure 19-44, click the Browse button and select your folder, then click Next.

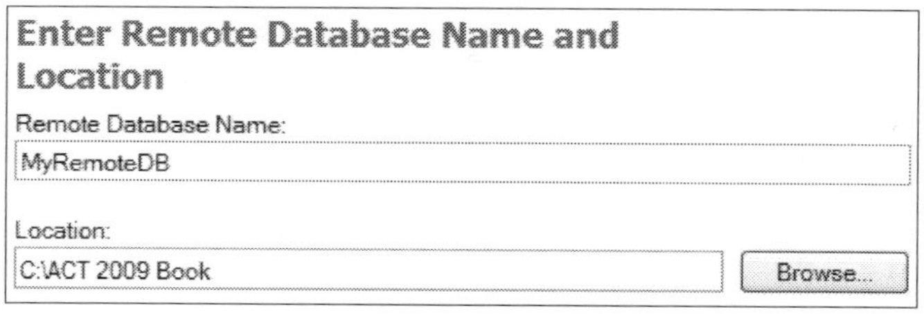

Figure 19-44 Remote Database Name and Location screen

4. Select the MyCustomers sync set, then click Next.

Database Synchronization Options

The options on this screen are used to set synchronization options for the database.

The **ALLOW DATABASE SUPPLEMENTAL FILES TO SYNCHRONIZE** option is used when you want the reports, documents, layouts and templates in the main database to be sent to the remote database.

The two attachment options determine whether or not attachments will be sent to the remote database or synchronized.

The **NUMBER OF DAYS THAT CAN PASS WITHOUT SYNCHRONIZATION** option determines when the remote database has to be synchronized.

If attachments are not needed in the remote copy of the database, it is best not to select them because they increase the synchronization time.

1. Clear the Allow database supplemental files to synchronize option.

2. Select the **DO NOT ALLOW THIS DATABASE TO SYNCHRONIZE ATTACHMENTS** option.

3. Open the drop-down list and select the option, **DO NOT INCLUDE ATTACHMENTS IN REMOTE DATABASE CREATION.**

   You should have the options selected that are shown in Figure 19-45. Click Next.

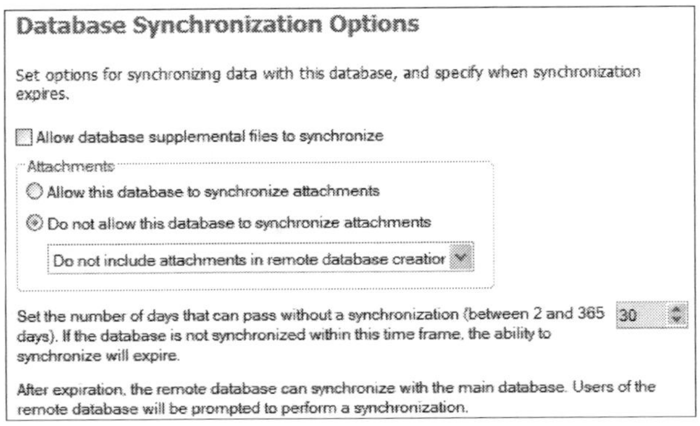

Figure 19-45 Database Synchronization Options screen

Sync Server Connection Options

The options shown on the screen in Figure 19-46 are used to select the Server Connection option.

Your machine name will automatically be filled in. I removed mine from the figure for security reasons.

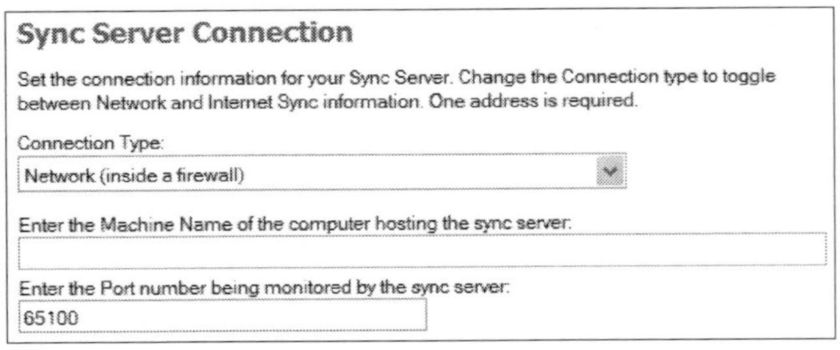

Figure 19-46 Sync Server Connection options

1. If necessary, select a different **CONNECTION TYPE**.

2. Enter the machine name if the correct one is not already filled in, then click Next.

Password Options

The options shown in Figure 19-47 only have to be filled in if the database has a password.

The databases in this exercise do not have a password, so you can skip the first step below.

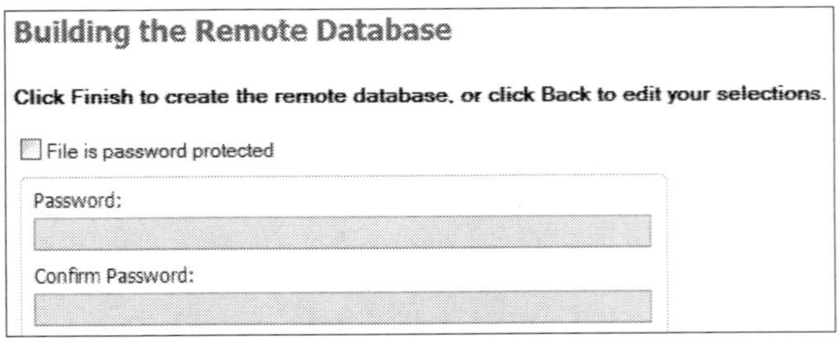

Figure 19-47 Remote database password options

1. Check the **FILE IS PASSWORD PROTECTED** option, then enter the password in both fields shown above in Figure 19-47.

2. Click Finish.

   You will see the screen shown in Figure 19-48.

   The remote database will be created.

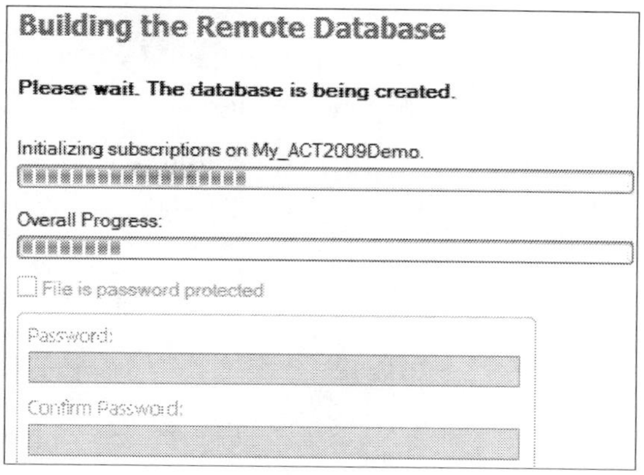

Figure 19-48 Building the Remote Database screen

3. Click No when you see the successfully created remote database message shown in Figure 19-49. The reason that you are clicking No is because you do not need to create another remote database.

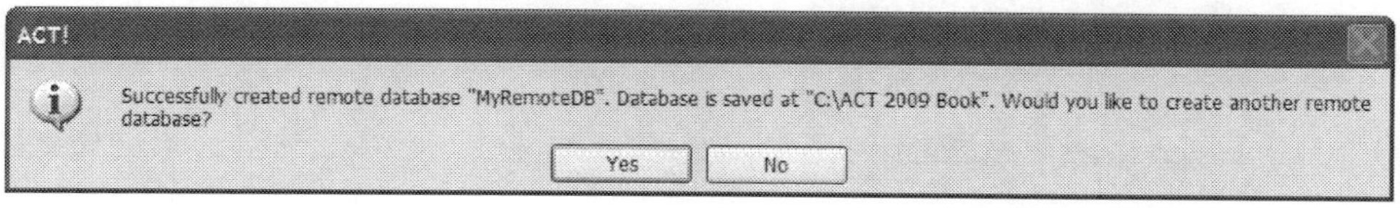

Figure 19-49 Remote database successful message

4. Close the Synchronization window.

Turning Synchronization On

Now that you have selected the sync options and created the remote database, the sync option needs to be turned on. When synchronization is turned on, the main database is set to listen for messages from the remote database. The synchronization will stay on until it is turned off. This is known as a communication.

1. Tools ⇒ Synchronize ⇒ Accept Incoming Syncs.

2. Accept the default port number.

   You may have a different port number then the one shown in Figure 19-50.

   Click OK twice to close both dialog boxes.

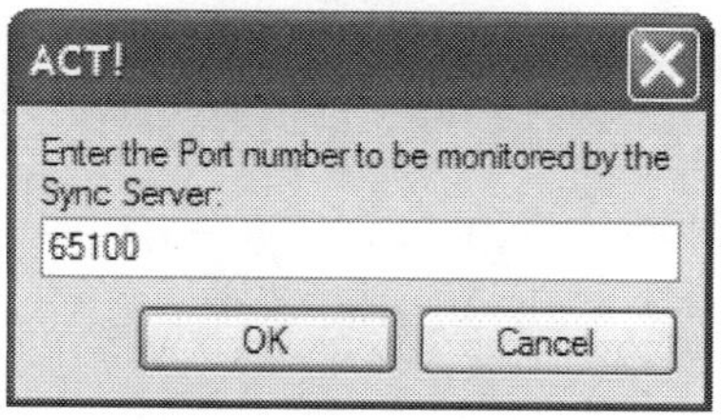

Figure 19-50 Port number dialog box

Using The Remote Database

The remote database must be unpacked and restored before it can be used and synchronized.

Exercise 19.9: How To Unpack And Restore The Remote Database

1. File ⇒ Restore ⇒ Database.

2. Select the **UNPACK AND RESTORE REMOTE DATABASE** option shown in Figure 19-51, then click OK.

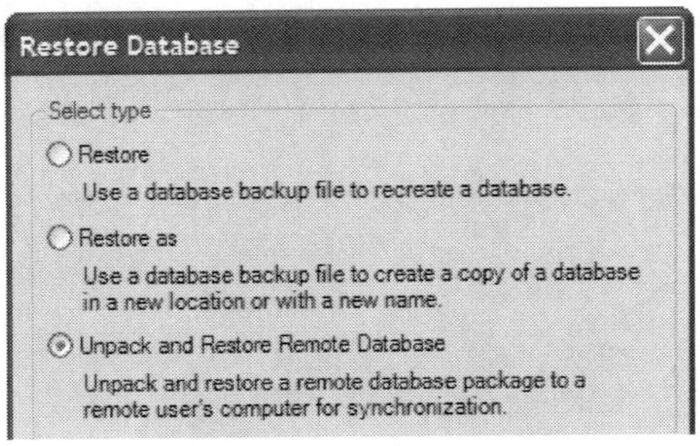

Figure 19-51 Restore Database dialog box

3. Click the first Browse button, then double-click on the MyRemoteDB.RDB file. The **RDB** file is not the actual database.

The folder in the **DATABASE LOCATION** field is where you want to place the restored database. The default folder that you set up on the General tab on the Preferences dialog box is what appears in this field by default. You can change the folder for the database by typing in a different location or by clicking the Browse button and selecting the folder.

4. Type `\Remote` at the end of the Restore Remote Database Location field.

5. Check the **SHARE THIS DATABASE WITH OTHER USERS** option.

   You should have the options shown in Figure 19-52.

   The Remote folder will be created.

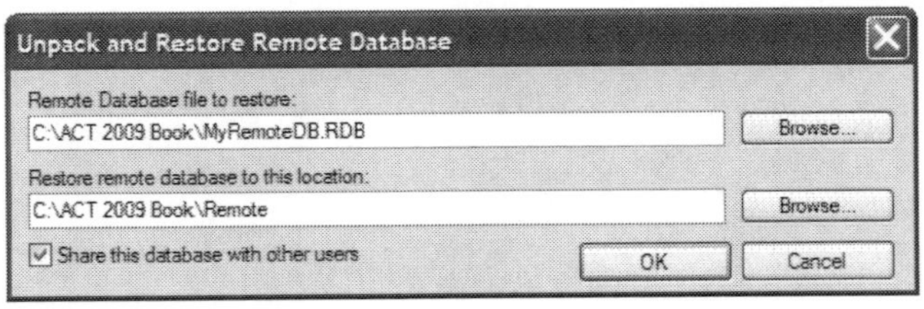

Figure 19-52 Unpack and Restore Remote Database dialog box

6. Click OK. You will see the Restore Database Progress window.

7. Click OK when the restore is complete.

Open And Use The Remote Database

The MyRemoteDB database will open automatically.

1. Click No when you see the Synchronize with main database message.

The remote database will open. At this point you can add and modify records in the remote database, just like you can any other database.

2. Go to the first record (Emily Dunn).

3. On the Notes tab, click the Select Users button, then select Chris Huffman and click OK.

4. Add a note. Type `This note was created in the remote database` in the Regarding field, then click OK. Leave the database open to complete the next exercise.

Using Subscription Lists To Add Contact Records

If you are using a remote database and realize that you need records that are in the main database, you can create a subscription list to get the contact records that you need from the main database. The contact records that are added to the remote database from a subscription list are always synchronized unless they are deleted from the subscription list or deleted from the database.

Exercise 19.10: Create A Subscription List

In this exercise you will create a subscription list that retrieves information for several contacts. You should have the remote database open. For this exercise, that is the **MYREMOTEDB** database.

1. Tools ⇒ Synchronization Panel.

2. Click the **MANAGE SUBSCRIPTION LIST** link in the User Tasks section. The contact records that you see on the Manage Subscription list screen are the records that you have access to.

3. Sort the records on the Sync Set column.

   The records that have a check mark in the **SYNC SET** column, as shown in Figure 19-53, are the contact records that are currently part of the sync set.

   The **VIEW SYNC SET QUERY** link will display the query shown earlier in Figure 11-42.

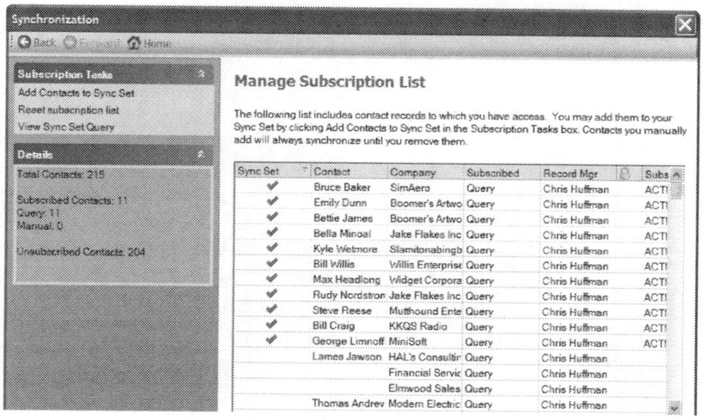

Figure 19-53 Manage Subscription List screen

4. Click the **ADD CONTACTS TO SYNC SET** link.

5. On the Contacts dialog box, add the first 10 companies shown in Figure 19-54, then click OK.

   Depending on the order that records are sorted in, you may have different companies displayed in the list. That's OK because this is practice. You will see the records in the Subscription list.

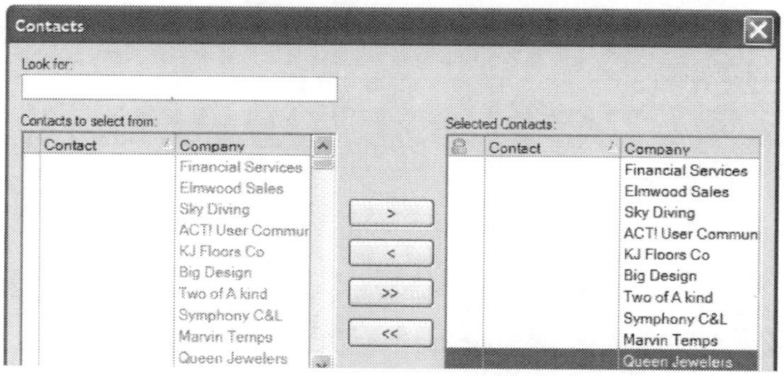

Figure 19-54 Contacts dialog box

6. Click Finish.

Manage Connection Information

There are two ways to move data between the main and remote databases as discussed below.

① **NETWORK (INSIDE A FIREWALL)** This option is used to synchronize through a virtual private network or remote application server.

② **APPLICATION SYNCHRONIZATION** This option requires ACT! and the main database to be open.

If you do not know if the sync will take place from behind a firewall, both connection types can be enabled.

1. Click the Home button if necessary, then click the **MANAGE CONNECTION INFORMATION** link in the User Tasks section.

2. Check the **PROMPT ME FOR WHICH ADDRESS TO USE** option at the bottom of the screen, then click Finish.

3. Close the Synchronization window.

Exercise 19.11: Synchronize The Database

So far in this lesson you have selected and designated a main database, turned the synchronization on, created a sync set, created a remote database and made changes to the remote database. The last step in the process is to sync the changes made in the remote database to the main database. There are two ways to sync a database as discussed below.

① **Manually** Synchronizes the database at any time.
② **Automatic** Synchronizes the database at pre-determined times.

In this exercise you will sync the remote database manually.

1. Tools ⇒ Synchronize ⇒ Synchronize Now.

   For this exercise select the Network option shown in Figure 19-55 unless you are working remotely, then click OK. Once the sync is completed, the 10 contacts that you just selected will be added to the remote database. There should be 30 records in the MyRemoteDB.

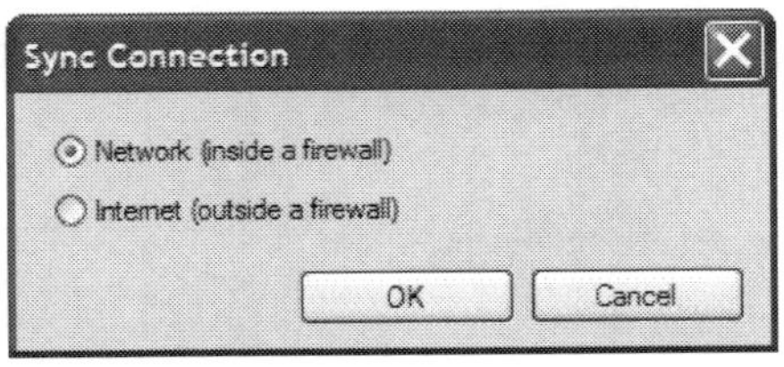

Figure 19-55 Sync Connection dialog box

DATABASE MAINTENANCE AND SECURITY

In this lesson you will learn how to use the following database maintenance tools and techniques:

- ☑ Delete database tool
- ☑ Backup tool
- ☑ Check and Repair tool
- ☑ Restoring databases
- ☑ Removing old data
- ☑ Using the Copy/Move Contact Data dialog box
- ☑ ACT! Scheduler
- ☑ ACT! Diagnostics

You will also learn the following security features:

- ☑ Creating, editing and deleting user accounts
- ☑ Password protecting a database
- ☑ Security roles and permissions
- ☑ Record access data security
- ☑ Password security and policies

LESSON 20

Database Maintenance

There are several things that you should do to keep a database working properly. If you are constantly adding and editing records in a database, you should back up the database frequently. Databases can become corrupt, which means that the database will not function properly and eventually may not open. It may run very slow or will not let you login. If you have a backup copy of the database you can restore it. You will have to re-enter any additions or changes that were made after the database was last backed up, but that is better than having to try to recreate the entire database. If you do not have a very recent backup, or worse, no backup at all, you will no longer have a database.

Many people say that they do not have time for maintenance. My thought is that it takes less time for maintenance then it does to type in all of the data again. More than likely, all of the notes and history records at the very least, cannot be recreated because you and anyone else that uses the database, probably cannot remember every note and activity that they created. Most companies create a backup of all files that are on servers every night. The majority of the ACT! maintenance tasks require administrator rights and that no other user has the database open when you are performing these tasks. The easy way to tell if you have administrator rights is if the options on the database maintenance submenu are enabled.

ACT! has several database maintenance tools that you can use to keep the database running smoothly. These tools are listed below.

① Backup
② Check and repair
③ Removing old data

Tools ⇒ Database Maintenance, will display the options shown in Figure 20-1.

I do not consider all of the options on this menu a maintenance tool, but all of the options on the menu are covered in this lesson.

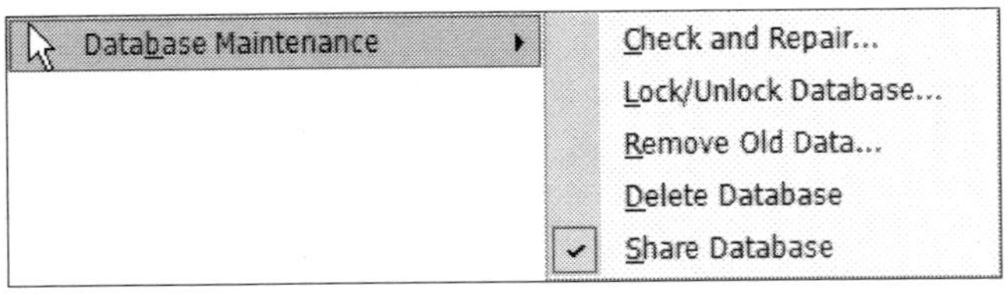

Figure 20-1 Database Maintenance tools

If your database is on a server, you may not have to do the database maintenance tasks discussed in this lesson because they will be handled by the computer department in your company.

Locking A Database

If you need to perform any type of maintenance like deleting, restoring, repairing or updating a database other than creating a back up, you must lock the database first. Locking a database means that you are the only person that can have the database open.

How To Lock A Database

1. Tools ⇒ Database Maintenance ⇒ Lock/Unlock Database.

If no users are in the database, it is locked automatically. When locked, you will see the word **(LOCKED)** in the Title bar after the database name.

If users have the database open, you will see the Lock Database dialog box which will list all of the users that have the database open. On this dialog box you can specify how long they can keep the database open before they are locked out. A warning message will then be sent to each user telling them to close the database.

Exercise 20.1: Using The Delete Database Tool

This tool is used to delete a database and all of the files associated with the database. The steps below will show you how to delete a database. You can just read these steps now, because you do not have a database to delete.

1. Open the database that you want to delete.

2. Tools ⇒ Database Maintenance ⇒ Delete Database. You will see the message shown in Figure 20-2.

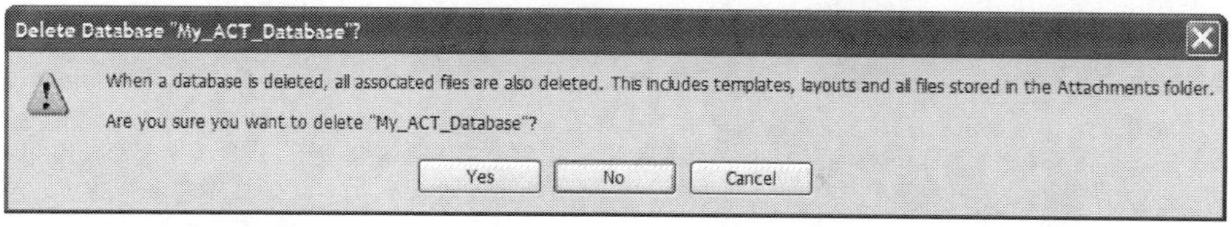

Figure 20-2 Delete Database message

3. Click Yes. You will see the message shown in Figure 20-3. Click Yes to delete the database. The database will now be deleted.

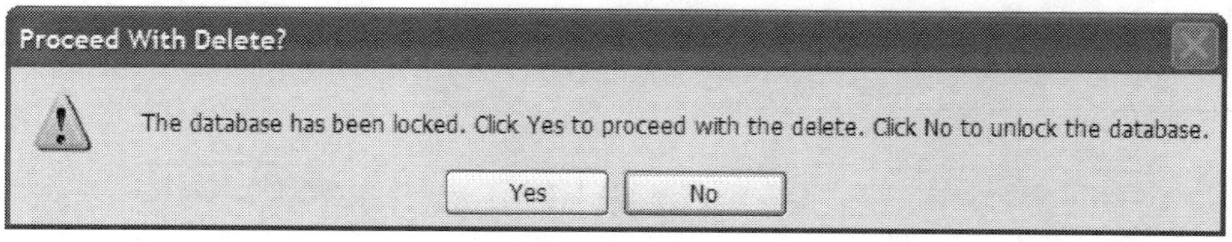

Figure 20-3 Proceed With Delete message

Once you delete a database, you cannot retrieve it.

The Backup Tool

There are three ways that you can create a back up copy of a database:

① Use Windows Explorer.
② Use the Save Copy As command.
③ Use the Back Up command.

Windows Explorer allows you to create a copy of the database. The **Save Copy As** command in ACT! also allows you to create a copy of the database, which you learned about in Lesson 1. Each database has additional files that the database needs and uses. Unless you select these files when using Windows Explorer, you will not make a complete back up of the database using this option. The Save Copy As command will automatically make a back up copy of the additional files.

The **Back Up** command has the same features as the Save Copy As command, plus it allows you to back up a database to disk, even if the database needs more than one disk. The back up files are saved in .zip format. The zip file format compacts files by removing the empty space in the file. The default file folder location for saving backups is:

C:\Documents and Settings\Your Username\My Documents\ACT\ACT for Windows 11\Backup.

In addition to being able to back up databases, **PERSONAL FILES** can also be backed up.
[See Lesson 12, What Are Supplemental Files?]

> When ACT! is installed, a backup folder is created on the same hard drive as the database. Please do not store your backups in this folder. There is nothing wrong with the folder, just hear me out. The goal of creating a backup is to have a copy of the database should something go wrong with the original one. If the "thing" that goes wrong is that the hard drive that the original database is on, dies or gets a virus, not only is the original database destroyed, so is the backup copy of the database if you store it on the same hard drive as the original database.
>
> This is why I do not understand the purpose of the Backup folder that is automatically created. The backup file should not be stored on the same hard drive as the original database. It should be stored on a different hard drive. This is also true for databases that are stored on a server.
>
> If your database is being backed up to the same server as the original database, do yourself a favor and start pricing an external hard drive if you do not already have one. Look for one that has the most space for $99 or less. You should be able to find a 500 or 650 GB drive for this price. There is an article on the web site for creating an image of the entire hard drive. www.tolana.com/tips/image.html

Exercise 20.2: How To Back Up A Database Using The Back Up Command

> Users with administrator or manager rights can back up a database, but only someone with administrator rights can restore a database.

In this exercise you will back up a database. You will save the backup file in the folder that you created. The reason that I am doing this is because I cannot guarantee that everyone that reads this book has an external device like an external hard drive, CD or DVD burner. The problem with CD's and DVD's in my opinion, is that for a reason that I do not understand, files that are copied to them are sometimes automatically set to **READ-ONLY**, which makes it difficult, if not impossible to use the file. CD-RW and DVD-RW formats work much better for me.

1. Open the RecordsToImport database.

2. File ⇒ Back Up ⇒ Database, then click the Browse button.

3. Navigate to and double-click on your folder, then click the Save button.

   You should see the folder that you selected in the field on the dialog box, as shown in Figure 20-4.

   Selecting the **INCLUDE ATTACHMENTS** option will back up the files in the Attachments folder.

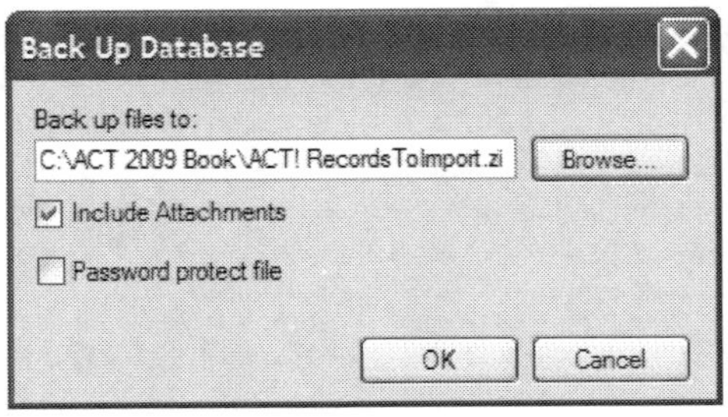

Figure 20-4 Back Up Database dialog box

4. Click OK. You will see the dialog box shown in Figure 20-5.

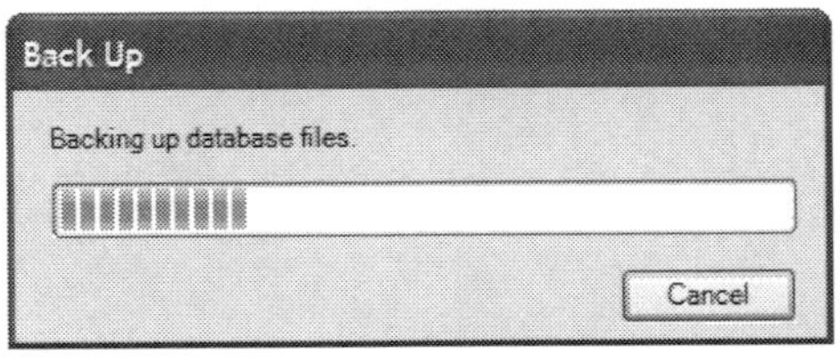

Figure 20-5 Back Up in progress dialog box

5. Click OK when you see the message that the backup completed successfully.

6. Close the RecordsToImport database, then open the My_ACT2009Demo database.

Password Protecting The Backup File

If checked, the password option shown earlier in Figure 20-4 will allow you to create a password for the back up file that will be created. Figure 20-6 shows the Backup Password dialog box.

Figure 20-6 Enter Backup Password dialog box

Exercise 20.3: How To Back Up Personal Files

Unlike backing up databases which requires administrator rights, anyone can back up personal files. You should give the personal backup file a different name then the file that it is being created from. This will prevent the original file from being overwritten if you have to restore it.

Tools ⇒ Preferences ⇒ General tab, will let you know where your personal files are stored. Look in the **PERSONAL FILE LOCATIONS** section and select the file type that you want to back up. The location of the files will be displayed. To complete the exercises in this book, the location for personal files is the folder that you created in Lesson 1. The steps below show you how to back up personal files.

1. File ⇒ Backup ⇒ Personal Files.

2. If your folder is not at the beginning of the **BACK UP FILES TO** field, click the Browse button, then double-click on your folder.

3. Change the file name to `ACT Dictionary Backup.zip`, as shown in Figure 20-7, then click the Save button. The reason that I had you change the file name is because you already created a backup of the custom menus and toolbars in Lesson 17 and used the default filename. Using the default file name now would overwrite that backup file.

   If you have to restore a file, it will be easier to find the right backup file if your backup files have meaningful names.

   If you want to password protect the back up file, check the **PASSWORD PROTECT FILE** option.

   The Backup personal zip file is stored in the folder that you selected in Step 2 above.

Figure 20-7 Back Up Personal Files dialog box

4. At the bottom of the dialog box shown above in Figure 20-7, select the types of files that you want to back up and clear the options for the file types that you do not want to back up. For this exercise check the **DICTIONARIES** option, then click OK to back up your personal files.

Check And Repair

This maintenance tool is used to improve database performance. Checking and repairing a database is a two step process as discussed below.

① **Integrity Check** Looks for errors in the database and repairs them when possible.

② **Re-Index** Reorganizes the records in the database. This allows the database to perform better. This step removes spaces from the database and defrags the database. This can take a long time to complete, especially the first time that it is run on the database. During the defrag process, the database is rewritten to the hard drive. Doing this makes the size of the database smaller, which allows it to perform tasks faster.

One way that performance is improved is by removing fragmentation. Fragmentation is caused when records are added or deleted in the database. It also occurs when other types of records like notes, history and opportunity records are deleted.

Reindexing Databases

Reindexing databases is another feature that the Check and Repair tool handles. Reindexing databases will make the database run more efficiently. Only deleting records does not give back disk space. Compressing a database will give back the disk space that deleted records and references to them take up in the index.

Reindexing a database will make queries and lookups run faster. Reindexing and compressing a database will take more time if the database is large. You should reindex and compress databases on a regular basis.

Figure 20-8 shows the current size of the My_ACT2009Demo database.

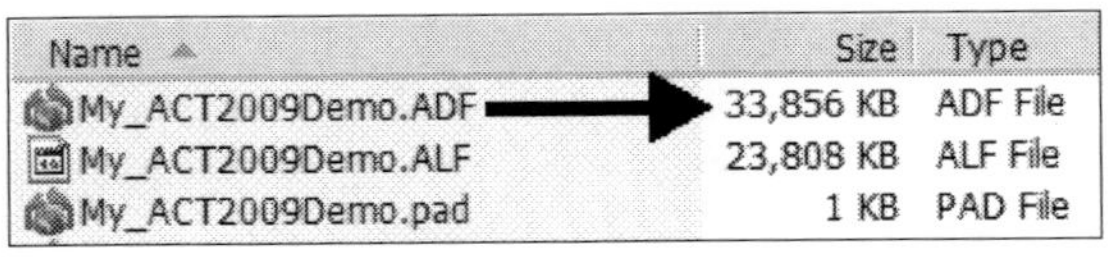

Figure 20-8 Size of database illustrated

Exercise 20.4: Check And Repair A Database

Before using this tool you should back up the database. You do not have to complete this exercise now because it will take at least 30 minutes for this process to run.

1. Back up the My_ACT2009Demo database.

2. Lock the database.

3. Tools ⇒ Database Maintenance ⇒ Check and Repair.

   You will see the dialog box shown in Figure 20-9.

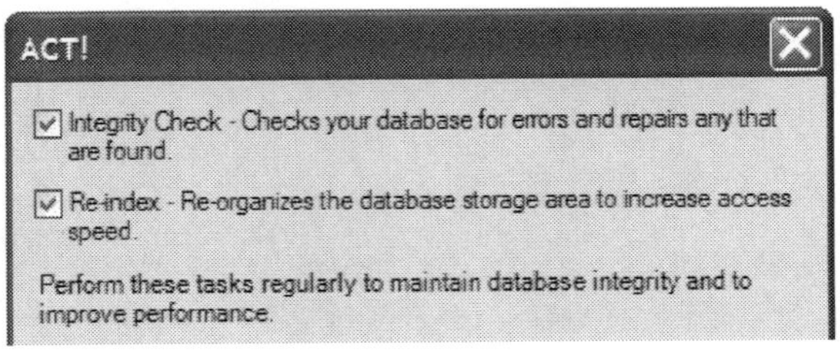

Figure 20-9 Database check and repair options

4. Both options should be checked to have the database perform at its best. Click OK. You will see the dialog box shown in Figure 20-10.

Figure 20-10 Check and Repair status dialog box

5. When the utility is finished click OK, then unlock the database.

Exercise 20.5: Restoring Databases

The backup database files are usually restored when the current version has been corrupted or is not working properly. Only administrators can restore databases. It is best to restore databases back to their original location, especially if it is a database that is part of a synchronization process. Not restoring a synchronized database back to its original location will break the synchronization between the two databases.

Restore Options

There are three ways that a database can be restored, as discussed below.

① **Restore** This option will restore all of the files to their original location. Select this option if the original database is corrupt or was deleted.
② **Restore As** This option is used to restore the database to a location other then the original location and to rename the database if necessary.
③ **Unpack And Restore Remote Database** This option is used to restore a remote database that has been synced back to the main database.

The steps below show you how to restore a database. For now you can read through the steps unless you have a backup copy of a database that could be restored.

1. File ⇒ Restore ⇒ Database.

2. Select the Restore option, then click OK.

3. Click the Browse button, then double-click on the zip file that contains the database that you want to restore.

4. Click OK on the dialog box shown in Figure 20-11.

   If prompted, enter your username and password, then click OK.

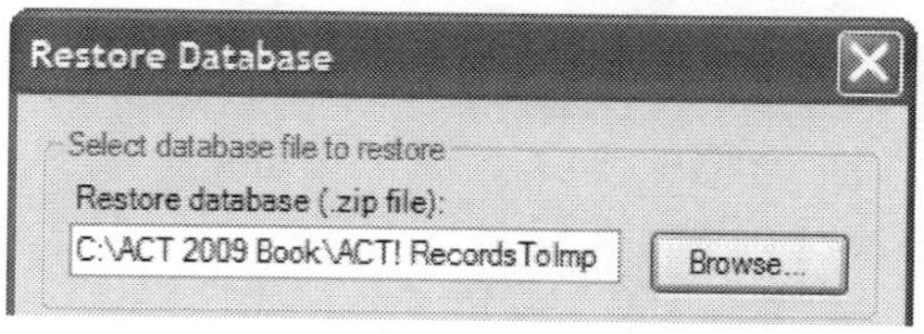

Figure 20-11 Restore Database (zip file) dialog box

5. Click Yes when prompted that files that were modified after the backup was created will be overwritten.

6. When the restore process is complete, open the database that was restored to make sure that it is working properly.

Removing Old Data

There may be data in the database that is no longer needed. If that is the case you can remove it. The following types of data can be removed: notes, attachments and activities. This is also known as **PURGING A DATABASE**. The main benefit of removing data that is not needed is that it will make the database smaller, which will allow it to run more efficiently. Only administrators can remove data. You should back up the database before deleting records and attachments.

> If you are using a Microsoft SQL Server 2005 Express database, from time to time you should check the file size to make sure that it is not close to the 4 GB limit. If it is, you should remove old data. To check the size of the database follow the steps below.

How To Check The File Size Of A Database

The instructions below only work if you have a database open.

1. Help ⇒ About ACT!.
2. Click the **DATABASE INFORMATION** button.

   You will see the dialog box shown in Figure 20-12.

   Look in the **DATABASE SIZE** section in the lower left corner of the dialog box.

   You can also see what security role your account has on this dialog box.

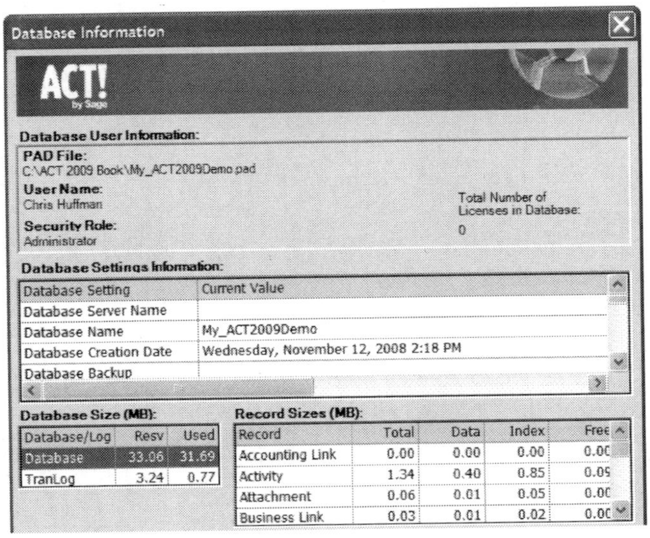

Figure 20-12 Database Information dialog box

Exercise 20.6: How To Remove Old Data

In this exercise you will create criteria that will be used to remove old data from the My_ACT2009Demo database.

1. Tools ⇒ Database Maintenance ⇒ Remove Old Data.
2. Check the options and number of days in Table 20-1.

   Your dialog box should have the options selected that are shown in Figure 20-13.

   The options shown in Figure 20-13 are used to select the type of data that you want to remove and select how far back to search for data that you want to remove.

Option	# Of Days
Notes older than	10
Cleared activities older than	5
Document tab entries older than	15

Table 20-1 Criteria for selecting old data

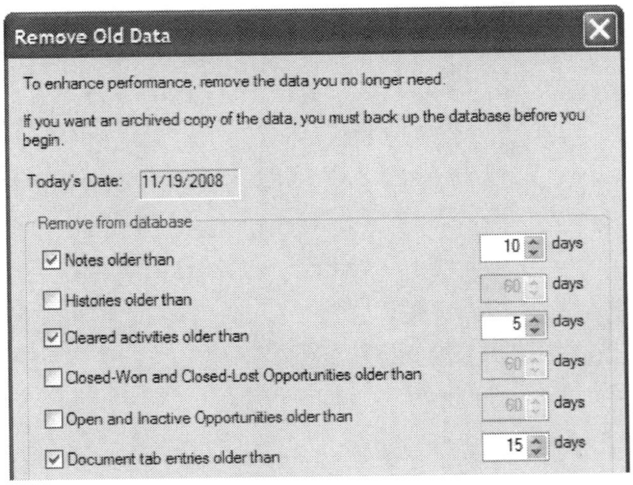

Figure 20-13 Remove Old Data dialog box

3. Click OK. You will see the message shown in Figure 20-14. You will see a different number of records to be removed because you are not running the utility on the same day that I am.

   Click Yes.

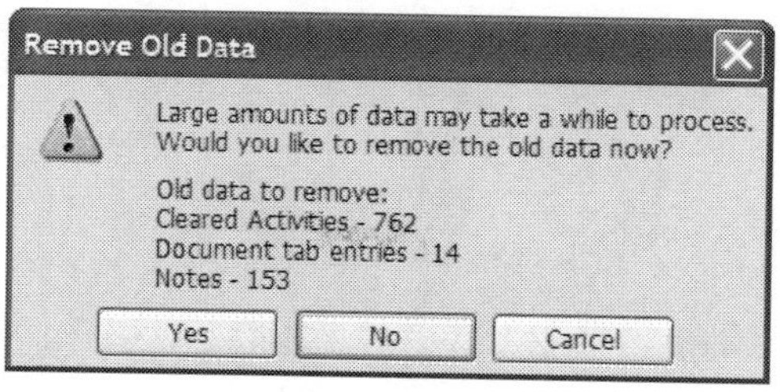

Figure 20-14 Remove Old Data message

4. When you see the purge message shown in Figure 20-15, you can click No.

   If this were a live database, you should reindex the database.

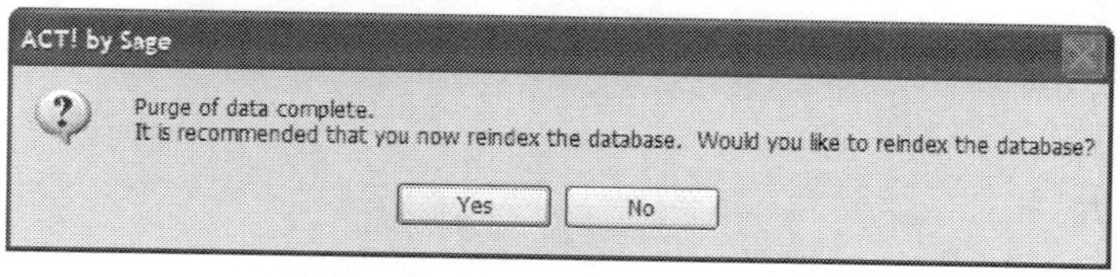

Figure 20-15 Purge message

Exercise 20.7: Finding And Deleting Duplicate Records

Deleting duplicate records will help keep the size of the database as small as possible. It will also keep the data more accurate. You can delete duplicate contact and group records. By default, **Contact** records are considered duplicate if they have the same Company, Contact and Phone number. You can select other fields on the dialog box shown in Figure 20-16 to use as criteria to determine duplicate contact records. **Group** records are considered duplicate if they have the same Record Creator (person that created the group) and group name.

1. Open the DuplicateRecords database.

2. Tools ⇒ Scan for Duplicates.

   The options on the Scan for Duplicate Contacts dialog box are used to select the fields that you want to use to determine what makes a contact record a duplicate.

   Often, duplicate contact records are caught when they are being created.

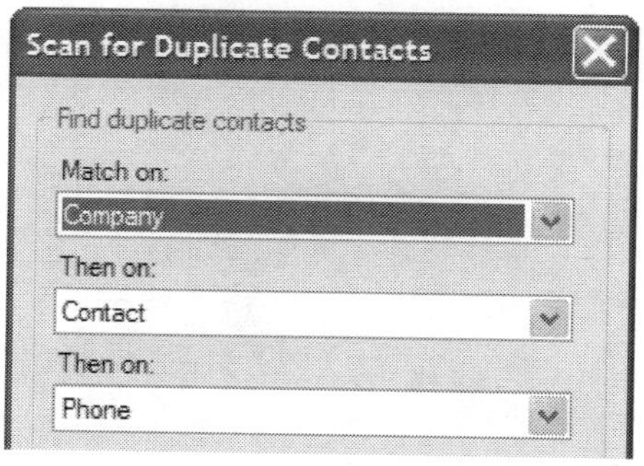

Figure 20-16 Scan for Duplicate Contacts dialog box

If you wanted to use different fields to determine if there are duplicate records, you would select them now. For this exercise you do not have to make any changes.

3. Click OK. You will see a message that says that there are duplicate contacts. Click Yes.

Using The Copy/Move Contact Data Wizard

If the scan for duplicate process finds duplicate contacts, this wizard will open automatically.

1. Click Next on the first wizard screen.

The options on the dialog box shown in Figure 20-17 are used to select what to do with the duplicate records.

The following options are available.

① Copy or move data from one record to another.
② Combine business and personal records for the same contact.
③ Merge the duplicate records for the same contact into one record.

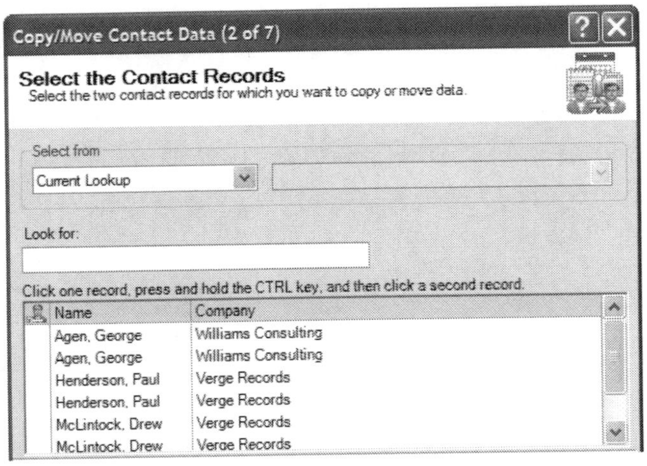

Figure 20-17 Select the Contact Records screen

Tools ⇒ Copy/Move Contact Data, will also open the dialog box shown above in Figure 20-17.

Take your time and be careful when merging records. Once they are merged, it cannot be undone. The good thing is that this process has to be completed for each set of duplicate records, so the worse case is that you would only have to restore a few records and not all of the duplicate records in the database.

2. Click on the first record for George Agen, then press and hold down the **CTRL** key and click on the second record for George Agen. Click Next.

On the screen shown in Figure 20-18, you have to decide which record you want to keep. It seems to me that this would be a great place to be able to delete a record from the main database, because enough information about each contact record is displayed.

You should scroll down and view the data in both records to determine which one you want to keep. Two contact information fields that I find helpful are the **EDIT DATE** and **IS IMPORTED** fields.

I tend to select the record that has more of the data that I want to keep as the target record.

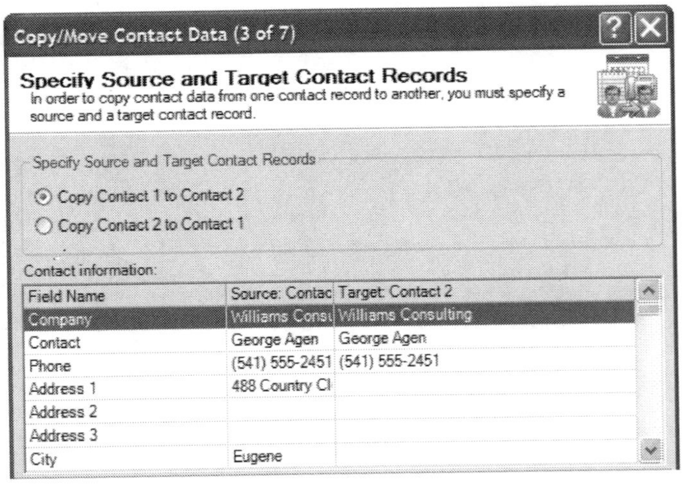

Figure 20-18 Specify Source and Target Contact Records screen

The **SOURCE** record contains the data that will be copied.
The **TARGET** record is where the data from the source record will be copied to.
The **COPY/MOVE DATA** options are used to copy or move data on a field by field basis, as shown below in Figure 20-19.
The **KEEP/DELETE DATA** options are used to keep or delete the source record. If you copy or move data from the source record, I think that the source record should be deleted. If you have a reason to keep it, then you should.

You can resize the columns on the wizard screens so that you can see the data better.

3. Select the **COPY CONTACT 2 TO CONTACT 1 OPTION**, then click Next.

The options on this screen are helpful if the source record has data in fields that the target record does not.

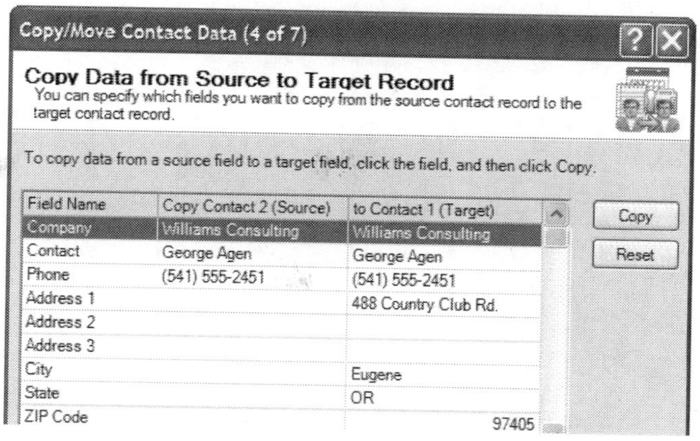

Figure 20-19 Copy Data from Source to Target Record screen

4. Click Next on screen 4 of 7. The options shown in Figure 20-20 are optional types of data that can be copied from the source record to the target record. Check the Notes, Histories and Activities options for this exercise, then click Next.

In a live database, you would probably select all of the items so that you would have a complete history of the contact.

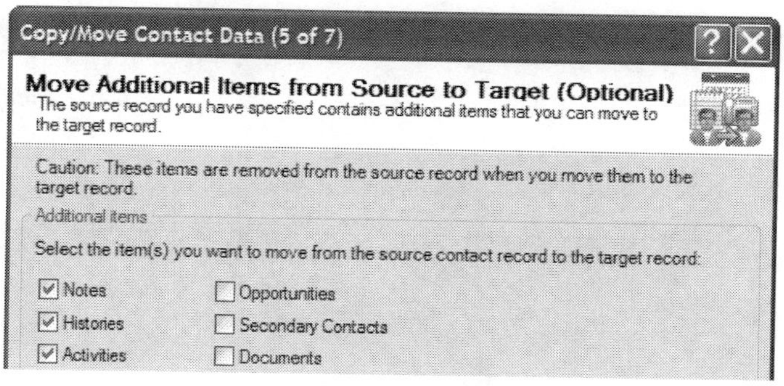

Figure 20-20 Move Additional Items from Source to Target screen

The options shown in Figure 20-21 are used to select whether or not to delete the record that you designated as the source record.

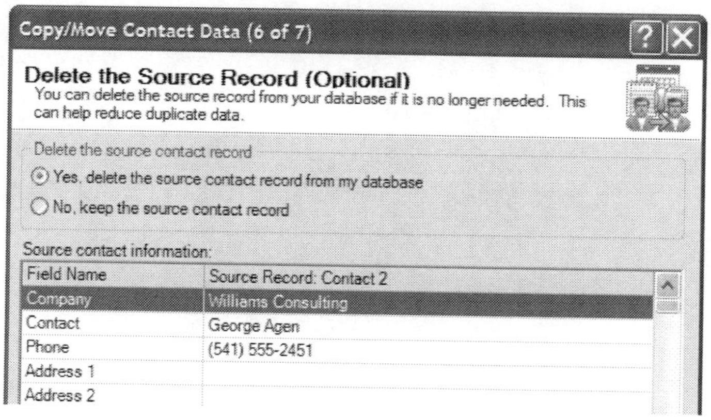

Figure 20-21 Delete the Source Record screen

5. Select the option Yes, delete the source record from my database, then click Next.

6. Click Yes when you see the message that says deleting a contact cannot be undone.

7. Click Finish to close the wizard. The changes to the record that you are keeping will be made. You have to repeat this process for all of the potential duplicate records displayed in the Contact List shown earlier in Figure 20-17.

Exercise 20.8: Deleting Duplicate Records From The Contact List View

After completing the exercise above, the database can still have duplicate records because the scan for duplicates process only checks for records that have identical information in up to three fields. If the contact name is spelled differently in two or more records, it would be skipped when the check for duplicate scan was run. Therefore, it is a good idea to visually view the records in the Contact List to see if there are other duplicate records.

When I do this, I first sort by the contact name, which is often the field that has duplicates due to typos. Then I sort the list by company to see if there are any company names that are spelled wrong. As you can imagine, as more records are added to the database the longer this can take, especially if it is not done on a regular basis.

If you do not want to merge data from one contact record to another, like you just learned how to do, you can delete the duplicate record(s) that you do not want to keep by following the steps below. Keep in mind that deleting the duplicate records from a view means that if you want to keep any data from the record that you will delete, you will have to type the information in the record that you want to keep.

1. Open the Duplicate Records database if it is not already open. In the Contact List view, right-click in the row of the record that you want to delete and select **DELETE CONTACT**.
2. Click the Delete Contact button when prompted that deleting contacts cannot be undone.
3. Click Yes. You are prompted twice to make sure that you want to delete the record.

View The Deleted Records

ACT! keeps a log of all records that are deleted on the History tab of the My Record.

1. Lookup ⇒ My Record.
2. Click on the History tab. The records that you deleted are at the top of the list, if the list is sorted in descending date order as shown in Figure 20-22.

   You will see today's date and time instead of the one shown in the figure.

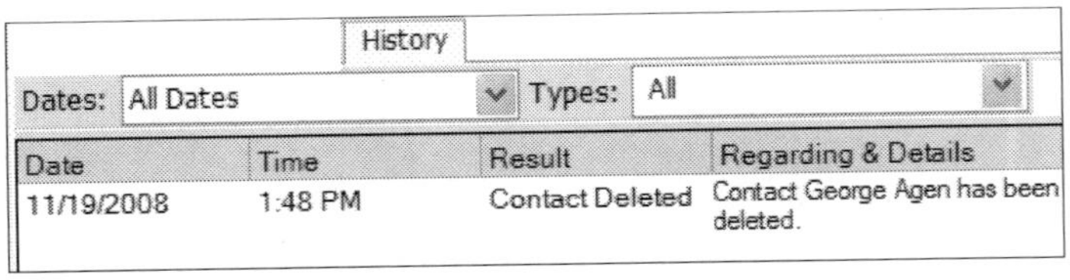

Figure 20-22 Deleted records on the History tab

Exercise 20.9: How To Select Other Fields To Check For Duplicates

In a previous exercise you used the default fields to check for duplicate records. You can select other fields.

1. Lookup ⇒ All Contacts.
2. Tools ⇒ Scan for Duplicates.
3. Open the **MATCH ON** drop-down list and select Department, then click OK. You will see a message that says duplicate contacts have been found. Click No.

ACT! Scheduler

So far in this lesson you have learned about a variety of maintenance tasks. If you are thinking that you will not remember to do them on a regular basis, you can set them up in the ACT! Scheduler, because this tool will run the tasks for you at the time that you select, even if ACT! is not open.

In addition to being able to run maintenance tasks, the scheduler can also be used to automatically run a synchronization process, including the process to sync ACT! and Outlook calendars.

Exercise 20.10: Schedule A Maintenance Task

In this exercise you will schedule the database maintenance utility to check and re-index the demo database that you created, once a week.

1. Tools ⇒ ACT! Schedule.

2. Click on the **CREATE A TASK** link.

3. Click the **BROWSE** button on the Select a Database screen, then double-click on the My_ACT2009Demo.pad file.

4. You should have the options selected, as shown in Figure 20-23.

   Click Next.

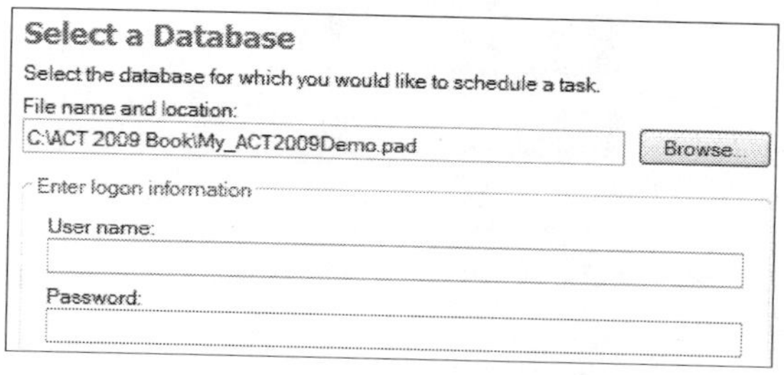

Figure 20-23 Select a Database screen

5. Open the **TASK** drop-down list and select Database Maintenance, as shown in Figure 20-24.

   Click Next.

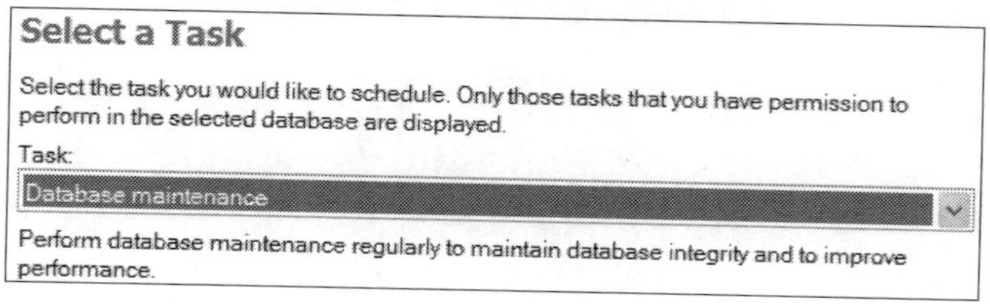

Figure 20-24 Select a Task screen

6. Check both options shown in Figure 20-25 if they are not already selected, then click Next.

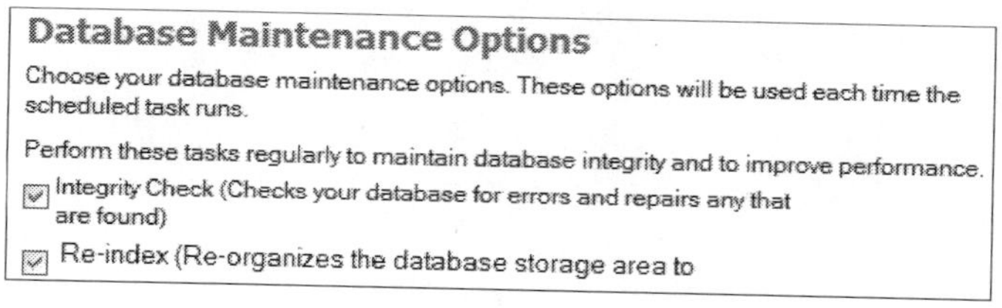

Figure 20-25 Database Maintenance Options screen

7. Select the weekly option, then select Thursday from the drop-down list on the right.

8. Change the **START TIME** to 10 PM, as shown in Figure 20-26, then click Finish.

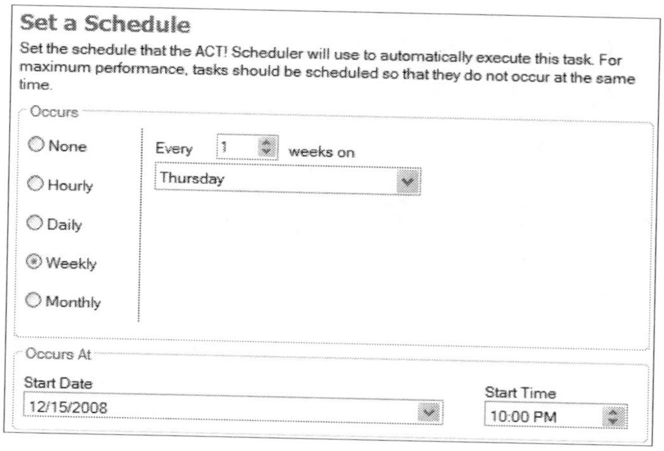

Figure 20-26 Set a Schedule screen

9. If you click on the task that you just created, you will see the details for it in the lower left corner, as shown in Figure 20-27.

   Click Exit.

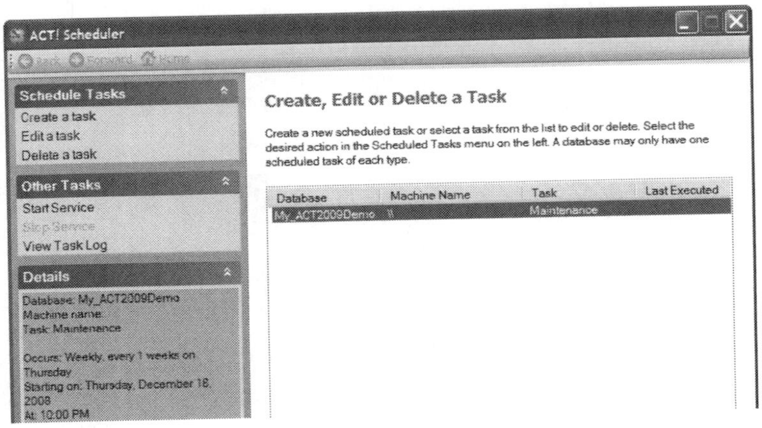

Figure 20-27 Create, Edit or Delete a Task screen

10. You should see the Scheduler icon in the Windows task bar. If not, open the ACT! Scheduler, then select the **START SERVICE** option, shown above in Figure 20-27.

Security

ACT! comes with several security options. With so many companies having their data stolen, it may be a good idea to implement as much security as possible, without going overboard.

> If you add a password to a user account or database, select one that you will remember. Using the word **PASSWORD** for a password is not a good idea, as this is the default password for some software packages. It is best to select passwords that have a combination of letters and numbers.

User Security

User security allows the administrator to create accounts so that other people can use the database. ACT! provides the following types of user level security.

① User accounts
② Security roles
③ Logon status
④ Permissions

Exercise 20.11: Creating User Accounts

In this exercise you will create a user account with your name.

1. Open the My_ACT2009Demo database. Tools ⇒ Manage Users. You will see a list of the users, their security role and log on status.

2. Click the **CREATE NEW USER** link.

> The Create New User option will create a new contact record. You should make sure that the person that you are creating the account for does not have a contact record in the database, so that you do not create a duplicate record.

There are two ways that you can create a new user account, as shown in Figure 20-28.

If you see the message shown in the **DETAILS** section, it means that only one person at a time can use the database. This is usually the case for home users. It does not mean that additional user accounts cannot be created.

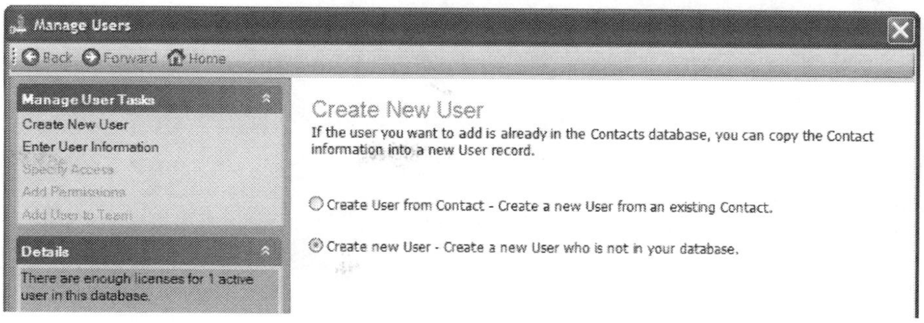

Figure 20-28 Create New User screen

The links in the **MANAGE USER TASKS** section are used to go to the screen that you want, instead of clicking the Next and Back buttons to get to another screen.

If you select the **CREATE USER FROM CONTACT** option and click Next, you will see the screen shown in Figure 20-29. It is used to select a name from the database to use for the user account that you want to create. When you click the Next button on this screen you will see the screen shown in Figure 20-30 with the Contact and User name fields filled in. From this point on, the screens are the same to finish creating the user account.

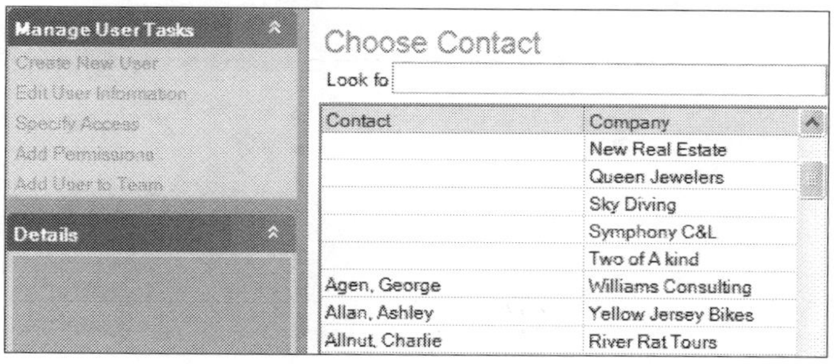

Figure 20-29 Choose Contact screen

If you select the **CREATE NEW USER** option shown above in Figure 20-28, you will see the screen shown in Figure 20-30. It is used to enter the information for the new user.

A contact record will be created for this user.

Figure 20-30 Enter User Information screen

User Account Creation Tips

① User names and passwords are not case sensitive.

② Passwords for user accounts are optional. If you leave the password field empty, the user will not have to enter a password unless the password policy option requires one.

3. Select the **CREATE NEW USER** option for this exercise, then click Next.

4. Type your first and last name in the Contact Name field, then press the Tab key. Your name should automatically be filled in the User Name field.

5. Select the **ADMINISTRATOR** Security Role and check the **PASSWORD NEVER EXPIRES** option. Security Roles are explained at the end of this exercise.

6. If you want to add a password, type your first name and the year in the **NEW PASSWORD** and **CONFIRM PASSWORD** fields (ie. Indera2007), then click Next.

> If you do not enter the same password in the New Password and Confirm Password fields, the **NEXT** and **FINISH** buttons will not be enabled.

If any of the password options discussed below are selected, they override the password policy options that are discussed later in this lesson.

① If you check the **USER MUST CHANGE PASSWORD AT NEXT LOG ON** option, you do not have to enter a password when setting up the account. This will cause the user to be prompted to create a password the first time that they log on.
② The **USER CANNOT CHANGE PASSWORD** option if checked, will disable the File ⇒ Set Password option, which is how users change their password.
③ If checked, the **PASSWORD NEVER EXPIRES** option will not require the user to change their password.

7. Select the **INACTIVE** option, then click Next.

The options shown in Figure 20-31 are used to select the logon access options.

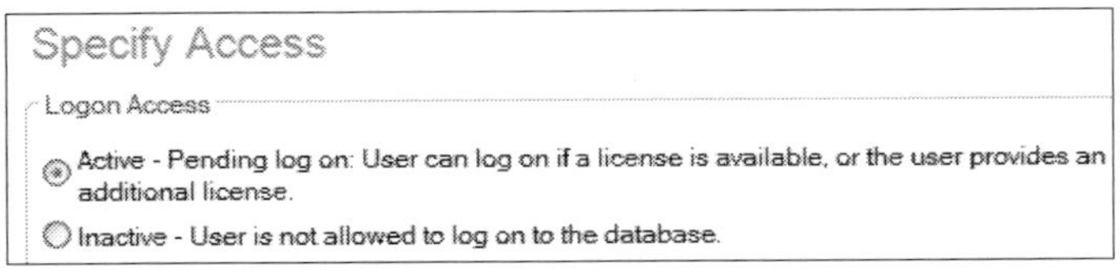

Figure 20-31 Specify Access screen

The options shown in Figure 20-32 are used to select the permissions for the user account.

The permissions available are based on the security role that is selected for the account.

Some security roles come with some of the permissions selected by default.

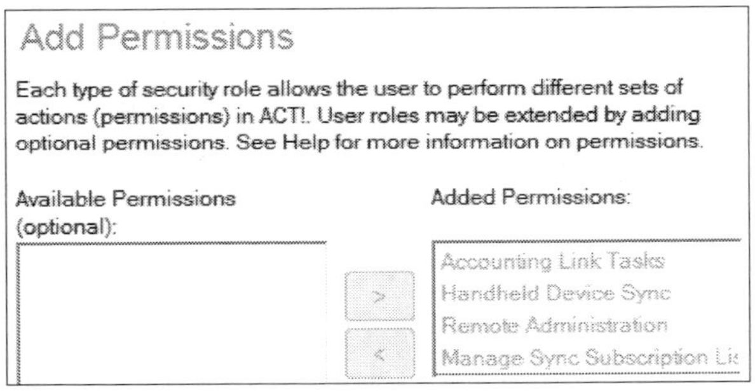

Figure 20-32 Add Permissions screen

Because you selected the Administrator security role, all of the permissions are available by default. They will appear in the **ADDED PERMISSIONS** column. These permissions are only available for Manager and Standard roles and are explained at the end of this exercise.

8. Click Finish.

The new user account and contact record will be created.

Leave the Manage Users window open to complete the next exercise.

Once the account is created you will see it on the screen shown in Figure 20-33.

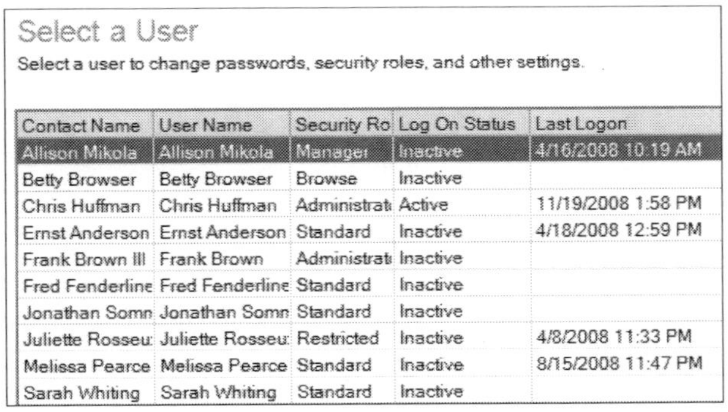

Figure 20-33 Select A User screen

Reset Passwords

The **RESET PASSWORD** button shown earlier in Figure 20-30 will let the administrator reset the password. This is helpful when a user forgets their password.

Once the password has been reset, you can tell the user to set up a new password on the dialog box shown in Figure 20-34.

File ⇒ Set Password, will open this dialog box.

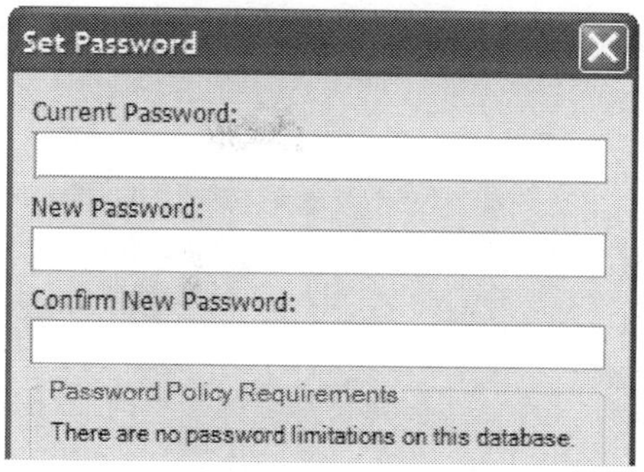

Figure 20-34 Set Password dialog box

Earlier I stated that I believe that there should be at least two administrator accounts per database. Resetting passwords is one reason. An administrator account cannot reset its own password because the account being reset cannot be logged on. If you do not know or remember the administrator account password and the database only has one administrator account set up, the only way that I know of to retrieve the password is to send the database to Sage.

Security Roles

As you saw earlier, there are five security roles (levels) that can be given to a user. The security roles determine what data a user has access to and what they can and cannot do to the records that they have access to. The goal of setting up security is to only give enough rights so that a user can get their job done. The five security levels that you can assign a user are discussed below.

Browse This level allows the user to view records and calendars of other users that they have access to. Users at this security level cannot edit or add any data, which includes sending an email or writing a letter from inside of ACT!. This is the most limited security level.

Restricted This level can only access public areas of the database. Users at this security level can create and edit contacts and opportunities, but cannot delete any data, even data that they create. Users cannot create groups or companies.

Standard This security level allows the user to view, edit, add and delete contacts and groups, as well as, synchronize databases. This is the most common security level. Users cannot delete other users data, create backups, import and export data, schedule activities for other users without being granted access to their calendar, modify layouts or perform database maintenance.

Manager This security level has access to the entire database, except for private records, but does not have administrator rights, which means users cannot create user accounts or perform database maintenance tasks.

Administrator This security level has full rights to the database. If the database is used by several people, there should be two administrator accounts, in my opinion, in case one account becomes corrupt or one person does something wrong. If there are other users and they mark records as private, people with administrator rights cannot view the records.

Permissions

These permissions give Standard and Manager level accounts additional rights. The available permissions are discussed below.

① **Accounting Link Tasks** The user can work on accounting tasks if an accounting software package like QuickBooks has been configured to work with ACT!.

② **Handheld Device Sync** Allows the user to synchronize ACT! data with a handheld device like a PDA (Personal Digital Assistant).

③ **Remote Administration** Allows the user to repair, back up, restore and check remote databases that they have rights to. This permission is primarily useful for remote users.

④ **Manage Sync Subscription List** Allows the user to make changes to the subscription (contact) list for a remote database.

Exercise 20.12: How To Edit User Account Information

In the previous exercise you created a new user account that had administrator rights and was inactive. In this exercise you will edit the user account and set up the permissions.

1. Open the Manage Users Utility.

2. Click on the user account with your name, then click the **EDIT USER INFORMATION** link.

3. Change the Security Role to Standard, then click the **ADD PERMISSIONS** link.

4. Add the Remote Administration permission to the account, then click the Back button.

5. Change the logon access to Active, then click Finish.

   You will see that your account is active, but pending log on, as illustrated in Figure 20-35.

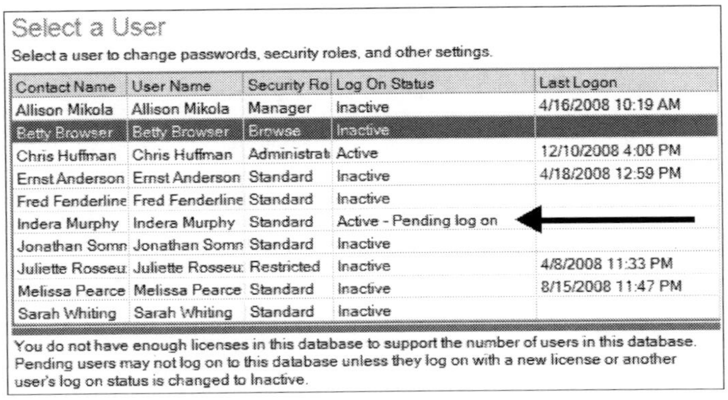

Figure 20-35 Select A User screen

How To Delete A User Account

Usually an account is deleted because the person will no longer use the database. There was a time that if you deleted a user account, all traces of the account would also be deleted. In an ACT! database, that would have meant that the attachments or notes that were added to the database by the user account, would also be deleted. The good news is that ACT! databases have evolved and now you can delete a user account and keep the work that was created under the account. You do not have to delete a user account. You can make the account inactive. The steps below show you how to delete a user account.

1. Click on the user account that you want to delete on the screen shown above in Figure 20-35. For this exercise, you can click on the account with your name.

2. Click the **DELETE USER** link.

   You will see the message shown in Figure 20-36 if the user did not add or modify any data. This message is asking if you want to keep the contact record for the account that you are about to delete.

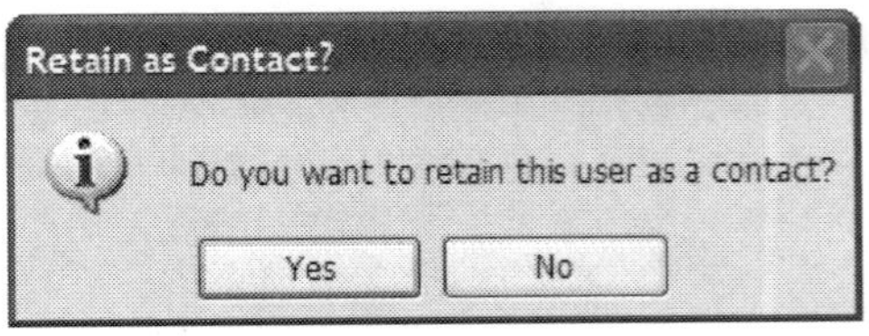

Figure 20-36 Retain as Contact message

3. Click Yes, when you see the message asking if you are sure that you want to remove the user.

   You will see the dialog box shown in Figure 20-37 if the user added or modified any data.

   The **DELETE RECORDS BELONGING TO THIS USER** option will do just that, delete the contact records that the user created, as well as, any notes for the contact, regardless of who created the note or activity.

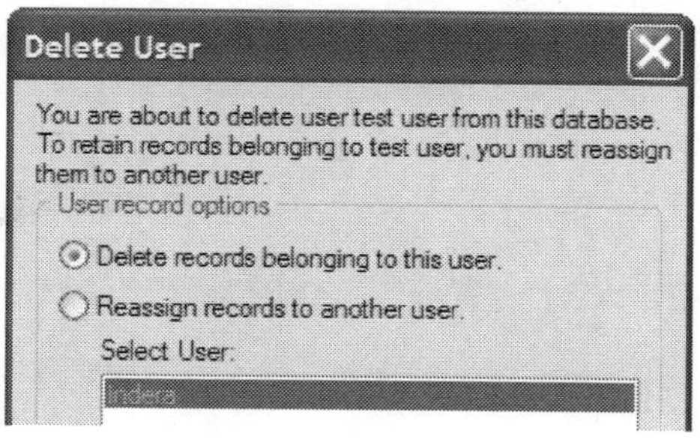

Figure 20-37 Delete User dialog box

   The **REASSIGN RECORDS TO ANOTHER USER** option moves the records to another user. This prevents the records from being deleted. In my opinion, this is the best option to select.

4. Select the appropriate options depending on which of the dialog boxes shown above that you see. When finished, the user account will be removed from the Select a User screen.

5. Close the Manage Users dialog box.

Data Security

Some of the data security options are handled under user security like security roles and permissions are. ACT! has the following types of data security.

① Record access
② Record Manager
③ Password policy

Record Access

This option determines which users can view the record. Access to records occurs on two levels as discussed below.

① Parent or Extended access
② Public or Private access

Parent Or Extended Access

Parent records are the contact, company and group records. Extended records are the notes, history, activity, opportunity and secondary contacts for the parent record. If a user does not have access to the parent record, they also do not have access to the extended records associated with the parent record. For example, if a user does not have access to the Jane Doe contact record, they will not have access to the records on the tabs for the contact Jane Doe.

Public Or Private Access

Records that are marked as public can be viewed by anyone that has access to the database. Records that are marked as private can only be viewed by the Record Manager (record owner). If you have the need for more functionality to limit access, you will have to upgrade to ACT! Premium Solutions. Like many of features in ACT!, there is more than one way to mark a record as public or private, as discussed below.

① On the Contact Detail view, click on the Contact Access tab and select Public or Private, as illustrated in Figure 20-38.
② On the Contact List view, Contacts ⇒ Edit Contact Access, as shown in Figure 20-39.
③ On the Contact List view, right-click on the record(s) that you want to change the access of and select Edit Contact Access. You will see the submenu options shown in Figure 20-39.

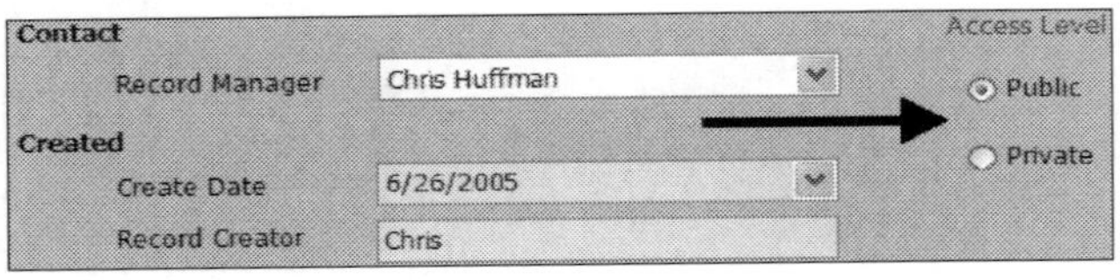

Figure 20-38 Public and private access options

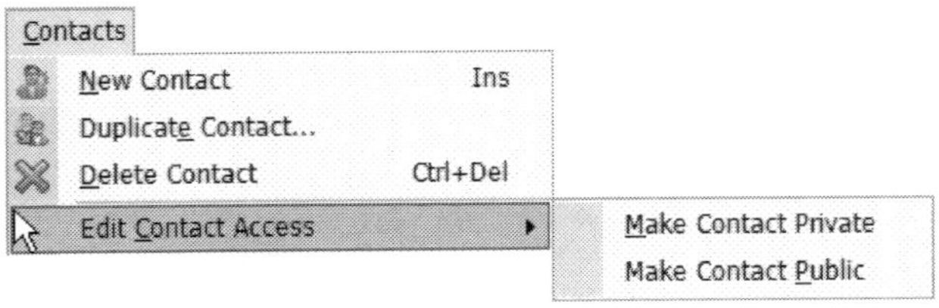

Figure 20-39 Edit Contact Access menu options

Company and group records can be marked as private. Data on some tabs can be marked as private by right-clicking on an item and selecting **MAKE <TAB NAME> PRIVATE**. On other tabs like Personal Info and User Fields, you can select the option shown above in Figure 20-39.

There was a time when there was no option to make company records private. They were always public.

Record Manager

The Record Manager is the user that creates the record. Anyone that adds or edits data should have their own login account that has Record Manager rights. The reason is so that ACT! can fill in certain system fields with the name of the person that made a change to the record. An example of this is who created an activity for a contact. If you created an activity, but are logged into the database as me, ACT! would enter my name as the person that created the activity. Record Managers and Administrators can change who the Record Manager is.

Field Security

In addition to being able to add security to specific records, you can add security to individual fields. The security on system fields cannot be changed. The two types of field security are discussed below. The steps in the next section show you how to change the field security.

① **Read Only** Users can view, select and copy the data in the field, but cannot edit or delete the data.
② **Full Access** This is the default security option for all fields. Users have all of the rights that Read Only users have, plus they can edit, add and delete data in the field.

Exercise 20.13: Assigning Field Security

In this exercise you will learn how to assign security to a field.

1. Tools ⇒ Define Fields.
2. Open the **VIEW FIELDS FOR** drop-down list and select the Record type that you need to secure.
3. Select the field, then click **FIELD SECURITY** link in the Field Tasks section of the screen.
4. Select the permission that you want, as shown in Figure 20-40, then click Finish.

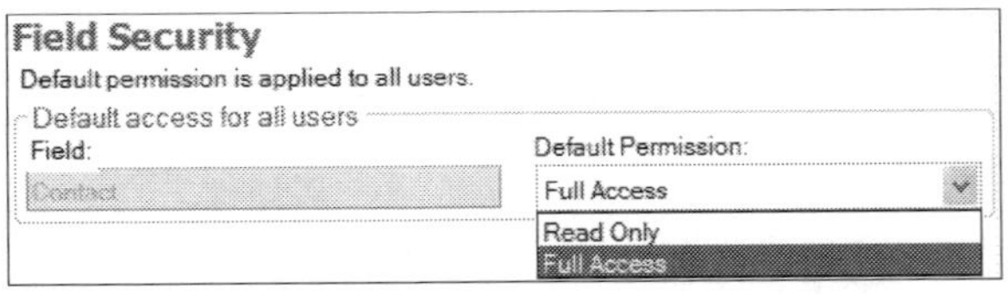

Figure 20-40 Field security options

With all of the attacks on data these days, you may be tempted to want to protect the database as much as possible. When applying field level security, there are some things to keep in mind when limiting access, as discussed below.

① Even with administrator or manager rights, if your rights to a field are read-only you cannot import or export data for the field.
② You cannot sync fields that you do not have full access to.
③ The data in the field with read-only access cannot be used for queries and will not appear in a report.

Password Security

User accounts have the option of having password security. Earlier in Exercise 20.11 when you created a user account, you saw the password options. These user options are managed by an administrator through a password policy for the database.

Exercise 20.14: How Users Change A Password

One of the policies that you can set is when passwords expire. If that option is enabled, users have to change their password. Later in this lesson you will learn how to set a password policy. The steps below show users how to change a password.

1. File ⇒ Set Password. You will see the dialog box shown earlier in Figure 20-34.

2. Type the existing password in the **CURRENT PASSWORD** field. If the account did not have a password, this field has to be left blank.

3. Type the new password in the **NEW PASSWORD** and **CONFIRM NEW PASSWORD** fields, then click OK.

Password Policy

Password policies are created to provide more security for a database. Whenever you change the password policy, users are prompted to enter a password the next time that they log in if their current password does not meet the new password policy. The options discussed below are the password policy options that can be set. The X in the option name represents the number that you select.

① **User cannot reuse last X passwords** This option is used to select how many of the previously used passwords cannot be reused. The maximum number that can be entered in this field is nine. For example, if this option is set to three, the last three passwords that were used, could not be used when the user creates the fourth password.
② **Password must change every X days** This option is used to select in days how often users must change their password. If this option is set to zero, users do not have to change the password. (1)
③ **Minimum duration between password changes is X days** This option is used to select the least number of days that a password has to be in use before the user can change it. (1)
④ **Password must be at least X characters in length** This option is used to select the minimum number of characters that a password must have. Setting this option to one is the same as requiring a password. A zero means that the user can enter a password up to 25 characters, which is the maximum number of characters.
⑤ **Password must contain X of 4 character groups** This option is used to select the type(s) of characters that the password has to have. The character groups are lower case, upper case, numbers and special characters. If the numbers option is selected, users must create a password that has at least one number in it.

(1) The maximum number for this field is 365 days.

Exercise 20.15: How To Create A Password Policy

In this exercise you will create a password policy.

1. Tools ⇒ Password Policy.

2. Select the options shown in Figure 20-41, then click OK.

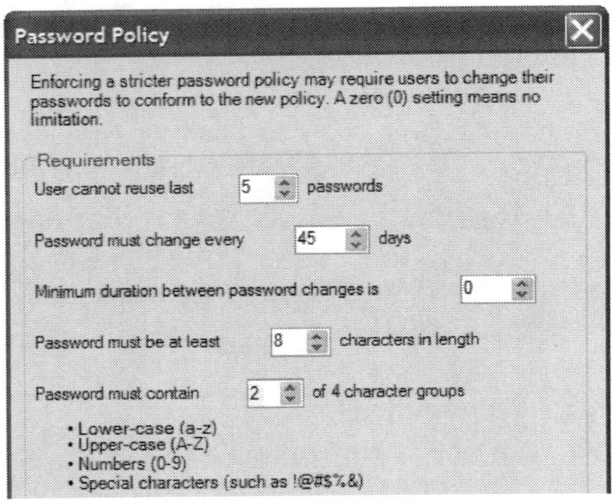

Figure 20-41 Password Policy dialog box

3. Open the Password Policy dialog box and reset all of the options back to zero, then click OK. That way, you will not have problems the next time that you open the database that you are using for this book.

ACT! Diagnostics

This is a utility that comes with ACT!. You can use it to maintain and repair databases, as well as, manage the local ACT! SQL server. Follow the steps below to run this utility.

1. Close ACT!.

2. Windows Start button ⇒ Run.

3. Type `actdiag` in the field, then press Enter. If you see the Diagnostics Disclaimer message, click OK.

4. Click on the **DATABASES** button and select Database List. You will see the dialog box shown in Figure 20-42. The menu options shown in Figure 20-43 are the database actions that you can use.

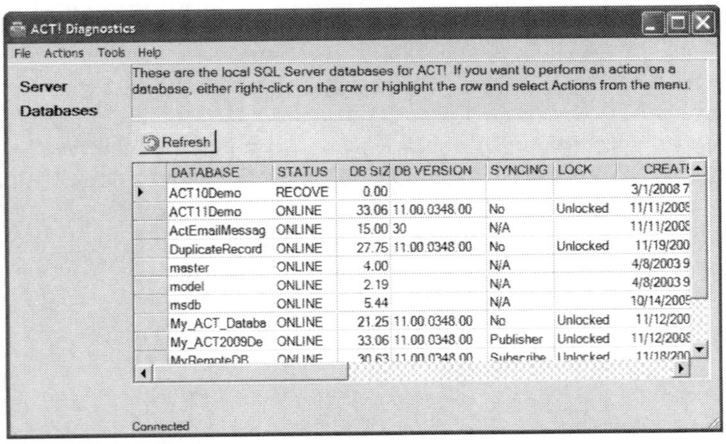

Figure 20-42 ACT! Diagnostics dialog box

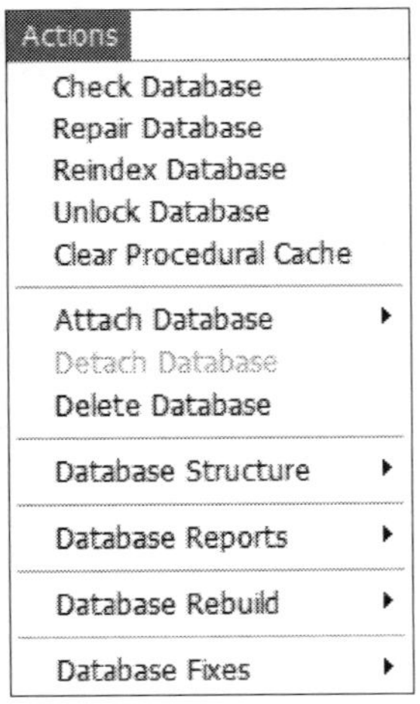

Figure 20-43 Database actions menu

The End!

If you are reading this paragraph, I hope that it means that you have completed all of the exercises in this book. If so, congratulations because you have covered a lot of material. If some topics seem a little fuzzy right now, that is to be expected. Hopefully you have gained some valuable ACT! skills and techniques. As you have probably figured out, there are a lot of options and features at your disposal. I hope that you enjoyed the book.

INDEX

A

D

T

U

No Stress Tech Guides

ISBN: 978-1-935208-18-1

ISBN: 978-1-935208-11-2

ISBN: 978-1-935208-15-0

ISBN: 978-1-935208-17-4

ISBN: 978-1-935208-16-7

ISBN: 978-1-935208-12-9

ISBN: 978-1-935208-14-3

ISBN: 978-1-935208-00-6

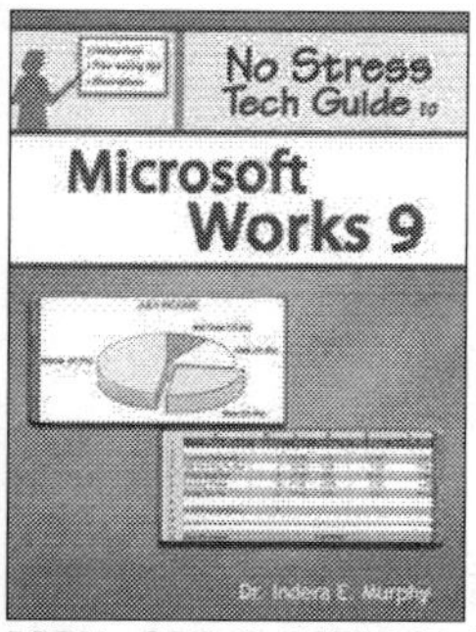

ISBN: 978-0-9773912-7-1

ISBN: 978-0-9773912-9-5

ISBN: 978-1-935208-10-5

ISBN: 978-1-935208-05-1

Visit us online to see the entire series www.tolanapublishing.com

Made in United States
Orlando, FL
05 November 2026

90231095R00219